KU-506-858

National Trust

Handbook 2012

The complete guide for
members and visitors.
1 January to 31 December 2012

For much more about
National Trust places, visit
www.nationaltrust.org.uk

Everything you can do with the National Trust

For enquiries contact 0844 800 1895

People and places, clockwise from top left: **discovering the garden at Buckland Abbey, Garden and Estate, Devon; walking at Sheringham Park, Norfolk; Dinefwr Park and Castle, Carmarthenshire, Wales; Sutton House, London; young farmer, Dyrham Park, South Gloucestershire; Lindisfarne Castle, Northumberland; dramatic view at Wasdale, Cumbria; proud mother at Llanerchaeron, Ceredigion, Wales.** *Previous page, clockwise from top left:* **Heddon Valley, Devon; Bradenham Village, Buckinghamshire; Bodiam Castle, East Sussex; Avebury, Wiltshire; peacock at Moseley Old Hall, Staffordshire.** *Cover:* **Brimham Rocks, North Yorkshire.**

2012

Outdoor nation

As one of the nation's biggest landowners, we are, and always have been, about the great outdoors.

But as each generation goes by, we spend less time in the outdoors, exploring and experiencing less of the natural world. Recent research shows that 64 per cent of children play outside less than once a week. One in five has never climbed a tree. Yet we also know that 80 per cent of Britain's happiest people have a strong connection with nature and the outdoors. Other studies have shown that as little as five minutes' 'green exercise' can have a significant effect on people's self-esteem.

Our glorious buildings, landscapes and coastlines belong to us all. They provide inspiration, fun, physical and intellectual challenges, companionship, joy, consolation and peace. The simple pleasures of a walk in the woods or time spent before a blazing hearth feel of greater value than anything you can buy. The Trust exists so that as many people as possible can share in these benefits, which refresh our spirits and help us thrive in an anxious, fast-changing and often confusing world.

Time well spent

Helping people enjoy life to the full has always been very important to us. For 117 years we have offered memorable

Emmetts Garden

Coniston and Tarn Hows

experiences in wonderful places protected for ever, for everyone, by the National Trust. But we know we can do even better and this year we're again making a special effort to open up our countryside and coastline. Come and sit in tranquil places to reflect and enjoy, challenge yourself to walk a single mile or many, rekindle your love for climbing trees or help your children or grandchildren experience new ways of having fun out of doors!

There are events of every type for all kinds of visitors, from the young in years to the young at heart, and wonderful sights and places to enjoy all year round.

So this year why not reconnect with nature and be truly inspired for life in the great outdoors of England, Wales and Northern Ireland?

Spring

Relish the early pleasures of snowdrop days (Anglesey Abbey, Gardens and Lode Mill, The Argory and Kingston Lacy) and bluebell woods (Emmetts Garden, Lanhydrock and Blickling Estate), and savour the progressive greening of great historic deer parks (Knole, Calke Abbey and Petworth House and Park).

Summer

Spend sunny summer days on your bike, cycling from Plymbridge to Dartmoor, around Clumber Park, along the Manifold Valley and around Erddig. Or try wild camping and den building (look for events at Fowey estuary, Coleton Fishacre and Holmwood Common). Woolbeding Gardens, Hidcote, Mottisfont and Sissinghurst Castle are among the musts for garden lovers, while fans of wide open spaces should head to Coniston and Tarn Hows or the moorlands of North Yorkshire, where they can enjoy great walking.

Autumn

Perfect for conkers, welly walks and treasure hunts. Enjoy superb autumn colours in the Clent Hills, Bodnant Garden, Sizergh Castle and Garden, Gibside, Belton House, Stourhead (tree-climbing activities also on offer!) and Winkworth Arboretum.

Winter

This is a great time to get together with family and friends to enjoy the winter garden at Dunham Massey and walks at Cragside, Chirk Castle, Stowe and Avebury. Christmas events abound, with National Trust shopping possibilities to boot, and for the properly prepared walker it's a fabulous time to be outdoors in the freshest of fresh air!

Be inspired by art

Our places have always been rich in artistic inspiration; however, 2012 is an especially important year as Trust New Art, our partnership with Arts Council England, which uses art to connect people with the stories of our places, reaches its climax.

Ham House and Garden, Tatton Park and Saltram have

Stourhead

Trust New Art

been centres of contemporary art for centuries and this year they welcome today's artists.

'Garden of Reason' at Ham House and Garden sees the 17th-century gardens taking centre stage with sculptures, installations and new films looking at the rich garden environment. The Tatton Park Biennial 'Flights of Fancy' celebrates the Egerton family's interests in early flight and radio with innovative new commissions in the park, gardens and house. Saltram uses its mysterious chinoiserie collections and works with Chinese, British and international artists to explore what these exchanges between the East and West mean today.

Five places are being brought to life with works from the Arts Council Collection. Antony Gormley's *Field for the British Isles*, a mass of thousands of small sculptural figures, occupies the Court House at Barrington Court. At Greyfriars' House and Garden delicate fabrics are contrasted with recent textile art, while Basildon Park complements its Graham Sutherland works with significant 1950s artists. Dyrham Park takes inspiration from the global connections of founder William Blathwayt, and there are a number of sites in West Cornwall which respond to the industrial history of the area.

For details of this exciting project visit **www.nationaltrust.org.uk/ trustnewart**

To find the places mentioned above, see the index, pages 405 to 415.

Using your Handbook

This *Handbook* gives details of the many National Trust places you can visit, including opening arrangements for 2012 from the start of January to the end of December, and available facilities. Property entries are arranged by area (see map on page 391) and are ordered alphabetically. Maps for each area appear on pages 392 to 404, and these show properties with a charge for entry, together with a selection of coast and countryside places plus three Historic House Hotels. Maps also show main population centres.

Property features are indicated by symbols. The key to the symbols is on the inside front cover.

Date at which the place (or first part of the place) was acquired by the National Trust.

To find places within a particular county/administrative area, please refer to the index on page 405.

A simple grid reference is given in each entry. These refer first to the number of the appropriate map in this *Handbook*, then to the grid square, for example ② D7.

Ordnance Survey (Landranger series or OSNI for Northern Ireland) grid references are given at the beginning of the 'Getting here' section.

Information regarding Access for all is shown using symbols. The key is on the inside front cover.

Hinton Ampner

Bramdean, near Alresford,
Hampshire SO24 0LA

Map ② D7   [⌂] [✿] [♠] [Y] [1986]

Getting here: 185:SU597275. Midway between Winchester and Petersfield. **Bus**: Winchester to Petersfield (passing close Winchester ≅ and passing Petersfield ≅). **Train**: Winchester 9 miles; Alresford (Mid-Hants Railway) 4 miles. **Road**: on A272, 1 mile west of Bramdean village, 8 miles east of Winchester. Leave M3 at exit 9 and follow signs to Petersfield. **Sat Nav**: use entrance off the A272, not village road as directed. **Parking**: free.

Finding out more: 01962 771305 or hintonampner@nationaltrust.org.uk

Access for all: [P♿] [wc] [♿] [⎙] [⎙] [⚫] [⊘]
Building [♿][♿] Grounds [♿][➡][♿]

For information on prices please telephone 0844 800 1895 or visit **www.nationaltrust.org.uk**

Opening arrangements

The information is given in table format, intended to show at a glance when places or parts of places are open and when they are closed.

Black type indicates that the place or facility is **open** on those days.

A grey dot indicates that the place or facility is **closed** on those days.

Opening period in date order.

Opening times.

Special notes or important information relating to opening arrangements.

Hinton Ampner		M	T	W	T	F	S	S
House								
11 Feb–4 Nov	11–5	M	T	W	T	F	S	S
5 Nov–28 Nov	11–5	M	T	W	·	·	S	S
1 Dec–9 Dec	10:30–4:30	M	T	W	T	F	S	S
Garden, shop and tea-room								
11 Feb–30 Mar	10–5	M	T	W	T	F	S	S
31 Mar–30 Sep	10–6	M	T	W	T	F	S	S
1 Oct–4 Nov	10–5	M	T	W	T	F	S	S
5 Nov–28 Nov	10–5	M	T	W	·	·	S	S
1 Dec–9 Dec	10–4:30	·	M	T	W	T	F	S	S

Last entry to house and tea-room 20 minutes before closing. 7 December: open to 7.

Please note the following points about this year's *Handbook*:

- areas are shown in hectares (1 hectare = 2.47 acres) with the acres equivalent in brackets. Short distances are shown in yards (1 yard = 0.91 metre); longer distances are measured in miles. Heights are shown in metres.

- although opening times and arrangements vary considerably from place to place and from year to year, most houses will be open during the period 1 March to 31 October inclusive, usually on three or more days per week between about noon and 5pm.

Please note that, unless otherwise stated in the property entry, last admission is 30 minutes before the stated closing time.

- we make every effort to ensure that property opening times and available facilities are as published, but very occasionally it is essential to change these at short notice. Always check the current *Handbook* for details and, if making a special journey, please telephone in advance for confirmation. You can also check our website **www.nationaltrust.org.uk**

- when telephoning a property, please remember that we can provide a better service if you call on a weekday morning, on a day when the property is open. Alternatively, call our Supporter Services Centre on 0844 800 1895, seven days a week (9 to 5:30 Monday to Friday, 9 to 4 at weekends and Bank Holidays).

Extra copies of the National Trust *Handbook* are available to buy, while stocks last.

Your visit

The following information will help you make the most of your visit. The questions and answers on page 382 also contain important information.

Admission fees
Trust members are admitted free to virtually all places (see information about membership, page 387); however, there may be a charge on special event days. For current admission prices visit **www.nationaltrust.org.uk** or telephone the Supporter Services Centre on 0844 800 1895. Please note that prices may vary during off-peak or busy times; our website always offers the definitive information. Admission fees include VAT and are liable to change if the VAT rate is altered. The prices for most places include a voluntary ten per cent donation under the Gift Aid on Entry scheme, see page 384.

Children: under-fives are free. Children aged five to 16 usually pay half the adult price. Seventeens and over pay the adult price. Children not accompanied by an adult are admitted at the Trust's discretion. Most places offer discounted family tickets (usually covering one or two adults and up to three children, unless stated otherwise).

Concessions: as a registered charity which has to raise all its own funds, we cannot afford to offer concessions on admission fees. Free entry is offered on Heritage Open Days

however (visit website for details) and very occasionally for other special events.

Group visits: please book in advance with each place. Admission discounts are usually available for groups of 15-plus people (this can vary so should be confirmed when booking). The Travel Trade team at the Trust's Heelis office (see page 416) can provide general groups information and details on special interest tours and activities for groups. For further information visit **www.nationaltrust.org.uk/groups**

Toilets
There is always one available, either onsite (when we are open), or nearby, unless the entry specifically indicates 'no toilet'.

Eating and shopping
Shops: times are given in the opening arrangements table. Many are open for Christmas shopping.

Restaurants and tea-rooms: we aim to offer the best local and seasonal produce, cooking and baking. At all cafés we offer facilities for families with children, either to warm baby food or provide children's portions.

For more details on shops and restaurants see page 378.

Children and families
We offer various facilities, from special parking areas to the loan of front slings and hip-seat carriers or reins, to help your visit run smoothly.

Some of the many events and activities for families and children are listed in the 'Making the most of your day' section of each entry. For details see page 378.

Dogs
Any restrictions are listed in the 'Making the most of your day' section. Assistance dogs are always welcome. For more details see page 378.

Guided tours
There is a range of guided tour options now available at many Trust places. Houses often offer 'taster' tours between 11 and 1, before opening for free-flow visiting. Many of our outdoor places – such as gardens, parks and coastal sites – also offer guided tours. Please telephone in advance or visit the website for details.

Events
A tremendous variety of events is on offer at our places throughout the year. Places may close for these events and members may have to pay on special event days. For more information see page 379.

Busy days
Bank Holidays and summer weekends are our busiest days and houses can be crowded. Although some places use timed tickets to smooth the flow of people, it is worth telephoning in advance if you are planning a long journey – and at some very small houses, booking is essential (for example, Mr Straw's House in Worksop, Nottinghamshire).

Your safety

You can help by:
- observing all notices and signs during your visit;
- following any instructions and advice given by Trust staff;
- ensuring that children are properly supervised at all times;
- wearing appropriate clothing and footwear in built places, the countryside and gardens.

At all our sites the responsibility for visitor safety should be seen as one that is shared between us and you. As the landscape becomes more rugged or remote, the balance of responsibility between the Trust and our visitors shifts. To help ensure your safety:
- take note of weather conditions and forecasts and be properly equipped for changes in the weather. Please note that some places (or parts of) may close in severe weather. It is always a good idea to check opening arrangements before setting out on your journey;
- make sure you are properly prepared, equipped and clothed for the terrain and the activity which you are planning on doing;
- tell other people of your intended route and estimated time of return;
- make sure you have the necessary skills and abilities for the location and activity and be aware of your own limitations.

For more information about safety please see page 380.

Access information

Details of access provisions for each place are shown using a range of symbols in each property entry – see key inside front cover.

We offer free entry, on request, to an essential companion or carer of a disabled visitor. The usual membership fee or admission cost applies to the disabled person. An Access for All Admit One Card can be issued in the name of the disabled visitor to make this easier – just telephone 01793 817634 or email enquiries@nationaltrust.org.uk

If you have a specific access requirement, we suggest you contact each place direct.

At some of our gardens and parks we offer powered vehicles (PMVs), either self-drive or volunteer-driven – see each entry for details. We recommend that you telephone in advance to check availability and any booking requirements. Wherever possible, we welcome users of powered wheelchairs and similar small vehicles to our buildings (subject to the physical limitations of the place and any other temporary constraints). Again, it is a good idea to check in advance.

Assistance dogs are welcome at our places.

For information on how to order the *Access Guide* please see page 379.

Your journey

The 'Getting here' section provides information regarding finding and travelling to a place, including non-car options. For more information see page 6 and 380.

You are strongly advised to check services and timetables before setting out.

See the box below for more information.

Further information to help plan your journey

Transport Direct: plan how to get there by public transport or car from any UK location or postcode using **www.transportdirect.info**

Sustrans: for NCN routes and cycling maps visit **www.sustrans.org.uk** or telephone 0117 929 0888.

National Rail Enquiries: for train times visit **www.nationalrail.co.uk** or telephone 08457 48 49 50.

Traveline: for bus routes and times for England, Wales and Scotland visit **www.traveline.info** or telephone 0871 200 2233.

Taxis from railway stations: **www.traintaxi.co.uk**

Public transport in Northern Ireland (train and bus): **www.translink.co.uk** or telephone 028 9066 6630.

Transport for London: for all travel information visit **www.tfl.gov.uk** or telephone 0843 222 1234.

The Trust online

You can find information about all the places in this Handbook at **www.nationaltrust.org.uk** (information is updated daily). To help you make the most of your visit, most places show additional information about their history and features. The website also includes regional news and events, information about volunteering and learning opportunities, as well as hiring a venue for corporate or private functions. In addition we have a dedicated holiday cottages website at **www.nationaltrustcottages.co.uk** and an online gift shop at **www.nationaltrust.org.uk/shop**

For monthly news, events information, details of things to do and places to visit, updates on our work and suggestions of how you might get involved, sign up for your free email newsletter via **www.nationaltrust.org.uk/email**

This Handbook contains email addresses for those places which can be contacted direct. General email enquiries should be sent to enquiries@nationaltrust.org.uk

All the property information in this Handbook is also available as an APP – available free for download on the iPhone, all Nokia phones and any Android devices. Users can find National Trust places near them, browse photo galleries and add future events to their calendars.

 Find us on Facebook at facebook.com/nationaltrust

 Follow us on Twitter at twitter.com/nationaltrust

South West

Canoeing on the sheltered waters
between the heavily wooded banks of
Pont Pill on the Fowey estuary

Outdoors in the South West

Is there anywhere in this country more blessed with a glorious variety of landscapes than the South West? Here are hundreds of beautiful places where you can refresh both body and soul: discover the simple pleasures of strolling across the moors or swimming in a deserted cove, picnicking on the cliffs or playing in the woods, cycling along country tracks or sitting in a quiet spot listening to birdsong.

Right:
drawing a huge sun on the sandy beach at Kynance Cove, Cornwall

Relaxation, inspiration, adventure
People are drawn to the South West for its breathtaking unspoilt coast and countryside: for many of us it's why we live here, or come on holiday here year after year. The Trust looks after a huge variety of landscapes throughout the South West's six counties. In fact some of the most striking and beautiful places in the South West are owned by the Trust, set in wonderful countryside which extends well beyond our boundaries.

We all need the outdoors to recharge our batteries, and there is nothing better for our body and soul than quiet relaxation in hidden places off the beaten track or the inspiration that a magnificent view provides. A blast of sea air, a carpet of wild flowers and the sheer joy of adventures and exercise in the open air: one of these will be perfect for you.

Clockwise from top right:
Rough Tor, Bodmin Moor, Cornwall. Avebury, Wiltshire. Dunkery Beacon, Somerset. Saltram Estate, Devon

Vital statistics

The Trust protects more than 50,000 hectares (123,500 acres) of countryside in the counties of Cornwall, Devon, Dorset, Somerset, Wiltshire and Gloucestershire, which includes nearly 6,000 hectares (14,826 acres) of woodland and 420 miles of coast (36 per cent of the total coastline of Devon and Cornwall alone).

Some of the South West's most iconic and wildlife-rich landscapes are partly owned and protected by the Trust: great swathes of Exmoor and Dartmoor, for example; the Jurassic Coast of Dorset and East Devon and the old mining areas of Cornwall and West Devon (both of which are World Heritage Sites); the famous cliffs of Cheddar Gorge in Somerset; the historic chalk downs of Wiltshire and Dorset; and the upland farms and woods of the northern Cotswolds; along with nature reserves, heathlands, meadows and ancient woodlands scattered across the counties.

Around the peninsula from Minehead in Somerset to Poole in Dorset runs the 630-mile South West Coast Path – the longest national trail in the country – 290 miles of which runs through Trust land.

How can you find out about all of this open country, and the many things you can do once you get there? Some of the best-known places have their own entries in this *Handbook* – see pages 18 to 98 – but there are hundreds more. To discover them, visit **www.nationaltrust.org.uk**

So much to do

Whether it's the beaches, coastal paths, countryside or the water itself that attracts you, we've got a lot to offer on our 420 miles of coastline and unspoilt swathes of countryside. From swimming and surfing to rock-climbing and outdoor gyms; mountain biking and running to kayaking and canoeing, this is the place for you.

Or maybe you yearn to enjoy the ultimate outdoor experience – spending a night under canvas? Camping brings you up close to nature and the outdoors, creating the chance to experience an altogether slower pace of life.

Walking is another excellent way to immerse yourself in some extraordinary Trust landscapes. Whether you prefer an amble, ramble or scramble, there is a Trust walk that is just right for you.

Then, of course, there is the bicycle. So many experiences are denied us when travelling by car: the sounds, the smells and primarily the ability to stop and enjoy a fleeting sight or wonderful view. The bicycle, often vaunted as man's most noble invention, allows us the opportunity to enjoy all these experiences.

Where to start

Car parks are often the first step into Trust countryside: there are simply too many to list them all here, but some key ones are listed on page 17. The website is the best place to find complete coverage of all our coast and countryside, along with details of access, activities and events.

Above:
snorkellers at South Milton Sands, Devon
Far right, top:
heading for the beach at Studland, Dorset
Far right, bottom: **off-road mountain biking in Plymbridge Woods, near Plymouth, Devon**

Clockwise from top right: **Teign Gorge, Devon. The Baden-Powell Outdoor Centre and red squirrel, both on Brownsea Island, Dorset**

Why not try...?

Walking – north, south, east and west

Try the walk along the coast from Godrevy towards Portreath in North Cornwall. The path along the wild clifftops here is teeming with birds and wildflowers, and there are secluded coves, sandy beaches and archaeology to discover as you walk.

Following the coast further north into Devon, spot seals and wonder at the wild seas crashing against rocks at Baggy Point, Morte Point and Heddon's Mouth – the steep-sided wooded valley here, with its tumbling river and stepping stones onto the pebble beach, will soon become a favourite walk.

Further along the Exmoor coast in Somerset, rugged heather moorland meets dramatic cliffs at Holnicote. There is some great moorland walking here, taking in wildlife-rich ancient wooded valleys, with the added challenge of climbing Dunkery Beacon, the highest point on Exmoor.

The south coast, too, is spectacular for walking. At the Jurassic Coast in Dorset, you can combine a walk with fossil hunting and rock-pooling. Golden Cap, with its panoramic clifftop views and miles of wide-open space, is particularly striking.

Inland, the picturesque landscape garden and countryside estate of Stourhead in Wiltshire is perfect for unwinding. An easy wander takes you around the beautiful lake and wooded garden, full of vibrant colours in autumn, or a longer walk encompasses rolling countryside, prehistoric hill forts, burial mounds, historic monuments and farmland.

Finally, north to Gloucestershire and the limestone grasslands of Minchinhampton and Rodborough Commons: a summer stroll here takes you through wildflower meadows bursting with butterflies, combined with an archaeological landscape and far-reaching views – well worth a good walk and picnic!

For downloadable walks visit
www.nationaltrust.org.uk/walks

The freedom of a bicycle

The South West offers cycling at all levels: amazing bridleway mountain-biking in the Quantock Hills and on Dartmoor; the disused railway track at Plymbridge near Plymouth (the perfect cycle route for beginners and tourers alike); and a gentle pedal along the beautiful Exe Estuary to visit A la Ronde.

These routes, along with others on the Holnicote Estate on Exmoor and family cycle tracks at Killerton in Devon, are a few of the brilliant rides on Trust land that cater for any rider. With opportunities to cycle to, and at, so many National Trust places, why not take the time to extend your adventure and make the journey part of the experience?

Visit **www.nationaltrust.org.uk/cycling**

Why not try...?

Life under canvas

Across the South West, from Golden Cap through Dartmoor to the Lizard, there is a range of ways to come camping with us. At Chyvarloe Campsite, between Loe Pool and Gunwalloe beach on the Lizard, you are right on the South West Coast Path. There are simple, basic facilities for tents and small campervans, and you can walk to the beaches or saunter to the pub in the evening.

Highertown Farm has a small campsite in a hallowed spot in the churchtown of Lansallos between Fowey and Polperro on Cornwall's south coast. Popular with families and couples, this eco-friendly site is a pleasant three quarters of a mile walk from a secluded beach, on the unspoilt sweep of Lantivet Bay. Here you can truly get away from it all and spend days walking, rock-pooling or lazing on Lantic beach.

In Devon, Prattshayes Campsite is popular with families, sun lovers, beachcombers, birdwatchers and walkers. A short stroll away lies Exmouth beach, well known for its fine sand and sea quality. A small and friendly place to stay – with special facilities for barbecues, food preparation and recycling – the campsite is down a quiet country lane among fields.

Find out about all of our campsites at **www.nationaltrust.org.uk/camping**

Wild swimming

We have a plethora of places to go for a dip around the South West. Look out for Cornwall's guided 'wild swimming' events down Frenchman's Creek and off Tremayne Quay on the Helford Estuary. Or take yourself for a splash at Knoll beach at Studland in Dorset, safe in the knowledge that it will just be you and your fellow crazy dippers in the zoned-off area, with not even a lifeguard to blow a whistle at you.

Paddle power

There are few things in life better than finding yourself up a creek with a paddle! Well, here's your chance. Spend a day with the Trust and Adventure Cornwall, exploring the creeks and harbour of the Fowey Estuary by canoe. Keep your eyes open for fleeting glimpses of kingfishers and egrets and – if you're really lucky – dormice. You can hire a kayak from one of our tenant businesses in Studland in Dorset, or at the watersports playground that is South Milton Sands in Devon.

Or get up close and personal with the riverbanks and wildlife of the Helford, and be guided by a Trust ranger and our business partner Waterborne: you could get buzzed by a heron or come nose-to-nose with a seal.

We have full-day expeditions in Canadian canoes, hosted by Singingpaddles, up the creeks of the Salcombe-Kingsbridge Estuary in South Devon, where you'll discover the wildlife and archaeology on Trust land, with a well-earned lunch on the shore.

For more details visit the downloadable canoe and kayak trails on our website.

Riding the waves

We have an ace up our sleeves: some of the best surfing beaches in the UK! Head down to Crantock beach on the North Cornwall coast, Godrevy beach further west on St Ives Bay, or Poldhu and Gunwalloe on the Lizard, and you'll be greeted by one of our ambassador surf schools. You'll be kitted out with all the gear and shown all the tricks... it'll be like living the endless summer.

Coastal and countryside car parks

The Trust provides hundreds of places to park throughout the South West: your thresholds to all that the outdoors has to offer. They range from inconspicuous parking spots leading to remote coves, cliffs, hills and undisturbed wildlife havens, to busy car parks for popular destinations, often manned in season, where you can buy walks guides and find facilities such as cafés and WCs. Listed below are the Ordnance Survey grid references of some of the busy ones (excluding those with main *Handbook* entries) and some of the quieter ones; there are too many to include them all, but you can find complete details on the South West pages of our website.

Right: **Golden Cap Estate, Dorset**
Left, top: **camping at Highertown Campsite, Lansallos, Cornwall**
Left, bottom: **surfing at Godrevy, Cornwall**

Cornwall		**St Anthony Head**	SW 847 313	Man Sands	SX 913 531
Morwenstow	SS 205 154	Porth Farm		Salcombe Hill	SY 148 889
Duckpool	SS 202 117	(Towan Beach)	SW 867 329	Branscombe	SY 197 887
Sandy Mouth	SS 203 100	Pendower Beach	SW 897 384	Plymbridge Woods	SX 524 585
Northcott Mouth	SS 204 084	Carne Beach	SW 905 384	Cadover Bridge	SX 533 636
Strangles Beach	SX 134 952	Nare Head	SW 922 380	Shaugh Prior	SX 554 645
Glebe Cliff, Tintagel	SX 050 884	Penare (Dodman)	SW 998 404		
Port Quin	SW 972 805	Lamledra (Vault Beach)	SW 011 411	**Dorset**	
Lundy Bay	SW 953 796	Coombe Farm	SX 110 512	Cogden, West Dorset	SY 503 883
Pentireglaze	SW 942 799	Pencarrow Head	SX 150 513	Stonebarrow Hill	SY 383 933
Park Head	SW 853 707	Frogmore	SX 157 517	Langdon Hill	SY 413 931
Crantock	SW 789 607	Lansallos	SX 174 518	Burton Bradstock	SY 491 888
Treago Mill (Polly Joke)	SW 778 601	Hendersick	SX 236 520	Ringstead Bay	SY 760 822
Holywell Bay	SW 767 586			Spyway	SY 996 785
St Agnes Beacon	SW 704 503	**Devon**		Studland: Shell Bay	SZ 035 864
Wheal Coates	SW 703 500	Countisbury	SS 747 497	Knoll Beach	SZ 035 836
Chapel Porth	SW 697 495	Combe Park	SS 740 477	Middle Beach	SZ 037 828
Reskajeage Downs	SW 623 430	Woody Bay	SS 676 486	South Beach	SZ 038 825
Derrick Cove	SW 620 429	Trentishoe Down	SS 635 480		
Hell's Mouth	SW 599 427	Torrs Walk, Ilfracombe	SS 511 475	**Gloucestershire**	
Trencrom	SW 517 359	Hartland: Brownsham	SS 285 259	Haresfield: Cripplegate	SO 832 086
Carn Galver	SW 422 364	and East Titchberry	SS 244 270	and Ash Lane	SO 824 066
Botallack	SW 366 334	Stoke	SX 558 466	Rodborough Common:	
Cape Cornwall	SW 353 318	Ringmore	SX 650 457	Hill Fort	SO 852 035
Cot Valley	SW 358 308	East Soar	SX 713 375	Minchinhampton:	
Penrose	SW 639 259	Snapes Point	SX 739 403	Reservoir	SO 855 013
Chyvarloe	SW 653 235	Prawle Point	SX 775 354	Mayhill	SO 691 221
Gunwalloe	SW 660 207	Little Dartmouth	SX 874 492		
Predannack	SW 669 162	Higher Brownstone	SX 905 510	**Somerset**	
Poltesco	SW 726 156	Coleton Camp	SX 909 513	Sand Point	ST 330 660
Bosveal (Durgan)	SW 775 276	Scabbacombe	SX 912 523		

A la Ronde

Summer Lane, Exmouth, Devon EX8 5BD

Map ① G7   1991

'**Excellent! It was inspirational – loved the wacky collection of objects. Amazing setting, lovely atmosphere, friendly, helpful staff. Love the tea-rooms.**'
Miss Fergusson, Drewsteignton

This unique 16-sided house, described by Lucinda Lambton as having 'a magical strangeness that one might dream of only as a child', was built for two spinster cousins, Jane and Mary Parminter, on their return from a European grand tour in the late 18th century. It contains many objects and mementoes of their travels, and the extraordinary interior decoration includes a feather frieze from many species of birds, including game birds, fowl, jays and parrots, laboriously stuck down with isinglass. The fragile shell-encrusted gallery, said to contain nearly 25,000 shells, is viewed via a 360-degree touchscreen virtual tour. **Note**: small, fragile rooms. Allow at least an hour to visit. Non-flash photography permitted.

Exploring	– Diamond windows in last Harry Potter film inspired by ours.
	– Discovery Room with dressing up, silhouette and shell activities.
	– Wildlife brass rubbing and spotter sheets for the grounds.

A 19th-century model of A la Ronde, Devon

Exploring
– Free garden activities – croquet, snakes and ladders, quoits and more.
– New art exhibition and sale of work every two weeks.
– Follow us on Facebook and Twitter.

Eating and shopping: buy local products in the shop. Plant sales. Licensed tea-room, home-cooked lunches and afternoon teas using local produce. Special diets catered for. Outside seating with stunning views. Buy a drink or ice-cream in the shop. Picnic area. Second-hand book sales.

Making the most of your day: full programme of events, exhibitions, rural skills, nature walks, school holiday craft activities. Self-guided themed tours and family trail in house. Stunning views over Exe estuary and local landscape panorama. **Dogs**: welcome on leads in car park and orchard picnic area.

Access for all: 🅿️ 🚐 🚻 ♿ 🔄 🖥️ ♿ 🔊 📷
House ♿♿ Tea-room ♿ Grounds ♿ ➡️

Getting here: 192:SY004834. 2 miles north of Exmouth. **Foot**: East Devon Way alongside. South West Coast Path 2 miles. **Cycle**: £1 shop or tea-room voucher for visitors arriving by green transport. **Bus**: Exeter to Exmouth and Budleigh Salterton, stops within ½ mile. **Train**: Lympstone village 1¼ miles; Exmouth 2 miles. **Road**: 2 miles north of Exmouth off A376. **Parking**: free. Caravans and trailers telephone in advance.

Finding out more: 01395 265514 (office). 01395 255918 (shop). 01395 278552 (tea-room) or alaronde@nationaltrust.org.uk

A la Ronde		M	T	W	T	F	S	S
7 Jan–5 Feb	12–4	·	·	·	·	·	S	S
11 Feb–19 Feb	11–5	M	T	W	·	·	S	S
25 Feb–4 Mar	11–5	·	·	·	·	·	S	S
10 Mar–27 Jun	11–5	M	T	W	·	·	S	S
29 Jun–31 Aug	11–5	M	T	W	T	F	S	S
1 Sep–4 Nov	11–5	M	T	W	·	·	S	S
10 Nov–16 Dec	12–4	·	·	·	·	·	S	S

Open Good Friday. Last admission to house 4. 11 February to 4 November: shop, tea-room and grounds open as house; shop and grounds 10:30 to 5:30, tea-room 10:30 to 5. 10 November to 16 December: house shown 'put to bed' by guided tours only (last tour 3:15); shop and grounds open 11:30 to 4:30, tea-room open 11:30 to 4.

The stately Yew Walk at Antony, Cornwall: home to the Carew Pole family for hundreds of years

Antony

Torpoint, Cornwall PL11 2QA

Map ① E8 1961

'It was magical, wonderful. My kids loved the grounds – finding the butterflies, the shapes of the hedges, the summer garden.'
Mrs Spatharis, Newbury, Berkshire

Still the home of the Carew Pole family after hundreds of years, this beautiful early 18th-century house contains fine collections of paintings, furniture and textiles. The grounds, landscaped by Repton, sweep down towards the Lynher estuary and include formal gardens with topiary, a knot garden, modern sculptures and the National Collection of Daylilies. The Woodland Garden has outstanding rhododendrons, azaleas, magnolias and camellias. The magic of Antony was recognised by Walt Disney when it was chosen as the set for the film *Alice in Wonderland*, directed by Tim Burton. **Note**: members admitted free to Woodland Garden (not National Trust) only when house is open.

Exploring
– Create stories inspired by our magical landscape.
– Soak up the unique atmosphere of a family home.
– Hunt for the modern sculpture installed throughout the gardens.
– Smell the delicious sea air and seasonal plant scents.
– Sit on the terrace and enjoy breathtaking river views.
– Explore the welcoming wide-open spaces.

Eating and shopping: enjoy a light lunch or afternoon tea in our self-service tea-room. Take home something special from our gift shop offering a range of souvenirs, plants and local produce.

Making the most of your day: full season of garden and family events, quizzes and trails; play croquet on the lawn. **Dogs**: assistance dogs only.

Access for all: ⃝⃝⃝⃝⃝⃝⃝⃝⃝
House ⃝⃝ **Tea-room** ⃝ **Grounds** ⃝⃝⃝

Getting here: 201:SX418564. 2 miles north-west of Torpoint. **Cycle**: NCN27, 2 miles.

Bus: from Plymouth, alight Great Park Estate, ¼ mile. **Train**: Plymouth 6 miles. **Road**: 6 miles west of Plymouth via Torpoint car ferry, 2 miles north-west of Torpoint, north of A374, 16 miles south-east of Liskeard. **Parking**: free, 250 yards.

Finding out more: 01752 812191 or antony@nationaltrust.org.uk

Antony		M	T	W	T	F	S	S
House								
3 Apr–31 May	1–5	·	T	W	T	·	·	
3 Jun–30 Aug	1–5	·	T	W	T	·	·	S
4 Sep–1 Nov	1–5	·	T	W	T	·	·	
Garden, shop and tea-room								
3 Apr–31 May	12–5	·	T	W	T	·	·	
3 Jun–30 Aug	12–5	·	T	W	T	·	·	S
4 Sep–1 Nov	12–5	·	T	W	T	·	·	
Woodland Garden								
1 Mar–1 Nov	11–5:30	·	T	W	T	·	S	S

Also open Good Friday, Easter Sunday, Sunday 6 May and Bank Holiday Mondays. Bath Pond House interior can only be seen by written application to the Property Manager, on days house is open. At peak times, timed tickets for entry to the house will be in operation.

Arlington Court and the National Trust Carriage Museum

Arlington, near Barnstaple, Devon EX31 4LP

Map ① F5

Arlington Court is an unexpected jewel: a complete family estate. The intimate Regency house contains treasures for all tastes, from model ships to shells, all collected by the Chichesters. Offering incident and contrast, the 19th-century picturesque garden is a perfect place to explore, picnic or play. The walled kitchen garden provides fruit and vegetables for the tea-room and flowers for

The elegant Morning Room, with White Drawing Room beyond, at Arlington Court, Devon

Entry is still possible at most places up to 30 minutes before closing

the house. The tranquil estate, abundant with wildlife, includes an ancient heronry. The Carriage Museum, in the stables, has a vehicle for every occasion – from cradle to grave. Our working horses and stables keep the story alive.

Exploring – Delve into a house full of treasures and secrets.
– Discover the romance of carriage travel in a bygone age.
– Explore three gardens in one: kitchen, flower and pleasure grounds.
– Experience the sights, sounds and smells of our working stables.
– Spy on our lesser horseshoe bats with the bat-cam.
– Don't miss this year's star: the spectacular Speaker's State Coach.

Eating and shopping: buy jams and preserves made locally from Arlington-grown produce. Taste local, seasonal fruit and vegetables in our tea-room, which serves gluten-free options every day. Stay longer in one of the estate's holiday cottages.

Making the most of your day: watch a harnessing demonstration, unpack souvenirs from a lady adventurer's travels, try a waymarked estate walk and borrow binoculars in the bird hide. **Dogs**: on leads in garden, Carriage Museum and the wider estate.

Access for all: [icons] **House** [icons] **Carriage Museum** [icons] **Grounds** [icons]

Getting here: 180:SS611405. 8 miles north of Barnstaple. **Bus**: infrequent service Barnstaple to Lynton. **Train**: Barnstaple, 8 miles. **Road**: A39 from Barnstaple; from east – A399 from South Molton. **Sat Nav**: from South Molton/east stay on A399 until turning for A39 (Arlington is signposted). Don't turn left into unmarked lane: this leads to deliveries' and residents' entrance only. **Parking**: free, 150 yards.

Ashleworth Tithe Barn, Gloucestershire

Finding out more: 01271 850296 or arlingtoncourt@nationaltrust.org.uk

Arlington Court		M	T	W	T	F	S	S
House, Carriage Museum and bat-cam								
13 Feb–19 Feb	11–3	M	T	W	T	F	S	S
25 Feb–4 Mar	11–3	.	.	.	.	.	S	S
10 Mar–4 Nov	11–5	M	T	W	.	F	S	S
10 Nov–23 Dec	11–3 *	.	.	.	.	.	S	S
Shop, tea-room and garden								
1 Jan–2 Jan	11–3	M	.	.	.	.	.	S
13 Feb–19 Feb	11–3	M	T	W	T	F	S	S
25 Feb–4 Mar	11–3	.	.	.	.	.	S	S
10 Mar–4 Nov	10:30–5	M	T	W	T	F	S	S
10 Nov–23 Dec	11–3	.	.	.	.	.	S	S
26 Dec–31 Dec	11–3	M	.	W	T	F	S	S

Limited access to house and Carriage Museum in February, 3 and 4 March, November and December. Shop and tea-room closed 24 and 25 December. Grounds open dawn till dusk, all year.

Ashleworth Tithe Barn

Ashleworth, Gloucestershire GL19 4JA

Map ① J2   [icon] 1956

The barn, with its immense stone-tiled roof, is picturesquely situated close to the banks of the River Severn. **Note**: no toilet.

Access for all: Building [icon]

Getting here: 162:SO818252. 6 miles north of Gloucester, south-east of Ashleworth.

Finding out more: 01452 814213 or ashleworth@nationaltrust.org.uk

Ashleworth Tithe Barn
Open every day all year from dawn to dusk

Avebury

near Marlborough, Wiltshire

Map ① K4

Avebury, Wiltshire: discovering the ancient stones

In the 1930s the pretty village of Avebury, partially encompassed by the stone circle of this World Heritage Site, was witness to the excavations of archaeologist Alexander Keiller. In re-erecting many of the stones, Keiller uncovered the true wonder of one of the most important megalithic monuments in Europe. His fascinating finds are on display in the 17th-century threshing barn and stables galleries of the Alexander Keiller Museum, where interactive displays and activities for children bring the landscape to life. The Manor, with notable Queen Anne alterations and Edwardian renovation, sits amongst tranquil gardens surrounded by topiary and garden 'rooms'. **Note**: English Heritage holds guardianship of Avebury Stone Circle, owned and managed by the National Trust.

Exploring
- Wander around the largest stone circle in the world.
- Discover Avebury's past secrets in our unique onsite museum.
- Explore the many prehistoric monuments of the World Heritage Site.
- Listen for voices of the past in the manor house.
- Don't miss the hidden gem of the tranquil Manor garden.

Eating and shopping: local, seasonal food at Circles, the only Trust vegetarian restaurant! Children's meals, homemade cakes and picnic food are also available. Buy a memento of your visit at the shop. Don't miss the Wessex range of locally sourced giftware.

Making the most of your day: come and spend a day at Avebury with world-renowned experts in archaeology on the Avebury team. Don't miss our calendar of lectures and events, from archaeology to wildlife walks.

Dogs: assistance dogs only in the Manor garden, elsewhere dogs on leads are welcome.

Access for all: ⬛⬛⬛⬛⬛⬛⬛⬛⬛⬛⬛⬛
Building ⬛⬛ Manor house ⬛⬛
Stone circle and gardens ⬛⬛➡

Getting here: 173:SU102699. 6 miles west of Marlborough. **Foot**: Ridgeway National Trail. **Cycle**: NCN4 and 45. **Bus**: frequent buses pass nearby. **Train**: Pewsey; Swindon. **Road**: 6 miles west of Marlborough on the A4361. **Parking**: pay and display. National Trust and English Heritage members free. Overnight parking prohibited.

Finding out more: 01672 539250 or avebury@nationaltrust.org.uk.
National Trust Estate Office, High Street, Avebury, Wiltshire SN8 1RF

Avebury		M	T	W	T	F	S	S
Stone circle								
Open all year	Dawn–dusk	M	T	W	T	F	S	S
Museum								
1 Jan–31 Mar	10–4*	M	T	W	T	F	S	S
1 Apr–31 Oct	10–6	M	T	W	T	F	S	S
1 Nov–31 Dec	10–4*	M	T	W	T	F	S	S
Shop and Circles restaurant								
1 Jan–31 Mar	10–4*	M	T	W	T	F	S	S
1 Apr–31 Oct	10–6	M	T	W	T	F	S	S
1 Nov–31 Dec	10–4*	M	T	W	T	F	S	S

*Or dusk if earlier. Museum, shop and restaurant closed 24 to 26 December. For opening times of manor house and garden visit nationaltrust.org.uk/avebury or telephone 01672 539250.

Baggy Point

Baggy Point, Moor Lane, Croyde,
Devon EX33 1PA

Map ① E5   1939

Baggy Point is the impressive headland at Croyde, one of the best surfing beaches in North Devon. With stunning coastal views, great walks along the South West Coast Path and opportunities to climb, surf and coasteer, it's a must-do destination for anyone visiting North Devon. **Note**: toilets (not National Trust) on main beach slipway, 500 yards from Trust car park.

Exploring – Stretch your legs on great coastal walks for all abilities.
– Use our car park as your base to explore Croyde.
– Have fun as a family with our activity pack.

Eating and shopping: our tenant-run Sandleigh Tea-room and Garden is a local gem. Sit in their secluded market garden and enjoy local and seasonal produce grown onsite. Located at the end of the car park, close to the beach slipway.

Making the most of your day: children can explore and learn about Baggy Point's wildlife and history with our free family activity pack (available to borrow). Pick up our walks leaflet to discover this area. **Dogs**: welcome on leads.

Access for all: Pⓓ

Getting here: SS433397. Outside Croyde village. **Foot**: on Moor Lane. Walk through Croyde village, and follow brown signs to Baggy Point car park. **Bus**: regular service from Barnstaple to Croyde, then follow brown signs. **Train**: Barnstaple. **Road**: A361 to Braunton, take Saunton Road B3231 to Croyde, then follow brown signs. **Parking**: free (manned from late March to October).

Finding out more: 01271 870555 or baggypoint@nationaltrust.org.uk

Baggy Point	Open every day all year

For opening times of Sandleigh Tea-room and Garden (not National Trust) telephone 01271 890930.

Barrington Court

Barrington, near Ilminster, Somerset TA19 0NQ

Map ① I6    1907

'**My favourite of all National Trust properties.**'
Miss R. Bailey, Taunton

This beautiful manor house has terraces leading out into walled garden rooms, orchards and parkland. The Trust's first large house, restored in the 1920s by Colonel Lyle (whose family firm became Tate & Lyle), it is completely empty, save for wonderful oak panelling. This peaceful space will house Turner Prize-winning artwork by Antony Gormley from April to August. The delightful flower gardens, designed in consultation with Gertrude Jekyll, adjoin the kitchen garden, producing fruit and vegetables for the restaurant. Try Barrington's handmade cider and apple juice, straight from the orchards. This is a place to relax and recharge.

Exploring – Experience Antony Gormley's *Field for the British Isles*.
– Taste our award-winning cider on the restaurant terrace.
– Sponsor a tree for the restored Chestnut Avenue.

The White Garden at Barrington Court, Somerset

Exploring — Admire the beautiful spring blossom in our apple orchards.
— Buy a unique gift from the craft workshops.
— Explore the parkland with carved golden Hamstone waymarks.

Eating and shopping: enjoy freshly cooked vegetables straight from the garden (telephone to book table). Buy Barrington's own cider and apple juice in the shop, along with beautiful gifts. Visit the craft workshops at the farm buildings – with furniture, pottery, quilts and bags.

Making the most of your day: daily programme of activities, family trails, as well as popular annual events – including Jazz on the Lawn, Chutfest and Apple Day. **Dogs**: assistance dogs only in the gardens. Shaded parking available.

Access for all: 🅿️ 🚻 📶 ♿ 🔄 🖥️ 📖 ♿ ⓐ
Building 🔃 **Grounds** 🔃 ➡️ ♿ ♿

Getting here: 193:ST396182. In Barrington village, 5 miles north-east of Ilminster.
Foot: numerous public footpaths.
Cycle: NCN30. Cycle hire in Langport (01458 250350). **Bus**: service from Ilminster to Martock, with connections from Taunton.
Train: Crewkerne, 7 miles. **Road**: on B3168. Signposted from A358 (Ilminster to Taunton) or off A303 (London to Exeter).
Sat Nav: incorrectly directs visitors to rear entrance – please follow brown tourist signs.
Parking: free.

Finding out more: 01460 242614 (Infoline). 01460 241938 or barringtoncourt@nationaltrust.org.uk

Barrington Court		M	T	W	T	F	S	S
House								
1 Mar–4 Nov	10–4	M	T	W	T	F	S	S
Garden, parkland, Orchard Café and shop								
1 Mar–4 Nov	10–5	M	T	W	T	F	S	S
Strode House Restaurant								
1 Mar–4 Nov	12–5	M	T	W	T	F	S	S
House, garden, parkland, shop, Strode House Restaurant								
10 Nov–2 Dec	10–4	·	·	·	·	·	S	S

The opulent ballroom at Bath Assembly Rooms, Somerset

Bath Assembly Rooms

Bennett Street, Bath, Somerset BA1 2QH

Map ① J4   🏢 🔔 🍽️ 1931

The Assembly Rooms were at the heart of fashionable Georgian society. When completed in 1771, they were described as 'the most noble and elegant of any in the kingdom'. The Fashion Museum (Bath and North East Somerset Council) is on the lower ground floor and is free to Trust members. **Note**: limited visitor access during functions.

Exploring — Holiday activities for families, on a fashion theme.
— Enjoy the summer exhibition in the Ballroom.
— New museum displays and exhibitions, visit www.fashionmuseum.co.uk.
— For concerts and music festivals, visit www.bathfestivals.org.uk.

Eating and shopping: café open nearly every day: coffee, light lunch or tea. Browse the extensive gift shop and renowned fashion bookshop. Savour an ice-cream in the garden café this summer.

Making the most of your day: stop for coffee, browse in the bookshop and enjoy the latest fashion exhibition.

Access for all:
Building Grounds [Å]

Getting here: 156:ST749653. In centre of Bath. **Cycle**: NCN4, ¼ mile. **Bus**: from Bath Spa ☒ and surrounding areas. **Train**: Bath Spa ¾ mile. **Road**: north of Milsom Street, east of the Circus. **Parking**: pay and display car parks (not National Trust), nearest Charlotte Street. Virtually no onstreet parking, park and ride recommended.

Finding out more: 01225 477789 or bathassemblyrooms@nationaltrust.org.uk

Rustic cottages at Blaise Hamlet, Bristol

Bath Assembly Rooms		M	T	W	T	F	S	S
1 Jan–29 Feb	10:30–5	M	T	W	T	F	S	S
1 Mar–31 Oct	10:30–6	M	T	W	T	F	S	S
1 Nov–31 Dec	10:30–5	M	T	W	T	F	S	S

Last admission one hour before closing. Closed when in use for booked functions and on 25 and 26.December. Access to all rooms guaranteed in August until 4:30, at other times some rooms may be closed. Visitors should telephone in advance.

Blaise Hamlet

Henbury, Bristol BS10 7QY

Map (1) I3   🏠🏠 1943

A delightful hamlet of nine picturesque cottages, designed by John Nash in 1809 to accommodate Blaise Estate pensioners. **Note**: access to green only; cottages not open. No toilet.

Getting here: 172:ST559789. 4 miles north of central Bristol.

Finding out more: 01275 461900 or blaisehamlet@nationaltrust.org.uk

Bolberry Down

near Salcombe, Devon

Map (1) F9   1938

Dramatic clifftop with far-reaching views. Bolberry Down has levelled circular trails through a breathtaking coastal landscape. **Note**: no toilet. Hotel and inn (not National Trust).

Access for all: [Pₐ][♿]

Getting here: SX689383. Between Hope Cove and Salcombe. Take the A381 towards Salcombe and turn right at Malborough. Go through the village and look out for a right-hand turn signposted Bolberry. **Sat Nav**: use TQ7 3DY.

Finding out more: 01752 346585 or bolberrydown@nationaltrust.org.uk. The Stables, Saltram House, Plymouth, Devon PL7 1UH

Blaise Hamlet	Open every day all year

Bolberry Down	Open every day all year

Boscastle

Cornwall PL35 0HD

Map ① D7 🏊🏰🏠 1955

Much of the land in and around Boscastle is owned by the National Trust. This includes the cliffs of Penally Point and Willapark, which guard the sinuous harbour entrance, Forrabury Stitches, high above the village and divided into ancient 'stitchmeal' cultivation plots, as well as the lovely Valency Valley. **Note**: toilet by main car park (not National Trust).

Exploring   –   Wander through the village and down to the picturesque harbour.
       –   Stroll along the peaceful Valency Valley to Minster church.
       –   Follow the coast path and discover Forrabury church.
       –   Enjoy a challenging walk along the coast path to Tintagel.

Looking down on Boscastle harbour, Cornwall

Eating and shopping: browse in the shop and visitor centre by the lower harbour. Visit the adjoining café and enjoy the courtyard seating area.

Making the most of your day: children's quiz/trail. Look out for family events in school holidays. **Dogs**: welcome in café courtyard.

Access for all: 🚾♿♿ Grounds ♿

Getting here: 190:SX097914. 5 miles north of Camelford, 3 miles north-east of Tintagel. **Bus**: services from Bude and Wadebridge (connections at Wadebridge for Bodmin Parkway 🚆). **Train**: Bodmin Parkway. **Road**: on B3263. **Parking**: pay and display, 100 yards (not National Trust).

Finding out more: 01840 250353 or boscastle@nationaltrust.org.uk

Boscastle		M	T	W	T	F	S	S
Open all year		M	T	W	T	F	S	S
Shop, café and visitor centre								
1 Jan–25 Mar	10:30–4	M	T	W	T	F	S	S
26 Mar–4 Nov	10–5	M	T	W	T	F	S	S
5 Nov–24 Dec	10:30–4	M	T	W	T	F	S	S
27 Dec–31 Dec	10:30–4	M	·	·	T	F	S	S

Shop and visitor centre sometimes open later than 5 in high season.

Bradley

Newton Abbot, Devon TQ12 6BN

Map ① G8 🏠🌳🏊 1938

Unspoilt and fascinating medieval manor house, still a relaxed family home, in a green haven of riverside meadows and woodland. **Note**: no toilet, shop or refreshments. Parking from 10.

Access for all: 🅿♿🖥♿👓📷
Building ♿♿ Grounds ♿♿➡

Getting here: 202:SX848709. ½ mile from Newton Abbot town centre on A381. From Totnes, gate lodge is on left just past Ogwell roundabout.

Finding out more: 01803 661907 or bradley@nationaltrust.org.uk

Bradley		M	T	W	T	F	S	S
3 Apr–27 Sep	10:30–5	·	T	W	T	·	·	·

Branscombe: the Old Bakery, Manor Mill and Forge

Branscombe, Seaton, Devon EX12 3DB

Map (1) H7  1965

Nestling in a valley that reaches down to the sea, these thatched buildings date back more than 200 years. Visit the working forge and mill, then enjoy a traditional cream tea in the Old Bakery. Explore the beach or woodlands – there are plenty of paths to choose from. **Note**: toilets at bakery and village hall.

Exploring
– Visit the Old Forge and watch the blacksmith in action.
– Enjoy open fires and a bit of baking history.
– Discover the restored water-powered Manor Mill along the millstream.
– Find out about the history of this old seaside community.

Eating and shopping: quality ironwork on sale – candlestick holders to log burners. Delicious homemade soups, ploughman's and sandwiches served all day.

Making the most of your day: walking along an extensive network of paths is the perfect way to enjoy this area. **Dogs**: on leads in garden and information room of Old Bakery and wider countryside area.

Access for all: ♿ **Building** 🏢♿
Manor Mill 🏢 **Grounds** ♿

Getting here: 192:SY198887. 8 miles from Honiton. **Foot**: South West Coast Path within ¾ mile. **Cycle**: public bridleway from Great Seaside to Beer. **Bus**: services from Sidmouth and Seaton. **Train**: Honiton, 8 miles. **Road**: off A3052, signposted Branscombe. **Parking**: small car park next to Old Forge (donations welcome); car park next to village hall (not National Trust: donations).

Finding out more: 01752 346585 (South and East Devon Countryside Office). 01297 680333/680481 (Old Bakery Tea-room/Old Forge) or branscombe@nationaltrust.org.uk. South and East Devon Countryside Office, The Stables, Saltram House, Plymouth, Devon PL7 1UH

Branscombe		M	T	W	T	F	S	S
Open all year		M	T	W	T	F	S	S
Old Bakery								
28 Mar–29 Jul	10:30–5			W	T	F	S	S
30 Jul–2 Sep	10:30–5	M	T	W	T	F	S	S
5 Sep–4 Nov	10:30–5			W	T	F	S	S
Manor Mill								
1 Apr–24 Jun	2–5							S
1 Jul–2 Sep	2–5			W				S
9 Sep–4 Nov	2–5							S
Old Forge*								
Open all year	10–5	M	T	W	T	F	S	S

*Old Forge: telephone 01297 680481 to confirm opening times.

Brean Down

Brean, North Somerset

Map (1) H4 🏢 1954

One of the most striking landmarks of the Somerset coastline, Brean Down projects dramatically into the Bristol Channel and offers magnificent views for miles around with fascinating wildlife and history. Explore the amazing ruined fort at the end of the Down or relax on the beach. **Note**: steep climbs and cliffs. Tide comes in quickly.

Splendid isolation at Brean Down, Somerset

Exploring — Explore the gun magazines, open most weekend afternoons in summer.
— Visit our new welcome beach hut.
— Have an ice-cream on the beach.
— Watch the sun go down over the Bristol Channel.

Eating and shopping: tempt your taste buds at the Cove Café. Enjoy a delicious cooked breakfast after a morning walk or treat yourself to a mouth-watering burger and chips. Visit the shop for an ice-cream or some games to play on the beach.

Making the most of your day: download the circular walk from our website and take a stroll to uncover Brean Down's secrets. Fly your kite or take part in one of our fantastic events. **Dogs**: welcome on leads.

Access for all: 🚻 **Building** 🐾

Getting here: 182:ST290590. Between Weston-super-Mare and Burnham-on-Sea. **Bus**: Highbridge to Weston-super-Mare, alight Brean, 1¾ miles. **Train**: Highbridge 8½ miles. **Road**: 8 miles from exit 22 of M5. **Parking**: 200 yards, at Cove Café at the bottom of Brean Down.

Finding out more: 01643 862452 or breandown@nationaltrust.org.uk

Brean Down		M	T	W	T	F	S	S
Countryside								
Open all year		M	T	W	T	F	S	S
Café and shop								
17 Mar–4 Nov	10–5	M	T	W	T	F	S	S
10 Nov–16 Dec	10–4	.	.	.	.	.	S	S
22 Dec–31 Dec	10–4	M	T	W	T	F	S	S

Café and shop opening hours vary according to weather. Closed 25 December.

Brownsea Island

Poole Harbour, Poole, Dorset BH13 7EE

Map ① K7 ✚ 🚻 ♿ 🏞 ♿ 🏠 | 1962

Brownsea Island is dramatically located in Poole Harbour, with spectacular views across to the Purbeck Hills. Thriving natural habitats – including woodland, heathland and a lagoon – create a haven for wildlife, such as the rare red squirrel and a wide variety of birds. Visitors will be fascinated by the island's rich history, for as well as boasting daffodil farming and pottery works, it was the birthplace of the Scouting and Guiding movement. So whether you love wildlife or just want to escape from the stresses of modern life, Brownsea is the perfect place to explore and enjoy throughout the year. **Note**: Dorset Wildlife Trust Nature Reserve subject to small entry fee. No public access to castle.

Exploring — Get wild about wildlife with a family Tracker Pack.
— Visit the Outdoor Centre and Scout stone.
— Look out for pottery remains on the seashore.
— Enjoy peace, tranquillity and breathtaking coastal views.
— Watch avocets, terns and godwits on the lagoon.
— Find out more about Brownsea Island in the Visitor Centre.

Eating and shopping: enjoy stunning views and delicious food in the Villano Café. Browse in the shop for Brownsea Island gifts and red squirrel souvenirs. Discover our new outdoors range, including outdoor clothing and binoculars. The shop also features old-fashioned sweets and ice-creams.

Making the most of your day: seasonal family activities and trails. Wildlife walks and talks. Brownsea open-air theatre. Daily introductory walks and guided tours for less mobile visitors (bookable).

View from the café on Brownsea Island, Dorset

Dogs: assistance dogs only, as island is a nature reserve.

Access for all: ♿ 🚻 📷 🅿 Ⓐ
Building ♿ 🦽 Grounds ♿ ➡ 🦽

Getting here: 195:SZ032878. In Poole Harbour, access by ferry. **Foot**: close to start/end of South West Coast Path at Shell Bay. **Ferry**: half-hourly boat service (not National Trust) from 10, departing Poole Quay (01202 631828/01929 462383) and Sandbanks (01929 462383). Wheelchair users: contact ferry operators. **Bus**: for Sandbanks: services from Bournemouth, Swanage and Poole. For Poole Quay: alight Poole Bridge. **Train**: Poole ½ mile to Poole Quay; Branksome or Parkstone 3½ miles to Sandbanks.

Finding out more: 01202 707744 or brownseaisland@nationaltrust.org.uk

Buckland Abbey, Garden and Estate, Devon

Brownsea Island	M	T	W	T	F	S	S
Boats from Sandbanks Jetty only							
11 Feb–18 Mar 10–4	·	·	·	·	·	S	S
Full boat service from Poole Quay and Sandbanks							
24 Mar–4 Nov 10–5	M	T	W	T	F	S	S
Booked organised youth, adult and community groups							
5 Nov–23 Dec 10–4	M	T	W	T	F	S	S

Shop and Villano Café open until last boat.

Buckland Abbey, Garden and Estate

Yelverton, Devon PL20 6EY

Map ① E8   🏠 🦇 ✛ ✿ ⚜ ☂ [1948]

'Wonderfully enjoyable, exceptionally informative, outstandingly friendly.'
Mrs Haydon, Delabole, Cornwall

Step into a tranquil valley, first chosen by Cistercian monks as a base from which to worship, farm their estate and trade. The Abbey was converted into a house by Sir Richard Grenville and later lived in by Sir Francis Drake. What you see now is part-museum and part-home. Outdoors, discover our newly acquired gem, the Cider House Garden, including a walled kitchen garden, open for the first time

this year. Visit community growing areas and the impressive Great Barn. Enjoy woodland and riverside walks with far-reaching views, orchards and late spring bluebells. **Note**: the Abbey interior is presented in association with Plymouth City Museum.

Exploring
 – Explore the newly acquired Cider House Garden.
 – Enjoy the peaceful estate on one of our walks.
 – Discover 700 years of history and change in the Abbey.
 – Take up the challenge of our letterbox trail!
 – See the famous Drake's Drum and learn the legend.
 – Full programme of events, from concerts to living history.

Eating and shopping: 14th-century Refectory Restaurant serving freshly cooked local produce. Enjoy your picnic in the beautiful grounds. Browse for that special gift or plant in our shop. Restaurant available to hire for private functions.

Making the most of your day: events include guided walks, in-depth tours, living history, music and family fun throughout the year. Christmas event in December. **Dogs**: for conservation and wildlife reasons, only assistance dogs allowed.

Access for all: 🅿️♿🚻🚹🅿️🔤🖼️🚹🔵🅰️
Abbey 🚻🏛️♿ **Reception, shop, restaurant** 🏛️♿
Garden and estate 🚻🏛️➡️♿

Getting here: 201:SX487667. 6 miles south of Tavistock, 11 miles north of Plymouth. **Cycle:** Drake's Trail, NCN27, 2 miles. **Bus:** from Yelverton (with connections from Plymouth 🚂), Monday to Saturday. **Train:** Plymouth 11 miles. **Road:** turn off A386, ¼ mile south of Yelverton. **Parking:** free, 150 yards.

Finding out more: 01822 853607 or bucklandabbey@nationaltrust.org.uk

Buckland Abbey		M	T	W	T	F	S	S
11 Feb–19 Feb	11–4:30	M	T	W	T	F	S	S
24 Feb–4 Mar	11–4:30	·	·	·	·	F	S	S
9 Mar–4 Nov	10:30–5:30	M	T	W	T	F	S	S
9 Nov–2 Dec	11–4:30	·	·	·	·	F	S	S
7 Dec–23 Dec	11–4:30	M	T	W	T	F	S	S

Carnewas and Bedruthan Steps

Bedruthan, near Padstow, Cornwall PL27 7UW

Map ① C8 🏛️ 1930

This is one of the most popular destinations on the Cornish coast. Spectacular clifftop views stretch across Bedruthan beach (not National Trust). The Trust has rebuilt the steep cliff staircase to the beach, but visitors need to be aware of the risk of being cut off by the tide. **Note:** it is unsafe to bathe at any time. Toilet not always available.

Exploring
- Enjoy magnificent walks along the coast path towards Park Head.
- Discover more in *Coast of Cornwall* leaflet, available in shop.

Eating and shopping: browse in the National Trust shop. Treat yourself in the popular café (National Trust-approved concession). Relax in the clifftop tea garden, adjoining the café.

Making the most of your day: children's quiz/trail, walks leaflet and information panel. Simple play area adjacent to a spot perfect for picnics. **Dogs:** allowed.

Access for all: 🅿️♿🚻🚹🅰️
Car park and clifftop 🏛️➡️

Getting here: 200:SW849692. 6 miles southwest of Padstow. **Foot:** ¾ mile of South West Coast Path runs through this site. **Bus:** Newquay to Padstow. **Train:** Newquay 7 miles. **Road:** just off B3276 from Newquay to Padstow. **Parking:** seasonal charge for non-members.

Finding out more: 01637 860563 or carnewas@nationaltrust.org.uk. Bedruthan, St Eval, Wadebridge, Cornwall PL27 7UW

Carnewas and Bedruthan Steps		M	T	W	T	F	S	S
Clifftop walks								
Open all year		M	T	W	T	F	S	S
Shop								
11 Feb–26 Feb	10:30–3:30	M	T	W	T	F	S	S
3 Mar–4 Mar	10:30–3:30	·	·	·	·	·	S	S
10 Mar–4 Nov	10:30–5	M	T	W	T	F	S	S
Café								
11 Feb–15 Apr	11–4	M	T	W	T	F	S	S
16 Apr–4 Nov	10:30–5	M	T	W	T	F	S	S
10 Nov–16 Dec	11–4	·	·	·	·	·	S	S
26 Dec–31 Dec	11–4	M	·	W	T	F	S	S

Cliff staircase closed from 1 November to 1 March. Telephone 01637 860701 to confirm café opening times in winter. Shop may open earlier in summer.

Castle Drogo

Drewsteignton, near Exeter, Devon EX6 6PB

Map ① F7 🏛️✝️🌀♿🏠🍴 1974

Inside this remarkable granite building, set above the Teign Gorge, is a surprisingly warm and comfortable family home. Commissioned by retail tycoon Julius Drewe, and designed by Sir Edwin Lutyens, the castle harks back to a romantic past, while its brilliant design heralds the modern era. Behind the imposing façade, poignant family keepsakes sit alongside 17th-century tapestries. The dramatic Dartmoor setting can be appreciated from the delightful formal garden and walks through the

Castle Drogo, Devon: looking west towards the wilds of Dartmoor

Teign Gorge. Tours and activities are arranged throughout the year. Our visitor centre, shop and café are open all year round.

Exploring — Within the austere granite castle, discover unexpected family comforts.
— Explore the Arts and Crafts-inspired garden.
— Enjoy the estate's changing landscapes, from moorland to woodland.
— Explore the Dartmoor orchard and wildflower meadow area.
— Follow in Mr Drewe's footsteps along the gorge edge.
— Discover Drogo's dramatic battle for survival.

Eating and shopping: café with open-air seating, public Wi-fi and play area (available for functions and parties). Try delicious Drogo breakfasts from 8:30 every morning (July to September) or roast lunches on Sundays. Shop sells local products and plants inspired by Drogo garden.

Making the most of your day: waymarked walks through the garden and surrounding countryside. Quizzes and trails. Play croquet on dry summer days. Events throughout the year. Enjoy a guided tour or activity, available

most days. **Dogs**: welcome on leads throughout the countryside and informal garden areas.

Access for all: 🅿️🐕♿🚾♿🔤📷🎒:📷
Building ♿♿♿ **Grounds** ♿♿♿➡️

Getting here: 191:SX721900. On Dartmoor: extreme weather may be experienced.
Foot: Two Moors Way. **Bus**: Exeter to Moretonhampstead (passing Exeter Central ➡️) Monday to Saturday. **Train**: Yeoford 8 miles. **Road**: 5 miles south of A30. Take A382 Whiddon Down to Moretonhampstead road; turn off at Sandy Park. Approach lanes narrow with tight corners. **Parking**: free, 400 yards.

Finding out more: 01647 433306 or castledrogo@nationaltrust.org.uk

Castle Drogo		M	T	W	T	F	S	S
Visitor centre, café, shop and garden*								
1 Jan–9 Mar	11–4	M	T	W	T	F	S	S
10 Mar–4 Nov	9–5:30	M	T	W	T	F	S	S
5 Nov–31 Dec	11–4	M	T	W	T	F	S	S
Castle								
11 Feb–19 Feb	11–4	M	T	W	T	F	S	S
25 Feb–4 Mar	11–4	·	·	·	·	·	S	S
10 Mar–4 Nov	11–5	M	T	W	T	F	S	S
10 Nov–23 Dec	11–4	·	·	·	·	·	S	S

Café: July to September opens 8:30. *Garden: closes dusk if earlier. Whole property closed 24 to 26 December.

Cheddar Gorge

The Cliffs, Cheddar, Somerset

Map ① I4   🏠🚻 1910

One of England's most iconic landscapes.
Take in the dramatic views and find out
more from the information centre/shop.
Note: downloadable walks available from
website and shop. Caves and car parks
privately owned, charge (including members).

Getting here: ST468543. 8 miles north-west of
Wells, signposted off the M5, A371 Axbridge to
Wells road and A38 Burnham to Bristol road.

Finding out more: 01643 862452 or
cheddargorge@nationaltrust.org.uk

Cheddar Gorge		M	T	W	T	F	S	S
Cliffs								
Open all year		M	T	W	T	F	S	S
Information centre and shop								
17 Mar–22 Jul	11–5	M	T	W		F	S	S
23 Jul–1 Sep	11–5	M	T	W	T	F	S	S
2 Sep–4 Nov	11–5	M	T	W		F	S	S

Information Centre and shop open Bank Holidays. Opening
times vary according to weather.

The dramatic Cheddar Gorge in Somerset

Chedworth Roman Villa

Yanworth, near Cheltenham,
Gloucestershire GL54 3LJ

Map ① K2   🏛 1924

'**Fantastic, very interesting, very well
documented. Extremely kind and helpful
staff, and amazing activities for children.
Thank you!**'
The Carré family, London

Unveiled this year, the extraordinary relics
of one of the country's largest Roman villas
reopen following a major project to bring to
life the golden age of Roman Britain.
Enjoy the fantastic new building, providing
all-weather access to the distinctive mosaics.
This wonderfully immersive experience will
transport you back to Roman times. The wider
site offers a tranquil setting where you can
explore outstanding Roman design features.
Also discover how the Victorians shaped the
site and see artefacts from past excavations
in the museum's new exhibition. This year the
visitor reception building offers a new café and
retail experience.

Exploring
- Discover some of the most spectacular mosaics in Britain.
- Explore fantastic examples of underfloor heating, bathhouses and latrines.
- Enjoy stunning Cotswold scenery and wonderful wildlife.
- Indulge in a decadent cake in our new café.
- Learn our Victorian story in the museum.
- Explore the villa with our family Tracker Packs.

Eating and shopping: our new café provides
indoor and outdoor seating with a selection of
light lunches, cakes, hot drinks and ice-creams.
The shop offers a range of Roman-themed
gifts, plus a unique selection of Roman and
archaeological books and seasonal plants.

Mosaic at Chedworth Roman Villa, Gloucestershire

Making the most of your day: see demonstrations of authentic Roman crafts. New audio guide and interpretation. Romano-British costumed interpreters on certain days throughout the season. Children's drop-in mosaic-making sessions, trails and quizzes during school holidays. **Dogs**: assistance dogs only.

Access for all: ⬚⬚⬚⬚⬚⬚
Reception, shop, café ⬚⬚⬚
West Range, museum ⬚⬚⬚ Grounds ⬚⬚

Getting here: 163:SP053135. 3 miles north-west of Fossebridge. **Foot**: on the 'Monarch's Way'. **Train**: Cheltenham Spa 14 miles. **Road**: on Cirencester to Northleach road (A429); approach from A429 via Yanworth, or from A436 via Withington. **Parking**: 15 yards from entrance. Overflow car park (April to September), 250 yards from entrance.

Finding out more: 01242 890256 or chedworth@nationaltrust.org.uk

Chedworth Roman Villa		M	T	W	T	F	S	S
4 Mar–24 Mar	10–4	M	T	W	T	F	S	S
25 Mar–27 Oct	10–5	M	T	W	T	F	S	S
28 Oct–2 Dec	10–4	M	T	W	T	F	S	S

The Church House

Widecombe-in-the-Moor, Newton Abbot, Devon TQ13 7TA

Map ① F7 🏠 1933

One of the finest examples of a 16th-century Church House, originally used for parish festivities or 'ales'. **Note**: used by the local community. Please check with National Trust shop next door to see if you can visit. No toilet.

Access for all: ⬚⬚⬚
Church House ⬚⬚ Shop ⬚⬚

Getting here: 191:SX718768. In centre of Widecombe, north of Ashburton, west of Bovey Tracey. On B3387 about 12 miles from A38, Bovey Tracey.

Finding out more: 01364 621321 or churchhouse@nationaltrust.org.uk

The Church House		M	T	W	T	F	S	S
Shop/information centre								
9 Feb–23 Dec	10:30–4	M	T	W	T	F	S	S

The Church House is open to visitors when not in use by the local community; telephone or ask at the shop for opening times. Opening and closing times dependent on weather conditions in winter.

Clevedon Court

Tickenham Road, Clevedon, North Somerset BS21 6QU

Map ① I4 🏠✿ 1961

Home to the lords of the manor of Clevedon for centuries, the core of the house is a remarkable survival from the medieval period. The house was bought by Abraham Elton in 1709 and it is still the much-loved family home of his descendants today. **Note**: the Elton family opens and manages Clevedon Court for the National Trust.

Light streams through the colourful stained glass in the chapel at Clevedon Court, Somerset

Exploring – Be delighted by the fascinating collection of Nailsea glass.
– Look at the wonderful collection of family portraits.
– Explore the delightful terraced garden.

Eating and shopping: quench your thirst at the National Trust tea kiosk.

Making the most of your day: family guide and children's quiz/trail.

Access for all: [icons] Building [icon] Grounds [icon]

Getting here: 172:ST423716. 1½ miles east of Clevedon. **Bus**: services from Clevedon to Bristol, and Yatton to Clevedon. **Train**: Yatton 3 miles. **Road**: on Bristol road (B3130), signposted from M5 exit 20. **Parking**: free, 50 yards. Unsuitable for trailer caravans or motor caravans. Alternative parking 100 yards east of entrance in cul-de-sac.

Finding out more: 01275 872257 or clevedoncourt@nationaltrust.org.uk

Clevedon Court		M	T	W	T	F	S	S
1 Apr–30 Sep	2–5	·	·	**W**	**T**	·	·	**S**

Car park open 1:15. House entry by timed ticket, not bookable. Open Bank Holiday Mondays.

Clouds Hill

Wareham, Dorset BH20 7NQ

Map (1) J7 [icon] 1937

This tiny isolated brick and tile cottage in the heart of Dorset was the peaceful retreat of T. E. Lawrence ('Lawrence of Arabia'). The austere rooms are much as he left them and reflect his complex personality and close links with the Middle East, as detailed in a fascinating exhibition. **Note**: no toilet.

Exploring – 'Lawrence Trail', three-mile circular walk, organised by Purbeck Council.
– Follow the trail to a perfect hilltop picnic spot.

Eating and shopping: the small shop features Lawrence memorabilia and books.

Making the most of your day: visit www. purbeck.gov.uk for information on 'Lawrence Trail'. **Dogs**: in the grounds on leads only.

Access for all: [icon] Building [icon] Grounds [icon]

Clouds Hill, Dorset: T. E. Lawrence's tiny retreat

Getting here: 194:SY824909. 9 miles east of Dorchester. **Train**: Wool 3½ miles; Moreton 3½ miles. **Road**: 1 mile north of Bovington Tank Museum, 9 miles east of Dorchester, 1½ miles east of Waddock crossroads (B3390), 4 miles south of A35 Poole to Dorchester. **Parking**: free in small car park.

Finding out more: 01929 405616 or cloudshill@nationaltrust.org.uk

Clouds Hill		M	T	W	T	F	S	S
14 Mar–31 Oct	11–5	·	·	**W**	**T**	**F**	**S**	**S**

Open Bank Holiday Mondays. Closes at dusk if earlier (no electric light).

Coleridge Cottage

35 Lime Street, Nether Stowey, Bridgwater, Somerset TA5 1NQ

Map ① H5   1909

Discover the former home of Romantic poet Samuel Taylor Coleridge and the place where he wrote *The Rime of the Ancient Mariner*. Following a major re-presentation project, some rooms are now dressed as they might have looked when Coleridge lived there. The garden is also open for the first time. **Note**: managed by Dunster Castle.

Exploring — Write poetry with a quill and ink in the cottage.
— Visit the garden and sit in the Lime Tree Bower.

Exploring — Enjoy tea and a delicious slice of cake.
— See our shop and its Coleridge range of souvenirs.

Eating and shopping: relax and enjoy a cup of tea and a slice of cake in the covered courtyard. Visit our shop for interesting and unusual gifts that reflect the life and work of Samuel Taylor Coleridge.

Making the most of your day: children's trail for cottage. Displays and poetry books in reading room. New information panels.

Access for all: ♿ 🅿 📶 ⦙⦙ 🅰
Building ♿ Garden ♿

Getting here: 181:ST191399. 8 miles west of Bridgwater. **Bus**: Bridgwater to Williton (passing close Bridgwater ≢). **Train**: Bridgwater 8 miles. **Road**: Lime Street, opposite Ancient Mariner pub. **Parking**: pub car park opposite, or village car park, 500 yards (neither National Trust).

Finding out more: 01278 732662 (Infoline). 01643 821314 or coleridgecottage@nationaltrust.org.uk

Coleridge Cottage		M	T	W	T	F	S	S
10 Mar–4 Nov	11–5	**M**	·	·	**T**	**F**	**S**	**S**

Desk and quills at Coleridge Cottage, Somerset

Coleton Fishacre

Brownstone Road, Kingswear, Devon TQ6 0EQ

Map ① G9 🏠🌸🏛🏠 | 1982 |

'I am lost for words, just wonderful!
Beautifully restored and such a fabulous
authentic feel, an absolute gem.'
Mrs Smith, Plymouth

Travel back in time to the Jazz Age in this
evocative country home of the D'Oyly Carte
family. Enjoy the 1920s' elegance of the Arts
and Crafts style, and glimpse life behind the
servants' doors. Experience the Savoy Theatre,
Hotel and Gilbert and Sullivan connections
through music playing in the Saloon. Inspiring
views add to the light, joyful atmosphere
in which you can lose yourself. Paths weave
through glades, past tranquil ponds and rare
tender plants from New Zealand and South
Africa. **Note:** narrow approach lane requires
some reversing at busy times (especially
between 1 and 2:30).

Coleton Fishacre, Devon: D'Oyly Carte's holiday home

Exploring
- Soak up the gorgeous Art Deco style in the house.
- Play the Blüthner piano in the Saloon.
- Explore the network of pathways through the valley garden.

Exploring
- Relax by the ponds or in the gazebo.
- Walk the coast path, parking at Coleton Camp or Brownstone.
- Seemly Hut open, with garden and Pudcombe Cove information.

Eating and shopping: we specialise in local
produce and products. Enjoy Café Coleton,
our licensed jazz tea-room serving delicious
home-cooked food. Visit our Deco-inspired
shop for china, music and gifts, plants and
garden furniture.

Making the most of your day: enjoy
ice-cream floats on the bowling green lawn
on hot, summer days or a daily guided garden
walk. Family quizzes and trails. Jazz, lecture
lunches and conservation master classes.
Dogs: welcome on leads around the dog route
in the garden (map in reception).

Access for all: 🅿️♿🚻♿♿♿🎧📷♿ 😊
Building 🔥♿♿ Grounds ♿➡️♿

Lady Dorothy's Saloon at Coleton Fishacre, Devon

Places may occasionally close for conservation, safety or events

Getting here: 202:SX910508. 3 miles from Kingswear. **Foot**: South West Coast Path within ¾ mile. **Bus**: services from Paignton or Brixham to Kingswear: alight ¾ mile south-west of Hillhead, 1½ miles walk to garden. **Train**: Paignton 8 miles; Kingswear (Dartmouth Steam Railway and Riverboat Company) 2¼ miles by footpath, 2¾ miles by road. **Road**: 3 miles from Kingswear: take Lower Ferry road, turn right at toll house. 6 miles from Brixham, take A3022 to Kingswear, turn left at toll house. **Parking**: for visitors to house and garden only.

Finding out more: 01803 842382 or coletonfishacre@nationaltrust.org.uk

Coleton Fishacre		M	T	W	T	F	S	S
3 Mar–28 Mar	10:30–5	M	T	W	·	·	S	S
31 Mar–26 Sep	10:30–5	M	T	W	T	·	S	S
29 Sep–31 Oct	10:30–5	M	T	W	·	·	S	S
3 Nov–23 Dec	11–4	M	·	·	·	·	S	S

Open Good Friday.

Compton Castle

Marldon, Paignton, Devon TQ3 1TA

Map ① G8 🖼️➕💠🏠 **1951**

A rare survivor, this medieval fortress with high curtain walls, towers and two portcullis gates, set in a landscape of rolling hills and orchards, is a bewitching mixture of romance and history. Home for nearly 600 years to the Gilbert family, including Sir Humphrey Gilbert, half-brother to Sir Walter Ralegh. **Note**: credit cards not accepted. Few rooms open. Restricted access for those with limited mobility.

Exploring   –   Feed your imagination among machicolations, spiral staircases and squints.
        –   Discover Sir Humphrey Gilbert, Elizabethan adventurer and explorer.
        –   Enjoy the lovely rose, knot and herb gardens.

Eating and shopping: refreshments available at Castle Barton restaurant (not National Trust). Table-top shop selling souvenirs, guidebooks, postcards and local produce. Seasonal plants for sale.

Making the most of your day: house, squirrel and garden trails. Walks with the gardener throughout the season and on National Gardens Scheme garden day. **Dogs**: assistance dogs only.

Access for all: 🅿️🗑️🖵🖊️🔅
Building 🖭🖰 Grounds 🖭🖰

Getting here: 202:SX865648. At Compton, 5 miles west of Torquay. **Bus**: Marldon to Paignton ☷; Dartmouth to Torquay (passing Totnes ☷), on both alight Marldon, 1½ miles. **Train**: Torquay 3 miles. Newton Abbot 6 miles. **Road**: 1½ miles north of Marldon. Signposted off A380 to Marldon or turn south from A381 Totnes road at Ipplepen – 2 miles to Compton. **Parking**: free, 30 yards. Additional parking at Castle Barton opposite entrance, 100 yards.

Finding out more: 01803 661906 or comptoncastle@nationaltrust.org.uk

Compton Castle		M	T	W	T	F	S	S
3 Apr–31 Oct	10:30–5	·	T	W	T	·	·	·

Open Bank Holiday Mondays: 9 April, 7 May, 4 June and 27 August.

The north front of Compton Castle, Devon

The romantic ruins of Corfe Castle, Dorset

Corfe Castle

The Square, Corfe Castle, Wareham,
Dorset BH20 5EZ

Map ① K7   1982

Enjoy one of Britain's most iconic and evocative
survivors of the English Civil War, partially
demolished in 1646 by the Parliamentarians.
A favourite haunt for adults and children
alike, you can't fail to be captivated by these
romantic castle ruins with breathtaking views
across Purbeck. Discover 1,000 years of our
history as a royal palace and fortress. With
fallen walls and secret places, there are tales
of treachery and treason around every corner.
Spot the 'murder holes' and count the arrow
loops. Feel history come to life and see the
wildlife that has set up home here. **Note**: steep,
uneven slopes, steps, sudden drops. All/parts
of castle may close in high winds.

Exploring
 – See our 'trebuchet' in action, a
   replica medieval siege engine.
 – Try on costumes and
   pose with helmets, shields
   and swords.
 – See conservation in action,
   ensuring the castle lives
   on forever.
 – Guided tours are often
   available during the
   main season.

Exploring
 – Try a downloadable trail
   around the surrounding
   Purbeck countryside.
 – Visit the pretty village, with
   its medieval church tower.

Eating and shopping: indulge in a homemade
Dorset cream tea in our 18th-century tea-room.
Enjoy the summer garden with unrivalled castle
views. In the village square, our shop offers a
range of products from pocket-money treats
to luxury locally made gifts.

Making the most of your day: events
throughout the year including living history,
open-air theatre and cinema, jester days and
family trails. Adventure across the Purbeck
countryside and explore glorious natural
coastline at Studland Beach. **Dogs**: welcome
on a short lead.

Access for all: 🅿️ ♿ 🚻 👜 🛗 📷 🏛️ 🚹 👓 🅰️
Grounds ♿ 🏔️

Getting here: 195:SY959824. In Corfe.
Bus: Poole to Swanage (passing Wareham
🚂). **Train**: Wareham 4½ miles. Corfe Castle
(Swanage Steam Railway) a few minutes walk
(park and ride from Norden station). **Road**: on
A351 Wareham to Swanage road. **Parking**: pay
and display at foot of castle, off A351 (800
yards walk uphill). Norden park and ride (all-
day parking, ½ mile walk) and West Street in
village (pay and display), neither National Trust.

Finding out more: 01929 481294 (ticket office).
01929 480921 (shop).
01929 481332 (tea-rooms) or
corfecastle@nationaltrust.org.uk

Corfe Castle		M	T	W	T	F	S	S
Castle, shop and tea-room								
1 Jan–29 Feb	10–4	M	T	W	T	F	S	S
1 Mar–31 Mar	10–5	M	T	W	T	F	S	S
1 Apr–30 Sep	10–6	M	T	W	T	F	S	S
1 Oct–31 Oct	10–5	M	T	W	T	F	S	S
1 Nov–31 Dec	10–4	M	T	W	T	F	S	S

Tea-room: closed for refurbishment 3 to 13 January.
Shop and tea-room: close 5:30 April to September.
Whole property closed 25 and 26 December, plus one
day in March (visit website for details). For extended
member opening hours, visit website.

Cornish Mines and Engines

See East Pool Mine, page 46.

Time seems to have stood still at Cotehele, Cornwall

Cotehele

St Dominick, near Saltash, Cornwall PL12 6TA

Map E8

'**What a fantastic place, so much to see and
do. The children loved the join-in activities.**'
The Clark family, Malmesbury

Cotehele's medieval origins provided a
perfect setting for the Edgcumbes to show
off their ancestral home to guests, such as
King George III in 1789. The interior tour has
changed little, although the furnishings were
titivated as Cotehele continued to inspire its
adoring owners. From early spring flowers, to
herbaceous borders in high season, to the
orchards in the autumn: there is something for
everyone all the year around in the garden.
The sailing barge *Shamrock* is moored at the
quay, where the Discovery Centre tells the
gripping story of the Tamar Valley, offering a
gateway to the wider estate.

Exploring – New this year: discover the Edgcumbes, their servants and tenants.
– 'CSI Friday': bring torch to view house in the dark.
– Savour the tranquillity of the Valley Garden and 16th-century dovecote.
– Nose around the cider press building in the Mother Orchard.
– Board *Shamrock*, the 1899 sailing barge. Sundays on the quay.
– Immerse yourself in Cotehele's extensive countryside on four highlighted walks.

Eating and shopping: buy Cornish food, gifts and local plants in our shop. Enjoy local produce in the Barn Restaurant and The Edgcumbe on Cotehele Quay. Browse through the exquisite arts and crafts in Cotehele Gallery. Stay in one of nine holiday cottages.

Making the most of your day: come early as exploring Cotehele will take a full day, packed with things to see and do. **Dogs**: welcome on the estate (assistance dogs only in the formal garden).

Access for all: 🄿 🄳 ♿ 🚼 ♿ 🄰 📷 🄰
👁🄰 **Building** ♿🅰️🅱️ **Grounds** ♿🅰️➡️

Getting here: 201:SX422685. On west bank of the Tamar, 1 mile west of Calstock.
Foot: 1½-mile riverside walk from Calstock.
Ferry: Calstock can be reached from Plymouth (contact Plymouth Boat Cruises Ltd 01752 822797). **Bus**: local daily service (01822 834571 for details). **Train**: Calstock, 1½-mile riverside walk (signposted from station). **Road**: 8 miles from Tavistock, 14 miles from Plymouth via Tamar Bridge. **Parking**: free.

Finding out more: 01579 351346. 01579 352711 (restaurant). 01579 352717 (Edgcumbe) or cotehele@nationaltrust.org.uk

Cotehele		M	T	W	T	F	S	S
House								
10 Mar–4 Nov	11–4	M	T	W	T		S	S
Hall of house and garland								
19 Nov–31 Dec	11–4	M	T	W	T	F	S	S
Garden and estate								
2 Jan–31 Dec	Dawn–dusk	M	T	W	T	F	S	S
Barn Restaurant, shop, plant sales and gallery								
11 Feb–9 Mar	11–4	M	T	W	T	F	S	S
10 Mar–4 Nov	11–5	M	T	W	T	F	S	S
5 Nov–31 Dec	11–4	M	T	W	T	F	S	S
The Edgcumbe								
7 Jan–9 Mar	11–4	M	T	W	T	F	S	S
10 Mar–4 Nov	11–5	M	T	W	T	F	S	S
5 Nov–31 Dec	11–4	M	T	W	T	F	S	S

House open Good Friday and special CSI-Friday openings 30 March and August (bring a torch). Barn Restaurant opens 10:30, 10 March to 4 November. Hall of house, The Edgcumbe, Barn Restaurant, shop and gallery closed on 25 and 26 December. Telephone for details of evening opening at The Edgcumbe.

Cotehele Mill

St Dominick, near Saltash, Cornwall PL12 6TA

Map ① E8   🏠🖼️🚽🔧🏠 1947

This working mill is an atmospheric reminder of the recent past when corn was ground here for the local community. A range of outbuildings includes a traditional chairmaker and a pottery, along with re-creations of wheelwrights', saddlers' and blacksmiths' workshops. **Note**: no toilets or parking (park at Cotehele Quay).

Exploring – Watch the watermill grind flour (Tuesdays and Thursdays).
– Learn how we make our own electricity using water power.
– Look out for the bakery demonstrations in the bakery.
– Stay in one of the mill's two holiday cottages.

The working waterwheel at Cotehele Mill, Cornwall

Imaginative planting and organically shaped topiary on the Yew Walk at The Courts Garden, Wiltshire

Eating and shopping: buy Cotehele flour, apple juice and gifts from our new retail outlet. A short walk to Cotehele Quay for a Cornish pasty or ice-cream is a must.

Making the most of your day: tours every day at 3. Family trails. **Dogs**: welcome, but assistance dogs only in the workshops.

Access for all: [Dj] [WC] [□] [Jl]
Building [≜] Grounds [♿]

Getting here: 201:SX417682. On west bank of the Tamar, 1 mile west of Calstock. **Ferry**: Calstock can be reached from Plymouth (contact Plymouth Boat Cruises Ltd 01752 822797). **Bus**: local daily service to Cotehele reception (01822 834571 for details). **Train**: Calstock, 2 miles. 1½-mile riverside walk to Cothele (signposted from station). **Road**: 8 miles from Tavistock, 14 miles from Plymouth. **Parking**: no parking, except by arrangement.

Finding out more: 01579 350606. 01579 351346 (property office) or cotehele@nationaltrust.org.uk

Cotehele Mill		M	T	W	T	F	S	S
10 Mar–30 Sep	11–5	M	T	W	T	F	S	S
1 Oct–4 Nov	11–4:30	M	T	W	T	F	S	S

The Courts Garden

Holt, near Bradford on Avon, Wiltshire BA14 6RR

Map ①J4   [1943]

Full of variety, this charming garden shows the English country style at its best. Peaceful water gardens and herbaceous borders, with organically shaped topiary, demonstrate an imaginative use of colour and planting, creating unexpected vistas. Stroll through the arboretum with its wonderful species of trees and naturally planted spring bulbs.

Exploring
– Relax in our tranquil garden, with topiary and colourful borders.
– See our productive small vegetable garden and orchard.
– Explore the arboretum with naturalised bulbs.
– See how the garden transforms with the changing seasons.

Eating and shopping: tea-room serving coffee, lunches and afternoon tea (not National Trust). Plants for sale, some grown here. Discover our new gallery shop 'trust' located in the Glove Factory Studios (not National Trust), next to the village hall car park.

Making the most of your day: events programme, guided tours (booking essential) and children's trail. Cross-country walk to Great Chalfield Manor and Garden (please check open days and times). **Dogs**: assistance dogs only.

Access for all:
Garden

Getting here: 173:ST861618. In centre Holt. **Cycle**: NCN254, 1¼ miles. **Bus**: Trowbridge to Melksham (passing close Trowbridge ≊). **Train**: Bradford on Avon 2½ miles; Trowbridge 3 miles. **Road**: 3 miles south-west of Melksham, 2½ miles east of Bradford on Avon, on south side of B3107. Follow signs to Holt. **Parking**: free (not National Trust), 80 yards, in village hall car park opposite, on B3107. Additional parking, when signed, at Tollgate Inn and Manor Farm, on B3107 towards Bath. No visitor parking on village streets.

Finding out more: 01225 782875 or courtsgarden@nationaltrust.org.uk

The Courts Garden		M	T	W	T	F	S	S
Garden and tea-room								
4 Feb–4 Mar	11–5:30	·	·	·	·	·	S	S
5 Mar–4 Nov	11–5:30	M	T	·	T	F	S	S
Shop: 'trust' at the Glove Factory Studios*								
7 Jan–4 Mar	11–4	·	·	·	·	·	S	S
5 Mar–4 Nov	11–5:30	M	T	W	T	F	S	S
5 Nov–24 Dec	11–4	M	T	W	T	F	S	S

Out of season by appointment only. *'trust' shop approximately 150 yards from the garden entrance.

Crickley Hill

Birdlip, Gloucestershire

Map ① K2   ≊ | 1935 |

Crickley Hill sits high on the Cotswold escarpment overlooking Gloucester and Cheltenham with far-reaching views toward the Welsh hills. **Note**: partly owned and managed by Gloucestershire County Council. Parking charges apply to all visitors, including members.

Access for all:

Getting here: 179:SO930165. 3½ miles from Gloucester; 2½ miles from Cheltenham on A417.

Finding out more: 01452 814213 or crickley@nationaltrust.org.uk

Crickley Hill		M	T	W	T	F	S	S
1 Jan–31 Mar	6–7	M	T	W	T	F	S	S
1 Apr–30 Sep	6–10	M	T	W	T	F	S	S
1 Oct–31 Dec	6–7	M	T	W	T	F	S	S

Information point (not National Trust) open 1 April to 30 September, afternoons only.

Dinton Park and Philipps House

Dinton, Salisbury, Wiltshire SP3 5HH

Map ① K5   🏠 ♣ | 1943 |

Excellent parkland walks throughout the year. Neo-Grecian house with fine Regency furniture, designed by Jeffry Wyatville for William Wyndham, 1820. **Note**: no toilet.

Access for all: ∷ Building 🦽 Grounds 🚶🦽

Getting here: 184:SU004319. 9 miles west of Salisbury, on north side of B3089.

Finding out more: 01722 716663 or sw.customerenquiries@nationaltrust.org.uk

Dinton Park	Open every day all year

For Philipps House opening arrangements please visit the website or telephone 01672 538014.

Dinton Park and Philipps House, Wiltshire

Dunster Castle

Dunster, near Minehead, Somerset TA24 6SL

Map (1) G5   🏰❄♠♣🔔🍴 1976

'**Wonderful! Stunning setting – marvellous castle and views. The morning room is an excellent idea!**'
Mrs Newport, Fareham, Hampshire

Dramatically sited on top of a wooded hill, a castle has existed here since at least Norman times, with an impressive medieval gatehouse and ruined tower giving a reminder of its turbulent history. The castle that you see today became a lavish country home during the 19th century, remodelled in 1868–72 by Antony Salvin. The fine oak staircase and plasterwork ceiling he adapted can still be seen. You can relax on the sunny south terrace, which is home to a variety of subtropical plants. Stunning panoramic views over the surrounding countryside and moorland complete the experience.

Exploring
- Enjoy breathtaking views across Exmoor and the Bristol Channel.
- Lose yourself in the subtropical terraced garden.
- Play the piano, enjoy snooker or handle a replica shotgun.
- Explore the serpentine path through the river garden.
- Visit the 17th-century stables and shop.
- See our fascinating new garden history exhibition.

Eating and shopping: browse in the 17th-century stables shop, with unusual local and regional gifts and pick up a guidebook. Visit Dunster village or the working watermill for places to eat.

Making the most of your day: a range of family trails available to help you explore the castle and garden. Behind-the-scenes tours and re-enactments, many costumed, and other events throughout the season. **Dogs**: welcome in parkland and garden on leads.

Dunster Castle, Somerset: turbulent past

Access for all:
Castle 🦽🪜 Stables 🦽 Grounds 🦽➡️🦽

Getting here: 181:SS995435. 3 miles south-east of Minehead. **Cycle**: cycle lane from Minehead along A39. **Bus**: services from Tiverton and Taunton to Minehead; alight Dunster Steep, ½ mile. **Road**: 3 miles south-east of Minehead, off A39. **Parking**: 300 yards, shuttle to entrance available. Enter from A39.

Finding out more: 01643 823004 (Infoline). 01643 821314 or dunstercastle@nationaltrust.org.uk

Dunster Castle		M	T	W	T	F	S	S
Castle								
10 Mar–4 Nov	11–5	M	T	W	T	F	S	S
Shop, garden and park*								
1 Jan–9 Mar	11–4	M	T	W	T	F	S	S
10 Mar–4 Nov	10–5	M	T	W	T	F	S	S
5 Nov–31 Dec	11–4	M	T	W	T	F	S	S

Last entry to castle one hour before closing (except 20 July to 2 September). *Shop: open weekends only in January and closed 25 and 26 December.

Dunster Working Watermill

Mill Lane, Dunster, near Minehead,
Somerset TA24 6SW

Map ① G5 1976

A restored working 18th-century watermill built on the site of a mill mentioned in the Domesday survey of 1086. **Note**: the mill is a private business, admission charge (including members).

Access for all: 🔲 Building 🦽🏛️

Getting here: 181:SS995435. On River Avill, beneath Castle Tor.

Finding out more: 01643 821759 (mill). 01643 821314 (Dunster Castle) or dunstercastle@nationaltrust.org.uk

Dunster Working Watermill		M	T	W	T	F	S	S
Mill								
1 Apr–4 Nov	11–4:45	M	T	W	T	F	S	S
Tea-room								
3 Mar–31 Mar	10:30–4:45	·	·	·	·	·	S	S
1 Apr–4 Nov	10:30–4:45	M	T	W	T	F	S	S

Dyrham Park

Dyrham, near Bath,
South Gloucestershire SN14 8ER

Map ① J4  1961

'Wow! I didn't know there was so much here, a beautiful park with stunning views, a real voyage of discovery.'
Jamie May, Bradford on Avon

Dyrham Park is a treasure to enjoy: set in a dramatic deer park on the edge of the stunning Cotswold escarpment, near the World Heritage Site City of Bath. Discover the beautiful late 17th-century home of William Blathwayt, a hard-working civil servant who thrived during the political upheaval of three monarchs. Explore how fashions changed over the centuries, from the original 17th-century Dutch-inspired interiors and formal garden, to the very different style of Victorian country squire Colonel Blathwayt. The elegant garden is a more recent restoration, recreating the spirit of what had been lost.

Exploring
– Discover the park and garden with Tracker Packs.
– Family fun in the Old Lodge play area.
– Look out for the historic herd of fallow deer.
– Step out on a guided park and garden tour.
– Enjoy spectacular views.

Eating and shopping: look out for local venison and perry pears on the menu in the newly refurbished tea-room. Quench your thirst and relax in the tea garden. A great range of plants, books and garden-related products in the shop.

Looking down towards the stately east front of Dyrham Park in South Gloucestershire

Making the most of your day: jazz on the lawn and open-air theatre in the summer, guided tours of the park, garden and house and seasonal activities for families. **Dogs**: welcome in car park only. Exercise area at the far end of car park.

Access for all: ♿🚿🚻🔊📷📱♿
Building 🔊♿ **Grounds** 🔊➡

Getting here: 172:ST743757. 8 miles north of Bath, 12 miles east of Bristol. **Foot**: Cotswold Way passes by. **Cycle**: Avon and Wiltshire cycleways. **Train**: Bath Spa 8 miles. **Road**: on the Bath to Stroud road (A46), 2 miles south of Tormarton interchange with M4, exit 18. **Sat Nav**: use SN14 8HY. **Parking**: free, 500 yards.

Finding out more: 0117 937 2501 or dyrhampark@nationaltrust.org.uk

Dyrham Park		M	T	W	T	F	S	S
Garden, shop and tea-room								
18 Feb–29 Jun	10–5	M	T	·	·	F	S	S
30 Jun–2 Sep	10–5	M	T	W	T	F	S	S
3 Sep–28 Oct	10–5	M	T	·	·	F	S	S
3 Nov–16 Dec	10–4	·	·	·	·	·	S	S
House								
10 Mar–29 Jun	11–5	M	T	·	·	F	S	S
30 Jun–2 Sep	11–5	M	T	W	T	F	S	S
3 Sep–28 Oct	11–5	M	T	·	·	F	S	S
Basement and kitchen only								
18 Feb–9 Mar	11–4	M	T	·	·	F	S	S
3 Nov–16 Dec	11–4	·	·	·	·	·	S	S
Park								
Open all year	10–5	M	T	W	T	F	S	S

Last admission one hour before closing. Whole property closed until 1 on 5 and 19 September, 7 and 21 November and 5 December. Closed 25 December.

East Pool Mine

Pool, near Redruth, Cornwall TR15 3ED

Map ① C9   1967

East Pool Mine lies at the very heart of the Cornish Mining World Heritage Site which celebrates the extraordinary technology that shaped the modern world. Exploring the site reveals many reminders of its innovative past, including two great beam engines, preserved in their towering engine houses. Each day, the restored winding engine springs into life as if beckoning you to work. Today nature has reclaimed this once-bustling industrial location, but the engines are still two of Cornwall's most important treasures. **Note:** Trevithick Cottage is nearby at Penponds (open April to October, Wednesdays 2 to 5).

Exploring
- Family activities and trails.
- Hands-on exhibits and working models.
- Massive working beam engine.
- Dress up as a balmaiden or miner.
- Watch our fascinating film about mining in Cornwall.
- Gateway to the World Heritage Site celebrating Cornish mining.

Eating and shopping: comprehensive selection of mining and local history books for sale. Spoil yourself with local fudge and chocolate from the Lizard. Local rocks, minerals and Cornish tin available from our shop.

Making the most of your day: engaging, knowledgeable guides bring the site to life, alongside hands-on exhibits and our working beam engine. Lots more to discover outside including trails and a picnic area.

Access for all: 🦽🧏♿📷👁️ⓐ
Taylor's engine house 🔼 Michell's engine house 🔼
Visitor centre and shop 🔼🦽➡️

Getting here: 203:SW672415. At Pool, on either side of A3047 midway between Redruth and Camborne. **Cycle**: NCN3, ½ mile. **Bus**: frequent services from Penzance, St Ives and Truro (passing Camborne and Redruth ≷). **Train**: Redruth 2 miles; Camborne 2 miles. **Road**: leave A30 at Camborne East or Redruth junctions. Site signposted on A3047, reached through Morrisons' car park. **Parking**: free at Morrisons' superstore, 50 yards. Secondary free car park (not National Trust) outside Michell's engine house off A3047.

Finding out more: 01209 315027 or eastpool@nationaltrust.org.uk. Trevithick Road, Pool, Cornwall TR15 3NP

East Pool Mine			M	T	W	T	F	S	S
19 Mar–31 May	11–5		M	·	W	T	F	·	S
1 Jun–2 Sep	11–5		M	·	W	T	F	S	S
3 Sep–4 Nov	11–5		M	·	W	T	F	·	S

Open for the Queen's Diamond Jubilee (5 June). November to end March: open by arrangement only.

East Pool Mine, Cornwall: winding engine in action

Finch Foundry

Sticklepath, Okehampton, Devon EX20 2NW

Map (1) F7   1994

Set amid beautiful Dartmoor countryside in the village of Sticklepath, this last remaining water-powered forge in England gives a unique insight into village life in the 19th century. In its heyday the foundry made 400 tools a day, including sickles, scythes and shovels for West Country farmers and miners. **Note:** narrow entrance to car park. Height restrictions apply.

Exploring
- Demonstrations and tours of the machinery every hour.
- Watch the large waterwheels driving the tilt hammer and grindstone.
- Learn about the lives of the foundry owners and workers.
- See Tom Pearse's summerhouse, of Widecombe Fair fame.

Eating and shopping: gifts and plants on sale in the shop. Try delicious local ice-cream at the tea-room.

Making the most of your day: family activities, vintage vehicle rallies and moorland walks.
Dogs: welcome in all areas except tea-room, shop and foundry during demonstrations.

Access for all: ⬚⬚⬚⬚⬚ Foundry ⬚
Upstairs gallery ⬚ Grounds ⬚

Heating metal in the forge at Finch Foundry, Devon

Getting here: 191:SX641940. In the centre of Sticklepath village. **Foot**: on 180-mile Tarka Trail. **Cycle**: on West Devon Cycle Route. **Bus**: regular services from Okehampton and Exeter. **Train**: Okehampton (Sunday, June to September only) 4½ miles. **Road**: 4 miles east of Okehampton off A30. **Parking**: free. Not suitable for high vehicles.

Finding out more: 01837 840046 or finchfoundry@nationaltrust.org.uk

Finch Foundry		M	T	W	T	F	S	S
17 Mar–4 Nov	11–5	M	T	W	T	F	S	S

Foundry and shop open for St Clement's Day (patron saint of blacksmiths) in November.

Fyne Court

Broomfield, Bridgwater, Somerset TA5 2EQ

Map (1) H5   ⬚⬚⬚⬚⬚ 1967

A real hidden Somerset gem. Although the house is no longer standing, Fyne Court is a wonderful place to spend a magical time walking through the estate's woodland garden and delightful meadows. A great place for families to explore.

Exploring
- New for 2012: have fun on our outdoor play trail.
- Uncover the stories about Andrew Crosse, 'thunder and lightning man'.
- Discover where the house was and how it burnt down.
- Play with the games box, climb trees, build a den.

Eating and shopping: the tea-room sells delicious homemade lunches, cream teas and cakes.

Making the most of your day: fantastic series of events throughout the year. From bush crafts to open-air theatre, there is something for everyone. Join us for our Wild Wednesdays in the school holidays. **Dogs**: on leads welcome.

Access for all: ⬚⬚⬚ Grounds

Getting here: 182:ST222321. 5 miles north of Taunton; 6 miles south-west of Bridgwater in Broomfield. **Train**: Taunton 5 miles, Bridgwater 6 miles. **Road**: follow signs to Broomfield. **Parking**: 150 yards.

Finding out more: 01643 862452 or fynecourt@nationaltrust.org.uk

Fyne Court		M	T	W	T	F	S	S
Estate								
Open all year		M	T	W	T	F	S	S
Tea-room								
17 Mar–22 Jul	10:30–4	M	·	·	T	F	S	S
23 Jul–2 Sep	10:30–4:30	M	T	W	T	F	S	S
3 Sep–4 Nov	10:30–4	M	·	·	T	F	S	S

Opening hours vary according to weather conditions (shorter in poor weather).

Glastonbury Tor

near Glastonbury, Somerset

Map (1) I5

Somerset's iconic tor, topped by a 15th-century tower: enjoy spectacular views and soak up its ancient history and mystical past.
Note: no toilet.

Exploring   –   Climb the Tor for spectacular views over three counties.
               –   Walk the public footpaths across the Tor.

Eating and shopping: enjoy the perfect picnic.

Access for all: [∷] Grounds [♿]

Getting here: 182/183:ST512386. On eastern edge of Glastonbury, off A361.

Finding out more: 01643 862452 or glastonburytor@nationaltrust.org.uk

Glastonbury Tor	Open every day all year

Glendurgan Garden

Mawnan Smith, near Falmouth,
Cornwall TR11 5JZ

Map (1) C9   [icons] 1962

'With the beach, the maze and so many places to sit and relax, we ended up spending all day here!'
Will and Tanya Lowther, Salisbury

Lose yourself in the three valleys of Glendurgan Garden – full of fun, natural beauty and amazing plants. Discover giant rhubarb plants in the jungle-like lower valley and spiky arid plants basking on the sunny upper slopes. Wander through the garden down to the beautiful hamlet of Durgan on the Helford River: a place to watch birds and boats, skim stones and build sandcastles. Find a boat-seat, gigantic tulip trees and ponds teeming with wildlife. Learn about the Fox family who created this 'small peace [sic] of heaven on earth'.

The laurel maze at Glendurgan Garden, Cornwall

Exploring   – Get lost in the 176-year-old cherry laurel maze.
   – Become airborne on the 'Giant's Stride' swing.
   – Explore three beautiful valleys leading to the Helford River.
   – Discover weird and wonderful plants from all around the world.
   – Find tranquillity among the many native wild flowers and wildlife.
   – Challenge yourselves to a stone-skimming competition on Durgan beach.

Eating and shopping: treat yourself to home-cooked locally sourced food from the tea-house (not National Trust). Indulge in an irresistible lunch, cream tea or slice of cake. Sample lots of Cornish produce from our shop. Find a living souvenir in the plant centre.

Making the most of your day: variety of coastal and inland walks from the car park and Durgan village. Information room in Durgan village with stories about the Helford River and its wildlife. **Dogs**: assistance dogs only in the garden.

Access for all: 🅿♿🚻🔽🐕📷🏠
Visitor reception ♿ Shop ♿♿

Getting here: 204:SW772277. 4 miles south-west of Falmouth. **Foot**: South West Coast Path within ¾ mile. **Ferry**: link between Helford Passage (1½-mile walk from Durgan) and Helford village on south side of Helford River. **Bus**: services from Helford Passage to Truro or Helston to Falmouth. **Train**: Penmere 4 miles. **Road**: ½ mile south-west of Mawnan Smith, on road to Helford Passage. **Parking**: free. Car park gates locked at 5:30.

Finding out more: 01326 252020. 01872 862090 (out of hours). 01326 250247 (tea-room) or glendurgan@nationaltrust.org.uk

Glendurgan Garden	M	T	W	T	F	S	S
11 Feb–3 Nov 10:30–5:30		T	W	T	F	S	

Garden closes dusk if earlier. Open Bank Holiday Mondays and all Mondays in August.

Bluebell wood at Godolphin, Cornwall

Godolphin

Godolphin Cross, Helston, Cornwall TR13 9RE

Map ① B9   2000

A beautiful and romantic place, with a long and fascinating history. Time has stood still here, giving the garden, house and surrounding estate buildings a haunting air of antiquity and peace. The garden is largely unchanged since the 16th century. The estate walks are rich in prehistoric and mining archaeology. **Note**: the house is open to visit between bookings as a holiday cottage: check opening dates.

Exploring — Enjoy the peace and calm of the ancient garden.
— Family trails and tours.
— Explore surrounding countryside, with many interesting archaeological features.
— Stay in the house: a place for very special holidays.

Eating and shopping: enjoy tea, coffee, biscuits, sandwiches and cakes in the Piggery. Small souvenirs and postcards on sale.

Making the most of your day: family activities, tours and guided walks. Bring a picnic. Borrow a blanket from the Piggery and picnic in the orchard, garden or estate. **Dogs**: welcome in the garden on short leads and under control throughout the estate.

Access for all: ♿🅿️🚻♿♿♿♿ Garden ♿

Getting here: 203:SW599321. 9 miles to Camborne. **Bus**: Camborne ▭ to Helston. **Train**: Camborne 9 miles. **Road**: from Helston take A394 to Sithney Common, turn right onto B3302 to Leedstown, turn left, follow signs. From Hayle B3302 to Leedstown, turn right, follow signs. From west, B3280 through Goldsithney, turn right at Townshend. **Parking**: free.

Finding out more: 01736 763194 or godolphin@nationaltrust.org.uk

Godolphin		M	T	W	T	F	S	S
Garden								
4 Feb–16 Dec	10–4	M	T	W	T	F	S	S
Estate								
Open all year		M	T	W	T	F	S	S
House								
4 Feb–9 Feb	10–4	M	T	W	T	·	S	S
3 Mar–8 Mar	10–4	M	T	W	T	·	S	S
7 Apr–12 Apr	10–4	M	T	W	T	·	S	S
5 May–10 May	10–4	M	T	W	T	·	S	S
2 Jun–7 Jun	10–4	M	T	W	T	·	S	S
7 Jul–12 Jul	10–4	M	T	W	T	·	S	S
1 Sep–6 Sep	10–4	M	T	W	T	·	S	S
6 Oct–11 Oct	10–4	M	T	W	T	·	S	S

Godrevy

Gwithian, near Hayle, Cornwall TR27 5ED

Map ① B9   🏞️ [1939]

Awe-inspiring expanse of sandy beaches around St Ives Bay. Wild cliffs, rich in wildlife and archaeology, with popular café. **Note**: beware of cliff edges, unstable cliffs and incoming tides. Toilet not always available.

Access for all: ♿ Grounds ♿

Getting here: 203:SW582430. Hayle 5 miles. Just off the B3301 north of Gwithian village.

Finding out more: 01208 265212 or godrevy@nationaltrust.org.uk

Godrevy	Open every day all year

Café open daily in main season; weekends out of season (visit www.godrevycafe.co.uk or telephone 01736 757999). Car parking fields open subject to weather and ground conditions.

The long, sandy beach at Godrevy, Cornwall

Yew topiary on the lawn of the 15th-century Great Chalfield Manor and Garden, Wiltshire

Great Chalfield Manor and Garden

near Melksham, Wiltshire SN12 8NH

Map (1) J4   1943

This beautiful medieval manor sits in peaceful countryside. Cross the upper moat, passing barns, gatehouse and delightful parish church to enjoy fine oriel windows and the soldiers, griffins and monkey adorning the rooftops. Romantic garden offers terraces, topiary houses, gazebo, lily pond, roses and views across the spring-fed fishpond. **Note**: home to donor family tenants, who manage it for the National Trust.

Exploring – Explore gardens designed by Alfred Parsons, replanted by the family.
– Elegant architecture and Edwardian restoration completed for the donor.
– Enjoy stone-looking masks, furniture, tapestries and Tropnell's Cartulary.
– Beautiful adjacent parish church (not National Trust), donations welcome.

Eating and shopping: enjoy tea/coffee in the Motor House (not National Trust). Buy plants grown on site from the garden and orchards.

Pick up a guidebook and postcards of the manor.

Making the most of your day: spot woodpeckers or nesting swallows. Enjoy history posters and slide show of the garden in the Edwardian Motor House. Walk to nearby Courts Garden for lunch or tea.

Access for all: [icons] Manor [icons] Garden [icons]

Getting here: 173:ST860631. 3 miles southwest of Melksham. **Foot**: 1-mile walk by public footpath from The Courts Garden (National Trust), Holt. **Cycle**: NCN254. On the Wiltshire Cycleway. **Bus**: Bradford-on-Avon to Holt. **Train**: Bradford-on-Avon, 3 miles. **Road**: off B3107 via Broughton Gifford Common, follow sign for Broughton Gifford (warning, narrow lane). Coaches must approach from Broughton Gifford (lanes from south too narrow). **Parking**: free, 100 yards, on grass verge outside manor gates.

Finding out more: 01225 782239 or greatchalfieldmanor@nationaltrust.org.uk

Great Chalfield		M	T	W	T	F	S	S
Manor*								
1 Apr–31 Oct	11–5		.	T	W	T	.	.	S
Garden								
1 Apr–28 Oct	2–5		.	.	.	.	.	.	S
3 Apr–31 Oct	11–5		.	T	W	T	.	.

*Admission to manor house by 45-minute guided tour only (places limited, not bookable). Tuesday to Thursday: at 11, 12, 2, 3 and 4. Sunday: at 2, 3 and 4. Additional timed manor tickets may be available on Sundays and other busy days. Part of house only open in November and December.

Greenway

Greenway Road, Galmpton, near Brixham,
Devon TQ5 0ES

Map ① G8  2000

'Thoroughly enjoyable, a most beautiful
house with a very warm, happy feel.
The grounds are really lovely with
wonderful views.'
Mrs Duke, Southampton

This is an extraordinary glimpse into the private
holiday home of the famous and much-loved
author Agatha Christie and her family. The
relaxed and atmospheric house is set in the
1950s and contains many of the family's
collections, including archaeology, Tunbridge
ware, silver, botanical china and books.
Outside you can enjoy the large and romantic
woodland garden, with restored vinery and
peach house, wild edges and rare plantings,
which drift down the hillside towards the
sparkling Dart estuary. Please consider 'green
ways' to get here to relieve pressure on
the lanes: for example ferry, bus, cycling or
walking. **Note**: steep uphill 800-yard walk from
Greenway Quay to visitor reception.

Exploring — Enjoy the adventure of
arriving by ferry at
Greenway Quay.
— Arrive in style on the
1950s vintage bus.

Exploring — Discover the garden and
estate on a network of paths.
— Stay here in the house
apartment, Lodge or
South Lodge.
— Visit the setting for
Dead Man's Folly.
— Theatre, literary and garden
events; resident local artists.

Eating and shopping: we specialise in local
products. Licensed Barn Café and House
Kitchen serving delicious award-winning
lunches and afternoon teas. Shop featuring
Agatha Christie books, souvenirs and
Greenway Nursery plants.

Making the most of your day: daily guided
garden tours in the afternoon. Regular events
include art exhibitions, artists in residence and
conservation master classes. Open-air theatre.
Family croquet, clock golf, trails and quizzes.
Dogs: welcome on short leads in garden.

Access for all: 🅿️ ♿ 🚾 ♿ ♿ 🎨 VT 👓 ♿
House 📖 Boathouse 📖 Garden 📖

Getting here: 202:SX876548. **Foot**: Dart Valley
Trail, Kingswear 3 miles, Dartmouth 6 miles.
Greenway walk from Broadsands or Churston
station 3½ miles. **Ferry**: from Dartmouth (use
park and ride), Totnes (tidal, Steamer Quay),
Brixham or Torquay (details from Greenway
Ferry Service, 01803 882811 or website).
Dartmouth ticket office opposite Trust
shop. Six hours minimum parking required.
Bus: daily from Torquay, Paignton and Brixham
park and ride (01803 882811).

Greenway, Devon: the much-loved holiday home of Agatha Christie and her family

Train: Paignton 4½ miles, Churston 2 miles (Dartmouth Steam Railway and River Boat Company 01803 555872). **Parking: spaces must be booked, unbooked cars may be refused** (telephone 01803 842382 or visit website) – same-day booking possible. No parking on Greenway road or in village.

Finding out more: 01803 842382 or greenway@nationaltrust.org.uk

Greenway		M	T	W	T	F	S	S
3 Mar–1 Apr	10:30–5		·	W	T	F	S	S
3 Apr–15 Apr	10:30–5	·	T	W	T	F	S	S
18 Apr–22 Jul	10:30–5		·	W	T	F	S	S
24 Jul–9 Sep	10:30–5	·	T	W	T	F	S	S
12 Sep–31 Oct	10:30–5		·	W	T	F	S	S

Also open Tuesday 5 June (Bank Holiday) and Tuesday 30 October. Timed entry tickets available upon arrival. On busy days there may be a delay during which time you are welcome to enjoy the gardens, boathouse, café, gallery and shop (Fridays and Saturdays tend to be quieter).

Hailes Abbey

near Winchcombe, Cheltenham, Gloucestershire GL54 5PB

Map ① K1   ✚ 🏛 1937

Once a Cistercian abbey, founded in 1246 by Richard of Cornwall and dissolved Christmas Eve 1539, Hailes never housed large numbers of monks but had extensive and elaborate buildings. It was financed by pilgrims visiting its renowned relic, 'the Holy Blood of Hailes' – allegedly a phial of Christ's blood. **Note:** financed, managed and maintained by English Heritage (0117 975 0700, www.english-heritage.org.uk/hailes).

Exploring – Explore the ruins of this 13th-century Cistercian abbey.
– Interpretation panels guide you around the abbey buildings.
– Sculptures, stonework and other finds are displayed in the museum.
– The adjacent parish church has medieval wall-paintings.

Eating and shopping: browse in the shop then choose a treat from the refreshments.

Making the most of your day: settle down for a picnic in the grounds. **Dogs:** on leads in grounds only.

Access for all: ⚫⚫ Building 🏛

Getting here: 150:SP050300. 2 miles north-east of Winchcombe. **Foot:** Cotswold Way within ¾ mile. **Bus:** Cheltenham to Willersey, alight Greet, 1¾ miles by footpath. **Train:** Cheltenham 10 miles. **Road:** 1 mile east of Broadway road (B4632, originally A46). **Parking:** free (not National Trust).

Finding out more: 01242 602398 or hailesabbey@nationaltrust.org.uk

Hailes Abbey		M	T	W	T	F	S	S
1 Apr–30 Jun	10–5	M	T	W	T	F	S	S
1 Jul–31 Aug	10–6	M	T	W	T	F	S	S
1 Sep–30 Sep	10–5	M	T	W	T	F	S	S
1 Oct–31 Oct	10–4	M	T	W	T	F	S	S

Opening times subject to change. Please visit website or telephone to confirm.

Hardy Country

near Dorchester, Dorset

Map ① J7   🏛 ❀ 1940

Hardy Country in Dorset is home to Thomas Hardy's Birthplace and his later home, Max Gate. In the small cob and thatch cottage where he was born, Hardy wrote his early novels. He later designed Max Gate and lived there from 1885 until his death in 1928. **Note:** no toilet.

Exploring – Be delighted by the charming cottage garden at Hardy's Birthplace.
– Visit Thomas Hardy's home.

Eating and shopping: we're sorry, but no catering is available at either place. Buy Thomas Hardy books, postcards and small gifts at Hardy's Birthplace.

Making the most of your day: programme of events runs at both places throughout the season.

Access for all: ⬛⬛

Hardy's Birthplace ⬛⬛ Max Gate ⬛⬛

Getting here: Hardy's Birthplace: 194:SY728925. Max Gate: 194:SY704899. Hardy's Birthplace: 3 miles north-east of Dorchester, ½ mile south of A35. From Kingston Maurward roundabout follow signs to Stinsford and Higher Bockhampton. Max Gate: from Dorchester follow A352 Wareham road to roundabout named Max Gate (at junction of A35 Dorchester bypass). Turn left and left again into cul-de-sac outside house. **Train:** Dorchester South 4 miles; Dorchester West 4 miles. **Sat Nav:** for Max Gate use DT1 2AB. **Parking:** Hardy's Birthplace: free (not National Trust), 600 yards. Max Gate: free (not National Trust), 50 yards. Drop-off point.

Finding out more: 01305 262366 (Hardy's Birthplace). 01297 489481 (Max Gate) or hardycountry@nationaltrust.org.uk

Hardy Country		M	T	W	T	F	S	S
Hardy's Birthplace								
14 Mar–31 Oct	11–5			W	T	F	S	S

Hardy's Birthplace: open Bank Holiday Mondays. **Max Gate: for opening times and further information telephone the West Dorset Office on 01297 489481 before visiting.**

Thomas Hardy was born in this small Dorset cottage

Hardy Monument

Black Down, Portesham, Dorset DT2 9HY

Monument has recently undergone major restoration; contact West Dorset Office 01297 489481 for opening details.

Heddon Valley

Parracombe, Barnstaple, Devon EX31 4PY

Map ① F5   ⬛⬛⬛⬛ 1963

The West Exmoor coast, favourite landscape of the Romantic poets, offers not only the Heddon Valley, but also Woody Bay and the Hangman Hills to explore. There are spectacular coastal and woodland walks, as well as a car park, shop and information centre in Heddon Valley itself.

Exploring – Discover the South West Coast Path and dramatic sea cliffs.
– Enjoy circular walks, guided by our walks leaflet.
– Feel free to use one of our car park barbecues.
– Discover the fantastic birdlife of Woody Bay.

Eating and shopping: outdoor wear, Exmoor products and great gifts in the shop. Delicious local ice-cream with flavours to suit all tastes.

Making the most of your day: two all-terrain children's buggies available for families to borrow at the Heddon Valley shop. **Dogs:** welcome.

Access for all: ⬛⬛⬛⬛⬛⬛

Shop ⬛ Heddon Valley ⬛⬛

Getting here: 180:SS655481. Halfway between Combe Martin and Lynton. **Foot:** South West Coast Path within ¾ mile. **Bus:** regular service from Barnstaple to Lynton (passing close Barnstaple ⬛), alight just north of Parracombe,

Looking down from the coast path towards the secluded Woody Bay near Heddon Valley, Devon

then 2 miles. **Road**: off A39 at Hunter's Inn. **Parking**: 50 yards.

Finding out more: 01598 763402 or heddonvalley@nationaltrust.org.uk

Heddon Valley		M	T	W	T	F	S	S
Countryside								
Open all year		M	T	W	T	F	S	S
Shop								
10 Mar–5 Apr	10:30–4:30	M	T	W	T	F	S	S
6 Apr–30 Sep	10:30–5	M	T	W	T	F	S	S
1 Oct–4 Nov	10:30–4:30	M	T	W	T	F	S	S

Heelis

Kemble Drive, Swindon, Wiltshire SN2 2NA

Map (1) K3   2005

The National Trust's award-winning central office is a remarkable example of an innovative and sustainable building. Timber from our woodlands and wool from Herdwick sheep grazed on Trust farmlands have been used in its construction, making Heelis a unique working environment.

Exploring — Tours every Friday, except Bank Holidays (small charge for non-members).

Eating and shopping: café serves a range of delicious local food. There is plenty of choice in our spacious, airy shop.

Making the most of your day: a virtual tour of Heelis is available at reception every day during normal opening hours.

Access for all: ⯑⯑⯑⯑⯑⯑⯑
Building ⯑ ⯑

Getting here: 173:SU141850. On Swindon's historic railway site, next door to the Designer Outlet. **Bus**: alight Rodbourne Road (200 yards). **Train**: Swindon, ¾ mile. **Road**: from M4 junction 16, follow signs for Outlet Centre North car park. Park and ride from Wroughton. **Parking**: 100 yards, not National Trust (charge including members).

Finding out more: 01793 817575 or heelisreception@nationaltrust.org.uk

Heelis

Admission to offices by booked guided tour only. Shop and café open daily throughout year, apart from 1 January, Easter Sunday, 25 and 26 December.

Hidcote

Hidcote Bartrim, near Chipping Campden, Gloucestershire GL55 6LR

Map ① L1 [symbols] 1948

Memories don't get any better than this. Relax and unwind in one of the country's great gardens and experience for yourself the fulfilment of a quiet American's English fantasy. You'll never forget the exquisite garden rooms, each with its own unique character. Discover rare shrubs and trees, herbaceous borders and unusual plants from around the world. The garden changes in harmony with the seasons, from vibrant spring bulbs to autumn's spectacular Red Border. Nestled in the Cotswolds with sweeping views across the Vale of Evesham, a visit to Hidcote is inspirational at any time of year.

Exploring
- Enjoy a game of croquet on the Theatre Lawn.
- Share a picnic with family or friends in the Wilderness.
- Capture the spirit of Lawrence Johnston in our planthouse.
- Discover great views on one of the many public footpaths.
- Be inspired by breathtaking garden design and planting.
- Children will love our new garden activity booklets.

Eating and shopping: enjoy a delicious meal in our Cedar Tree Restaurant and conservatory, with seasonal menus inspired by our fresh kitchen garden produce. Browse the largest plant centre in the National Trust and buy exclusive Hidcote souvenirs in the shop.

Making the most of your day: daily introductory talks, programme of exclusive evening Head Gardener tours, open-air theatre, themed family trails and workshops.

Access for all: [symbols]
Visitor reception [symbols] Grounds [symbols]

Getting here: 151:SP176429. 4 miles north-east of Chipping Campden. **Foot**: 1½ miles by steep uphill footpath from Mickleton. **Cycle**: NCN5, 1¼ miles. **Train**: Honeybourne 4½ miles. **Road**: close to Mickleton village, 1 mile east of B4632 (originally A46), off B4081. **Parking**: free, 100 yards.

Finding out more: 01386 438333 or hidcote@nationaltrust.org.uk

Hidcote		M	T	W	T	F	S	S
18 Feb–4 Mar	11–4	·	·	·	·	·	S	S
10 Mar–29 Apr	10–6	M	T	W	·	·	S	S
30 Apr–2 Sep	10–6	M	T	W	T	F	S	S
3 Sep–30 Sep	10–6	M	T	W	·	·	S	S
1 Oct–4 Nov	10–5	M	T	W	·	·	S	S
10 Nov–16 Dec	11–4	·	·	·	·	·	S	S

Open Good Friday. All facilities close at the same time as last admission (one hour before closing). Barn Café closed during November and December.

The Old Garden at Hidcote, Gloucestershire

High Cross House, Devon: this Modernist gem was built as a 'machine for living'

High Cross House

Dartington, near Totnes, Devon TQ9 6ED

Map (1) G8   🏠 ✤ 2011

Built as a 'machine for living in' for William Curry, headmaster of Dartington Hall School, this Modernist gem was commissioned by Leonard Elmhirst and designed by William Lescaze in 1932. The house still evokes the 'serenity, clarity and a kind of openness' described by Curry.
Note: owned by Dartington Hall but managed by the National Trust.

Exploring   – A showcase for contemporary art exhibitions and sales.
   – Wonderful views from the roof terraces to open countryside.
   – Talks and demonstrations, musical evenings.
   – One of Britain's most celebrated Modern residences.

Eating and shopping: café gallery on the first floor serving cakes and coffee; wine and nibbles in the evening. Contemporary art sales.

Making the most of your day: wonderful day out combined with a visit to Greenway for Studio Pottery, or Coleton Fishacre for Art Deco interiors. Visit Dartington Hall and shops at Dartington (not National Trust).
Dogs: welcome on leads in the garden.

Access for all: Pᴅ Dᴅ 🚻 **Grounds** ♿ ♿ ➡ ♿

Getting here: 202:SX796627. On the right, off driveway to Dartington Hall. **Foot**: walk along the River Dart to the Dartington Hall drive from Totnes railway station. **Cycle**: Sustrans cycle path from Totnes to Dartington Hall estate. **Bus**: services from Buckfastleigh and Totnes to Dartington Hall. **Train**: Totnes 1½ miles. **Road**: from Plymouth A38 take the A385 exit signposted Dartington 4 miles.
Parking: parking at shops at Dartington.

Finding out more: 01803 842382 or highcrosshouse@nationaltrust.org.uk

High Cross House		M	T	W	T	F	S	S
7 Mar–30 Dec	10:30–5	·	·	**W**	**T**	**F**	**S**	**S**

Closed 25 December. Late night opening on Friday evenings until 8:30.

Holnicote Estate

Selworthy, Minehead, Somerset TA24 8TJ

Map (1) G5 ⊞🏠🏖🎨🌳🏡 [1944]

This stunning estate, within Exmoor National Park, offers breathtaking views and spectacular coastline. Miles of footpaths through unspoilt rural landscapes, woods, moors, farmland and villages. **Note**: toilets at Bossington, Horner and Selworthy. Also at Allerford (not National Trust).

Exploring — Climb to the highest point on Exmoor at Dunkery Beacon.
— Explore the unspoilt villages with their cob and thatched cottages.
— Enjoy coastal, woodland, village and moorland walks.
— Share a BBQ with friends at Bossington car park.

Eating and shopping: visit our new tea-room on picturesque Selworthy Green and enjoy a delicious cream tea. Pop into our shop, a haven for walkers, and find out more about exploring the estate.

Making the most of your day: discover our orienteering trail at Selworthy. Explore the estate by mountain bike or download a walk. Take part in one of our wonderful events. **Dogs**: welcome on leads.

Access for all: 🚻 Grounds 🚶🏔

Getting here: 181:SS920469. Near Selworthy. **Foot**: 3¾ miles of South West Coast Path; Coleridge Way; Macmillan Way. **Bus**: services from Minehead to Porlock, and Taunton to Lynmouth. **Train**: West Somerset Railway, 5 miles. **Road**: off A39, Minehead. **Parking**: free: Allerford, North Hill, Dunkery, Webbers Post, Selworthy. Charge: Bossington, Horner. Coaches: Horner.

Finding out more: 01823 451587 or holnicote@nationaltrust.org.uk

Sweeping view on the Holnicote Estate, Devon

Holnicote Estate		M	T	W	T	F	S	S
Countryside								
Open all year		M	T	W	T	F	S	S
Tea-room								
17 Mar–15 Apr	10:30–5	M	T	W	T	F	S	S
17 Apr–22 Jul	10:30–5	·	T	W	T	F	S	S
23 Jul–1 Sep	10:30–5	M	T	W	T	F	S	S
2 Sep–4 Nov	10:30–5	·	T	W	T	F	S	S
Shop								
17 Mar–4 Nov	10:30–5	·	·	W	T	F	S	S

Estate office open Monday to Friday, 8:30 to 5. Shop and tea-room open Bank Holidays. Opening hours vary according to weather.

Horton Court

Horton, near Chipping Sodbury, South Gloucestershire BS37 6QR

Visit website or telephone 01225 833977 for details of limited special openings in 2012.

Places may occasionally close for conservation, safety or events

Jurassic Coast

Dorset

Map ① H-J7  1961

England's only natural World Heritage Site, this spectacular swathe of Jurassic coastline traces almost 185 million years of the Earth's history, creating a unique 'walk through time'. Why not come and visit us at our new shop on the Marine Parade in Lyme Regis, Dorset?

Exploring   — Explore the 95 miles of unspoilt cliffs and beaches.
            — Safely search for fossils on the beach.

Getting here: visit www.nationaltrust.org.uk for transport details. **Parking**: pay and display car parks at various points.

Finding out more: 01297 489481 or jurassiccoast@nationaltrust.org.uk

Jurassic Coast	Open every day all year

Killerton

Broadclyst, Exeter, Devon EX5 3LE

Map ① G6 1944

'Very enjoyable visit. The house is imaginatively presented, gardens are beautiful and lunch in the Killerton Kitchen was yummy.'
Heather Williams, Hungerford

Would you give away your family home for your political beliefs? Sir Richard Acland did just this with his estate, at 2,590 hectares (6,400 acres) one of the largest the Trust has acquired (it includes 20 farms and 200-plus cottages). Killerton House, built in 1778–9, brings to life generations of the Aclands, one of Devon's oldest families. 'Gems', our new historic fashion exhibition, features drop-dead

gorgeous dresses in the collection. The garden, created by John Veitch, is the highlight of Killerton, beautiful year round. Marvel at the ancient rhododendrons, magnolias and rare trees surrounded by rolling Devon countryside.

Exploring   — Feel at home in the relaxed atmosphere of the house.
            — Escape into the garden, with majestic trees and sloping lawns.
            — Discover the summerhouse where Tom, the family pet bear, lived.
            — Have fun and find out more at our many events.
            — Explore over 60 miles of footpaths on the Killerton Estate.
            — See the sparkling costume exhibition; try on gorgeous replica dresses.

The west front at Killerton, Devon

Eating and shopping: buy award-winning Killerton cider, chutney, flour or honey in the gift shop or visit the plant centre. Enjoy morning coffee, lunch or afternoon tea in the Stable tea-room or the lovely Killerton Kitchen restaurant in the house.

Making the most of your day: discover 'Killerton's Characters'. Try on replica costumes. Browse in the second-hand bookshop. For families: Tracker Packs, play area, Discovery Centre (school holidays), trails. Waymarked walks, cycle track, orienteering routes. **Dogs**: welcome on leads in park and estate walks only. Dog bowls and posts available.

Access for all:
House ⬛⬛⬛ Shop ⬛⬛⬛
Grounds ⬛➡⬛

Getting here: 192:SS973001. 7 miles north-east of Exeter. **Cycle**: NCN52. **Bus**: services from Exeter to Tiverton, alight Killerton Turn ¾ mile. **Train**: Pinhoe (not Sunday), 4½ miles; Whimple, 6 miles; Exeter Central and St David's, both 7 miles. **Road**: off Exeter to Cullompton road (B3181); from M5 northbound, exit 30 via Pinhoe and Broadclyst; from M5 southbound, exit 28. **Parking**: free, 280 yards. Follow signs (do not go up drive to house).

Finding out more: 01392 881345 or killerton@nationaltrust.org.uk

Killerton		M	T	W	T	F	S	S
Park and garden								
Open all year	10:30–7	M	T	W	T	F	S	S
House								
11 Feb–9 Mar	11–3	M	T	W	T	F	S	S
10 Mar–4 Nov	11–5	M	T	W	T	F	S	S
1 Dec–23 Dec	2–4	M	T	W	T	F	S	S
Tea-room								
7 Jan–5 Feb	11–5	·	·	·	·	·	S	S
11 Feb–4 Nov	11–5	M	T	W	T	F	S	S
Restaurant								
10 Mar–4 Nov	11–5:30	M	T	W	T	F	S	S
Shop and plant sales								
7 Jan–5 Feb	11–5	·	·	·	·	·	S	S
11 Feb–4 Nov	11–5:30	M	T	W	T	F	S	S
5 Nov–31 Dec	11–5	M	T	W	T	F	S	S

Stable tea-room and shop close at 3 on 24 December and all day 25 and 26 December. In winter, shop and tea-room may not open in bad weather. Booked Christmas lunches, teas and special events available in Killerton Kitchen restaurant in house.

Killerton: Budlake Old Post Office

Broadclyst, Killerton, Exeter, Devon EX5 3LW

Map ① G7   ⬛⬛ 1944

Close to Killerton, this small thatched cottage was the village post office, serving Killerton House and the local community until the 1950s. The cottage has a delightful cottage garden including rose borders, herb and vegetable plots. **Note**: nearest toilets at Killerton.

Exploring
 – Discover the double-seated privy and pigsty.
 – Listen to reminiscences of life in the post office.
 – Step back in time amid the 1950s memorabilia.
 – Imagine doing washing in the Victorian wash-house.

Eating and shopping: visit nearby Killerton for tea-rooms, shop and plants.

Making the most of your day: footpath to Killerton along old carriage drive. **Dogs**: on leads in garden only.

Access for all: ⬛ Building ⬛ Grounds ⬛

Getting here: 192:SS973001. **Cycle**: NCN52. **Bus**: Services from Exeter to Tiverton Parkway ⬛ (passing close Exeter Central ⬛), alight Killerton Turn ¾ mile. **Train**: Pinhoe, not Sunday, 4½ miles; Whimple, 6 miles; Exeter Central and St David's, both 7 miles. **Road**: off Exeter to Cullompton road (B3181); from M5 northbound, exit 30 via Pinhoe and Broadclyst; from M5 southbound, exit 28. **Parking**: limited parking. Ample parking for cars and coaches at Killerton, 800 yards.

Finding out more: 01392 881690 or budlakepostoffice@nationaltrust.org.uk

Budlake Old Post Office		M	T	W	T	F	S	S
1 Apr–30 Oct	2–5	M	T	·	·	·	·	S

Last admission 10 minutes before closing.

Killerton: Clyston Mill

Broadclyst, Exeter, Devon EX5 3EW

Map ① G7   🏛️🔼 1944

Historic water-powered mill in a picturesque setting by the River Clyst, surrounded by farmland and orchards. Grain is still ground here to make flour, keeping alive traditional skills. Discover more about what life would have been like for the miller, with hands-on activities and interpretation. **Note:** nearest parking and toilets in Broadclyst.

Exploring – Wander through Broadclyst's old churchyard to visit the mill.
– Working mill: watch the flour being ground.
– See where the mill boy slept.
– Picnic by the river and listen to the birds.

Eating and shopping: buy a bag of Clyston Mill flour. Visit Killerton for produce made from Clyston Mill flour.

Making the most of your day: children's trail and hands-on activities. **Dogs:** welcome on a lead.

Access for all: Building 🔲 Grounds 🔲

Getting here: 192:SX981973. In Broadclyst village. **Foot:** from village car park, walk towards church and follow signs through churchyard. **Cycle:** NCN52. **Bus:** Exeter to Tiverton, alight Broadclyst village. **Train:** Pinhoe, not Sunday, 4½ miles; Whimple, 6 miles; Exeter Central and St David's, both 7 miles. **Road:** off Exeter to Cullompton Road (B3181). **Parking:** free (not National Trust), 450 yards.

Finding out more: 01392 462425 or clystonmill@nationaltrust.org.uk

Clyston Mill	M	T	W	T	F	S	S
1 Apr–30 Oct 2–5	M	T	.	.	.	.	S

Telephone Killerton 01392 881345/462425 for further information.

The simple hall at Marker's Cottage, Devon

Killerton: Marker's Cottage

Townend, Broadclyst, Exeter, Devon EX5 3HX

Map ① G7   🏠🔼 1944

An intriguing medieval cob cottage with a thatched roof and smoke-blackened timbers. Discover the fascinating history of the cottage, including the unusual painted decorative screen showing St Andrew. A cross passage opens out onto a garden with a contemporary cob summerhouse and blacksmith's workshop. **Note:** nearest parking and toilets in Broadclyst.

Exploring – Find the painting of St Andrew and his boat.
– Discover the art of pargeting.
– Spot the dead rat.

Eating and shopping: visit nearby Killerton for tea-rooms, shop and plant centre.

Making the most of your day: handling collection and trail. Follow the Broadclyst village trail.

Access for all: 🔲 Building 🔲 Grounds 🔲

Getting here: 192:SX985973. In Broadclyst village. **Cycle:** NCN52. **Bus:** Exeter to Tiverton, alight Broadclyst village. **Train:** Pinhoe, not Sunday, 2½ miles; Whimple, 4½ miles; Exeter Central and St David's, both 6 miles.

Road: from village car park turn left, then right and right again onto Townend. Marker's Cottage is second cottage on left. **Parking**: free (not National Trust), 250 yards.

Finding out more: 01392 461546 or markerscottage@nationaltrust.org.uk

Marker's Cottage	M	T	W	T	F	S	S
1 Apr–30 Oct	2–5	M	T	·	·	·	·	S

King John's Hunting Lodge

The Square, Axbridge, Somerset BS26 2AP

Map ⓵ I4   1968

This early Tudor timber-framed wool merchant's house (*circa* 1500) provides a fascinating insight into local history. **Note**: run as local history museum by Axbridge and District Museum Trust. Small entry charge (including members).

Exploring – Explore inside the building by visiting the museum.
– Wander round Axbridge town in search of more local history.

Eating and shopping: visit the shop in the museum (not National Trust).

Making the most of your day: occasional tours of historic Axbridge start from the museum.

Access for all: 🗎 Building 👣

Getting here: 182:ST431545. In the Square, Axbridge, on corner of High Street. **Bus**: Weston-super-Mare to Wells (passing close Weston-super-Mare ≋). **Train**: Worle 8 miles. **Parking**: 100 yards (not National Trust).

Finding out more: 01934 732012 or kingjohns@nationaltrust.org.uk

King John's Hunting Lodge	M	T	W	T	F	S	S
1 Apr–30 Sep	1–4	M	T	W	T	F	S	S

Kingston Lacy

Wimborne Minster, Dorset BH21 4EA

Map ⓵ K7    1982

Home of the Bankes family for more than 300 years, this striking 17th-century house is noted for its lavish interiors. The outstanding art collection includes paintings by Rubens, Van Dyck, Titian and Tintoretto, with the largest private collection of Egyptian artefacts in the UK. Outside, stroll across the beautiful lawns towards the restored Japanese tea garden. There are several waymarked walks through the surrounding parkland, with its fine herd of North Devon cattle, and the 3,443-hectare (8,500-acre) estate is dominated by the Iron Age hill fort of Badbury Rings, home to 14 varieties of orchid.

Exploring – Outstanding art collection, including works by Rubens and Titian.
– View the restored Tintoretto in the dining room.
– Explore the Edwardian Japanese Garden.
– Discover the new Winter Garden in the Shelter Belt.
– Seek out the Egyptian obelisk and sarcophagus.
– Enjoy Eyebridge riverside walk (hard, level surface) and Badbury Rings.

Eating and shopping: be sure to sample our prize-winning scones. Try our beef, from the Kingston Lacy North Devon herd. Treat yourself to regional and local foods and wines. Take home some National Trust-grown plants, high quality gifts or souvenirs.

Making the most of your day: 'Putting the House to Bed' tours and lecture lunches in November (booking essential). Throughout year: farmers' markets, open-air theatre, tractor-trailer tours, children's crafts and 'Above and Below Stairs' days. **Dogs**: on leads in restaurant courtyard, park and woodlands only.

Kingston Lacy, Dorset: a stately avenue of cedars leads up to the striking 17th-century house

Access for all: 🅿️🏠♿🚻🐕🔊🎧📷🎥🎒
👁️📱 Building 🔁 Grounds 🏠➡️🗺️🔁

Getting here: 195:ST980019. 1½ miles west of Wimborne Minster. **Bus**: services from Bournemouth and Poole, alight Wimborne Square. **Train**: Poole 8½ miles. **Road**: on B3082 Blandford to Wimborne road. **Sat Nav**: data unreliable, follow B3082. **Parking**: free. Charge at Badbury Rings on point-to-point race days.

Finding out more: 01202 883402 or kingstonlacy@nationaltrust.org.uk

Kingston Lacy		M	T	W	T	F	S	S
House								
17 Mar–28 Oct	11–5			W	T	F	S	S
Garden, park, shop and restaurant								
2 Jan–16 Mar	10:30–4	M	T	W	T	F	S	S
17 Mar–28 Oct	10:30–6	M	T	W	T	F	S	S
29 Oct–23 Dec	10:30–4	M	T	W	T	F	S	S
27 Dec–30 Dec	10:30–4				T	F	S	S

Open Bank Holiday Mondays. Timed tickets may operate on Bank Holiday Sundays and Mondays. Last admission to house one hour before closing. Garden, park, shop and restaurant closed 24, 25, 26 and 31 December; open 27 to 30 December. Shop and restaurant close 30 minutes earlier than main property closing time.

Knightshayes Court

Bolham, Tiverton, Devon EX16 7RQ

Map ① G6   🏛️❄️🌳🏠🍽️ 1973

One of the finest surviving Gothic Revival houses, built in the lush landscape of mid-Devon, Knightshayes Court is a rare example of the work of the eccentric and inspired architect William Burges. Built for the grandson of pioneer lace-maker John Heathcoat in 1869, the house is an exciting architectural experience, with extraordinary 'medieval' romantic interiors, rich decoration and ceramics. The restored and fully productive organic kitchen garden is a treat for everyone who enjoys local produce. The vast garden, which was the Heathcoat Amory family's great passion, is renowned for its rare trees, shrubs and seasonal colours.

Exploring
– Enjoy the wonderfully re-created 'Burges Bedroom'.
– Relax in the peaceful and glorious garden.
– Discover the Seven Deadly Sins in the billiard room.

Exploring – Search for the Talbot dogs in the house and garden.
– Explore the celebrated 'Garden in the Wood'.
– Discover how to grow your own in the kitchen garden.

Eating and shopping: enjoy organic kitchen garden produce in the restaurant. Children's menu available. Opening hours may vary in October, but light refreshments are always available. Exceptionally well-stocked plant and outdoor centre. Gift shop. Produce for sale in kitchen garden.

Making the most of your day: daily introductory talks in the house and introductory garden walks. Programme of open-air, family, Christmas, gardening and restaurant events. Picnics in parkland only. **Dogs**: on leads in woodland and park. Assistance dogs only in kitchen or formal gardens.

Access for all: �🅿 🅿 ♿ 🚻 🅣 🎧 📖 🚹 Ⓐ
House 🔥 ♿ 🔥 Restaurant ♿ Gardens ➡ ♿

Getting here: 181:SS960151. 1½ miles north of Tiverton. **Cycle**: NCN3. **Bus**: Tiverton to Minehead, alight Bolham ¾ mile. Otherwise from Tiverton Parkway ≋; Exeter to Tiverton (passing close Exeter Central ≋), alight Tiverton 1¾ miles. **Train**: Tiverton Parkway 8 miles. **Road**: 7 miles from M5 exit 27 (A361); turn right off Tiverton to Bampton road (A396) at Bolham. **Sat Nav**: turn off on reaching Tiverton and follow signs. **Parking**: free.

Finding out more: 01884 254665 (office). 01884 257381 (visitor reception) or knightshayes@nationaltrust.org.uk

Knightshayes Court		M	T	W	T	F	S	S
House								
11 Feb–19 Feb	11–4	M	T	W	T	·	S	S
3 Mar–4 Nov	11–5	M	T	W	T	·	S	S
10 Nov–23 Dec	11–3	·	·	·	·	·	S	S
26 Dec–31 Dec	11–3	M	·	W	T	F	S	S
Garden, shop, plant centre and restaurant								
11 Feb–19 Feb	11–4	M	T	W	T	F	S	S
3 Mar–4 Nov	11–5	M	T	W	T	F	S	S
8 Nov–23 Dec	11–4	·	·	·	T	F	S	S
26 Dec–31 Dec	11–3	M	·	W	T	F	S	S

House closed Fridays. Access restricted in November, December and February, during events, weddings and in adverse weather conditions.

Productive kitchen garden at Knightshayes Court, Devon

Entry is still possible at most places up to 30 minutes before closing

North cloister walk at Lacock Abbey, Wiltshire

Lacock Abbey, Fox Talbot Museum and Village

Lacock, near Chippenham, Wiltshire SN15 2LG

Map ① K4 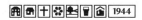 1944

Set in rural Wiltshire, Lacock village is famous for its picturesque streets, historic buildings and its more recent role as a television and film location. The Abbey, located at the heart of the village within its own woodland grounds, is a quirky country house of various architectural styles, built upon the foundations of a former nunnery. Visitors can experience the atmosphere of the medieval rooms and cloister court, giving a sense of the Abbey's monastic past. The museum celebrates the achievements of former Lacock resident William Henry Fox Talbot, famous for his contributions to the invention of photography.

Exploring
- Discover stories of the Abbey's fascinating past residents.
- Explore the Abbey grounds, for a tranquil stroll or picnic.

Exploring
- Wander the historic village streets, enjoying shopping and a meal.
- See wonderful exhibitions in the upper gallery of the museum.
- Experience Lacock life with a stay in our holiday cottage.
- Visit the location of films like *Harry Potter* and *Cranford*.

Eating and shopping: enjoy browsing in the many village shops and food outlets, including our National Trust shop and tea-room. Take home a souvenir or plant from our museum shop and pick up your next read in the Abbey's second-hand bookshop.

Making the most of your day: enjoy daily family trails and plenty of places to play. A full programme of events runs throughout the year, including family fun days, themed activities, open-air theatre, exhibitions and walks.
Dogs: welcome in the Abbey grounds from 1 November to 31 March (Easter if earlier).

Access for all:
Abbey Museum
Grounds

Getting here: 173:ST919684. 3 miles south of Chippenham. **Foot**: beside Wilts/Berks Canal. **Cycle**: NCN4, 1 mile. **Bus**: Chippenham to Frome (passing Melksham, close to Chippenham and Trowbridge stations). **Train**: Melksham 3 miles; Chippenham 3½ miles. **Road**: M4 exit 17, signposted Chippenham, Poole, Warminster then Lacock (A350). **Parking**: 220 yards (pay and display). No visitor parking on village streets.

Finding out more: 01249 730459 or lacockabbey@nationaltrust.org.uk

Lacock Abbey		M	T	W	T	F	S	S
Village*								
Open all year		M	T	W	T	F	S	S
Cloisters, grounds, museum, exhibition, museum shop**								
2 Jan–10 Feb	11–4	M	T	W	T	F	S	S
11 Feb–4 Nov	10:30–5:30	M	T	W	T	F	S	S
5 Nov–31 Dec	11–4	M	T	W	T	F	S	S
Abbey rooms**								
7 Jan–5 Feb	12–4	·	·	·	·	·	S	S
11 Feb–4 Nov	11–5	M	·	W	T	F	S	S
10 Nov–30 Dec	12–4	·	·	·	·	·	S	S
Tea-room and High Street shop**								
2 Jan–10 Feb	11–4	M	T	W	T	F	S	S
11 Feb–4 Nov	10–5:30	M	T	W	T	F	S	S
5 Nov–31 Dec	11–4	M	T	W	T	F	S	S

Last admission 45 minutes before closing. *Village businesses open at various times. **All (excluding village) closed 1 January, 25 and 26 December.

The 17th-century gatehouse at Lanhydrock, Cornwall

Lanhydrock

Bodmin, Cornwall PL30 5AD

Map ① D8  1953

'What an insight into Victorian life! A place with everything – gorgeous gardens and parkland and a home people have loved.'
Liz Finlayson, Edinburgh

Lanhydrock is the perfect country house and estate, with the feel of a wealthy but unpretentious family home. Follow in the footsteps of generations of the Robartes family, walking in the 17th-century Long Gallery among the rare book collection under the remarkable plasterwork ceiling. After a devastating fire in 1881 the house was refurbished in the high-Victorian style, with the latest mod cons. Boasting the best in country-house design and planning, the kitchens, nurseries and servants' quarters offer a thrilling glimpse into life 'below stairs', while the spacious dining room and bedrooms are truly and deeply elegant.

Exploring
– There are 50 rooms to explore; allow plenty of time!
– Play the Steinway piano in the Long Gallery.
– Look out for our second-hand bookshop and family museum.
– Explore the extensive garden and estate, colourful all year.
– Discover the network of woodland, park and riverside paths.
– Don't miss our picnic area and adventure playground.

Eating and shopping: we serve local seasonal food in our friendly licensed restaurants. Go Cornish and have an Oggie pasty and cream tea. Local food and gifts available in the shop. Plant centre in car park outside the tariff area.

We welcome dogs assisting visitors with disabilities

Making the most of your day: open-air theatre, garden tours and children's activities throughout the year. **Dogs**: welcome on leads in park and woods but assistance dogs only in formal garden.

Access for all:

Getting here: 200:SX088636. 2½ miles south-east of Bodmin. **Foot**: 1¾ miles from Bodmin Parkway via original carriage-drive to house, signposted in station car park. **Cycle**: NCN3 runs past entrance. **Train**: Bodmin Parkway 1¾ miles by cycle or foot; 3 miles by road. **Road**: signed from A30, A38 Bodmin to Liskeard, and B3268 off A390 at Lostwithiel. **Parking**: free, 600 yards.

Finding out more: 01208 265950 or lanhydrock@nationaltrust.org.uk

Lanhydrock		M	T	W	T	F	S	S
House								
1 Mar–31 Mar	11–5	·	T	W	T	F	S	S
1 Apr–30 Sep	11–5:30	·	T	W	T	F	S	S
2 Oct–4 Nov	11–5	·	T	W	T	F	S	S
Garden and estate								
Open all year	10–6	M	T	W	T	F	S	S
Shop and refreshments*								
1 Jan–5 Feb	11–4	·	·	·	·	·	S	S
11 Feb–29 Feb	11–4	M	T	W	T	F	S	S
1 Mar–31 Mar	11–5	M	T	W	T	F	S	S
1 Apr–30 Sep	11–5:30	M	T	W	T	F	S	S
1 Oct–4 Nov	11–5	M	T	W	T	F	S	S
5 Nov–31 Dec	11–4	M	T	W	T	F	S	S

House also open Bank Holiday Mondays and Mondays during state school holidays (telephone for dates). Church, plant centre and second-hand bookshop open as house, plus Mondays April to October. Refreshments open from 10:30, 11 February to 4 November. Shop and refreshments are inside the tariff area. *Closed 25 and 26 December.

Lawrence House

9 Castle Street, Launceston, Cornwall PL15 8BA

Map ① E7   1964

A Georgian town house, Lawrence House was built in 1753 in Launceston, once the county town of Cornwall. **Note**: Lawrence House is leased to Launceston Town Council and used as a local museum and civic centre.

Access for all: Building Garden

Getting here: 201:SX330848. 1 mile approximately north of the A30 in the oldest part of Launceston.

Finding out more: 01566 773277 or lawrencehouse@nationaltrust.org.uk

Lawrence House		M	T	W	T	F	S	S
2 Apr–2 Nov	10:30–4:30	M	T	W	T	F	·	·

Leigh Woods

Leigh Woods, near Bristol, Avon

Map ① I4   1909

A beautiful haven on Bristol's doorstep. A tranquil and diverse woodland with wonderful views of Avon Gorge and suspension bridge. Great for walking or cycling with an excellent network of paths including a 1¾-mile easy-access trail and link to the National Cycle Network. **Note**: no toilets.

Exploring
- Look out for Red Devon cattle grazing part of site.
- Let off steam in the natural play area.
- Track down many rare species, including whitebeam trees.
- Discover Stokeleigh Camp Iron Age hill fort.

Eating and shopping: picnics welcome as there are no catering facilities.

Making the most of your day: look out for the natural play area. Explore the permanent orienteering course (please contact the office for a map). **Dogs**: welcome (but be aware of the cattle).

Getting here: 172:ST555730. 2 miles south-west of Bristol. **Foot**: River Avon Trail (Pill to Bristol) links with footpath up Nightingale Valley. **Cycle**: blue trail through woods connects with NCN41. **Bus**: Bristol to Portishead (alight Beggar Bush Lane and follow Valley Road). **Train**: Clifton Down ⊠ 2½ miles,

Bristol Temple Meads 3 miles. **Road**: off A369 Bristol to Portishead road: from Bristol via Clifton Suspension Bridge; from M5 junction 19 take A369. **Parking**: roadside parking on North Road off A369, or Forestry Commission car park.

Finding out more: 0117 973 1645 or leighwoods@nationaltrust.org.uk. Reserve Office, Valley Road, Leigh Woods, Bristol, Avon BS8 3PZ

Leigh Woods	Open every day all year

Levant Mine and Beam Engine

Trewellard, Pendeen, near St Just, Cornwall TR19 7SX

Map ① A9 1967

'Unbelievable. The tour this morning was the best we've ever done. Made our membership cost worth it alone today. Brilliant.'
John and Anita Farnell, Ruyton, North Shropshire

In its dramatic clifftop setting on the edge of the Atlantic Ocean, Levant was, for 110 years, 'the queen of Cornwall's submarine mines', with undersea levels stretching more than a mile out under the sea. Today, as part of the Cornwall and West Devon Mining World Heritage Site, Levant embodies an atmospheric and awe-inspiring landscape that has made the local mining district famous worldwide. The surviving buildings and ruins offer a moving glimpse into the lives and stories of the men and women who toiled to extract the riches of the earth from beneath the crashing waves.

Exploring
- Watch the 1840 beam engine come to life under steam.
- Follow the miners' footsteps through the tunnel to Man-Engine Shaft.
- Discover the stories of our mining ancestors.
- Explore a patchwork of enigmatic ruins.
- Join our guides to uncover the site's secrets.
- Downloadable walks help you experience more of the mining landscape.

Eating and shopping: hot and cold drinks and light refreshments are available from the kiosk. Small shop with mining-related goods and books.

Making the most of your day: steam engine and guided tours daily. 'Tales from the mine under the sea' in school holidays. Downloadable walks to Geevor and Botallack. **Dogs**: welcome on leads.

Access for all: ⓟ 🅱️ ♿ 🔄 📷 🚶 ∴ 🅿️
Building ♿ ♿ ➡️ ♿

Getting here: 203:SW368346. 1 mile west of Pendeen. **Foot**: South West Coast Path passes entrance. **Bus**: hourly service from Penzance to Trewellard (1 mile from site). **Train**: Penzance, 7 miles. **Road**: on B3306 St Just to St Ives road. **Parking**: free, 100 yards.

Finding out more: 01736 786156 or levant@nationaltrust.org.uk

Levant Beam Engine		M	T	W	T	F	S	S
Steaming								
12 Feb–2 Nov	11–5		M	T	W	T	F	·	S
Not steaming								
6 Jan–10 Feb	11–4		·	·	·	·	F	·	·
9 Nov–14 Dec	11–4		·	·	·	·	F	·	·

Atmospheric Levant Mine and Beam Engine, Cornwall

Little Clarendon

Dinton, Salisbury, Wiltshire SP3 5DZ

Map (1) K5

Late 15th-century stone house and curious 20th-century chapel adjoining. **Note**: no toilet.

Access for all: 👓 **Building** 🔾

Getting here: 184:SU015316. On B3089, 9 miles west of Salisbury. Close to Dinton post office.

Finding out more: 01985 843600 or littleclarendon@nationaltrust.org.uk

Little Clarendon		M	T	W	T	F	S	S
9 Apr	2–5	M	·	·	·	·	·	·
7 May	2–5	M	·	·	·	·	·	·
4 Jun	2–5	M	·	·	·	·	·	·
27 Aug	2–5	M	·	·	·	·	·	·

The Lizard and Kynance Cove

The Lizard, near Helston, Cornwall

Map (1) C10

Lizard Point, Britain's most southerly mainland point, offers dramatic cliff walks, wild flowers and geological features. Two miles north lies Kynance Cove, considered one of the most beautiful beaches in the world. Marconi's historic wireless experiments are celebrated at the Lizard Wireless Station and the Marconi Centre at Poldhu. **Note**: Kynance car park toilets closed in winter (cove toilets open all year). Some sheer cliffs.

Exploring – At the Point, watch Cornish choughs fledge and fly.
– Hire a kayak and explore the creeks around the Helford.
– Take to the waves and learn to surf at Poldhu.

The beautiful Kynance Cove, Cornwall

Exploring – Enjoy the view with a picnic at Kynance.

Eating and shopping: café at Kynance Cove (March to October), café at Lizard Point (March to October) – both Trust-approved concessions. Café open all year at Poldhu (not National Trust).

Making the most of your day: visit in May and June to see the wild flowers at their best; you may even spot basking sharks. Surfing at Poldhu or join a kayak event on the Helford. **Dogs**: seasonal day-time dog bans on some beaches, including Kynance and Poldhu.

Access for all: 🅿️🚽♿🚻🎧 **Mullion Cove** ♿
Poldhu Beach ♿ **Kynance Cove** ➡️

Getting here: 203:SW688133. 11 miles southeast of Helston. **Foot**: South West Coast Path around peninsula. **Cycle**: visit website for trails. **Bus**: Helston to Lizard (Kynance Cove 1 mile, Lizard Point ½ mile). **Road**: A3083 from Helston to Lizard. Mullion and Poldhu: signposted. Helford and Gillan: follow B3293 (to St Keverne) until signs to Helford. **Parking**: car parks at Lizard and Kynance. Limited parking around Helford and Gillan (not National Trust). Council car park at Poldhu.

Finding out more: 01326 561407 or lizard@nationaltrust.org.uk. The Stables, Penrose, Helston, Cornwall TR13 0RD

The Lizard	Open every day all year

Telephone for opening times of the Lizard Wireless Station at Bass Point and the Marconi Centre at Poldhu.

Lodge Park and Sherborne Estate

Lodge Park, Aldsworth, near Cheltenham, Gloucestershire GL54 3PP

Map ① K/L2 🏛️🌳🏠🔔🍴 1983

17th-century grandstand created in 1634 by John 'Crump' Dutton, inspired by his passion for gambling, banqueting and entertaining. The National Trust's first restoration project relying on archaeological evidence. Enjoy the impressive views of the deer course and park (designed by Charles Bridgeman in the 1720s). Note: repairs may require scaffolding. Toilet at Lodge Park only.

Exploring
- England's only surviving 17th-century deer course and grandstand.
- Dramatic views from the grandstand of Charles Bridgeman's landscape.
- Explore the windswept and romantic countryside.
- Plenty of space for picnics and ball games.

Eating and shopping: small shop. Hot and cold drinks available, including local apple juice, as well as ice-cream and sandwiches.

Lodge Park, Gloucestershire: 17th-century grandstand

Making the most of your day: open-air theatre and living history during the summer. Walks around the surrounding Sherborne Estate. **Dogs**: welcome under close control.

Access for all: 🅿️🅳🚾🖥️📶 Building 🦽🔼

Getting here: 163:SP146123. 3 miles east of Northleach. **Road**: approach from A40 only. **Parking**: Ewe Pen Barn car park 163:SP158143, Water Meadows 163:SP175154 (off A40 towards Sherborne).

Finding out more: 01451 844130 or lodgepark@nationaltrust.org.uk

Lodge Park and Sherborne Estate	M	T	W	T	F	S	S
Lodge Park							
16 Mar–4 Nov 11–4	·	·	·	·	·	**F**	**S S**
Sherborne Estate							
Open all year	**M**	**T**	**W**	**T**	**F**	**S**	**S**

Lodge Park open Bank Holiday Mondays. Occasionally closes for weddings (telephone to confirm opening times). Access to Sherborne Estate from Ewe Pen car park.

Loughwood Meeting House

Dalwood, Axminster, Devon EX13 7DU

Map ① H7 ✚ 1969

Set in the beautiful East Devon countryside, this atmospheric 17th-century thatched Baptist meeting house is dug into the hillside. **Note**: no toilet. Door handle turns backwards.

Access for all: Building 🦽🔼

Getting here: 192/193:SY253993. 4 miles west of Axminster, 1 mile south of Dalwood, 1 mile north-west of Kilmington.

Finding out more: 01752 346585 or loughwood@nationaltrust.org.uk. South and East Devon Countryside Office, The Stables, Saltram House, Plymouth, Devon PL7 1UH

Loughwood Meeting House	
Open every day all year from 11 to 5	

Services held twice yearly (details at Meeting House).

Lundy

Bristol Channel, Devon EX39 2LY

Map ① D5   1969

Undisturbed by cars, the island encompasses a small village with an inn and Victorian church, and the 13th-century Marisco Castle. For nature-lovers there is a variety of flora and fauna. Designated the first Marine Conservation Area, Lundy offers opportunities for diving and seal watching. **Note**: Lundy is financed, administered and maintained by the Landmark Trust. Holiday cottages available (not National Trust).

Exploring   − A unique island experience.
− Sail from Ilfracombe or Bideford on board MS *Oldenburg*.
− Peaceful and remote − a world apart.

Eating and shopping: Marisco Tavern serves hot and cold food and drinks. Island shop sells souvenirs, Lundy stamps, snacks and ice-creams.

Making the most of your day: there is a wealth of things to do, including walking, letterboxing, birdwatching and discovering the varied wildlife. **Dogs**: assistance dogs only.

Access for all: [icons]
Building [icon] Grounds [icon]

Getting here: 180:SS130450. In the Bristol Channel 11 miles north of Hartland Point, 25 miles west of Ilfracombe. **Ferry**: sea passages from Bideford or Ilfracombe according to tides up to four days a week, end of March to end October. **Bus**: regular services from Barnstaple to Ilfracombe and Bideford. **Train**: Barnstaple: 8 miles to Bideford, 12 miles to Ilfracombe. **Sat Nav**: Ilfracombe booking office: EX34 9EQ. Bideford office: EX39 2EY. **Parking**: at Bideford or Ilfracombe for ferries (pay and display).

Finding out more: 01271 863636 or lundy@nationaltrust.org.uk. The Lundy Shore Office, The Quay, Bideford, Devon EX39 2LY

Lundy
MS *Oldenburg* sails from Bideford or Ilfracombe up to four times a week from the end of March until the end of October carrying both day and staying passengers. A helicopter service operates from Hartland Point from November to mid-March, Mondays and Fridays only, for staying visitors.

Lundy, in the Bristol Channel, Devon: dramatic coastline (top) and lighthouse

Lydford Gorge

Lydford, near Tavistock, Devon EX20 4BH

Map ① F7 1947

This lush oak-wooded steep-sided river gorge (the deepest in the South West), with its natural beauty, fascinating history and many legends, can be explored through a variety of exhilarating short or long walks. Around every corner the River Lyd plunges, tumbles, swirls and gently meanders as it travels through the gorge. Throughout the seasons there is an abundance of wildlife and plants to see, from woodland birds to wild garlic (you can smell it too) in the spring and fungi in the autumn. **Note**: strenuous walking, rugged terrain, vertical drops. Unsuitable for visitors with heart complaints or walking difficulties.

Exploring – Discover the magical 30-metre-high Whitelady Waterfall.

Whitelady Waterfall at Lydford Gorge, Devon

Exploring – Walk out over the bubbling Devil's Cauldron.
– Watch woodland birds from the bird hide.
– See the water tumble through Tunnel Falls.
– Learn about the myths of the Gubbins and Whitelady Waterfall.
– Find out about natural remedies in the Wild Garden.

Eating and shopping: look out for wildlife books and outdoor clothing in the shop. Enjoy Devon cream teas at one of two tea-rooms. Add to your picnic with takeaway drinks and food.

Making the most of your day: school holiday and family events, wildlife-themed activities, wild food area, children's play area, bird hide. **Dogs**: welcome on leads.

Access for all: 🅿️🚻♿🔉📷🅰️ ⚫⚫🅰️
Buildings 🏠 Gorge 🚶

Getting here: 191/201:SX509845. At the end of Lydford village. **Foot**: as road directions or via Blackdown Moor from Mary Tavy. **Cycle**: NCN27 and 31. **Bus**: regular service from Tavistock. **Road**: 7 miles south of A30. Halfway between Okehampton and Tavistock, 1 mile west off A386 opposite Dartmoor Inn: main entrance at west end of Lydford village; waterfall entrance near Manor Farm. **Parking**: free.

Finding out more: 01822 820320 or lydfordgorge@nationaltrust.org.uk

Lydford Gorge		M	T	W	T	F	S	S
Gorge*								
10 Mar–7 Oct	10–5	M	T	W	T	F	S	S
8 Oct–4 Nov	10–4	M	T	W	T	F	S	S
Shop and tea-room (main entrance)**								
11 Feb–19 Feb	10–4	M	T	W	T	F	S	S
10 Mar–7 Oct	10–5	M	T	W	T	F	S	S
8 Oct–4 Nov	10–4	M	T	W	T	F	S	S
7 Nov–23 Dec	10–3	·	·	W	T	F	S	S
Waterfall tea-room (waterfall entrance)								
10 Mar–7 Oct	11–5	M	T	W	T	F	S	S
8 Oct–4 Nov	11–4	M	T	W	T	F	S	S

*Majority of gorge closed January, February, November and December due to weather conditions, higher river levels, reduced daylight hours and maintenance work (there is still access to Whitelady Waterfall from the waterfall entrance). 11 to 19 February: top path also open to the Whitelady Waterfall, 11 to 4. ** 7 November to 23 December: opening dependent on weather (telephone to check).

Apostles topiary at Lytes Cary Manor, Somerset

Lytes Cary Manor

near Somerton, Somerset TA11 7HU

Map ① I5  1949

An intimate medieval manor house with beautiful Arts and Crafts garden that you can imagine living in. Originally the family home of Henry Lyte, where he translated the unique *Niewe Herball* book on herbal remedies, Lytes Cary was then lovingly restored in the 20th century by Sir Walter Jenner. The garden rooms contain a magical collection of topiary and herbaceous borders, while tranquil walks on the estate take you along the River Cary. To complete your visit take a stroll among our community allotments and discover their creative and colourful designs.

Exploring   — Explore the enchanting garden rooms.
- Play a game of croquet on the lawn.
- Stroll through cherry blossom on the estate's White Walk.
- Have fun in the children's natural outdoor play area.
- Walk through the 12 Apostles to the house gates.
- See the *Lytes Herbal* dedicated to Queen Elizabeth I.

Eating and shopping: relax in our peaceful courtyard with a light lunch and a cream tea from our food kiosk. Our rustic shop has a wide range of gifts, plants, garden tools and accessories.

Making the most of your day: enjoy croquet on the lawn, garden talks and tours, family trails, explorer backpacks and outdoor games. **Dogs**: welcome on leads on estate walks only.

Access for all: 🅿️🅿️♿🚻🏷️🎬 ᠄᠄
Building 🏠♿ Grounds 🏠♿

Getting here: 183:ST529269. Near Somerton. **Bus**: Wells to Yeovil; Taunton to Yeovil (passing close Taunton ✇). Both pass within ¾ mile Yeovil Pen Mill ✇. Alight Kingsdon, 1 mile. **Train**: Yeovil Pen Mill 8 miles; Castle Cary 9 miles; Yeovil Junction 10 miles. **Road**: off A372. Signposted, 1 mile from A303 (London to Exeter). **Parking**: free, 40 yards.

Finding out more: 01458 224471 or lytescarymanor@nationaltrust.org.uk

Lytes Cary Manor		M	T	W	T	F	S	S
House								
17 Mar–4 Nov	10–4	M	T	W	·	F	S	S
Garden, parkland, food kiosk and shop								
17 Mar–4 Nov	10–5	M	T	W	·	F	S	S

Max Gate

See Hardy Country, page 53.

Mompesson House

The Close, Salisbury, Wiltshire SP1 2EL

Map ① K5   1952

When walking into the celebrated Cathedral Close in Salisbury, visitors step back into a past world, and on entering Mompesson House, featured in the award-winning film *Sense and Sensibility*, the feeling of leaving the modern world behind deepens. The tranquil atmosphere is enhanced by the magnificent plasterwork, fine period furniture and graceful oak staircase, which are the main features of this perfectly proportioned Queen Anne house. In addition, the Turnbull collection of 18th-century drinking glasses is of national importance. The delightful walled garden has a pergola and traditionally planted herbaceous borders.

Exploring – View the exceptional Turnbull collection of 18th-century drinking glasses.
– Fantasise about living in this townhouse in the 18th century.

Eating and shopping: locally baked scones and cakes served in the tea-room. Light lunches and teas can be eaten in the garden. Salisbury National Trust shop is only 60 yards away. Catalogue of Turnbull Glass Collection for sale.

Making the most of your day: regular croquet sessions on the lawn for people of every age and ability. Music includes pianists playing our 1790s Broadwood square piano and Northumbrian Pipers' sessions. **Dogs**: assistance dogs only.

Access for all: 🚻🧷♿🗺️📷📖🦽👓📷
Building 🦽🏠 Grounds 🦽🏠

Getting here: 184:SU142297. On north side of Choristers' Green in the Cathedral Close, near High Street Gate. **Foot**: from city centre follow signs to the Cathedral. **Bus**: buses from surrounding area. **Train**: Salisbury ½ mile. **Road**: park and ride on all main routes into city. **Parking**: 260 yards in city centre (not National Trust, pay and display).

The gracious façade of Mompesson House in Salisbury Cathedral Close, Wiltshire

Exploring – Perch on the window seats to admire the fine plasterwork.
– Children, seek out all the human faces in the mouldings.
– In cooler weather, sit in the library by the fire.
– Treat yourself to a delicious cream tea in the garden.

Finding out more: 01722 420980 (Infoline). 01722 335659 or mompessonhouse@nationaltrust.org.uk

Mompesson House			M	T	W	T	F	S	S
10 Mar–4 Nov	11–5		M	T	W	·	·	S	S
Open Good Friday.									

Montacute House

Montacute, Somerset TA15 6XP

Map (1) I6   🏛️ ✿ ♠ 🏠 🔔 🍷 | 1931 |

A magnificent golden mansion surrounded by terraced formal gardens, grand trees and garden pavilions. This Elizabethan house is full of oak-panelled rooms with period furniture and tapestries. It has the longest gallery in England, displaying more than 50 Tudor portraits (including Henry VIII and Elizabeth I) on permanent loan from London's National Portrait Gallery. The garden's roses, flower borders and famous old wobbly hedges are delightful; you can relax on the lawns and explore the parkland, with its ancient trees. From our car park, discover the surrounding countryside, including St Michael's Hill, where King Harold's holy cross was allegedly discovered.

The many-windowed Montacute House, Somerset

Exploring
- Discover the bed used by Johnny Depp in *The Libertine*.
- See the unique Goodhart collection of embroidery samplers spanning centuries.
- Use the easy touch-screens to learn about the portraits.
- Speak to the experts in new conservation-in-action rooms.
- Play a game of croquet on Cedar Lawn.
- Stroll the famous West Drive used in *Sense and Sensibility*.

Eating and shopping: tasty local home-cooked food, fresh coffee and hot chocolate in the Courtyard Café. Children's menu and lunch boxes. Separate tea-room to book for private hire or for groups to eat together. Large, well-stocked shop with Tudor theme and plant sales.

Making the most of your day: programme of events and activities, including farmers' markets, open-air theatre, free family activity backpacks and Tudor visits for schools. Licensed for civil weddings and private functions. **Dogs**: under control in parkland. On leads in garden 2 November to 9 March.

Access for all: 🅿️ 🎧 ♿ 🛏️ 🚶 ⠿ 📷
Building 🔼 ♿🔽 Grounds 🔼 ➡️ 🔽

Getting here: 183/193:ST499172. In Montacute village, 4 miles west of Yeovil. **Bus**: Yeovil bus station to South Petherton. **Train**: Yeovil Pen Mill 5 miles; Yeovil Junction 7 miles. **Road**: 3 miles south of, and signed from, A303 (London to Exeter). Take A3088 towards Yeovil. **Parking**: free.

Finding out more: 01935 823289 or montacute@nationaltrust.org.uk

Montacute House		M	T	W	T	F	S	S
House								
10 Mar–4 Nov	10–4	M	·	W	T	F	S	S
Garden, parkland, café and shop								
1 Jan–16 Mar	10–4	·	·	W	T	F	S	S
17 Mar–4 Nov	10–5	M	·	W	T	F	S	S
7 Nov–23 Dec	10–5	M	·	W	T	F	S	S

Opens every day in August.

Newark Park

Ozleworth, Wotton-under-Edge,
Gloucestershire GL12 7PZ

Map (1) J3    1949

Overlooking the splendid Ozleworth Valley, Newark Park commands breathtaking, unspoilt views to the Mendips. The house and grounds are steeped in history, from Tudor beginnings to their dramatic rescue by a Texan architect in the 20th century.

Newark Park, Gloucestershire: once a hunting lodge

Exploring   – Discover 450 years of life at Newark Park.
– Enjoy tranquil countryside walks.
– Marvel at the magnificent views.
– Relax in the serene, peaceful garden.

Eating and shopping: snack and shop in the basement rooms of the house.

Making the most of your day: waymarked countryside walks and footpath link to the Cotswold Way. Family events and children's quiz. Garden games for hire. Picnics welcome in garden. **Dogs**: on leads in grounds only.

Access for all: [icons]
Building [icons] Grounds [icon]

Getting here: 172:ST786934. 1½ miles east of Wotton-under-Edge. **Foot**: Cotswold Way passes property. **Bus**: Bristol to Thornbury, connecting Thornbury to Dursley, alight Wotton-under-Edge, 1¾ mile. **Train**: Stroud 10 miles. **Road**: 1¾ miles south of junction of A4135 and B4058, follow signs for Ozleworth. House signposted from main road. **Parking**: free, 100 yards.

Finding out more: 01793 817666 (Infoline). 01453 842644 or newarkpark@nationaltrust.org.uk

Newark Park		M	T	W	T	F	S	S
1 Mar–28 Oct	11–5			**W**	**T**	·	**S**	**S**

Open Bank Holidays. Closes dusk if earlier.

Overbeck's

Sharpitor, Salcombe, Devon TQ8 8LW

Map (1) F9   1937

'Lovely peaceful garden, just to sit down and let the working week drift away, helped by delicious crab sandwiches… Bliss.'
Mr G. Mumford, Much Wenlock

An exotic and fascinating hidden treasure perched high on the cliffs above Salcombe. Explore the banana garden, meander through the woodland, or relax beneath the palms and soak up the spectacular panorama across miles of beautiful coastline and estuary. Continue your journey of discovery into the Edwardian seaside home of eccentric scientist Otto Overbeck. See his amazing invention: the 'rejuvenator'; hear the polyphon, a giant Victorian music box; and be intrigued by the eclectic collections of natural and maritime history. The perfect day out for families who enjoy exploring, or the keen gardener who wants to be inspired and excited.
Note: entrance path and grounds are very steep in places.

Exploring   – Enjoy the monthly garden newsletter, produced by our Head Gardener.
– Join the gardeners and encounter plants from around the world.

Finding out more: 01548 842893 or overbecks@nationaltrust.org.uk

Overbeck's		M	T	W	T	F	S	S
Garden and tea-room								
7 Jan–4 Mar	11–3	·	·	·	·	·	S	S
Garden, museum, tea-room and shop								
10 Mar–4 Nov	11–5	M	T	W	T	F	S	S
Garden and tea-room								
10 Nov–30 Dec	11–3	·	·	·	·	·	S	S

Tea-room: March to October closes 4:15.
Museum closes 4:30.

View over the estuary from Overbeck's, Devon

Exploring
- Discover our range of family trails and self-guided tours.
- Hunt for Fred, the friendly ghost, in the museum.
- Listen to the melodious sounds of the polyphon.
- Check out our website for special events throughout the year.

Eating and shopping: enjoy local crab in a freshly prepared sandwich. Kick off those boots and relax by a warming fire. Book a luxury picnic hamper to make the day complete. Select a plant to rejuvenate your garden or take away a gift.

Making the most of your day: pick up a walks leaflet and enjoy even more views. Select a melody to be played on the polyphon. Flick through our local pictures and shipwreck albums. **Dogs**: assistance dogs only.

Access for all: ⬛⬛⬛⬛⬛⬛⬛⬛
Building 🏚 Grounds 🔲➡️

Getting here: 202:SX728374. Above Salcombe. **Foot**: South West Coast Path within ¾ mile. **Ferry**: Salcombe to South Sands, then ½-mile strenuous walk. **Bus**: from Totnes or Kingsbridge, alight Salcombe. **Road**: narrow and unsuitable for large vehicles. **Sat Nav**: ignore in Malborough; follow brown signs. **Parking**: small car park. Alternative, East Soar, then 2-mile walk.

Parke

Parke, Bovey Tracey, Devon TQ13 9JQ

Map (1) G7

Set on the south-eastern edge of Dartmoor, this tranquil country park contains numerous delights. Enjoy a gentle amble along the banks of the River Bovey, as it meanders through woodlands and meadows rich in plant and wildlife, then discover the medieval weir, walled garden and orchard with historic apple trees.

Exploring
- Walk through riverside meadows to the medieval weir.
- Explore the orchard and see the walled garden.
- Try orienteering or cycle along the old railway track.
- Enjoy the woodland and parkland through a maze of paths.

Parke, Devon, sits on the edge of Dartmoor

Eating and shopping: enjoy a light lunch, cream tea or ice-cream at the café. Outdoor seating area. Local products for sale.

Making the most of your day: try out our orienteering trails. Don't miss the wildlife events and apple days. Visit the Dartmoor Pony Heritage Visitor and Education Centre. **Dogs**: on leads where stock grazing. Welcome in the café.

Access for all: ♿ Café 🏛 Countryside ⚑

Getting here: 191:SX805786. In Bovey Tracey. **Cycle**: Newton Abbot to Bovey Tracey cycleway. **Bus**: Exeter bus station to Newton Abbot, alight at Bovey Tracey (1 mile). Also Widecombe to Bovey Tracey, May to October Saturdays only. **Train**: Newton Abbot 6 miles. **Road**: 2 miles north of A38, Exeter to Plymouth. Take the A382 towards Bovey Tracey. **Parking**: free.

Finding out more: 01626 834748 or parke@nationaltrust.org.uk. Home Farm, Parke, Bovey Tracey, Devon TQ13 9JQ

Parke		M	T	W	T	F	S	S
Parkland, woodland and walks								
Open all year	Dawn–dusk	M	T	W	T	F	S	S
Café and shop*								
1 Mar–31 Oct	8–4:30	M	T	W	T	F	S	S
1 Nov–23 Dec	10–4	·	·	W	T	F	S	S

*Opening and closing times in winter dependent on weather: please telephone to check.

A National Trust holiday cottage sits on the edge of Loe Pool, on the Penrose Estate, Cornwall

Penrose Estate: Gunwalloe and Loe Pool

Penrose Estate, Helston, Cornwall TR13 0RD

Map ① B10

Loe Bar separates Cornwall's largest freshwater pool, Loe Pool, from the sea. At Gunwalloe, beautiful beaches frame a medieval church. **Note**: cliff edges and coast path subject to erosion. Seasonal dog ban on Gunwalloe Church Cove. Seasonal refreshments kiosk at Gunwalloe. 'Outdoor gym' alongside Loe Pool. Gunwalloe parking: free (pay and display charges for non-members).

Access for all: ♿ Penrose Estate (parkland) 🏛 Gunwalloe beach ➡

Getting here: 203:SW639259. Just outside Porthleven, 2 miles south-west of Helston.

Finding out more: 01326 561407 or penroseestate@nationaltrust.org.uk. The Stables, Penrose, Helston, Cornwall TR13 0RD

Penrose Estate	Open every day all year

Beach refreshments kiosk (not National Trust) at Gunwalloe during peak summer season only. Toilets at Gunwalloe (not National Trust) also only during peak season.

The graceful Palladian Bridge at Prior Park Landscape Garden, Bath, Somerset

Priest's House

Muchelney, Langport, Somerset TA10 0DQ

Map (1) I6   1911

This medieval hall-house, built in 1308 for the parish priest, has been little altered since the early 17th century. **Note**: house is tenanted. No toilet.

Access for all: 🔲📷 Building 🔣

Getting here: 193:ST429250. 1 mile south of Langport.

Finding out more: 01458 253771 or priestshouse@nationaltrust.org.uk

Priest's House		M	T	W	T	F	S	S
4 Mar–22 Oct	2–5	M	·	·	·	·	·	S

Admission by guided tour, last tour 4:30.

Prior Park Landscape Garden

Ralph Allen Drive, Bath, Somerset BA2 5AH

Map (1) J4   1993

'Beautiful! Staff very friendly and helpful. Gorgeous coffee.'
Lynda Jones, Bath

One of only four Palladian bridges of this design in the world can be crossed at Prior Park, which was created in the 18th century by local entrepreneur Ralph Allen, with advice from 'Capability' Brown and the poet Alexander Pope. The garden is set in a sweeping valley where visitors can enjoy magnificent views of Bath. Restoration of the 'Wilderness' has reinstated the Serpentine Lake, Cascade and Cabinet. A five-minute walk leads to the Bath

Skyline, a six-mile circular route encompassing beautiful woodlands and meadows, an Iron Age hill fort, Roman settlements, 18th-century follies and spectacular views. **Note**: mansion not accessible. There are steep slopes, steps and uneven paths in the garden.

Exploring – A green tourism site with disabled parking only.
– Beautiful and intimate 18th-century garden.
– Fabulous views of the city of Bath.
– Serpentine Lake and cascade.
– One of only four Palladian bridges in the world.
– Free family activity packs.

Eating and shopping: revive yourself at our tea kiosk by the lakes.

Making the most of your day: free family activity packs throughout the year. Open-air events programme. Guided tours of the Wilderness. **Dogs**: on leads only.

Access for all:
Grounds

Getting here: 172:ST760633. **Foot**: 1 mile uphill (very steep) walk from rear of railway station: cross river, pass Widcombe shopping parade, turn right onto Prior Park Road at White Hart pub, proceed uphill, garden on left. Kennet & Avon Canal path ¾ mile. **Cycle**: NCN4, ¾ mile. **Bus**: frequent services from Bath Spa ▶, Abbey and Dorchester Street by the bus station. **Train**: Bath Spa 1 mile. **Road**: no brown signs. **Parking**: for disabled visitors only.

Finding out more: 01225 833422 or priorpark@nationaltrust.org.uk

Prior Park Landscape Garden		M	T	W	T	F	S	S
Garden								
1 Jan–29 Jan	10–5:30	·	·	·	·	·	S	S
1 Feb–4 Nov	10–5:30	M	T	W	T	F	S	S
10 Nov–30 Dec	10–5:30	·	·	·	·	·	S	S
Tea kiosk								
4 Feb–1 Apr	11–5	·	·	·	·	·	S	S
6 Apr–4 Nov	11–5	M	T	W	T	F	S	S
10 Nov–30 Dec	11–5	·	·	·	·	·	S	S

Last admission one hour before closing. Closes dusk if earlier than 5:30. Tea kiosk also open school holidays, events and Bank Holidays.

Purbeck Countryside

Purbeck, near Corfe Castle, Dorset

Map ① K7

From the dinosaur-era Purbeck limestones to the recent sand dunes of Studland, nowhere else packs such a variety of habitats into such a small area. As a result, Purbeck is the richest place for plant life in Britain. Discover these landscapes through 54 miles of paths and bridleways.

Exploring – Waymarked off-road family cycle route between Hartland and Studland.
– Variety of downloadable walks, rides and adventures from Trust website.
– Relax and take in the heathland wildlife at Middlebere.
– Rock climbing on the cliffs west of Swanage.

Eating and shopping: look out for the shops and cafés at Studland beach and Corfe Castle village. Throughout Purbeck there are other suitable facilities to start or finish your visit. Purbeck's own 'Old Volunteer Cider' available in summer at Trust outlets.

Making the most of your day: enjoy the 'best view in the kingdom' at viewpoint by Purbeck Golf Club. Horse riding over Ballard Down and Godlingston Heath from Studland Stables. Discover carving at Burngate Stone Centre. **Dogs**: welcome under close control, some restrictions may apply (see signs).

Getting here: OL15:SY9615. **Foot**: South West Coast Path begins at Shell Bay, Studland; many other footpaths. **Cycle**: NCN2 between Hartland and Studland, plus 23 miles of bridleways. **Ferry**: Sandbanks car ferry for access to Studland. **Bus**: Wareham to Swanage bus serves Hartland Moor, Corfe Castle and Spyway. Bournemouth to Swanage bus for Studland Heath and Dunes, plus Ballard Down.

Places may occasionally close for conservation, safety or events

Parking: free at Durnford Drove, Langton and Slepe road verges. Pay and display (free to members) at Castle View by Corfe Castle; Studland.

Finding out more: 01929 450123 or purbeck@nationaltrust.org.uk. Purbeck Office, Currendon Farm, Ulwell Road, Swanage, Dorset BH19 3AA

Purbeck Countryside	Open every day all year

Bird hides at Studland and Hartland and free parking sites open all year.

St Michael's Mount

Marazion, Cornwall TR17 0HT

Map ① B9  1954

Still home to the St Aubyn family (which runs and maintains it in partnership with the Trust) as well as to a small community, this iconic rocky island is crowned by a medieval church and castle – the oldest buildings dating from the 12th century. Immerse yourself in history, wonder at the architecture and discover the legend of Jack the Giant Killer. Look down on the subtropical terraced garden and enjoy breathtaking views of spectacular Mount's Bay. If the weather is favourable, take a short evocative boat trip to the island, or at low tide enjoy the walk across the causeway. **Note**: steep climb to the castle up an uneven, cobbled pathway. Narrow passageways in castle.

Exploring
 – Enjoy the adventure of getting here – by foot or boat.
 – Find the giant's heart in the path to castle.
 – Discover the amazing plaster frieze showing medieval hunting scenes.
 – See the model of the Mount made from champagne corks!
 – Explore the exotic subtropical garden.
 – Guided tours of the castle in the winter months.

Eating and shopping: Island Café: (licensed) enjoy a cream tea or Cornish pasty. Sail Loft Restaurant (licensed): local food freshly produced and sustainably sourced. National Trust shop: contemporary gifts, Cornish produce and art. The Island Shop offers local gifts and artwork.

Making the most of your day: children's quiz for castle and garden. Live music most Sundays during summer. Garden tours

Romantic St Michael's Mount, off Marazion in Cornwall, is crowned by a medieval church and castle

(by arrangement). Sunday church services: Whitsun to end September. Winter guided tours. **Dogs**: assistance dogs only in castle and garden.

Access for all: 🚾♿♿ Castle 🏰 Village 🏘

Getting here: 203:SW515298. Off coast at Marazion. **Foot**: South West Coast Path within ¾ mile. Access to Mount on foot over the causeway at low tide only. **Cycle**: NCN3, ¾ mile. **Ferry**: small boats make the crossing at high tide. Occasionally, the boats don't run in bad weather (please telephone). **Bus**: Penzance to Helston or St Ives. All pass Penzance ➧. **Train**: Penzance 3 miles. **Road**: ½ mile south of A394 at Marazion. **Parking**: ample parking in Marazion opposite St Michael's Mount (not National Trust, charge including members).

Finding out more: 01736 710265/710507 (general enquiries/tide information). 01736 711067 (shop). 01736 710748 (restaurant) or stmichaelsmount@nationaltrust.org.uk

St Michael's Mount		M	T	W	T	F	S	S
Castle								
26 Mar–29 Jun	10:30–5	M	T	W	T	F	·	S
1 Jul–31 Aug	10:30–5:30	M	T	W	T	F	·	S
2 Sep–2 Nov	10:30–5	M	T	W	T	F	·	S
Garden								
16 Apr–29 Jun	10:30–5	M	T	W	T	F	·	·
5 Jul–31 Aug	10:30–5:30	·	·	·	T	F	·	·
6 Sep–28 Sep	10:30–5	·	·	·	T	F	·	·

Last admission 45 minutes before castle closing (enough time should be allowed for travel from the mainland). Castle winter opening: Tuesday and Friday, entry by guided tour only, 11 and 2 (subject to weather conditions). Please telephone in advance.

Saltram

Plympton, Plymouth, Devon PL7 1UH

Map ① F8   🏛🏠❖♣💺🍴 1957

Still a largely undiscovered treasure, and the result of centuries of sophistication and extravagance, Saltram is the perfect family day out: close to Plymouth and yet in a world of its own. Home to the Parker family for nearly 300 years, the house with its original contents provides a fascinating insight into country-estate life throughout the centuries. Fine Robert Adam interiors and beautiful collections bring the 'age of elegance' to life at Saltram. Learn about some of the fascinating characters and family stories, including the correspondence between Frances, the first Countess, and Jane Austen.

Exploring
- Escape the Plymouth hustle and bustle in this green haven.
- Be blown away by the grandeur of the impressive Saloon.
- Peek behind the scenes with an eye opener guided tour.
- Transform yourself into a gorgeous Georgian with the dressing-up clothes.
- Hunt out the romantic follies in the magnificent garden.
- Ride your bike or fly a kite in the parkland.

The west front of Saltram, Devon, stands out against a grey menacing sky

Eating and shopping: enjoy the local and seasonal food in the Park Restaurant, which is available for special occasions and private functions. Browse the gift and garden shops. Visit the Chapel Gallery for local arts and crafts.

Making the most of your day: varied year-round family events programme, open-air theatre, craft fairs, costumed Georgian evenings. Special themed guided tours available for no extra charge, revealing family stories and some behind-the-scenes access. **Dogs**: welcome in woods and parkland.

Access for all: 🅿️🆔♿🚻🔊📷🖨️ House ♿🦽 Restaurant ♿🦽 Grounds ♿➡️🦽

Getting here: 201:SX520557. 3½ miles east of Plymouth city centre. **Foot**: South West Coast Path within 4 miles. **Cycle**: NCN27. **Bus**: service from city centre will drop off within one mile. **Train**: Plymouth 3½ miles. **Road**: 3½ miles east of Plymouth city centre. Travelling south (from Exeter): exit from A38 is signed Plymouth City Centre/Plympton/Kingsbridge. At roundabout take centre lane, then third exit for Plympton. Take right-hand lane and follow brown signs. Travelling north (from Liskeard): leave A38 at Plympton exit. From roundabout as before. **Sat Nav**: enter Merafield Road. **Parking**: free, 50 yards.

Finding out more: 01752 333503 or saltram@nationaltrust.org.uk

Saltram		M	T	W	T	F	S	S
Park								
Open all year	Dawn–dusk	M	T	W	T	F	S	S
House 🙿								
11 Feb–19 Feb	12–4:30	·	·	·	·	·	S	S
10 Mar–4 Nov	12–4:30	M	T	W	T	·	S	S
Park Restaurant								
1 Jan–9 Mar	10–4	M	T	W	T	F	S	S
10 Mar–4 Nov	10–5	M	T	W	T	F	S	S
5 Nov–31 Dec	10–4	M	T	W	T	F	S	S
Garden, shops and gallery								
2 Jan–9 Mar	11–4	M	T	W	T	F	S	S
10 Mar–4 Nov	11–5	M	T	W	T	F	S	S
5 Nov–31 Dec	11–4	M	T	W	T	F	S	S

Last admission to house 45 minutes before closing. Parts of house open for special Christmas events, see website for details. Garden, gallery and shops closed 24 to 26 December. Park Restaurant closed 25 and 26 December. Gallery closed 1 January to 10 February and opening hours may vary during the winter: telephone to check.

Shute Barton

Shute, near Axminster, Devon EX13 7PT

Map ① H7  1959

A fascinating medieval manor house, with a later Tudor gatehouse and battlemented turrets, set in pretty grounds. **Note**: limited opening. Shute has been converted into a National Trust premium holiday property.

Access for all: Building 🏠

Getting here: 177/193:SY253974. 3 miles south-west of Axminster, 2 miles north of Colyton on Honiton to Colyton road (B3161).

Finding out more: 01752 346585 or shute@nationaltrust.org.uk. South and East Devon Countryside Office, The Stables, Saltram House, Plymouth, Devon PL7 1UH

Shute Barton		M	T	W	T	F	S	S
12 May–13 May	11–5	·	·	·	·	·	S	S
16 Jun–17 Jun	11–5	·	·	·	·	·	S	S
15 Sep–16 Sep	11–5	·	·	·	·	·	S	S
13 Oct–14 Oct	11–5	·	·	·	·	·	S	S

Entrance by guided tours only (last tour 4:30).

Snowshill Manor and Garden

Snowshill, near Broadway, Gloucestershire WR12 7JU

Map ① K1 🏠♿🏠 1951

Charles Wade was a treasure-seeker who loved buying and restoring beautifully made objects. His family motto was 'Let nothing perish', and he spent his inherited wealth doing just that, amassing a spectacular collection of everyday and extraordinary objects from across the globe. He restored the ancient Cotswold manor house specifically to display these unlikely treasures. Laid out with creative flair, just as Mr Wade intended, the house is literally packed to the rafters with thousands of unusual objects – from tiny toys to splendid suits of Samurai armour. The manor house is surrounded by an equally characterful hand-crafted terraced garden.

Exploring
– Be fascinated by the story of collector Charles Wade.
– Be amazed by his vast and astonishing collection.
– Be intrigued by stunning examples of craftsmanship.
– Relax in the 'outdoor rooms' of the peaceful hillside garden.
– Have a go at one of our children's trails.
– Visit the Priest's House, the home of Charles Wade.

Eating and shopping: enjoy a delicious home-cooked lunch in the restaurant. Try one of our legendary cream teas or homemade cakes on the terrace. Treat yourself to local produce in our gift shop. Pick up a bargain in the second-hand bookshop.

Making the most of your day: children's trails indoors and around garden. History weekend in July. Apple weekend 13 and 14 October. Winter weekend events in November. **Dogs**: assistance dogs only in garden and manor house.

Access for all: 🅿♿🚻🖊♿🚾🔼🔽🖥🎥👓🅰
Manor 🔼 Garden 🔼🔽

Getting here: 150:SP095341. 2½ miles south-west of Broadway. **Foot**: Cotswold Way within ¾ mile. **Bus**: Evesham to Broadway, then 2½ miles uphill. **Train**: Moreton-in-Marsh 7 miles, Evesham 8 miles. **Road**: turn off A44 Broadway bypass into Broadway village; at green turn right uphill to Snowshill. **Parking**: free, 500 yards. Walk from car park to manor house and garden along undulating country path. Transfer available.

Finding out more: 01386 852410 or snowshillmanor@nationaltrust.org.uk

Snowshill Manor and Garden		M	T	W	T	F	S	S
Manor								
31 Mar–1 Jul	12–5	·	·	W	T	F	S	S
2 Jul–26 Aug	11:30–4:30	M	·	W	T	F	S	S
29 Aug–28 Oct	12–5	·	·	W	T	F	S	S
Garden, shop and restaurant								
31 Mar–1 Jul	11–5:30	·	·	W	T	F	S	S
2 Jul–26 Aug	11–5	M	·	W	T	F	S	S
29 Aug–28 Oct	11–5:30	·	·	W	T	F	S	S
3 Nov–25 Nov	12–4	·	·	·	·	·	S	S
Priest's House								
31 Mar–1 Jul	11–5	·	·	W	T	F	S	S
2 Jul–26 Aug	11–4:30	M	·	W	T	F	S	S
29 Aug–28 Oct	11–5	·	·	W	T	F	S	S

Admission by timed ticket (numbers limited). Last admission to Manor one hour before closing. Open all Bank Holidays between April and October. Limited opening by guided tour in November.

Fascinating corner at Snowshill Manor, Gloucestershire

South Milton Sands

Thurlestone, near Kingsbridge, Devon TQ7 3JY

Map ① F9   1980

Long sandy beach and dunes with spectacular sunsets. Discover great rock-pooling, kayaking and snorkelling. On South West Coast Path. **Note**: Beach House café.

Fun at South Milton Sands, Devon

Access for all: Beach House

Getting here: SX677414. 4 miles outside Kingsbridge. From Kingsbridge take the A381 towards Salcombe. Turn right to South Milton village, then left in the village centre (signposted) to the beach.

Finding out more: 01548 561144 (Beach House café) or southmiltonsands@nationaltrust.org.uk. South Devon Countryside Office, The Stables, Saltram House, Plymouth, Devon PL7 3UH

South Milton Sands	Open every day all year

Café open throughout summer and at various times out of season, weather dependent (telephone 01548 561144).

Stoke-sub-Hamdon Priory

North Street, Stoke-sub-Hamdon, Somerset TA14 6QP

Map (1) I6   1946

The priests who lived here served the Chapel of St Nicholas (now destroyed). The Great Hall is open to visitors. **Note**: no toilet.

Access for all: Grounds

Getting here: 193:ST473175. 2 miles west of Montacute between Yeovil and Ilminster.

Finding out more: 01935 823289 or stokehamdonpriory@nationaltrust.org.uk

Stoke-sub-Hamdon Priory		M	T	W	T	F	S	S
1 Mar–28 Oct	11–5	M	T	W	T	F	S	S

Stembridge Tower Mill

High Ham, Somerset TA10 9DJ

Map (1) I5   1969

Built in 1822, this is the last remaining thatched windmill in England – the last survivor of five in the area. **Note**: holiday cottage on site, please respect the tenants' privacy. No toilet. Parking limited.

Getting here: 182:ST432305. 2 miles north of Langport, ½ mile east of High Ham.

Finding out more: 01935 823289 or stembridgemill@nationaltrust.org.uk

Stembridge Tower Mill		M	T	W	T	F	S	S
1 Mar–28 Oct	10–5	M	T	W	T	F	S	S

Interior open Sundays 15 April, 17 June and 12 August, 12 to 5.

Stonehenge Landscape

near Amesbury, Wiltshire

Map (1) K5   1927

Within the Stonehenge World Heritage Site, the Trust manages 827 hectares (2,100 acres) of downland surrounding the famous stone circle. On the ridges all around Stonehenge are fine Bronze Age round barrows, the resting places of the privileged. The shallow banks of Stonehenge's Great Cursus enclosure are 5,500 years old, pre-dating the stone circle. The massive henge of Durrington Walls, 4,500 years ago the site of feasting and huge gatherings, encloses a natural valley. Large areas of arable land are being restored as chalk grassland, habitat for a diverse range of insects, birds and wild flowers. **Note**: stone circle managed by English Heritage (admission free to Trust members).

Exploring – Explore the monuments on foot with our downloadable walk leaflets.
– Check out our events, walks and workshops before you visit.
– Family activities and trails downloadable from our website.
– Listen for skylarks and keep an eye out for hares.
– Enjoy a picnic while admiring the Stonehenge views.

Eating and shopping: catering kiosk at the stone circle (not National Trust).

Making the most of your day: walks and workshops available throughout the year – visit our website to find out more. **Dogs**: welcome under close control (assistance dogs only at stone circle).

Access for all: ⓟ♿♿

Getting here: 184:SU120420. 2 miles west of Amesbury. **Bus**: Stonehenge Tour bus Salisbury ➔ to Stonehenge. **Train**: Salisbury 9½ miles. **Road**: on A344, off A303. **Parking**: 50 yards (not National Trust). Charge may apply June to October (National Trust members free).

Finding out more: 01980 664780 or stonehenge@nationaltrust.org.uk.
3 Stonehenge Cottages, King Barrows, Amesbury, Wiltshire SP4 7DD

Stonehenge Landscape	Open every day all year

Perfect spot for daydreaming at Stourhead, Wiltshire

Stourhead

near Mere, Wiltshire BA12 6QD

Map ① J5

'A living work of art' is how a magazine described Stourhead when it first opened in the 1740s. The world-famous landscape garden, with a magnificent lake reflecting classical temples, mystical grottoes and rare and exotic trees, offers a day of fresh air and discovery. Experience Italian grand tour adventures at Stourhead House – with its unique Regency library, Chippendale furniture and inspirational paintings, set amid 'picnic perfect' lawns and parkland. The garden and house are at the heart of a 1,072-hectare (2,650-acre) estate, where chalk downs, ancient woods and farmland are managed for wildlife and for you to explore.

Exploring – Have fresh air fun with a walk in the woods.
– Climb 205 steps to the top of King Alfred's Tower.
– Get closer to nature with our family Tracker Packs.
– Discover secrets of the garden on a free tour.
– Pack a picnic and find a place to relax.
– Experience an Italian adventure at Stourhead House.

Eating and shopping: take home a Stourhead memento from our extended shop and plant centre. Taste delicious dishes in our award-winning restaurant. Visit the farm shop, drink or dine in the Spread Eagle Inn. Enjoy tea, coffee and ices from the ice-cream parlour.

Making the most of your day: enjoy a grand day out full of simple pleasures, from climbing trees and hands-on conservation to behind-the-scenes glimpses and fresh-air workouts. Get the latest news at stourheadnt.wordpress.com. **Dogs**: landscape garden, November to February only (short fixed leads). Welcome in countryside all year.

Access for all: ⃞⃞⃞⃞⃞⃞⃞⃞⃞
Building ⃞⃞⃞ **Grounds** ⃞⃞⃞⃞

Getting here: 183:ST780340. Stourton, 3 miles north-west of Mere, 8 miles south of Frome. **Cycle**: Wiltshire Cycle Way. **Bus**: from Warminster and Shaftesbury, alight Zeals, 1¼ miles. **Train**: Gillingham 6½ miles; Bruton 7 miles. **Road**: brown signs off A303. B3092 from Frome. **Parking**: 400 yards. King Alfred's Tower 50 yards.

Finding out more: 01747 841152 or stourhead@nationaltrust.org.uk.
Stourhead Estate Office, Stourton, Warminster, Wiltshire BA12 6QD

Stourhead		M	T	W	T	F	S	S
Garden								
Open all year	9–6	M	T	W	T	F	S	S
House*								
18 Feb–4 Mar	11–3	·	·	·	·	·	S	S
House								
10 Mar–17 Jul	11–5	M	T	·	·	F	S	S
20 Jul–4 Sep	11–5	M	T	W	T	F	S	S
7 Sep–9 Oct	11–5	M	T	·	·	F	S	S
12 Oct–4 Nov	11–5	M	T	W	T	F	S	S
House**								
30 Nov–16 Dec	11–3	·	·	·	·	F	S	S
Restaurant and shop								
Open all year	10–5	M	T	W	T	F	S	S
Farm shop								
1 Jan–23 Dec	10–4	M	T	W	T	F	S	S

Garden, shop and restaurant open 1 January. Closed 25 December. *Selection of rooms open with chance to see and take part in conservation. **Selection of rooms decorated for Christmas. Please call for King Alfred's Tower opening times. Shop, restaurant and farm shop closing times vary according to season.

Running to the beach at Studland, Dorset

Studland Beach and Nature Reserve

Studland, near Swanage, Dorset

Map ① K7   ⃞⃞⃞⃞ 1982

A glorious slice of natural coastline in Purbeck featuring a four-mile stretch of golden, sandy beach, with gently shelving bathing waters and views of Old Harry Rocks and the Isle of Wight. Ideal for watersports and includes the most popular naturist beach in Britain. The heathland behind the beach is a haven for native wildlife and features all six British reptiles. Designated trails through the sand dunes and woodlands allow for exploration and spotting of deer, insects and bird life as well as a wealth of wild flowers. Studland was the inspiration for Toytown in Enid Blyton's *Noddy*. **Note**: Shell Bay toilets are low-water flush, only other toilets at Knoll Beach and Middle Beach.

Exploring – The start of the South West Coast Path.
– Try the summer watersports, including boat hire, kayaking and windsurfing.

Exploring
- Picnic in the dunes watching the activities in Poole Bay.
- Discover the bird life on Little Sea in the winter.
- Rent a wooden beach hut.
- Enjoy a BBQ in the designated beach areas.

Eating and shopping: seaside-themed shop selling beach goods, as well as gifts from Dorset. Indoor and open-air seating with a spectacular sea view at Knoll Beach Café. Local Purbeck ice-creams and daily seasonal specials. Serving local meat dishes from the wider estate.

Making the most of your day: wide range of events year round, including children's trails, wildlife guided walks, food events and Discovery Centre. Coastal change interpretation hut open all year. **Dogs**: restrictions from 1 May to 30 September.

Access for all: �📶🚻♿ Grounds ♿🅿️

Getting here: 195:SZ036835. 5 miles south of Poole and north of Swanage. **Foot**: 5 miles of South West Coast Path. **Ferry**: car ferry from Sandbanks, Poole, to Shell Bay. **Bus**: Bournemouth to Swanage. **Train**: Branksome or Parkstone, both 3½ miles to Shell Bay (via vehicle ferry) or Wareham 12 miles. **Parking**: Shell Bay and South Beach, 9 to 11; Knoll Beach and Middle Beach, 9 to 8 or dusk if earlier. Prices vary through season. Most car parks are pay and display.

Finding out more: 01929 450500 or studlandbeach@nationaltrust.org.uk. Purbeck Estate Office, Studland, Swanage, Dorset BH19 3AX

Studland Beach		M	T	W	T	F	S	S
Beach								
Open all year		M	T	W	T	F	S	S
Shop and café								
1 Jan–24 Mar	10–4	M	T	W	T	F	S	S
25 Mar–1 Jul*	9:30–5	M	T	W	T	F	S	S
2 Jul–2 Sep	9–6	M	T	W	T	F	S	S
3 Sep–28 Oct*	9:30–5	M	T	W	T	F	S	S
29 Oct–31 Dec	10–4	M	T	W	T	F	S	S

*Shop and café open one hour later at weekends. Shop and café opening hours may be longer in fine weather and shorter in poor. Visitor centre, shop and café closed 25 December. **Car parks can be very full in peak season.**

Tintagel Old Post Office

Fore Street, Tintagel, Cornwall PL34 0DB

Map ①D7   🏠♣ 1903

Built around 1380 as a farmhouse, this building never actually sold stamps, but has had various uses across the centuries. The homely rooms are mostly furnished with 16th-century oak furniture, whilst the cottage garden at the back provides a peaceful retreat from the bustling high street. **Note**: nearest toilet, 54 yards.

Exploring
- Discover Victorian postal memorabilia and 19th-century samplers.
- A tranquil cottage garden offers respite from the busy street.
- Experience the glow of the open fire on wintry days.
- Enjoy the handmade rag rugs, and have a go yourself.

Eating and shopping: visit the shop in the Post Room and get a special decorative hand stamp from the Old Post Office.

Hall of Tintagel Old Post Office, Cornwall

We welcome dogs assisting visitors with disabilities

Making the most of your day: family trail available. Have a go at making a rag rug. Challenge someone to a garden game, during good weather. **Dogs**: assistance dogs only.

Access for all: 🏠📷♿🅿️📷
Building 🔵🔵 Grounds 🔵🔵

Getting here: 200:SX056884. On high street, opposite King Arthur's car park. **Foot**: South West Coast Path within ¾ mile. **Bus**: services from Wadebridge to Boscastle. **Road**: follow signs off A39 for Tintagel. **Parking**: no onsite parking. Pay and display (not National Trust).

Finding out more: 01840 770024 or tintageloldpo@nationaltrust.org.uk

Tintagel Old Post Office		M	T	W	T	F	S	S
11 Feb–19 Feb	11–4	M	T	W	T	F	S	S
10 Mar–1 Apr	11–4	M	T	W	T	F	S	S
2 Apr–30 Sep	10:30–5:30	M	T	W	T	F	S	S
1 Oct–4 Nov	11–4	M	T	W	T	F	S	S

Water lilies at Tintinhull Garden, Somerset

Tintinhull Garden

Farm Street, Tintinhull, Yeovil, Somerset BA22 8PZ

Map (1) I6   1953

This delightful garden, described as one of the most harmonious small gardens in Britain, surrounds a charming manor house that you can rent as a holiday cottage. The garden rooms have secluded lawns, pools and colourful herbaceous borders, and the lovely kitchen garden provides fruit and vegetables for the restaurant at nearby Montacute House. The house has two ground-floor rooms you can visit, whilst the courtyard has a fascinating exhibition about Tintinhull. You can explore the orchards and the surrounding countryside on the woodland walk, and even the car park is set among picturesque orchards, where sheep graze contentedly.

Exploring
- Sit and relax by the tranquil pools and water lilies.
- Play croquet on the lawn under the magnolia trees.

Exploring
- Relax on the sofa in the garden room.
- Stay in the beautiful holiday cottage in Tintinhull House.
- Have your wedding day in the romantic garden pavilion.
- Discover interesting stories about Tintinhull in the village exhibition.

Eating and shopping: small, pretty tea-room serving delicious cakes and cream teas. Sit outside and enjoy your food in the sunshine. Take home a plant or a postcard, available in reception.

Making the most of your day: summer family activities. Pick up an explorer sheet from the exhibition and explore the beautiful village of Tintinhull. Play a game of croquet on the lawn.

Access for all: 🅿️📷♿♿♿♿⋯🅰️
Building 🔵🔵 Gardens 🔵➡️🔵

Getting here: 183:ST503198. In Tintinhull village, 4 miles west of Yeovil. **Bus**: Yeovil bus station to South Petherton. **Train**: Yeovil Pen Mill 5 miles; Yeovil Junction 7 miles. **Road**: 1 mile south of A303 (London to Exeter). Follow signs to Tintinhull village. **Parking**: free, 150 yards.

Finding out more: 01935 823289 or tintinhull@nationaltrust.org.uk

Tintinhull Garden		M	T	W	T	F	S	S
17 Mar–4 Nov	10–5			W	T	F	S	S

Open Bank Holiday Mondays. House closes at 4.

Treasurer's House

Martock, Somerset TA12 6JL

Map (1) I6   🏠 | 1971 |

Medieval house with Great Hall, completed 1293, and kitchen added in the 15th century. Upstairs room contains an unusual wall-painting. **Note**: tenanted house, directly opposite All Saints' parish church and war memorial. No toilet or parking on site.

Access for all: Building 🖳 Grounds 🖳🖳

Getting here: 193:ST462191. 1 mile north-west of A303, between Ilminster and Ilchester.

Finding out more: 01935 825015 or treasurersmartock@nationaltrust.org.uk

Treasurer's House		M	T	W	T	F	S	S
4 Mar–23 Sep	2–5	M	T	·	·	·	·	S

Note: Copeland family china collection admission and introductory talk – additional charge of £5 per person (including members).

Exploring
- Discover not one, but four, summerhouses dotted around the garden.
- See a variety of unusual shade and sun-loving plants.
- Find the perfect place to picnic in the sheltered garden.
- Explore the magical *Cryptomeria* tree on the main lawn.
- Get close to nature on the riverside woodland walks.
- Relax in the spacious parkland overlooking the River Fal.

Eating and shopping: enjoy lunch at Crofters café or fresh grilled produce at the Blackrock restaurant. Shop for local food, plants and souvenirs. Discover Cornish art in the gallery. Browse for second-hand books or stay longer in one of six holiday cottages.

Trelissick Garden

Feock, near Truro, Cornwall TR3 6QL

Map (1) C9   🏠🏛️❀🌷♠🐚
🏞️🏠🍸| 1955 |

'We really enjoyed exploring all the different areas and seeing how well both the garden and little summerhouses are kept.'
The Davies Family, Coventry

Starting in a complex of former farm buildings and garden walls, explore this elevated garden with its views of deep-wooded valleys and flashes of blue water. Trelissick sits on its own peninsula in an unspoiled stretch of the River Fal. Picturesque planting is heightened by the folding contours and the informal wooded setting. There are places in both sun and shade to discover a wide range of plants growing and also to sit down and recharge the batteries. All of Trelissick's many owners have made their mark and built on the framework that their predecessors laid out before them.

Spring at Trelissick Garden, Cornwall

Making the most of your day: walks in the parkland and woodland, open-air theatre in summer, exhibitions and shows held in the stables by local groups, extensive calendar of events for visitors of all ages. **Dogs**: welcome on woodland walks surrounding garden. Assistance dogs only in garden.

Access for all: ⊞🚾♿👁🦻📷📷
Visitor reception ♿ Shop ♿
Garden ♿♿➡♿♿

Getting here: 204:SW837396. 5 miles south of Truro. **Cycle**: NCN3. **Ferry**: from Falmouth, Truro and St Mawes: Enterprise boats (01326 374241), K&S Cruisers (01326 211056), Newman's Cruises/Tolverne Ferries (01872 580309). Steep uphill walk from ferry pontoon. **Bus**: Truro to Trelissick and Feock. **Train**: Truro 5 miles; Perranwell 4 miles. **Road**: on B3289 above King Harry ferry. **Parking**: 50 yards.

Finding out more: 01872 862090 or trelissick@nationaltrust.org.uk

Trelissick Garden		M	T	W	T	F	S	S
2 Jan–10 Feb	11–4	M	T	W	T	F	S	S
11 Feb–4 Nov	10:30–5:30	M	T	W	T	F	S	S
5 Nov–23 Dec	11–4	M	T	W	T	F	S	S
26 Dec–31 Dec	11–4	M		W	T	F	S	S

Allow an hour to enjoy this large garden. Garden closes dusk if earlier. Copeland China Collection open Thursdays in September, 2 to 4.

Trengwainton Garden

Madron, near Penzance, Cornwall TR20 8RZ

Map ① B9   ❄🏠 1961

Trengwainton's ten hectares (25 acres) invite you to explore – and come back for more. Discover a garden where the spirit of the plant hunters lives on. Enjoy breathtaking spring displays of magnolias, rhododendrons and camellias, then visit a walled kitchen garden that will inspire creativity with your own growing space. The wide-open views across Mount's Bay will have you reaching for your camera, before you lose yourself among winding wooded paths, picnic by the stream or simply find a quiet corner to breathe in the peace of this special place.

Exploring
– Imagine dinosaurs lurking as you explore giant tree fern glades.
– Enthuse the children with our family trails.
– Find your bearings with the toposcope.

Kitchen garden at Trengwainton Garden, Cornwall

Eating and shopping: enjoy some retail therapy in the shop and plant centre, indulging yourself with our range of Cornish products. Sample mouth-watering cakes in the award-winning tea-room (National Trust-approved concession) or light meals that include ingredients sourced from the kitchen garden.

Making the most of your day: find creative ways for you and your family to enjoy the garden with our full programme of events and activities throughout the year. **Dogs**: welcome on leads throughout.

Access for all:
Tea-room **Shop/reception** **Grounds**

Getting here: 203:SW445315. 2 miles north-west of Penzance. **Foot**: from Penzance via Heamoor village. **Cycle**: NCN3, 2½ miles. **Bus**: Penzance to St Just (from Penzance). **Train**: Penzance 2 miles. **Road**: follow signs from A30 or A3071 St Just to Penzance road. **Parking**: free, 150 yards.

Finding out more: 01736 363148 or trengwainton@nationaltrust.org.uk

Trengwainton Garden		M	T	W	T	F	S	S
12 Feb–1 Nov	10:30–5	**M**	**T**	**W**	**T**	·	·	**S**
6 Dec–16 Dec	11–4	·	·	·	**T**	**F**	·	**S**

Open Good Friday. Tea-room opens 10. Last admission 15 minutes before closing.

Trerice

Kestle Mill, near Newquay, Cornwall TR8 4PG

Map (1) C8 1953

'We just sat in the sun on the terrace overlooking the house and just admired its sheer beauty and survival.'
Valerie French, Exeter

Narrow lanes with high hedges suddenly reveal the exquisite beauty of the intimate Elizabethan manor house. Behind 576 panes of glass is the Arundell family's magnificent Great Hall with its refined plasterwork ceiling. Upstairs the Great Chamber has an even finer ceiling and views out to lands once part of the extensive estate. The story of the Trust's tenants in the 1950s – who rebuilt a fallen part of the house and devoted themselves to the restoration of Trerice – unfolds in the North Wing. Tudor defence and entertainment are brought to life by visitors trying on armour and playing traditional games.

Playing in the orchard at Trerice, Cornwall

Exploring
- Handle replica artefacts and armour and make a brass rubbing.
- Play house detective and uncover the building's eventful life.
- Relax in the tranquillity of the terraced garden and orchard.
- Try the Tudor garden games of 'kayling' (bowls) and 'slapcock'.
- Imagine how the Arundell family lived in their new house.
- Learn about the Trust's tenants' restoration work in the 1950s.

Eating and shopping: taste lemon meringue pie in the Barn tea-room and garden. Enjoy lunch overlooking the Tudor vegetable garden or in the lofty Barn. In the shop, buy gifts, souvenirs, books, local food and drink, and items inspired by Tudor times.

Making the most of your day: look out for Tudor-themed family and adult workshops, family trails and special 'living history' days. Open-drawers events, conservation surgeries, behind-the-scenes and evening opening at certain times of year. **Dogs**: welcome in the car park only.

Access for all: 🅿️♿🔔♿🚻♿♿🖼️📷♿♿
House ♿♿ Barn tea-room ♿
Garden ♿♿➡️♿

Getting here: 200:SW841585. 3 miles south-east of Newquay. **Cycle**: NCN32. **Bus**: Newquay 🚆 to St Austell 🚆, alight Kestle Mill, ¾ mile. **Train**: Quintrell Downs, 1½ miles. **Road**: south-east of Newquay via A392 and A3058, signed from Quintrell Downs (turn right at Kestle Mill), or signed from A30 at Summercourt via A3058. **Parking**: free, 300 yards.

Finding out more: 01637 875404 or trerice@nationaltrust.org.uk

Trerice		M	T	W	T	F	S	S
House								
11 Feb–4 Nov	11–5	M	T	W	T	F	S	S
Garden, shop and tea-room								
11 Feb–4 Nov	10:30–5	M	T	W	T	F	S	S
Great Hall only								
9 Nov–23 Dec	11–4	·	·	·	·	F	S	S

Atmospheric evening opening at certain times of the year. Visit the website for more information.

Tyntesfield

Wraxall, Bristol, North Somerset BS48 1NX

Map ① I4
🏠🐕✚✳️♠️
♿🏠🍽️ 2002

'It was wonderful to come back and view this glorious house post-scaffolding! An absolutely marvellous café and shop.'
Mrs Mandsfield, Weston-super-Mare

'Tyntesfield Unpacked!' 2012 celebrates ten years of National Trust ownership as 1,000 items are unpacked and 100 stories are told. Discover the glory of this Victorian home lived in by four generations of the Gibbs family, all

The flamboyant Tyntesfield, Somerset

making their mark and never throwing anything away. Find out how Tyntesfield became the Trust's largest conservation project. Be inspired by flower-filled terraces, the enchanting rose garden and productive kitchen garden. Experience the great outdoors on the wider estate and let the views take your breath away. Enjoy delicious food at Home Farm and browse in the gift shop, garden and bookshops.

Exploring
    – Come and see our newly restored walled garden.
    – Be inspired by the flamboyant Gothic architecture of the chapel.
    – Wonder at the Trust's largest recorded collection of fascinating objects.
    – Get active with the garden 'play trail' for family fun.
    – Become a wildlife detective when you 'focus on the wild'.
    – Take part in exciting events throughout the year.

Eating and shopping: enjoy estate-grown ingredients at the Home Farm restaurant or café, and sit in original Victorian cattle stalls. Visit the gift shop selling locally made gifts, be inspired in the garden shop or pick up a second-hand book.

Making the most of your day: explore the whole estate to enjoy the fascinating story of the rise, decline and rediscovery of Tyntesfield and the Gibbs family. **Dogs**: welcome on woodland estate walks. Assistance dogs only in house and garden.

Access for all:
House ▣▣▣▣ Home Farm ▣▣
Grounds ▣▣▣▣

Getting here: ST502724. 7 miles south-west of Bristol. **Bus:** frequent services from Bristol bus station. **Train:** Nailsea and Backwell station 2 miles. **Road:** on B3128. M5 southbound exit 19 via A369 (towards Bristol), B3129, B3128. M5 northbound exit 20, B3130 (towards Bristol), B3128. **Parking:** at visitor centre (transfer to house and garden available).

Finding out more: 0844 800 4966 (Infoline). 01275 461900 or tyntesfield@nationaltrust.org.uk

Tyntesfield		M	T	W	T	F	S	S
House and chapel								
11 Feb–19 Feb	11–3	M	T	W	·	·	S	S
10 Mar–4 Nov	11–5	M	T	W	·	·	S	S
Garden and estate								
1 Jan–9 Mar	10–5*	M	T	W	T	F	S	S
10 Mar–4 Nov	10–6	M	T	W	T	F	S	S
5 Nov–31 Dec	10–5*	M	T	W	T	F	S	S
Restaurant, shop and café								
1 Jan–9 Mar	10:30–4:30	M	T	W	T	F	S	S
10 Mar–4 Nov	10:30–5:30	M	T	W	T	F	S	S
5 Nov–31 Dec	10:30–4:30	M	T	W	T	F	S	S

Last admission to house one hour before closing. Timed tickets to house on busy days (limited numbers). *Garden and estate: close 5 or dusk if earlier. House: open Good Friday. December weekends: Christmas events in house. Garden and estate: closed 25 December. 24 and 31 December: closes 3.

Watersmeet

Watersmeet Road, Lynmouth, Devon EX35 6NT

Map ① F5 🏠🏛️🏞️🏡🍴 1955

A haven for wildlife with waterfalls and excellent walking, where the lush valleys of the East Lyn and Hoar Oak Water tumble together. At the heart of this area sits Watersmeet House, a 19th-century fishing lodge, which is now a tea garden, shop and information point. **Note:** deep gorge with steep walk down to house.

Exploring – Treat yourself to a delicious cream tea in the garden.

Exploring – Explore this walkers' paradise with our local walks leaflet.
– Dramatic clifftop walks, from Countisbury to Foreland Point.
– Enjoy fishing the best salmon river in England.

Eating and shopping: enjoy local and seasonal food in Watersmeet's riverside setting. Local produce, walking gear and gifts available in the shop.

Making the most of your day: buy the *Exmoor Coast of Devon* walks leaflet to help you explore and enjoy the beautiful coast and countryside of West Exmoor. Family and nature events throughout the season. **Dogs:** allowed in tea garden.

Access for all: 🅿️👁️📷 Building 🐾 Grounds 🐾

Getting here: 180:SS744487. 1½ miles east of Lynmouth. **Foot:** South West Coast Path within ¾ mile. 1½ miles from Lynmouth. **Bus:** regular services from Barnstaple (passing close Barnstaple ₮), and Minehead, alight Lynmouth. **Road:** on east side of Lynmouth to Barnstaple road (A39). **Parking:** pay and display (not National Trust), steep walk to house. Free car parks at Combe Park and Countisbury.

Finding out more: 01598 753348 or watersmeet@nationaltrust.org.uk

Watersmeet		M	T	W	T	F	S	S
Countryside								
Open all year		M	T	W	T	F	S	S
Tea-room and tea garden								
10 Mar–5 Apr	10:30–4:30	M	T	W	T	F	S	S
6 Apr–30 Sep	10:30–5	M	T	W	T	F	S	S
1 Oct–4 Nov	10:30–4:30	M	T	W	T	F	S	S

Watersmeet House shop opens 30 minutes after tea-room and tea garden.

Watersmeet, Devon: a haven for wildlife

Wembury

Wembury Beach, Wembury, Devon PL9 0HP

Map (1) F9 🏠🖼️🏖️⛵🏛️ | 1939 |

A coastal village with a small, pretty beach and a charming 19th-century mill, which is now a tea-room. With beautiful views, excellent rock-pooling and a great starting point for coastal and inland walks, Wembury, near the Yealm estuary, is a popular place to visit.

Exploring – Join a rock-pool ramble discovering life under the sea.
– Enjoy miles of coastal trails.
– Simply relax and enjoy the beautiful sunsets.
– Treat yourself to a cream tea at the Old Mill.

Eating and shopping: morning coffees, homemade cakes, soups, pasties and ice-creams. Local arts and crafts. Beach shop sells everything from spades and wetsuits to windbreaks. Deckchairs, body boards and wetsuits for hire at weekends and school holidays.

Making the most of your day: discover a wide variety of activities at Wembury, including rock-pooling (01752 862538), sailing, surfing, kayaking, walking and horse riding (visit www.oldmillwembury.co.uk for more details). **Dogs**: welcome on coast path. Banned on beach 1 May to 30 September.

Access for all: 🅿️♿🚻📠 Old Mill Café 🔽
Marine Centre 🚻 Wembury Beach 🔽

Getting here: 201:SX517484. On edge Wembury village. **Foot**: South West Coast Path. **Ferry**: seasonal ferries to Noss Mayo and Bantham. **Bus**: Plymouth to Wembury daily (limited on Sunday). For Wembury Point: Plymouth to Heybrook Bay. **Train**: Plymouth 10 miles. **Road**: Wembury Point and beach follow the A379 from Plymouth, turn right at Elburton, follow signs to Wembury. At Wembury follow the road until you see Wembury primary school, turn left where you see a brown sign for café. **Parking**: free (charge for non-members). Manned during busy times.

The sun sets over Wembury Point, Devon

Finding out more: 01752 346585 (South Devon Coast and Countryside Office). 01752 862314 (Old Mill Café) or wembury@nationaltrust.org.uk. South and East Devon Countryside Office, The Stables, Saltram House, Plymouth, Devon PL7 1UH

Wembury		M	T	W	T	F	S	S
Beach and coast								
Open all year		M	T	W	T	F	S	S
Old Mill Café								
1 Jan–2 Jan	11–3	M	·	·	·	·	·	S
11 Feb–19 Feb	10:30–4	M	T	W	T	F	S	S
31 Mar–4 Nov	10:30–5	M	T	W	T	F	S	S
26 Dec–31 Dec	11–3	M	·	W	T	F	S	S

Café opening hours may vary depending on weather.

Westbury College Gatehouse

College Road, Westbury-on-Trym,
Bristol BS9 3EH

Map ① I3   🏛 1907

15th-century gatehouse to the 13th-century
College of Priests – where the 14th-century
theological reformer John Wyclif lived.
Note: access by key. No toilet.

Access for all: Building 🐾

Getting here: 172:ST572775. 3 miles north of
Bristol centre.

Finding out more: 01275 461900 or
westburycollege@nationaltrust.org.uk

Westbury College Gatehouse
Access (Monday to Friday) by key to be collected by
appointment from Holy Trinity Parish Church Office, Church
Road, Westbury-on-Trym, Bristol BS9 3EQ. 0117 950 8644
(mornings only).

Westbury Court Garden

Westbury-on-Severn, Gloucestershire GL14 1PD

Map ① J2   ✿ 1967

'We so enjoyed our visit. Such a beautiful
and well kept garden. It is a great credit
to the staff.'
Mr E. Jones, Worcester

Originally laid out between 1696 and 1705,
this is the only restored Dutch water garden
in the country. Visitors can explore canals,
clipped hedges and working 17th-century
vegetable plots and discover many old
varieties of fruit trees.

Parterre at Westbury Court Garden, Gloucestershire

Exploring – See the gardening style of
 the late 18th century.
– The huge tulip tree flowers at
 the end of June.
– One of the oldest holm oaks
 in the country.
– Historic fruit and vegetables
 grown and sold throughout
 the year.
– Footpath access to the
 River Severn.
– Lovely picnicking spot.

Making the most of your day: evening
garden tours, Easter Egg trails, Apple Day.
Dogs: welcome on short leads at all times.

Access for all: 🅿️♿️🚻🖼👓 Grounds ♿️♿️♿️

Getting here: 162:SO718138. 9 miles
south-west of Gloucester. **Foot**: River
Severn footpath runs from garden to river.
Bus: Gloucester ⊞ to Chepstow or Coleford.
Train: Gloucester 9 miles. **Road**: on A48.
Parking: free, 300 yards.

Finding out more: 01452 760461 or
westburycourt@nationaltrust.org.uk

Westbury Court Garden		M	T	W	T	F	S	S
14 Mar–1 Jul	10–5	·	·	W	T	F	S	S
2 Jul–2 Sep	10–5	M	T	W	T	F	S	S
5 Sep–28 Oct	10–5	·	·	W	T	F	S	S

Open Bank Holiday Mondays. Open other times
by appointment.

Westwood Manor

Westwood, near Bradford-on-Avon,
Wiltshire BA15 2AF

Map (1) J4   🏠➕❀ 1960

This beautiful small manor house, built over three centuries, has late Gothic and Jacobean windows, decorative plasterwork and two important keyboard instruments. There is also some fine period furniture, as well as 17th- and 18th-century tapestries and a modern topiary garden. **Note**: administered for the National Trust by the tenant. No toilet.

Exploring — Enjoy an elegant manor house with a friendly, domestic atmosphere.
— The country's earliest Italian keyboard instrument in playing order.
— A variety of woods, colours and textiles in the furniture.
— Sit in the peaceful green garden surrounded by yew topiary.

Eating and shopping: buy a CD of atmospheric musical recordings of the recently restored virginal and spinet.

Making the most of your day: children's quizzes for five to eight year olds, plus eight and aboves. House unsuitable for under-fives.

Access for all: 🅿️🔴🅰️ Manor 🔵🔵 Garden 🔵

Getting here: 173:ST812590. 1½ miles south-west of Bradford-on-Avon, in Westwood village, beside church. **Cycle**: NCN254, ¾ mile. **Bus**: Bath ➡ to Trowbridge (passing close Trowbridge ➡). **Train**: Avoncliff 1 mile; Bradford-on-Avon 1½ miles. **Road**: Westwood village signed off B3109 Bradford-on-Avon to Rode. Turn left opposite the New Inn towards the church. **Parking**: free, 90 yards.

Finding out more: 01225 863374 or westwoodmanor@nationaltrust.org.uk

Westwood Manor		M	T	W	T	F	S	S
1 Apr–30 Sep	2–5		**T**	**W**				**S**

Small groups at other times by written application with stamped addressed envelope.

Westwood Manor, Wiltshire: from church roof

White Mill

Sturminster Marshall, near Wimborne Minster, Dorset BH21 4BX

Map ① K6   🏠🔧⚙️ 1982

Corn mill with original wooden machinery in a peaceful riverside setting.

Access for all: 🅿️🔧♿
Building ♿♿ Grounds ♿

Getting here: 195:ST958006. On the River Stour in the parish of Shapwick, close to Sturminster Marshall.

Finding out more: 01258 858051 or whitemill@nationaltrust.org.uk

White Mill		M	T	W	T	F	S	S
24 Mar–28 Oct	12–5	·	·	·	·	·	**S**	**S**

Admission by guided tour. Open Bank Holiday Mondays: 12 to 5, last tour 4.

Old kennels at Woodchester Park, Gloucestershire

Woodchester Park

Nympsfield, near Stonehouse, Gloucestershire GL10 3TS

Map ① J3   🌳♿ 1994

The tranquil wooded valley contains a 'lost landscape': remains of an 18th- and 19th-century landscape park with a chain of five lakes. The restoration of this landscape is an ongoing project. Waymarked trails (steep in places) lead through picturesque scenery, passing an unfinished Victorian mansion (not National Trust). **Note**: toilet not always available.

Exploring — Families will enjoy discovering our new 'play' trail.
— Don't miss Woodchester Mansion Open Days (01453 861541).

Making the most of your day: follow the waymarked trails through the valley. **Dogs**: under close control, on leads where requested.

Access for all: Grounds ♿

Getting here: 162:SO797012. 4 miles south-west of Stroud. **Foot**: Cotswold Way within ¾ mile. **Bus**: Stroud to Nympsfield (passing close Stroud ≋). **Train**: Stroud 5 miles. **Road**: off B4066 Stroud to Dursley road. **Parking**: £2 (pay and display), no change given from ticket machine. Accessible from Nympsfield road, 300 yards from junction with B4066. Last admission one hour before dusk.

Finding out more: 01452 814213 or woodchesterpark@nationaltrust.org.uk. The Ebworth Centre, The Camp, Stroud, Gloucestershire GL6 7ES

Woodchester Park
Open every day all year from dawn to dusk

South East

In the lap of a giant: an awe-inspiring sequoia
at Sheffield Park and Garden

Outdoors in the South East

The South East of England is one of the country's most densely populated areas; however, thanks to the National Trust and similar organisations, it still boasts extensive and beautiful green spaces and miles of dramatic coastline – perfect places to enjoy some fun out of doors.

Right:
on the beach at
East Head,
West Sussex
Below:
Slindon Estate,
South Downs,
West Sussex

Explore the newest national park

The newest national park, in the South Downs, offers a host of exciting activities, including zorbing (rolling down a hill in a giant blow-up hamster ball), mountain boarding, cycling, kayaking and power kiting. But it's not all about sport – there are fabulous places for everyone to enjoy, take a stroll with a picnic and just admire the views. There are also plenty of downloadable walks and trails on our website.

Take the Surrey Hills challenge

The rolling hills of Surrey offer equally exciting opportunities, with some of the best cycling anywhere to be had at Box Hill – the hairpin bends of the famous zigzag road are a real challenge. With the visitor centre and servery at the top, you can always stop for a well-deserved break. For the younger explorers, Box Hill is also home to a new natural play trail, with plenty of exciting obstacles and challenges to tackle.

Clockwise from top right:
**mountain-biking at Black
Down, West Sussex.
View from Coombe Hill,
Buckinghamshire.
Walking along the clifftop
on the South Downs Way,
Seven Sisters, East Sussex**

Experience a reunited landscape

One of the highlights of this year is certainly the newly reunited Hindhead Commons. With no noisy road to interrupt the views and disturb the peace, you can make the most of this stunning landscape with new waymarked walks and trails. At the Devil's Punch Bowl café choose between a traditional English breakfast or delicious cream tea.

Step back in time

Our countryside is full of reminders of the past, from Iron Age hill forts to neolithic burial chambers. One place not to miss is the ancient Saddlescombe Farm. Although not far from Brighton, this unique place feels a world away. With 3,000 years of history tied up within it, there is so much to see – including a 17th-century threshing barn, Tudor scullery and donkey wheel. Visit on one of the special open days or as part of a group on a booked tour.

The Garden of England

Kent is famous for the iconic White Cliffs of Dover and now, for the first time, we are working with the British Mountaineering Council to offer experienced climbers the amazing opportunity to climb these giants (on restricted routes). There are also many lovely walks you can enjoy in this glorious county – it is not called the Garden of England for nothing. You can follow a number of trails through Knole Park, spotting the resident deer along the way, or visit Old Soar Manor, then follow the trail to Ightham Mote, where you can refuel with a cream tea.

Take in the Chilterns

We look after a group of popular beauty spots in the picturesque Chiltern Hills, where there are many fabulous walking opportunities. Spend a pleasant day exploring this attractive landscape of woods, farms and hamlets, stopping for a spot of lunch at a pub. Or set off on an adventure by bike along the Chilterns Cycleway. If you follow the famous Ridgeway long-distance path you will find yourself at Coombe Hill – the highest viewpoint in the Chilterns. You could even pay a visit to Watlington Hill and spot the magnificent red kites. These graceful birds have been brought back from the edge of extinction.

How will you discover Ashridge?

There are many ways to explore the 2,000 hectares (5,000 acres) of woodland, open countryside and hills of the Ashridge Estate. See the sights by bike on one of our family-friendly cycle routes. Children can explore the woodland and discover our orienteering and eye-spy trails. Take one of our powered mobility vehicles around the meadow, into the woodland or try our new route offering beautiful views of Aldbury and into the Vale. With such a range of walks, there is something to suit everyone.

Down the Wey in a day

The River Wey, the largest stretch of waterway the Trust cares for, is a green corridor through Guildford and out into the Surrey countryside. You can hire a boat and escape the hustle and bustle for a day or take a longer break and really get used to the relaxed pace of river life.

Right, top:
woodland on the Ashridge Estate, Hertfordshire
Right, bottom:
the River Wey Navigations, Surrey

Why not try...?

Leaving the car at home

If you want to get outdoors and go a little further afield, but don't fancy sitting in traffic, then here are our top suggestions. 'Walk the Chalk' is a new waymarked trail from Dorking West to Gomshall railway stations. It leads you up onto the ridge of the Surrey Hills, taking in some wonderful views. For those further south, the Breeze up to the Downs bus service from Brighton railway station, takes you to Devil's Dyke, where you can spend the day picnicking or walking – if you really want to explore the area, you could even hire a bike. Also starting in Brighton is the National Cycle Network route 20 cycle path, which takes you right past the entrance to Nymans. Finally, a new riverside walk and circular cycle trail from Richmond railway station leads straight to the delightful Ham House and Garden.

Rock-pool rambles

We look after some of the magnificent coastline of East Sussex and the Isle of Wight – places where wildlife is abundant. From the birds that make their home on the cliffs of the Seven Sisters, to the creatures that hide in the pools left by the sea at Birling Gap and St Helen's beach, there's a new world waiting to be explored.

Pedal power

Cycling is a great way to stay fit and enjoy the outdoors. You can now take advantage of even more opportunities to participate in this fun activity at our places. Hire a bike at the Devil's Dyke, or go to Stowe, where there is a new free cycling route which runs around the edge of the landscape gardens. It is just over three miles long and covers easy terrain, so is perfect for all the family.

Alfriston Clergy House

The Tye, Alfriston, Polegate,
East Sussex BN26 5TL

Map ② H8   🏠 ❄️ 1896

This rare 14th-century Wealden 'hall-house' was the first building to be acquired by the National Trust, in 1896. The thatched, timber-framed house is in an idyllic setting, with views across the River Cuckmere and surrounded by a delightful, tranquil cottage garden featuring a magnificent Judas tree. **Note**: no toilet, nearest in village car park.

Exploring — Admire the first house the National Trust saved.
— Enjoy the tranquillity of our English cottage garden.
— Discover the chalk and sour milk floor in the hall.
— Soak up the atmosphere of this 650-year-old house.

Eating and shopping: browse in the shop for a souvenir of your visit.

Making the most of your day: children's quizzes and trails. Varied events programme all year. Short circular walks and longer distance hikes over South Downs. Situated in the interesting and historic medieval village of Alfriston.

Access for all: 🦽🔍🏠♿🅿
Building 🦽 Grounds 🦽🏞

Getting here: 189:TQ521029. In Alfriston village. **Foot**: South Downs Way within ¾ mile. **Cycle**: NCN2. **Bus**: services from Lewes, Eastbourne and Seaford (pass close Lewes 🚆 and Seaford 🚆). **Train**: Berwick 2½ miles. **Road**: 4 miles north-east of Seaford, just east of B2108, in Alfriston village, adjoining The Tye and St Andrew's church. **Parking**: 500 yards at other end of village (not National Trust).

Finding out more: 01323 871961 or alfriston@nationaltrust.org.uk

Alfriston Clergy House		M	T	W	T	F	S	S
25 Feb–4 Mar	11–4						**S**	**S**
10 Mar–31 Jul	10:30–5	**M**	**T**	**W**			**S**	**S**
1 Aug–31 Aug	10:30–5	**M**	**T**	**W**		**F**	**S**	**S**
1 Sep–4 Nov	10:30–5	**M**	**T**	**W**			**S**	**S**
5 Nov–19 Dec	11–4	**M**	**T**	**W**			**S**	**S**

Open Good Friday. Special Friday openings in August.

Alfriston Clergy House, East Sussex: Wealden 'hall-house'

Ascott

Wing, near Leighton Buzzard,
Buckinghamshire LU7 0PR

Map ② E3   🏛️ ❄️ 1949

This half-timbered Jacobean farmhouse,
transformed by the de Rothschilds towards
the end of the 19th century, now houses
an exceptional collection of paintings, fine
furniture and superb oriental porcelain. The
extensive gardens are an attractive mix of
formal and natural, with specimen trees and
shrubs and some unusual features.

Exploring   —   See one of the best small
                picture collections in Britain.
          —   Tell the time by the unusual
                topiary sundial.
          —   Relax in the Dutch Garden,
                admiring the Eros Fountain.

Making the most of your day: spot
the unusual features in the gardens.
Dogs: assistance dogs only.

Access for all: 🅿️♿🚻📷👀📷
Building ♿♿♿ **Grounds** ♿♿➡️

Getting here: 165:SP891230. ½ mile east of
Wing, 2 miles south-west of Leighton Buzzard.
Bus: from Aylesbury to Milton Keynes (passing
close Aylesbury 🚇 and Leighton Buzzard 🚇).
Train: Leighton Buzzard 2 miles. **Road**: on
south side of A418. **Parking**: free, 220 yards.

Finding out more: 01296 688242 or
ascott@nationaltrust.org.uk

Ascott		M	T	W	T	F	S	S
20 Mar–29 Apr	2–6	·	T	W	T	F	S	S
1 May–26 Jul	2–6	·	T	W	T	·	·	·
31 Jul–7 Sep	2–6	·	T	W	T	F	S	S

Open Bank Holiday Mondays and Good Friday. Last
admission one hour before closing. *Gardens open in aid
of National Gardens Scheme on 7 May and 27 August
(charges including members). Some areas of the gardens
may be roped off when ground conditions are bad.

Topiary sundial at Ascott, Buckinghamshire

Ashdown House

Lambourn, Newbury, Berkshire RG17 8RE

Map ② C5   🏛️🏛️❄️🔑 1956

Extraordinary chalk-block house with
doll's-house appearance and fine portrait
collection built for the Queen of Bohemia
in the 17th century. **Note**: access is via a
staircase of 100 steps. Changes to opening
arrangements may apply from April to July
due to conservation work.

Access for all: 🅿️♿🚻📷📷📷
Building ♿ **Grounds** ♿

Getting here: 174:SU282820. 2½ miles south
of Ashbury, 3½ miles north of Lambourn, on
west side of B4000.

Finding out more: 01494 755569 (Infoline).
01793 762209 or
ashdownhouse@nationaltrust.org.uk

Ashdown House		M	T	W	T	F	S	S
House								
4 Apr–31 Oct	2–5	·	·	W	·	·	S	·
Woodland								
Open all year		M	T	W	T	·	S	S

Admission by guided tour to house at 2:15, 3:15 and 4:15
(places limited). Woodland walks open every day except
Fridays. Due to major conservation work planned from April
to July tour times and type may vary (portrait collection
cannot be seen during this period).

Ashridge Estate

Visitor Centre, Moneybury Hill, Ringshall,
Berkhamsted, Hertfordshire HP4 1LT

Map ② E3   1926

This wonderful countryside estate runs along the main ridge of the Chiltern Hills. Discover its breathtaking scenery, from ancient oak and beech woodland to the rolling chalk grassland of Ivinghoe Beacon. There is a huge network of paths to explore, with the chance to spot wildlife including wild fallow deer and red kites. Find ideas for walks and family days out at the Visitor Centre near to the Bridgewater Monument. Visit throughout the year to enjoy carpets of bluebells in spring, beautiful orchids and butterflies in summer, spectacular leaf colour in autumn and frost-covered trees in winter. **Note:** toilets only available when Visitor Centre open. No bins, please take your rubbish home.

Ashridge Estate, Hertfordshire: Bridgewater Monument

Exploring – Escape to 2,000 hectares (5,000 acres) of fresh air.
– Climb the Bridgewater Monument for wonderful panoramic views.
– Experience a landscape rich in history and archaeology.
– Visit nearby Pitstone Windmill, one of the oldest in Britain.

Eating and shopping: buy local maps and self-guided walks leaflets in the Trust shop. Treat yourself to a delicious selection of food at Brownlow Café (National Trust-approved concession).

Making the most of your day: events include wildlife walks, talks and countryside festival. Children's activities in Discovery Room. **Dogs**: allowed under close control (deer roam freely).

Access for all: ⓟ🖉♿♿🅿🖉
Visitor Centre 🅱 Grounds 🖉▶🖉

Getting here: 181:SP970131. Between Berkhamsted and Dagnall. **Foot**: Visitor Centre is a short detour from Ridgeway footpath at Ivinghoe Beacon. **Bus**: services to Monument Drive, Aldbury (½ mile uphill walk) and Tring (1¾ mile walk). **Train**: Tring ≊ 1¾ miles. Ivinghoe Beacon: Cheddington ≊ 3½ miles. **Road**: off B4506 between Berkhamsted and Dagnall. **Parking**: free.

Finding out more: 01494 755557 (Infoline). 01442 851227 or ashridge@nationaltrust.org.uk

Ashridge Estate		M	T	W	T	F	S	S
Estate								
Open all year	Dawn–dusk	M	T	W	T	F	S	S
Visitor Centre and shop*								
13 Feb–16 Dec	10–5	M	T	W	T	F	S	S
Bridgewater Monument (weather dependent)**								
31 Mar–28 Oct	12–4:30	·	·	·	·	·	S	S
Brownlow Café**								
1 Jan–24 Mar	8–4	M	T	W	T	F	S	S
25 Mar–27 Oct	8–6	M	T	W	T	F	S	S
28 Oct–31 Dec	8–4	M	T	W	T	F	S	S

*Visitor Centre, shop and café may close at dusk if earlier than published closing time. **Last entry 4:15.
***Café closed 25 December.

The west front of Basildon Park, Berkshire

Basildon Park

Lower Basildon, Reading, Berkshire RG8 9NR

Map ② D5  1978

The Basildon Park you see today is a re-creation and restoration of the 18th-century mansion, brought back to life in the 1950s by Lord and Lady Iliffe. The collection includes important 18th- and 19th-century paintings and antiques. Explore our waymarked trails through the historic parkland and gravel paths around the gardens. Don't miss our newly opened 1950s office and family activity space. **Note**: main show rooms are on the first floor – 21 steps up from ground level.

Exploring – Be inspired by the Iliffes' remarkable restoration in the 1950s.
– Take a guided tour with one of our expert guides.
– Revel in the nostalgia of Basildon Park's 1950s kitchen.
– Relax in the gardens with a picnic on the lawns.
– Discover our new accessible parkland trails.
– Enjoy a special afternoon tea in Lady Iliffe's sitting room.

Eating and shopping: enjoy traditional English fare in our tea-room, especially our Sunday roast. Treat yourself to a cream tea, with homemade cakes and scones. Don't miss the range of foods in our gift shop. Browse in our second-hand bookshop with a coffee.

Making the most of your day: guided house tours, walks in the parkland, Gardener's Workshop, baking demonstrations in 1950s kitchen, grand piano for visitors to play, waymarked trails, family activity space, garden toys. Exciting events programme. **Dogs**: welcome in grounds, on leads only.

Access for all: ♿ Mansion ♿ Stables ♿ Grounds ♿

Getting here: 175:SU611782. Between Pangbourne and Streatley. **Bus**: service from Reading to Goring & Streatley. **Train**: Pangbourne 2½ miles; Goring 3 miles. **Road**: 7 miles north-west of Reading, on west side of A329. Leave M4 at exit 12 and follow signs for Beale Park and Pangbourne, then signs to Basildon Park. **Sat Nav**: use main entrance from A329. **Parking**: free, 400 yards from mansion (buggy available).

Finding out more: 0118 984 3040 or basildonpark@nationaltrust.org.uk

Basildon Park		M	T	W	T	F	S	S
Ground-floor exhibition area, tea-room, shop and grounds								
6 Feb–9 Mar	10–4	M	T	W	T	F	S	S
10 Mar–4 Nov	10–5	M	T	W	T	F	S	S
5 Nov–21 Dec	10–4	M	T	W	T	F	S	S
House (main show rooms)								
10 Mar–4 Nov	11–5	M	T	W	T	F	S	S
1 Dec–16 Dec	11–4	M	T	W	T	F	S	S

House opens 11 for guided tours only, free-flow from 12.
Tuesday: entry by guided tour only. Timed tickets may apply.

Bateman's

Bateman's Lane, Burwash,
East Sussex TN19 7DS

Map ② H7   ♿🏠🗝️🍴♣️🛍️☂️ 1940

'We've been here before and will return
again and again. The place is just lovely.
The scones aren't bad either!'
Mrs Mills, Bromley

Eating and shopping: buy Kipling books and
souvenirs in the shop. Eat in the restaurant
with its wonderful garden setting. Relax and
have fun in the picturesque picnic glen.

Making the most of your day: events, family
fun days, storytelling, re-enactment weekends,
garden and countryside walks. Virtual tour of
watermill and first floor of house. Children's
quizzes and trails. **Dogs**: on leads in car park
only. Dog crèche available.

Access for all: 🅿️♿🚻👶🚽🔖🚗📶♿..♿🅰️
Building 🔢♿♿ Grounds ♿➡️♿

'That's She! The Only She! Make an honest
woman of her – quick!' was how Rudyard
Kipling and his wife, Carrie, felt the first
time they saw Bateman's. Surrounded by
the wooded landscape of the Sussex Weald,
this 17th-century house, with its mullioned
windows and oak beams, provided a much
needed sanctuary for this world-famous writer.
Don't miss Kipling's 1928 Rolls-Royce Phantom
1 or the working watermill near the river that
runs through the garden. **Note**: the garden,
shop and restaurant are open free of charge
in November.

Exploring
– Soak up the atmosphere in
  Kipling's book-lined study.
– Enjoy the serenity of the
  Formal Garden.
– Walk by the river as it flows
  through the meadow.
– Watch the watermill grind
  flour most Wednesday and
  Saturday afternoons.
– Experience 'Kipling Country'
  with a walk through the estate.
– Discover Kipling's 1928
  Rolls-Royce Phantom 1.

Having fun at Bateman's, East Sussex

Getting here: 199:TQ671238. ½ mile south
of Burwash. **Bus**: hourly service from
Uckfield to Etchingham (weekdays) – less
frequent at weekends. **Train**: Etchingham
3 miles. **Road**: ½ mile south of Burwash.
A265 west from Burwash, first turning on left.
Parking: free, 30 yards. Coaches: tight left
turn into first bay.

Finding out more: 01435 882302 or
batemans@nationaltrust.org.uk

Bateman's		M	T	W	T	F	S	S
Garden, shop and tea-room								
25 Feb–4 Mar	11–4	·	·	·	·	·	S	S
10 Mar–4 Nov	10–5	M	T	W	·	·	S	S
5 Nov–19 Dec	11–4	M	T	W	·	·	S	S
House								
10 Mar–4 Nov	11–5	M	T	W	·	·	S	S
1 Dec–19 Dec	11:30–3:30	M	T	W	·	·	S	S

Open Good Friday: 10 to 5. **Shop and garden close 5:30, 10
March to 4 November.** Mill grinds corn most Wednesdays
and Saturdays at 2. House: downstairs rooms decorated for
traditional Edwardian Christmas 1 to 19 December.

Bembridge Fort

Bembridge Down, near Bembridge,
Isle of Wight PO36 8QY

Map ② D9   1967

In a commanding position on top of
Bembridge Down, this derelict Victorian
fort is now opening for volunteer-run guided
tours. **Note**: access by guided tour (booking
essential). No toilets or other facilities.
Tours £3.50, including members.

Getting here: 196:SZ624861. Off B3395
Sandown to Bembridge road.

Finding out more: 01983 741020 or
bembridgefort@nationaltrust.org.uk.
c/o Longstone Farmhouse, Strawberrry Lane,
Mottistone, Isle of Wight PO30 4EA

Bembridge Fort
Guided tours on first and third Tuesdays of the month
from April to October and other days in August. Additional
weekday tours for groups of 10-plus may be possible
on request.

Bembridge Windmill

High Street, Bembridge,
Isle of Wight PO35 5SQ

Map ② D9   1961

This little gem, the only surviving windmill
on the Isle of Wight, is one of its most iconic
images. Built around 1700, it last operated in
1913 but still has most of its original machinery
intact. Climb to the top and follow the milling
process back down its four floors.

Exploring – Feel the wooden machinery
worn smooth by the years.
– See how the windmill
operated with our
working model.
– Watch a short film to discover
the milling process.

Bembridge Windmill, Isle of Wight

Exploring – Enjoy the countryside that
inspired J. M. W. Turner.

Eating and shopping: treat yourself in the
kiosk to an ice-cream or a hot or cold drink,
including tea, different coffees and hot
chocolate. Buy a gift or souvenir as a
reminder of your visit.

Making the most of your day: try milling
with our hand quern. Find the hidden millers.
Children's discovery trail sheet. Nature trails
during school holidays. Countryside walks
including the start of the Culver Trail.
Dogs: on leads are welcome in the grounds
but not in the windmill.

Access for all: Building 🏠

Getting here: 196:SZ639874. On outskirts of
village where High Street becomes Mill Road.
Cycle: NCN67, ½ mile. **Ferry**: Ryde (Wightlink)
6 miles (0871 376 1000); East Cowes (Red
Funnel) 13 miles (0844 844 9988). **Bus**: from
Ryde Esplanade ⧼ to within ½ mile; Newport
and Sandown to within ¼ mile. **Train**: Brading
2 miles by footpath. **Road**: ½ mile south of
Bembridge on B3395. **Sat Nav**: do not use
postcode, look for brown signs. **Parking**: free
(not National Trust), 100 yards in lay-by.

Finding out more: 01983 873945 or
bembridgemill@nationaltrust.org.uk

Bembridge Windmill		M	T	W	T	F	S	S
17 Mar–4 Nov	10:30–5	**M**	**T**	**W**	**T**	**F**	**S**	**S**

Closes dusk if earlier. Conducted school groups and special
visits March to end October by written appointment.

Birling Gap and the Seven Sisters

East Dean, near Eastbourne,
East Sussex BN20 0AB

Map ② H9   1931

Stretching between Birling Gap and Cuckmere Haven are the gleaming white cliffs of the Seven Sisters, eroded continuously by the sea. They are an impressive sight, both from the clifftops and from the beach below. There are some lovely walks across rolling downland with spectacular views out to sea.

Exploring   — Explore over 600 acres (242 hectares) of Trust open-access land.
— Variety of walks; access to South Downs Way (steep paths).
— Range of events and activities throughout the year, including rock-pooling.
— Pick up a Tracker Pack to help you explore.

Eating and shopping: treat yourself to fish and chips by the sea – just one of a range of hot snacks available throughout the day.

Making the most of your day: close to Cuckmere Haven and Alfriston Clergy House.

Getting here: 189:TQ554961. 5 miles west of Eastbourne and 6 miles east of Seaford.

Crisp white cliffs at the Seven Sisters, East Sussex

Foot: on the South Downs Way. **Bus**: times vary throughout year. **Train**: Eastbourne ≋ 6 miles, Seaford ≋ 7 miles. **Road**: between Eastbourne and Seaford, south of A259 and East Dean village. **Parking**: at Birling Gap, £2 for half day, £4 for whole day (pay and display). No lorries. Coaches £5 for half day, £10 for whole day (pay and display).

Finding out more: 01323 423197 or birlinggap@nationaltrust.org.uk.
Birling Gap Café, Birling Gap, East Dean, near Eastbourne, East Sussex BN20 0AB

Birling Gap and the Seven Sisters		M	T	W	T	F	S	S
Countryside								
Open all year		M	T	W	T	F	S	S
Café and bar*								
1 Jan–29 Feb	10–4	M	T	W	T	F	S	S
1 Mar–30 Jun	10–5	M	T	W	T	F	S	S
1 Jul–31 Aug	10–6	M	T	W	T	F	S	S
1 Sep–31 Oct	10–5	M	T	W	T	F	S	S
1 Nov–31 Dec	10–4	M	T	W	T	F	S	S

*Bar: times vary (telephone for details). Café and bar closed 24 and 25 December.

Boarstall Duck Decoy

Boarstall, near Bicester,
Buckinghamshire HP18 9UX

Map ② D3   1980

One of only three duck decoys left in the country. Picturesque pathways around a secluded lake. Unspoilt natural environment.

Access for all: Exhibition hall 🏛♿

Getting here: 164/165:SP624151. Signposted from B4011 midway between Bicester and Thame. Entrance through Manor Farm, Boarstall.

Finding out more: 01296 730349 or boarstalldecoy@nationaltrust.org.uk

Boarstall Duck Decoy		M	T	W	T	F	S	S
7 Apr–26 Aug	10–4	·	·	·	·	·	S	S
11 Apr–22 Aug	3:30–6	·	·	W	·	·	·	·

Open on all public and Bank Holidays from 6 April to 27 August inclusive, 10 to 4.

Boarstall Tower

Boarstall, near Bicester,
Buckinghamshire HP18 9UX

Map (2) D3  1943

Charming 14th-century moated gatehouse set in beautiful gardens. Discover seven centuries of history on a guided tour – a special experience. **Note**: this year marks this building's 700th birthday.

Access for all: [symbols] Building [symbol] Grounds [symbol]

Getting here: 164/165:SP624141. Signposted from B4011 midway between Bicester and Thame.

Finding out more: 01296 730349 or boarstalltower@nationaltrust.org.uk

Boarstall Tower	M	T	W	T	F	S	S
2 May–26 Sep 2–5	.	.	**W**	.	.	.	.

Also open 11 to 5 on: 7, 9 April, 5, 7 May, 2, 4 June and 25, 27 August.

Boarstall Tower, Buckinghamshire: 700th birthday

Bodiam Castle

Bodiam, near Robertsbridge,
East Sussex TN32 5UA

Map (2) I7 1926

'A very romantic small castle and beautifully maintained.'
Mrs Elliott, British Columbia, Canada

One of the most famous and evocative castles in Britain, Bodiam was built in 1385 as both a defence and a comfortable home. The exterior is virtually complete and the walls rise dramatically above the moat. Enough of the interior survives to give an impression of castle life. There are spiral staircases and battlements to explore, and wonderful views of the Rother Valley from the top of the towers. In the impressive gatehouse is the castle's original wooden portcullis, an extremely rare example of its kind. **Note**: toilets in car park only. Property often used by educational groups during term time.

Exploring
– Explore the courtyard and battlements and imagine medieval castle life.
– 'Bodiam Household' interpreters in courtyard daily from April to October.
– Discover Bodiam's story through a film and exhibition.
– Children's discovery challenges available, plus seasonal trails and events.
– Climb the towers for wonderful views of the Rother Valley.
– See the original portcullis – probably the oldest in England.

Eating and shopping: the shop has a range of exciting gifts and local produce. Try local honey and Bodiam-grown herbs, plus much more. The Wharf tea-room serves seasonal, local food cooked onsite. Ice-creams, snacks and drinks available from castle kiosk (seasonal).

Finding out more: 01580 830196 or
bodiamcastle@nationaltrust.org.uk

Bodiam Castle		M	T	W	T	F	S	S
7 Jan–5 Feb	11–4	·	·	·	·	·	S	S
11 Feb–4 Nov	10:30–5	M	T	W	T	F	S	S
7 Nov–23 Dec	11–4	·	·	W	T	F	S	S
29 Dec–30 Dec	11–4	·	·	·	·	·	S	S

12 February to 30 October, gift shop and tea-room close at
5 most days but at 5:30 during school summer holidays.

The evocative Bodiam Castle, East Sussex

Making the most of your day: exciting events
programme throughout the year – from the
mid-February challenge to Santa's Christmas
Grotto. Also evening events and medieval-
themed weekends. Activities for all the family
daily throughout August. **Dogs**: welcome on
leads in grounds only.

Access for all: 🅿️ 🐕 🏢 🚻 ♿ 📷 🖼️ 📹 💺 👶
👁️ ⬇️ Castle 👣 👣 👣 ♿ Grounds 👣 ➡️ 👣 ♿

Getting here: 199:TQ785256. 3 miles south
of Hawkhurst. **Foot**: on Sussex Border path.
Ferry: Bodiam Ferry (seasonal) from Newenden
Bridge (A28). **Bus**: 349 from Hastings 🚆 to
Hawkhurst. **Train**: steam railway (seasonal)
from Tenterden ¼ mile; Robertsbridge 5 miles;
Battle 10 miles. **Road**: 3 miles east of A21 Hurst
Green, between Tunbridge Wells and Hastings.
Parking: 400 yards, £2. Coaches £5.

Box Hill

The Old Fort, Box Hill Road, Box Hill, Tadworth,
Surrey KT20 7LB

Map ② F6   🏠 👥 👣 1914

A great place to visit whatever you are looking
for: stunning countryside, wildlife, history,
far-reaching views, a place for fun or quiet
contemplation. The busy shop, servery and
Discovery Zone on the hilltop are in contrast
to the peaceful woodlands off the beaten path.
Note: 27 to 29 July: no vehicle access, due to
Olympic cycle races (details on website).

Exploring — Visit the new Discovery Zone
and 'Bee' amazed.
— Explore Box Hill by following
our four new guided walks.
— Have fun on the new
Natural Play trail.

Eating and shopping: homemade sandwiches
and delicious cakes, including famous 'Rider's
Revival' flapjack. Treat your children to a lunch
box. Awarded Gold standard in Eat Out
Eat Well scheme. Visit our shop for special
gifts or pick up a jar of local honey.

Making the most of your day: children's
quiz/trail. Special Christmas shopping day on
Friday 14 December. Suitable for school groups.
Education room/centre. **Dogs**: under close
control where sheep grazing.

Access for all: 🅿️ 🚻 💺 📷 🏢 🖼️ 👁️
Building 👣 ♿ Grounds ➡️

Getting here: 187:TQ171519. North of Dorking.
Bus: services to top and foot of Box Hill.
Train: Box Hill and Westhumble station
1½ miles. **Road**: off A24. **Parking**: £3 (machine or RingO by mobile). Coaches must only approach from east side of hill B2032/B2033; parking at summit.

Finding out more: 01306 885502 or boxhill@nationaltrust.org.uk

Box Hill	M	T	W	T	F	S	S
Countryside							
Open all year	M	T	W	T	F	S	S
Servery							
1 Jan–24 Mar	10–4	M	T	W	T	F	S	S
25 Mar–27 Oct	9–5	M	T	W	T	F	S	S
28 Oct–31 Dec	10–4	M	T	W	T	F	S	S
Shop/Discovery Zone							
1 Jan–24 Mar	11–4	M	T	W	T	F	S	S
25 Mar–27 Oct	11–5	M	T	W	T	F	S	S
28 Oct–31 Dec	11–4	M	T	W	T	F	S	S

Shop, Discovery Zone and servery closed 25 December. In summer, the servery may be open for longer, weather permitting. **27 to 29 July: no vehicle access, due to Olympic cycle races (details on website).**

Bradenham Village

near High Wycombe, Buckinghamshire

Map ② E4

Scenic village with cottages clustered around a village green. 17th-century manor house (not open) and church provide impressive backdrop. **Note**: designated parking at the village green above the cricket pavilion. Contact property to arrange group garden tours.

Access for all: Grounds 🏞

Getting here: 165:SU825970. 4 miles north-west of High Wycombe, off A4010.

Finding out more: 01494 755573 or bradenham@nationaltrust.org.uk

Bradenham Village	Open every day all year

Contact property for garden tours.

Buckingham Chantry Chapel

Market Hill, Buckingham,
Buckinghamshire MK18 1JX

Map ② D2

Peruse second-hand books while enjoying a coffee in this atmospheric 15th-century chapel, restored by Gilbert Scott in 1875. **Note**: available to hire for functions and events.

Access for all: 🚾♿🏛🅿 Building 🏞

Getting here: 152/165:SP693340. On Market Hill, Buckingham, tucked away opposite the post office.

Finding out more: 01296 730349 or buckinghamchantry@nationaltrust.org.uk

Buckingham Chantry Chapel		M	T	W	T	F	S	S
3 Jan–22 Dec	10–3	·	T	W	T	F	S	·

Maintained by volunteers, opening is subject to their availability. Please contact property before visiting.

The Buscot and Coleshill Estates

Coleshill, near Swindon, Wiltshire

Map ② B4

These countryside estates on the western borders of Oxfordshire include the attractive, unspoilt villages of Buscot and Coleshill, each with a thriving village shop and tea-room. There are circular walks of differing lengths and a series of footpaths criss-crossing the estates. **Note**: toilets in Coleshill estate office yard and next to village shop and tea-room in Buscot.

Exploring – Enjoy countryside walks across Coleshill Park.
– From Buscot enjoy access to the River Thames.

Schoolchildren study flora at Coleshill Farm on the Coleshill Estate, Wiltshire

Exploring — See the Iron Age hill fort at Badbury Hill.
— Visit the restored watermill and see the milling process.

Eating and shopping: Buscot tea-rooms offer lunches and afternoon tea. The Radnor Arms uses locally sourced produce and has a wide range of award-winning ales including its own microbrewery. The Coleshill shop and tea-room also offer locally sourced produce.

Making the most of your day: range of guided walks throughout the year. **Dogs**: on leads only.

Getting here: SU239973. **Cycle**: NCN45, 10 miles. Regional Route 40: Oxfordshire Cycleway. **Bus**: Swindon to Carterton (passing close Swindon ⊜), alight Highworth, 2 miles. **Train**: Swindon 10 miles. **Road**: Coleshill village on B4019 between Faringdon and Highworth. Buscot village on A417 between Faringdon and Lechlade. **Parking**: at Buscot village and Badbury Clump; for Coleshill at Estate Office.

Finding out more: 01793 762209 or buscotandcoleshill@nationaltrust.org.uk. Coleshill Estate Office, Coleshill, Swindon, Wiltshire SN6 7PT

The Buscot and Coleshill Estates	Open every day all year

Coleshill Mill open second Sunday of the month: April to October, 2 to 5.

Buscot Old Parsonage

Buscot, Faringdon, Oxfordshire SN7 8DQ

Map ② C4   🏠 ✿ 1949

Beautiful early 18th-century house with small walled garden, situated on the banks of the River Thames next to Buscot Church. **Note**: administered on the National Trust's behalf by a tenant. Prior booking is required. No toilets.

Access for all: Building ♿

Getting here: 163:SU231973. 2 miles from Lechlade, 4 miles from Faringdon on A417.

Finding out more: 01793 762209 or buscot@nationaltrust.org.uk

Buscot Old Parsonage		M	T	W	T	F	S	S
4 Apr–31 Oct	2–6	·	·	**W**	·	·	·	·

Admission is by advance booking only. Admission by written appointment with the tenant. Please mark envelope 'National Trust booking'.

Buscot Park

Estate Office, Buscot Park, Faringdon,
Oxfordshire SN7 8BU

Map ② C4 1949

'Buscot is exciting, vibrant and
constantly being improved.'
Stuart Richmond-Watson, Northamptonshire

The Peto Water Garden at Buscot Park, Oxfordshire

Family home of Lord Faringdon, who continues
to care for the property as well as the
Faringdon Collection, the family art collection,
which is displayed in the house. Consequently,
despite the grandeur of their scale, both
the house and grounds remain intimate and
idiosyncratic and very much a family home.
They also continue to change and develop –
nothing is preserved in aspic here! Outside,
discover the water feature, 'Faux Fall', by David
Harber, and 17 life-size terracotta warriors from
China. Inside, view contemporary paintings
by Eileen Hogan and Amelia Roberts, and
glassware by Colin Reid and Sally Fawkes.

Note: administered on behalf of the National
Trust by Lord Faringdon.

Exploring – Explore one of England's finest
water gardens.
– Discover the Faringdon
Collection of Art.
– Enjoy the scents of the Four
Seasons Walled Garden.
– Marvel at Burne-Jones' *Legend
of the Briar Rose*.
– Revisit your childhood in the
Swinging Garden.

Eating and shopping: savour a delicious
homemade tea in the tea-room (not National
Trust). Pick up some local honey, peppermints,
cider, plants and kitchen garden produce
(when available). Treat yourself to an ice-cream.
Enjoy a picnic lunch (bring your own from 1).

Making the most of your day: occasional
events in grounds and theatre (available for
hire). **Dogs**: allowed only in the Paddock (the
overflow car park).

Access for all: 🅿️ 🚻 🚻 🏠 🎨 🏠 🔘 Ⓐ
House 🔽 Tea-room 🏠 Grounds 🔽 🏠 ➡️ 🏠

Getting here: 163:SU239973. Between
Faringdon and Lechlade. **Foot**: 4 miles
by footpath from Faringdon, 3½ miles
from Lechlade. **Bus**: services from Oxford
and Swindon to Faringdon and Swindon
to Lechlade (passing close Swindon ➤).
Train: Oxford 18 miles, Swindon 12 miles.
Road: on south side of A417. **Parking**: free.

Finding out more: 01367 240932 (Infoline).
01367 240786 or
buscotpark@nationaltrust.org.uk.
www.buscotpark.com

Buscot Park		M	T	W	T	F	S	S
House, grounds and tea-room*								
4 Apr–28 Sep	2–6	·	·	**W**	**T**	**F**	·	·
Grounds only								
2 Apr–25 Sep	2–6	**M**	**T**	·	·	·	·	·

Last admission to house one hour before closing. Open
Bank Holidays. Closed for Queen's Diamond Jubilee (4 and
5 June). ***House, grounds and tea-room weekend opening**:
7 and 8, 21 and 22 April, 5 and 6, 12 and 13, 26 and 27 May,
9 and 10, 23 and 24 June, 14 and 15, 28 and 29 July, 11 and
12, 25 and 26 August, 8 and 9, 22 and 23 September 2 to 6
(tea-room 2:30 to 5:30).

Chartwell

Mapleton Road, Westerham, Kent TN16 1PS

Map ② G6    1946

Chartwell was the much-loved Churchill family home and the place from which Sir Winston drew inspiration from 1924 until the end of his life. The rooms remain much as they were when he lived here, with pictures, books and personal mementoes evoking the career and wide-ranging interests of this great statesman, writer, painter and family man. The hillside gardens reflect Churchill's love of the landscape and nature. They include the lakes he created, Lady Churchill's Rose Garden, the kitchen garden, and the Marycot, a playhouse built especially for the youngest Churchill daughter. **Note**: entrance by timed ticket only.

Exploring
- Knowledgeable room stewards introducing you to Sir Winston's family home.
- Wander through the beautiful, tranquil garden.
- Discover Sir Winston's paintings in his fascinating studio.
- Picnic by the lake and look for the black swans.
- Enjoy family trails and play in the Marycot.
- Visit our working kitchen garden – with bees and chickens too!

Eating and shopping: large, popular self-service restaurant with regular special events and function services available. Enjoy fresh produce from the Chartwell kitchen garden. Beautiful shop stocking Churchill memorabilia and interesting local ranges. Kiosk serving light bites, drinks and snacks on busy days.

Making the most of your day: year-round events programme, free talks and tours on selected days, daily studio talks, children's trails and activities, walk sheets available from car park. **Dogs**: on short leads in gardens only.

Chartwell, Kent, seen from the rose garden

Access for all:
Building Shop and restaurant
Grounds

Getting here: 188:TQ455515. 2 miles south of Westerham. **Foot**: Greensand Way. **Bus**: services from Bromley North and Sevenoaks (Sundays and Bank Holidays only). **Train**: Edenbridge 4½ miles. **Road**: left off B2026 after 1½ miles. **Parking**: pay and display. Gates locked at 5, March to October; 4:30 November to 31 December.

Finding out more: 01732 868381 or chartwell@nationaltrust.org.uk

Chartwell		M	T	W	T	F	S	S
House and studio								
10 Mar–4 Nov	11–5		·	W	T	F	S	S
3 Jul–28 Aug	11–5		T	W	T	F	S	S
Studio								
1 Jan–8 Jan	11–4		·	W	T	F	S	S
1 Feb–9 Mar	11–4		·	W	T	F	S	S
10 Mar–31 Dec	12–4	M	T	W	T	F	S	S
Garden, exhibition, shop and restaurant								
1 Jan–9 Mar	11–4		·	W	T	F	S	S
10 Mar–4 Nov	10–5	M	T	W	T	F	S	S
5 Nov–31 Dec	10:30–4	M	T	W	T	F	S	S
Car park								
Open all year	9–5	M	T	W	T	F	S	S

*Car park closes at 4 from January to March, November and December, dusk if earlier. Admission to house by timed ticket (places limited), purchase on arrival. Last admission 45 minutes before closing. All winter opening weather permitting. Closed 24 and 25 December. Exhibition closed until 11 January and 1 to 17 November. Studio closed 9 to 29 January.

Chastleton House

Chastleton, near Moreton-in-Marsh,
Oxfordshire GL56 OSU

Map ② C3   1991

A rare gem of a Jacobean country house, Chastleton House was built between 1607 and 1612 by a prosperous wool merchant as an impressive statement of wealth and power. Owned by the same increasingly impoverished family until 1991, the house remained essentially unchanged for nearly 400 years as the interiors and contents gradually succumbed to the ravages of time. With virtually no intrusion from the 21st century, this fascinating place exudes an informal and timeless atmosphere in a gloriously unspoilt setting. There is no shop or tea-room, so you can truly believe you have stepped back in time.

Exploring
– Discover rooms full of rare objects, without ropes or barriers.
– Enjoy the garden, with Jacobean topiary and a vegetable plot.
– Explore using free family trails and children's activity packs.
– Admire the spectacular Long Gallery.
– See rare 17th-century wall coverings, still in place.

Eating and shopping: picnics welcome (in car park only). Garden produce available (subject to season). Second-hand bookshop.

Making the most of your day: free Family Explorer packs; seasonal concerts; out-of-hours private views each Wednesday; themed events; free garden tours from end of April to September; conservation in action most Wednesdays and Thursdays. **Dogs**: assistance dogs only in garden; welcome on leads in car park and field opposite house.

Access for all: [icons]
Building [icons] Garden [icon]

Getting here: 163:SP248291. 4 miles from Moreton-in-Marsh. **Train**: Moreton-in-Marsh 4 miles. **Road**: approach only from A436 between A44 and Stow-on-the-Wold. **Sat Nav**: follow brown signs not directions to Chastleton village. **Parking**: free, 270 yards (including a short steep hill). No parking outside church.

Finding out more: 01494 755560 (Infoline). 01608 674981 or chastleton@nationaltrust.org.uk

Chastleton House		M	T	W	T	F	S	S
10 Mar–31 Mar	1–4	·	·	W	T	F	S	·
4 Apr–29 Sep	1–5	·	·	W	T	F	S	·
3 Oct–3 Nov	1–4	·	·	W	T	F	S	·

Entrance by timed ticket system (not bookable, places limited). Ticket office opens at 12:30. Last admission one hour before closing.

Chastleton House, Oxfordshire, exudes an informal and timeless atmosphere

Chiddingstone Village

near Edenbridge, Kent TN8 7AH

Map ② 7H 🏠 ✝ 🚻 1939

One of the prettiest villages in Kent, Chiddingstone is a beautiful example of a Tudor village. **Note**: the village is owned by the National Trust and is open all year; however, the houses are not open to view.

Getting here: 188:TQ501451. 4 miles east of Edenbridge, signed from the B2027.

Finding out more: 01304 207326 or chiddingstone@nationaltrust.org.uk

Chiddingstone Village	Open every day all year

The white marble hall at Clandon Park, Surrey

Clandon Park

West Clandon, Guildford, Surrey GU4 7RQ

Map ② F6 🏛 🏠 ❋ 🔔 🍴 1956

'**Clandon House is a beautiful building with an awe-inspiring marble hall, impressive collections and a fascinating history.**'
K. Williams, Surrey

Built *circa* 1730 for the 2nd Lord Onslow by Venetian architect Giacomo Leoni, Clandon Park is one of England's most complete examples of a Palladian mansion. It contains a superb collection of 18th-century furniture, porcelain and textiles, much of which was acquired in the 1920s by connoisseur Mrs Gubbay. The wider parkland – still owned by the Onslow family – surrounds the mansion which is set in intimate gardens, home to a Maori meeting house brought back from New Zealand in 1892. The Onslow family is unique in providing three Speakers of the House of Commons. Surrey Infantry Museum is based here. **Note**: Olympic cycle races, 28 and 29 July: open but local road closures (details on website).

Exploring
– Be amazed by the stunning two-storey white marble hall.
– Explore the sunken Dutch garden or picnic on the lawn.
– Take in a wealth of ceramics, tapestries and furniture.
– Discover the Maori meeting house – unique in the UK.
– Come on a Wednesday to learn more about 'Clandon Discovered'.
– Enjoy a children's trail around the house or garden.

Eating and shopping: visit our shop in the 19th-century kitchen. Enjoy a meal in the vaulted undercroft restaurant (approved concession).

Making the most of your day: events include conservation demonstrations, behind-the-scenes tours, children's activities, re-enactors, art exhibitions and much more. **Dogs**: assistance dogs only.

Access for all: 🅿️♿️🚾♿️📷📖🖼️

Building ♿️⬆️♿️ Grounds ♿️🖼️

Getting here: 186:TQ042512. 3 miles east of Guildford. **Foot:** follow the drive to reception. **Bus:** services from Guildford to Epsom (passing Leatherhead ⮂, close Guildford ⮂) and Woking ⮂. **Train:** Clandon 1 mile. **Road:** at West Clandon on A247; from A3 follow signposts to Ripley to join A247 via B2215. **Sat Nav:** may be incorrect – make sure you enter from A247. **Parking:** free, 300 yards.

Finding out more: 01483 222482. 01483 222502 (restaurant) or clandonpark@nationaltrust.org.uk

Clandon Park		M	T	W	T	F	S	S
House, garden, museum, shop and restaurant*								
26 Feb–4 Mar	11–4	.	.	.	.	.	.	S
House, garden, museum, shop and restaurant								
11 Mar–29 Jul	11–5	.	T	W	T	.	.	S
30 Jul–27 Aug	11–5	M	T	W	T	.	.	S
28 Aug–4 Nov	11–5	.	T	W	T	.	.	S
Shop and restaurant								
6 Nov–29 Nov	12–4	.	T	W	T	.	.	S
Shop								
2 Dec–23 Dec	12–4	M	T	W	T	.	.	S
Restaurant**								
2 Dec–23 Dec	12:15–10	M	T	W	T	.	.	S
Surrey Infantry Museum								
6 Nov–20 Dec	12–4	.	T	W	T	.	.	.

*'Waking Up the House' event 26 February and 4 March, garden closed on these days if waterlogged. Open Bank Holiday Mondays, Good Friday and Easter Saturday.
**Restaurant bookings essential for Christmas meals in December. Lift availability restricted (booking essential).

Claremont Landscape Garden

Portsmouth Road, Esher, Surrey KT10 9JG

Map ② F6   ❇️ 1949

Claremont is not a typical garden of herbaceous borders, but a tranquil, 19.8-hectare (49-acre) landscape garden. It is a green oasis of trees and shrubs that offers colourful views throughout the year. Garden enthusiasts may recognise some of the famous names from garden history involved in Claremont's creation – Sir John Vanbrugh, Charles Bridgeman, William Kent and 'Capability' Brown. Central to the garden is a serpentine lake, home to a variety of waterfowl, which is overlooked by a grass amphitheatre and grotto. There are many hidden features to discover as well as lovely garden walks and a children's play area. **Note: Olympic cycle races**, 28, 29 July, 1 August: open – restricted road access (details on website).

Exploring
  – Camellia Terrace is a mass of blooms, December to May.
  – Don't miss the rhododendrons and azaleas flowering in late spring.
  – Marvel at the stunning autumn colour.

Claremont Landscape Garden, Surrey: tranquil oasis, colourful throughout the year

Exploring – Enjoy the constantly changing views around the lake.
– Children will love their exciting play area.
– Special children's trails and activities during school holidays.

Eating and shopping: licensed tea-room serving tasty homemade cakes, cream teas, soup, sandwiches and light lunches. New outside terrace eating area with view across lake.

Making the most of your day: open-air theatre events in July. Children's craft workshops, storytelling and trails during school holidays. Guided walks April to October. Full yearly programme of walks, talks and activities. **Dogs**: allowed between 1 November and 31 March only (on short leads).

Access for all: 🅿️♿🚻🔛🔆👁️ⓐ
Grounds 🏔️➡️♿

Getting here: 187:TQ128631. 1 mile south of Esher. **Bus**: Kingston to Guildford (passing close Esher 🚉). **Train**: Esher 2 miles. **Road**: on east side of A307. **Parking**: free, at entrance.

Finding out more: 01372 467806 or claremont@nationaltrust.org.uk

Claremont Landscape Garden		M	T	W	T	F	S	S
Garden								
1 Jan–31 Jan	10–4	·	T	W	T	F	S	S
1 Feb–12 Feb	10–5	·	T	W	T	F	S	S
13 Feb–31 Mar	10–5	M	T	W	T	F	S	S
1 Apr–31 Oct	10–6	M	T	W	T	F	S	S
1 Nov–30 Dec	10–4	·	T	W	T	F	S	S
Tea-room and shop								
1 Jan–31 Jan	10–3:30	·	T	W	T	F	S	S
1 Feb–12 Feb	10–4:30	·	T	W	T	F	S	S
13 Feb–31 Mar	10–4:30	M	T	W	T	F	S	S
1 Apr–31 Oct	10–5:30	M	T	W	T	F	S	S
1 Nov–30 Dec	10–3:30	·	T	W	T	F	S	S

Open Bank Holiday Monday 2 January. Closed 25 December. Belvedere Tower open 1 January, 12 to 2, and first weekend each month April to October, 2 to 5. Late night openings 2, 9, 16, 23 and 30 June until 9. **Olympic cycle races**, 28 and 29 July, 1 August: open – restricted road access (visit website for details).

Claydon

Middle Claydon, near Buckingham, Buckinghamshire MK18 2EY

Map ②D3 🏛️✝️❄️🌳🎿🔔🍸 1956

'**The house is an historical and architectural gem. We were enchanted by it and the setting.**'
J. Kiasnichik, Thunder Bay, Canada

State rooms within a grand country house that never quite was. Claydon's dazzling 18th-century interiors are amongst the finest to be found anywhere in England. Chinoiserie, Rococo, Palladian and Neo-classical styles all jostle for position in a house designed to impress. More than 500 years of Verney family history has been played out within these walls. Heroes of the English Civil War, Barbary Coast buccaneers, eccentric 19th-century collectors and Florence Nightingale have all called Claydon home. Set amidst 21 hectares (52 acres) of peaceful parkland, with tranquil lake walks and views, Claydon is an inspirational place for all the family. **Note**: the gardens are maintained by the Claydon Estate, additional entry charges apply (including members).

Ornate chimneypiece at Claydon, Buckinghamshire

Exploring
- New: exhibition of Sir Edmund's gold doublet, *circa* 1633.
- Discover how we care for Claydon at our 'Conservation Station'.
- New: from the Verney archive, 'The Cost of Showing Off'.
- Visit the glorious gardens (run by the Claydon Estate).
- A perfect place for picnics.
- Wander along walks through picturesque parkland and around the lakes.

Eating and shopping: Trust shop. Second-hand bookshop. Courtyard craft shops and galleries (not National Trust). Relax in the Carriage House Restaurant and Courtyard Tea-room (not National Trust). Vegetables for sale from kitchen garden, when in season.

Making the most of your day: discover more through our family activity worksheets. **Dogs**: welcome in the park on leads.

Access for all: ⬛⬛⬛⬛⬛⬛⬛⬛⬛⬛ ⬛⬛
Main House ⬛⬛⬛ Grounds ⬛⬛ ➡

Getting here: 165:SP720253. In Middle Claydon 13 miles north-west of Aylesbury, 4 miles south-west of Winslow. **Foot**: Bernwood Jubilee Way. **Cycle**: NCN51. **Train**: Aylesbury Parkway 13 miles, Bicester North 13½ miles, and Milton Keynes Central, 17 miles. **Road**: signposted A413 (Buckingham), A41 (Waddesdon crossroads). M40 junction 9 (Bicester) follow A41, turn off to Grendon Underwood and Calvert, signposted from Calvert Crossroads. **Parking**: free.

Finding out more: 01494 755561 (Infoline). 01296 730349 or claydon@nationaltrust.org.uk

Claydon		M	T	W	T	F	S	S
House*								
17 Mar–31 Oct	11–5	M	T	W	·	·	S	S
Tea-room, church and bookshop								
17 Mar–31 Oct	11–5	M	T	W	·	·	S	S
Garden, restaurant and shops								
17 Mar–31 Oct	12–5	M	T	W	·	·	S	S

*House entry by 'Taster Tours' between 11 and 1 daily. Visitors are taken through a selection of rooms by an experienced guide. Tours start every 30 minutes (and last approximately 30 minutes). Open Good Friday. The Carriage House Restaurant: last lunch orders at 3.

Cliveden

Taplow, Maidenhead, Buckinghamshire SL6 0JA

Map ② E5   ⬛⬛⬛⬛⬛ 1942

A country retreat on a grand scale, Cliveden's magnificent gardens and breathtaking views have been admired for centuries. Visited by virtually every British monarch since George I, in the early 20th century it became home to Waldorf and Nancy Astor. As the glittering hub of society, numerous parties and political gatherings were hosted here and later Cliveden became infamously associated with the Profumo Affair. Today, you can experience the relaxed grandeur of Cliveden as you explore the beautiful gardens and woodlands. The house is a hotel, and tours of part of the interior are available on certain days. **Note**: mooring charge on Cliveden Reach, £7.50 per 24 hours (including members), does not include entry.

The yew maze at Cliveden, Buckinghamshire

Exploring
- Don't get lost in the 2-metre high yew maze!
- Be inspired by stunning seasonal floral displays.
- Admire the famous parterre, beautifully restored with colourful bedding.
- Stretch your legs with a riverside or woodland walk.
- Let imaginations run wild in the storybook-themed play area.
- Discover more with our full events programme and guided walks.

Eating and shopping: enjoy home-cooked lunches and snacks at The Orangery. Morning coffee and afternoon tea served in Dovecote Coffee House. Kiosk in car park at peak times. Picnic areas available. Wide selection of products and plants for sale in the gift shop.

Making the most of your day: don't miss the introductory film 'Cliveden: Camelot on Thames'. Take a relaxing boat trip on the River Thames (additional charge, call for schedule). **Dogs**: welcome under close control in the woodlands only.

Access for all:
Cliveden House (hotel)
Garden

Getting here: 175:SU915851. 2 miles north of Taplow. **Train**: Taplow (not Sunday) 2½ miles; Burnham 3 miles. £1 voucher for shop or café for those arriving by 'green transport', visit website for details. **Road**: from M4 take exit 7 onto A4 to Maidenhead, or from M40 take exit 4 onto A404 to Marlow and follow brown signs. Entrance opposite Feathers Inn. **Sat Nav**: enter Cliveden Road and SL1 8NS. **Parking**: free.

Finding out more: 01628 605069 (Estate office) or cliveden@nationaltrust.org.uk

Cliveden		M	T	W	T	F	S	S
Garden and shop*								
11 Feb–28 Oct	10–5:30	M	T	W	T	F	S	S
29 Oct–31 Dec	10–4	M	T	W	T	F	S	S
Woodlands*								
1 Jan–10 Feb	10–4	M	T	W	T	F	S	S
11 Feb–28 Oct	10–5:30	M	T	W	T	F	S	S
29 Oct–31 Dec	10–4	M	T	W	T	F	S	S
Coffee shop								
11 Feb–28 Oct	10–5	M	T	W	T	F	S	S
29 Oct–23 Dec	10–3:30	M	T	W	T	F	S	S
The Orangery (café)								
11 Feb–2 Nov**	10–5	M	T	W	T	F	S	S
3 Nov–23 Dec	10–3:30	·	·	·	·	·	S	S
House (part), chapel								
1 Apr–25 Oct	3–5:30	·	·	·	T	·	·	S

*Shop closed 24 to 31 December. Garden and woodlands closed 24 to 26 December. **Orangery closes 3:30 29 October to 2 November. Admission to house limited (timed ticket only) from information centre. Some areas of formal garden may close when ground conditions are poor. Last admission to maze 30 minutes before closing. No toilet in woodlands.

Cobham Wood and Mausoleum

South Lodge Barn, Lodge Lane, Cobham, Kent DA12 3BS

Map (2) H5 2012

The Darnley Mausoleum at Cobham Wood, Kent

Absorb the atmosphere at the wonderfully restored Darnley Mausoleum, designed by James Wyatt and so memorably featured in the BBC's *Restoration* programme. Then follow in the footsteps of the Darnley family while walking through the peaceful woodland, once part of their extensive estate and recently acquired by the National Trust. **Note**: no vehicle access or parking. No toilets.

Exploring
- Discover the beautifully restored Grade I listed mausoleum.
- Explore the varied habitats of Cobham Park's ancient woodland.
- Enjoy far-reaching, commanding views over the Thames.
- Learn about the people who shaped this unique landscape.

Eating and shopping: refreshments and toilets available at Shorne Wood Country Park.

Making the most of your day: enjoy guided walks (visit website for details). **Dogs**: under control in the wood (stock grazing).

Access for all: **Mausoleum**

Getting here: 178:TQ694683. At the east end of Cobham village. **Foot**: 2 miles from Shorne Wood Country Park via waymarked footpath to South Lodge and mausoleum. **Train**: Sole Street 1 mile. **Road**: ½ mile from the M2 and A2. Exit A2 at Shorne/Cobham, follow signs to Shorne Wood Country Park. **Sat Nav**: do not use South Lodge Barn postcode, instead enter DA12 3HX (Shorne Wood Country Park). **Parking**: at Shorne Wood Country Park, pay and display (not National Trust), charge including members, then follow waymarked footpath.

Finding out more: 01474 816764 or cobham@nationaltrust.org.uk

Cobham Wood and Mausoleum
Visit website for opening information.

Dorneywood Garden

Dorneywood, Dorney Wood Road, Burnham, Buckinghamshire SL1 8PY

Map ② E5   1942

1930s-style garden, with herbaceous borders, rose garden, cottage garden and lily pond. Afternoon tea available. **Note**: upkeep funded by Dorneywood Trust, at no cost to National Trust or public. **No photography please**. Charge including members.

Access for all: Grounds 🏞️➡️

Getting here: 175:SU938848. On Dorney Wood Road, south-west of Burnham Beeches, 1½ miles north of Burnham village, 2 miles east of Cliveden.

Finding out more: or dorneywood@nationaltrust.org.uk

Dorneywood Garden		M	T	W	T	F	S	S
In aid of National Gardens Scheme								
25 Apr	2–4:30	·	·	W	·	·	·	·
29 May–30 May	2–4:30	·	T	W	·	·	·	·
18 Jul	2–4:30	·	·	W	·	·	·	·
In aid of Dorneywood Trust								
25 Jul	2–4:30	·	·	W	·	·	·	·
Visit by appointment only (email for tickets).								

Emmetts Garden

Ide Hill, Sevenoaks, Kent TN14 6BA

Map ② H6   1965

Bluebells at Emmetts Garden in Kent

Charming Emmetts – an Edwardian estate owned by Frederic Lubbock – was a plantsman's passion and a much-loved family home. Influenced by William Robinson, the delightful garden was laid out in the late 19th century and contains many exotic and rare trees and shrubs from across the world. Explore the rose and rock gardens, take in the spectacular views and enjoy glorious shows of spring flowers and shrubs, followed by vibrant autumn colours.

Exploring
- Stunning rock garden returned to its original design.
- Charming formal rose garden.
- Unique collection of exotic shrubs.
- Beautiful woodland, spectacular views and lovely picnic meadow.
- New this year: visitor reception and enlarged shop.
- Traditional children's games available.

Eating and shopping: Stable tea-room, with delicious homemade cakes. New enlarged shop opening this year with wide variety of plants for sale.

Making the most of your day: year-round events programme, guided tours on selected days, children's activities, walks sheets for surrounding countryside. **Dogs**: on short leads only.

Access for all:

Grounds 🏔️➡️♿

Getting here: 188:TQ477524. 4½ miles from Sevenoaks. **Foot**: from Ide Hill (½ mile). Weardale walk from Chartwell (3 miles) – guide leaflet available. **Bus**: from Sevenoaks (Monday to Friday only), alight Ide Hill, 1½ miles. **Train**: Sevenoaks 4½ miles; Penshurst 5½ miles. **Road**: 1½ miles south of A25 on Sundridge to Ide Hill road, 1½ miles north of Ide Hill off B2042, leave M25 exit 5, then 4 miles. **Parking**: free, 100 yards.

Finding out more: 01732 751509 (Infoline). 01732 868381 or emmetts@nationaltrust.org.uk. Chartwell Office, Mapleton Road, Westerham, Kent TN16 1PS

Emmetts Garden		M	T	W	T	F	S	S
10 Mar–4 Nov	10–5	M	T	W			S	S

Open Bank Holiday Mondays and Good Friday. Last admission 45 minutes before closing.

Great Coxwell Barn

Great Coxwell, Faringdon, Oxfordshire SN7 7LZ

Map ② C4 🏠 1956

Former monastic barn, a favourite of William Morris, who would regularly bring his guests to wonder at its structure. **Note**: no toilet, narrow access lanes leading to property.

Access for all: ♿

Getting here: 163:SU269940. 2 miles south-west of Faringdon between A420 and B4019.

Finding out more: 01793 762209 or greatcoxwellbarn@nationaltrust.org.uk

Great Coxwell Barn
Open every day all year from dawn to dusk

Greys Court

Rotherfield Greys, Henley-on-Thames, Oxfordshire RG9 4PG

Map ② D5 🏠 🏠 ✣ 🍀 ⚑ 1969

An intimate family home and peaceful estate set in the rolling hills of the Chilterns. This picturesque 16th-century mansion and tranquil gardens were home to the Brunner family until recent years. The house exudes a welcoming atmosphere, with a well-stocked kitchen and homely living rooms. The series of walled gardens is a colourful patchwork of interest set amidst medieval ruins. Other buildings from earlier eras include the 12th-century Great Tower and a rare Tudor donkey wheel, in use until the early 20th century.

Greys Court, Oxfordshire: intimate family home

Exploring
- Soak up the atmosphere of a real family home.
- Stroll around the enchanting gardens.
- Burn off some energy in the beech woodlands.
- Find out how the donkey drew water from the well.
- Follow your food from plot to plate.

Eating and shopping: treat yourself to a light lunch or tea and cake in the tea-room. Browse our family-inspired shop. Pick up seasonal organic produce from the gardens (when available).

Making the most of your day: programme of open-air events and garden days. Wider estate walk, taking in the interesting ice-house. Family activities, including explorer packs and garden and house trails. **Dogs**: on the estate walk only.

Access for all: P♿🚻♿🚼📷📱🏠🎨
House 🏠 Tea-room 🏠 Grounds 🏠

Getting here: 175:SU725834. 2½ miles west of Henley-on-Thames. **Cycle**: on Oxfordshire cycleway. **Train**: Henley-on-Thames 3 miles. **Road**: from Nettlebed mini-roundabout on A4130 take B481. Property is signed to the left after about 3 miles. From Henley-on-Thames town centre, follow signs to Badgemore Golf Club towards Peppard (approximately 3 miles from Henley). **Parking**: free, 220 yards.

Finding out more: 01494 755564 (Infoline). 01491 628529 or greyscourt@nationaltrust.org.uk

Greys Court		M	T	W	T	F	S	S
House								
21 Mar–4 Nov*	1–5	·	·	W	T	F	S	S
1 Dec–16 Dec	1–4	·	·	·	·	·	S	S
Garden								
21 Mar–4 Nov	11–5	·	·	W	T	F	S	S
Tea-room								
21 Mar–4 Nov	11–4:30	·	·	W	T	F	S	S
Shop								
21 Mar–4 Nov	11–5	·	·	W	T	F	S	S
1 Dec–16 Dec	1–4	·	·	·	·	·	S	S

Open Bank Holiday Mondays and Queen's Diamond Jubilee (5 June). Closed Good Friday. Village fête day (2 September) special opening arrangements apply (charge including members); contact property for details. *Entry by timed ticket only, including members (places limited), only available from ticket office from 11 on day.

Ham House and Garden

Ham Street, Ham, Richmond-upon-Thames, Surrey TW10 7RS

Map ② F5 🏠♣️♿🍴 1948

This atmospheric Stuart mansion nestles on the banks of the river in leafy Richmond-upon-Thames. It has remained virtually unchanged for 400 years and is internationally recognised for its superb collection of textiles, furniture and art which have remained in the house for centuries. Largely the vision of Elizabeth Murray, Countess of Dysart, who was deeply embroiled in the politics of the English Civil War and subsequent restoration of the monarchy, Ham House and Garden is an unusually complete survival of the 17th century. It is also reputed to be one of the most haunted houses in Britain. **Note**: for conservation reasons, some rooms have low light levels.

Exploring
- Discover our outstanding collection of furniture and textiles.
- Explore the Wilderness – our visitors' favourite area of the garden.
- Enjoy family house and garden trails and play areas.
- Taste produce from our kitchen garden in the Orangery Café.
- Find out about Disney's new 2012 blockbuster, filmed at Ham.
- Experience our hands-on basement area.

Eating and shopping: the Orangery Café serves seasonal dishes, made using produce from the kitchen garden, as well as delicious cakes, baked onsite. Our shop stocks local crafts and gifts and a range of books, toys, plants and gardening accessories.

The atmospheric, and very haunted, Ham House and Garden in Surrey

Making the most of your day: regular free garden tours, confirm in advance. Interactive discovery room, family house and garden trails, bookstall. Programme of events throughout the year; check *What's On* leaflet or website. **Dogs**: assistance dogs only.

Access for all: [icons]
Building [icons] **Orangery Café** [icons]
Grounds [icons]

Getting here: 176:TQ172732. On south bank of Thames, between Richmond, 1½ miles, and Kingston, 3 miles. **Foot**: Thames Path passes entrance. **Cycle**: NCN4. **Ferry**: seasonal foot/bike ferry across river from Twickenham towpath (by Marble Hill House). **Bus**: services from Richmond ≥ and Kingston ≥. **Train**: Richmond, 1½ miles. **Underground**: Richmond, 1½ miles. **Road**: west of A307. From Richmond Park take Ham gate exit. Accessible from M3, M4 and M25. **Sat Nav**: directs to stables on Ham Street, carry straight on to car park. **Parking**: free, 400 yards (not National Trust).

Finding out more: 020 8940 1950 or hamhouse@nationaltrust.org.uk

Ham House and Garden		M	T	W	T	F	S	S
House tours, selected rooms only*								
20 Feb–8 Mar	12–4	M	T	W	T	·	S	S
House**								
10 Mar–31 May	12–4	M	T	W	T	·	S	S
2 Jun–16 Sep	12–5	M	T	W	T	·	S	S
17 Sep–1 Nov	12–4	M	T	W	T	·	S	S
Garden, shop and café								
1 Jan–19 Feb	11–3	·	·	·	·	·	S	S
20 Feb–8 Mar	11–4:30	M	T	W	T	·	S	S
10 Mar–31 May	11–5	M	T	W	T	·	S	S
2 Jun–16 Sep	11–6	M	T	W	T	·	S	S
17 Sep–1 Nov	11–4:30	M	T	W	T	·	S	S
3 Nov–16 Dec	11–3	·	·	·	·	·	S	S

*30-minute guided tours of selected rooms only (every 30 minutes), no free-flow. Entry by timed ticket (places limited). Last tour 3:30. Book on arrival, normal admission charges apply. **Free-flow visit only. House and garden open Good Friday. Special Christmas event 1, 2, 8, 9, 15 and 16 December gardens, shop and café open 11 to 5. Please note: some rooms occasionally close for essential conservation work.

Hartwell House Hotel, Restaurant and Spa

Oxford Road, near Aylesbury,
Buckinghamshire HP17 8NR

Map ② E3  2008

The most famous resident of this elegant Grade I listed stately home (held on long lease from The Ernest Cook Trust) was Louis XVIII, the exiled King of France, who lived here with his Queen and members of his court for five years from 1809. Only one hour from central London, the magnificent grounds include a romantic ruined church, lake, bridge and 36 hectares (90 acres) of parkland.

The house and gardens are already accessible to the public as a hotel, and welcome guests to stay, to dine in the restaurants and to have afternoon tea (booking strongly advised). Please contact hotel directly for best available offer. **Note**: all paying guests to the hotel are welcome to walk in the garden and park.

Finding out more: 01296 747444. 01296 747450 (fax) or info@hartwell-house.com. www.hartwell-house.com

The elegant Hartwell House Hotel in Buckinghamshire

Hatchlands Park

East Clandon, Guildford, Surrey GU4 7RT

Map ② F6   1945

'The bluebell woods are stunningly beautiful, within magnificent parkland. We have also enjoyed the Stable exhibition and house keyboard collection.'
R. Robson, Surrey

Hatchlands Park was built in the 1750s for Admiral Boscawen, hero of the Battle of Louisburg. Robert Adam ceilings decorate the house, appropriately featuring nautical motifs. Today the mansion is a family home, containing tenant Alec Cobbe's superb collection of paintings. Our six rooms also display the Cobbe Collection, Europe's largest collection of keyboard instruments, associated with famous composers such as J. C. Bach, Chopin and Elgar. The mansion is set in informal grounds, with one small parterre garden designed by Gertrude Jekyll. The surrounding parkland provides a number of waymarked walks in a tranquil and beautiful setting. **Note: Olympic cycle races**, 28 and 29 July: open but restricted road access (details on website).

Exploring – An intimate mansion with an exemplary collection.
– Listen to the instruments with an audio guide (charge applies).
– More than 161 hectares (400 acres) of parkland to explore.
– Discover the stunning bluebell wood in April and May.
– Fun trails and activities for children, both inside and out.
– Join a guided tour of the mansion on Thursdays.

Eating and shopping: homely tea-room (Trust-approved concession) in the original kitchen. Visit the friendly shop for a memento of your visit.

Making the most of your day: walk in the parkland, visit the stable exhibition, come for a 'Conservation in Action' demonstration or

Hatchlands Park, Surrey: fabulous collections

a Cobbe Collection Trust concert (telephone 01483 211474 for details). **Dogs**: welcome under close control in designated parkland areas only.

Access for all: ⬛⬛⬛⬛⬛⬛⬛⬛⬛⬛
Building ⬛⬛⬛ Grounds ⬛⬛⬛

Getting here: 187:TQ063516. 2 miles from Clandon. **Bus**: Guildford to Leatherhead (passing Leatherhead ⊠ and close Guildford ⊠). **Train**: Clandon 2 miles, Horsley 2½ miles. **Road**: entry off the A246 between Guildford and Leatherhead. **Sat Nav**: recommend following brown signs to main entrance on A246. **Parking**: free, 300 yards.

Finding out more: 01483 222482 or hatchlands@nationaltrust.org.uk

Hatchlands Park		M	T	W	T	F	S	S
House and garden*								
1 Apr–31 Oct	2–5:30	·	T	W	T	·	·	S
Park walks								
1 Apr–7 May	10–6	M	T	W	T	F	S	S
8 May–31 Oct	11–6	M	T	W	T	F	S	S
Shop								
1 Apr–31 May	10–5:30	M	T	W	T	F	S	S
3 Jun–31 Oct	11–5:30	·	T	W	T	·	·	S
2 Jun–27 Oct	11–4:30	·	·	·	·	·	S	·
Tea-room								
1 Apr–31 Oct	11–5	·	T	W	T	·	·	S
7 Apr–27 Oct	12–4:30	·	·	·	·	·	S	·

*Garden open 11 to 6 on house open days. **Olympic cycle races**, 28 and 29 July: visit website for opening arrangements. **Fridays in August**: house, shop and tea-room open usual times. Timed tickets may be used on Bank Holidays and busy periods. Open Bank Holiday Mondays. Please telephone for Christmas events information.

Hindhead Commons and the Devil's Punch Bowl

London Road, Hindhead, Surrey GU26 6AB

Map ② E7   ⬛⬛ 1906

Since the opening of the A3 tunnel last year, peace has returned to this dramatic landscape after 100 years of road traffic noise. Explore the commons, reunited at last, enjoy the sweeping views and experience the tranquillity of this very special place.

Exploring
  – Experience peace and quiet at this new 'destination'.
  – Extensive new views from café and old A3.
  – See both portals of new A3 tunnel from viewing platforms.
  – Self-guided trails from café into Punch Bowl and Hindhead Commons.

Eating and shopping: treat yourself to an 'all-day' breakfast from 9 to 2:30, lunches with two daily specials until 2:30. Homemade cakes, including delicious shortbread, and sandwiches throughout the day. Seating inside or out. Plenty of peace and quiet at last!

Making the most of your day: extensive programme of guided walks throughout the year – contact the wardens for details. Maps, books and walks on sale from the Devil's Punch Bowl café. Souvenir postcards. **Dogs**: allowed (under very close control during bird-nesting season, March to October).

Access for all: ⬛⬛⬛⬛⬛ Café ⬛ Grounds ➡

Getting here: 186:SU890357. Access via A333 from Hazel Grove roundabout, just south of the tunnel. **Bus**: from Farnham, Haslemere alight Hindhead crossroads. **Train**: Haslemere 3 miles. **Parking**: £3 (pay and display or RinGo pay by mobile). No lorries.

Finding out more: 01428 681050 (wardens).
01428 608771 (café) or
hindhead@nationaltrust.org.uk

Hindhead Commons		M	T	W	T	F	S	S
Countryside								
Open all year		**M**	**T**	**W**	**T**	**F**	**S**	**S**
Café								
1 Jan–24 Mar	9–4	**M**	**T**	**W**	**T**	**F**	**S**	**S**
26 Mar–26 Oct	9–5	**M**	**T**	**W**	**T**	**F**	·	·
25 Mar–27 Oct	9–6	·	·	·	·	·	**S**	**S**
28 Oct–31 Dec	9–4	**M**	**T**	**W**	**T**	**F**	**S**	**S**
Café closed 25 December.								

Hinton Ampner

Bramdean, near Alresford,
Hampshire SO24 0LA

Map (2) D7   1986

Best known for its magnificent garden and
stunning views to the south, Hinton Ampner
is an elegant country house remodelled in
1960 by Ralph Dutton, the 8th and last Lord
Sherborne, after a devastating fire. It contains
his fascinating collection of Georgian and
Regency furniture, Italian pictures and *objets
d'art*. The gardens were also laid out by Ralph
Dutton and are widely acknowledged as a
masterpiece of 20th-century design, mixing
formal and informal planting and providing
year-round interest.

Exploring
– Admire elegant interiors and
  fine furnishings.
– Visit the upstairs rooms.
– Stroll through different areas
  of the formal gardens.
– Discover the seasonal produce
  growing in the walled garden.
– Enjoy fine views of the
  South Downs.

Eating and shopping: enjoy homemade cakes
and light lunches in the tea-room, and look
out for seasonal dishes using produce from
the walled garden. Browse in the shop for gifts,
books, plants and garden products. Property
plants and produce on sale, when available.

Making the most of your day: our
gardeners are always on hand to answer your
questions. Free guided walk in the garden
and conservation demonstrations in the
house on Tuesdays. Children's quiz sheets.
Dogs: assistance dogs only.

Access for all: [icons]
Building [icons] Grounds [icons]

Getting here: 185:SU597275. Midway between
Winchester and Petersfield. **Bus**: Winchester
to Petersfield (passing close Winchester ≣
and passing Petersfield ≣). **Train**: Winchester
9 miles; Alresford (Mid-Hants Railway) 4 miles.
Road: on A272, 1 mile west of Bramdean village,
8 miles east of Winchester. Leave M3 at exit 9
and follow signs to Petersfield.

A stunning border and topiary in the Sunken Garden at Hinton Ampner, Hampshire

Sat Nav: use entrance off the A272, not village road as directed. **Parking**: free.

Finding out more: 01962 771305 or hintonampner@nationaltrust.org.uk

Hinton Ampner		M	T	W	T	F	S	S
House								
11 Feb–4 Nov	11–5	M	T	W	T	F	S	S
5 Nov–28 Nov	11–5	M	T	W	·	·	S	S
1 Dec–9 Dec	10:30–4:30	M	T	W	T	F	S	S
Garden, shop and tea-room								
11 Feb–30 Mar	10–5	M	T	W	T	F	S	S
31 Mar–30 Sep	10–6	M	T	W	T	F	S	S
1 Oct–4 Nov	10–5	M	T	W	T	F	S	S
5 Nov–28 Nov	10–5	M	T	W	·	·	S	S
1 Dec–9 Dec	10–4:30	M	T	W	T	F	S	S

Last entry to house and tea-room 20 minutes before closing. 7 December: open to 7.

The Homewood

Portsmouth Road, Esher, Surrey KT10 9JL

Map ② F6   1999

20th-century house and garden designed by the architect Patrick Gwynne reflecting the style and ethos of the Modern Movement. **Note**: administered on behalf of the National Trust by a tenant. No toilet.

Access for all: [icons]
Building [icons] Grounds [icons]

Getting here: 187:TQ130635.
Access is via minibus from Claremont Landscape Garden only.

Finding out more: 01372 476424 or thehomewood@nationaltrust.org.uk.
c/o Claremont Landscape Garden, Portsmouth Road, Esher, Surrey KT10 9JG

The Homewood

Entrance by booked guided tours only. Open first and third Friday and the second and fourth Saturday of every month April to October. Five guided tours (45 minutes approximately), 10:30, 11:30, 12:30, 2 and 3. Garden open day: Wednesday, 10 October.

Hughenden

High Wycombe, Buckinghamshire HP14 4LA

Map ② E4   [icons] 1947

'I love a warm friendly house. Hughenden ticked all the boxes!'
Ingrid Finch, Ketley, Telford

Amid rolling Chilterns countryside, discover the hideaway and colourful private life of Benjamin Disraeli, the most unlikely Victorian Prime Minister. Follow in his footsteps: stroll through his German forest, relax in his elegant garden and imagine dining with Queen Victoria in the atmospheric manor. Uncover the Second World War story of Operation Hillside, for which unconventional artists painted maps for bombing missions – including the famous Dambusters raid. Experience Sergeant Hadfield's wartime living room. Outdoors, get tips for growing your own vegetables in our walled garden. Don't miss our ancient woodland, where you may spot red kites soaring overhead.

Exploring
– Get to know Queen Victoria's favourite Prime Minister.
– Discover why Hughenden was top of Hitler's hit list.
– Explore the flourishing walled garden.
– Watch the busy bees at work in our new hives.
– Enjoy a stunning view of the Chilterns from the Monument.

Eating and shopping: enjoy home-grown produce in many of our dishes in our Stables Restaurant. Browse in the gift shop and second-hand bookshop. Choose a plant from our volunteer-run stall.

Making the most of your day: varied events programme, woodland trails, introductory film, morning guided tour of manor at 11:20 and free introductory talks during the day. Children's hands-on activities and I-Spy sheets. **Dogs**: welcome under close control in park and woodland.

Children busy planting seeds in the vegetable garden at Hughenden, Buckinghamshire

Access for all: ♿🅿🚻🔊🔉📷🏛🅿⌛🅰

Building 🦽♿👁 Grounds 🦽🏛

Getting here: 165:SU866955. 1½ miles north of High Wycombe. **Foot**: 1½ miles from High Wycombe. **Bus**: High Wycombe to Aylesbury (passing close High Wycombe ≋). Note: long, steep walk to house entrance. **Train**: High Wycombe 2 miles. **Road**: on west side of Great Missenden road (A4128). From M40 exit 4, take A404 towards High Wycombe, follow signs to Eden shopping centre, then take A4128 towards Great Missenden. Follow brown signs. **Parking**: free, 200 yards; overflow car park, 400 yards (waiting possible at peak times).

Finding out more: 01494 755565 (Infoline). 01494 755573 or hughenden@nationaltrust.org.uk

Hughenden		M	T	W	T	F	S	S
Garden, shop and restaurant								
11 Feb–16 Mar	11–4	M	T	W	T	F	S	S
17 Mar–31 Oct	11–5:30	M	T	W	T	F	S	S
1 Nov–30 Dec	11–4	M	T	W	T	F	S	S
House								
11 Feb–16 Mar	11–3	M	T	W	T	F	S	S
17 Mar–31 Oct	12–5	M	T	W	T	F	S	S
1 Nov–30 Dec	11–3	M	T	W	T	F	S	S
Park								
Open all year		M	T	W	T	F	S	S

Timed tickets may be in operation on Bank Holidays and other busy days (available from ticket office from 11 on day). Occasional early closing for special events and weddings. Special Christmas opening during December. Closed 24, 25 and 31 December.

Ightham Mote

Mote Road, Ivy Hatch, Sevenoaks, Kent TN15 0NT

Map ② H6   🏛✝🌸🍴🏠 1985

'The jewel in the National Trust crown.'
Mrs Jean Hewitson, Sutton, Surrey

Lose yourself in this romantic moated manor house, described by David Starkey as 'one of the most beautiful and interesting of English country houses'. Built nearly 700 years ago, this house has seen many changes – having been owned by medieval knights, courtiers to Henry VIII and high-society Victorians. Highlights include the picturesque courtyard, Great Hall, crypt, Tudor painted ceiling, Grade I listed dog kennel and the private apartments of Charles Henry Robinson, who gave Ightham Mote to the National Trust in 1985. The building is surrounded by peaceful gardens with an orchard, water features, lakes and woodland walks. **Note**: very steep slope from reception (lower drop-off point available).

Exploring
- Enjoy a free introductory talk.
- See the Tudor royal emblems and 18th-century Chinese wallpaper.
- Join a free garden tour and discover the South Lake.
- Learn about the Trust's largest conservation project.

Exploring – See for miles from the top of the tower (weather-permitting).

Eating and shopping: shop for gifts, local produce and a wide variety of shrubs and herbaceous plants. Enjoy locally sourced food in the Mote Restaurant or attend one of our events.

Making the most of your day: there are plenty of quizzes, activities and events to keep the children busy. Enjoy one of the many walks around the estate. **Dogs**: welcome on leads on estate walks only.

Access for all: Building Grounds

Getting here: 188:TQ584535. Between Sevenoaks and Borough Green 1¾ miles south of A25. **Bus**: service from Sevenoaks ≋ Thursday and Friday only, other days alight Ivy Hatch, ¾ mile. Autocar 222 Tonbridge to Borough Green, alight at Ightham, 2 miles. Arriva 306/8 Sevenoaks ≋ to Gravesend, alight Ightham Common, 1½ miles. **Train**: Borough Green & Wrotham 3½ miles; Hildenborough 4 miles; Sevenoaks 6 miles.

Road: 6 miles north of Tonbridge on A227; 6 miles south of Sevenoaks on A25; 16 miles west of Maidstone on A20/A25.
Parking: free, 200 yards.

Finding out more: 01732 810378 (extension 100) or ighthammote@nationaltrust.org.uk

Ightham Mote		M	T	W	T	F	S	S
House*								
10 Mar–4 Nov	11–5	**M**	·	·	**T**	**F**	**S**	**S**
6 Jun–29 Aug	11–5	**M**	·	**W**	**T**	**F**	**S**	**S**
8 Nov–23 Dec	11–3	·	·	·	**T**	**F**	**S**	**S**
Shop, restaurant and garden**								
4 Feb–4 Mar	11–3	·	·	·	·	·	**S**	**S**
10 Mar–4 Nov	10:30–5	**M**	·	·	**T**	**F**	**S**	**S**
6 Jun–29 Aug	10:30–5	**M**	·	**W**	**T**	**F**	**S**	**S**
8 Nov–23 Dec	11–3	·	·	·	**T**	**F**	**S**	**S**
Restaurant								
27 Dec–31 Dec	11–3	**M**	·	·	**T**	**F**	**S**	**S**
Estate								
Open all year	Dawn–dusk	**M**	**T**	**W**	**T**	**F**	**S**	**S**

*November and December, 11 to 3: partial gardens, courtyard, library, ground-floor access, visitor reception and conservation exhibition. Dressed for Christmas.
**Restaurant may not fully open during private functions. February weekends and 3 and 4 March: restaurant, partial gardens, shop, visitor reception and conservation exhibition. Shop: telephone 01732 811203 for additional opening times. Restaurant: for opening times, themed evenings booking, functions and Christmas lunch telephone 01732 811314.

The Formal Garden at Ightham Mote, Kent: a delightful moated manor house

King's Head

King's Head Passage, Market Square, Aylesbury, Buckinghamshire HP20 2RW

Map (2) E3   1925

Historic public house with a pleasant family atmosphere. The King's Head is one of England's best-preserved coaching inns. Dating back to 1455, the building has many fascinating architectural features, including rare stained-glass windows, exposed wattle and daub and the original stabling for the inn. **Note**: The Farmers' Bar is leased by Chiltern Brewery.

Exploring – Visit The Farmers' Bar for local beer and fine foods.
– Relax with a drink in the peaceful courtyard.
– Take afternoon tea in the Great Hall.
– Learn about the history of the site in the Stable.

Eating and shopping: award-winning Farmers' Bar, run by local Chiltern Brewery, provides excellent local food and fine ales.

Access for all: [symbols] Building [symbol]

Getting here: 165:SP818137. At top of Market Square in the centre of Aylesbury. **Foot**: access through cobbled lane near the war memorial. **Train**: Aylesbury 400 yards. **Parking**: no onsite parking. Car parks in town centre (not National Trust).

Finding out more: 01296 718812 (Farmers' Bar). 01296 730349 (National Trust) or kingshead@nationaltrust.org.uk

King's Head		
Farmers' Bar*		
Open every day all year from 11 to 11		

*Normal pub opening hours apply. Closed 25 December. For Great Hall tea-room opening times telephone 01296 718812.

Knole

Sevenoaks, Kent TN15 0RP

Map (2) H6   1946

Knole, one of our most important and complete historic houses, this year launches an exciting project to secure its future. Expect everything to look and feel a bit different as we carry out urgent repairs to save the house from rapid decline, with scaffolding on our east front. It's the first phase in a huge programme which aims to engage all our visitors in our continuing history. Once at the centre of court life, Knole was the inspiration for Virginia Woolf's *Orlando*, and contains extraordinary furniture from the royal palaces, alongside superb portraits, textiles and silver.

Exploring – See how a grand estate was run.
– Hear new stories in the estate office from June.
– Understand Knole's whole history in our stunning visitor centre.
– Sit and dream among the lemon trees in the Orangery.
– Walk among the deer in the park.
– Discover the treasures of kings.

Eating and shopping: discover local produce in the shop and browse through the large selection of books, gifts and children's pocket-money toys. Visit the Brewhouse tea-room, Knole's original brewery, for great food made fresh and served in a Grade I listed building.

Making the most of your day: extensive programme of guided park walks. Holiday family trails and activities, including historic crafts, skittles and Tudor dressing-up days. Conservation demonstrations, evening candelit tours, Christmas workshops and carol concerts. **Dogs**: welcome in the park on leads.

Access for all: [symbols] House [symbols] Grounds [symbols]

Playing at Knole, Kent: the forgotten palace

Lamb House

West Street, Rye, East Sussex TN31 7ES

Map ② J8   1950

Fine brick-fronted house with literary associations – both Henry James and E. F. Benson lived here. Surprisingly large beautiful town garden. **Note:** administered and largely maintained on the National Trust's behalf by a tenant. No toilets.

Access for all: ⬚ Building 🔣 Grounds 🔣

Getting here: 198:TQ920202. In West Street, facing west end of church.

Getting here: 188:TQ532543. 1½ miles from Sevenoaks. **Foot:** entrance by Sevenoaks Library, or as road details. **Bus:** from surrounding area to Sevenoaks, ¾-mile walk. **Train:** Sevenoaks 1½ miles. **Road:** leave M25 at exit 5 (A21). Park entrance south of Sevenoaks town centre off A225 Tonbridge Road (opposite St Nicholas church). **Sat Nav:** use TN13 1HU for church opposite park entrance. **Parking:** 60 yards, available when house, visitor centre or tea-room open, otherwise parking in nearby town centre.

Finding out more: 01732 450608 (Infoline). 01732 462100 or knole@nationaltrust.org.uk

Finding out more: 01580 762334 or lambhouse@nationaltrust.org.uk

Lamb House	M	T	W	T	F	S	S
24 Mar–27 Oct	2–6		·	T	·	·	S

Knole		M	T	W	T	F	S	S
House								
10 Mar–4 Nov	12–4		·	·	W	T	F	S	S
Tea-room								
7 Jan–26 Feb	11–4		·	·	·	·	·	S	S
Visitor centre, Orangery, tea-room, shop								
3 Mar–4 Mar	11–4		·	·	·	·	·	S	S
Visitor centre, Orangery, tea-room, shop, estate office								
10 Mar–1 Apr	10:30–5		·	·	W	T	F	S	S
3 Apr–30 Sep	10:30–5		·	T	W	T	F	S	S
3 Oct–4 Nov	10:30–5		·	·	W	T	F	S	S
7 Nov–23 Dec	11–4		·	·	W	T	F	S	S
Garden								
3 Apr–25 Sep	11–4		·	T	·	·	·	·	·

Open Bank Holiday Mondays. Great Hall will be open selected dates in December. Car park: gates open 10:15, close 6. Vehicles not admitted when whole of property is closed. Park: open daily for pedestrians.

Lamb House, East Sussex: Henry James's home

Leith Hill

Leith Hill, near Coldharbour village,
Dorking, Surrey

Map ② F7 1923

Climb the spiral staircase and, at more than
1,000 feet, become the highest person
in south-east England. Enjoy panoramic
views and see how many landmarks can be
spotted with the aid of the telescope. Follow
circular nature trails and then reward yourself
with refreshments from the tea servery.
Note: Olympic cycle races, 28 and 29 July: open
but local road closures (details on website).

Exploring
— New 360-degree panoramic
leaflet/quiz available
from tower.
— Child entry includes
panoramic leaflet/quiz, pencil
and telescope token.
— New guide to Rhododendron
Wood available from
car-park noticeboard.
— New Frank's Walk leaflet
around spectacular
bluebell wood.

Eating and shopping: light refreshments sold
from tower (opening hours only). Reward
yourself with something delicious and
homemade. Please note: no toilet.

Making the most of your day: programme
of guided walks and activities, including
children's fun afternoons throughout the year.
Three circular waymarked nature trails, with
accompanying leaflet, available from Tower,
Rhododendron Wood and Landslip car-park
noticeboards. **Dogs**: under close control in
Rhododendron Wood, heathland and farmland
during March to July.

Access for all: Tower 👍

Getting here: 187:TQ139432. 1 mile south-west
of Coldharbour. **Bus**: Holmbury St Mary
2½ miles. **Train**: Holmwood 2½ miles, Dorking
5½ miles. **Road**: off A29/B2126.

Leith Hill, Surrey: panoramic views

Parking: designated areas along road at
foot of hill (no vehicle access to summit).
Rhododendron Wood £3 per car.

Finding out more: 01306 712711 or
leithhill@nationaltrust.org.uk

Leith Hill		M	T	W	T	F	S	S
Countryside								
Open all year		M	T	W	T	F	S	S
Tower								
1 Jan–24 Mar	10–3:30	·	·	·	·	·	S	S
14 Feb–19 Feb	10–3:30	·	T	W	T	F	S	S
25 Mar–27 Oct	10–5	·	·	·	·	F	S	S
4 Jun–10 Jun	10–5	M	T	W	T	F	S	S
28 Oct–30 Dec	10–3:30	·	·	·	·	·	S	S
30 Oct–4 Nov	10–3:30	·	T	W	T	F	S	S

Open Bank and Public Holidays, except 25 December
(tower/servery). Now open half-term weeks, except Monday
(unless a Bank Holiday).

Long Crendon Courthouse

Long Crendon, Aylesbury,
Buckinghamshire HP18 9AN

Map ② D4 🏠 1900

Visit the second building acquired by the National Trust, a 14th-century Court House with a wealth of local history. **Note**: village exhibition on display. Extremely steep stairs. No toilet.

Access for all: Building 🔉

Getting here: 165:SP698091. Next to the parish church at the end of High Street. Limited parking.

Finding out more: 01296 730349 or longcrendon@nationaltrust.org.uk

Long Crendon Courthouse	M	T	W	T	F	S	S
4 Apr–26 Sep	2–6		·	·	W	·	·	·
7 Apr–30 Sep	11–6		·	·	·	·	·	S	S

Managed by volunteers, so sometimes only open subject to availability (telephone before making a special journey). Open Bank Holiday Mondays, 11 to 6.

Monk's House

Rodmell, Lewes, East Sussex BN7 3HF

Map ② G8 🏠 ✿ 1980

Novelist Virginia Woolf's country retreat, a charming 18th-century weatherboarded cottage – featuring the room where she created her best-known works.

Access for all: 🚻 Building 🔉 Grounds 🔉🔉

Getting here: 198:TQ421063. In Rodmell village, near church, 4 miles south of Lewes.

Finding out more: 01273 474760 or monkshouse@nationaltrust.org.uk

Monk's House	M	T	W	T	F	S	S
4 Apr–28 Oct	1–5:30	·	·	W	T	F	S	S

Garden: opens 12. House: opens 1 (last entry to house 5). Open Bank Holiday Mondays during season.

The writing shed at Monk's House, East Sussex: Virginia Woolf's country retreat

Mottisfont

near Romsey, Hampshire SO51 0LP

Map (2) C7    1957

At the heart of this tranquil rural estate is Mottisfont, set in glorious grounds alongside the fast-flowing River Test. There are many layers of history for the visitor to explore, including the Gothic remains of the original 13th-century Augustinian priory. In the mid-20th century the final private owner, society hostess and patron of the arts Maud Russell, used the Abbey as a base for her racy and intriguing life. The River Test is one of the finest chalk streams in the world, and the walled gardens house the National Collection of Old-fashioned Roses. **Note**: during the rose season in June weekday and/or evening visits are recommended.

Exploring
- Discover changing exhibitions in the art gallery.
- See Rex Whistler's *trompe l'oeil* design in the drawing room.
- Winter garden, 60,000 spring bulbs, late summer borders.
- Picnic on the lawn, under our majestic plane trees.
- Build dens, run, jump or enjoy our creative play space.
- Explore Mottisfont's wider estate by bike or on foot.

Eating and shopping: taste Mottisfont's locally sourced homemade food, including 'cake of the month'. Cool down in the Angel Ice-cream Parlour, serving a delicious choice of local ice-creams. Browse and buy in our Coach House shop. Find a bargain in the second-hand bookshop.

Making the most of your day: comprehensive events programme runs throughout the year. Enjoy our popular open-air theatre, guided walks and talks, changing exhibitions and take part in activity days and trails. **Dogs**: welcome on specially designed route around grounds and estate walks only.

Access for all: [symbols]
Building [symbols] Grounds [symbols]

Getting here: 185:SU327270. 4½ miles north of Romsey. **Foot**: on Hampshire's long-distance path, Testway. Clarendon Way 2 miles north. **Cycle**: on Testway. **Train**: Dunbridge 1½ miles. **Road**: signposted off A3057 Romsey to Stockbridge. Also signposted off B3087 Romsey to Broughton. **Parking**: free.

Finding out more: 01794 340757 or mottisfont@nationaltrust.org.uk

Mottisfont		M	T	W	T	F	S	S
Garden, shop and café								
Open all year	10–5	M	T	W	T	F	S	S
Art gallery								
Open all year	11–5	M	T	W	T	F	S	S
House								
1 Mar–4 Nov	11–5	M	T	W	T	F	S	S

Closes dusk if earlier. Contact property for late opening in June. Gallery closes for short periods to change exhibitions. Closed 25 December.

Mottisfont, Hampshire: layers of history

Magical Mottistone Manor Garden, Isle of Wight

Mottistone Manor Garden

Mottistone, near Brighstone,
Isle of Wight PO30 4EA

Map ② C9   1965

'A beautiful, peaceful garden. It was lovely to sit and reflect with friends. And I got some handy planting tips!'
Jill Genders, Overstrand

Set in a sheltered valley this magical garden is full of surprises, with shrub-filled banks, hidden pathways and colourful herbaceous borders. Surrounding an attractive Elizabethan manor house (tenanted so not open) this 20th-century garden is experimenting with a Mediterranean-style planting scheme to take advantage of its southerly location. Other surprises include a young olive grove, a small organic kitchen garden and a traditional tea garden set alongside The Shack, a unique cabin retreat designed as their summer drawing office by architects John Seely (2nd Lord Mottistone) and Paul Paget. There are also delightful walks across the adjoining Mottistone Estate. **Note**: the manor house is only open on 3 and 4 June.

Exploring — Enjoy this hillside garden throughout the seasons.
— Relish the informality – a bit on the wild side.
— Discover our resident flowerpot people.

Exploring — Explore the garden with a family discovery trail.
— Venture inside The Shack, a unique 1930s garden cabin.
— Extend your visit with a walk to the Long Stone.

Eating and shopping: browse in our gift shop. Take home a plant from the plant stall. Snap up a second-hand book bargain. Relax in the tea garden (not National Trust).

Making the most of your day: programme of family events and garden tours. Flowerpot trail and walks across the surrounding estate. **Dogs**: welcome on leads.

Access for all: ⬛⬛⬛⬛⬛⬛⬛⬛⬛
Grounds ⬛⬛➡⬛

Getting here: 196:SZ406838. At Mottistone. **Foot**: 1 mile north of coastal path; 1 mile south of Tennyson Trail. **Cycle**: NCN67. On the 'Round the Island' cycle route. **Ferry**: Yarmouth (Wightlink) 5 miles (0871 376 1000); East Cowes (Red Funnel) 16 miles (0844 844 9988). **Bus**: Newport to Totland. **Road**: between Brighstone and Brook on B3399. **Parking**: free, 50 yards.

Finding out more: 01983 741302 or mottistonemanor@nationaltrust.org.uk

Mottistone Manor Garden		M	T	W	T	F	S	S
18 Mar–1 Nov	11–5	M	T	W	T	·	·	S

Closes dusk if earlier. Special two-day opening of house to mark the Queen's Diamond Jubilee: Sunday 3 June (members only). Guided tours 9:30 to 12 by timed ticket (available on day), free-flow 1:30 to 5. Monday 4 June open 11 to 12 then 1:30 to 5 (additional charges apply).

The Needles Old Battery and New Battery

West High Down, Alum Bay,
Isle of Wight PO39 0JH

Map (2) C9 1975

'We came for the view, but found so much more.'
Elaine Lindow, Bolton

Perched high above the Needles, amid acres of unspoilt countryside, is the Needles Old Battery, a Victorian fort built in 1862 and used throughout both World Wars. The Parade Ground has two original guns and the Fort's fascinating military history is brought to life with new displays and models plus a series of vivid cartoons by acclaimed comic book artist Geoff Campion. An underground tunnel leads to a searchlight emplacement with dramatic views over the Needles rocks. The New Battery, further up the headland, has an exhibition on the secret British rocket tests carried out there during the Cold War. **Note**: steep paths and uneven surfaces. Spiral staircase to tunnel. Toilet at Old Battery only.

Exploring
- Enjoy dramatic sea views from the clifftop walk.
- Discover the rooms where soldiers worked with gunpowder.
- Explore the site with a family activity pack.
- See the Needles from our wheelchair-friendly viewing platform.
- Don't miss one of our most unusual tea-rooms.
- Discover recently revealed secrets of Britain's rocket test programme.

Eating and shopping: enjoy homemade food in our clifftop tea-room. Treat yourself to a gift or souvenir in the guardroom shop. Hot and cold drinks, take-away snacks and ice-creams available at the New Battery kiosk.

Bird spotting at The Needles Old Battery, Isle of Wight

Making the most of your day: programme of family events. Family activity packs and soldier trail. Clifftop walks to Tennyson Monument and beyond. **Dogs**: welcome on leads although assistance dogs only in tea-room.

Access for all:
Building **Grounds**

Getting here: 196:SZ300848. In Alum Bay. **Foot**: Alum Bay ¾ mile, well-surfaced path. **Cycle**: NCN67, ½ mile. 'Round the Island' route. **Ferry**: Yarmouth (Wightlink) 5 miles (0871 376 1000); East Cowes (Red Funnel) 16 miles (0844 844 9988). **Bus**: services from Newport to Alum Bay, then ¾ mile. Needles Breezer from Yarmouth and Alum Bay (March to October), member discount with card. **Road**: no vehicular access. West of Freshwater Bay (B3322). **Parking**: no onsite parking. Limited disabled parking by arrangement. Alum Bay ¾ mile (not National Trust, minimum £4). Freshwater Bay 3½ miles (not National Trust), or Highdown (SZ325856) 2 miles, both across Downs.

Finding out more: 01983 754772 or needlesoldbattery@nationaltrust.org.uk

The Needles Batteries		M	T	W	T	F	S	S
Tea-room								
7 Jan–4 Mar	11–3	·	·	·	·	·	**S**	**S**
10 Nov–16 Dec	11–3	·	·	·	·	·	**S**	**S**
Old Battery and tea-room								
17 Mar–4 Nov	10:30–5	**M**	**T**	**W**	**T**	**F**	**S**	**S**
New Battery*								
17 Mar–4 Nov	11–4	·	**T**	·	·	·	**S**	**S**

Old Battery closes dusk if earlier. Property closes in high winds, telephone on day of visit to check. *Open other days where possible, telephone to check. 30 June: Old Battery early opening (6:30) for Round the Island Yacht Race.

Why not visit us on foot or by public transport? See pages 10 and 380

Newtown Old Town Hall

Newtown, near Shalfleet,
Isle of Wight PO30 4PA

Map ② C9 🏠 1933

Tucked away in a tiny hamlet adjoining the National Nature Reserve, the 17th-century Old Town Hall is the only remaining evidence of Newtown's former importance. It's hard to believe that this tranquil corner of the island once held often turbulent elections before sending two Members to Parliament. **Note**: nearest toilet in car park.

Newtown Old Town Hall, Isle of Wight: now tranquil

Exploring — Discover the surprising local and political history.
— Learn about the mysterious Ferguson Gang who saved the Hall.
— Enjoy regular exhibitions.
— Take a delightful estuary walk.

Eating and shopping: treat yourself to a small memento of your visit.

Making the most of your day: children's quiz sheet. Programme of countryside family activities (bookable) run by the Newtown Warden from a nearby Visitor Point. Nature Reserve information, 01983 531622.

Access for all: 🚻♿📷📖🖼 Building ♿

Getting here: 196:SZ424905. Between Newport and Yarmouth. **Cycle**: NCN67½ mile. **Ferry**: Yarmouth (Wightlink) 5 miles (0871 376 1000); East Cowes (Red Funnel) 11 miles (0844 844 9988). **Bus**: Newport to Yarmouth, alight Barton's Corner, Shalfleet 1 mile. **Road**: 1 mile north of A3054. **Parking**: free 15 yards.

Finding out more: 01983 531785 or oldtownhall@nationaltrust.org.uk

Newtown Old Town Hall		M	T	W	T	F	S	S
18 Mar–28 Jun	2–5	·	T	W	T	·	·	S
1 Jul–30 Aug	2–5	M	T	W	T	·	·	S
2 Sep–25 Oct	2–5	·	T	W	T	·	·	S

Last admission 15 minutes before closing. Closes dusk if earlier than 5. Open Bank Holiday Mondays, 2 to 5.

Nuffield Place

Huntercombe, near Henley-on-Thames, Oxfordshire RG9 5RY

Map ② D5 🏠♿❋ 2011

Home of the philanthropist William Morris, Lord Nuffield, the founder of Morris Motor Cars and one of the richest men in the world. The house and complete collection have recently been saved for the nation. Despite his vast fortune Morris's house reflects a modest lifestyle comprising everyday objects. **Note**: new property, so will be busy with ongoing work taking place (booking essential).

Exploring — Marvel at William Morris's tool cupboard in his bedroom.
— Enjoy the woodland walks.
— Relax in the unspoilt gardens.

Making the most of your day: explore the gardens and woodland trails. **Dogs**: on leads in woodland.

Access for all:

Getting here: 175:SU679878. At Huntercombe, between Wallingford and Henley-on-Thames. **Foot:** Ridgeway National Trail adjacent to property. **Bus:** Wallingford to Henley-on-Thames. **Train:** Henley-on-Thames, 7 miles and Reading, 12 miles. **Road:** on A4130 between Wallingford and Henley-on-Thames. **Parking:** free.

Finding out more: 01491 641224 or nuffieldplace@nationaltrust.org.uk

Nuffield Place	M	T	W	T	F	S	S
4 Apr–4 Nov 11-4				W	T	F	S	S

Closed 8 April and 24 June. This property is new so opening arrangements may be subject to change. **Booking essential on 01491 641224.**

Nuffield Place, Oxfordshire: everyday objects hint at a simple life

Nymans

Handcross, near Haywards Heath, West Sussex RH17 6EB

Map ② G7

'Nymans is too lovely a place for people to miss. I visit often and love it.'
Dame Vera Lynn, Ditchling

In the late 19th century an unusually creative family bought the Nymans Estate in the picturesque High Weald landscape of Sussex, to make a home in the country. Inspired by the setting and the soil, the Messels created one of the greatest gardens, with experimental designs and new plants from around the world. Here they entertained family and friends, enjoyed relaxing times, strolled in the garden, played, picnicked and walked in the woods. Enjoy Nymans as they did. We are reinventing Nymans for the 21st century by running the estate in a new, greener way. **Note:** now open seven days a week.

Exploring
- Beauty and colour all year round.
- Fascinating and rare plants.
- Green gardening and living in action.
- Anne Messel's house filled with flowers.
- Creative Messel family including Oliver (designer) and Lord Snowdon (photographer).
- Ancient woodland and splendid South Downs and Sussex Weald views.

Eating and shopping: large shop supporting local products. Plant centre and nursery sell plants propagated from the garden. Restaurant and tea garden serving locally sourced food. Refresh yourself at the garden catering buggy.

Nymans, West Sussex: colourful borders in the Walled Garden, with the Italian marble fountain beyond

Making the most of your day: adult programme: theatre, creative workshops, guided walks, croquet evenings, second-hand bookshop, art exhibitions. Family programme: audio guides, schools, bamboo jungle, art days, trails. **Dogs**: welcome in the woodland only.

Access for all: ⃤⃤⃤⃤⃤⃤⃤⃤⃤⃤⃤⃤⃤
House ⃤⃤⃤ Garden ⃤⃤⃤⃤

Getting here: 187:TQ265294. In Handcross, 5 miles south of Crawley. **Foot**: 5 miles from Balcombe. **Cycle**: NCN20. **Bus**: services from Brighton to Crawley and Haywards Heath to Crawley. All stop outside Nymans. **Train**: Balcombe 4 miles, Crawley 5 miles. **Road**: off London to Brighton M23/A23. **Parking**: free.

Finding out more: 01444 405250 or nymans@nationaltrust.org.uk

Nymans		M	T	W	T	F	S	S
Garden, woods, restaurant, shop and plant centre								
1 Jan–24 Dec	10–5	M	T	W	T	F	S	S
House								
1 Mar–31 Oct	11–3	M	T	W	T	F	S	S

Nymans closes at 4 from 1 November to 31 December. Closed 25 to 31 December.

Oakhurst Cottage

Hambledon, near Godalming, Surrey GU8 4HF

Map ② E7   ⃤⃤ [1952]

A delightfully restored and furnished simple labourer's cottage, containing artefacts reflecting four centuries of continual occupation, and beautiful cottage garden. **Note**: no toilet. Nearest visitor facilities, including tea-room and toilets, at Winkworth Arboretum (5 miles approximately).

Access for all: ⃤⃤⃤⃤⃤

Getting here: 186:SU965380. Off A283 between Wormley and Chiddingfold.

Finding out more: 01483 208936 or oakhurstcottage@nationaltrust.org.uk

Oakhurst Cottage		M	T	W	T	F	S	S
4 Apr–26 Sep	2–5			W				
7 Apr–29 Sep	1–5						S	S
3 Oct–31 Oct	2–4			W				
6 Oct–28 Oct	1–4						S	S

Wednesday: admission by guided tour only (booked in advance – up to 12 noon on day of visit). Open Bank Holiday Mondays, 2 to 5. Open Saturdays and Sundays, no appointment required but advance booking recommended.

Old Soar Manor

Plaxtol, Borough Green, Kent TN15 0QX

Map (2) H6   [🏠] 1947

Rare remaining structure of a late 13th-century knight's dwelling, including solar chamber, barrel-vaulted undercroft, chapel and garderobe. **Note:** no toilet or restaurant. Narrow lanes, limited off-road parking.

Access for all: Building [♿]

Getting here: 188:TQ619541. 2 miles south of Borough Green (A25); approached via A227 and Plaxtol.

Finding out more: 01732 810378 or oldsoarmanor@nationaltrust.org.uk

Old Soar Manor	M	T	W	T	F	S	S
1 Apr–30 Sep	10–6	M	T	W	T	·	S	S

Owletts

The Street, Cobham, Gravesend, Kent DA12 3AP

Map (2) H5   1938

Discover untold stories at the family home of Sir Herbert Baker, the architect who redesigned the Bank of England.

Access for all: Main House [♿][♿]

Getting here: 177:TQ665687. 1 mile south of A2/M2 at west end of the village, at junction of roads from Dartford and Sole Street.

Finding out more: 01304 207326 or owletts@nationaltrust.org.uk

Owletts

Expected to re-open April following conservation work. Visit website for details.

Petworth House and Park

Petworth, West Sussex GU28 0AE

Map (2) E7   1947

'It was absolutely wondrous!'
Mabel Taylor, Oxted

Nestling in the South Downs National Park, discover one of Britain's finest stately homes, set within a beautiful deer park landscaped by 'Capability' Brown. Immerse yourself in the grandeur of the house and its world-famous paintings, many by J. M. W. Turner, Van Dyck, Reynolds and Blake, together with ancient and Neo-classical sculpture and intricate woodcarvings by Grinling Gibbons. In contrast to the opulence of the house, follow in the servants' footsteps and see what life was like 'below stairs' in the servants' quarters. Additional private rooms open on weekdays by kind permission of Lord and Lady Egremont. **Note:** additional charge for Christmas fair (including members).

Exploring
– Discover the house with a multimedia tour or downloadable App.
– Look out for our new films.
– Enjoy one of our family trails or fun family events.
– Glimpse the deer among ancient trees in Petworth Park.
– Indulge in a programmed Connoisseur Tour.
– See extraordinary objects from an internationally important collection.

Eating and shopping: enjoy a delicious cappuccino and homemade cake in our new Servants' Hall coffee shop, or a home-cooked lunch (using locally sourced ingredients) in our Audit Room restaurant. The gift shop offers seasonal inspiration, ideal presents, and children's books and toys.

Making the most of your day: varied programme of talks, guided walks,

behind-the-scenes tours, family trails, children's activity baskets in house, family multimedia guide, and events for all ages and interests. **Dogs**: under close control in Petworth Park. Assistance dogs only in Pleasure Ground.

Access for all: 🅿️🅳♿🚻🚹🖐️👁️📷💻VT♿ ⊙⊙Ⓐ Building 🔤📖♿

Getting here: 197:SU976218. In centre of Petworth. **Foot**: access from Petworth and A272. **Bus**: services from Worthing to Midhurst (passing Pulborough ≥), and Horsham to Petworth (passing Horsham ≥). **Train**: Pulborough 5¼ miles, Horsham 15 miles. **Road**: in centre of Petworth (A272/A283); house and park car parks on A283. **Sat Nav**: use GU28 9LR. **Parking**: 700 yards. Petworth Park car park: £2 charge for non-members.

Finding out more: 01798 343929 (Infoline). 01798 342207 or petworth@nationaltrust.org.uk

Petworth House and Park		M	T	W	T	F	S	S
House								
10 Mar–7 Nov	11–5	M	T	W	·	·	S	S
Shop and restaurant								
11 Feb–7 Mar	10:30–3:30	M	T	W	·	·	S	S
10 Mar–7 Nov	10:30–5	M	T	W	·	·	S	S
14 Nov–23 Dec	10:30–3:30	·	·	W	T	F	S	S
Pleasure Ground								
11 Feb–7 Mar	10:30–3:30	M	T	W	·	·	S	S
10 Mar–7 Nov	10:30–6	M	T	W	·	·	S	S
14 Nov–23 Dec	10:30–3:30	·	·	W	T	F	S	S

Open Good Friday. **Extra rooms shown weekdays from 1:** Monday (not Bank Holiday Mondays), White and Gold Room and White Library; Tuesday and Wednesday, three bedrooms on first floor.

Exploring Petworth House and Park, West Sussex

Pitstone Windmill

Ivinghoe, Buckinghamshire

Map ② E3   🚫♿ 1937

Discover one of the oldest windmills in the UK and explore the surrounding Ivinghoe hills for stunning views. **Note**: no toilet. Located at the end of a rough track.

Access for all: Building 🔤

Getting here: 181:SP945157. ½ mile south of Ivinghoe, 3 miles north-east of Tring, just west of the B488.

Finding out more: 01442 851227 or pitstonemill@nationaltrust.org.uk

Pitstone Windmill		M	T	W	T	F	S	S
27 May–26 Aug	2:30–6	·	·	·	·	·	·	S

Open Bank Holiday Mondays 4 June and 27 August. Due to staffing restrictions, property may not open as publicised (telephone to check).

Polesden Lacey

Great Bookham, near Dorking, Surrey RH5 6BD

Map ② F6    1942

An Edwardian country estate designed as the perfect setting for the famous Edwardian hostess Mrs Greville to entertain royalty, politicians and the cream of society. Polesden Lacey has stunning interiors and collections, delightful gardens and superb views across the rolling Surrey Hills all waiting to be explored. Immerse yourself in a lifestyle where nothing was too much trouble for your hostess, and discover all the gossip from Mrs Greville's country house parties. Wander through the beautiful walled gardens, before strolling the extensive grounds and landscape walks. **Note**: Olympic cycle races, 28 and 29 July: open but local road closures (details on website).

Exploring — Feel like one of Mrs Greville's party guests.
  — Enjoy the stunning formal gardens, including the famous Rose Garden.
  — Take in the beautiful countryside on a landscape walk.

Exploring — Discover nature and history with family activities and play area.
  — Events, including Tulip Festival and Music Festival (July).

Eating and shopping: savour home-cooked seasonal menus in the Courtyard Restaurant. Treat yourself to homemade cakes in our coffee shop. Enjoy a unique shopping experience, purchase items from Surrey artists and live the Polesden Lacey life in our holiday cottage.

Making the most of your day: welcome talks and guided tours, extensive events programme including specialist tours and opening of the house weekends November to February. Shops and restaurant located outside the pay perimeter. **Dogs**: on leads in designated areas, under close control on landscape walks, estate and farmland.

Access for all: [icons] Building [icons] Grounds [icons]

Getting here: 187:TQ136522. 5 miles north-west of Dorking. **Foot**: North Downs Way within ¾ mile. **Bus**: Guildford to Epsom, alight Great Bookham, 1½ miles. **Train**: Boxhill & Westhumble 2 miles; Dorking 4 miles. **Road**: 2 miles south of Great Bookham, off A246 Leatherhead to Guildford road. **Parking**: 200 yards (pay and display).

Polesden Lacey in Surrey has stunning interiors and collections, as well as delightful gardens

Finding out more: 01372 458203 (Infoline). 01372 452048 or polesdenlacey@nationaltrust.org.uk

Polesden Lacey	M	T	W	T	F	S	S
House – limited guided tours							
7 Jan–12 Feb	11–3:30						S	S
15 Feb–26 Feb	11–4:30			W	T	F	S	S
10 Nov–25 Nov	11–3:30						S	S
House							
29 Feb–28 Oct	11–5			W	T	F	S	S
31 Oct–4 Nov	11–4			W	T	F	S	S
1 Dec–16 Dec	11–4						S	S
Gardens, restaurant, gift/garden shop and coffee shop*							
1 Jan–10 Feb	10–4	M	T	W	T	F	S	S
11 Feb–28 Oct	10–5	M	T	W	T	F	S	S
29 Oct–31 Dec	10–4	M	T	W	T	F	S	S
Car park							
Open all year	7:30–6:30	M	T	W	T	F	S	S

January, February and November house entry limited and by guided tour only. Open Bank Holiday Mondays and Tuesday 5 June. *Closed 13 March. Olympic cycle races, 28 and 29 July: open but local road closures (details on website). Closed 24 and 25 December.

Priory Cottages

1 Mill Street, Steventon, Abingdon, Oxfordshire OX13 6SP

Map ② C5 | 1939 |

Now converted into two houses, these former monastic buildings were gifted to the National Trust by the famous Ferguson's Gang. **Note**: Priory Cottage South only open. No toilet.

Getting here: 164:SU466914. 4 miles south of Abingdon.

Finding out more: 01793 762209 or priorycottages@nationaltrust.org.uk

Priory Cottages	M	T	W	T	F	S	S
5 Apr–27 Sep	2–6			T			

Admission by written appointment with the tenant. Please allow sufficient time for your booking enquiry to be dealt with.

Quebec House

Quebec Square, Westerham, Kent TN16 1TD

Map ② G6 | 1918 |

Visit this little treasure and experience the intimacy of living in Quebec House, James Wolfe's boyhood home. Uncover the glory of General Wolfe's great victory at Quebec, explore both sides of the conquest of Canada and reflect on the tragedy of Wolfe's death and the art it inspired.

Exploring
- Discover this intimate 18th-century family home.
- Enjoy the pretty garden, with new vegetable and herb beds.
- Exhibition telling the story of Wolfe's life and Quebec.
- See our progress as we open the bedroom.

Quebec House in Kent: a little treasure

Eating and shopping: enjoy tea, coffee, biscuits and ice-cream in the delightful garden. Range of local foods, Quebec House-themed products and gifts are on sale in the Coach House.

Making the most of your day: exciting events programme, including special talks, children's activities, living history and family trails.

Access for all: 🚻♿🏠🎦🎧👓📷

Building 🏠♿ Grounds ♿➡️♿

Getting here: 187:TQ449541. At east end of Westerham. **Bus**: services from Bromley North 🚃 (passing Bromley South 🚃) and Sevenoaks 🚃; also from Tunbridge Wells 🚃 (Sundays only). **Train**: Sevenoaks 4 miles; Oxted 4 miles. **Road**: on north side of A25, facing junction with B2026 Edenbridge road. M25 exit 5 or 6. **Parking**: 80 yards east of Quebec House on A25 (not National Trust). Follow footpath beside A25 to house.

Finding out more: 01732 868381 or quebechouse@nationaltrust.org.uk

Quebec House		M	T	W	T	F	S	S
House								
10 Mar–4 Nov	1–5	·	·	**W**	**T**	**F**	**S**	**S**
10 Nov–23 Dec	1–4	·	·	·	·	·	**S**	**S**
Garden and exhibition								
10 Mar–4 Nov	12–5	·	·	**W**	**T**	**F**	**S**	**S**
10 Nov–23 Dec	12–4	·	·	·	·	·	**S**	**S**

Open Bank Holiday Mondays.

River Wey and Godalming Navigations and Dapdune Wharf

Navigations Office and Dapdune Wharf, Wharf Road, Guildford, Surrey GU1 4RR

Map ② F6   🏠🚻♿🍴 1964

'A favourite place. Don't miss the most interesting chat with Jim, the Old Seadog – wonderful, thank you!'
Mike, Jane and Margaret Guillem, Fetcham, Surrey

Explore one of the first British rivers to be made navigable. The Wey opened to barge traffic in 1653, and this 15½-mile waterway linked Guildford to Weybridge on the Thames, and so to London. The Godalming Navigation opened in 1764 and enabled barges to work a further four miles upriver. Our award-winning visitor centre at Dapdune Wharf in Guildford tells the story of the Navigations and the people who lived and worked on them. See where the huge Wey barges were built and climb aboard *Reliance*, one of three surviving barges.

A crisp winter's day on the River Wey, Surrey: one of the first British rivers to be made navigable

Note: Olympic cycle races, 28 and 29 July: open but local road closures (details on website). Mooring and fishing fees (including members).

Exploring
- Take a boat trip on our electric launch.
- Climb aboard *Reliance*, one of the last surviving Wey barges.
- Enjoy the peace and tranquillity of a towpath walk.
- Have a go at pond dipping in the creek.
- Schools can enjoy our river studies workshop.

Eating and shopping: small tea-room serves sandwiches, cakes, ice-cream and drinks. Small shop with plant sales. Picnic areas at Dapdune Wharf.

Making the most of your day: year-round events programme, including events for children at Dapdune and programme of guided walks along the towpath and beyond. Annual Guildford Festival Boat Gathering in July. Overnight moorings available. **Dogs:** on leads at Dapdune Wharf and lock areas; elsewhere under control.

Access for all: P♿🚻♿🚻⬛.⬛📷♿
Grounds ♿

Getting here: 186:SU993502. **River:** visiting craft can enter from the Thames at Shepperton. Slipways at Guildford/Pyrford. **Foot:** access to Dapdune Wharf from town centre via towpath. **Bus:** frequent services, alight at the Cricket Ground on Woodbridge Road. **Train:** Addlestone ➤, Byfleet and New Haw, Guildford, Farncombe and Godalming all close to the Navigations. **Road:** Dapdune Wharf is on Wharf Road to rear of Surrey County Cricket Ground, off Woodbridge Road, A322 (only accesible from the northbound carriageway), Guildford. **Parking:** at Dapdune Wharf.

Finding out more: 01483 561389 or riverwey@nationaltrust.org.uk

River Wey and Dapdune Wharf		M	T	W	T	F	S	S
Dapdune Wharf								
24 Mar–28 Oct	11–5	M			T	F	S	S
4 Jun–10 Jun	11–5	M	T	W	T	F	S	S
29 Oct–4 Nov	11–5	M	T	W	T	F	S	S

River trips 11 to 4 (conditions permitting). Access to towpath during daylight hours all year.

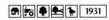

Runnymede

Egham, near Old Windsor, Surrey

Map ② F5   🏠🛶♿🛶🚻 1931

In 1215 Runnymede was witness to King John's sealing of the Magna Carta, on the banks of the River Thames. Set within the beautiful natural landscape are various memorials by Maufe, Jellicoe and Lutyens, commemorating moments in world history. The perfect countryside setting in which to remember and reflect. **Note:** toilets available during standard opening hours. Mooring and fishing fees apply (including members).

Exploring
- Reflect on world history at the memorials.
- Stroll along the path by the River Thames.
- Wander through the historic meadows.
- Explore the ancient woodlands and their venerable veteran trees.

Eating and shopping: tea-room (not National Trust). Runnymede Art Gallery open all year (for upcoming artists, exhibitions and opening times visit www.runnymedegallery.com). River boat trips available from Runnymede (contact French Brothers for more information at www.frenchbrothers.co.uk).

Making the most of your day: guided walk programme throughout the year, plus Easter Egg trail. **Dogs:** under close control or on leads near livestock.

Access for all: P♿🚻🚻 Tea-room ♿
Art gallery/estate office ♿♿ Grounds ♿♿♿

Getting here: SU996731. Adjacent to River Thames, between Egham and Old Windsor on A308. **Foot:** 1¼ miles of Thames Path, National Trail. **Cycle:** 1¼ miles of Thames Path, National Trail. **Bus:** Heathrow to Slough, via Staines. Alight Old Windsor, Bells of Ouzeley, walk back along A308 towards Egham for ¼ mile. **Train:** Egham ➤, 1½ miles. **Road:** 2 miles from M25, junction 13: A308 towards Old Windsor.

Parking: either side of A308, adjacent to Lodges, pay and display. Riverside grass car park open seasonally, weather dependent.

Finding out more: 01784 432891 or runnymede@nationaltrust.org.uk. Runnymede Estate Office, North Lodge, Windsor Road, Egham, Old Windsor, Berkshire SL4 2JL

Runnymede		M	T	W	T	F	S	S
Countryside								
Open all year		M	T	W	T	F	S	S
Memorials car park (hard-standing)								
2 Jan–1 Mar	8:30–5	M	T	W	T	F	S	S
2 Mar–28 Sep	8:30–7	M	T	W	T	F	S	S
29 Sep–31 Dec	8:30–5	M	T	W	T	F	S	S
Riverside car park (grass/seasonal)								
2 Mar–28 Sep	10–7	M	T	W	T	F	S	S

Car parks: may close dusk if earlier; closed 25 and 26 December. Riverside grass car park open when ground and weather conditions permit.

St John's Jerusalem

Sutton-at-Hone, Dartford, Kent DA4 9HQ

Map ② H5   ✚ ❊ 1943

A beautiful 13th-century chapel, surrounded by a tranquil moated garden, once part of the former Commandery of the Knights Hospitallers. **Note**: occupied as a private residence, maintained and managed by a tenant on behalf of the National Trust.

Access for all: Chapel Grounds

Getting here: 177:TQ558703. 3 miles south of Dartford at Sutton-at-Hone.

Finding out more: 01732 810378 (c/o Ightham Mote) or stjohnsjerusalem@nationaltrust.org.uk

St John's Jerusalem		M	T	W	T	F	S	S
4 Apr–26 Sep	2–6	·	·	W	·	·	·	·
3 Oct–31 Oct	2–4	·	·	W	·	·	·	·

Sandham Memorial Chapel

Harts Lane, Burghclere, near Newbury, Hampshire RG20 9JT

Map ② C6   ✚ ❊ 1947

Unexpected treasure can be found in this modest red-brick building – an outstanding series of large-scale paintings by acclaimed artist Stanley Spencer. Inspired by his experiences as a First World War medical orderly and soldier, and peppered with personal and unexpected details, these paintings are considered among his finest achievements. **Note**: no toilet. No credit card facilities.

Exploring
– Revel in the details of these extraordinary works of art.
– Wander through the orchard to spot wild flowers.
– Enjoy the surroundings, with walks and views to Watership Down.
– Learn more about the life and work of Stanley Spencer.

Eating and shopping: browse through the selection of books and postcards available for purchase, as well as home-grown plants in the garden.

Making the most of your day: bring a picnic and enjoy the garden. Reference folders, children's quiz and handling kit available. No artificial lighting, so bright days are best for viewing. **Dogs**: in grounds on leads only.

Access for all: 🅳♿🖼️👓📷
Building 🔤♿ Grounds 🔤♿

Getting here: 174:SU463608. 4 miles south of Newbury. **Bus**: 'demand-responsive' service from Newbury (telephone 0845 602 4135). **Train**: Newbury 4 miles. **Road**: ½ mile east of A34. From M4, follow A34, then brown signs. From A339 (Basingstoke to Newbury) follow brown and white signs. Exit A34 at Tothill services. **Parking**: no onsite parking. Parking in public lay-by opposite chapel, roadway

between village church and village hall or
village car park (¼ mile).

Finding out more: 01635 278394 or
sandham@nationaltrust.org.uk

Sandham Memorial Chapel		M	T	W	T	F	S	S
3 Mar–25 Mar	11–3						S	S
31 Mar–30 Sep	11–4:30		·	W	·	F	S	S
3 Oct–28 Oct	11–3		·	W	·	F	S	S
11 Nov	10–3							S

Open Bank Holiday Mondays, 11 to 4:30. Visit website for
additional special openings.

Scotney Castle

Lamberhurst, Tunbridge Wells, Kent TN3 8JN

Map ② I7    1970

'We had a fantastic day out and the whole
family enjoyed it. We will be back soon!'
Ditton family, Cornwall

The 14th-century moated Scotney Castle in Kent

Scotney Castle is quite simply one of the most
stunning, picturesque gardens in England,
with two celebrated former homes on one
site. You can enjoy the newly opened rooms
in the Victorian mansion or simply explore the
stunning ruins of the 14th-century moated
castle, which is the magnificent focal point
of this truly romantic garden. Spectacular
displays of rhododendrons, azaleas and kalmia
can be seen in May and June with trees and
shrubs providing brilliant autumnal colour. The
310-hectare (770-acre) estate is open all year,
offering a variety of wonderful walks through
beautiful parkland, woodland and farmland.

Exploring
– Voted among the top ten best
  English gardens to visit.
– Superb display of
  rhododendrons and azaleas.
– Explore the beautiful estate,
  woodland and parkland.
– The only National Trust-
  owned working hop farm.
– Discover the fantastic rooms
  in the country mansion.
– Garden and estate
  designated a Site of Special
  Scientific Interest.

Eating and shopping: our tea-room serves
delicious sandwiches, glorious cream teas, plus
hot and cold lunches. The picnic area kiosk
serves light refreshments. Seek out Scotney ale,
Scotney honey and peat-free plants for sale.
New estate explorer for purchase with
lovely walks.

Making the most of your day: a wide range
of activities and events throughout the year
– including open-air theatre/cinema, music,
lecture lunches and family activities. Estate
and wildlife walks – a full events programme
is available. **Dogs**: welcome on leads around
estate, assistance dogs only in the garden.

Access for all: ⊞⊞⊞⊞⊞⊞⊞⊞⊞
House ⊞⊞⊞ **Grounds** ⊞⊞⊞

Getting here: 188:TQ688353. Outskirts
of Lamberhurst village. **Foot**: links to local
footpath network. **Cycle**: NCN18, 3 miles.
Bus: service from Tunbridge Wells to
Lamberhurst. **Train**: Wadhurst 5½ miles.
Road: signposted from A21 at Lamberhurst.
Parking: main car park 130 yards (limited
parking), overflow 440 yards.

Finding out more: 01892 893820 (Infoline).
01892 893868 or
scotneycastle@nationaltrust.org.uk

Scotney Castle		M	T	W	T	F	S	S
Garden								
15 Feb–2 Nov*	11–4:30	·	·	W	T	F	S	S
3 Nov–23 Dec	11–2	·	·	·	·	·	S	S
House								
15 Feb–2 Nov	11–4	·	·	W	T	.F	S	S
3 Nov–23 Dec**	11–2	·	·	·	·	·	S	S
Shop and tea-room								
15 Feb–2 Nov	11–5	·	·	W	T	F	S	S
3 Nov–23 Dec	11–3	·	·	·	·	·	S	S
Estate walks								
Open all year		M	T	W	T	F	S	S

Open Bank Holiday Mondays and Good Friday. House
and garden open one hour after last admission. All visitors
require timed ticket to visit house (places limited, early sell-
outs possible). Property may close during adverse weather.
*Access to Old Castle restricted during weddings. **Access to
house during November and December by guided tour only
– booking essential (01892 893868).

Shalford Mill

Shalford, near Guildford, Surrey GU4 8BS

Map (2) E6   1932

Large timber watermill on the Tillingbourne
with well-preserved machinery. Although the
mill no longer works, the atmosphere is very
evocative. **Note**: Olympic cycle races, 28 and
29 July: open but local road closures (details on
website). No toilet. No parking. Regular guided
tours.

Access for all: VT •• Building 🦽

Getting here: 186:TQ001476. 1½ miles south of
Guildford on A281 opposite Seahorse Inn.

Finding out more: 01483 561389 or
shalfordmill@nationaltrust.org.uk

Shalford Mill		M	T	W	T	F	S	S
1 Apr–4 Nov	11–5	·	·	W	·	·	·	S

Also open Saturday, Sunday and Monday on
Bank Holiday weekends and Saturday and Sunday on
National Mills Weekend (early May) and Heritage
Open Weekend (September).

Sheffield Park and Garden

Sheffield Park, East Sussex TN22 3QX

Map (2) G7   1954

Sheffield Park and Garden, East Sussex

This magnificent informal landscape garden
was laid out in the 18th century by 'Capability'
Brown and further developed in the early
years of the 20th century by its owner, Arthur
G. Soames. The original four lakes form the
centrepiece. There are dramatic shows of
daffodils and bluebells in spring, and the
rhododendrons and azaleas are spectacular in
early summer. Autumn brings stunning colours
from the many rare trees and shrubs, and
winter walks can be enjoyed in this garden for
all seasons. Visitors can now also explore South
Park and East Park, areas of historic parkland
with stunning countryside views.

Exploring – Visit our new Coach House
          tea-room for lunch or tea.
        – Enjoy a cricket match on our
          historic cricket pitch.

Exploring – Enjoy the mirror-like reflections in the lakes.
– Go on a tour, Tuesdays and Thursdays in May/October.
– Take home a locally produced souvenir from our shop.

Eating and shopping: enjoy cream teas, selection of hot and cold lunches from our Coach House tea-room. In the garden you can visit our catering buggy. Local products available in our shop. Browse through our plants for sale, sourced from National Trust properties.

Making the most of your day: activities and special events throughout the year (telephone or visit website for details). Family activities available for garden and parkland – just pop into our reception to find out more. **Dogs:** allowed under close control in parkland. Assistance dogs only in garden. Please observe restrictions.

Access for all: ⃞⃞⃞⃞⃞⃞⃞⃞⃞⃞
Reception/shop ⃞ ⃞ Coach House tea-room ⃞
Garden ⃞ ⃞ ⃞ ⃞

Getting here: 198:TQ415240. Midway between East Grinstead and Lewes. **Bus**: Bluebell Railway link from near East Grinstead ⃞ to Kingscote ⃞, service from close Lewes ⃞ (Saturday only) and Uckfield (Monday, Wednesday, Friday only). **Train**: Sheffield Park (Bluebell Railway) ¾ mile; Uckfield 6 miles; Haywards Heath 7 miles. **Road**: 5 miles north-west of Uckfield, on east side of A275 (between A272 and A22). **Parking**: free.

Finding out more: 01825 790231 or sheffieldpark@nationaltrust.org.uk

Sheffield Park and Garden		M	T	W	T	F	S	S
Garden, restaurant and shop								
Open all year	10:30–5:30	M	T	W	T	F	S	S
Parkland								
Open all year	Dawn–dusk	M	T	W	T	F	S	S

Garden closed 25 December. Last admission into garden one hour before closing. Closes dusk if earlier (see board on entry). Tea-room last food orders 5.

Sissinghurst Castle

Biddenden Road, near Cranbrook, Kent TN17 2AB

Map ② I7   🏠 🐘 📷 ✳ ⚓ ⌂ ⊤ 1967

Sissinghurst Castle is a ruin of an Elizabethan manor house gently seated in the beautiful Weald of Kent. Once a prison to captured French seamen during the Seven Years War, a poor house and latterly a working farm, it gained international fame in the 1930s when Vita Sackville-West and Harold Nicolson created a garden here. The estate, perfect for wildlife spotting and walking, also comprises our organic vegetable garden.

The Elizabethan Tower at Sissinghurst Castle, Kent

Exploring — Visit the garden and discover the intimate atmosphere.
— See the new exhibition on Sissinghurst Castle's prisoners of war.
— Explore the estate walks, open all year.
— Visit our organic vegetable garden between May and September.
— Enjoy home-grown food in the Granary Restaurant.

Eating and shopping: fruit and vegetables grown in our extensive vegetable garden are used in our restaurant and coffee shop. Meat and eggs are produced by our tenant farmer, John. The gift shop sells local products and crafts.

Making the most of your day: look out for late night summer opening in the garden and afternoon events. **Dogs**: welcome in the woods. Assistance dogs only in garden.

Access for all:  Building 🦽♿🦼 Grounds 🦽♿➡

Getting here: 188:TQ810380. 1 mile east of Sissinghurst village. **Foot**: from Sissinghurst village past church to footpath on left signposted Sissinghurst Castle. **Cycle**: NCN18. **Bus**: from Maidstone to Hawkhurst (passing Staplehurst train station) alight Sissinghurst. **Train**: Staplehurst 5 miles. **Road**: on Biddenden Road, off A262. **Parking**: 315 yards, £2.

Finding out more: 01580 710701 (Infoline). 01580 710700 or sissinghurst@nationaltrust.org.uk

Sissinghurst Castle		M	T	W	T	F	S	S
Garden, shop and restaurant								
17 Mar–28 Oct	10:30–5:30	M	T	·	·	F	S	S
Shop and restaurant								
29 Oct–22 Dec	11–4	M	T	·	·	F	S	S
Vegetable garden								
1 May–30 Sep	10:30–5:30	M	T	·	·	F	S	S
Estate								
Open all year	Dawn–dusk	M	T	W	T	F	S	S

Last garden admission 45 minutes before closing.
Special late night openings: 25 May, 1, 8, 15, 22 and 29 June, 10:30 to 8.

Smallhythe Place

Smallhythe, Tenterden, Kent TN30 7NG

Map ② I7   🏠 ❀ ♿ 1939

Home of the Victorian actress Ellen Terry from 1899 to 1928 and containing her fascinating theatre collection, this half-timbered house was built in the early 16th century when Smallhythe was a thriving shipbuilding yard. Explore Ellen Terry's rose garden, the orchard, nuttery and working Barn Theatre in the cottage grounds.

Exploring — Fabulous costume exhibition, including Ellen Terry's famous beetle-wing dress.
— Pick up an events programme at the wonderful Barn Theatre.
— Discover Smallhythe's shipbuilding heritage through our fascinating exhibition.
— Explore Ellen Terry's informal cottage garden, a tranquil retreat.

Eating and shopping: atmospheric tea-room attached to the Barn Theatre where you can purchase freshly produced sandwiches, cakes and a wide range of drinks. Look out for our garden produce on sale in the autumn at our Orchard Day.

Making the most of your day: enjoy our unique open-air theatre, indoor plays and music in the Barn Theatre. Experience our special event for the Queen's Diamond Jubilee. Don't miss the Smallhythe Music and Beer Festival in September. **Dogs**: allowed on leads in grounds.

Access for all: 🔊 🏠 ♿ •• Ⓐ
Building 🦽🏠 Grounds 🏠➡

Getting here: 189:TQ893300. 2 miles south of Tenterden. **Bus**: from Rye to Tenterden. **Train**: Rye 8 miles; Appledore 8 miles; Headcorn 10 miles. **Road**: on east side of Rye road (B2082). **Parking**: free (not National Trust), 50 yards.

Finding out more: 01580 762334 or smallhytheplace@nationaltrust.org.uk

Smallhythe Place		M	T	W	T	F	S	S
House								
3 Mar–31 Oct	11–5	M	T	W			S	S
Tea-room								
3 Mar–31 Oct	11:30–4	M	T	W			S	S

Open Good Friday. Last admission 4:30 or dusk if earlier. Look out for our special Christmas event over one weekend in December.

Getting here: 179:TR359433. On coast, 1 mile from St Margaret's. **Foot**: from Dover 2½ miles, or St Margaret's 1 mile. **Cycle**: NCN1, ½ mile. **Bus**: from Dover to Deal, alight Bay Hill 1 mile via Lighthouse Road. **Train**: Dover 3 miles. **Road: no vehicular access. Parking**: no onsite parking. Nearest at White Cliffs, 2-mile clifftop walk, or St Margaret's village and bay, 1 mile.

Finding out more: 01304 852463 or southforeland@nationaltrust.org.uk

South Foreland Lighthouse

The Front, St Margaret's Bay, Dover, Kent CT15 6HP

Map ② K6  1989

Enjoy a walk along the White Cliffs to visit this distinctive, historic landmark with unrivalled views. The building has a fascinating tale to tell: a beacon of safety, guiding ships past the infamous Goodwin Sands; the first lighthouse powered by electricity and the site of the first international radio transmission. **Note**: no access for cars.

Exploring – New exhibition, including interactive display about channel navigation.
– Accompanied tours for all visitors.
– Astonishing 360-degree views of the Kent countryside and English Channel.

Eating and shopping: shop selling gifts, souvenirs and ice-creams. New this year, Mrs Knott's Tea-room, offering freshly prepared food and an outstanding view.

Making the most of your day: children's events during school holidays. Guided walks programme throughout the year, in conjunction with The White Cliffs of Dover, a 2-mile walk. **Dogs**: allowed in grounds.

Access for all: 🏠📷🦽📷 **Building** 🏠
Visitor reception/shop 🏠 **Grounds** 🏠

South Foreland Lighthouse, Kent

South Foreland Lighthouse		M	T	W	T	F	S	S
16 Mar–1 Apr	11–5:30	M				F	S	S
2 Apr–15 Apr	11–5:30	M	T	W	T	F	S	S
16 Apr–3 Jun	11–5:30	M				F	S	S
4 Jun–10 Jun	11–5:30	M	T	W	T	F	S	S
11 Jun–22 Jul	11–5:30				T	F	S	S
23 Jul–9 Sep	11–5:30	M	T	W	T	F	S	S
10 Sep–21 Oct	11–5:30	M				F	S	S
22 Oct–28 Oct	11–4	M				F	S	S
29 Oct–4 Nov	11–4	M	T	W	T	F	S	S

Admission by guided tour, last tour 5.

Sprivers Garden

Horsmonden, Kent TN12 8DR

Telephone Scotney Castle (01892 893820) for information.

Standen

West Hoathly Road, East Grinstead,
West Sussex RH19 4NE

Map ② G7  1973

'Beautiful home, clearly enjoyed by its family,
and enjoyed by our own family today.'
Joe and Becky Sutton, Crawley

Discover a family home in this gem of the Arts
and Crafts Movement. Standen is hidden at the
end of a quiet Sussex lane with breathtaking
views over the High Weald and Weirwood
Reservoir. The design of the house is a
monument to the combined genius of architect
Philip Webb and his friend William Morris. All
the big names of the Arts and Crafts period are
represented, including ceramics by William
De Morgan and metalwork by W. A. S. Benson.
The beautiful hillside gardens provide
year-round interest and the woodlands,
a number of easily accessible walks.

Exploring
- Discover the family who lived here in the 1920s.
- Explore the Sussex countryside through our picturesque woodland walks.
- Enjoy the designs of Morris and Co. throughout the house.
- Create your own adventures with our family woodland play area.
- See our garden grow as the restoration gets underway.

Eating and shopping: discover our unique
shop with gifts inspired by William Morris.
Enjoy delicious meals, or grab a snack in the
Barn Restaurant. Fresh produce from the
barrow in our kitchen garden. Add colour to
your garden with our Standen plants collection.

Making the most of your day: open-air
theatre, guided walks, family play area and
activities, regular temporary exhibitions and
workshops, introductory talks, conservation
demonstrations, lecture lunches, special
Christmas programme of festive events
and activities.

Dogs: welcome on leads in designated areas,
including the extensive woodland walks.

Access for all: [icons]
Building [icons] Grounds [icons]

Getting here: 187:TQ389356. 2 miles south
of East Grinstead. **Cycle**: NCN21, 1¼ miles.
Bus: from East Grinstead ⮕ to Crawley
(passing Three Bridges ⮕), alight at the end
of drive (request stop, just north of Saint
Hill), ½ mile footpath. **Train**: East Grinstead
2 miles; Kingscote (Bluebell Railway) 2 miles.
Road: signposted from town centre and B2110
(Turners Hill Road). **Parking**: free, 200 yards.

Finding out more: 01342 323029 or
standen@nationaltrust.org.uk

Standen		M	T	W	T	F	S	S
House								
11 Feb–26 Feb	11–4:30						S	S
29 Feb–25 Mar	11–4:30			W	T	F	S	S
28 Mar–15 Apr	11–4:30	M	T	W	T	F	S	S
18 Apr–27 May	11–4:30			W	T	F	S	S
30 May–2 Sep	11–4:30	M	T	W	T	F	S	S
5 Sep–21 Oct	11–4:30			W	T	F	S	S
24 Oct–4 Nov	11–4:30	M	T	W	T	F	S	S
10 Nov–23 Dec	11–3						S	S

Garden, shop and restaurant all open same days as house
but opening/closing times vary: gardens 10:30 to 5:30;
restaurant 10:30 to 5; shop 11 to 5. Please note 10 November
to 23 December: gardens, restaurant and shop all close 3:30.
Major repairs may affect opening from October (please
contact Standen before travelling or visit website for
up-to-date details).

Comfortable corner at Standen, West Sussex

Following in the footsteps of 18th-century tourists at Stowe, Buckinghamshire

Stoneacre

Otham, Maidstone, Kent ME15 8RS

Map ② I6   🏠 ❄ [1928]

Captivating 15th-century timber-framed house restored by the Arts and Crafts designer Aymer Vallance, surrounded by a beautiful garden. **Note**: administered by tenants on behalf of the National Trust. During fine weather, homemade cakes and teas served outside in the former stableyard. No toilets.

Access for all: 🅿 🅳 ⠿
Building 🦽🔼 Grounds ➡

Getting here: 188:TQ800535. At north end of Otham village, 3 miles south-east of Maidstone, 1 mile south of A20.

Finding out more: 01622 863247 or stoneacre@nationaltrust.org.uk

Stoneacre		M	T	W	T	F	S	S
17 Mar–29 Sep	11–5:30	·	·	·	·	·	S	·

Open Bank Holiday Mondays. Last admission one hour before closing.

Stowe

Buckingham, Buckinghamshire MK18 5EQ

Map ② D2   🏠 ❄ ♣ ♠ ♠ 🍽 [1990]

Step back in time at Stowe and follow in the footsteps of 18th-century tourists. Visit our recently restored coaching inn to experience an 18th-century inn for yourself. Head into the gardens and explore new trail maps; there are lots of fun play elements for children to enjoy and new guided tours. With more than 40 temples and monuments, the gardens have beautiful lakes and vistas with ever-changing scenes throughout the seasons. There's an endless variety of walks to enjoy. **Note**: new entrance from Stowe Avenue by Corinthian Arch.

Exploring — New circular lakeside walk.
— Visit our newly restored 18th-century parlour rooms.
— Enjoy local produce in our shop and café.
— Let children discover Stowe's secrets with their own map.

Exploring – Vice, virtue, liberty: which tour will you take?
– Discover the seasons of Stowe with ever-changing trails.

Eating and shopping: using local ingredients our new menu includes seasonal meals, cakes, soups and Stowe's famous scones, all freshly cooked every day. New gift shop stocks local products including a Stowe Ale and plants grown on the estate, along with seasonal blooms.

Making the most of your day: family activity packs available and special events throughout the year. Visitors can also enjoy Stowe House's magnificent state rooms (not National Trust). Free family cycle trail in the parkland. **Dogs**: welcome on leads.

Access for all: �P⅃ D⅃ 🌡️ 🅦🅒 🔉 ⟳ Ⓐ
New Inn and visitor centre 🏔️ ⬍ ♿
Grounds 🏔️ ➡️ 🌿

Getting here: 152:SP665366. 1½ miles north-west of Buckingham. **Foot**: 1½ miles from Buckingham. **Cycle**: 1½ miles from Buckingham. **Bus**: Cambridge to Oxford, stops Buckingham, 1½ miles. **Train**: Bicester North 9 miles; Milton Keynes Central 14 miles. **Road**: off A422 Buckingham to Banbury road. From M40 take exits 9 to 11, from M1 exits 13 or 15a. **Parking**: £2 non-members.

Finding out more: 01280 822850 (weekdays). 01280 818825 (weekends). 01280 818166 (Stowe House) or stowe@nationaltrust.org.uk

Stowe		M	T	W	T	F	S	S
Gardens, shop and café								
1 Jan–26 Feb	10–4	M	T	W	T	F	S	S
27 Feb–28 Oct	10–6	M	T	W	T	F	S	S
29 Oct–31 Dec	10–4	M	T	W	T	F	S	S
Parkland								
Open all year	Dawn–dusk	M	T	W	T	F	S	S

Last entry is recommended 90 minutes before closing or dusk if earlier. 2 June: landscape gardens closed; visitor centre, parkland, café and shop open. Closed 24, 25 and 26 December. May close in severe weather conditions.

Uppark House and Garden

South Harting, Petersfield, West Sussex GU31 5QR

Map ② E8 🏠 ✿ 🍴 ⟨1954⟩

Uniquely placed in a stunning hilltop location on the South Downs, Uppark was built in the 17th century and restored to its former glory after a fire in 1989. The elegant Georgian interior houses a famous Grand Tour collection. Discover the world of Sir Harry Fetherstonhaugh, Lady Emma Hamilton and the dairymaid who married her master. The complete servants' quarters in the basement are shown as they were in Victorian days, when H. G. Wells' mother was housekeeper. The garden is adorned with wonderfully scented shrubs and fine specimen trees, all planted within a naturalistic framework with breathtaking sea views.

Exploring – Complete and astonishing doll's house – more than 270 years old.
– Fascinating servants' tunnels to explore.
– Woodland walk with eco seat.
– House and garden trails. Outdoor toy box.
– Lecture lunch programme in March and December.
– Garden tours and welcome talks.

Eating and shopping: our shop stocks a range of local food products, including honey, jams and pickles. This complements the restaurant which serves seasonal homemade dishes with local breads and cheeses. Freshly baked cakes and scones from our own kitchen are a speciality.

Making the most of your day: to enhance your visit there are introductory talks on the house. Free garden history tours every Thursday. **Dogs**: on leads on woodland walk only. Please note: no shaded parking.

Getting here: 197:SU775177. 5 miles south-east of Petersfield. **Foot**: South Downs Way within ¾ mile. **Bus**: Petersfield ≥ to Chichester ≥ (warning, service under review). **Train**: Petersfield 5½ miles. **Road**: on B2146, 1½ miles south of South Harting. **Parking**: free, 300 yards.

Finding out more: 01730 825857 (Infoline). 01730 825415 or uppark@nationaltrust.org.uk

Uppark House and Garden		M	T	W	T	F	S	S
Garden, shop and restaurant								
18 Mar–1 Nov	11–5	M	T	W	T	·	·	S
House								
18 Mar–1 Nov	11–4:30	M	T	W	T	·	·	S
House, garden, shop and restaurant								
18 Nov–16 Dec	11–3	·	·	·	·	·	·	S
8 Dec–9 Dec	11–3	·	·	·	·	·	S	S

House 11 to 12:30: open for guided tours only. Open Good Friday. Open Sundays 18 November to 16 December. Also open Saturday 8 December. Garden tours every Thursday from April to October. Print Room open first Wednesday of each month (times as house).

Kitchen at Uppark House and Garden, West Sussex

The Vyne

Vyne Road, Sherborne St John, Basingstoke, Hampshire RG24 9HL

Map ② D6   🏠 ✚ ✿ 🌳 ♨ ✝ ☂   1956

While away your day following in the footsteps of Henry VIII amidst The Vyne's tranquil majesty. Experience an intimate family home surrounded by beauty and steeped in history, with royal connections dating from Tudor times. The Vyne has inspired and housed art, architecture and literature, with names such as Jane Austen and Tolkien gracing our story. The gardens provide a peaceful escape. Stroll around the lake, picnic on the lawn or explore the restored walled garden – now a working kitchen garden. The woodlands are of year-round interest; explore the Hampshire countryside on waymarked walks, abundant in wildlife and adventure. **Note**: no handrail on the *circa* 18th-century staircase to first floor.

Exploring
– Discover 500 years of history in one family home.
– Try our free fun-filled family trails.
– Find out about the restoration of our walled garden.
– Explore our woodlands and wetlands, a rich haven for wildlife.
– New this year – orienteering course for all the family.
– Enjoy events from outdoor cinema to re-enactment days.

Eating and shopping: visit the Coach House shop for gifts and local produce. Plants and garden-related products available from the new retail outlet in the car park. Delicious home-cooked food available in the Tudor Brewhouse tea-room. Refreshment kiosk in the car park.

Making the most of your day: free children's activities. Waymarked woodland walks and permanent orienteering course. Changing exhibitions within the house. Exciting new garden projects. Comprehensive events programme with something for everyone.

The Vyne, Hampshire: once a Tudor 'power house'

Dogs: welcome on leads in woodlands. Assistance dogs only in house and gardens.

Access for all: [icons] [icons] Building [icons] Grounds [icons]

Getting here: 175/186:SU639576. 4 miles north of Basingstoke, between Bramley and Sherborne St John. **Cycle**: NCN23, 1 mile. **Train**: Bramley 2½ miles; Basingstoke 4 miles. **Parking**: free, 40 yards, ⅓-mile walk through gardens from visitor reception to house.

Finding out more: 01256 883858 or thevyne@nationaltrust.org.uk

The Vyne		M	T	W	T	F	S	S
House								
11 Feb–2 Mar	11–3	M	T	W	T	F	S	S
3 Mar–4 Nov*	11–5	M	T	W	T	F	S	S
8 Nov–25 Nov	11–3	·	·	·	T	F	S	S
Gardens, shop and tea-room								
11 Feb–2 Mar	11–3	M	T	W	T	F	S	S
3 Mar–4 Nov	11–5	M	T	W	T	F	S	S
8 Nov–25 Nov	11–3	·	·	·	T	F	S	S
Christmas house (part), gardens, shop and tea-room								
1 Dec–22 Dec	11–3	M	T	W	T	F	S	S

*House closed weekdays 11 to 1. Low light-levels in house on overcast days.

Waddesdon Manor

Waddesdon, near Aylesbury, Buckinghamshire HP18 0JH

Map (2) D3   [icons] 1957

'The jewel in the National Trust's crown, something for everyone all year round. Our grandson loves the fantastic woodland playground.'
Mrs G. Hayes, Great Missenden

This Renaissance-style château was built by Baron Ferdinand de Rothschild to display his outstanding collection of art treasures and to entertain the fashionable world. The 45 rooms on view combine the highest quality French furniture and decorative arts from the 18th century, with superb English portraits and Dutch Old Masters. The Victorian garden is considered one of the finest in Britain, with its parterre, seasonal displays, fountains and statuary. At its heart lies the aviary, stocked with species once part of Baron Ferdinand's collection. Visit the contemporary art gallery in the Coach House at the Stables. **Note**: managed by a Rothschild family charitable trust. House entrance by timed tickets only.

Exploring — Visit the new Chardin exhibition, April to June, in house.
— See one of the finest collections of Sèvres porcelain.
— Discover contemporary sculptures in the gardens.
— Relax in the rose garden, aviary glade and parterre.
— Enjoy the wildlife interpretation trail and woodland playground.
— Visit the contemporary art gallery at the Stables.

Eating and shopping: enjoy a meal in one of the two licensed restaurants (not National Trust). Have a snack or drink at the Summerhouse. Browse and buy in the shops and plant centre. Visit the old-fashioned sweet shop at the Stables.

Making the most of your day: family events and free activities, children's quiz/trail, wine tastings, Christmas opening and events, garden workshops, plant centre. Visit www.waddesdon.org.uk for more information. **Dogs**: assistance dogs only.

Access for all: ♿🅿️♿🅳♿🚻♿🍴♿🐾🄰
Building 🅰♿🅱 Grounds 🅰➡️

Breathtaking Waddesdon Manor, Buckinghamshire

Getting here: 165:SP740169. 6 miles north-west of Aylesbury. **Bus**: from Aylesbury (passing close Aylesbury ≋). **Train**: Aylesbury Vale Parkway 4 miles; Aylesbury 6 miles; Haddenham & Thame Parkway 9 miles. **Road**: access via Waddesdon village, on A41; M40 (westbound) exit 6 or 7 via Thame and Long Crendon or M40 (eastbound) exit 9 via Bicester. **Parking**: free.

Finding out more: 01296 653226 or waddesdonmanor@nationaltrust.org.uk

Waddesdon Manor		M	T	W	T	F	S	S
Gardens, aviary, woodland playground, shops, restaurants								
7 Jan–12 Feb	10-5						S	S
15 Feb–17 Feb	10-5			W	T	F		
18 Feb–25 Mar	10-5						S	S
28 Mar–30 Dec	10-5			W	T	F	S	S
House, wine cellars, gardens, shops and restaurants*								
1 Apr–28 Oct	11-4						S	S
28 Mar–26 Oct	12-4			W	T	F		
14 Nov–28 Dec	12-4			W	T	F		
17 Nov–30 Dec	11-4						S	S
Bachelors' Wing								
28 Mar–26 Oct	12-4			W	T	F		

Recommended last admission to house one hour before closing. Open Bank Holiday Mondays. Open 10 April, 5 June and 31 December, 11 to 4 and 17 to 18 December. Closed 24 to 26 December. Sculpture in garden uncovered week before Easter (weather permitting). East Wing and Bachelors' Wing decorated for Christmas 14 November to 23 December and 27 to 31 December. House operates by timed ticket system (including members), available from ticket office or online www.waddesdon.org.uk (tickets limited). *Admission to house must include a garden ticket; also open Tuesday 10 April, 12 to 4; gardens 10 to 5.

Wakehurst Place

Ardingly, Haywards Heath,
West Sussex RH17 6TN

Map ② G7 1964

Open throughout the year, Wakehurst is the country estate of the Royal Botanic Gardens, Kew, and is the National Trust's most visited property. This beautiful botanic garden is internationally significant for its collections and also its vital scientific research and plant conservation. Enjoy visiting woodland and lakes, formal gardens, the Elizabethan house and Kew's Millennium Seed Bank. In 2010, Wakehurst marked an international conservation milestone, conserving the seeds of 10 per cent of the world's plant species for the future. It now embarks on the target of conserving a quarter of the world's plant species by 2020. **Note**: funded and managed by the Royal Botanic Gardens, Kew. Free for National Trust members.

Exploring — Journey through changing landscapes of garden, wetland and woodland.
— Discover and enjoy plants from all around the world.
— Explore the nature reserves.
— Watch science in action at the Millennium Seed Bank.
— Join a free guided tour.

Exploring — Be inspired as each season brings something new.

Eating and shopping: enjoy a lunch of seasonal and local produce at the Stables Café. Fresh homemade sandwiches and cakes at the Seed Café. Take home the perfect gift from the Kew-run shop. Enhance your own garden with something from the plant centre.

Making the most of your day: spring and autumn colour weekend events, Christmas celebrations, children's trail. Kingfisher and badger-watching evenings. Loder Valley nature reserve with wetland and meadowland (admission limited to 50 people per day). **Dogs**: assistance dogs only.

Access for all: 🅿️ 🚾 ♿ 🏠
Building ♿ 🚻 Grounds ♿ ➡️ ♿ 🚻

Getting here: 187:TQ339314. 3 miles south of Turners Hill. **Foot**: footpath from Balcombe (4 miles). **Bus**: from Haywards Heath to Crawley, passing Haywards Heath ≣ and Three Bridges ≣. **Train**: Haywards Heath 6 miles; East Grinstead 6 miles. **Road**: M23 junction 10, on B2028 near Ardingly. **Parking**: 50 yards from visitor centre.

Finding out more: 01444 894066 or wakehurst@kew.org. www.kew.org

Wakehurst Place		M	T	W	T	F	S	S
1 Jan–29 Feb	10–4:30	M	T	W	T	F	S	S
1 Mar–31 Oct	10–6	M	T	W	T	F	S	S
1 Nov–31 Dec	10–4:30	M	T	W	T	F	S	S

Last admission to Seed Bank and house 90 minutes before closing. In winter, café closes at 3:45. Closed 24 and 25 December. Shop closed Easter Sunday.

Kew's Millennium Seed Bank at Wakehurst Place, West Sussex: vital research and conservation

Entry is still possible at most places up to 30 minutes before closing

The Palladian villa at West Wycombe Park,
Buckinghamshire

West Wycombe Park

West Wycombe, Buckinghamshire HP14 3AJ

Map (2) E4 🏛️🌳 1943

The lavishly decorated Palladian villa and
exquisite, tranquil landscape garden –
featuring temples, lake and streams – were
created by the infamous 2nd Baronet,
Sir Francis Dashwood, founder of the Dilettanti
Society and Hellfire Club. It is still home to the
Dashwood family today. Step into the world of
the gorgeous Georgians.

Exploring	– View the unique wall-paintings on south and east porticos.
	– Investigate the village and its centuries of vernacular architecture.
	– Visit the intriguing Hellfire Caves nearby.
	– New this year: the exciting exhibition of Windsor chairs (May).

Eating and shopping: refreshments available
at the George and Dragon public house,
community library, Plant and Harvest Garden
Centre and Hellfire Caves (none National Trust).
Enjoy the variety of shops in the vibrant and
bustling National Trust village adjacent to
the park.

Making the most of your day: take a picnic
and enjoy the vistas on West Wycombe Hill.
View the church of St Lawrence and the unique

West Green
House Garden

West Green, Hartley Wintney,
Hampshire RG27 8JB

Map (2) D6 ♣ 1957

A delightful series of walled gardens
surrounding a charming 18th-century house.
Note: maintained on behalf of the National
Trust by a tenant and opened on a limited basis.
Dogs: assistance dogs only.

Access for all: 🦽🅿️ Grounds 🦽🔋

Getting here: 175:SU745564. 1 mile west
of Hartley Wintney, 10 miles north-east of
Basingstoke, 1 mile north of A30.

Finding out more: 01252 845582 or
westgreenhouse@nationaltrust.org.uk

West Green House Garden		M	T	W	T	F	S	S
Garden, tea-room and shop								
18 Mar	1–4	·	·	·	·	·	·	S
7 Apr–30 Sep	11–4:30	·	·	**W**	·	·	S	S

Opening and closing times will differ on 22 April, 18 May, 7,
8, 14, 15, 21 and 22 July, plus 22 September. Please contact
property for further details and for dates of Christmas Fair.

architecture of the golden ball and Dashwood family mausoleum. **Dogs**: assistance dogs only in park but welcome on West Wycombe Hill.

Access for all: 🅿️🅳♿🔊🚻👁️

Building ♿🔾

Getting here: 175:SU828947. 2 miles west of High Wycombe. **Foot**: circular walk links West Wycombe, Bradenham, Hughenden Manor. **Bus**: services from High Wycombe. **Train**: High Wycombe 2½ miles. **Road**: at west end of West Wycombe village, south of Oxford road (A40). **Parking**: 250 yards.

Finding out more: 01494 755571 (Infoline). 01494 513569 or westwycombe@nationaltrust.org.uk

West Wycombe Park		M	T	W	T	F	S	S
Grounds only								
1 Apr–2 May	2–6	M	T	W	T	·	·	S
House and grounds								
3 May–30 Aug	2–6	M	T	W	T	·	·	S

Last admission 45 minutes before closing. House is free-flow in May for the Windsor chair exhibition and by guided tour/timed ticket in June through to August (except for Sundays and Bank Holidays, which are also free-flow).

West Wycombe Village and Hill

West Wycombe, Buckinghamshire

Map ② E4    1934

Historic village with cottages and inns of architectural interest dating from the 16th century. Far-reaching views from West Wycombe Hill. **Note**: church, mausoleum and caves are not National Trust. Nearest toilets in village.

Access for all: Grounds 🔾

Getting here: 175:SU828946. 2 miles west of High Wycombe, on both sides of A40.

Finding out more: 01494 755573 or westwycombe@nationaltrust.org.uk

West Wycombe Village	Open every day all year

The White Cliffs of Dover

Langdon Cliffs, Upper Road, Dover, Kent CT16 1HJ

Map ② K7    1968

There can be no doubt that The White Cliffs of Dover are one of this country's most spectacular natural features. They are an official icon of Britain and have been a symbol of hope and freedom for centuries. You can appreciate their beauty and enjoy their special appeal through the seasons by taking one of the dramatic clifftop walks, which offer unrivalled views of the busy English Channel and the French coast. Whilst here, learn more about the fascinating military and penal history of The White Cliffs and savour the rare flora and fauna only found on this chalk grassland. **Note**: toilets only available when Visitor Centre is open.

Exploring
– Spectacular cross-Channel panorama to France.
– View the world's busiest shipping lanes.
– Dramatic clifftop countryside walks.
– Search out rare chalk grassland flora and fauna.
– Explore the hidden wartime heritage of Hellfire Corner.
– Learn about life as a convict in the former prison.

Eating and shopping: browse in our two shops for a great range of gifts to suit all ages, including outdoor goods, local produce/items and White Cliffs souvenirs. Enjoy seasonal light lunches, afternoon teas and unique cross-Channel views in the coffee shop.

Making the most of your day: self-guided walks for adults and activity sheets for children. Range of events and guided walks throughout the year, including Easter Trails and the spring plant fair. **Dogs**: under close control at all times (stock grazing).

Access for all: 🅿️ 🚻 ♿ 🏠 📶 ••🌀

Visitor Centre ♿🔽 Grounds ♿

Getting here: 138:TR336422. **Foot**: signed pathways from the port, station and town centre. On the Saxon Shore Way path. **Cycle**: NCN1. **Bus**: Canterbury to Deal, via Dover, alight Castle Hill then 1 mile along Upper Road (no footpath). Alternatively alight Dover Docks. **Train**: Dover Priory 2½ miles. **Road**: A2/A258 roundabout: take A258 towards Dover town. After 1 mile turn left into Upper Road. Entrance on right after 1 mile. A20: go straight over four roundabouts, left at second lights, right at lights, right into Upper Road (see above). **Sat Nav**: use CT15 5NA.

Finding out more: 01304 202756 or whitecliffs@nationaltrust.org.uk

The White Cliffs of Dover		M	T	W	T	F	S	S
Visitor Centre								
1 Jan–12 Feb	10:30–4	M	T	W	T	F	S	S
13 Feb–1 Apr	10–5	M	T	W	T	F	S	S
2 Apr–15 Apr	9:30–5:30	M	T	W	T	F	S	S
16 Apr–15 Jul	10–5	M	T	W	T	F	S	S
16 Jul–9 Sep	9:30–5:30	M	T	W	T	F	S	S
10 Sep–31 Oct	10–5	M	T	W	T	F	S	S
1 Nov–31 Dec	10:30–4	M	T	W	T	F	S	S
Car park								
1 Jan–12 Feb	8–5	M	T	W	T	F	S	S
13 Feb–31 Oct	8–7	M	T	W	T	F	S	S
1 Nov–31 Dec	8–5	M	T	W	T	F	S	S

Visitor Centre closed 24, 25 and 26 December. Car park closed 24 and 25 December.

Langdon Cliffs, part of The White Cliffs of Dover, Kent

White Horse Hill

Uffington, Oxfordshire

Map ② C4   🏛️♿🐾 [1979]

The oldest dated chalk figure in the country and an Iron Age hill fort, two of many local ancient sites. **Note**: archaeological monuments under English Heritage guardianship. No toilet.

Access for all: 🅿️

Getting here: SU299863. South-west Oxfordshire, on the Ridgeway between Swindon and Wantage.

Finding out more: 01793 762209 or whitehorsehill@nationaltrust.org.uk

White Horse Hill		M	T	W	T	F	S	S
Countryside								
Open all year		M	T	W	T	F	S	S
National Trust information trailer*								
7 Apr–28 Oct	11–4						S	S

*Information trailer may be closed at short notice.

Winchester City Mill

Bridge Street, Winchester,
Hampshire SO23 0EJ

Map ② D7   1929

A rare surviving example of an urban working
corn mill, Winchester City Mill is powered by
the fast-flowing River Itchen, which can be
seen passing underneath, thrilling our visitors.
Rebuilt in 1743 on a medieval mill site, it
remained in use until the early 20th century.
The National Trust undertook an ambitious
restoration project and the mill resumed
grinding flour in March 2004. With hands-on
activities for families and audio-visual displays
about milling and the rich wildlife in the area,
the City Mill is a lively and informative place for
all ages to enjoy. **Note**: nearest toilet 220 yards
(not National Trust).

Getting here: 185:SU487294. At foot of High
Street, beside City Bridge. **Foot**: South Downs
Way, King's Way, Itchen Way – all pass through
or finish at Winchester. **Bus**: from surrounding
areas. **Train**: Winchester 1 mile. **Road**: junction
9 from north M3. Junction 10 from south M3.
Sat Nav: do not use postcode. **Parking**: at
Chesil car park or park and ride, St Catherine's
to Winchester.

Finding out more: 01962 870057 or
winchestercitymill@nationaltrust.org.uk

Winchester City Mill		M	T	W	T	F	S	S
1 Jan–12 Feb	11–4	M	·	·	·	F	S	S
13 Feb–30 Nov	10–5	M	T	W	T	F	S	S
1 Dec–22 Dec	10:30–4	M	T	W	T	F	S	S

Exploring
- Discover a millennium of milling history.
- Enjoy our weekend milling demonstrations.
- Have a go at milling flour using hand querns.
- Watch CCTV footage of Winchester's resident otters.
- Escape to the nearby Winnall Moors Nature Reserve.
- Programme of baking demonstrations.

Eating and shopping: browse in our shop for
gifts and books. Buy local produce, such as
award-winning cheeses, wine and beer, as well
as a bag of our freshly milled wholemeal flour.

Making the most of your day: wide-ranging
programme of events. Family activities and
children's activities during school holidays.
Regular milling demonstrations. Programme of
baking demonstrations and workshops.

Access for all:
Building

Charming Winchester City Mill, Hampshire

Winkworth Arboretum

Hascombe Road, Godalming, Surrey GU8 4AD

Map ② F7 1952

Eating and shopping: delicious home-prepared light lunches. Afternoon teas with homemade cakes and biscuits. Visit our small, friendly tea-room.

Making the most of your day: programme of events, walks and talks throughout the year (send stamped addressed envelope for details). **Dogs**: welcome on leads.

Fiery colours light up Winkworth Arboretum in Surrey: spectacular all year

Established in the 20th century, this stunning natural landscape houses more than 1,000 different shrubs and trees, many of them rare. There is year-round colour, with the most impressive displays being in spring, when the magnolias, bluebells and azaleas flower, and autumn, when the colour of the foliage is stunning. In summer this tranquil place is ideal for the family to explore and picnic. **Note**: steep slopes and banks of lake and wetlands are only partially fenced.

Exploring
- Arboretum offers peace and tranquillity.
- Superb display of English bluebells in springtime.
- Magnolias, cherry blossom and azaleas.
- Famed for stunning autumn colour.
- Inspiring landscape and views.
- Award-winning collection: more than 1,000 different shrubs and trees.

Access for all: ⃞ ⃞ ⃞ ⃞ Grounds ⃞ ⃞

Getting here: 169/170/186:SU990412. 2 miles south-east of Godalming. **Bus**: Guildford to Cranleigh (passing close Godalming ≋). **Train**: Godalming 2 miles. **Road**: near Hascombe, on east side of B2130. **Parking**: free, 100 yards.

Finding out more: 01483 208477 or winkwortharboretum@nationaltrust.org.uk

Winkworth Arboretum		M	T	W	T	F	S	S
Arboretum								
1 Jan–31 Jan	10–4	M	T	W	T	F	S	S
1 Feb–31 Mar	10–5	M	T	W	T	F	S	S
1 Apr–31 Oct	10–6	M	T	W	T	F	S	S
1 Nov–31 Dec	10–4	M	T	W	T	F	S	S
Tea-room								
1 Jan–12 Feb	10–4	·	·	·	·	·	S	S
13 Feb–19 Feb	10–4	M	T	W	T	F	S	S
22 Feb–31 Oct	10–5	·	·	W	T	F	S	S
1 Nov–30 Nov	10–4	·	·	W	T	F	S	S
1 Dec–23 Dec	10–4	·	·	·	·	·	S	S

Tea-room opens Bank Holiday Mondays and additional days during school holidays, when bluebells bloom and in autumn. Arboretum may be closed in bad weather. Closed 25 December. Car park gates locked at 6.

Woolbeding Gardens

Midhurst, West Sussex GU29 9RR

Map ② E7/8 ✿ 1956

Woolbeding is a modern garden masterpiece, with constantly evolving colour-themed garden rooms surrounding the house, plus a woodland garden. A gentle walk over open pastureland provides views of the River Rother and leads to the landscape garden, which includes a Chinese-style bridge, waterfall and stumpery. **Note: booking essential**. Access by minibus only (booking essential).

Exploring — Be inspired by the colourful borders and rich plant collection.
— Learn about the travels of the Woolbeding fountain.

Exploring — See the monument to Europe's largest tulip tree.
— Admire the birds fishing in the River Rother.

Access for all: 🅿 ♿ 🚾 ♨
Reception ♿🔽 Garden ♨➡🔽

Getting here: SU872227. 8¾ miles from Petersfield and Haslemere. **Foot:** various footpaths to gardens. **Bus:** services from Petersfield ⮐ to Midhurst. **Train:** Petersfield ⮐ 8¾ miles. **Parking:** no onsite or local parking. Access by minibus only (booking essential).

Finding out more: 01730 825415 or woolbedinggardens@nationaltrust.org.uk. South Harting, Petersfield, Hampshire GU31 5QR

Woolbeding Gardens	M	T	W	T	F	S	S
12 Apr–28 Sep	10:30–4:30	·	·	·	**T**	**F**	·	·

Advance booking essential. Access by minibus only (booking essential on 01730 825415).

Woolbeding Gardens in West Sussex: a masterpiece of modern garden design

London

Twin cupolas frame the symmetrical
splendour of the perfectly formed
Osterley Park and House

Outdoors in London

Despite being one of the world's major conurbations, London still contains numerous green and relatively tranquil areas. Many are fragments of the city's once extensive common land and have been saved thanks, in part, to the efforts of the National Trust.

Working with the community

The phenomenal growth of the capital over the centuries has meant that several of our places, which once stood in open countryside, now fall within the Greater London area. Sutton House in Hackney, for example, was once part of a small village, but now sits within a densely populated area. This has advantages, however, as it is ideally placed for carrying out our work with local communities and inner-city schools.

The perfect retreat

Another place which has been subsumed by the city is Osterley Park. This large estate was originally created as a retreat from the hustle and bustle of urban life. Since then, of course, the city has crept up on it, and it now stands in the midst of suburbia – providing a welcome green retreat for local residents and visitors.

A safe haven for all

There is another unexpected oasis in South West London. Morden Hall Park is a picturesque and historic park with meadows, waterways and lovely old buildings. It also has an impressive rose garden, and is the perfect safe haven for families, walkers and cyclists.

Everyone can explore

Visitors with walking difficulties will find a trip to Morden Hall Park or Osterley Park particularly rewarding, as both have extremely accessible paths. Osterley Park boasts numerous routes suitable for wheelchair users – encircling the lake as well as through the wider parkland – while Morden Hall Park's routes run through the rose garden and along the River Wandle.

Above: this year we are launching an exciting tie-up with a selection of small museums. The stunning Leighton House Museum (page 171) in Holland Park, is the first place to open under this new partnership

Why not try...?

Getting out and about

There are plenty of ways to enjoy and explore these urban gems. Osterley's bike racks give cyclists a chance to lock up and relax with refreshments before choosing one of two routes around the estate. Also suitable for walkers, the routes take in Osterley's glorious woodland and lakes. Discover Morden Hall Park by bike too, via the National Cycle Network route 20. There is also an orienteering course, a new geocaching route, a downloadable trail and regular Monday 'Walk for Health' guided walks.

Blewcoat School Gift Shop

23 Caxton Street, Westminster,
London SW1H 0PY

Map ② G5   1954

Built in 1709 as a school for poor children, this hidden architectural gem now houses a coffee house and shop.

Access for all:  Building 🏠

Getting here: 176:TQ295794. Near the junction of Caxton Street and Buckingham Gate.

Finding out more: 020 7222 2877 or blewcoat@nationaltrust.org.uk

Blewcoat School Gift Shop	M	T	W	T	F	S	S
3 Jan–31 Dec	10–5:30	**M**	**T**	**W**	**T**	**F**	·	·

Closed Bank Holiday Mondays and Good Friday.

Carlyle's House

24 Cheyne Row, Chelsea, London SW3 5HL

Map ② F5   1936

The extraordinarily evocative Victorian home of Thomas and Jane Carlyle, a celebrity couple of 19th-century London's literary scene. Get to know 'the crazy Carlyles' as you look round their Chelsea house, and learn about their remarkable relationships with contemporaries such as Charles Dickens, Robert Browning and George Eliot.

Exploring   – Learn about Carlyle's influence on William Morris and the Pre-Raphaelites.
  – Enjoy the Carlyles' walled garden, just minutes from King's Road.
  – Located in the heart of London's most famous creative quarter.

Access for all: Building 🏠 Grounds 🏠

Getting here: 176:TQ272777. Signposted on Oakley Street and Cheyne Walk, near Carlyle's statue. **Bus:** frequent services along King's Road to Carlyle Square, then walk down Bramerton Street or Glebe Place to Cheyne Row. **Underground:** Sloane Square or South Kensington, 1 mile. **Parking:** no onsite parking. Limited metered street parking (charge including members).

Finding out more: 020 7352 7087 or carlyleshouse@nationaltrust.org.uk

Carlyle's House	M	T	W	T	F	S	S
7 Mar–4 Nov	11–5	·	·	**W**	**T**	**F**	**S**	**S**

Open Bank Holiday Mondays, 11 to 5.

Eastbury Manor House

Eastbury Square, Barking, London IG11 9SN

Map ② G5   🏠 ✿ ♠ 1918

Fascinating brick-built Tudor house, completed about 1573 and little altered since. Early 17th-century wall-paintings showing fishing scenes and a cityscape grace the former Great Chamber. Evocative exposed timbers in attic, fine original spiral oak staircase in turret, soaring chimneys, cobbled courtyard, peaceful walled garden with bee-boles.
Note: managed by the London Borough of Barking and Dagenham.

Exploring   – Discover Eastbury through attic displays and fresh interpretation.
  – Fun events first and second Saturdays of month.
  – Marvel at the skills of the Tudor builders and craftsmen.
  – Consider intriguing Gunpowder Plot connections.

Eating and shopping: relax in our garden tea-room, or at tables outside. Enjoy hot and cold drinks, sandwiches and snacks. Drop in to the Old Buttery gift shop (not National Trust).

Making the most of your day: guided tours. Themed family days first Saturday of the month – homemade cakes and costumed guides. School holiday activities. Children's workshops (Saturdays). Candlelit tours (last Tuesday of month, October to March). **Dogs**: in grounds only on leads.

Access for all: [icons]
Building [icons] Courtyard [icons] Grounds [icon]

Getting here: 177:TQ457838. In Eastbury Square. **Cycle**: LCN15 ¾ mile, local link. **Bus**: frequent services. **Train**: Barking, 1½ miles. **Underground**: Upney, 750 yards. **Road**: A13, then signposted from A123 Ripple Road. **Parking**: free, in adjacent street.

Finding out more: 020 8724 1002 or eastburymanor@nationaltrust.org.uk

Eastbury Manor House		M	T	W	T	F	S	S
House and grounds								
9 Jan–18 Dec	10–4	M	T	·	·	·	·	·
Tea-room and shop								
9 Jan–18 Dec	10–3:30	M	T	·	·	·	·	·

Also open every first and second Saturday of the month. Closed Bank Holiday Mondays, 2, 3 and 7 January and 24, 25 and 31 December.

19th centuries and are still played regularly. Don't miss the acclaimed walled gardens, featuring a formal garden, rose garden, 300-year-old orchard and kitchen garden – an unexpected oasis in the busy city.

Exploring
– Enjoy panoramic views of London from the top-floor balcony.
– Hear beautiful period music, performed on the early keyboard instruments.
– Relax in the garden or enjoy a game of croquet.
– Walking and cycling routes across Hampstead Heath – five minutes away.

Eating and shopping: our café opens later in the year, serving delicious light refreshments in the old stable building. Small shop area with a select range of local and National Trust items, garden plants and produce.

Fenton House and Garden

Hampstead Grove, Hampstead, London NW3 6SP

Map (2) G4   [icons] [1952]

'**Magnificent views of London – lovely to get out onto the balcony! What a gem of a house.'**
G. Gore, Lewisham

Explore this enchanting 17th-century townhouse and its world-class collection of decorative and fine art, amassed by a host of eccentric collectors. A cabinet of curiosities, the house includes collections of ceramics, needlework, furniture, paintings by the Camden Town Group of artists and musical instruments – these range from the 15th to

Fenton House and Garden, Hampstead

Making the most of your day: extensive programme of musical, learning and social events including recitals, celebrity lectures, talks and tours, annual Easter Egg Trail and Apple Weekend. Joint tickets with 2 Willow Road available. **Dogs**: assistance dogs only.

Access for all: 🖼️🔲📱⚙️📷
Building 🔲🖼️ Grounds 🔲🖼️

Getting here: 176:TQ262860. In Hampstead village, near Whitestone Pond. **Bus**: frequent services pass nearby. **Train**: Hampstead Heath (Overground) 1 mile. **Underground**: Hampstead (Northern Line) 300 yards. **Parking**: very limited parking, pay and display (including members).

Finding out more: 020 7435 3471 or fentonhouse@nationaltrust.org.uk. Fenton House, Windmill Hill, London NW3 6RT

Fenton House and Garden		M	T	W	T	F	S	S
3 Mar–4 Nov	11–5			W	T	F	S	S
1 Dec–16 Dec	11–4						S	S

Open Bank Holiday Mondays.

George Inn

The George Inn Yard, 77 Borough High Street, Southwark, London SE1 1NH

Map ② G5

This public house, dating from the 17th century, is London's last remaining galleried inn. **Note**: leased to a private company (please telephone to book a table).

Getting here: 176:TQ326801. On east side of Borough High Street, near London Bridge ➹.

Finding out more: 020 7407 2056 or georgeinn@nationaltrust.org.uk

George Inn		M	T	W	T	F	S	S
2 Jan–31 Dec	11–11	M	T	W	T	F	S	
1 Jan–30 Dec	12–10:30							S

Closed 25 and 26 December. Sunday opening hours also apply on Bank Holidays.

Ham House and Garden

See South East section, page 124.

Leighton House Museum

12 Holland Park Road, London W14 8LZ

Map ② G5

The recently restored Leighton House was the home of eminent Victorian painter Frederic, Lord Leighton (1830-96), and is one of the most remarkable houses of the 19th century. Built to designs by George Aitchison, it was extended and embellished over a period of 30 years to create a private palace of art. The Arab Hall houses Leighton's priceless collection of more than 1,000 Islamic tiles and important works by Leighton and his contemporaries are on display. **Note**: owned and operated by the Royal Borough of Kensington and Chelsea – www.rbkc.gov.uk

Access for all: 🔲📱⚙️📷 House 🔲

Getting here: 176:TQ247792. North of Kensington High Street, off Melbury Road. **Bus**: many local services. **Train**: Kensington Olympia. **Underground**: High Street Kensington; Holland Park. **Parking**: no onsite parking.

Finding out more: 020 7602 3316. www.rbkc.gov.uk/museums

Entry charges: £5/£3 (£2.50/£1.50 per National Trust member on presentation of valid membership card).

Leighton House Museum		M	T	W	T	F	S	S
House								
Open all year	10–5:30	M		W	T	F	S	S
Garden*								
2 May–30 Sep	10–5:30	M		W	T	F	S	S

*Open weather permitting. House: closed 1 January plus 25, 26 and 27 December.

The bridge over the River Wandle at Morden Hall Park: a green oasis in South London

Morden Hall Park

Morden Hall Road, Morden, London SM4 5JD

Map (2) G5   🏠🚻🅿️♣️♠️📷♿📍 1942

With diverse landscapes and hidden histories, Morden Hall Park is a green oasis in suburbia, giving visitors a glimpse back to a country estate with an industrial heart. This tranquil former deer park is one of the few remaining estates that lined the River Wandle during its industrial heyday. The river meanders through the park, creating a haven for wildlife, and snuff mills still survive – one is now a Learning Centre. The Victorian Stableyard has been restored and is now open to visitors for the first time. It is powered using renewable energy and has an interactive visitor centre. **Note**: May Fair and other special events, admission charges apply (including members).

Exploring
- Enjoy the two miles of paths around the park.
- Discover wetland wildlife and wildflower meadows.
- Relax in the rose garden and enjoy its unusual design.
- Learn how to grow your own with our engagement garden.
- Let the kids run free in the new play area.
- Follow the Wandle Trail to Deen City Farm.

Eating and shopping: eat in the riverside café or the ice-cream parlour in the Stables. Browse through our extensive range of gifts in the shop. Spot a bargain in our second-hand bookshop. Major garden centre (not National Trust). Craft workshops.

Making the most of your day: selection of trails. Extensive events programme, including walks, talks and open-air theatre. Snuff Mill open first and third Sunday from April to October. Thursday family activities in the school holidays. **Dogs**: welcome on leads around buildings and mown grass; under close control elsewhere.

Access for all: 🅿️♿🚻♿💺🔍📷🚶‍♀️:•:🅰️
Building 🦽♿♿ Grounds ♿➡️

Getting here: 176:TQ261684. Near Morden town centre. **Foot**: Wandle Trail from Croydon or Carshalton to Wandsworth. **Cycle**: NCN20 passes through. **Bus**: frequent services from surrounding areas. **Train**: Tramlink to Phipps Bridge, on park boundary ½ mile. **Underground**: Morden, 500 yards. **Road**: off A24, and A297 south of Wimbledon, north of Sutton. **Parking**: free, 25 yards (not National Trust), next to garden centre.

Finding out more: 020 8545 6850 or mordenhallpark@nationaltrust.org.uk

Morden Hall Park		M	T	W	T	F	S	S
Shop								
2 Jan–31 Dec	10–5	M	T	W	T	F	S	S
Café*								
2 Jan–31 Dec	10–5	M	T	W	T	F		
Second-hand bookshop								
2 Jan–31 Dec	11–3	M	T	W	T	F	S	S

*Café: open weekends 9:30 to 5 March to October inclusive, 10 to 5 in winter. Stable-yard café: open 10 to 5 March to October; November to February weekends only 10 to 4. All closed 7 February and 25 to 26 December. Snuff Mill open first and third weekends April to October.

Osterley Park and House

Jersey Road, Isleworth, Middlesex TW7 4RB

Map ② F5 🏠 🏚 ✾ ♣ ▲ ᵀ 1949

'Very interesting. Beautifully kept house with enthusiastic and informative guides.'
Pam Teather, Surrey

Once described as 'the palace of palaces' and surrounded by gardens, park and farmland, Osterley is one of the last surviving country estates in London. Created in the late 18th century by architect and designer Robert Adam for the wealthy Child family to entertain and impress their friends and clients, it continues to impress today.

Osterley Park and House in Middlesex

Explore the dazzling interior with handheld audio-visual guides or downloadable iPhone App which bring the house to life in a completely new way. Retreat from urban life in the delightful gardens and park which are perfect for picnics and leisurely strolls.

Exploring – Opening this year: don't miss the newly created Winter Garden.
– Atmospheric film in the Tudor stables brings Osterley to life.
– Varied events programme, including walks, tours and themed weeks.
– Explore domestic life in the 'below stairs' area.
– Dressing up, tours and lots of hands-on activities for children.
– Beautiful and tranquil gardens, carefully restored to their 18th-century glory.

Eating and shopping: enjoy a hearty lunch or afternoon tea in the Stables Café and Tea Garden. Find the perfect gift in the shop or plant- and second-hand bookshop. Farm shop selling fresh vegetables. Lakeside ice-cream and snack kiosk open throughout the year.

Making the most of your day: family activities and trails for the house and garden. Walks around park and lake; free leaflet available. Cycling in park on shared paths. **Dogs**: allowed in park only, on leads (unless indicated otherwise).

Access for all: 🅿️ 🅓 �ᴴ 🚾 🏛 🅛 🎨 🖼 ⱱᵀ
🦽 ⦂ⓐ House 🅛🅛 Café and shop 🅛🅛
Garden 🅛 ➡ 🅛🅛

Getting here: 176:TQ146780. Between Hammersmith and Hounslow. **Cycle**: links to London Cycle Network. **Bus**: services to within 1 mile. **Train**: Isleworth 1½ miles. **Underground**: Osterley (Piccadilly Line) 1 mile. **Road**: A4 between Hammersmith and Hounslow. Follow brown signs between Gillette Corner and Osterley Underground; from west M4, exit 3 then A312/A4 towards London. Main gates on Jersey Road. **Parking**: 400 yards.

Finding out more: 020 8232 5050 or
osterley@nationaltrust.org.uk

Osterley Park and House		M	T	W	T	F	S	S
House tours								
11 Feb–4 Mar	12–3:30	·	·	W	T	F	S	S
House								
7 Mar–4 Nov*	12–4:30	·	·	W	T	F	S	S
1 Dec–16 Dec	12–3:30	·	·	·	·	·	S	S
Café and shop								
11 Feb–4 Nov**	11–5	·	·	W	T	F	S	S
7 Nov–16 Dec	12–4	·	·	W	T	F	S	S
Garden								
11 Feb–29 Apr	11–5	·	·	W	T	F	S	S
2 May–2 Sep	11–6	·	·	W	T	F	S	S
5 Sep–4 Nov	11–5	·	·	W	T	F	S	S
Second-hand bookshop								
11 Feb–16 Dec	12–4	·	·	W	T	F	S	S
Park and car park*								
Open all year	8–6	M	T	W	T	F	S	S

Open Bank Holiday Mondays. *House: 2 May to 2 September, closes 5. **Shop: opens 12. Café and shop: 2 May to 2 September, open to 6 at weekends. Additional snack and ice-cream kiosk: spring to autumn, open every day; winter, weekends only. ***Car park: closed 1 January, 25 and 26 December. Park: 26 March to 28 October, closes 7:30.

Rainham Hall

The Broadway, Rainham, Havering,
London RM13 9YN

Map ② H5 1949

Charming Georgian house with some surprising features, quality materials and fine craftmanship. Awaiting conservation. Newly restored garden and orchard. **Note**: no toilet.

Getting here: 177:TQ521821. 5 miles east of Barking. Just south of the church.

Finding out more: 020 7799 4552 or
rainhamhall@nationaltrust.org.uk

Rainham Hall		M	T	W	T	F	S	S
7 Apr–3 Nov	2–5	·	·	·	·	·	S	·

Open Bank Holiday Mondays, April to October, 2 to 5. Open for May Day event and Rainham Christmas Fair.

Red House

Red House Lane, Bexleyheath, Kent DA6 8JF

Map ② H5 2003

'Amazingly special place – wonderful design, welcoming staff and charming tea-room. Absolutely love it!'
Barbara Moffatt, Truro

The only house commissioned, created and lived in by William Morris, founder of the Arts and Crafts movement, Red House is a building of extraordinary architectural and social significance. When it was completed in 1860, it was described by Edward Burne-Jones as 'the beautifullest place on earth'. Only recently acquired by the Trust, the house is not fully furnished, but the original features and furniture by Morris and Philip Webb, stained glass and paintings by Burne-Jones, the bold architecture and a simple garden (originally designed to 'clothe the house') add up to a fascinating and rewarding place to visit.

Exploring
– Truly iconic architecture of worldwide fame.
– Wonderful design features surviving from the time of William Morris.
– Relaxing garden – a real oasis in the midst of suburbia.
– March and April – display of original Red House artefacts.
– New exhibition of Red House plans and architects' drawings.
– Coach House tea-room serves light refreshments daily.

Eating and shopping: Morris-related gifts and Red House souvenirs – textiles, books, china, homeware. Second-hand bookshop in the old stables. Light refreshments available in the Coach House.

Making the most of your day: Easter Fun, summer arts and crafts fair, autumn Apple Day and carols at Christmas. Family fun in school holidays. Games in the garden and picnicking in the orchard always available. **Dogs**: assistance dogs only.

Getting here: 177:TQ481750. In Bexleyheath.
Bus: services from central London. All stop
at Upton Road. **Train**: Bexleyheath 🚃, ¾ mile.
Road: M25 junction 2 to A2 for Bexleyheath.
Exit Danson interchange and follow A221
Bexleyheath. **Sat Nav**: DA6 8HL – Danson Park
car park. **Parking**: nearest parking at Danson
Park 1 mile. Charge at weekends and
Bank Holidays.

Finding out more: 020 8304 9878 or
redhouse@nationaltrust.org.uk

Red House		M	T	W	T	F	S	S
29 Feb–4 Nov	11–5	·	·	W	T	F	S	S
9 Nov–23 Dec	11–5	·	·	·	·	F	S	S

Open Bank Holiday Mondays. Booked guided tours at 11,
11:30, 12, 12:30 and 1 (booking essential, 020 8304 9878).
Free-flow 1:30 until 5 (booking not required). Last admission
45 minutes before closing. Last serving in tea-room 4:30.

Quirky window at Red House, Bexleyheath

Sutton House

2 and 4 Homerton High Street, Hackney,
London E9 6JQ

Map ② G4   🏠🔔🍷 1938

Built in 1535 by Sir Ralph Sadleir, prominent
courtier of Henry VIII, Sutton House retains
much of the atmosphere of a Tudor home
despite some alterations by later occupants,
including a succession of merchants, Huguenot
silkweavers and squatters. There are oak-
panelled rooms, original carved fireplaces and a
charming courtyard.

Exploring – Discover a hidden gem in the
heart of East London.
– Experience the sights and
smells of a real Tudor kitchen.
– Relax in our tranquil and
stunning courtyard.
– Enjoy our family treasure
chests, representing our
unusual residents.

Eating and shopping: charming, fully licensed
tea-room. Browse in the second-hand
bookshop. Small shop, stocking limited range
of local and National Trust goods.

Making the most of your day: lively and
varied programme of events for all tastes and
ages. Craft fairs, fantastic themed family days.
Monthly Sunday guided tours, February to
November. **Dogs**: assistance dogs only.

Access for all: 🅿🚻♿🔌📷🖼🔌⋮🖼

Building ♿🖼🖼

Getting here: 176:TQ352851. At the
corner of Isabella Road and Homerton
High Street. **Cycle**: NCN1, 1¼ miles.
Bus: frequent local services. **Train**: Hackney
Central ¼ mile; Hackney Downs ½ mile.
Underground: Bethnal Green. **Parking**: no
onsite parking. Limited metered parking on
adjacent streets.

Finding out more: 020 8986 2264 or
suttonhouse@nationaltrust.org.uk

Exploring — Modern art by Max Ernst,
Henry Moore and Bridget Riley.
— Changing exhibition
programme of contemporary
responses to Goldfinger's work.

Eating and shopping: interesting range of
property-related cards, books and CDs available.

Making the most of your day: 20th-century
art and architecture walks and events
programme. Joint tickets with nearby Fenton
House available. Children's quizzes, playground
and Hampstead Heath just 20 yards.
Dogs: assistance dogs only.

Sutton House, Hackney, was built in 1535

Sutton House		M	T	W	T	F	S	S
Historic rooms								
2 Feb–14 Dec	10:30–4:30	·	·	·	T	F	·	·
4 Feb–16 Dec	12–4:30	·	·	·	·	·	S	S
23 Jul–29 Aug	10:30–4:30	M	T	W	·	·	·	·
Café, gallery and shops								
2 Feb–14 Dec	10:30–5	·	·	·	T	F	·	·
4 Feb–16 Dec	12–5	·	·	·	·	·	S	S
23 Jul–29 Aug	10:30–5	M	T	W	·	·	·	·

Open Bank Holiday Mondays and Good Friday. Property
is regularly used by local community groups – the rooms
will always be open as advertised, but telephone if you
would like to visit during a quiet time. Occasional
'Museum Lates' opening.

Access for all: 🅿️ ♿ 🖼️ 🖥️ 🎵 👓 🎨
Building 🦽 🪜

Getting here: 176:TQ270858. On the
corner of Willow Road and Downshire
Hill. **Foot**: signposted walks from
Hampstead Heath Overground station
¼ mile, or from Hampstead Underground
½ mile. **Bus**: frequent services pass
nearby. **Train**: Hampstead Heath ¼ mile.
Underground: Hampstead (Northern Line)
½ mile. **Parking**: very limited parking nearby
(pay and display, charge including members).

Finding out more: 020 7435 6166 or
2willowroad@nationaltrust.org.uk

2 Willow Road		M	T	W	T	F	S	S
3 Mar–4 Nov	11–5	·	·	W	T	F	S	S

Open Bank Holiday Mondays. 11 to 2, entry by guided tour
on the hour (places limited). 3 to 5, self-guided viewing
(timed entry when busy). Morning tours Wednesday to
Friday occasionally booked by groups, so telephone before
making specific journey.

2 Willow Road

Hampstead, London NW3 1TH

Map ② G5 1994

Designed by acclaimed architect Ernö
Goldfinger in 1939, this unique and surprising
Modernist home was inhabited by four
generations of his family. The house paints a
vivid picture of the urban creative and social
circles of the mid-20th century through
Goldfinger's modern art collection, innovative
designs and intriguing personal possessions.
Note: nearest toilet at local pub.

Exploring — From 11 to 2, join an hourly
expert-led guided tour.
— From 3 to 5, explore the
house at your leisure.

2 Willow Road, Hampstead: unique and surprising

East of England

Making friends – of the bovine variety
– at Home Farm on the Wimpole Estate

Outdoors in the East of England

Whatever you want from the great outdoors, and however you like to enjoy it, in the East of England you are spoilt for choice. We've got so much space, so whether you want to explore, spread out a picnic rug, ride a bike, take a stroll, check out the wildlife, or even just soak up the peace and quiet, then this stunning corner of England is the place for you. Do as much, or as little, as you want.

Clockwise from top right: a gentle stroll beside the coast at Dunwich Beach, Suffolk. Blakeney Point in Norfolk. The wet grassland area at Blakeney Point

Delights for all the senses

The wealth of landscapes, gardens, coast and habitats we boast is, in our view, second to none. And as for the flora and fauna, there's plenty to find, whether you have an expert interest or are taking your first steps in nature appreciation.

From Dunstable Downs in the west to Orford Ness on the Suffolk coast, Blakeney Point on the North Norfolk coast and Rayleigh Mount in south Essex, the range is awe-inspiring and the beauty unmistakable and unmissable.

Every month of the year brings different delights for all the senses. Wherever you choose to go, we've got great places where you can stop and refuel, to recharge yourself after your exertions, or simply reflect on your encounter with the outdoors.

Left:
**riding out
on Danbury
Common, Essex**

Cambridgeshire countryside

We are probably best known for our mansions in Cambridgeshire. But there is so much more to choose from if you want to venture outside. Be prepared to be bowled over by the vibrant colours of a rose garden, herbaceous border or formal parterre.

Our gardening teams ensure that lawns are manicured to perfection and that pleasure grounds are just that. And they are always happy to share their knowledge and experience if you happen to come across them staking, dead-heading or pruning. Ask about composting, for instance, and you'll discover just what passion and care goes into keeping our gardens so special.

But it's not all about order and neatness. Just a little further afield at Anglesey Abbey you cross the boundary between tamed formality and wilderness. The Wildlife Discovery Area is the perfect place to find freedom in nature. Build a den, create sculptures, check out the inhabitants of the bug hotel, or let your imagination run riot in the story circle.

Wimpole's gardens lead seamlessly to its gently undulating parkland. Find your own oasis of tranquillity, contrasting with Cambridge's corporate and commercial whirl. If you make it up as far as the folly, take time to enjoy the views and perspective they offer.

Rare breed cattle and sheep grace the parkland, and this connection with where your food comes from continues as you explore Wimpole Home Farm. This is no petting farm, but a place which demonstrates the realities of farming. Chickens enjoy their free-range lifestyle, and conversion to organic production is nearing completion, as the masses of butterflies and bees clouding the fields attest.

Humans exert different levels of control over the landscape, leaving intriguing traces of lives and livelihoods. For another step closer to the rule of nature, head for Wicken Fen National Nature Reserve, where we are working hard to re-establish more of the fenland habitats as they would have been.

It's impossible to put your finger on what is so special about Wicken Fen, but it seems to reflect changes of mood. We'll help you find your place here, with hides, cycle routes, and places to sit and take in the views of ponies across the wide open space.

Escape from it all in Essex

If you're not from Essex, you may have preconceptions. Much of it is urban and, arguably, overpopulated. But many people who live and work in this county of contrasts love the secret green spaces on their doorsteps.

Our places hint at the county's rich history of battles, protection and defence, hunting, forestry, common rights and waterway navigation for industrial supplies. For centuries our land has been worked hard to provide for the needs we've placed on it, and now we get to enjoy the spaces that have been shaped by this passage of time.

Quite apart from its isolated beauty, Northey Island's claim to fame is being the site of the Battle of Maldon in AD991. Here the course of history was changed dramatically as the resident Vikings were ousted by the East Saxons.

Venture onwards to medieval times, when King Henry VIII established Hatfield Forest as his hunting ground. Some of the trees are more than 1,000 years old, and if you stay still enough, you may spot fallow deer, descendants from King Henry's animals.

Danbury and Lingwood Commons, not far from the market town bustle of Chelmsford, form the largest area of common land in Essex. Now, they are a haven for wildlife and people alike, as they coexist amicably. Walking, cycling and horse riding are popular pursuits.

Left:
**Blakes Wood,
Essex, in spring**
Right, bottom:
**an ancient
hornbeam at
Hatfield Forest,
Essex**

Norfolk on your doorstep

Norfolk's enduring popularity as a holiday destination is well deserved. It has it all in shades of gold, brown and blue – golden sandy beaches, nature reserves, woodland, heaths, not forgetting the stunning gardens and houses.

If you're walking the Norfolk Coast Path, you'll come into contact with many of the places in our care. Start at Brancaster, with its sand dunes and busy quay – so essential to the most local of economies. Mussels anyone?

Head east and you can take in Stiffkey Marshes, on your way to the shingle of Blakeney National Nature Reserve, which has been in the care of the Trust for a century as of this year. You could take one of the local seal boats from Morston Quay and check out the grey and common seal populations which haul out to breed on Blakeney Point.

Further east, the Repton landscape of Sheringham Park is justifiably famous for its dazzling display of rhododendrons. It is well worth the walk, or bike ride, as far as the sea, where there is the added charm of a steam train gently progressing across the view.

Then on into the Broads, where Horsey Windpump affords unbeatable views across this quintessential Norfolk scene, reminiscent of many happy family holidays.

We haven't even mentioned our great estates inland – Blickling, Felbrigg and Oxburgh – with their lakes, moats, formal gardens, quiet woods and colour.

If you're lucky enough to live in Norfolk, why would you even think about going anywhere else?

Why not try...?

Staying longer and getting closer
Our holiday cottages are set within some of our most stunning places. Once our gates close at the end of the day, you have exclusive behind-the-scenes access, alongside the wildlife which calls our estates home. Explore from your doorstep.

Taking to two wheels
More and more of our places are opening up new routes for cycling, and linking in with national cycle routes. Cycling gives a different perspective on our countryside, whether you want to raise your heart rate as you race along, or take a more gentle pace. If you've arrived without bikes, you can now hire them at Blickling, Dunstable Downs and Wicken Fen. You can even charge your electric bike at Dunwich Heath, if that is your two-wheel choice.

A canvas adventure
For some, camping is the only way to holiday, getting up close to nature and all its glories. Look out for more opportunities to experience our places in the raw, whether it's wild camping at Wicken Fen or building your own shelter under the stars at Hatfield Forest.

Anglesey Abbey, Gardens and Lode Mill

Quy Road, Lode, Cambridge,
Cambridgeshire CB25 9EJ

Map ③ G7  1966

'So homely – I could live here! What an incredible collection and wonderful gardens – there's a surprise around every corner.'
Pat Newberry, Maidenhead

Anglesey Abbey, Cambridgeshire: tradition and style

A passion for tradition and style inspired Lord Fairhaven to transform a rundown country house and desolate landscape. Step into his elegant home and journey back to the golden age of country house living. A generous host, Lord Fairhaven loved to entertain, and enjoyed a life of horse racing and shooting. His guests were treated to a luxurious stay, surrounded by rare and fabulous objects. The celebrated garden, with its working watermill and wildlife discovery area, offers captivating views, vibrant colour and delicious scents in every season. Delight in the sweeping avenues, classical statuary and beautiful flower borders.

Exploring
– Visit our Inspiration Station for family activities.
– Catch the chime of one of our 37 rare clocks.
– Transform yourself into a country gentleman with our dressing-up clothes.

Exploring
– Be wowed by the Himalayan silver birches.
– Spot nature from the dizzy heights of our tree house.
– Unwind with a peaceful stroll through the glorious gardens.

Eating and shopping: visit the plant centre and recreate the look of Anglesey's gardens at home. Buy yourself a bag of our specially ground Lode Mill flour from the shop. Enjoy delicious food in the tranquil setting of Redwoods Restaurant, overlooking the garden.

Making the most of your day: exhibitions, activities and events all year round. Family trails and adventure packs. Experience 1930s living and discover fascinating facts with the help of room cards and volunteer room guides. **Dogs**: assistance dogs only.

Access for all: 🅿️ 🏠 🚻 👂 💺 📷 🎥 ♿ 👁 📷
House 👥📷 Mill 👥📷 Grounds 📷➡️♿👥

Getting here: 154:TL533622. 6 miles north-east of Cambridge. **Foot**: Harcamlow Way from Cambridge. **Cycle**: NCN51, 1¼ miles. **Bus**: from Cambridge (frequent services link Cambridge ➹ and bus station). Alight at Lode Crossroads. **Train**: Cambridge 6 miles. **Road**: on B1102. Signposted from A14, junction 35. **Parking**: free, 50 yards.

Finding out more: 01223 810080 or angleseyabbey@nationaltrust.org.uk

Anglesey Abbey		M	T	W	T	F	S	S
Garden, restaurant, shop and plant centre								
1 Jan–11 Mar	10:30–4:30	M	T	W	T	F	S	S
12 Mar–28 Oct	10:30–5:30	M	T	W	T	F	S	S
29 Oct–31 Dec	10:30–4:30	M	T	W	T	F	S	S
House								
14 Mar–28 Oct	11–5			W	T	F	S	S
31 Oct–4 Nov	11–3:30			W	T	F	S	S
House (guided tours only)								
12 Mar–30 Oct	12–3	M	T					
5 Nov–31 Dec	12–3	M	T	W	T	F	S	S
Lode Mill								
1 Jan–11 Mar	11–3:30			W	T	F	S	S
14 Mar–28 Oct	11–4			W	T	F	S	S
31 Oct–30 Dec	11–3:30			W	T	F	S	S

House: open completely on Bank Holiday Mondays. Spaces limited on guided tours. Property closed 24 to 26 December. Some areas of the garden may be closed due to season. Snowdrop season: 23 January to 26 February.

A sweep of sky at the haunting Blakeney National Nature Reserve in Norfolk

Blakeney National Nature Reserve

Morston Quay, Quay Road, Morston, Norfolk NR25 7BH

Map ③ I3    1912

Wide open spaces and uninterrupted views of this unspoilt coastline make for an inspiring visit, especially in 2012, our centenary year. The ebb and flow of the tide, covering pristine salt-marsh or exposing the harbour, combined with the constantly changing light of Norfolk's big skies, create beautiful and memorable scenery. **Note**: nearest toilet at Morston Quay and Blakeney Quay (not National Trust).

Exploring
- Special 2012 events to mark 100th anniversary of Blakeney Point.
- Blakeney Point – internationally important for seabirds and seals.
- Walk the Norfolk Coast Path for great views and wildlife.
- Learn about marine life at Stiffkey, Morston and Blakeney.

Eating and shopping: refreshments and seafood stall (not National Trust) at Morston Quay. Seafood, including Morston mussels from local suppliers (not National Trust). Nearby pubs and hotels (not National Trust) offering locally themed menus.

Making the most of your day: learn more about this dynamic coastal environment – Information Centres at Morston Quay and at the Lifeboat House on Blakeney Point. Download a walk from our website. **Dogs**: welcome, some restrictions apply (particularly Blakeney Point) from 1 April to mid-August.

Access for all: [VT] Lifeboat House and toilets [♿]
Morston Quay Information Centre [♿]

Getting here: 133:TG000460. **Foot**: Norfolk Coast Path passes property. **Cycle**: NCN30 runs along ridge above the coast. **Ferry**: to Blakeney Point. **Bus**: Cromer ⇌ to Hunstanton. **Train**: Sheringham 8 miles. **Road**: Morston Quay, Blakeney and Cley are all off A149 Cromer to Hunstanton road. **Parking**: pay and display (members free) at Morston Quay and also at Blakeney Quay (administered by Blakeney Parish Council). Quayside car parks are liable to tidal flooding.

Finding out more: 01263 740241 or blakeneypoint@nationaltrust.org.uk. Norfolk Coast Office, Friary Farm, Cley Road, Blakeney, Norfolk NR25 7NW

Blakeney	M	T	W	T	F	S	S
Nature Reserve							
Open all year	M	T	W	T	F	S	S
Lifeboat House (Blakeney Point)							
2 Apr–30 Sep	Dawn–dusk	M	T	W	T	F	S	S

*Lifeboat House and toilets (Blakeney Point) open dawn to dusk. Refreshment kiosk (not National Trust) and Information Centre at Morston Quay open according to tides and weather.

Blickling Estate

Blickling, Norwich, Norfolk NR11 6NF

Map ③ J4

For four centuries, Blickling Estate has been home to many, from the Boleyn family to the RAF, stationed here in the Second World War. Many have worked here, from cooks and butlers to gardeners and scullery maids. All have made their mark on this beautiful country estate. Now you can walk in their footsteps – through the Long Gallery with its nationally important book collection, make jam tarts in the kitchen, relax in the stunning garden or ramble through the parkland to find the hidden pyramid. Make your own mark and come back to discover something new every time.

Exploring
- See how the spectacular gardens change throughout the seasons.
- Discover over 400 years of fascinating history.
- Explore with our children's trails and tracker packs.
- Listen to the actual voices of Blickling's servants.
- Enjoy the tranquillity of the lake and parkland.
- Follow Blickling's wartime history in the RAF Museum.

Eating and shopping: visit our two cafés or the restaurant, with menus featuring local seafood and produce from the estate. Bag yourself a bargain in the second-hand bookshop, then pop into the East Wing gift shop or the garden shop.

Making the most of your day: house highlight tours (Mondays and Tuesdays at 1, 2 and 3, other days 10:45). Garden tours, RAF Museum, croquet, cycle hire and children's trails. Exhibitions throughout the year.
Dogs: welcome in park and woods, on leads at all times.

Access for all: ⛔♿🚻🏛️📷🅿️♿
Building 🏛️🏠♿ Grounds ♿➡️♿

Getting here: 133:TG178286. 1½ miles north-west of Aylsham. **Foot**: Weavers' Way (Aylsham, 2 miles). **Cycle**: permitted path alongside Bure Valley Railway. **Bus**: services from Norwich to Holt and Sheringham, alight Aylsham 1½ miles. **Road**: on B1354, signposted off A140 Norwich/Cromer. **Parking**: 400 yards.

Finding out more: 01263 738030 or blickling@nationaltrust.org.uk

Blickling Estate		M	T	W	T	F	S	S
House								
11 Feb–4 Nov	11–5	M	T	W	T	F	S	S
Garden, shop, restaurant and bookshop								
5 Jan–10 Feb	11–4				T	F	S	S
11 Feb–4 Nov	10–5:30	M	T	W	T	F	S	S
7 Nov–30 Dec	11–4			W	T	F	S	S
Plant centre								
10 Mar–4 Nov	11–5:30	M	T	W	T	F	S	S
Cycle hire								
31 Mar–4 Nov	10–4						S	S
Park								
Open all year	Dawn–dusk	M	T	W	T	F	S	S

On quiet days hall open for guided tours only at 12, 1, 2 and 3 (other days guided tour available 10:45) – spaces limited to 12, telephone for details. 1 January to 10 February: Hobarts restaurant closed; Estate Barn café open seven days a week. Cycle hire available daily during local school holidays. Closed 25 and 26 December.

Blickling Estate, Norfolk: 400 years of history

Bourne Mill

Bourne Road, Colchester, Essex CO2 8RT

Map ③ I8   1936

A delightful piece of late Elizabethan playfulness. Built for banquets and converted into a mill, still with working waterwheel. **Note**: small gifts available from the new shop area. No toilet. Limited parking in mill grounds.

Access for all: ⌂ ♿ ••
Building 🏛 Grounds ♿🏛

Getting here: 168:TM006238. 1 mile south of centre of Colchester, on Bourne Road, off Mersea Road (B1025).

Finding out more: 01206 572422 or bournemill@nationaltrust.org.uk

Bourne Mill		M	T	W	T	F	S	S
3 Jun–24 Jun	2–5		·	·	·	·	·	S
28 Jun–26 Aug	2–5		·	·	·	T	·	S

Open Easter, May and August Bank Holidays, Sundays and Mondays.

Bourne Mill, Essex: Elizabethan playfulness

Brancaster Estate

Car Park, Beach Road, Brancaster, Norfolk P31 8AX

Map ③ H3  1923

Famous for its mussels, the fishing village of Brancaster Staithe lies on the shores of the beautiful North Norfolk coast. Find out about the history of the fishing industry at Brancaster Quay, visit Branodunum Scheduled Ancient Monument or stroll along Brancaster beach. **Note**: nearest toilet (not National Trust) Brancaster beach. Scolt Head Island NNR managed by Natural England.

Exploring
 – Relax and picnic at Brancaster beach.
 – Follow the Norfolk Coast Path for great views and wildlife.
 – Enjoy the harbour and spectacular salt-marsh views from Brancaster Staithe.
 – Step back in time at the Roman fort of Branodunum.

Eating and shopping: try the fabulous Brancaster mussels or locally caught fresh fish. Quench your thirst at Brancaster Staithe's pubs (not National Trust).

Making the most of your day: visit our website and download one of our walks or sign up for a family adventure day or week at Brancaster Millennium Activity Centre during holiday periods. **Dogs**: welcome, but some restrictions apply at Brancaster beach from May to mid-August.

Access for all: Grounds 🏛

Getting here: 132:TF800450. Halfway between Wells and Hunstanton. **Foot**: Norfolk Coast Path passes property. **Cycle**: Regional Route 30 runs along ridge above coast. **Bus**: service Sheringham ⊒ to Hunstanton. **Road**: on A149. **Sat Nav**: use PE31 8AX (Beach Road), P31 8BW (Brancaster Staithe). **Parking**: Beach Road, Brancaster (not National Trust), charge including members. Limited parking at Brancaster Staithe, subject to tidal flooding.

A fishing boat at Brancaster Staithe in Norfolk

Finding out more: 01263 740241 or brancaster@nationaltrust.org.uk. Norfolk Coast Office, Friary Farm, Cley Road, Blakeney, Norfolk NR25 7NW

Brancaster Estate	Open every day all year

Brancaster Millennium Activity Centre

Dial House, Harbour Way, Brancaster Staithe, Norfolk PE31 8BW

Map ③ H3   1984

The 400-year-old Dial House was once a pub but later became a family home. Now a residential activity centre for schoolchildren and families, visitors can enjoy outdoor activities like sailing, kayaking and orienteering, and take part in team challenges, at the same time developing a better understanding of sustainable living. **Note**: contact the centre for activity programmes, prices and availability.

Exploring — Group and family accommodation available during school holidays.
— Curious about sailing? Budding artist? All sorts of courses available.

Exploring — Develop skills in the outdoors – kayak, cycle, sail and more.
— Explore the coastline and its wildlife with our expert guides.

Eating and shopping: meals are prepared by our head cook, who uses locally sourced produce whenever possible (some of which is grown in our garden and looked after by our visitors). We have a small ethical gift shop for residents.

Making the most of your day: accommodation and activities for families during holiday periods, adult courses and school day and residential weeks focusing on outdoor pursuits and field studies; contact us for availability and choice. **Dogs**: seasonal restrictions apply, telephone for details.

Access for all: ♿

Brancaster Millennium Activity Centre ♿♿

Getting here: 132:TF792444. Halfway between Wells and Hunstanton. **Foot**: Norfolk Coast Path passes property. **Cycle**: Regional Route 30 runs along ridge above the coast. **Bus**: service from Sheringham ≥ to Hunstanton. **Road**: on A149 coast road. **Parking**: limited parking within Harbour Way, Brancaster Staithe.

Finding out more: 01485 210719 or brancaster@nationaltrust.org.uk

Brancaster
Please contact the centre for more information on residential group bookings, courses and activities.

Fun at Brancaster Millennium Activity Centre, Norfolk

Coggeshall Grange Barn

Grange Hill, Coggeshall, Colchester, Essex CO6 1RE

Map ③ I8 1989

One of Europe's oldest timber-framed buildings, with an astonishing cathedral-like interior housing an exhibition of local woodcarving and tools.

Access for all: 🅿♿️🚻👓 Building 🏛 Grounds 🏛

Getting here: 168:TL848223. Off A120 Coggeshall bypass, on B1024 ¼ mile south of centre of Coggeshall.

Finding out more: 01376 562226 or coggeshall@nationaltrust.org.uk

Coggeshall Grange Barn	M	T	W	T	F	S	S
1 Apr–4 Nov	1–5		·	·	W	T	F	S	S

Open Bank Holiday Mondays. May be closed some days for private functions (telephone for details).

Coggeshall Grange Barn, Essex: vast interior

Dunstable Downs, Chilterns Gateway Centre and Whipsnade Estate

Whipsnade Road, Dunstable, Bedfordshire LU6 2GY

Map ③ E8 1928

Acres of space to enjoy with fabulous views over the Vale of Aylesbury and along the Chiltern Ridge. Dunstable Downs is an Area of Outstanding Natural Beauty because of its chalk grassland, rich in wildlife. The windswept ridge makes this a kite-flying hotspot, and there are often gliders soaring overhead. **Note:** Chilterns Gateway Centre is owned by Central Bedfordshire Council and managed by the National Trust.

Exploring
- Enjoy the views from the comfort of our visitor centre.
- Have fun flying kites from the top of Dunstable Downs.
- Explore the chalk grassland habitat with its fascinating archaeological features.
- Take part in our guided nature walks.

Eating and shopping: try local foods, such as the Bedfordshire Clanger, in the café. Our shop sells an excellent range of kites. The visitor centre sells leaflets describing circular walks on Dunstable Downs.

Making the most of your day: waymarked routes (leaflets available from visitor centre or via website), kite flying, multi-user trail to Five Knolls and regular guided walks. Events throughout the year, including annual kite festival. **Dogs:** under close control, on leads near livestock.

Access for all: 🅿♿️🚻🚻🥤🚶

Chilterns Gateway Centre 🏛♿️ Dunstable Downs ➡

We welcome dogs assisting visitors with disabilities

Getting here: 165/166:TL002189. 7 miles from Luton. **Foot**: from West Street and Tring Road, Dunstable. **Cycle**: bridleway from West Street, Dunstable, and Whipsnade. **Bus**: services from Hemel Hempstead ➡ and St Albans ➡, all Sundays only; otherwise from Aylesbury to Luton ➡, to within 1½ miles. **Train**: Luton 7 miles. **Road**: on B4541 west of Dunstable. **Sat Nav**: for older equipment use LU6 2TA. **Parking**: Dunstable Downs, off B4541 (pay and display); Whipsnade crossroads (Whipsnade Heath), junction of B4541 and B4540.

Finding out more: 01582 500920 or dunstabledowns@nationaltrust.org.uk

Dunstable Downs		M	T	W	T	F	S	S
Chilterns Gateway Centre								
1 Jan–29 Feb	10–4	M	T	W	T	F	S	S
1 Mar–31 Oct	10–5	M	T	W	T	F	S	S
1 Nov–31 Dec	10–4	M	T	W	T	F	S	S
Downs								
Open all year		M	T	W	T	F	S	S

Chilterns Gateway Centre closes dusk if earlier and closed 24 and 25 December. Car park adjacent to Centre locked dusk in winter and 6 in summer. Opening times extended in summer (contact Visitor Centre for details).

Dunwich Heath: Coastal Centre and Beach

Dunwich, Saxmundham, Suffolk IP17 3DJ

Map ③ K6    1968

'Beautifully unspoilt – I've had time to walk, relax and find me again. It's a true oasis in a mad world.'
Gill Thurgood, Essex

Tucked away on the Suffolk coast, Dunwich Heath offers peace and quiet and a true sense of being at one with nature. A rare and precious habitat, the heath is in an Area of Outstanding Natural Beauty, and home to species such as the Dartford warbler, nightjar, woodlark, ant-lion, adder and much more. Quiet and serene, wild and dramatic, this is an inspiring visit whatever the time of year. From July to September, the heath is alive with colour – the patchwork of pink and purple heather and coconut-scented yellow gorse is an unmissable experience. **Note**: parking restrictions may operate at times of extreme fire risk.

Exploring
– Follow three waymarked nature trails linking beach and heath.
– Explore our children's trails.
– Visit the SeaWatch lookout – spot porpoises, seals and birds.
– Try and spot the rare Dartford warbler.
– Free to use, solar-powered charging point for electric cycles.
– Holiday in our three clifftop flats or a village cottage.

Exploring the great outdoors in this region of space, sea, sky and unspoilt nature

Eating and shopping: clifftop tea-room with outside seating area where you can relax and enjoy the coastal views; homecooked lunches and cakes with gluten-free choices and children's menu. Coastal-themed gifts in the shop.

Making the most of your day: warden-led guided walks, family events, nature, smugglers and history trails, Tracker Packs for families, tea-room events, sea-watching and wildlife identification charts and telescopes. Children's play area next to tea-room. **Dogs**: allowed under close control, restrictions apply.

Access for all: P♿ D♿ 🚻 🐕 🔌 🏛
Tea-room and gift shop ♿ 🔌
SeaWatch building ♿ 🔌 Grounds ➡ ♿

Getting here: 156:TM476685. 1 mile south of Dunwich. **Foot**: Suffolk Coast and Heaths Path and Sandlings Walk. **Cycle**: on Suffolk coastal cycle route. **Bus**: demand-responsive bus from Darsham 🚃 and Saxmundham (booking essential, 01728 833526). **Train**: Darsham 6 miles. **Road**: signposted from A12. From Westleton/Dunwich road, turn right 1 mile before Dunwich village into Minsmere road, then 1 mile to Dunwich Heath. **Parking**: 150 yards (pay and display). Limited to three coaches.

Finding out more: 01728 648501 or dunwichheath@nationaltrust.org.uk

Dunwich Heath		M	T	W	T	F	S	S
Heath								
Open all year		M	T	W	T	F	S	S
Tea-room and shop								
1 Jan–5 Feb	10:30–3:30	·	·	·	·	·	S	S
11 Feb–19 Feb	10:30–3:30	M	T	W	T	F	S	S
25 Feb–4 Mar	10:30–3:30	·	·	·	·	·	S	S
7 Mar–1 Apr	10–4	·	·	W	T	F	S	S
2 Apr–30 Sep	10–5	M	T	W	T	F	S	S
6 Oct–28 Oct	10–4	·	·	W	T	F	S	S
29 Oct–4 Nov	10–4	M	T	W	T	F	S	S
10 Nov–23 Dec	10:30–3:30	·	·	·	·	·	S	S
27 Dec–31 Dec	10:30–3:30	M	·	·	T	F	S	S

Open Bank Holiday Mondays. *Tea-room and shop closing times vary and limited service during weekdays early and late season.

Elizabethan House Museum

4 South Quay, Great Yarmouth, Norfolk NR30 2QH

Map ③ K5   🏛 1943

An amazing hands-on museum to enthrall and fascinate all ages. The museum reflects the life and times of the families who lived in this 16th-century quayside building, from Tudor right through to Victorian times. **Note**: house is managed by Norfolk Museums and Archaeology Service.

Exploring
– See how the Tudors lived in the 16th century.
– Discover what Victorian life was like, upstairs and downstairs!
– Enjoy a stroll along Great Yarmouth's historic South Quay.

Eating and shopping: small shop on ground floor.

Making the most of your day: Tudor costumes to try on; activity-packed toy room for children and hands-on activities.

Access for all: 🔌 🎨 🖥 🔌 ∶ Building ♿ ♿

Getting here: 134:TG523073. On Great Yarmouth's South Quay. **Train**: Great Yarmouth ½ mile. **Road**: from A47 follow town centre signs, then brown South Quay signs. From A12 follow brown signs. **Parking**: free on South Quay or in town centre (pay and display), none National Trust.

Finding out more: 01493 855746 or elizabethanhouse@nationaltrust.org.uk

Elizabethan House Museum		M	T	W	T	F	S	S
2 Apr–31 Oct	10–4	M	T	W	T	F	·	·
1 Apr–28 Oct	12–4	·	·	·	·	·	S	S

Felbrigg Hall, Gardens and Estate

Felbrigg, Norwich, Norfolk NR11 8PR

Map ③ J4 🏛🏠➕♿♠ ♿🏠☕ 1969

'Serenity, thrill, detail.'
Stephen Fry

Felbrigg Hall in Norfolk: a place of surprises

Truly a hidden gem, Felbrigg Hall is full of delights, a surprising mixture of opulence and homeliness where every room has something to feed the imagination. Outside, this 'bountiful estate' really lives up to its name. The decorative and productive walled garden is a gardener's delight, providing fruit and vegetables for the brasserie, flowers for the Hall and inspiration to visitors. The rolling landscape park with a lake, 211 hectares (520 acres) of woods and miles of waymarked trails, is a great place to explore nature, spot wildlife or just to get away from it all.

Exploring
– See the dining room laid for an 1860s dinner party.
– Don't miss the kitchen, the 'engine room' of the house.

Exploring
– Soak up the atmosphere in our wonderful library.
– In the Cabinet, see the 'Grand Tour' in one room.
– If you feel energetic, walk around the estate and woodlands.
– Relax in the magnificent garden.

Eating and shopping: Carriages Brasserie, using seasonal produce from the walled garden and estate – enjoy our four-mile menu. Tea-room serving homemade cakes and snacks. Gift shop and plant sales. Browse through the second-hand bookshop for that book you never thought you would find.

Making the most of your day: ask about our indoor and outdoor children's trails. Chilli Fiesta 1 August, the Hall at Harvest 6 to 10 October and Hall at Christmas 14, 15 and 16 December. **Dogs**: on leads in parkland when stock grazing, under close control in woodland.

Access for all: 🅿️🔄♿🚻👶🔊📷📖📹☺️♿
Hall ♿🔄 Shop and catering ♿
Grounds ♿♿▶️♿

Getting here: 133:TG193394. Felbrigg village, 2 miles from Cromer. **Foot**: Weavers' Way runs through property. **Cycle**: Regional Route 30. **Train**: Cromer or Roughton Road, both 2½ miles. **Road**: 2 miles from Cromer; off B1436, signposted from A148 and A140. **Sat Nav**: gives poor directions, follow 'brown signs'. **Parking**: 100 yards, £2.50 non-members.

Finding out more: 01263 837444 or felbrigg@nationaltrust.org.uk

Felbrigg Hall		M	T	W	T	F	S	S
House and bookshop								
3 Mar–4 Nov	11–5	M	T	W	·	·	S	S
19 Jul–31 Aug	11–5	M	T	W	T	F	S	S
Refreshments, shop and bookshop								
1 Jan–26 Feb	11–3	·	·	·	·	·	S	S
Gardens, refreshments and shop								
3 Mar–4 Nov	11–5	M	T	W	T	F	S	S
8 Nov–30 Dec	11–3	·	·	·	T	F	S	S
Parkland								
Open all year	Dawn–dusk	M	T	W	T	F	S	S

Open Good Friday 11 to 5. 19 July to 31 August: access to some areas of house may be limited on Thursdays and Fridays.

Flatford: Bridge Cottage

Flatford, East Bergholt, Suffolk CO7 6UL

Map ③ I8 🏠♿ 1943

In the heart of the beautiful Dedham Vale, the charming hamlet of Flatford is the location for some of John Constable's most famous pastoral paintings. Find out more about Constable at the updated exhibition in Bridge Cottage. Relax in the riverside tea-room and browse in the gift shop. **Note**: no public access to Flatford Mill, Valley Farm and Willy Lott's house.

Exploring
– Visit the location of Constable's famous paintings.
– Discover more about Constable in Bridge Cottage.
– Escape on foot and explore the peaceful Dedham Vale.
– Visit the restored Valley Farm kitchen garden.

Eating and shopping: enjoy homemade food in the lovely riverside tea-room. Local gifts and Constable souvenirs in the thatched shop.

Making the most of your day: guided tours of Constable's painting locations, programme of longer rambles in the Dedham Vale, special tours of Flatford Mill buildings, family activity trail.

Access for all: 🅿♿🚻♿♿🎨♿⋯🅰
Building ♿♿ Grounds ♿♿♿

Getting here: 168:TM075333. ½ mile south of East Bergholt. **Foot**: accessible from East Bergholt, Dedham and Manningtree. **Bus**: frequent services from Colchester bus station. **Train**: Manningtree 1¾ miles by footpath, 3½ miles by road. **Road**: south of East Bergholt off B1070. **Parking**: 200 yards, pay and display (not National Trust), charge for members.

Finding out more: 01206 298260 or flatfordbridgecottage@nationaltrust.org.uk

Flatford: Bridge Cottage		M	T	W	T	F	S	S
7 Jan–26 Feb	11–3:30						S	S
1 Mar–31 Mar	11–5			W	T	F	S	S
1 Apr–30 Apr	11–5	M	T	W	T	F	S	S
1 May–30 Sep	10:30–5:30	M	T	W	T	F	S	S
1 Oct–31 Oct	11–5	M	T	W	T	F	S	S
1 Nov–23 Dec	11–3:30			W	T	F	S	S

Open Bank Holiday Mondays. May close early October to March if weather is bad. Visitor information centre closed weekdays in March, November and December.

Flatford: Bridge Cottage, Suffolk, inspired some of John Constable's most famous paintings

Please display current sticker for free parking (and show card when asked)

Hatfield Forest

near Bishop's Stortford, Essex

Map ③ G8 🏛️🔧🛶🎣🍽️ 1924

No other forest on Earth evokes the atmosphere of a medieval hunting forest so completely. The ancient trees, some of which are 1,200 years old, are like magnificent living sculptures. These gentle giants each have a unique shape and support a unique ecosystem. Just imagine what these trees have lived through and the stories they could tell. Whether you want somewhere for the children to let off steam, somewhere you can exercise to keep fit, or somewhere tranquil to walk where you can quietly reflect, you are sure to find your own special place in Hatfield Forest.

Exploring
- Explore the hidden depths of the woods on foot.
- Marvel at the half a billion buttercups in spring.
- Relax in beautiful surroundings and browse the new guidebook.
- Be inspired by the intricacies of the Shell House.
- See the conservation team at work in the forest.
- Discover the forest on horseback (permit required) or by bike.

Eating and shopping: discover beautiful locally produced gifts in our shop. Stop for a bite to eat at the Forest Café. Try some healthy Hatfield Forest venison (seasonal), now available in individual cuts. Buy our sustainable woodland products, from firewood to beanpoles.

Making the most of your day: full programme of family events. Tracker Packs and trail guides available to help you explore. Batricar and all-terrain pushchair available. **Dogs**: on leads near livestock and lake.

Access for all: 🅿️♿🚾♿◎
Grounds ♿➡️♿♿

The tranquil Hatfield Forest, Essex

Getting here: 167:TL547203. 4 miles east of Bishop's Stortford. **Foot**: Flitch Way from Braintree. Three Forests Way and Forest Way pass through the forest. **Cycle**: Flitch Way. **Bus**: Saffron Walden to Stansted Airport, alight Takeley Street (Green Man), 1 mile. **Train**: Stansted Airport 3 miles. **Road**: from M11 exit 8, take B1256 towards Takeley and follow signs. **Parking**: limited parking, November to March. Charge per car (non-members).

Finding out more: 01279 874040 (Infoline). 01279 870678 or hatfieldforest@nationaltrust.org.uk. Hatfield Forest Estate Office, Takeley, Bishop's Stortford, Hertfordshire CM22 6NE

Hatfield Forest		M	T	W	T	F	S	S
Forest								
Open all year	Dawn–dusk	M	T	W	T	F	S	S
Shop								
1 Jan–11 Mar	10–3:30	·	·	·	·	·	S	S
12 Mar–4 Nov	10–5	M	T	W	T	F	S	S
10 Nov–30 Dec	10–3:30	·	·	·	·	·	S	S
Forest Café								
1 Jan–11 Mar	10–3:30	·	·	W	T	F	S	S
12 Mar–4 Nov	10–5	M	T	W	T	F	S	S
7 Nov–30 Dec	10–3:30	·	·	W	T	F	S	S
Elgins and Shell House car parks*								
1 Jan–11 Mar	10–3:30	·	·	·	·	·	·	S
12 Mar–4 Nov	10–5	M	T	W	T	F	S	S
10 Nov–30 Dec	10–3:30	·	·	·	·	·	S	S

Forest Café and shop: open daily during February and December school holidays, 10 to 3:30. Elgins and Shell House car parks exit closes 8. Café closed 25 December. Shop closed 25 and 26 December. *Opening of Elgins car park is subject to ground conditions.

Heigham Holmes

Martham Staithe, Ferrygate Lane,
Martham, Norfolk

Map ③ K5 1987

A remote island nature reserve with grazing
marshes and ditches supporting wildlife typical
of this important and vast broadland landscape.
Note: access by foot only, via floating river-
crossing over River Thurne. No toilet. Limited
parking. Major construction work to replace
Heigham Holmes River Crossing.

Getting here: 134:TG445194. 1 mile north-west
of Martham.

Finding out more: 01263 740241 or
heighamholmes@nationaltrust.org.uk.
Norfolk Coast Office, Friary Farm, Cley Road,
Blakeney, Norfolk NR25 7NW

Heigham Holmes	M	T	W	T	F	S	S
1 Apr–28 Oct	10–2		·	**W**	·	·	**S**

Group visits only, by prior written arrangement via Norfolk
Coast Office. Closed Bank Holidays.

The impressive Horsey Windpump, Norfolk

Horsey Windpump

Horsey, Great Yarmouth, Norfolk NR29 4EF

Map ③ K4  1948

Built 100 years ago, this striking windpump
offers stunning views over Horsey Mere and
this mysterious broadland landscape, full of
exceptional wildlife. Here you'll find a great
introduction to the Broads – whether you want
to go for a walk, visit the beach or just enjoy a
cup of tea. **Note**: surrounded by Horsey Estate
– managed by the Buxton family. Building work
to replace stock/sails.

Exploring   – Visit Horsey Staithe Stores to
                discover more about the area.
                – Climb the five-storey
                windpump for unmissable
                views over Horsey Mere.

Exploring   – Take a walk from the Broads
                to the beach.
                – Discover the workings of
                this broadland drainage
                windpump.

Eating and shopping: enjoy a friendly welcome
and light refreshments at Horsey Staithe Stores
(next to Horsey Windpump), which also sells
local gifts, souvenirs and books. Eat outside
and relax before or after your walk.

Making the most of your day: get ideas for
your visit from the staff at Horsey Staithe
Stores (right next to Horsey Windpump). Take
a boat trip (not National Trust) across Horsey
Mere in holiday periods. **Dogs**: welcome on
leads (wildlife and livestock).

Access for all: 🅿️♿🚻♿♿📖♿🅿️

Horsey Windpump ♿♿♿ Horsey Staithe Stores ♿

Grounds ♿➡️

Getting here: 134:TG457223. 15 miles north of Great Yarmouth; 4 miles north-east of Martham. **Road**: off B1159 south of Horsey village. **Parking**: 50 yards, pay and display (members free).

Finding out more: 01263 740241 or horseywindpump@nationaltrust.org.uk. Norfolk Coast Office, Friary Farm, Cley Road, Blakeney, Norfolk NR25 7NW

Horsey Windpump		M	T	W	T	F	S	S
Horsey Windpump								
3 Mar–31 Mar	10–4:30	·	·	·	·	·	S	S
1 Apr–4 Nov	10–4:30	M	T	W	T	F	S	S
Horsey Staithe Stores								
3 Mar–31 Mar	10–4:30	·	·	·	·	·	S	S
1 Apr–4 Nov	10–4:30	M	T	W	T	F	S	S

Open all Bank Holidays between 3 March and 4 November. Car park open all year, dawn to dusk.

Houghton Mill

Houghton, near Huntingdon, Cambridgeshire PE28 2AZ

Map (3) F6 1939

Situated in a stunning riverside setting and full of excellent hands-on activities for all the family, this five-storey historic building is the last working watermill on the Great Ouse. You can watch a milling demonstration and even buy flour, ground in the traditional way by water-powered millstones. **Note**: milling demonstrations (Sundays and Bank Holidays, 1 to 5) subject to river levels.

Exploring
- Come and watch one of our milling demonstrations.
- Find out more with our touch-screen display.
- Wander or cycle through the neighbouring water meadows.

Eating and shopping: have a snack or try our famous Houghton scones in the delightful riverside tea-room. Spend some time browsing in the second-hand bookshop. Take home some of our freshly ground Houghton Mill wholemeal flour.

Making the most of your day: family events programme, including open-air theatre and hands-on baking days. Visit our website for children's summer holiday events. Follow the family Cat and Rat trail around the mill. **Dogs**: on leads in grounds only.

Access for all:
Building **Grounds**

Getting here: 153:TL282720. 3½ miles from Huntingdon. **Foot**: on the Ouse Valley Way. **Cycle**: NCN51. **Bus**: services Cambridge to Huntingdon (passing close Huntingdon). **Train**: Huntingdon 3½ miles. **Road**: signposted off A1123. **Parking**: 20 yards, pay and display.

Finding out more: 01480 301494 or houghtonmill@nationaltrust.org.uk

Houghton Mill		M	T	W	T	F	S	S
Mill								
17 Mar–28 Oct	11–5	·	·	·	·	·	S	S
2 Apr–11 Apr	1–5	M	T	W	·	·	·	·
30 Apr–26 Sep	1–5	M	T	W	·	·	·	·
Tea-room								
17 Mar–28 Oct	11–5	·	·	·	·	·	S	S
2 Apr–11 Apr	11–5	M	T	W	·	·	·	·
30 Apr–26 Sep	11–5	M	T	W	·	·	·	·

Open Bank Holiday Mondays and Tuesdays, plus Good Friday 11 to 5. Caravan and campsite: open March to October; managed by the Caravan Club (01480 466716). Car park closes 8 or dusk if earlier. **Toilets: as tea-room but closed Thursday and Friday**.

Finding out more at Houghton Mill, Cambridgeshire

Ickworth

The Rotunda, Horringer, Bury St Edmunds,
Suffolk IP29 5QE

Map ③ H7   1956

Step inside Ickworth and uncover the story
of the impressive central 'rotunda' and the
4th Earl of Bristol, who built this magnificent
showcase to house his priceless treasures,
collected on his tours around Europe in the
18th century. For 200 years the infamous and
eccentric Hervey family continued to add
to the treasures inside and out, creating the
first and finest Italianate garden in England.
Experience the lives of the servants and
workers who kept this country estate running
and share their memories of domestic life by
visiting our innovative display of the basement
servants' quarters. **Note:** for wedding,
conference and banqueting facilities telephone
01284 735957; Ickworth Hotel 01284 735350.

Exploring
- Experience 'Ickworth Lives', a fascinating representation of Edwardian life.
- Admire spectacular paintings, including some by Velasquez and Gainsborough.
- Tour the basement and learn about upstairs downstairs life.
- Enjoy the Hervey's magnificent Georgian silver collection.
- Creep amongst the ferns in the magical Victorian stumpery.
- Relax amid acres of idyllic parkland, then explore the vineyard.

Eating and shopping: sample our seasonal
menu in the West Wing restaurant. Ickworth
wines and locally sourced products are
available from the gift shop. Visit our attractive
plant and garden centre. Spend time browsing
in the second-hand bookshop at
Honeyballs Cottage.

Making the most of your day: year-round
events and activities, including house, park,
garden and vineyard tours; 'Ickworth Lives'
exhibition; waymarked walks and cycle routes;
play areas; walk guides available from visitor
reception. **Dogs**: welcome (on leads
near livestock).

Access for all: House West Wing
Grounds

Getting here: 155:TL810610. 3 miles south-
west of Bury St Edmunds. **Foot**: 4½ miles via
footpaths from Bury St Edmunds. **Bus**: from
Bury St Edmunds to Haverhill. **Train**: Bury St
Edmunds 3 miles. **Road**: from A14 take junction
42 towards Westley; on west side of A143.
Parking: 200 yards.

The 'rotunda' at Ickworth, Suffolk

Finding out more: 01284 735270 or
ickworth@nationaltrust.org.uk

Ickworth		.M	T	W	T	F	S	S
Parkland, woods and children's playground								
Open all year	8–8	M	T	W	T	F	S	S
Gardens								
Open all year	8–5	M	T	W	T	F	S	S
Rotunda (house and basement)								
2 Mar–22 Jul	11–5	M	T	·	·	F	S	S
23 Jul–2 Sep	11–5	M	T	W	T	F	S	S
3 Sep–2 Nov	11–5	M	T	·	·	F	S	S
3 Nov–16 Dec	11–3	·	·	·	·	·	S	S
Plant and garden shop								
1 Mar–4 Nov	11–5	M	T	W	T	·F	S	S
Shop, restaurant* and West Wing reception								
1 Jan–29 Feb	11–4	M	T	W	T	F	S	S
1 Mar–2 Nov	10–5	M	T	W	T	F	S	S
3 Nov–31 Dec	11–4	M	T	W	T	F	S	S

Open all Bank Holidays except 25 December. *Limited
catering available 24 and 26 December. Parkland, woods
and gardens close 8 or dusk if earlier. Last entry to Rotunda
is 60 minutes before closing.

The Guildhall of Corpus Christi at Lavenham, Suffolk

Lavenham Guildhall

Market Place, Lavenham, Sudbury,
Suffolk CO10 9QZ

Map ③ l7   🏠 ✤ 1951

**'A truly most absorbing building.
It oozes history and magnifies the
life and times of the past. Wonderful!'**
Mr Hawks, Shefford, Bedfordshire

Set the scene for your day in the lovely
village of Lavenham by visiting the Guildhall
of Corpus Christi. Lavenham is famed for its
wealth of timber-framed buildings, which
make it one of the best-preserved medieval
villages in England. Step inside the Guildhall of
Corpus Christi to experience one of the finest
examples of these buildings. During your visit
you'll learn about the changing fortunes of
Lavenham, from the boom times of the cloth
industry to the poverty of the 19th century,
before going on to explore this remarkably
preserved small medieval town that has
changed little in five centuries.

Exploring
– Learn about timber-framed
  construction and
  medieval guilds.
– Browse the exhibits on
  cloth working, local railways
  and agriculture.
– See Ramesses, the mummified
  cat, discovered in a nearby roof.
– Visit the walled garden to see
  traditional dye plants.
– Join one of our guided walks
  and talks during summer.
– Pop into Lavenham church,
  one of Suffolk's finest.

Eating and shopping: ploughman's lunches with
local bread, regional cheeses and Norfolk ham.
Mouthwatering cream teas, with the famous
Guildhall scones. A wide range of local gifts,
souvenirs, books and plants for sale in the shop.

Making the most of your day: identify
mystery objects from the museum's collections,
follow children's trails around the house or
try on children's Tudor dressing-up costumes.
Programme of walks, talks and events, local
history exhibition.

Access for all: 🏛️🔼🅿️📖♿👓🅰️
Guildhall and garden 🔼♿ Shop ♿ Tea-room 🔼♿

Getting here: 155:TL916493. Market Place, off the main High Street. **Foot**: 4 mile Railway Walk links Lavenham with Long Melford. **Cycle**: South Suffolk Cycle Route A1. **Train**: Sudbury 7 miles. **Road**: A1141 and B1071. **Parking**: free throughout the village.

Finding out more: 01787 247646 or lavenhamguildhall@nationaltrust.org.uk

Lavenham Guildhall		M	T	W	T	F	S	S
Shop								
7 Jan–26 Feb	11–4	·	·	·	·	·	S	S
1 Nov–23 Dec	11–4	·	·	·	T	F	S	S
Tea-room								
1 Dec–23 Dec	11–4	·	·	·	·	·	S	S
Guildhall, tea-room and shop								
3 Mar–25 Mar	11–4	·	·	W	T	F	S	S
26 Mar–31 Oct	11–5	M	T	W	T	F	S	S
3 Nov–25 Nov	11–4	·	·	·	·	·	S	S

Parts of the Guildhall may be closed occasionally for community use.

Croquet on the lawn at Melford Hall, Suffolk

Melford Hall

Long Melford, Sudbury, Suffolk CO10 9AA

Map ③ I7   1960

'A real sense of a family home – as welcoming and friendly as it is impressive.'
Giles Dixon, Bishops Stortford

For almost five centuries the picturesque turrets of Melford Hall have dominated Long Melford's village green. Devastated by fire in 1942, the house was brought back to life by the Hyde Parker family and it remains their much-loved family home to this day. Their interior decoration and furnishings chart the changing tastes and fashions of two centuries, but it is the stories of family life at Melford – from visits by their relation Beatrix Potter with her menagerie of animals, to children sliding down the grand staircase on trays – that make this house more than just bricks and mortar.

Exploring
– See Beatrix Potter's Jemima Puddleduck toy and her bedroom.
– Relax on the comfy sofas in the Great Hall.
– Play traditional games like croquet in the garden.
– Chat to our friendly volunteers and uncover Melford's stories.
– Discover 250 years of naval service and ancient captured treasure.

Eating and shopping: relax in the Old Kitchen or Park Room over a cream tea or a sandwich. Browse the souvenirs, gifts, second-hand books and plants in the Gatehouse shop. Take home our souvenir story book to delve deeper into Melford's history.

Making the most of your day: wide programme of walks, talks and family events April to October. Children's treasure hunt in the house and garden trails. Some annual events in the park are not National Trust. **Dogs**: on leads in car park and park walk only.

Access for all:
Building 🔳🔳🔳🔳 Grounds 🔳🔳

Getting here: 155:TL867462. 3 miles from Sudbury. **Foot**: 4 mile Railway Walk linking Long Melford with Lavenham. **Bus**: Mondays to Saturdays from Sudbury and Bury St Edmunds ➡. **Train**: Sudbury 4 miles. **Road**: off A134, 14 miles from Bury St Edmunds. **Parking**: free at car park and throughout village.

Finding out more: 01787 376395 (Infoline). 01787 379228 or melford@nationaltrust.org.uk

Melford Hall		M	T	W	T	F	S	S
31 Mar–8 Apr	1–5						S	S
9 Apr–15 Apr	1–5	M		W	T	F	S	S
21 Apr–29 Apr	1–5						S	S
2 May–30 Sep	1–5			W	T	F	S	S
6 Oct–28 Oct	1–5						S	S

Also open on Bank Holiday Monday and Bank Holiday Tuesday afternoons. Closed Good Friday.

Orford Ness National Nature Reserve

Orford, Woodbridge, Suffolk

Map ③ K7   🔳🔳🔳🔳🔳 1993

Take a boat trip to this wild remote shingle spit, the largest in Europe. Follow trails through a stunning landscape and a history that will both delight and intrigue. Although an internationally important nature reserve, the site is littered with unusual, often forbidding, buildings from a sometimes disturbing past. **Note**: charge for ferry (including members). Steep, slippery steps. 'Pagodas' accessible on guided events only. Ferry charge applies to members.

Exploring
- Explore this 'top secret' site with our self-guiding booklet.
- Experience the wild, wide open spaces and the big skies.
- Children's trail – become a spy for the day.
- Come face to face with a nuclear bomb!

Eating and shopping: visit the quay and try some freshly caught fish; take home a flavour of the coast from local smokehouses.

Making the most of your day: guided tours and events (booked only). Crossings limited, arrive early to avoid disappointment. Bring own food and drink (and suitable clothing). Sorry no cycling permitted. **Dogs**: assistance dogs only.

Access for all: 🔳🔳🔳🔳🔳
All buildings 🔳 Grounds 🔳➡

Getting here: 169:TM425495. Orford, Suffolk coast, east of Ipswich. **Foot**: Suffolk Coast Path and Sandlings Walk pass nearby on mainland. **Cycle**: Regional Route 41, 1 mile. No cycling onsite (no cycle parking). **Ferry**: only access to Ness via National Trust ferry *Octavia*. See opening arrangements. **Bus**: local service from Woodbridge (passing Melton ➡). Bookable demand-responsive service (0845 604 1802). **Train**: Wickham Market 8 miles. **Road**: 10 miles east of A12 (B1094/1095), 12 miles north-east of Woodbridge (B1152/1084). **Parking**: Quay Street, 150 yards, not National Trust (pay and display).

Distant 'Pagoda' at Orford Ness in Suffolk

Finding out more: 01728 648024 (Infoline). 01394 450900 or orfordness@nationaltrust.org.uk. Quay Office, Orford Quay, Orford, Woodbridge, Suffolk IP12 2NU

Orford Ness		M	T	W	T	F	S	S
7 Apr–30 Jun	10–2	·	·	·	·	·	**S**	·
3 Jul–29 Sep	10–2	·	**T**	**W**	**T**	**F**	**S**	·
6 Oct–27 Oct	10–2	·	·	·	·	·	**S**	·

The only access is by National Trust ferry from Orford Quay, with boats crossing regularly to the Ness between 10 and 2 only, the last ferry leaving the Ness at 5. Some routes only open seasonally.

Oxburgh Hall

Oxborough, near Swaffham, Norfolk PE33 9PS

Map ③ H5   1952

'I enjoyed my visit very much. Oxburgh is a fascinating house in a beautiful setting.'
Mr Coleman, Swaffham

No one ever forgets their first sight of Oxburgh. This romantic, moated manor house was built by the Bedingfeld family in the 15th century and they have lived here ever since. Inside, learn about the family's Catholic history, complete with a secret priest's hole. See the astonishing needlework by Mary, Queen of Scots, and the private chapel, built with reclaimed materials. Outside, you can enjoy panoramic views from the Tudor gatehouse roof and follow the woodcarving trails in the gardens and woodlands. **Note**: major electrical rewiring February/March, so access to parts of house restricted (visit website for updates).

Exploring
– Marvel at the amazing needlework by Mary, Queen of Scots.
– Explore secret doors and climb inside the hidden priest's hole.
– Discover a wealth of heraldry, including painted ceilings.
– Climb the original spiral stairs to the gatehouse roof.
– Stroll in the kitchen garden, orchard and meadow.
– Enjoy drifts of late winter snowdrops in the woodlands.

Eating and shopping: Old Kitchen tea-room; picnic area and seasonal kiosk serving light refreshments in the car park. Well-stocked gift shop, including local Norfolk products, and plant sales for the green-fingered. Browse in the second-hand bookshop in the Gun Room.

Making the most of your day: free garden tours every open day. Free children's trails in the house and garden. Year-round events

Oxburgh Hall in Norfolk: a romantic, moated manor house with many secrets and stories

programme. Woodland walks and nature trails. **Dogs**: assistance dogs only in both grounds and house.

Access for all: 🅿️♿🚾♿🔄📷📹🚶
Hall ♿♿♿ Chapel ♿ Garden ♿➡️♿

Getting here: 143:TF742012. In Oxborough village. **Train**: Downham Market, 10 miles, then taxi; no public transport. **Road**: 7 miles south-west of Swaffham and 3 miles from A134 at Stoke Ferry; 17 miles south of King's Lynn. **Parking**: free onsite parking.

Finding out more: 01366 328258 or oxburghhall@nationaltrust.org.uk

Oxburgh Hall		M	T	W	T	F	S	S
House, garden, shop and tea-room								
25 Feb–28 Mar*	11–4	M	T	W	·	·	S	S
31 Mar–18 Apr	11–5	M	T	W	T	F	S	S
21 Apr–30 May	11–5	M	T	W	·	·	S	S
2 Jun–13 Jun	11–5	M	T	W	T	F	S	S
16 Jun–25 Jul	11–5	M	T	W	·	·	S	S
28 Jul–5 Sep	11–5	M	T	W	T	F	S	S
8 Sep–30 Sep	11–5	M	T	W	·	·	S	S
1 Oct–4 Nov*	11–4	M	T	W	·	·	S	S
Garden, shop and tea-room								
7 Jan–19 Feb	11–4	·	·	·	·	·	S	S
10 Nov–23 Dec	11–4	·	·	·	·	·	S	S

*House: 25 February to 7 March admission by timed tours only on weekdays. House, garden, shop and tea-room: open all week for October half-term (27 October to 4 November). February and March: due to essential electrical rewiring works access to parts of the house may be restricted (check in advance of visit).

Paycocke's

25 West Street, Coggeshall, Colchester, Essex CO6 1NS

Map ③ I8 🏠✿ 1924

Marvel at the stunning woodcarving and elaborate panelling inside this fine half-timbered merchant's house. Built around 1500 for Thomas Paycocke, this house is evidence of the great wealth generated by the East Anglian cloth trade in the 16th century. Outside, there is a beautiful and tranquil cottage garden. **Note**: nearest toilet at Grange Barn.

Exploring – Discover the intriguing history of this house and its residents.
– See the new vegetable beds in the cottage garden.
– Soak up the atmosphere of this remarkable 500-year-old building.

Paycocke's, Essex, was built around 1500

Making the most of your day: children's trail in the house and garden, children's activities during events, guided tours on request. **Dogs**: in the garden only.

Access for all: 🅿️📷🚶♿🔄
Building ♿ Grounds ♿

Getting here: 168:TL848225. 5½ miles east of Braintree. **Foot**: close to Essex Way. **Bus**: from Colchester to Braintree (passing Marks Tey ➡️). **Train**: Kelvedon 2½ miles. **Road**: signposted off A120. On south side of West Street, 400 yards from centre of Coggeshall, on road to Braintree next to the Fleece Inn. **Parking**: Grange Barn (½ mile) until 4:30. Very limited roadside parking.

Finding out more: 01376 561305 or paycockes@nationaltrust.org.uk

Paycocke's		M	T	W	T	F	S	S
1 Apr–4 Nov	11–5	·	·	W	T	F	S	S

Open Bank Holiday Mondays.

Peckover House and Garden

North Brink, Wisbech, Cambridgeshire PE13 1JR

Map ③ G5  1943

Peckover House is a secret gem, an oasis hidden away in an urban environment. A classic Georgian merchant's town house, it was lived in by the Peckover family for 150 years. The Peckovers were staunch Quakers, which meant they had a very simple lifestyle, yet at the same time they ran a successful private bank. Both facets of their life can be seen as you wander through the house and gardens. The gardens themselves are outstanding – a huge area of sensory delight, complete with orangery, summerhouses, croquet lawn and rose garden with more than 60 varieties of rose.

Exploring – Learn about the Quaker history of the Peckover family.
– Examine the Cabinet of Curiosities – both old and new.
– Take a peek inside the unrestored butler's pantry.

Exploring – Admire the Rococo plasterwork in the drawing room and landing.
– See oranges growing in the orangery – where else!

Eating and shopping: tea-room in the thatched 17th-century barn, with a charming courtyard seating area. The gift shop in the old banking wing offers a range of local products. Pick up a bargain in the second-hand bookshop. Plant sales for the green-fingered.

Making the most of your day: play our Bechstein piano. Free garden tours most days, croquet in summer. Children's handling collection and trails. Behind-the-scenes tours on selected days. Octavia Hill's birthplace is nearby. **Dogs**: assistance dogs only.

Access for all: 🅿️♿🚻♿🐕📷🎥♿
Main house ♿🅐 Tea-room ♿ Garden ♿➡️♿

Getting here: 143:TF458097. West of Wisbech town centre on north bank of River Nene. **Foot**: from Chapel Road car park walk up passageway to left of W-Four restaurant, turn right by river. Peckover House is 164 yards on right. **Cycle**: NCN1, ¼ mile. **Bus**: from Peterborough 🚇 to Lowestoft; and King's Lynn (passing close King's Lynn 🚇). **Train**: March 9½ miles. **Road**: B1441.

Stunning colour in the exuberant Rose Garden at Peckover House in Cambridgeshire

Sat Nav: enter PE13 1RG for nearest car park.
Parking: free in town, nearest is Chapel Road (not National Trust), 273 yards.

Finding out more: 01945 583463 or peckover@nationaltrust.org.uk

Peckover House and Garden		M	T	W	T	F	S	S
Garden and tea-room								
11 Feb–4 Mar	12–4	·	·	·	·	·	S	S
10 Mar–1 Apr	12–5	M	T	W	·	·	S	S
2 Apr–15 Apr	12–5	M	T	W	T	F	S	S
16 Apr–4 Nov	12–5	M	T	W	·	·	S	S
House								
10 Mar–1 Apr	1–5	M	T	W	·	·	S	S
2 Apr–15 Apr	1–5	M	T	W	T	F	S	S
16 Apr–4 Nov	1–5	M	T	W	·	·	S	S
Whole property								
8 Dec–16 Dec	12–6	·	·	·	·	·	S	S

Open all week during spring Bank Holiday, 4 to 10 June, Wisbech Rose Fair, 4 to 7 July (garden and tea-room open 11 and house 12), plus half-term, 29 October to 4 November. Christmas opening: 8 and 9, plus 15 and 16 December. Gift shop and second-hand bookshop open as house.

Ramsey Abbey Gatehouse

Abbey School, Ramsey, Huntingdon, Cambridgeshire PE17 1DH

Map ③ F6   1952

This charming former gatehouse is all that remains of the once great Benedictine abbey at Ramsey. **Note**: on school grounds, please respect school security. Exterior can be seen all year.

Access for all: ⓟ Gatehouse 🐾 Grounds 🐾🦽

Getting here: 142:TL291851. At south-east edge of Ramsey, at point where Chatteris road leaves B1096, 10 miles south-east of Peterborough.

Finding out more: 01480 301494 or ramseyabbey@nationaltrust.org.uk

Ramsey Abbey Gatehouse
Open first Sunday of the month, April to September, 1 to 5. Combine your visit with Ramsey Rural Museum and walled garden.

Rayleigh Mount

Rayleigh, Essex

Map ③ I10   1923

Enjoy amazing views at this medieval motte and bailey castle site, now abundant with wildlife. Adjacent windmill houses historical exhibition. **Note**: exhibition in windmill operated by Rochford District Council.

Access for all: Grounds 🐾

Getting here: 178:TQ805909. 100 yards from High Street, next to Mill Hall car park.

Finding out more: 01284 747500 or rayleighmount@nationaltrust.org.uk

Rayleigh Mount
Open every day all year from 7 to 6
Mount closes at 2 on Saturdays and 5 in winter, other opening times may vary. For windmill exhibition opening times telephone 01702 318120.

St George's Guildhall

29 King Street, King's Lynn, Norfolk PE30 1HA

Map ③ H5   1951

The largest surviving medieval guildhall in England, with many original features. The guildhall is now a working theatre. **Note**: managed by local Council and King's Lynn Arts Centre Trust.

Access for all: Building 🐾 Grounds 🦽

Getting here: 132:TF616202. On west side of King Street close to the Tuesday Market Place.

Finding out more: 01553 765565 or stgeorgesguildhall@nationaltrust.org.uk

St George's Guildhall		M	T	W	T	F	S	S
3 Jan–21 Dec	10–2	·	T	W	T	F	·	·
Closed on Bank Holidays.								

Shaw's Corner

Ayot St Lawrence, near Welwyn,
Hertfordshire AL6 9BX

Map ③ F9   1944

Home to playwright George Bernard Shaw for more than 40 years, Shaw's Corner is a 1902 Arts and Crafts house set in a quintessentially English garden. It feels like Shaw has just left – his clothes are still in the wardrobe and his typewriter and glasses sit on his study desk. **Note**: access roads are very narrow.

Exploring – Discover Shaw's unique revolving writing hut in the garden.
– See the 1938 Oscar for *Pygmalion*.
– Get up close to some of Shaw's personal belongings.

Eating and shopping: enjoy ice-creams and soft drinks in the garden. Take time to browse in the second-hand bookshop. Pre-1950s varieties of plants for sale.

Making the most of your day: open-air performances of George Bernard Shaw's plays each summer in the garden. Regular events. **Dogs**: assistance dogs only.

Access for all: 🅿️ 🏛️ 🖥️ 🚻 ⚠️ 🅰️
Building 🔽🔽🔽 Grounds 🔽🔽🔽

Getting here: 166:TL194167. 5 miles from Harpenden. **Cycle**: NCN12, 1 mile. **Bus**: nearest bus stops Blackmore End (infrequent) and Wheathampstead, both a 2-mile walk down narrow country lanes without pavements. **Train**: Welwyn North 4½ miles; Welwyn Garden City 6 miles; Harpenden 5 miles. **Road**: A1(M) exit 4 or M1 exit 10. Signposted from B653 Welwyn Garden City to Luton road near Wheathampstead, and from B656 at Codicote. **Parking**: free small car park, 30 yards (unsuitable for large vehicles).

Finding out more: 01438 829221 (Infoline). 01438 820307 or shawscorner@nationaltrust.org.uk

Shaw's Corner		M	T	W	T	F	S	S
House								
10 Mar–28 Oct	1–5		·	·	**W**	**T**	**F**	**S**	**S**
Garden								
10 Mar–28 Oct	12–5:30		·	·	**W**	**T**	**F**	**S**	**S**

Open Bank Holiday Mondays. Closes earlier when there are evening events.

Shaw's Corner, Hertfordshire: Arts and Crafts house set in a quintessentially English garden

Sheringham Park

Upper Sheringham, Norfolk NR26 8TL

Map ③ J4   🎴🌸♨️🏛️🏠 1987

'What a wonderful park, with such a wide variety of walks, constantly changing scenery and far-reaching views.'
Lesley Gwynn, Sheringham

Sheringham Park is renowned for its rhododendron collection, which reaches its peak in early May into June. But Sheringham has so much more to offer – come and enjoy glorious countryside walks, with stunning views of the North Norfolk coast. As you stroll along the main drive admire the landscape created by Humphry Repton and see why he described it as his favourite work. **Note**: Sheringham Hall is privately occupied. April to September: limited access by written appointment with leaseholder.

Strolling through Sheringham Park, Norfolk

Exploring
– Enjoy woodland walks disturbed only by birdsong.
– Climb the gazebo for an unforgettable coastal view.
– Hire a Tracker Pack and become a wildlife detective.
– Listen to the song of the skylark by the cliffs.
– Look out for white admiral butterflies in the summer.
– Visit in the autumn for spectacular foliage.

Eating and shopping: take home a souvenir of Sheringham Park from our well-stocked shop or buy a rhododendron from our plant table. Relax in the courtyard with a cream tea, ice-cream or perhaps a bacon sandwich.

Making the most of your day: explore the 'Bower', an ideal place for families to enjoy. Adults can relax by the pond while children create their own environmental art or hunt for minibeasts. **Dogs**: on leads near livestock and visitor facilities.

Getting here: 133:TG135420. 2 miles south-west of Sheringham. **Foot**: on Norfolk Coast Path. **Cycle**: Regional Route 30, 1½ miles south. **Bus**: services stop on request at main entrance. **Train**: Sheringham 2 miles. **Road**: 5 miles west of Cromer, 6 miles east of Holt. Main entrance at junction A148/B1157. **Parking**: 60 yards, £4.70 (pay and display).

Finding out more: 01263 820550 or sheringhampark@nationaltrust.org.uk. Visitor Centre, Wood Farm, Upper Sheringham, Norfolk NR26 8TL

Sheringham Park		M	T	W	T	F	S	S
Park								
Open all year	Dawn–dusk	M	T	W	T	F	S	S
Visitor centre								
1 Jan–11 Mar	11–4	·	·	·	·	·	S	S
17 Mar–30 Sep	10–5	M	T	W	T	F	S	S
1 Oct–4 Nov	10–5	M	·	·	T	F	S	S
10 Nov–30 Dec	11–4	·	·	·	·	·	S	S
Refreshment kiosk								
17 Mar–30 Sep	10–5	M	T	W	T	F	S	S
1 Oct–4 Nov	10–5	M	·	·	T	F	S	S

Visitor centre and refreshment kiosk: open daily 11 to 19 February and 27 October to 4 November, 10 to 5; 27 to 31 December, 11 to 4.

Access for all: 🅿️♿🚐🚻♿🍴♿🏛️🎧♿📷
Building 🏛️♿ Grounds 🏛️➡️♿

Sutton Hoo

Tranmer House, Sutton Hoo, Woodbridge, Suffolk IP12 3DJ

Map (3) J7 1998

'I have come to a place of mystery that fires the imagination. Wonderful!'
Mrs Vicky Wardrope, Norwich

This hauntingly beautiful estate, with far-reaching views over the River Deben, is home to one of the greatest archaeological discoveries of all time. Walk around the ancient burial mounds and discover the incredible story of the ship burial of an Anglo-Saxon king and his treasured possessions. Explore our award-winning exhibition, the atmospheric full-size reconstruction of the burial chamber, stunning replica treasures and original finds from one of the mounds, including a prince's sword. Sit, touch, relax and explore inside Edith Pretty's beautiful Edwardian house, or enjoy the beautiful seasonal colours on a walk around the estate.

Exploring
- New burial chamber experience! Sights, sounds and smells of AD625.
- Enjoy the beautiful period interiors of Edith Pretty's country home.
- Take a guided tour of the royal burial mounds.
- Explore beautiful woodland and heathland walks with fine estuary views.
- Meet a 1930s archaeologist and help them unearth the past.
- Stay for longer in one of our Edwardian holiday flats.

Eating and shopping: relax in our contemporary licensed café, with its views towards the River Deben. Discover exclusive ceramics and jewellery in our gift shop. Browse through the books in our well-stocked second-hand bookshop.

Making the most of your day: family events, living history, exclusive behind-the-scenes tours and changing exhibitions. Wildlife/nature walks. Children's play area, 'Let's Dig It' archaeology trench, quiz/trails and dressing-up box. **Dogs**: welcome on leads in park and café terrace area only.

Access for all:
Building **Grounds**

Getting here: 169:TM288487. 1¼ miles from Melton. **Bus**: from Ipswich to Framlingham (passing Melton). **Train**: Melton 1¼ miles, Woodbridge 3 miles. **Road**: on B1083 Melton to Bawdsey, follow signs from A12. **Parking**: 30 yards (pay and display when exhibition closed). Motorcycle parking, cycle racks, lockers.

Finding out more: 01394 389700 or suttonhoo@nationaltrust.org.uk

Sutton Hoo		M	T	W	T	F	S	S
1 Jan–5 Feb	11–4	·	·	·	·	·	S	S
11 Feb–19 Feb	11–4	M	T	W	T	F	S	S
25 Feb–18 Mar	11–4	·	·	·	·	·	S	S
21 Mar–1 Apr	10:30–5	·	·	W	T	F	S	S
2 Apr–28 Oct	10:30–5	M	T	W	T	F	S	S
29 Oct–4 Nov	11–4	M	T	W	T	F	S	S
10 Nov–23 Dec	11–4	·	·	·	·	·	S	S
27 Dec–31 Dec	11–4	M	·	·	T	F	S	S

Open Bank Holiday Mondays. Estate walks open daily all year, 9 to 6 (except for some Thursdays, November to end December).

Burial mound at Sutton Hoo, Suffolk

Theatre Royal, Bury St Edmunds

Westgate Street, Bury St Edmunds,
Suffolk IP33 1QR

Map ③ I7   🏛 | 1974 |

Getting here: 155:TL856637. In Bury St
Edmunds. **Foot**: easily accessible from town
centre. **Train**: Bury St Edmunds ¾ mile.
Road: on Westgate Street on south side
of A134 from Sudbury (one-way system).
Parking: free on road and short-term parking
(charges including members) nearby.

Finding out more: 01284 769505 or
theatreroyal@nationaltrust.org.uk

Theatre Royal, Bury St Edmunds		M	T	W	T	F	S	S
31 Jan–15 May	2–4	·	T	·	T	·	·	·
4 Feb–13 May	10:30–1	·	·	·	·	·	S	S
16 May–29 Jul	10–5	·	·	W	T	F	S	S
5 Aug–18 Aug	10–5	·	·	W	T	F	S	S
21 Aug–22 Nov	2–4	·	T	·	T	·	·	·
25 Aug–18 Nov	10:30–1	·	·	·	·	·	S	S

Closed 6 and 7 June, plus 11 August. Please visit website or
telephone 01284 769505 for more details.

The stage at the Theatre Royal, Suffolk

This Grade I listed theatre is one of the
country's most significant theatre buildings
and the only surviving Regency playhouse in
Britain. From May until August actors bring the
whole theatre to life. For the rest of the year,
discover the theatre through the open-doors
season or performances.

Exploring   – Booking available May to
August for actor-led tours.
– Free-flow visits available as
well as tours.
– For programme of period and
contemporary productions
please visit website.

Eating and shopping: gifts and souvenirs on
sale. Light snacks available in the Greene Room.

Making the most of your day: new this year
– during summer you can meet some of the
characters who played a part in the theatre
through the years, as they guide you through
the playhouse's story.

Whipsnade Tree Cathedral

Whipsnade, Dunstable, Bedfordshire LU6 2LL

Map ③ E8   ♿ | 1960 |

This incredible tree cathedral was created
after the First World War in a spirit of 'faith,
hope and reconciliation'. **Note**: owned by
the National Trust and administered by the
Trustees of Whipsnade Tree Cathedral.
An annual service is held on the second
Sunday in June.

Getting here: 165/166:TL008180. 4 miles south
of Dunstable, off B4540 (signposted). Free
parking (spaces limited).

Finding out more: 01582 872406 or
whipsnadetc@nationaltrust.org.uk.
Trustees c/o Chapel Farm, Whipsnade,
Dunstable, Bedfordshire LU6 2LL

Whipsnade Tree Cathedral

Car park: 1 January to 26 March, locked at 5; 27 March
to 30 October, locked at 7; 31 October to 31 December,
locked at 5.

Wicken Fen National Nature Reserve

Lode Lane, Wicken, Ely,
Cambridgeshire CB7 5XP

Map ③ G6 🏠🏕️♿👶🍽️ 1899

Wicken Fen is Britain's oldest nature reserve and one of Europe's most important wetlands. It supports some amazing wildlife, including more than 8,000 species of plants, birds and dragonflies. The raised boardwalk and lush grass droves allow easy access to a lost landscape of flowering meadows, sedge and reedbeds, where you may see rarities such as hen harriers, water voles and bitterns. The Wicken Fen Vision, an ambitious landscape-scale conservation project, is opening up new areas of land to explore. Our grazing herds of Highland cattle and Konik ponies are helping to create a diverse range of new habitats.

Exploring   –   See the last working windpump in the fens.
  –   Walk through this unique fenland wilderness and look for wildlife.
  –   Enjoy an open boat trip along Wicken Lode.

Exploring   –   Spot spectacular harriers hunting over the sedge fields at dusk.
  –   Explore these ancient fens on flat and easy cycle routes.

Eating and shopping: our shop specialises in local crafts and books on wildlife. Try delicious homemade soup or 'Fen Docky'. Reward yourself after your walk or bike ride with some delicious cake.

Making the most of your day: family events such as pond-dipping all year; guided boat trips; cycle hire; walking trails with nine wildlife observation hides. On summer weekends, visit Fen Cottage and the Dragonfly Centre. **Dogs**: welcome on leads on the reserve and in the visitor centre.

Access for all: 🅿️ 🚻♿🚼♿🖼️ 🅰️ 📷 🔆 🅰️
Building ♿🚶 Grounds ♿🚶

Getting here: 154:TL563705. 3 miles west of Soham. **Cycle**: NCN11 from Ely; Lodes Way from Anglesey Abbey and local villages. **Train**: Ely 9 miles. **Road**: south of Wicken (A1123), 3 miles west of Soham (A142), 9 miles south of Ely, 17 miles north-east of Cambridge via A10. **Parking**: 120 yards (£2 for non-members).

Finding out more: 01353 720274 or
wickenfen@nationaltrust.org.uk

Wicken Fen		M	T	W	T	F	S	S
Reserve, visitor centre and shop								
Open all year	10–5	M	T	W	T	F	S	S
Café								
1 Jan–12 Feb	10–4:30	·	·	W	T	F	S	S
13 Feb–4 Nov	10–5	M	T	W	T	F	S	S
7 Nov–30 Dec	10–4:30	·	·	W	T	F	S	S
31 Dec	10–4:30	M	·	·	·	·	·	·
Fen Cottage								
24 Mar–22 Jul	2–5	·	·	·	·	·	S	S
28 Mar–18 Jul	11–3	·	·	W	·	·	·	·
25 Jul–29 Aug	11–5	·	·	W	T	F	S	S
1 Sep–4 Nov	2–5	·	·	·	·	·	S	S
Cycle hire								
31 Mar–4 Nov	10–5	·	·	·	·	·	S	S

Closed 25 December. Access on and off the reserve available
dawn to dusk. Visitor centre closes dusk in winter. Some
paths may be closed in very wet conditions. Fen Cottage
also open Bank Holiday Mondays. Cycle hire: last hire 3:30;
open every day during Cambridgeshire school holidays
March to November.

Willington Dovecote and Stables

Willington, Church End, near Bedford,
Bedfordshire MK44 3PX

Map ③ F7   1914

Enjoy the tranquil setting of these outstanding
Tudor stone-built dovecote and stable
buildings, built for Henry VIII's 1541 visit.
Note: no toilet.

Access for all: 🧏 Dovecote 🦽
Stables 🦽🦽 Grounds 🦽🦽

Getting here: 153:TL107499. In Willington
village, off the A603.

Finding out more: 01480 301494 or
willingtondovecote@nationaltrust.org.uk

Willington Dovecote and Stables

Open space accessible all year. Dovecote and stables open
last Sunday afternoon of the month April to September,
1 to 5. Admission to buildings also by appointment with
the Voluntary Custodian, Mrs J. Endersby, 21 Chapel Lane,
Willington MK44 3QG (01234 838278).

Wimpole Estate

Arrington, Royston, Cambridgeshire SG8 0BW

Map ③ G7   1976

'**What a great asset to the National Trust – it's
a wonderful property.'**
Mr P. Weaving, Maldon

A unique working estate still guided by the
seasons, with an impressive mansion at its
heart. Uncover the stories of the people who
shaped Wimpole, soak up the atmosphere,
take in the spectacular views and find your own
special place. Explore the hall, where intimate
rooms contrast with beautiful Georgian
interiors. Stroll through the pleasure grounds
to the walled garden, bursting with seasonal
produce and glorious herbaceous borders. At
Home Farm, contrast the traditional farmyard
with the noisy modern piggery and cattle
sheds. Ask our stockman about our rare breeds
and learn more about your food and our
farming. **Note**: half-price entry to Home Farm
for members (under-threes free).

The chapel at Wimpole Hall, Cambridgeshire

Exploring
- Explore the basement corridor to glimpse life below stairs.
- Get some gardening advice from our knowledgeable gardeners.
- Walk under the gasolier in the Yellow Drawing Room.
- Stroll to the serpentine lakes or through the shady woodland.
- See tiny piglets – usually trying to escape from their pigsties!
- Check out the ducks and chickens, help collect their eggs.

Eating and shopping: enjoy delicious dishes made with produce from our walled garden and Home Farm in the Stable Café. Buy local pottery, plants, toys, gifts, Wimpole rare-breed meat and free-range eggs! Pick up a good read in the second-hand bookshop.

Making the most of your day: daily farm activities, free family trails and Tracker Packs, living history days, open-air theatre, bat and wildlife walks, monthly seasonal market, craft fair, Christmas events. **Dogs**: welcome on leads in the park.

Access for all: 🅿️ 🔧 🔊 🔉 🔈 ✏️ 📷 📺 📏 🖼️
Hall 🔧🔊 Farm 🔧🔊 Gardens 🔧➡️🔧🔊

Getting here: 154:TL336510. 6 miles north of Royston. **Foot**: Wimpole Way from Cambridge. **Bus**: alight Arrington (1 mile) or Orwell (2 miles). **Train**: Shepreth 5 miles. Taxi service from Royston 8 miles. **Road**: 8 miles south-west of Cambridge (A603), 6 miles north of Royston (A1198). Entrance via A603. **Parking**: 275 yards, £2 (non-members).

Finding out more: 01223 206000 or wimpolehall@nationaltrust.org.uk

Wimpole Estate		M	T	W	T	F	S	S
Hall								
11 Feb–4 Nov*	11–5	M	T	W	T	·	S	S
Home Farm								
1 Jan–5 Feb	11–4	·	·	·	·	·	S	S
11 Feb–4 Nov	10:30–5	M	T	W	T	F	S	S
10 Nov–23 Dec	11–4	·	·	·	·	·	S	S
Garden, restaurant and shop								
1 Jan–8 Feb	11–4	M	T	W	·	·	S	S
11 Feb–4 Nov	10:30–5	M	T	W	T	F	S	S
5 Nov–24 Dec	11–4	M	T	W	·	·	S	S
Park								
Open all year	Dawn–dusk	M	T	W	T	F	S	S

Home Farm, garden, restaurant and shops: 1 to 4 January and 27 to 31 December, open daily, 11 to 4. Stable shop and café: open 26 December, 11 to 4. Bookshop open same days as shop but times may vary.

Home Farm sheep graze peacefully in front of Wimpole Hall, on the Wimpole Estate, in Cambridgeshire

Entry is still possible at most places up to 30 minutes before closing

Midlands

Why not lose yourself among the magnificent yew topiary at Packwood House?

Outdoors in the Midlands

Above:
looking down from the escarpment, Wenlock Edge at Hill Top, Shropshire

Situated in the very heart of England, the Midlands offers a huge diversity of countryside to explore and enjoy. There is something for everyone, from the dramatic landscapes of the Peak District, with its deep grassland gorges, soaring limestone cliffs and tumbling streams, to the sweeping hills of Shropshire and panoramic views from the Clent Hills – just 12 miles from the city of Birmingham.

Iconic landscapes in the Peak District
We care for about 15,000 hectares (37,000 acres) of land within the Peak District National Park, so there is plenty of this iconic landscape to discover. Challenge yourself with a brisk walk to the top of Mam Tor, where you'll be rewarded by a truly amazing view, or enjoy a leisurely stroll around the picturesque White Peak Estate.

The Trust has joined forces with the RSPB to manage the Eastern Moors – a stunning upland on the outskirts of Sheffield, which is a major gateway to the Peak District National Park. Covering almost ten square miles, the area comprises five moors: Clod Hall, Leash Fen, Ramsley Moor, Big Moor and Totley Moss. The popular walking and climbing areas of Curbar, Froggatt and Birchen Edges also fall within the Eastern Moors.

Near to the Peak District are the Staffordshire moorlands, including the lowland heath of Downs Bank, near Stone, where cattle graze the heathland.

Kinver Edge, also in Staffordshire, has a fascinating history and dramatic views towards Worcestershire and the Malvern Hills. The nearby Rock Houses tea-room provides well-earned refreshments after a relaxing walk.

Enjoy landscaped woodlands at the Dudmaston Estate in Shropshire, where there are miles of paths to explore, and discover the south Shropshire countryside. Alternatively, a litte further north, near Shrewsbury, you can enjoy a peaceful walk through the dappled woodland at Attingham Park.

Rare and special fauna

Whether you like a long ramble, a brisk walk or gentle stroll there are endless opportunities. The Long Mynd (Long Mountain) in Shropshire, a Site of Special Scientific Interest, offers excellent walking, riding and cycling. An ancient track, the Portway, extends for ten miles and is home to a variety of flora and fauna, including an increasing number of ground-nesting birds– such as snipe, curlew and red grouse.

Wenlock Edge is another rare and special landscape that stretches 19 miles through Shropshire. This thickly wooded limestone escarpment offers panoramic views, historic quarries, limekilns as well as rare flowers. There are several varieties of orchids to spot, such as the rare bee orchid, as well as a huge variety of birds and insects – including the dingy skipper butterfly.

Clockwise from top right: Dovedale, on the South Peak Estate, Derbyshire. Mam Tor, Derbyshire. The Long Mynd, Shropshire

The ancient woodland at Hawksmoor Nature Reserve in the Churnet Valley is an excellent place to spot green woodpeckers, spotted flycatchers and ravens. The wild flowers and archaeology of Gibridding Wood at Hawksmoor are so special that they have attracted artists and photographers for many years.

Kinder Scout is an iconic part of the Peak District in Derbyshire, with a dramatic landscape that is home to several upland breeding birds. At Dovedale in Derbyshire, the flower-rich grasslands support rare plants, including Jacob's ladder, and many invertebrates live in the large areas of woodland. Look hard enough, and you might even find beetles which have become nationally scarce.

The park at Calke Abbey in Derbyshire is home to some of the oldest trees in Europe, including a 1,000-year-old oak tree affectionately known as 'the old man of Calke'. Even the decaying wood of the parkland trees plays a valuable role here, providing a home to several endangered species of beetles.

Left:
Wilderhope Manor Farm, Wenlock Edge, Shropshire
Right:
enjoying the parkland at Clumber Park, Nottinghamshire

Fresh air on your doorstep

For great activities and lots to see both indoors and out, our historic houses cannot be beaten. But remember our parklands are open all year round, so are perfect for the autumn and winter months.

Hardwick Hall in Derbyshire offers beautifully preserved gardens in a series of courtyards, and a vast parkland, with circular walks and trails, where you can spot a variety of wildlife. In the stableyard, we are transforming a collection of estate buildings into brand new visitor facilities, including a shop, restaurant and reception, due to be completed this year.

For family adventure, look no further than Calke Abbey in Derbyshire, which offers 'I spy' sheets and Tracker Packs to keep the children entertained. There's also fun to be had in Squirt the Stallion's stables throughout the year.

In Herefordshire, tuck into the award-winning local food produced on the Brockhampton Estate after enjoying a walk through the traditionally farmed landscape – where there are miles of orchards, woodlands and pathways to explore.

The parkland at Croft Castle in Herefordshire is open throughout the year. It offers a feast for the eyes as the seasons change, as well as a feast for the senses in the tea-room, which serves a wide range of local produce.

At Croome in Worcestershire, take a gentle stroll to the outer eye-catchers and see James Wyatt's and Robert Adam's designs for these follies in their former 18th-century splendour. On certain days you can climb to the top of the Panorama Tower and take in the stunning Worcestershire countryside. An experience not to be missed.

Why not try...?

Kite-flying in Calke Abbey's park
Grab your kite and head for the parkland at Calke Abbey in Derbyshire. The vast park is an ideal spot to catch the wind and watch your kite as it flies majestically through the sky.

A picnic at Belton House
Get together with friends and family and enjoy a picnic in the grounds of Belton House in Lincolnshire. Throw down a rug, unwrap the sandwiches and sit and watch the world go by.

Geocaching in the Clent Hills
Become an adventure seeker and try out geocaching in the Clent Hills in Worcestershire. But be warned, this high-tech treasure hunt, where you search for containers using GPS, is highly addictive.

Camping in the Peak District
Get back to basics and have a camping holiday in Derbyshire's Peak District this year. The Trust runs a campsite at Upper Booth Farm in Edale – perfect for enjoying the Peak District's spectacular scenery and getting away from it all.

Walking at Hanbury Hall
Pull on your walking boots and enjoy a walk at Hanbury Hall and Gardens in Worcestershire. There are routes to suit all abilities and you can take in the countryside and wildlife while you ramble.

Cycling at Clumber Park
There are more than 20 miles of cycle routes to explore at Clumber Park in Nottinghamshire, with the chance to take in spectacular scenery and amazing wildlife on the way. Bicycles are available to hire, including those suitable for children.

Attingham Park

Atcham, Shrewsbury, Shropshire SY4 4TP

Map (4) H4   1947

Attingham Park, built for the 1st Lord Berwick in 1785, was owned by the same family for over 160 years. As their fortunes rose and fell, they proved themselves to be spenders, savers and saviours. Highlights include the atmospheric dining room, set for an evening banquet, and the contrasting decoration of the delicate feminine Boudoir with the rich, opulent textiles of the masculine Octagon Room. Outside, the walled garden and many park walks offer further delights. The mansion, set in beautiful parkland and designed to impress, is at the heart of this great estate between Shrewsbury and the River Severn. **Note**: major roofing project – watch the work to the Nash staircase and picture gallery.

Exploring
- Enjoy 'Mansion Regency Wednesdays' – all room guides in costume.
- Experience exclusive 1930s afternoon tea in the mansion's Lady B's.
- 'House of Beasts' – major contemporary art exhibition to July.
- Witness the continuing mansion transformation through the Attingham Re-discovered project.
- Enjoy something new each season with the walled garden restoration.
- Make the most of park walks on beautiful summer evenings.

Eating and shopping: the Carriage House Café and Stables shop are open daily all year. On days that the mansion is open, visit the Mansion tea-room or indulge in our exclusive 1930s afternoon tea in the heart of the mansion in Lady B's.

The picture gallery at Attingham Park, Shropshire: so much to see and enjoy for every age

Making the most of your day: witness ongoing developments in the mansion and walled garden. Family trails throughout local school holidays. Extensive all-year-round events programme. Follow us on YouTube and Twitter. **Dogs**: welcome on leads in deer park and near mansion. Identified off-lead areas.

Access for all: 🅿️♿🚻♿♿📷🦽⚫🅿
Mansion ♿⬆♿
Shop, bookshop and café ♿♿
Grounds ♿➡♿♿

Getting here: 126:SJ550099. In Atcham village. **Foot**: ½ mile along park road from main drive. **Bus**: Shrewsbury to Telford. **Train**: Shrewsbury 5 miles. **Road**: on B4380, 4 miles southeast of Shrewsbury. **Parking**: free, 25 yards approximately from visitor reception.

Finding out more: 01743 708123 (Infoline). 01743 708162 or attingham@nationaltrust.org.uk

Attingham Park		M	T	W	T	F	S	S
Park, walled garden, café, shop, bookshop and playground*								
Open all year	9–7	M	T	W	T	F	S	S
Mansion and mansion tea-room**								
10 Mar–4 Nov	11–5:30	M	T	W	T	F	S	S
Lady B's Afternoon Tea in the mansion								
10 Mar–4 Nov	1–4	M	T	W	T	F	S	S
8 Dec–9 Dec	11:30–3	·	·	·	·	·	S	S
15 Dec–23 Dec	11:30–3	M	T	W	T	F	S	S
Mansion tours and mansion tea-room**								
7 Jan–4 Mar	11–2	·	·	·	·	·	S	S
10 Nov–25 Nov	11–2	·	·	·	·	·	S	S
Mansion and mansion tea-room**								
8 Dec–9 Dec	11–4	·	·	·	·	·	S	S
15 Dec–23 Dec	11–4	M	T	W	T	F	S	S

*Park, walled garden, café, shop, bookshop, playground: January, February, November, December close 5 or dusk if earlier; March, April, October, close 6. **Mansion: tours only 11 to 12:30, free-flow from 12:30; last admission one hour before closing. Bank Holiday weekends: free-flow from 11. ***Mansion tea-room: open 10:30 to 4:30. Mansion Butler's Pantry shop: 10 March to 4 November open daily, 12:30 to 4:30. Mansion winter tours: 12, tour bookable (01743 708170, Monday to Friday). Frost Fair: 30 November to 2 December. Snowdrop walk evenings: 10 to 12 February. Closed 25 December.

Attingham Park Estate: Cronkhill

near Atcham, Shrewsbury, Shropshire SY5 6JP

Map ④ H5 ⟨🏠⟩ ⟨✿⟩ 1947

Delightful Italianate villa designed by Regency architect John Nash. Stands proudly on a hillside with views across the Attingham Estate. **Note**: property contents belong to the tenants.

Access for all: 🅿️🦽 Building ♿
Grounds 🦽♿➡

Getting here: 126:SJ535083. From Attingham Park take road to Cross Houses; Cronkhill is located on the right-hand side.

Finding out more: 01743 708162 or cronkhill@nationaltrust.org.uk

Attingham Park Estate: Cronkhill		M	T	W	T	F	S	S
27 Apr–29 Apr	11–4	·	·	·	·	F	·	S
22 Jun–24 Jun	11–4	·	·	·	·	F	·	S
28 Sep–30 Sep	11–4	·	·	·	·	F	·	S

Cronkhill, Shropshire: John Nash Regency villa

The atmospheric Baddesley Clinton in Warwickshire has been a sanctuary since the 15th century

Baddesley Clinton

Rising Lane, Baddesley Clinton,
Warwickshire B93 0DQ

Map ④ K6    1980

From refuge to haven, this atmospheric moated house has been a sanctuary since the 15th century, hiding persecuted Catholics in its three priest holes, and was home to the Ferrers family for 500 years. The peaceful gardens include fish pools, romantic lake and walled garden filled with colours for every season – from daffodils in spring, to the magnificent dahlia border in the autumn.

Exploring – Soak up the feel of this well-loved home.
– Relax in the gardens and stroll along the lakeside walk.
– Stretch your legs on our estate walks.
– Murder most foul, investigate the evidence in the library.
– Browse for bargains in the second-hand bookshop.
– Family trails in the house – become a priest hunter.

Eating and shopping: try our homemade bread – straight from the oven. Savour seasonal food, using produce from our own vegetable garden. Our varied menu will delight all diners. Locally sourced products and plants available in the shop.

Making the most of your day: set the scene with an introductory talk. Brunch lectures in the restaurant in spring and autumn. Family events, living history and outdoor theatre. **Dogs**: welcome on leads in the car park and on public footpaths across the estate.

Access for all: [icons]
Building [icons] **Grounds** [icons]

Getting here: 139:SP199723. 7½ miles north-west of Warwick. **Foot**: Heart of England Way crosses property. **Train**: Lapworth, 1½ miles; Birmingham International 9 miles. **Road**: ¾ mile west of A4141 Warwick to Birmingham road, 6 miles south of M42 exit 5; 15 miles south-east of central Birmingham. **Parking**: free, 100 yards.

Finding out more: 01564 783294 or baddesleyclinton@nationaltrust.org.uk

Baddesley Clinton		M	T	W	T	F	S	S
House, grounds, shop and restaurant								
1 Jan–10 Feb	12–4	M	T	W	T	F	S	S
11 Feb–4 Nov	11–5	M	T	W	T	F	S	S
5 Nov–31 Dec	12–4	M	T	W	T	F	S	S

Admission to house by timed ticket on Bank Holidays and busy days – tickets available from reception (not bookable). Closed 25 December.

Belton House

Belton House, Grantham,
Lincolnshire NG32 2LS

Map ③ E4  1984

'Superb scenery, whatever the season! There really is something for everyone at Belton, both indoors and out!'
Gordon Lockwood, Manthorpe, near Grantham

The 'perfect' English country-house estate, set in delightful gardens and its own magnificent deer park, Belton was designed to impress. Built in the late 17th-century for 'Young' Sir John Brownlow, its honey-coloured symmetry, opulent décor, fine furnishings, stunning silverware and gorgeous gardens provided the perfect setting for lavish hospitality and entertainment on a grand scale. Each generation left its mark, employing top designers, craftsmen and portrait painters. Did they achieve perfection? Judge for yourself as you explore and discover all that Belton has to offer. **Note**: we are extending and developing our gift and coffee shop facilities.

Exploring
- Explore magnificent parkland and discover a wealth of wildlife.
- Enjoy the seasonal delights of the garden and tranquil lakeshore.
- Burn off steam in Lincolnshire's largest adventure playground.
- Enjoy Discovery Centre family activities (weekends/holidays, April to October).
- Explore 'below stairs' – daily tours during main season (timed tickets).
- Enjoy garden tours, walks with a ranger, family fun trails.

Eating and shopping: find year-round inspiration in our plant and garden shop. Enjoy local, seasonal dishes in our restaurant – our speciality Belton venison casserole features on the winter menu. Visit our gift shop for seasonal inspiration and perfect presents.

Making the most of your day: varied events programme, Easter and Hallowe'en trails, 'Paint the Garden', open-air theatre, living history weekends, Food Fayre, Christmas craft market, Wildlife Explorers' Club (monthly). **Dogs**: on leads in parkland and stableyard only.

Belton House, Lincolnshire: this 'perfect' English country house and estate were designed to impress

Please display current sticker for free parking (and show card when asked)

Access for all:
House Grounds

Getting here: 130:SK930395. 3 miles
north-east of Grantham. **Bus**: Grantham
to Lincoln (passing close to Grantham ⮆).
Train: Grantham 3 miles. **Road**: on A607
Grantham to Lincoln road, signposted from
A1. **Parking**: free, 250 yards. Please note: all
visitors (including members) must obtain a
ticket from visitor reception.

Finding out more: 01476 566116 or
belton@nationaltrust.org.uk

Belton House		M	T	W	T	F	S	S
House								
3 Mar–11 Mar	12:30–4	·	·	·	·	·	S	S
14 Mar–4 Nov	12:30–5	·	·	W	T	F	S	S
Basement								
3 Mar–4 Nov	11–3	M	T	W	T	F	S	S
5 Nov–31 Dec	11–2	M	T	W	T	F	S	S
Garden, park, restaurant and shop								
1 Jan	10:30–4	·	·	·	·	·	·	S
4 Feb–26 Feb	10:30–4	·	·	·	·	·	S	S
3 Mar–4 Nov	10:30–5:30	M	T	W	T	F	S	S
5 Nov–31 Dec	10:30–4	M	T	W	T	F	S	S
Adventure playground								
3 Mar–4 Nov	10:30–5:30	M	T	W	T	F	S	S

Open Bank Holiday Mondays (March to October). House
conservation talks 11:30 selected days (March to October).
House open for free-flow from 12:30. Guided tours replace
free-flow some days. Timed tickets likely at busy times.
Basement entrance by guided tour only (every 15 minutes).
Below stairs area closes occasionally for maintenance.
Bellmount Woods: open daily, access from separate car park.
Bellmount Tower and Boathouse open occasionally (contact
Belton for details). Please note: Whole property closed
25 December. Property likely to close early in poor weather
or light conditions and on Spitfire Prom Concert Day
(date on website).

Benthall Hall

Broseley, Shropshire TF12 5RX

Map ④ I5   1958

This fine stone house situated near the River
Severn has mullioned and transomed windows,
a stunning interior with carved oak staircase,
decorated plaster ceilings and oak panelling.
There is an intimate and carefully restored
plantsman's garden, old kitchen garden and
interesting Restoration church.

The attractive Benthall Hall in Shropshire

Note: Benthall Hall is the home of Edward and
Sally Benthall.

Exploring – Relax in the
picturesque gardens.
– Enjoy a walk along the
woodland edge.
– Discover the George Maw tiles
hidden under the hall floor.
– Find the priest's hole from the
period of Charles II.

Making the most of your day: guided walks
and tours of the Hall available by arrangement.
There is a wonderful crocus display in the spring.
Dogs: in the parkland and woodland only.

Access for all:
Building Grounds

Getting here: 127:SJ658025. 1 mile south-west
of Ironbridge. **Bus**: services from Telford and
Wellington to Much Wenlock. **Train**: Telford
Central 7½ miles. **Road**: 1 mile north-west of
Broseley (B4375), 4 miles north-east of Much
Wenlock, 1 mile south-west of Ironbridge.
Parking: free, 100 yards. Space for one
coach only.

Finding out more: 01952 882159 or
benthall@nationaltrust.org.uk

Benthall Hall		M	T	W	T	F	S	S
House*								
4 Feb–26 Feb	1–4	·	·	·	·	·	S	S
House								
3 Mar–31 Oct	1–5	·	T	W	·	·	S	S
Garden								
4 Feb–26 Feb	12–4:30	·	·	·	·	·	S	S
3 Mar–31 Oct	12–5:30	·	T	W	·	·	S	S

*Ground floor only open. Open Good Friday and Bank
Holiday Mondays. Closes dusk if earlier.

www.nationaltrust.org.uk

Berrington Hall

near Leominster, Herefordshire HR6 0DW

Map ④ H6 🏚️❀♣🏠⛱️ 1957

Created as the perfect house in the perfect setting, Berrington has many secrets to uncover. In this, one of Henry Holland's first houses, you can explore the family rooms and see how the servants moved around the house unseen by the family and guests. Find out what happened to William Kemp, Lord Cawley's butler, discover the anguish of a grieving mother during the First World War, or join a below-stairs tour to see if you would have liked to have been a servant at Berrington.

Making the most of your day: family events throughout the year, as well as house quizzes and a play area. Costume collection on view by appointment. Waymarked estate walks. **Dogs**: on leads on the estate and in parts of the garden.

Access for all: P♿ D♿ WC ♿ ♿ ⬛ VT ♿ ::
Building ♿⬛ Grounds ♿⬛➡️⬛

Getting here: 137:SO510637. 3 miles north of Leominster. **Bus**: Ludlow to Hereford (passing close Ludlow ⚏ and Leominster), alight Luston, 2 miles. **Train**: Leominster 4 miles. **Road**: 7 miles south of Ludlow on west side of A49. **Parking**: free, 30 yards to visitor reception. Mobile homes: telephone for details.

Finding out more: 01568 615721 or berrington@nationaltrust.org.uk

Berrington Hall, Herefordshire: one of 'Capability' Brown's final landscapes

Exploring
– Walk through one of 'Capability' Brown's final landscapes.
– Join a garden, parkland or architecture tour.
– Learn more about the servants on a below-stairs tour.
– Relax in the gardens, including traditional Herefordshire orchards.
– Get creative in our den-building area.
– See a display of items from the Wade Costume Collection.

Eating and shopping: browse in the shop for gifts, local products and preserves made from our own fruit. Relax in the tea-room over a light lunch, afternoon tea or a cake made by our baker.

Berrington Hall		M	T	W	T	F	S	S
Below stairs, gardens, park, tea-room and shop								
11 Feb–19 Feb	10–4	M	T	W	T	F	S	S
3 Mar–4 Nov	10–5	M	T	W	T	F	S	S
10 Nov–16 Dec	10–4	·	·	·	·	·	S	S
Mansion tours								
11 Feb–19 Feb	10:30–1	M	T	W	T	F	S	S
3 Mar–4 Nov	10:30–1	M	T	W	T	F	S	S
10 Nov–16 Dec	10:30–1	·	·	·	·	·	S	S
Mansion								
11 Feb–19 Feb	1–4	M	T	W	T	F	S	S
3 Mar–4 Nov	1–5	M	T	W	T	F	S	S
10 Nov–16 Dec	1–4	·	·	·	·	·	S	S
Mansion, below stairs, garden, park, tea-room and shop								
17 Dec–23 Dec	10–4	M	T	W	T	F	S	S

Below stairs, gardens, park, tea-room and shop: 28 January to 26 February, open weekends 10 to 4; 27 to 31 December, open daily 10 to 4. House: ground floor only 10 November to 23 December. Shop: opens 11. 25 April, Red Cross event, charge (including members), telephone for details.

Biddulph Grange Garden

Grange Road, Biddulph, Staffordshire ST8 7SD

Map ④ J2 ❖ 1988

Amazing Victorian garden created by Darwin contemporary, James Bateman, as an extension of his beliefs and scientific interests. His plant collection comes from all over the world – a visit takes you on a global journey from an Italian terrace to an Egyptian pyramid, via a Himalayan glen and Chinese-inspired garden. Discover the fabulous collection of rhododendrons, dahlia walk and the oldest surviving golden larch in Britain, brought from China by the great plant hunter Robert Fortune. Explore the Geological Gallery: as you travel through time the biblical story of creation unfolds against a backdrop of science. A garden for all seasons. **Note:** many steps throughout the garden and from the car park.

Exploring
- Take a look at the kitchen garden.
- Wander along the new Woodland Walk.
- Explore the hidden tunnels and pathways.

Exploring
- The unique Geological Gallery tells the story of creation.
- Relax by the lake.
- Exhibition and audio-visual room tell the garden's story.

Eating and shopping: taste local food, some freshly picked from our kitchen garden, in the tea-room. Browse the world-themed gift shop and plant centre.

Making the most of your day: talks, guided tours, events and children's trails throughout the year. Summer activities programme.

Access for all: P⅃ 🗾 🖳 ⠃
Building 🏬 Grounds 🏬

Getting here: 118:SJ895591. 1 mile north of Biddulph. **Bus:** from Congleton (passing Congleton ≋). **Train:** Congleton 2½ miles. **Road:** 3½ miles south-east of Congleton, 7 miles north of Stoke-on-Trent. Access from A527 (Tunstall to Congleton road). Entrance on Grange Road. **Parking:** free, 50 yards.

Finding out more: 01782 517999 or biddulphgrange@nationaltrust.org.uk

Biddulph Grange Garden		M	T	W	T	F	S	S
13 Feb–31 Mar	11–3:30	M	T	W	T	F	S	S
1 Apr–4 Nov	11–5:30	M	T	W	T	F	S	S
9 Nov–23 Dec	11–3:30	M	·	·	·	F	S	S

Open Bank Holiday Mondays. Closes dusk if earlier.

Travel all over the world at Biddulph Grange Garden, Staffordshire: an astonishing Victorian creation

Step back in time at the Birmingham Back to Backs and find out how ordinary people lived

Birmingham Back to Backs

55-63 Hurst Street/50-54 Inge Street, Birmingham, West Midlands B5 4TE

Map ④ J5 🏠 ♿ 🏠 ▼ 2004

An atmospheric glimpse into the lives of the ordinary people who helped make Birmingham an extraordinary city. On a fascinating guided tour, step back in time at Birmingham's last surviving court of back to backs: houses built literally back-to-back around a communal courtyard. Moving from the 1840s through to the 1970s, discover the lives of some of the former residents who crammed into these small houses to live and work. With fires alight in the grates, and sounds and smells from the past, experience an evocative and intimate insight into life at the Back to Backs. **Note**: visits by guided tour only (advance booking advised).

Exploring – The guided tour brings the houses and characters to life.
– Make yourself at home, warm up by the fire.
– Learn more in the thought-provoking exhibition.
– A programme of events brings Birmingham's diverse heritage to life.

Exploring – Find out about life with communal privies and wash-houses.
– Discover stories about the people who lived and worked here.

Eating and shopping: buy mementoes of your visit in our reception. Traditional 1930s sweetshop (not National Trust).

Making the most of your day: exciting year-round events programme. Ground-floor tour also available.

Access for all:
Building ♿ 🏠

Getting here: 139:SP071861. In the centre of Birmingham next to the Hippodrome Theatre.
Foot: within easy walking distance of bus and railway stations (follow signs for Hippodrome Theatre). **Cycle**: NCN5. **Bus**: services from Birmingham city centre. **Train**: Birmingham New Street ¼ mile. **Parking**: nearest in Arcadian Centre, Bromsgrove Street (not National Trust).

Finding out more: 0121 666 7671 (booking line). 0121 622 2442 or backtobacks@nationaltrust.org.uk

Birmingham Back to Backs		M	T	W	T	F	S	S
7 Feb–21 Dec	10–5	·	T	W	T	F	S	S

Admission by timed ticket and guided tour only, **booking essential**. Open Bank Holiday Mondays (but closed next day). **During term time property closed 10 to 1 on Tuesdays, Wednesdays and Thursdays for schools.** Last tour times vary in winter, telephone to check. **Closed September 1 to 7.**

Brockhampton Estate

Greenfields, Bringsty, near Bromyard,
Herefordshire WR6 5TB

Map ④ I7
🏠🕴🏯 1946

This beautiful medieval manor house,
surrounded by a moat, is entered via
a charming timber-framed gatehouse.
Experience the Great Hall where feasts and
celebrations have been held throughout
the centuries. Learn about the last owner
of Brockhampton, Colonel Lutley, who
bequeathed the entire 687-hectare (1,700-acre)
estate to the Trust in 1946. Enjoy the peace
and tranquillity as you sit by the moat in the
damson orchard. There are miles of walks
through the park and woodland, featuring
ancient trees and a rich variety of wildlife,
along with historic farming breeds.

Exploring   – Experience life as lived in
       a medieval moated
       manor house.
       – Follow the nature trail and
       spot wildlife from our
       bird-hide.
       – Discover new areas of
       the estate on our
       orienteering course.
       – Enjoy the stunning views from
       the parkland.
       – Have fun in the natural
       play area.
       – See the blossom in April, then
       pick damsons in September.

Eating and shopping: enjoy local produce
in the Old Apple Store tea-room and try
our delicious cakes made by estate tenants.
Browse for something unique in our Granary
shop and take home award-winning jams,
honey and beer from the estate. New
second-hand bookshop.

Making the most of your day: year-round
events and family activities including Living
History re-enactments, ranger-led walks and
a medieval Christmas. Guided tours most
weekends. Picnics welcome. **Dogs**: welcome on
leads in grounds, woods and parkland.

Access for all: 🅿♿♿♿♿♿♿🖼♿ ••
Building 🔼♿♿ Grounds ♿➡♿

Getting here: 149:SO682546. 2 miles east
of Bromyard. **Bus**: Worcester to Hereford
(passing Worcester Foregate Street ⇌ and
close Hereford ⇌). **Road**: on Worcester road
(A44); house reached by a narrow road through
1½ miles of woods and park. **Parking**: 50 yards
and 1½ miles.

Finding out more: 01885 488099 (Infoline).
01885 482077 or
brockhampton@nationaltrust.org.uk

Brockhampton Estate		M	T	W	T	F	S	S
Estate								
Open all year	10–5	M	T	W	T	F	S	S
Tea-room								
1 Jan–3 Jan	10–4	M	T	·	·	·	·	S
11 Feb–19 Feb	10–4:30	M	T	W	T	F	S	S
3 Mar–4 Nov	10–5	M	T	W	T	F	S	S
10 Nov–16 Dec	10–4:30	·	·	·	·	·	S	S
27 Dec–31 Dec	10–4:30	M	·	·	T	F	S	S
House, grounds and shop								
11 Feb–19 Feb	11–4:30	M	T	W	T	F	S	S
3 Mar–4 Nov	11–5	M	T	W	T	F	S	S
10 Nov–16 Dec	11–4	·	·	·	·	·	S	S

Tea-room: 7 January to 5 February open weekends,
10 to 4:30; 17 to 23 December open daily, 10 to 4:30.

Brockhampton Estate, Herefordshire: the Great Hall

Calke Abbey

Ticknall, Derby, Derbyshire DE73 7LE

Map ③ C4 🏠🐿️➕🌄❄️🌷
🐾🏚️🍴 1985

With peeling paintwork and overgrown courtyards Calke Abbey tells the story of the dramatic decline of a grand country-house estate. The house and stables are little restored, with many abandoned areas vividly portraying a period in the 20th-century when numerous country houses did not survive to tell their story. Discover the tales of an eccentric family who amassed a vast collection of hidden treasures. Visit the beautiful, yet faded, walled gardens and explore the orangery, auricula theatre and kitchen gardens. Escape into the ancient and fragile habitats of Calke Park and its National Nature Reserve. **Note:** all house and garden visitors require admission tickets (free for members).

Calke Abbey, Derbyshire: the 'unstately home'

Access for all: 🅿️♿🚻👁️🦻🔉📷📖📹‥
Building 🔼♿♿ Grounds 🔼♿➡️

Getting here: 128:SK367226. 10 miles south of Derby. **Bus:** Swadlincote, alight Ticknall, 1½-mile walk through park. **Train:** Derby 9½ miles; Burton-on-Trent 10 miles. **Road:** on A514 at Ticknall between Swadlincote and Melbourne. Access from M42/A42 exit 13 and A50 Derby South. Entry via Ticknall main entrance only. **Parking:** per person park admission for all visitors. 3.6-metre height restriction on archway.

Exploring — Discover Calke Abbey – the 'unstately home'.
— Follow the twists and turns of the Brewhouse Tunnel.
— Stroll in the beautiful walled garden and see the orangery.
— Explore Calke Park and its National Nature Reserve.
— Discover 'the old man of Calke', a 1,000-year-old oak.
— Have fun with Tracker Packs and our Discovery Trails.

Finding out more: 01332 863822 or calkeabbey@nationaltrust.org.uk

Eating and shopping: shop and restaurant open all year. Enjoy local produce, including meat reared on the estate. The shop is full of wonderful gifts; buy local food in the Pantry. Refreshments available from the coffee shop kiosk at peak times.

Making the most of your day: enjoy the West Wing conservation tour. Discover our family events programme, available throughout the year. Tracker Packs, Discovery Trails and family activities in Squirt's Stable, weekends March to October. **Dogs:** welcome on leads in park and stables. Assistance dogs only in garden area.

Calke Abbey		M	T	W	T	F	S	S
Calke Park National Nature Reserve								
Open all year	7:30–7:30	M	T	W	T	F	S	S
House								
25 Feb–4 Nov	11–5	M	T	W	·	·	S	S
Themed house tours								
1 Mar–2 Nov	11–4	·	·	·	T	F	·	·
Garden and stables								
25 Feb–4 Nov	11–5	M	T	W	T	F	S	S
Restaurant and shop								
Open all year	10:30–5	M	T	W	T	F	S	S

House: Saturday to Wednesday, 11 to 12, entry by guided conservation tour (places limited); house opens fully at 12:30. House admission by timed ticket for all visitors (including members); delays may occur at peak times. Open for themed tours Thursday and Friday. Restaurant and shop: closed 25 December; January, February, November and December closes 4. Calke Park closes 7:30 or dusk if earlier.

Members may have to pay on special events days

Canons Ashby

Daventry, Northamptonshire NN11 3SD

Map ③ D7 🏠 ✝ 🏛 ❀ 🌺 1981

Canons Ashby has been the Dryden family home since Elizabethan times and the family atmosphere remains today. Largely unaltered since 1710, stunning Jacobean plasterwork and tapestries in the grand rooms contrast with the domestic detail of the kitchen and servants' quarters. Canons Ashby is presented as seen through the eyes of Sir Henry Dryden, an eminent Victorian antiquarian. The atmospheric house is warmly welcoming, and the garden is restored to its delightful Victorian style. Strolling in the wider parkland offers a glimpse of the earlier medieval history, while the church explores the medieval story of the canons of Canons Ashby.

Exploring
- Enjoy the friendly home of the Dryden family.
- Explore the newly opened private apartment.
- Relax in the recently restored gardens.
- Discover acres of historic parkland.
- Follow a children's trail or grab a Tracker Pack.
- Enjoy the delights of the garden tea-room.

Eating and shopping: visit the new Victorian Stable shop for gifts and ideas for the home and garden. Sample delicious home-cooked treats in the tea-room and, in fine weather, enjoy the beautiful tea-garden. Why not discover a bargain in the second-hand bookshop?

Making the most of your day: many events throughout the year, including a 'step back in time' weekend, live music in the garden, guided walks, family fun activities, Christmas market and Victorian Family Christmas weekends.
Dogs: on leads in Home Paddock, car park and parkland only.

Access for all: 🅿️ ♿ ♿ ♿ ♿ 🏛 📷 📖 🍴 👓 🖼
Building 🏛 ♿ 🔄 Grounds 🏛 ♿ ➡️ 🔄

Getting here: 152:SP577506. In Canons Ashby village, 11 miles south of Daventry.
Foot: on Macmillan long-distance footpath.
Cycle: NCN70. **Train**: Banbury 10 miles.
Road: from M40 exit 11, M1 exit 16. M1 take A45 (Daventry) and at Weedon crossroads turn left onto A5, then follow brown signs.
Parking: 218 yards.

Finding out more: 01327 861900 or canonsashby@nationaltrust.org.uk

Canons Ashby		M	T	W	T	F	S	S
18 Feb–22 Feb*	12–4	M	T	W	·	·	S	S
25 Feb–11 Mar*	12–4	·	·	·	·	·	S	S
17 Mar–30 May**	11–5	M	T	W	·	·	S	S
1 Jun–31 Aug***	11–5	M	T	W	·	F	S	S
1 Sep–31 Oct**	11–5	M	T	W	·	·	S	S
3 Nov–16 Dec****	12–4	·	·	·	·	·	S	S

*House open for tours only. **17 March to 31 October: Taster Tours only before 1, house open for free-flow visits from 1.
***House open Fridays for tours only in June, July and August.
****House open, some weekends have special events, 15 and 16 December tours only. Open Good Friday, 11 to 5.

Canons Ashby, Northamptonshire: Dryden family home

Looking towards the Shropshire Hills in this Area of Outstanding Natural Beauty

Carding Mill Valley and the Shropshire Hills

Shropshire

Map ④ H5   🏛️ 🅿️ ⛵ 👣 ☕ 1965

Covering as much as 2,000 hectares (4,942 acres) of heather-covered hills with iconic views of the Shropshire Hills Area of Outstanding Natural Beauty. An important place for wildlife, geology, landscape and archaeology, with excellent visitor facilities and information in Carding Mill Valley.

Exploring
- Some of the best walking in the Marches.
- Take a picnic and sit, relax and enjoy Shropshire's food.
- Horse-riding and cycling routes across a variety of terrains.
- Join us for pond-dipping, birdwatching, volunteering and much more.

Eating and shopping: Chalet Pavilion tea-room serves excellent local food, including hot lunches, drinks and ice-cream. The shop next to the tea-room sells maps, guides and gifts.

Making the most of your day: year-round events programme and more than 50 walks and talks each year run by rangers. Use the shuttle bus to extend or enhance your walk. **Dogs**: under close control (grazing livestock).

Access for all: 🅿️ 📶 🚻 🔔 ♿ 🚶
Building ♿ Grounds ♿

Getting here: 137:SO443945. 15 miles south of Shrewsbury. **Foot**: many long-distance routes, including Jack Mytton Way and Shropshire Way. **Cycle**: 10 miles of off-road tracks and bridleways. **Bus**: Shrewsbury to Ludlow, alight Church Stretton, ½ mile. Shuttle bus weekends and Bank Holidays (Easter to October), plus shuttle to Stiperstones. **Train**: Church Stretton 1 mile. **Road**: west of Church Stretton Valley and A49; approached from Church Stretton or from Ratlinghope or Asterton. **Sat Nav**: SY6 6JG. **Parking**: 50 yards (pay and display). Open daily all year.

Finding out more: 01694 725000 or cardingmill@nationaltrust.org.uk. Chalet Pavilion, Carding Mill Valley, Church Stretton, Shropshire SY6 6JG

Carding Mill Valley		M	T	W	T	F	S	S
Countryside								
Open all year		M	T	W	T	F	S	S
Tea-room and shop*								
1 Jan–12 Feb	11–4	.	.	.	.	.	S	S
13 Feb–4 Nov	10–5	M	T	W	T	F	S	S
5 Nov–23 Dec	11–4	M	.	.	.	F	S	S
26 Dec–31 Dec	11–4	M	.	W	T	F	S	S

Toilet and information hut open 9 to 7 summer; 9 to 4:15 winter. *Shop opens 12 on weekdays. Tea-room and shop close dusk if earlier.

Charlecote Park

Wellesbourne, Warwick,
Warwickshire CV35 9ER

Map ④ K7  1946

Charlecote Park has been home to the Lucy
family since the 12th century. Their stories are
told throughout the house by their portraits,
the objects they collected from around the
world and the design influence they had on the
house and parkland. See how Mary Elizabeth
Lucy remodelled the house in Victorian
times. The gardens include a formal parterre,
woodland walk and the wider parkland
(inspired by 'Capability' Brown), which offers
walks with picturesque views across the River
Avon. A herd of fallow deer has been in the
park since Tudor times.

Exploring
 – Seasonal access to the wider parkland.
 – Bring a picnic to enjoy with your family and friends.
 – Enjoy one of our guided walks or talks.
 – Try your hand at a game of croquet.
 – Experience this 'Capability' Brown landscape all year round.

Exploring Charlecote Park in Warwickshire

Exploring
 – See the house festively decorated during weekends in December.

Eating and shopping: enjoy a range of hot
meals and light snacks – we use local produce
whenever possible in the restaurant. Look out
for our main shop and also the gatehouse shop
selling locally sourced produce.

Making the most of your day: year-round
programme of events. Plenty of outdoor
space for children to enjoy. Bring a picnic
with you and enjoy the scenery. Please note
there are gravel paths around the grounds.
Dogs: assistance dogs only.

Access for all: 🅿️🚌♿🚻🐕🔡🔉🎧📷🎦♿
♿♿ **Building** ♿♿♿ **Outbuildings** ♿♿♿
Grounds ♿➡️♿

Getting here: 151:SP263564. 1 mile west
of Wellesbourne, 5 miles east of Stratford-
upon-Avon. **Bus**: Leamington Spa to Stratford-
upon-Avon. **Train**: Stratford-upon-Avon,
5 miles; Warwick 6 miles; Leamington Spa
8 miles. **Road**: 6 miles south of Warwick on
north side of B4086. **Parking**: free, 300 yards.

Finding out more: 01789 470277 or
charlecotepark@nationaltrust.org.uk

Charlecote Park		M	T	W	T	F	S	S
Park, gardens and outbuildings								
Open all year	10:30–5:30	M	T	W	T	F	S	S
House								
11 Feb–28 Feb*	12–3:30	M	T	·	·	F	S	S
2 Mar–4 Nov*	11–4:30	M	T	·	·	F	S	S
10 Nov–23 Dec	12–3:30	·	·	·	·	·	S	S
Restaurant								
1 Jan–2 Mar	10:30–4	M	T	W	T	F	S	S
3 Mar–30 Oct	10:30–5	M	T	W	T	F	S	S
31 Oct–31 Dec	10:30–4	M	T	W	T	F	S	S
Shop and Gatehouse shop								
1 Jan–5 Feb*	10:30–4	·	·	·	·	·	S	S
11 Feb–4 Nov*	10:30–5	M	T	·	·	F	S	S
10 Nov–30 Dec	10:30–4	·	·	·	·	·	S	S

Closed 24 and 25 December. *House and shop: open
Thursdays in Warwickshire school holidays. Parts of the
ground floor only in February, November and December.
Park, garden, outbuildings: close 4 in January, November
and December. May close dusk if earlier. Admission by
timed tickets available from visitor reception during busy
times (not bookable).

Clent Hills

Romsley, Worcestershire

Map ④ J6   🏛️🚻♿ 1959

The Clent Hills, on the edge of Birmingham and the Black Country, offer a green oasis with panoramic views. **Note**: café (not National Trust) and toilets open Tuesday to Sunday (10 to 4) and Bank Holiday Mondays. Visit our website for events programme.

Access for all: 🅿️♿🧠👜➡️

Getting here: 139:SO938807 (Nimmings Wood car park). South-west of Birmingham, close to M5 (junction 4).

Finding out more: 01562 712822 or clenthills@nationaltrust.org.uk. Waseley Hills Office, Gannow Green Lane, Birmingham, West Midlands B45 9AT

Clent Hills	Open every day all year

Nimmings car park gates close at dusk.

Panoramic view at the Clent Hills, Worcestershire

Clumber Park

Worksop, Nottinghamshire S80 3AZ

Map ③ D2   🏠➕♿♿♿🍴 1946

This stunning park, with hints of a grand past, is a haven for wildlife. With 1,537 hectares (3,800 acres) of glorious parkland and gardens, Clumber has the space for you to explore and relax with family and friends all year round. Whether you enjoy walking, cycling or spotting wildlife, there's plenty to make a trip to Clumber your perfect day out. The mansion, which was home to the Dukes of Newcastle, no longer exists, but the Walled Kitchen Garden, chapel and pleasure ground are clues to the Park's grand past.

Exploring
- Explore the vast and picturesque parkland and gardens.
- Discover 20 miles of cycle routes through spectacular scenery.
- Go wild at our new Discovery Centre.
- Hang out on the climbing forest in the play park.
- Unearth tastes of the past in the Walled Kitchen Garden.
- Enjoy a night under the stars in our new campsite.

Eating and shopping: enjoy a snack, lunch or afternoon tea in our café or newly opened Barkers Restaurant, which offers a unique fine-dining experience. Browse through a treasure trove of toys, gifts and souvenirs, and search a wide selection of quality unusual plants.

Making the most of your day: year-round packed family events programme (visit www.nationaltrust.org.uk/clumberpark). Hands-on wildlife exhibitions and activities in the Discovery Centre. Family Tracker Packs. Cycle hire centre. **Dogs**: welcome throughout – on leads in Walled Kitchen Garden, pleasure ground and grazed areas.

Bird-spotting at Clumber Park, Nottinghamshire

Access for all: ♿🅿️🚾♿🔊📷🎫👁️🅰️
Chapel ♿🔊 Glasshouse ♿🔊
Grounds ♿➡️♿🔊

Getting here: 120:SK629752. 4½ miles south-east of Worksop. **Cycle**: NCN6. **Bus**: from Worksop to Ollerton, alight Carburton, ¾ mile. **Train**: Worksop 4½ miles; Retford 6½ miles. **Road**: 6½ miles south-west of Retford, 1 mile from A1/A57, 11 miles from M1 exit 30. **Parking**: throughout park. Main parking 200 yards from visitor facilities and 250 yards from Walled Kitchen Garden.

Finding out more: 01909 476592 or clumberpark@nationaltrust.org.uk

Clumber Park		M	T	W	T	F	S	S
Park								
Open all year	7–dusk	M	T	W	T	F	S	S
Walled Kitchen Garden								
25 Mar–30 Sep	10–5	M	T	W	T	F	S	S
17 Mar–24 Mar	10–4	M	T	W	T	F	S	S
1 Oct–28 Oct	10–4	M	T	W	T	F	S	S
Barkers Restaurant								
1 Jan–24 Mar	10–4	·	·	W	T	F	S	S
25 Mar–27 Oct	10–5	·	·	W	T	F	S	S
28 Oct–30 Dec	10–4	·	·	W	T	F	S	S
Visitor facilities*								
1 Jan–24 Mar	10–4	M	T	W	T	F	S	S
25 Mar–27 Oct	10–5	M	T	W	T	F	S	S
28 Oct–31 Dec	10–4	M	T	W	T	F	S	S

*Visitor facilities include: café, shop, plant sales, cycle hire, chapel, Discovery Centre and woodland play park. 25 March to 27 October: open weekends and Bank Holidays (all facilities open 10 to 6). Last hiring of cycles two hours before closing. Chapel open as visitor facilities except 12 January to 28 March, when closed for conservation cleaning. Park and all facilities closed 25 December.

Coughton Court

near Alcester, Warwickshire B49 5JA

Map ④ K6   🏛️➕♣️🎫 1946

Coughton has been home to the Throckmorton family for 600 years. Facing persecution for their Catholic faith, they were willing to risk everything. Follow the family on their journey from plotting to destroy Parliament to taking a seat within it, and explore a fascinating story through the 'family album' of portraits and Catholic treasures around the house. Coughton is still very much a family home with an intimate feel: in fact the Throckmorton family still live here. They created and manage the stunning gardens, which include a riverside walk, bog garden and beautiful display of roses in the walled garden. **Note**: entrance charge for the walled garden (including members).

Glorious Coughton Court, Warwickshire

Exploring
- Discover the stories of Coughton through the family's eyes.
- Relax in the gardens and stroll along the river.
- Gunpowder plots and priest holes; see how the family survived.
- Explore the grounds with a family adventure pack.
- Stretch your legs on a walk through the woods.
- Take in the views from the Tudor tower.

Eating and shopping: treat yourself to delicious local ice-cream from the parlour or afternoon tea in the Pewter Room. Try home-baked cakes or hot lunches in the restaurant. Take home locally sourced gifts from the shop, and plants from the Throckmorton plant centre.

Making the most of your day: set the scene with an introductory talk. Children's play area, house trail and outdoor family adventure packs. Volunteer tourism days. Family events, open-air theatre and Winter Festival. **Dogs**: welcome on leads in car park.

Access for all: 🅿🅳♿🚻🔊🎧📷📹👁
Building 🏚🏚♿ Grounds 🏚▶♿

Getting here: 150:SP080604. 2 miles north of Alcester. **Foot**: Arden Way passes close by. **Cycle**: NCN5, ½ mile. **Bus**: services from Redditch, Evesham and Stratford upon Avon. **Train**: Redditch 6 miles. **Road**: on A435. **Parking**: free, 150 yards.

Finding out more: 01789 400777 or coughtoncourt@nationaltrust.org.uk

Coughton Court		M	T	W	T	F	S	S
House, shop, restaurant and garden*								
10 Mar–25 Mar	11–5						S	S
31 Mar–30 Jun	11–5			W	T	F	S	S
1 Jul–31 Aug	11–5		T	W	T	F	S	S
1 Sep–30 Sep	11–5			W	T	F	S	S
4 Oct–4 Nov	11–5				T	F	S	S
House, shop and restaurant**								
24 Nov–2 Dec	11–5	M	T	W	T	F	S	S

Open Bank Holidays. **Closed Good Friday and 9 June and 7 July**. Admission by timed ticket at weekends and busy days. No hot food on Tuesdays. Shop open to 5:30. *Parts of the garden may be closed March and October to December. **Coughton Winter Festival, find out more online.

Croft Castle and Parkland

Yarpole, near Leominster, Herefordshire HR6 9PW

Map ④ H6

'Very refreshing, as the house and grounds have a warm, comfortable and lived-in feeling.'
Mr Tweed, Stratford upon Avon

Croft Castle is informal, relaxed and very family friendly. Home of the Croft family for nearly 1,000 years, Croft is the place to stroll through miles of woodland trails, picnic on the lawns, enjoy the beautiful scenery of the 607-hectare (1,500-acre) estate and be delighted by the splendid Georgian interiors. Learn about the family who have made Croft so special, relax in the walled garden and walk to the Iron Age hill fort at Croft Ambrey, past some of our 300 veteran trees. Homemade locally sourced food and a shop selling local gifts add to the enjoyment. **Note**: parts of the property may close in high winds.

Exploring
- Walk through miles of beautiful, tranquil woodland trails and glades.
- Go wild in our castle-themed play area (under 11s).
- Explore the walled garden, its flowers, shrubs, apples and vines.
- Discover the 1,000-year history of the Croft family.
- Try out the new menu guides around the property.
- Experience Georgian life, play cards or read in the Saloon.

Eating and shopping: local food and drink freshly prepared in our own kitchen. Local beers, fruit juices, ciders, delicious homemade cakes and scones. Local gifts in shop, including the Heart of England range. Plant sales, second-hand bookshop, wildlife and gardening gifts.

Parking charges for non-members may apply

Croft Castle, Herefordshire, is surrounded by beautiful gardens, all set within spectacular parkland

Making the most of your day: castle-inspired play area, family room, events and activities. Waymarked walks across the estate. Try out the new menu options to make the most of your day. **Dogs**: on leads in parkland only.

Access for all: 🅿️♿🔄♿🚻👁️📷📹♿
Building 🔄♿♿ **Grounds** ♿➡️♿

Getting here: 137:SO455655. 5 miles north-west of Leominster, 9 miles south-west of Ludlow. **Bus**: from Ludlow to Hereford (passing close Ludlow ➡️ and Leominster), alight Gorbett Bank, 2¼ miles. **Train**: Leominster 7 miles. **Road**: approach from B4362, turning north at Cock Gate between Bircher and Mortimer's Cross; signposted from Ludlow to Leominster road (A49) and from A4110 at Mortimer's Cross. **Sat Nav**: use HR6 0BL. **Parking**: 100 yards.

Finding out more: 01568 782120 or croftcastle@nationaltrust.org.uk

Croft Castle and Parkland		M	T	W	T	F	S	S
Tea-room. shop, garden and play area								
11 Feb–19 Feb	10–4:30	M	T	W	T	F	S	S
3 Mar–4 Nov	10–5	M	T	W	T	F	S	S
10 Nov–23 Dec	10–4:30	·	·	·	·	·	S	S
Castle tours*								
11 Feb–19 Feb	10:30–1	M	T	W	T	F	S	S
3 Mar–4 Nov	10:30–1	M	T	W	T	F	S	S
10 Nov–23 Dec	10:30–1	·	·	·	·	·	S	S
Castle								
11 Feb–19 Feb	1–4:30	M	T	W	T	F	S	S
3 Mar–4 Nov	1–5	M	T	W	T	F	S	S
10 Nov–16 Dec	1–4:30	·	·	·	·	·	S	S
17 Dec–23 Dec	1–4:30	M	T	W	T	F	S	S

*Castle: admission between 10 and 1 by tour only (free with entry, book on arrival). Shop: opens 11. Tea-room: open winter weekends 10 to 4. Countryside: open daily to 7, closes dusk if earlier. Castle, tea-room, shop, gardens and countryside: open 17 to 20 December. Tea-room, play area and countryside: open 27 to 31 December 10 to 4. Parkland and woods may close in high winds. Whole property may be closed in snow (telephone before travelling).

Croome

near High Green, Worcester,
Worcestershire WR8 9DW

Map (4) J7 1996

Croome, Worcestershire: ever-changing splendour

Explore the ever-changing splendour of Croome, a place with dramatic open spaces and fascinating stories to discover – from the 17th century right up to the 21st. The serene lakeside garden – with its sumptuous shrubberies, miles of winding paths, enchanting temples, bridges and statues – makes Croome the perfect place to relax with family and friends. Or why not let the children go wild? Step into Croome Court, the family-friendly mansion house, and discover its chequered past, then explore the evocative spaces which have been home to a diverse range of characters and communities for more than 400 years. **Note:** house owned by Croome Heritage Trust and leased to the National Trust.

Exploring – Discover newly opened Home Shrubbery and recently restored Rotunda folly.
– Enjoy fresh air and changing seasons with parkland walks.
– Escape to the eye-catcher follies – see Croome from different perspectives.
– Check out our extended winter opening times.
– Everyone will enjoy our year-round events.
– Let off steam with the family in our play area.

Eating and shopping: visit our 1940s-style restaurant or indulge yourself in the Tapestry Room tea-room inside Croome Court. A new shop awaits you with all the gift ideas you could wish for and a wider range of local produce.

Making the most of your day: variety of family events and trails in school holidays, RAF-themed play area, eye-catcher follies

open on special days. Grand ground floor and vaulted basement to explore in Croome Court. **Dogs:** welcome on leads. Assistance dogs only inside house, restaurant and shop (waiting areas provided).

Access for all: 🅿️♿🚻👶🦽📷🚐👓📱
House 🔆♿ Garden ➡️♿

Getting here: 150:SO887452. 9 miles south of Worcester. **Bus:** from Worcester to Pershore, alight Ladywood Road/Rebecca Road crossroads, 2 miles. From Worcester to Malvern, alight Kinnersley, 2 miles. **Train:** Worcester/ Pershore. **Road:** from M5 take Junction 7. Follow brown signs off B4084 from Pershore or off A38 from Worcester/Upton. **Parking:** free.

Finding out more: 01905 371006 or croomepark@nationaltrust.org.uk. National Trust Estate Office, The Builders' Yard, High Green, Severn Stoke, Worcestershire WR8 9JS

Croome		M	T	W	T	F	S	S
Garden, park, restaurant and shop								
1 Jan–12 Feb	10–4:30	·	·	·	·	·	S	S
13 Feb–2 Nov	10–5:30	M	T	W	T	F	S	S
3 Nov–23 Dec	10–4:30	·	·	·	·	·	S	S
Park, restaurant and shop								
5 Nov–23 Dec	10–4:30	M	T	W	T	F	S	S
House								
1 Jan–12 Feb	11–4	·	·	·	·	·	S	S
13 Feb–2 Nov	11–4:30	M	·	W	T	F	S	S
3 Nov–23 Dec	11–4	·	·	·	·	·	S	S
House, garden, park, restaurant and shop								
26 Dec–31 Dec	11–4	M	·	W	T	F	S	S

*Parkland, restaurant and shop now open every day through winter (garden closed on winter weekdays). Park and garden last admission 45 minutes before closing.

Cwmmau Farmhouse

Brilley, Whitney-on-Wye,
Herefordshire HR3 6JP

Map ④ G7   1965

Unique early 17th-century 'black and white' timbered farmhouse with many original features, including stone-tiled roofs and vernacular barns. **Note**: open occasionally. Available at other times as holiday cottage (0844 800 2070). Tea, coffee and cake available on open days.

Access for all: 🖊 **Building** 🔊📖

Getting here: 148:SO267514. 4 miles south-west of Kington between A4111 and A438. From Kington take Brilley road at junction opposite church, 3½ miles. Turn left at National Trust signpost. From A438 between Winforton and Whitney on Wye take Brilley road at junction opposite Stowe Farm, straight on for 2 miles. Turn right, approximately ¾ mile turn right at Trust signpost. Farmhouse is approximately ½ mile at end of 'no through road'.

Finding out more: 01568 782120 or cwmmaufarmhouse@nationaltrust.org.uk

Cwmmau Farmhouse		M	T	W	T	F	S	S
28 Jun–1 Jul	1–5		·	·	T	F	S	S
4 Oct–7 Oct	1–5		·	·	T	F	S	S

Cwmmau Farmhouse, Herefordshire

Dudmaston Estate

Quatt, near Bridgnorth, Shropshire WV15 6QN

Map ④ I5 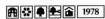 1978

'The children loved the play area and running around in the orchard.'
Thomas Birtwhistle, Worcester

Dudmaston offers something unexpected in the Shropshire countryside, a house that provides a classical setting for a collection of modern and contemporary art. The modern art galleries were assembled by diplomat Sir George Labouchere, while his wife Rachel showed off her collections of botanical drawings and watercolours. Outside the gardens and orchard provide the perfect backdrop for sculptures. A walk around the Big Pool and Dingle offers stunning views of the house, while the wider estate, covering 1,200 hectares (2,965 acres) of woodland and farmland, provides extensive walking and cycling routes which can be enjoyed all year round. **Note**: this is the family home of Colonel and Mrs James Hamilton-Russell.

Exploring
- Don't miss the kitchen garden.
- Have fun in our extended children's play area.
- Discover one family's varied art collection.
- Explore the wider estate, including the Dingle and Comer Wood.
- Enjoy the breathtaking gardens as the seasons change.
- Relax in the comfortable Oak Room and enjoy the view.

Eating and shopping: in our shop we sell everything from gifts to our own charcoal and logs. Our refurbished tea-room and stables café offer a variety of home-baked cakes and meals.

Making the most of your day: garden games, guided tours around the gardens, a variety of events going on throughout the open season and in-depth booked tours in the house on

Dudmaston Estate, Shropshire: unexpected

Duffield Castle

Milford Road, Duffield, Derbyshire DE56 4DW

Map ③ C4 🖼 🏛 1899

The remains of one of England's largest 13th-century castles. The foundations, the story and views are all that remain today. **Note:** unmanned. No toilets. Steep steps.

Getting here: SK508440. On the northern edge of Duffield village. A6 passes directly in front.

Finding out more: 01332 844052 or duffieldcastle@nationaltrust.org.uk. c/o Kedleston Hall, near Quarndon, Derbyshire DE22 5JH

Duffield Castle	Open every day all year

Mondays. **Dogs:** on leads on footpaths in the park and on the estate only.

Access for all: 🅿️🚻♿👶🔁📷📶📱📖

Building 🔼🔁♿ **Grounds** 🔼➡️

Getting here: 138:SO746887. 4 miles south-east of Bridgnorth. **Foot:** walks from Hampton Loade car park to property. **Ferry:** from Severn Valley Railway, via river ferry. **Bus:** from Bridgnorth to Kidderminster (passing close Kidderminster 🚆). **Train:** Hampton Loade (Severn Valley Railway) 1½ miles; Kidderminster 10 miles. **Road:** on A442. **Parking:** at the house and at Hampton Loade and The Holt (both pay and display).

Finding out more: 01746 780866 or dudmaston@nationaltrust.org.uk

Dudmaston Estate		M	T	W	T	F	S	S
Garden								
1 Apr–30 Sep	12–6	**M**	**T**	**W**	·	·	·	**S**
House								
1 Apr–30 Sep	2–5:30	·	**T**	**W**	·	·	·	**S**
Tea-room and shop*								
1 Apr–30 Sep	11:30–5:30	**M**	**T**	**W**	·	·	·	**S**

Open Bank Holiday Mondays. Snowdrop walks: 11, 12, 18 and 19 February. *Shop opens 12. St Andrew's church, Quatt: open as house. Tours of the house are available on the first and third Mondays of the month, telephone for details.

Farnborough Hall

Farnborough, near Banbury, Oxfordshire OX17 1DU

Map ④ L7 🏛 ❄ 🌳 1960

Honey-coloured stone house, with stunning library and treasures collected during the Grand Tour, surrounded by landscape garden with country views. **Note:** occupied and administered by the Holbech family.

Access for all: 🅿️ **Building** 🔼 **Grounds** 🔼

Getting here: 151:SP430490. 6 miles north of Banbury, ½ mile west of A423.

Finding out more: 01295 690002 or farnboroughhall@nationaltrust.org.uk

Farnborough Hall		M	T	W	T	F	S	S
4 Apr–29 Sep	2–5:30	·	·	**W**	·	·	**S**	·
6 May–7 May	2–5:30	**M**	·	·	·	·	·	**S**

The Fleece Inn

Bretforton, near Evesham,
Worcestershire WR11 7JE

Map ④ K7   1978

The Fleece Inn is a half-timbered medieval farmhouse which originally sheltered a farmer and his stock. The Inn was first licensed in 1848. Fully restored to its former glory, with witches' circles and precious pewter collection, it has developed a reputation for traditional folk music, morris dancing and asparagus.

Exploring
– Annual Asparagus Auctions and Festival Day – spring Bank Holiday.
– Medieval thatched barn licensed for civil weddings, functions and events.
– Weekly folk session, regular gigs and other events.
– Annual Apple and Ale Festival in October.

Eating and shopping: mouthwatering menu using the finest local produce. Quality cask ales, including landlord's own. Local ciders and wines. Special asparagus menu between 23 April and 21 June.

Making the most of your day: traditional folk music and morris dancing throughout the year. Vintage and classic car events May to September.

Access for all: ⬚⬚⬚⬚ Building ⬚⬚

Getting here: 150:SP093437. In the village square in the centre of Bretforton.
Bus: from Evesham to Chipping Campden.
Train: Evesham 2½ miles. **Road**: 4 miles east of Evesham, on B4035. **Parking**: in village square only (not National Trust).

Finding out more: 01386 831173 or fleeceinn@nationaltrust.org.uk

The Fleece Inn							
Open every day all year from 11 to 11							
September: may close Monday and Tuesday, 3 to 6. June, July, August and Bank Holidays: open all day.							

Grantham House

Castlegate, Grantham, Lincolnshire NG31 6SS

Map ③ E4   1944

A handsome town house and one of the oldest buildings in Grantham. Architectural features from various eras; riverside walled garden.
Note: the house is leased by the National Trust and the lessee is responsible for arrangements and facilities. Appointments may be needed on some dates.

Access for all: ⬚⬚⬚
House ⬚⬚ Grounds ⬚

Getting here: 130:SK916362. In the centre of Grantham, immediately east of St Wulfram's church.

Finding out more: 01476 564705 or granthamhouse@nationaltrust.org.uk

Grantham House		M	T	W	T	F	S	S
4 Apr–31 May*	By appointment			W	T			
6 Jun–28 Jun	2–5			W	T			
4 Jul–31 Oct*	By appointment			W	T			

*By written appointment. The property is leased by the National Trust and the house and garden are open to visitors at various times, as advertised. The lessee is responsible for all arrangements and facilities. Entrance via gates opposite Church Street.

Greyfriars' House and Garden

Friar Street, Worcester, Worcestershire WR1 2LZ

Map ④ J7   1966

Set in the heart of historic Worcester, Greyfriars is a stunning timber-framed merchant's house where you can get away from the hustle and bustle. This unique house and garden were rescued by two extraordinary people with a vision to rescue this medieval gem and create a peaceful oasis.

Exploring – Modern art exhibition in the house, visit website for details.
– Discover how Greyfriars was saved from demolition.
– See how the house has changed over the centuries.
– Explore the delightful walled garden.

Eating and shopping: enjoy a light lunch or afternoon tea in the tranquil setting of the walled garden. Buy plants grown at nearby Hanbury Hall.

Making the most of your day: garden games for all ages, conservation tours every Friday morning, family events throughout the year. **Dogs**: welcome in the garden.

Access for all: 🖼️🖥️·· Building 🏛️🏞️

Getting here: 150:SO852546. In centre of Worcester on Friar Street. **Bus**: from surrounding areas. **Train**: Worcester Foregate Street ½ mile. **Parking**: at Corn Market, Kings Street and Cathedral Plaza (pay and display). No onsite parking, park and ride service from city outskirts.

Finding out more: 01905 23571 or greyfriars@nationaltrust.org.uk

Greyfriars	M	T	W	T	F	S	S
House and garden							
14 Feb–15 Dec	1–5	·	T	W	T	F	S	·
Conservation tours							
17 Feb–14 Dec	11:30–12:30	·	·	·	·	F		

Admission by timed ticket on busy days. Open Bank Holiday Mondays. Closes dusk if earlier.

Gunby Hall

Gunby, Spilsby, Lincolnshire PE23 5SS

Map ③ G3 🏠🎎🌰🏚️🔔🍵 1944

A splendid red-brick house, dating from 1700. With Victorian walled gardens containing hundreds of specimen plants, flowers and trees.

Access for all: 🅿️🖥️🖨️·· Building 🏛️🏞️ Grounds 🏞️

Getting here: 122:TF467668. 2½ miles north-west of Burgh le Marsh, 7 miles west of Skegness on south side of A158 (access off roundabout).

Finding out more: 01754 890102 or gunbyhall@nationaltrust.org.uk

Gunby Hall	M	T	W	T	F	S	S
Hall							
7 Mar–28 Oct	2–5	·	·	W	·	·	·	S
Gardens and tea-room							
4 Jan–23 Dec	11–5	·	·	W	T	F	S	S

Gardens open Bank Holidays. Closed 25 to 31 December.

Gunby Hall Estate: Monksthorpe Chapel

Monksthorpe, near Spilsby, Lincolnshire PE23 5PP

Map ③ G3 ✝️ 2000

Remote late 17th-century Baptist chapel.

Access for all: 🅿️🖥️ Building 🏛️🏞️ Grounds 🏞️

Getting here: 122:TF450654. From A158 in Candlesby, turn off main road opposite Royal Oak pub, following signs to Monksthorpe. Follow road for about 1½ miles and turn left. After 50 yards turn left at dead-end sign. Parking is on the left at entrance to avenue.

Finding out more: 01526 342543 or monksthorpe@nationaltrust.org.uk

Monksthorpe Chapel

April to September: admission Wednesday and Thursday, 11 to 4, by key only – obtained from Gunby Hall (£20 deposit required, fully refundable). For information about services, open days and events, please check the Friends of Monksthorpe Chapel website: www.monksthorpe.org.uk.

Hanbury Hall and Gardens

School Road, Hanbury, Droitwich Spa,
Worcestershire WR9 7EA

Map ④ J6  1953

'A wonderfully welcoming house. Beautifully tended gardens. The staff and volunteers were superb and very knowledgeable. A definite treat!'
Janet Peggs, St Ives, Cambridgeshire

Hanbury Hall is a beautiful William and Mary-style house built in 1701 by Thomas Vernon, a lawyer and whig MP for Worcester. Inside a mix of interiors await to be discovered, from the restored Hercules rooms and recreated Gothic corridor, to the Smoking Room and magnificent recently restored staircase wall paintings by Sir James Thornhill. Surrounding the house are eight hectares (20 acres) of recreated early 18th-century gardens and 162 hectares (400 acres) of park. Features include the intricately laid out parterre, fruit garden, grove, orangery, orchard and bowling green. Park walks enable you to explore the surrounding countryside.

Exploring
- Discover more about the travels of the Vernon family.
- Find out about the stunning award-winning wall-paintings.
- Stroll through the gardens and enjoy a game of bowls.
- Relax and enjoy a picnic on the peaceful orangery lawn.
- Have fun and games in our children's play area.
- Enjoy the beautiful Worcestershire countryside on a bracing park walk.

Eating and shopping: browse through our new extended gardening range and buy a plant grown in the Walled Garden. Enjoy delicious meals, cooked using local produce, in the tea-room overlooking the parterre. Relax and enjoy a snack in the open-air Stables Kiosk.

The elegant William and Mary-style Hanbury Hall, Worcestershire, was built in 1701

Making the most of your day: regular garden tours and introductory talks. Year-round varied events programme, including family activity days, concerts, open-air theatre productions, art exhibitions and themed weekends. Park walks leaflet available. **Dogs**: in car park and park only.

Access for all:
Building 🏠🏠♿ Grounds 🏠🏠➡

Getting here: 150:SO943637. 4 miles east of Droitwich Spa. **Foot**: public footpaths cross the park. **Bus**: Worcester to Birmingham (passing close Droitwich Spa ➤), alight Wychbold, 2 miles. **Train**: Droitwich Spa 4 miles. **Road**: from M5 exit 5 follow A38 to Droitwich; from Droitwich 4 miles along B4090. **Parking**: free, 150 yards.

Finding out more: 01527 821214 or hanburyhall@nationaltrust.org.uk

Hanbury Hall and Gardens		M	T	W	T	F	S	S
House*, gardens, park, shop and tea-room								
1 Jan–5 Feb	11–4	·	·	·	·	·	S	S
House*, gardens, park, shop, tea-room and play area								
11 Feb–4 Nov	11–5	M	T	W	T	·	S	S
10 Nov–23 Dec	11–4	·	·	·	·	·	S	S
Gardens, park, shop and tea-room								
26 Dec–31 Dec	11–4	M	·	W	T	F	S	S

*11 February to 4 November: house admission by guided tour from 11 to 1 (limited places), 1 to 5 free-flow. January to 5 February and 10 to 25 November: house admission by tour 11:30 to 3:30 (limited access and places). December: limited free-flow access. Tour tickets allocated on arrival (non-bookable). Admission by timed tickets on busy days. Bank Holiday Mondays: free-flow access, 11 to 5. Whole property open Good Friday. Stables Kiosk open at busy times. Property closes dusk if earlier.

Note: nearest toilet at Hardwick Hall.

Exploring — Discover the secrets of a 13th-century watermill.
— Children's trail and activity sheets available.
— Have a go at milling your own flour.

Eating and shopping: buy Stainsby freshly milled flour, then visit the restaurant and shop at nearby Hardwick Hall.

Making the most of your day: join us to celebrate National Mills weekend in May.
Dogs: on leads in Hardwick Park only.

Access for all: 🔊🔲♿..🅰
Building 🏠 Grounds 🏠🏠

Getting here: 120:SK455653. 6½ miles west of Mansfield. **Foot**: Rowthorne Trail and Teversal Trail nearby. **Bus**: from Chesterfield, alight Glapwell 'Young Vanish', 1½ miles. **Train**: Chesterfield 7 miles. **Road**: M1 exit 29, A6175 signposted to Clay Cross, first left and left again to Stainsby Mill. **Parking**: free, limited (not National Trust).

Finding out more: 01246 850430 or stainsbymill@nationaltrust.org.uk

Hardwick Estate: Stainsby Mill		M	T	W	T	F	S	S
11 Feb–3 Jun	10–4	·	·	W	T	F	S	S
6 Jun–2 Sep	10–5	·	·	W	T	F	S	S
5 Sep–4 Nov	10–4	·	·	W	T	F	S	S

Open Bank Holiday Mondays and Tuesday 5 June.

Hardwick Estate: Stainsby Mill

Doe Lea, Chesterfield, Derbyshire S44 5QJ

Map ③ D3 🏠 1976

Come and explore the workings of a fully operational watermill, which gives a vivid evocation of the workplace of a 19th-century miller. Flour is ground regularly and is for sale throughout the season.

Stainsby Mill, Derbyshire: a working watermill

Hardwick Hall

Doe Lea, Chesterfield, Derbyshire S44 5QJ

Map ③ D3

'Very enjoyable! I intend to bring my granddaughter, as I thought that the activities for the children were very good.'
Mrs Jackson, Chesterfield

The Hardwick Estate is made up of stunning houses and beautiful landscapes that have been created by a cast of thousands. It was the formidable Bess of Hardwick who first built Hardwick Hall in the late 16th century. In the centuries since then gardeners, builders, decorators, embroiderers and craftsmen of all kinds have contributed and made Hardwick their creation. We want you to explore and enjoy Hardwick and in the process discover the lives, loves and adventures of the builders of Hardwick. **Note**: Old Hall is owned by the National Trust and administered by English Heritage (01246 850431).

Exploring
- New visitor facilities and car park opening this spring.
- See Hardwick come to life on costumed days.
- Get your 'Hands on Hardwick' with family activities.
- Experience sensory delight in the herb garden.
- Don't miss our new outdoors and garden shop (opening spring).
- Explore the picturesque parkland on one of our circular walks.

Eating and shopping: eat, shop and explore in style at The Stableyard, which opens this spring. Savour a delicious meal in the new Great Barn Restaurant, then discover the beautiful range of gifts in the Ox House Shop. Treat yourself and your family.

Making the most of your day: family trails, Tracker Packs, activities and events, Living History days, Conservation in Action days,

The splendid Hardwick Hall, Derbyshire

garden tours, fishing, circular walks. **Dogs**: on leads and in the park and car park only.

Access for all: 🅿️♿🚻♿👶📷🏠📺♿👓
Hardwick Hall ♿♿♿ Garden ➡️♿♿

Getting here: 120:SK463638. 6½ miles west of Mansfield. **Foot**: Rowthorne Trail; Teversal Trail. **Bus**: from Chesterfield, alight Glapwell 'Young Vanish', 1½ miles. **Train**: Chesterfield. **Road**: 8 miles south-east of Chesterfield; via A6175. Leave M1 exit 29, follow brown signs. **Parking**: new car park opening this year.

Finding out more: 01246 850430 or hardwickhall@nationaltrust.org.uk

Hardwick Hall		M	T	W	T	F	S	S
Park, garden, shop and restaurant								
11 Feb–1 Apr	11–5	·	·	W	T	F	S	S
2 Apr–31 Dec*	9–6	M	T	W	T	F	S	S
Hall								
11 Feb–4 Nov**	12–4:30	·	·	W	T	F	S	S
1 Dec–16 Dec	11–3	·	·	·	·	·	S	S

*Closed 25 December. **Hall: also open Bank Holiday Mondays (April to August) and Tuesday 5 June, 12 to 4:30. Stone Centre opens daily all year round. Hall, gardens, shop, restaurant and park may close early if weather is bad during winter months.

Hawford Dovecote

Hawford, Worcestershire WR3 7SG

Map (4) J6 1973

The picturesque Hawford Dovecote has survived virtually unaltered since the late 16th-century and retains many of its nesting boxes. **Note**: no toilet or tea-room. Please park carefully to one side of the lane.

Access for all: Building 🏛

Getting here: 150:SO846607. 3 miles north of Worcester, ½ mile east of A449.

Finding out more: 01527 821214 or hawforddovecote@nationaltrust.org.uk

Hawford Dovecote	
Open every day all year from 9 to 6	
Closes dusk if earlier. Out of hours visits by appointment.	

High Peak Estate

See Peak District: Dark Peak, page 245.

Ilam Park and South Peak Estate

See Peak District: White Peak, page 247.

Kedleston Hall

near Quarndon, Derby, Derbyshire DE22 5JH

Map (3) C4  1987

Celebrate the National Trust's 25th year of opening at this spectacular Neo-classical mansion, framed by historic parkland. Designed for lavish entertaining and displaying an extensive collection of paintings, sculpture and original furnishings, Kedleston is a stunning example of the work of architect Robert Adam. The Curzon family have lived at the Hall since the 12th century and continue to live here. Lord Curzon's Eastern Museum is a treasure trove of fascinating objects acquired on his travels in Asia and while Viceroy of India (1899 to 1905). Used as a key location for *The Duchess*, the recent Hollywood blockbuster. **Note**: medieval All Saints church, containing many family monuments, is run by the Churches Conservation Trust.

Exploring
- Experience the stunning Adam interiors.
- Discover Britain's colonial connections in the Eastern Museum.
- Follow in the footsteps of *The Duchess*, using our trail.
- Explore the parkland and see what wildlife you can spot.
- New room opening this year.

Kedleston Hall, Derbyshire: looking through the dressing-room columns into the ante-room in the State Apartments

Eating and shopping: buy a Kedleston souvenir and local products. Peat-free plants for sale. Seasonal recipes made using local produce, including Kedleston Park lamb.

Making the most of your day: available most house open days at selected times – introductory talk, tours of fishing pavilion, great west stable or pleasure grounds, and brief talks by 18th-century housekeeper Mrs Garnett. **Dogs**: on leads in park and pleasure grounds.

Access for all: 🅿️🚐♿♿🚹♿🖼️
🏠📺♿♿📷 Ground floor 🪑♿
State floor 🪑♿ Grounds ➡️

Getting here: 128:SK312403. 5 miles north-west of Derby; 12 miles south-east of Ashbourne. **Cycle**: on parkland roads only. **Bus**: service from Derby to Ashbourne, calls at the Hall summer Saturdays only, otherwise alight the Smithy, 1 mile. **Train**: Duffield 3½ miles; Derby 5½ miles. **Road**: aim for intersection of A52/ A38, and follow A38 (north). Take first exit (by Derby University) and continue along Kedleston Road towards Quarndon. **Parking**: 200 yards, admission fees apply.

Finding out more: 01332 842191 or kedlestonhall@nationaltrust.org.uk

Kedleston Hall		M	T	W	T	F	S	S
Park								
1 Jan–17 Feb	10–4	M	T	W	T	F	S	S
18 Feb–28 Oct	10–6	M	T	W	T	F	S	S
29 Oct–31 Dec	10–4	M	T	W	T	F	S	S
Pleasure Grounds								
18 Feb–28 Oct	10–6	M	T	W	T	F	S	S
House*								
18 Feb–28 Oct	12–5	M	T	W	·	·	S	S
Restaurant and shop								
1 Jan–12 Feb	11–3	·	·	·	·	·	S	S
18 Feb–28 Oct	11–5	M	T	W	·	·	S	S
26 Jul–31 Aug	11–5	M	T	W	T	F	S	S
3 Nov–30 Dec	11–3	·	·	·	·	·	S	S
6 Dec–21 Dec	11–3	·	·	·	T	F	S	S

*Last entry to house 45 minutes before closing. 18 February to 19 March: house entry by guided tour only, every 30 minutes from 12 to 3 (spaces limited). Open Good Friday. Park closes occasionally November to February. Closed 25 December.

Holy Austin Rock Houses at Kinver Edge, Staffordshire

Kinver Edge and the Rock Houses

Holy Austin Rock Houses, Compton Road, Kinver, near Stourbridge, Staffordshire DY7 6DL

Map ④ I5   🏠🏚️🚻❀♿ 1917

Step back in time and explore the Holy Austin Rock Houses, learn about the extraordinary people who carved a home for themselves in this famous sandstone ridge. Take a walk onto Kinver Edge and discover the dramatic views stretching across three counties.

Exploring – An atmospheric glimpse into a bygone age.
– Explore the newly restored Martindale Caves.
– Miles of woodland and heathland walks to discover.
– Completely new events and activities programme on offer.

Eating and shopping: be sure to sample delicious locally made cakes at the Rock Houses tea-room.

Making the most of your day: hire one of our Family Explorer Backpacks, jammed full of activities, trails and information to help you get the most out of the countryside. **Dogs**: on leads within grounds of Rock Houses.

Access for all: 🅿️🚐♿🖼️🏠📷
Building 🪑 Grounds 🪑

Getting here: 138:SO836836. On edge Kinver village, 4 miles west of Stourbridge. **Bus**: Merry Hill bus station to Kinver. **Train**: Stourbridge town 5 miles. **Road**: 4 miles north of Kidderminster. The Rock Houses are signposted from Kinver High Street. **Parking**: at the Warden's lodge on Comber Road for the Edge and on Compton Road for the Rock Houses.

Finding out more: 01384 872553 or kinveredge@nationaltrust.org.uk

Kinver Edge and the Rock Houses		M	T	W	T	F	S	S
Countryside								
Open all year		M	T	W	T	F	S	S
Rock Houses								
1 Mar–23 Nov	2–4	·	·	·	T	F	·	·
3 Mar–25 Nov	11–4	·	·	·	·	·	S	S
Tea-room								
1 Mar–25 Nov	11–4	·	·	·	T	F	S	S

Open Bank Holiday Mondays. Lower Rock Houses open for guided weekday tours (March to November), by arrangement (groups of ten or over).

Kinwarton Dovecote

Kinwarton, near Alcester, Warwickshire B49 6HB

Map (4) K7   1958

A lovely and rare 14th-century circular dovecote with metre-thick walls, hundreds of nesting holes and original rotating ladder. **Note**: farm stock may be grazing in field. No toilet.

Access for all: Building

Getting here: 150:SP106585. 1½ miles north-east of Alcester, just south of B4089. 3½-mile walk from Coughton Court.

Finding out more: 01789 400777 or kinwartondovecote@nationaltrust.org.uk

Kinwarton Dovecote		M	T	W	T	F	S	S
1 Mar–31 Oct	11–6	M	T	W	T	F	S	S

Closes dusk if earlier. Other times by appointment.

Knowles Mill

Dowles Brook, Bewdley, Worcestershire DY12 2LX

Map (4) I6   1938

The mill dates from the 18th century and retains much of its machinery, including the frames of an overshot waterwheel. **Note**: Mill Cottage is not open to visitors, please respect the resident's privacy. No toilets or tea-room. No parking at Mill Cottage.

Access for all: Mill

Getting here: 138:SO762765. Next to Dowles Brook in the centre of the Wyre Forest, Bewdley. Nearest parking at Natural England car park, near foot of Dry Mill Lane, Bewdley, ¾ mile.

Finding out more: 01527 821214 or knowlesmill@nationaltrust.org.uk. Hanbury Hall, School Road, Droitwich Spa, Worcestershire WR9 7EA

Knowles Mill	
Open every day all year from 9 to 6	

Closes dusk if earlier.

Letocetum Roman Baths and Museum

Watling Street, Wall, near Lichfield, Staffordshire WS14 0AW

Map (4) K5   1934

Explore the remains of this once-important Roman staging post and settlement, including *mansio* (Roman inn) and bathhouse. **Note**: in the guardianship of English Heritage.

Access for all: Open-air site   Museum

Getting here: 139:SK099067. In the village of Wall on the north side of A5, 3 miles south of Lichfield.

Finding out more: 0121 625 6820 (English Heritage) or letocetum@nationaltrust.org.uk

Letocetum Roman Baths
Open-air site accessible at all reasonable times. March to end of October: site and Roman finds museum manned by volunteers on the last weekend of each month, 11 to 4. 15 July to 2 September and Bank Holiday weekends: site and museum also manned by volunteers on Saturday, Sunday and Monday, 11 to 4. Guided walks some afternoons.

Lyveden New Bield

near Oundle, Northamptonshire PE8 5AT

Map ③ E6   🏛️➕✨🔆🏠⬆️ 1922

'A wonderful place to bring a picnic – the children loved the freedom to explore, we loved the tranquillity!'
Mrs Wright, Kettering

Lyveden New Bield, Northamptonshire

Lyveden is a remarkable story of survival. One of England's oldest garden landscapes, Lyveden was abandoned in 1605 when its creator Sir Thomas Tresham died and his son became embroiled in the Catholic Gunpowder Plot. Today you can enjoy an experience of an Elizabethan garden with moats, mounts, terracing and intriguing garden lodge. Period fruit trees recreate what was described as 'one of the fairest orchards in England', and the circular labyrinth reflects Tresham's original garden design. Lyveden is a place where you can relax in peace, explore with the new audio guide or venture further and discover Rockingham Forest.

Exploring
– Discover Lyveden through our audio guide.
– Uncover the mysteries of Sir Thomas's symbolic garden lodge.
– Relax with a picnic in the peaceful setting of Lyveden.
– Enjoy stunning wildflower meadows between April and August.
– Explore the garden labyrinth and Elizabethan orchard.
– Enjoy the Lyveden Way – and discover Rockingham Forest.

Eating and shopping: enjoy an ice-cream sitting by the moated garden. Hot and cold drinks sold in the shop. Local honey (seasonal).

Making the most of your day: garden tours every Saturday and Sunday from May to October. The freedom to explore makes Lyveden a great place for a family visit and an ideal setting for a picnic. **Dogs**: welcome on leads only.

Access for all: ♿🚻👓👁️ Building 🔆 Grounds 🏞️

Getting here: 141:SP983853. 3 miles east of Brigstock and 4 miles south-west of Oundle. **Foot**: Lyveden Way passes though Lyveden and connects with Wadenhoe and Fermyn Woods. **Bus**: from Northampton 🚆 to Peterborough 🚆. **Train**: Kettering 10 miles. **Road**: off A6116. From Oundle take A427. **Parking**: free, 100 yards.

Finding out more: 01832 205358 or lyveden@nationaltrust.org.uk

Lyveden New Bield		M	T	W	T	F	S	S
4 Feb–11 Mar	11–4						S	S
14 Mar–31 Oct	10:30–5			W	T	F	S	S
1 May–30 Sep	10:30–5	M	T	W	T	F	S	S
3 Nov–25 Nov	11–4						S	S

Open Bank Holidays. Open Good Friday, 10:30 to 5.

Middle Littleton Tithe Barn

Middle Littleton, Evesham,
Worcestershire WR11 8LN

Map (4) K7 1975

Discover the largest and finest fully restored
13th-century tithe barn in the country.
Note: no toilet.

Access for all: Building ⓙ

Getting here: 150:SP080471. 3 miles north-
east of Evesham, signposted off the B4085.

Finding out more: 01905 371006 or
middlelittleton@nationaltrust.org.uk

Middle Littleton Tithe Barn	M	T	W	T	F	S	S
1 Apr–31 Oct	2–5	**M**	**T**	**W**	**T**	**F**	**S**	**S**

Access instructions on barn door interior.

Morville Hall

Morville, near Bridgnorth,
Shropshire WV16 5NB

Map (4) I5 1965

This beautiful stone-built house set in
attractive gardens is of Elizabethan origin
and was enlarged and expanded around 1750.
Note: Dower House garden also open (not
National Trust).

Access for all: 🖼 Building ⓙ Grounds 🖼

Getting here: 138:SO668940. 3 miles west of
Bridgnorth, off A458.

Finding out more: 01746 780838 or
morvillehall@nationaltrust.org.uk

Morville Hall

Admission by guided tour. By written appointment
only with the tenants, please contact Dr and
Mrs C. Douglas directly.

Moseley Old Hall

Moseley Old Hall Lane, Fordhouses,
Wolverhampton, Staffordshire WV10 7HY

Map (4) J5  1962

'Whole day was brilliant. We shall certainly be
visiting again with our grandchildren, who
we know will love the experience.'
Linda Henshall, Warrington

This atmospheric Elizabethan farmhouse
conceals a priest's hole and hiding places, in
one of which Charles II hid while on the run
after being defeated at the Battle of Worcester
in 1651. You can also see the bed on which the
royal fugitive slept. Follow the story of the
King's dramatic escape from Cromwell's troops
and find out about 17th-century domestic life
in this friendly and fascinating historic home.
The Hall is an integral part of the Monarch's
Way Trail. The garden has plant varieties in
keeping with the period and has a striking knot
garden following a 17th-century design.

Exploring
- Follow in the footsteps of a king.
- Take a fascinating guided tour of the house.
- Sit by the fire and immerse yourself in 17th-century life.
- Discover the delights of the walled garden and the 'knot'.
- Children will love to explore with our Tracker Packs.
- Walk in our newly opened wood.

Eating and shopping: enjoy delicious light
lunches and homemade cakes in our very
popular tea-room. We regularly use locally
sourced ingredients. Browse for gifts and
plants in our shop. Find bargains galore in the
second-hand bookshop.

Making the most of your day: events and
activities throughout the year including family
events, demonstrations and re-creations
of 17th-century life. Children's activities
on family event days and Mondays and
Tuesdays in August (events leaflet available).

A corner of the delightful walled garden at the Elizabethan Moseley Old Hall in Staffordshire

Dogs: welcome on leads in the garden and grounds.

Access for all: [icons] House [icons] Shop and tea-room [icons] Grounds [icons]

Getting here: 127:SJ932044. 4 miles north of Wolverhampton. **Bus**: regular service from Wolverhampton or Cannock; both ½ mile. **Road**: south of M54; from north on M6 leave at exit 11, then A460; from south on M6 and M54 take exit 1. **Parking**: free, no coach parking.

Finding out more: 01902 782808 or moseleyoldhall@nationaltrust.org.uk

Moseley Old Hall		M	T	W	T	F	S	S
3 Mar–1 Jul	12–5	·	·	W	·	·	S	S
2 Jul–9 Sep	12–5	M	T	W	·	·	S	S
12 Sep–31 Oct	12–5	·	·	W	·	·	S	S
3 Nov–16 Dec	12–4	·	·	·	·	·	S	S

House: entry 12 to 1 by guided tour only (free-flow or tour from 1). Open Bank Holiday Mondays, 11 to 5 (no tours). **Open Saturday to Wednesday during autumn half-term.** 3 November to 16 December: guided tour only. Christmas events.

The Old Manor

Norbury, Ashbourne, Derbyshire DE6 2ED

Map (3) B4   [icons] [1987]

Medieval hall featuring a rare king post, Tudor door and 17th-century Flemish glass. Gardens include a parterre herb garden. **Note**: limited parking (cars only).

Access for all: [icons] Building [icon] Grounds [icons]

Getting here: 128:SK125424. 4 miles from Ashbourne; 9 miles from Sudbury Hall.

Finding out more: 01283 585337 or oldmanor@nationaltrust.org.uk

The Old Manor		M	T	W	T	F	S	S
30 Mar–26 Oct	11–1	·	·	·	·	F	·	·
31 Mar–27 Oct	2–4	·	·	·	·	·	S	·

Property is tenanted and visits are only available during opening hours.

Packwood House

Packwood Lane, Lapworth,
Warwickshire B94 6AT

Map ④ K6   1941

Originally built in the 16th-century, Packwood was lovingly restored between the world wars by Graham, Baron Ash, creating his perfect vision of a Tudor home. The house contains a wonderful collection of 16th-century furniture and textiles. The gardens include renowned herbaceous borders and a famous collection of yews. **Note**: some areas of the garden may be closed for ongoing maintenance.

The Yew Garden, Packwood House, Warwickshire

Exploring
- Follow the spiral path to view the unique Yew Garden.
- Explore the park and woodland.
- Discover how Baron Ash reinvented the house.
- Family trails for the house and garden.
- Relax among the beautiful flower borders.
- Check your watch against the sundials.

Eating and shopping: locally sourced products available in the shop. Garden plants for sale, many grown in our own nursery. Light refreshments available from our new kiosk.

Making the most of your day: set the scene with an introductory talk. Family events, outdoor theatre and Meet the Gardener evening tours. Adventure walk for families through the woodland. **Dogs**: welcome on leads in car park and on public footpaths.

Access for all: 🅿️ 🅳 🚾 🏠 👓
Building 🔩 ♿ Grounds 🔩 🏠 ♿

Getting here: 139:SP174723. 1½ miles from Lapworth. **Foot**: Millennium Way crosses the park. **Bus**: from Birmingham to Stratford-upon-Avon, alight Hockley Heath, 1¾ miles. **Train**: Lapworth 1½ miles; Birmingham International 8 miles. **Road**: 2 miles east of Hockley Heath (on A3400), 11 miles south-east of central Birmingham. **Parking**: free 100 yards.

Finding out more: 01564 782024 or packwood@nationaltrust.org.uk

Packwood House		M	T	W	T	F	S	S
House, garden and shop								
11 Feb–22 Jul	11–5	·	T	W	T	F	S	S
23 Jul–2 Sep	11–5	M	T	W	T	F	S	S
4 Sep–4 Nov	11–5	·	T	W	T	F	S	S
Park								
Open all year		M	T	W	T	F	S	S

Admission to the house by timed ticket on Bank Holidays, tickets available from reception (not bookable). Open Bank Holiday Mondays.

Peak District: Dark Peak

Edale, Hope Valley, Peak District,
Derbyshire S33 6RF

Map ③ B2 🏛️🚻♿👕🏠 1936

Mountain-biking at Dark Peak, Derbyshire

The estate stretches from the heather-clad moors of Kinder to the gritstone tors of Derwent Edge, from the peat bogs of Bleaklow to the limestone crags of Winnats Pass. The wild Pennine moorlands are of international importance for their populations of breeding birds and mosaic of habitats. Sites of particular interest include Mam Tor, with spectacular views, landslip and prehistoric settlement, and the famous Snake Pass. Kinder Scout, where the Mass Trespass of 1932 took place, is the highest point for 50 miles. The Trust also owns several farms and a café in the beautiful Edale Valley. **Note**: nearest toilet in adjacent villages and at visitor centres at Ladybower Reservoir, Edale, Castleton.

Exploring

– Follow one of the ancient routes across wild moorland.
– Wander through the oak woods of the Derwent Valley.
– Explore the limestone caves and caverns of Winnats Pass.
– Climb Kinder Scout, the highest point in the Peak District.
– Discover the beautiful hay meadows in the Edale Valley.
– Learn about wildlife and history by booking onto an event.

Eating and shopping: enjoy breakfast, lunch or tea at Penny Pot Café in Edale. Camp and enjoy local food at Upper Booth Farm, Edale. Discover more about our moorlands at Edale Visitor Centre.

Making the most of your day: programme of events throughout the year. New downloadable walking trails, audio trails, geocaching and podcasts from www.nationaltrust.org.uk/peakdistrict.

Various waymarked walks and information barns on the estate. **Dogs**: must be on a lead at all times from early March to end July.

Access for all: ♿🚻♿♿ Penny Pot Café ♿

Getting here: 110:SK100855. Within the Peak District National Park. **Foot**: Pennine Way and many miles of footpaths. **Cycle**: Pennine Bridleway and many other routes. **Bus**: from Sheffield, Bakewell and Manchester to

Castleton, Edale and Hope Valley. **Train**: Edale for Kinder Scout and Mam Tor; Chinley for Kinder Scout west; Hope for Losehill; Bamford for Upper Derwent Valley. **Road**: A57 Sheffield to Manchester, A625 through Hope Valley. **Parking**: pay and display at Mam Nick (SK123833). Other pay and display at Edale, Castleton, Bowden Bridge, Upper Derwent Valley and Hayfield (not National Trust).

Finding out more: 01433 670368 or peakdistrict@nationaltrust.org.uk. Dark Peak Estate Office, Edale End, Hope Valley, Derbyshire S33 6RF

Dark Peak		M	T	W	T	F	S	S
Estate								
Open all year		M	T	W	T	F	S	S
Penny Pot Café								
1 Jan–11 Mar	10–4:30		·	·	·	·	S	S
14 Mar–4 Nov	10–4:30		·	·	W	T	F	S	S
19 May–16 Sep	8:30–4:30	·	·	·	·	·	S	S
10 Nov–23 Dec	10–4		·	·	·	·	S	S
27 Dec–31 Dec	10–4	M	·	·	T	F	S	S

Information shelters open all year: Lee Barn (110:SK096855) and Dalehead (110:SK101843) in Edale; South Head (SK060854) at Kinder; Edale End (SK161864); Grindle Barns above Ladybower Reservoir (SK189895). Dalehead bunkhouse available to let; camping and bed and breakfast available at some farms. For accommodation visit website.

Spectacular view at Longshaw and Eastern Moors in the Peak District

Peak District: Longshaw and Eastern Moors

Longshaw, near Sheffield, Derbyshire

Map ③ C2

Longshaw offers spectacular views of the Peak District, with ancient woods, meadows, parkland, heather moorland and many unusual sites – from millstone quarries to packhorse routes. The adjacent Eastern Moors, managed in partnership with the RSPB, offers a good network of footpaths and fantastic views. **Note**: Moorland Discovery Centre only open to the public for certain events and during school holidays.

Exploring
   – Follow walking trails through the ancient woods and hay meadows.
   – Enjoy spectacular views over the Derwent Valley and Peak District.

Exploring – Discover more with the guidebook and Hairy Wood Ant trail.
– Check out our new Granby Information Barn.

Eating and shopping: browse in the shop for local and wildlife-themed products. Enjoy delicious homemade food using produce from the kitchen garden, the wider estate and the Peak District, including daily specials. All food comes with wonderful views.

Making the most of your day: year-round events programme, including seasonal family events and trails. Circular, waymarked walks to explore the park and woodland and new geocaching trail. Wildlife webcams in the Visitor Centre. **Dogs**: on estate on-leads from early March to end of July.

Access for all: ⓟⒹ♿🚾👶📷🅰️ Building 🏢 Grounds 🚶♿➡️

Getting here: 110/119:SK266800. 7½ miles from Sheffield. **Foot**: 2 miles Grindleford, 3 miles Hathersage. **Cycle**: from Sheffield via Moss Road and Houndkirk bridleways. **Bus**: services from Sheffield to Castleton 🚃, Matlock and Buxton 🚃. **Train**: Grindleford 2 miles. **Road**: A625 Sheffield to Hathersage road; Woodcroft car park off B6055, near junction with A625. **Parking**: at Haywood (110/119: SK256778), Wooden Pole (110/119: SK267790), Woodcroft (110/119: SK267802). All pay and display.

Finding out more: 01433 637904 (Longshaw). 01433 630316 (Eastern Moors) or peakdistrict@nationaltrust.org.uk. Estate Office, Longshaw Estate, Longshaw, Sheffield, Derbyshire S11 7TZ

Longshaw and Eastern Moors		M	T	W	T	F	S	S
Estate								
Open all year	Dawn–dusk	M	T	W	T	F	S	S
Visitor Centre								
1 Jan–12 Feb	10:30–4	·	·	·	·	·	S	S
13 Feb–4 Nov	10:30–5	M	T	W	T	F	S	S
10 Nov–23 Dec	10:30–4	·	·	·	·	·	S	S
27 Dec–31 Dec	10:30–4	M	·	·	T	F	S	S

Open Bank Holiday Mondays. Lodge is not open to the public. Closed 24 to 26 December. White Edge Lodge available as holiday let throughout year (visit website for details).

Peak District: White Peak

White Peak Estate, Ilam, Ashbourne, Derbyshire and Peak District

Map ③ B3

White Peak Estate is situated in the spectacular setting of the Staffordshire and Derbyshire Peak District. Explore the rich daleside grasslands and ash woodlands in dramatic Dovedale. Enjoy Ilam Park's beautiful location beside the River Manifold, relax in the tea-room with amazing views of Dovedale, browse in the shop and discover the visitor centre with changing exhibitions. You can stay on our caravan site at Ilam Park, or our holiday cottages at Wetton Mill in the magnificent Manifold Valley. Use it as a base to explore the other parts of the White Peak Estate, such as Winster Market House. **Note**: Ilam Hall is let to the Youth Hostel Association.

Exploring – Discover the dramatic limestone dalesides of Dovedale.
– Enjoy historic Ilam Park's gardens, park and walks.
– Manifold Valley – walks and cycling on the old railway line.
– Be reminded of local life in Winster Market House.
– Climb to the top of Thorpe Cloud for fantastic views.
– Explore the wide open spaces of the southern Peak District.

Eating and shopping: enjoy homemade dishes at Manifold tea-room at Ilam Park. Find great gifts in the Ilam Park shop and the mobile barn at Dovedale. Buy award-winning meat at the Peak District farm shop. Tea-room also at Wetton Mill (not National Trust).

Making the most of your day: varied programme of guided walks, talks and exhibitions. New walks postcards in the shop, downloadable walking trails, geocaches, audio trails and podcasts from the Peak District website. **Dogs**: under close control and on leads in areas with livestock.

Access for all:

Ilam Park stableyard 🏃‍♿ Winster Market House ♿

Ilam Park grounds 🏃🏃🏃➡️♿

Getting here: 119:SK132507 (Ilam Park), 119:SK152514 (Dovedale), 119:SK241606 (Winster Market House). Ilam Park and Dovedale are 4½ miles north-west of Ashbourne. Winster Market House is in Winster village, 4 miles west of Matlock. **Cycle**: NCN68, 2 miles. **Bus**: for Ilam and Dovedale: services from Buxton ₪ to Ashbourne, daily, alight Thorpe, 2 miles (Monday to Saturday, Ilam village Sunday and Bank Holidays). For Winster Market House from Bakewell to Matlock ₪, daily. **Parking**: in Ilam Park (pay and display).

Finding out more: 01335 350503 or peakdistrict@nationaltrust.org.uk. White Peak Estate Office, Home Farm, Ilam, Ashbourne, Derbyshire DE6 2AZ

White Peak		M	T	W	T	F	S	S
Ilam Park								
Open all year	Dawn–dusk	M	T	W	T	F	S	S
Dovedale mobile barn								
6 Apr–30 Sep	11–5	M	T	W	T	F	S	S
Ilam Park shop								
13 Feb–4 Nov	11–5	M	T	W	T	F	S	S
10 Nov–23 Dec	11–4	·	·	·	·	F	S	S
26 Dec–31 Dec	11–4	M	·	W	T	F	S	S
Ilam Park tea-room								
13 Feb–4 Nov	10:30–5	M	T	W	T	F	S	S
10 Nov–23 Dec	11–4	·	·	·	·	·	S	S
24 Dec–31 Dec	11–4	M	·	W	T	F	S	S
Ilam Park shop and tea-room								
1 Jan–12 Feb	11–4	·	·	·	·	·	S	S
Winster Market House								
31 Mar–4 Nov	11–5	M	T	W	T	F	S	S

For shop and tea-room Christmas opening telephone 01335 350503. Closed 25 December. Ilam Hall: available for overnight accommodation via the Youth Hostel Association (telephone 01335 350212). Ilam Park caravan site: open 31 March to 4 November, daily 8 to 8.

Priest's House

Easton on the Hill, near Stamford, Northamptonshire PE9 3LS

Map ③ E5   🏠 1966

A delightful small late 15th-century building, with interesting local architecture and a museum exploring Easton's industrial past.

Access for all: Building ♿🏃

Getting here: 141:TF009045. Approximately 2 miles south-west of Stamford off A43.

Finding out more: 01780 762619 or priestshouse2@nationaltrust.org.uk

Priest's House
Unmanned. Open by appointment daily throughout year. Names of keyholders on property noticeboard. Appointments for groups may be made through volunteer custodian Mr Paul Way, 39 Church Street, Easton on the Hill, Stamford PE9 3LL.

Rosedene

Victoria Road, Dodford, near Bromsgrove, Worcestershire B61 9BU

Map ④ J6   1997

Restored 1840s cottage, organic garden and orchard illustrating the mid-19th-century Chartist movement – a time of remarkable British political change. **Note**: available to hire as a 'back to basics' holiday cottage.

Rosedene, Worcestershire, was home to Chartists from the mid-19th century

Places may occasionally close for conservation, safety or events

The fine Georgian mansion which is the centrepiece of the Shugborough Estate in Staffordshire

Access for all: Building  Grounds 🏠

Getting here: 150:SO929730. Follow signs for Dodford off A448, left into Priory Road, left into Church Road, then left into Victoria Road.

Finding out more: 01527 821214 or rosedene@nationaltrust.org.uk

---

Rosedene
Admission by guided tours, first Sunday of the month only, from 4 March to 2 December (booking essential). Tours available 10, 11:30, 1 and 2:30. Limited group visits at other times by arrangement (not in July or August).

Shugborough Estate

Milford, near Stafford, Staffordshire ST17 0XB

Map ④ J4   🏠🏚🖼️🐾❄️🌺
🎣🌳🏚🍵 1966

Shugborough is the ancestral home of the Earls of Lichfield. With rumoured connections to the Holy Grail, the 364-hectare (900-acre) classical landscape is peppered with unusual monuments. The fine Georgian mansion house, with magnificent views over riverside garden terraces, features stunning collections of porcelain. Costumed characters work in the servants' quarters and farmstead: doing laundry, cheese-making, milling, brewing and baking. In these areas the Staffordshire County Council Museum collections are held, including reconstructed chemist shop, tailors' shop, Victorian schoolroom and puppet collection. In addition, the newly restored walled garden grows historic varieties of fruit and vegetables. **Note**: Shugborough is run by Staffordshire County Council. Only house and gardens are free to members.

Exploring
- Enjoy the whole estate: purchase a reduced estate ticket.
- New: Patrick Lichfield's private apartments are now open.
- Enjoy new museum galleries – toys, costumes, health, trades and wildlife.
- Try out the beds in the new servants' bedroom.
- Uncover the art of historic gardening in the walled garden.
- Visit Patrick Lichfield's private island arboretum.

Eating and shopping: licensed tea-room serving homemade, locally sourced food. Seek out the perfect present in our gift shop. Treat yourself in the ice-cream parlour. Old-fashioned sweet shop and craft outlets making and selling handmade goods.

Making the most of your day: year-round varied events programme, concerts, open-air theatre productions, themed weekends and family fun. **Dogs**: on leads in parkland and gardens only.

Access for all: 🅿️🚻♿🛗🪑📷📹👓🔊
Building 🏚 Grounds 🏠➡️

Getting here: 127:SJ992225. 6 miles east of Stafford. **Foot**: access from east, from the canal/Great Haywood side of the estate. Estate walks link to towpaths along Trent & Mersey Canal and Staffordshire & Worcestershire Canal and to Cannock Chase trails. On Staffordshire Way. **Bus**: Stafford ⊟ to Lichfield (passing close Lichfield City ⊟). **Train**: Rugeley 5 miles; Rugeley Trent Valley 5 miles; Stafford 6 miles. **Road**: on A513, entrance at Milford. Signposted from M6 exit 13. **Parking**: £3 (pay and display, including members). Refunded on purchase of an all-sites ticket.

Finding out more: 0845 459 8900 or shugborough@nationaltrust.org.uk

Shugborough Estate		M	T	W	T	F	S	S
House, farm, servants' quarters, grounds and tea-room								
16 Mar–28 Oct	11–5	M	T	W	T	F	S	S
Shop								
16 Mar–28 Oct	11–5	M	T	W	T	F	S	S
29 Oct–23 Dec	11–4	M	T	W	T	F	S	S

Staunton Harold Church

Staunton Harold, Ashby-de-la-Zouch, Leicestershire LE65 1RW

Map ③ C4   ✚ 1954

This is one of the few churches built between the outbreak of the English Civil War and the Restoration period. **Note**: toilets 500 yards (not National Trust). Staunton Harold Estate not National Trust so parking charges apply.

Access for all: 🅿♿ **Building** ♿♿

Getting here: 128:SK380209. 5 miles north-east of Ashby-de-la-Zouch, west of B587. Access from M42/A42 exit 13, follow Ferrers Centre brown signs – anvil symbol.

Finding out more: 01332 863822 (Calke Abbey) or stauntonharoldchurch@nationaltrust.org.uk

Staunton Harold Church		M	T	W	T	F	S	S
31 Mar–28 Oct	1–4:30	·	·	·	·	·	S	S
30 May–31 Aug	1–4:30	·	·	W	T	F	S	S

Church open Good Friday and Bank Holidays April to October. Services: Easter to December, second and fourth Sundays.

Mr Straw's House

5-7 Blyth Grove, Worksop, Nottinghamshire S81 0JG

Map ③ D2   🏠 ❖ 1990

Step back in time to the early 20th-century and find out how a grocer's family lived in this market town. This ordinary semi-detached house, with original interior decorations from 1923, was the home of the Straw family. For 60 years the family threw little away and chose to live without many of the modern comforts we take for granted. Be intrigued by stories of the family who made an extraordinary home in this ordinary house – hear about the times they lived in and see the everyday objects they treasured.

Exploring
– Get to know the Straw family with an introductory video.
– Explore three floors of an Edwardian house with informative guides.
– See the annual exhibition of items not usually on display.

Mr Straw's House, Nottinghamshire: intriguing

Mr Straw's House, Nottinghamshire: hats and coats

Exploring – Visit the garden and replica greenhouse with the cacti collection.
– Discover an extraordinary family home in an ordinary house.
– Occasional activity days and events.

Eating and shopping: small shop area with snacks and souvenirs.

Making the most of your day: tea and cakes, usually on first Saturday in month in orchard car park (provided by Friends group).

Access for all: [icons]
No 5 [icon] No 7 [icon] Back garden [icon]

Getting here: 120:SK592802. In private road in suburbs north of Worksop town centre. **Cycle**: NCN6, ¾ mile. **Bus**: services from Worksop. **Train**: Worksop ½ mile. **Road**: follow signs for Bassetlaw Hospital and Blyth Road (B6045). Blyth Grove is a small private road off B6045, just south of Bassetlaw Hospital A&E entrance. House signposted with black and white sign at the entrance to Blyth Grove. **Parking**: free, across the road.

Finding out more: 01909 482380 or mrstrawshouse@nationaltrust.org.uk

Mr Straw's House		M	T	W	T	F	S	S
13 Mar–27 Oct	11–5	·	**T**	**W**	**T**	**F**	**S**	·

Admission by timed ticket only, including members – must be booked in advance by telephone or letter (with sae), not email, to property. On quiet days a same-day telephone call is often sufficient. Last admission one hour before closing. Closed Good Friday.

Sudbury Hall and the National Trust Museum of Childhood

Sudbury, Ashbourne, Derbyshire DE6 5HT

Map ③ B4   [icons]  [1967]

'Great fun, staff were friendly, great with parents and children alike – you offer great value for money. Thank you.'
Mrs E. Wood, Ashbourne

Sudbury, 'two days out in one'. The country home of the Lords Vernon, a delight of 17th-century craftsmanship, featuring exquisite plasterwork, wood carvings and classical story-based murals. Has this fashion stood the test of time? The Museum of Childhood is a delight for all ages with something for everyone. Explore the childhoods of times gone by, make stories, play with toys and share your childhood with others. You can be a chimney sweep, a scullion or a Victorian pupil. How has childhood changed over time?

Exploring – Visitors love our morning taster tours of the Hall.
– Be amazed by our magnificent Long Gallery.
– Was George Vernon's vision an enduring fashion or fleeting fad?
– Have a birthday party with a difference here at Sudbury.
– Use your imagination to create a magical story.
– Come and 'rock the boat' in our woodland play area.

Eating and shopping: looking for toys or gifts? We offer both at Sudbury. Relax and take time out in tranquil surroundings with a latte or cappuccino, and indulge in our delicious seasonal menus.

Sudbury Hall and the National Trust Museum of Childhood, Derbyshire: two days out in one

Making the most of your day: join in our family crafts in the school holidays. Find our upside-down bedrooms. Play billiards and pretend to be a 'gentleman'. Follow in the footsteps of Mr Darcy. **Dogs**: assistance dogs only.

Access for all: [icons] Sudbury Hall [icons]
Museum of Childhood [icons] Grounds [icons]

Getting here: 128:SK158322. 6 miles east of Uttoxeter. **Cycle**: NCN54. **Bus**: from Burton to Uttoxeter. **Train**: Tutbury & Hatton 5 miles. **Road**: 6 miles east of Uttoxeter at junction of A50 Derby to Stoke and A515 Ashbourne. **Parking**: free, 500 yards.

Finding out more: 01283 585305 (Infoline). 01283 585337 or sudburyhall@nationaltrust.org.uk

Sudbury Hall		M	T	W	T	F	S	S
Hall								
11 Feb–4 Nov	1–5	·	·	W	T	F	S	S
Museum, restaurant and shops								
11 Feb–1 Apr	11–5	·	·	W	T	F	S	S
2 Apr–4 Nov	11–5	M	T	W	T	F	S	S
8 Nov–9 Dec	11–4	·	·	·	T	F	S	S
Hall tours								
11 Feb–4 Nov	11–12	·	·	W	T	F	S	S
3 Apr–30 Oct	11–2	·	T	·	·	·	·	·
Christmas event								
1 Dec–9 Dec	11–4	M	T	W	T	F	S	S
Grounds								
11 Feb–9 Dec	10–5	M	T	W	T	F	S	S

Open Bank Holiday Mondays. Last admission 45 minutes before closing (Hall will close early if light level is poor). Hall tours available Wednesdays to Sundays between 11 and 12 and Tuesdays between 11 and 2 (please note that not all rooms are open as part of these tours). Average length of visit to both Hall and Museum of Childhood is three hours. School bookings: 01283 585022.

Sunnycroft

200 Holyhead Road, Wellington, Telford, Shropshire TF1 2DR

Map ④ I4 1999

Tucked away in Wellington is this rare suburban villa and mini estate. This Edwardian time capsule, with original contents and features, transports you back to the pre-First World War 'country-house' lifestyle. Sunnycroft tells the story of a brewer, a widow, and three generations of a local industrialist family. **Note**: no credit or debit card facilities.

Exploring – Open every weekend in November and December.
– Take a free guided tour of the house or garden.
– Play croquet or badminton and picnic on the lawn.
– Have a go at our children's trails.

Eating and shopping: take afternoon tea or a light lunch in the Smoking Room or out on the veranda. Pick up a bargain in the second-hand bookshop and – new this year – buy a Sunnycroft souvenir.

Making the most of your day: events programme reflects Sunnycroft's heyday, including a traditional Easter Egg hunt, garden fête in July, harvest-themed Michaelmas Fair in September and Edwardian Christmas. **Dogs**: welcome on leads in grounds only.

Access for all: ⓅⒹ🚾◻♿
Building ⬆ Grounds 🚶➡

Getting here: 127:SJ652109. In Wellington. **Cycle**: NCN81, 1 mile. **Bus**: from Telford (passing Wellington ≥). **Train**: Wellington ½ mile. **Road**: M54 exit 7, follow B5061 towards Wellington. **Sat Nav**: enter address not postcode. **Parking**: free, 150 yards in orchard. Additional free parking in Wrekin Road car park (not National Trust).

Finding out more: 01952 242884 or sunnycroft@nationaltrust.org.uk

Sunnycroft		M	T	W	T	F	S	S
2 Mar–5 Nov*	10:30–5	M	·	·	·	F	S	S
10 Nov–9 Dec**	10:30–2	·	·	·	·	·	S	S
15 Dec–23 Dec	10:30–4	M	T	W	T	F	S	S

*Timed tickets with ten-minute introductory talk, then free-flow (not bookable). Three guided tours daily (places limited). **Winter entry by guided tour only starting on the hour. Free-flow throughout house for Bank Holiday weekends, Christmas and event days. Open for the Queen's Diamond Jubilee (5 June). Last admission one hour before closing.

Sunnycroft in Shropshire: an Edwardian 'country-house' lifestyle in suburbia

Tattershall Castle

Sleaford Road, Tattershall,
Lincolnshire LN4 4LR

Map ③ F3 1925

Explore all six floors of this stunning red-brick medieval castle built by Ralph Cromwell, Lord Treasurer of England in 1434. Let the audio guide create a picture of what life was like at Tattershall Castle in the 15th century. Climb the 150 steps from the basement to the battlements and enjoy the magnificent views of the Lincolnshire countryside from the roof. Keep an eye out on summer weekends for a passing Spitfire, Hurricane or even a Lancaster Bomber! Then explore the grounds, moats, Guardhouse gift shop and neighbouring church – the largest parish church in the country!

Exploring
- Explore all six floors, from the basement to the battlements.
- Enjoy amazing views from the roof.
- Follow the audio tour (family and children's versions).
- Picnic in the moated grounds.
- Explore the church, also built by Ralph Cromwell.
- Visit the neighbouring RAF Battle of Britain Centre (weekdays only).

Eating and shopping: buy presents for all the family in our fully refurbished Guardhouse gift shop. Relax and enjoy light refreshments, also available from the shop.

Making the most of your day: major events, audio guides, family activities and 'have a go' sessions. **Dogs:** assistance dogs only.

Access for all: 🅿️♿👆♿📷📱📲
Building ♿🏠🅱️ **Grounds** ♿🏠

Getting here: 122:TF211575. 10 miles south-west of Horncastle. **Cycle:** NCN1 passes within 1 mile. **Bus:** from Lincoln to Boston (passing close Lincoln ➤). **Train:** Ruskington 10 miles. **Road:** on south side of A153, 15 miles north-east of Sleaford. **Parking:** free, 150 yards.

Vaulted ceiling at Tattershall Castle, Lincolnshire

Finding out more: 01526 342543 or tattershallcastle@nationaltrust.org.uk

Tattershall Castle		M	T	W	T	F	S	S
3 Mar–11 Mar	11–4	·	·	·	·	·	**S**	**S**
12 Mar–31 Oct	11–5	**M**	**T**	**W**	·	·	**S**	**S**
3 Nov–16 Dec	11–4	·	·	·	·	·	**S**	**S**

Open Good Friday. Last audio guide issued one hour before closing. Opens 1 some Saturdays if hosting a wedding (please ring in advance to confirm).

Town Walls Tower

Shrewsbury, Shropshire SY1 1TN

Map ④ H4 1930

This last remaining 14th-century watchtower sits on what were once the medieval fortified, defensive walls of Shrewsbury. **Note:** no toilet or car parking and 40 extremely steep steps to top floor of property.

Access for all: **Building** ♿

Getting here: 126:SJ492122. Close to town centre between English and Welsh Bridges, on south of town wall.

Finding out more: 01743 708162 or townwallstower@nationaltrust.org.uk

Town Walls Tower		M	T	W	T	F	S	S
28 Apr	11–3	·	·	·	·	·	S	·
20 May	11–3	·	·	·	·	·	·	S
23 Jun	11–3	·	·	·	·	·	S	·
8 Jul	11–3	·	·	·	·	·	·	S
12 Aug	11–3	·	·	·	·	·	·	S
29 Sep	11–3	·	·	·	·	·	S	·

Tours between 11 and 3. Last admission 20 minutes before closing.

Ulverscroft Nature Reserve

Ulverscroft, Copt Oak, near Loughborough, Leicestershire

Map ③ D5 1945

Part of the ancient forest of Charnwood, Ulverscroft is especially beautiful during the spring bluebell season. Heathland and woodland habitats. **Note**: no toilet. Access by permit only from Leicestershire and Rutland Wildlife Trust, 0116 272 0444.

Access for all: Grounds 🧑‍🦽

Getting here: 129:SK493118. 6 miles south-west of Loughborough.

Finding out more: 01332 863822 or ulverscroftnaturereserve@nationaltrust.org.uk

Ulverscroft Nature Reserve

Access by permit only from The Secretary, Leicestershire and Rutland Wildlife Trust, Brocks Hill Environment Centre, Washbrook Lane, Oadby, Leicestershire LE2 5JJ (0116 272 0444). Please allow a week to receive permit.

Upton House and Gardens

near Banbury, Warwickshire OX15 6HT

Map ④ L7   🏠 ❀ 🏠 🔔 🍴 1948

Join the guests of Lord and Lady Bearsted and experience a weekend house party of a 1930s millionaire. Surrounded by internationally important art and porcelain collections, hear and discover more about family life and soak up the atmosphere of the party. See the red and silver art deco bathroom and get close to art works by El Greco, Stubbs and Bosch. The stunning gardens – being returned to their 1930s heyday – have a sweeping lawn which gives way to a series of terraces and herbaceous borders leading to a kitchen garden, tranquil water garden and spring bulb displays. **Note**: some areas of the gardens may be closed for ongoing maintenance.

Exploring
- 2012 Year of Art: discover the stories behind our paintings.
- Preview the house and collections on our daily Taster Tours.
- New for families: activity packs, dressing up and play spaces.
- Wander among the colourful 1930s herbaceous borders.
- The kitchen garden flourishes in summer and supplies the restaurant.
- Winter opening – with new art exhibition and more.

Eating and shopping: visit the shop for a wide range of memorabilia, gifts and books, locally sourced food and plants inspired by Upton's beautiful garden. Enjoy homemade cakes and local produce in the restaurant. Book the restaurant or squash court for your function.

Making the most of your day: read family papers, taste cooking in the kitchen, play snooker or listen to 1930s broadcasts. Family events, jazz concerts and garden tours. National Collection of Asters in bloom in September.

Long Gallery at Upton House, Warwickshire

Access for all: ⬛⬛⬛⬛⬛⬛⬛⬛⬛ ⬛⬛ Building ⬛⬛⬛ Grounds ⬛⬛⬛

Getting here: 151:SP371461. On the edge of the Cotswolds, between Banbury and Stratford-upon-Avon. **Foot**: footpath SM177 runs adjacent to property, Centenary Way ½ mile, Macmillan Way 1 mile. **Cycle**: NCN5, 5 miles. Oxfordshire Cycle Way 1½ miles. **Train**: Banbury 7 miles. **Road**: on A422, 7 miles north of Banbury, 12 miles south-east of Stratford-upon-Avon. Signed from exit 12 of M40. **Parking**: free, 300 yards, on grass.

Finding out more: 01295 670266 or uptonhouse@nationaltrust.org.uk

Upton House and Gardens		M	T	W	T	F	S	S
Servants exhibition, spring walk, shop and restaurant*								
11 Feb–5 Mar	11–4	M	·	·	·	F	S	S
House**								
9 Mar–5 Nov	1–5	M	T	W	·	F	S	S
9 Nov–23 Dec	12–4	M	·	·	·	F	S	S
Taster tours***								
9 Mar–5 Nov	11–1	M	T	W	·	F	S	S
Garden, restaurant, shop and plant centre								
9 Mar–5 Nov	11–5	M	T	W	·	F	S	S
Art exhibition, winter walk, shop and restaurant*								
9 Nov–23 Dec	12–4	M	·	·	·	F	S	S
26 Dec–31 Dec	12–4	M	·	W	T	F	S	S

*Short guided tours throughout day, timed tickets available on arrival only. **Open Thursdays during summer holidays; admission from 11 on Bank Holidays by timed ticket (visitors may stay to 5); part of house only open in November and December. ***Tours last 35 minutes and focus on part of the collection, timed tickets available on arrival only. **20 July to 5 September: open every day.**

The Weir

Swainshill, Hereford, Herefordshire HR4 7QF

Map ④ H7   🏛 ✸ ⛵ 1959

Stunning riverside garden with sweeping views along the River Wye and Herefordshire countryside. The garden is spectacular all year round – drifts of spring bulbs give way to wild flowers, followed by autumn colour, and the walled garden is full of fruit and vegetables. Worth a visit any time of year. **Note**: sturdy footwear recommended.

Exploring
– New: visit the walled garden.
– Enjoy the carpets of spring flowers and summer wild flowers.
– Stunning views across the River Wye.
– The mature trees provide an array of autumn colour.

Eating and shopping: take a hamper to one of the riverside picnic sites.

Making the most of your day: children's days in school holidays (check for details). Open-air theatre. **Dogs**: assistance dogs only in garden – may be exercised on leads in the car park.

Access for all: ⬛ Grounds ⬛⬛

Getting here: 149:SO438418. 5 miles west of Hereford. **Bus**: to Hereford and then taxi. **Train**: Hereford 5 miles. **Road**: on A438. **Parking**: free.

Finding out more: 01981 590509 (Infoline). 01568 782120 (Croft office) or theweir@nationaltrust.org.uk

The Weir		M	T	W	T	F	S	S
11 Feb–19 Feb	11–4	M	T	W	T	F	S	S
25 Feb–4 Nov	11–5	M	T	W	T	F	S	S

Last admission 45 minutes before closing.

Wichenford Dovecote

Wichenford, Worcestershire WR6 6XY

Map ④ I7 1965

A charming 17th-century half-timbered dovecote at Wichenford Court. The building, although small, is very striking. **Note**: no access to Wichenford Court (privately owned). No toilet or tea-room. Please consider local residents when parking.

Access for all: Building 👤

Getting here: 150:SO788598. 5 miles north-west of Worcester, north of B4204.

Finding out more: 01527 821214 or wichenforddovecote@nationaltrust.org.uk

Wichenford Dovecote
Open every day all year from 9 to 5
Closed dusk if earlier. Open other times by appointment.

Wightwick Manor and Gardens

Wightwick Bank, Wolverhampton, West Midlands WV6 8EE

Map ④ J5 1937

A vision of the house beautiful and one family's passion for Victorian art. In 1884 Wolverhampton politician and industrialist Theodore Mander heard the Oscar Wilde lecture on the 'House Beautiful' and was inspired to commission a house in the old English style. The new house of red brick and timber beams was then furnished with pieces by William Morris to create a sumptuous interior. Theodore's son Geoffrey added a garden of yew hedges and roses, and filled the house with paintings and sketches by Rossetti, Burne-Jones and ceramics by William De Morgan, as well as enlarging the Morris collection. **Note**: entry by timed tickets only

(including members) – from reception. Tea-rooms unable to accept card payment.

Exploring
- Paintings by the finest artists of the Pre-Raphaelite movement.
- Rare surviving Arts and Craft garden by Thomas Mawson.
- Our Edwardian kitchen garden supplies produce for the tea-room.
- Games for adults in the billiards room.
- Games for children in the day nursery.
- Award-winning Carribean community herb garden.

Eating and shopping: William Morris and Arts and Crafts-inspired shop – now available online at www.shop.nationaltrust.org.uk/williammorris. Tea-room serves food from our kitchen garden (currently unable to accept card payment). New stable block restaurant planned for this year.

Making the most of your day: house entry by combination of full or partially guided tour and free-flow (all with timed entry) depending on day and time of year. Full and varied calendar of events. **Dogs**: welcome on leads in garden.

Wightwick Manor and Gardens, West Midlands: delightful

Access for all: [icons]
Building [icons] Grounds [icons] ➡

Getting here: 139:SO869985. 3 miles west of Wolverhampton. **Bus**: regular service from Wolverhampton to Bridgnorth Road, alight Wightwick Bank on Bridgnorth Road beside Mermaid pub. **Train**: Wolverhampton 3 miles. **Road**: access A454 from junction with A4150 (ring road). From A41 follow brown signs on the B4161. **Sat Nav**: on approach please follow brown signs. **Parking**: off A454.

Finding out more: 01902 761400 or wightwickmanor@nationaltrust.org.uk

Wightwick Manor and Gardens		M	T	W	T	F	S	S
Garden, tea-room and shop								
11 Feb–19 Feb	11–4	M	T	W	T	F	S	S
3 Mar–4 Nov	11–5	M	·	W	T	F	S	S
10 Nov–25 Nov	11–4	·	·	·	·	·	S	S
1 Dec–23 Dec	11–4	M	·	W	T	F	S	S
House								
11 Feb–19 Feb	12–4	M	T	W	T	F	S	S
3 Mar–4 Nov	12–5	M	·	W	T	F	S	S
10 Nov–25 Nov	12–4	·	·	·	·	·	S	S
1 Dec–23 Dec	12–4	M	·	W	T	F	S	S

House: entry by timed ticket only (including free-flow days), available from visitor reception on day of visit (delays possible during peak times). Average house visit one hour to 90 minutes. February half-term and November: house will be shown during conservation cleaning – not all rooms and objects will be visible.

Wilderhope Manor

Longville, Much Wenlock, Shropshire TF13 6EG

Map ④ H5 [icons] 1936

Beautiful Elizabethan manor house restored by John Cadbury in 1936. Surrounding farmland managed for landscape and wildlife with permissive access. **Note**: manor is a popular youth hostel, so access to some rooms may be restricted.

Access for all: [icon] Building [icons] Grounds [icon]

Getting here: 138:SO545929. 7 miles south-west of Much Wenlock, 7 miles east of Church Stretton, ½ mile south of B4371.

Finding out more: 01694 771363 (Hostel Warden YHA) or wilderhope@nationaltrust.org.uk

Wilderhope Manor		M	T	W	T	F	S	S
8 Jan–1 Apr	2–4	·	·	·	·	·	·	S
4 Apr–30 Sep	2–4	·	·	W	·	·	·	S
7 Oct–23 Dec	2–4	·	·	·	·	·	·	S

The beautiful Elizabethan Wilderhope Manor, Shropshire, sits in a gently undulating landscape

Entry is still possible at most places up to 30 minutes before closing

Winster Market House

See Peak District: White Peak, page 247.

Woolsthorpe Manor

Water Lane, Woolsthorpe by Colsterworth,
near Grantham, Lincolnshire NG33 5PD

Map ③ E4   🏠 🏠 ❀ 1943

A small manor house but the birthplace of a
great mind – Isaac Newton, world-famous
scientist, mathematician, alchemist and Master
of the Royal Mint. During the plague years of
1665–7, he returned from Cambridge University
and produced some of his most important
work on physics and mathematics here,
including his crucial experiment to split white
light into a spectrum of colours. Meanwhile
family life and the work of the farm went
on. Today you can still see the famous apple
tree and explore some of Newton's ideas for
yourself in the Science Discovery Centre.

Newton's telescope at Woolsthorpe Manor, Lincolnshire

October and summer holiday workshops for
children. **Dogs**: welcome in car park only.

Access for all: 🅿️ 🅳 🚾 🏠 🔗 💻 ♿ ⦂ 🖼
Building 🔗 🏠 ♿ **Science Discovery Centre** 🏠 ♿
Grounds 🔗 🏠

Exploring
– Be inspired by the house where a genius grew up.
– Experiment in the hands-on Science Discovery Centre.
– Contemplate the apple tree with a place in history.
– See the short film about Newton's experiments at Woolsthorpe.
– Hear the inside stories as told by our volunteers.
– Say hello to our rare breed sheep.

Eating and shopping: refuel with tea, coffee
and cake in our small café. Visit the small shop
in the Goat House ticket office.

Making the most of your day: programme
of events, including regular 'Tales from
Woolsthorpe' and Conservation in Action.
National Science Week in March, Apple Day in

Getting here: 130:SK924244. 8 miles south of
Grantham, ½ mile north-west of Colsterworth.
Foot: footpath from Colsterworth; Viking Way
3 miles. **Bus**: from Grantham to South Witham
(passes close Grantham ≢). **Train**: Grantham,
8 miles. **Road**: at Woolsthorpe by Colsterworth
(not Woolsthorpe near Belvoir). Follow brown
signs from A1. From Melton take B676 towards
Colsterworth; 1 mile after Stainby turn left
onto Old Post Lane, then left into Water Lane.
Parking: free, 50 yards.

Finding out more: 01476 860338 or
woolsthorpemanor@nationaltrust.org.uk.
23 Newton Way, Woolsthorpe by Colsterworth,
near Grantham, Lincolnshire NG33 5NR

Woolsthorpe Manor		M	T	W	T	F	S	S
2 Mar–11 Mar	11–5						F	S	S
14 Mar–4 Nov	11–5			W	T	F	S	S

Open Bank Holiday Mondays, 11 to 5. Timed tickets may be
in operation at busy times.

The Workhouse, Southwell

Upton Road, Southwell,
Nottinghamshire NG25 0PT

Map ③ D3   2002

Discover the most complete workhouse in existence. Find out about the Reverend Becher, the founder of The Workhouse, and immerse yourself in the unique atmosphere of the building. Learn about the true stories of the 19th-century poor, brought vividly to life by archive evidence. Discover how society dealt with poverty through the centuries, right up to the modern day. Explore the segregated work yards, day rooms, dormitories, master's quarters and cellars, then see the recreated working 19th-century garden and find out what food the paupers may have eaten.

Exploring — Take a thought-provoking look
at hidden histories of the poor.
— Decide for yourself whether
The Workhouse offered hope
or despair.
— Enjoy the drama of our Living
History events.
— Discover the challenges
of conserving an
'empty' property.
— Enjoy some quiet time in the
recreated vegetable garden.

Eating and shopping: our shop sells specialist publications and unique Workhouse souvenirs. We also sell fresh, seasonal produce from our vegetable garden.

Making the most of your day: programme of family activities, special events, tours and exhibitions. Children's trails and games to play.

Access for all: 🅿️🄳🚽🖐️🎧📷🎦🎵❗🅰️
Building 🦽🏠♿ Grounds ♿➡️

Getting here: 120:SK712543. 13 miles from Nottingham. **Foot**: Robin Hood Trail. **Cycle**: National Byway (Heritage Cycle Route). **Bus**: regular services from Newark, Nottingham and Mansfield bus stations. **Train**: Newark Castle 7 miles; Newark North Gate 7½ miles; Nottingham 13 miles. **Road**: 13 miles from Nottingham on A612 and 8 miles from Newark via A617 and A612. **Parking**: free, 200 yards.

Finding out more: 01636 817260 or theworkhouse@nationaltrust.org.uk

The Workhouse, Southwell	M	T	W	T	F	S	S
Workhouse*							
29 Feb–28 Oct 12–5				W	T	F	S	S

*Guided tour of the outside and other buildings at 11. No booking is required but numbers are limited. Open Bank Holidays. Last admission one hour before closing.

The Workhouse, Southwell, Nottinghamshire

North West

A magical moment as sunlight glances through the trees at Ennerdale

Outdoors in the North West

Visit the North West and discover some of Britain's finest landscapes, wildlife and fascinating industrial heritage, while enjoying amazing hospitality, as well as great food and drink.

Right:
Derwentwater, Cumbria
Below:
Wasdale, Cumbria

The unbeatable Lake District

For pure drama and internationally renowned beauty, the Lake District is unbeatable.

Whether you like a gentle stroll with friends around a tarn, a hike in the fells to a picnic spot, or a challenging cycle ride on rugged terrain, you'll have plenty of chance to share your experiences here, capture memories and return home spiritually refreshed.

The Trust looks after one quarter of the Lake District, encouraging access and enjoyment of this magnificent place. We care for England's highest mountain, Scafell Pike, and our deepest lake, Wastwater, and most of the central fells and major valley heads, together with 24 lakes and tarns. The Lake District Appeal exists to help fund this work.

Beatrix Potter, whose love of the area is legend, left us 1,600 hectares (4,000 acres) and 14 farms when she died in 1943. This great estate had already begun to be purchased piece by piece – beginning in 1902 with Brandelhow on the shore of Derwentwater, funded by local people who wanted to save it from development by wealthy Victorian merchants.

You'll find a huge variety of plants, trees and other wildlife, all thriving in our valleys and woodlands and on our crags. Look out for meadow flowers and the rare small-leaved lime, fine sessile oak woodlands and internationally important lichens, mosses and insects as well as many different bird species, including wildfowl and waders.

Why not stay in one of our holiday cottages, ranging from luxurious large cottages to small cosy hideaways – some right on the lakeshores, some with sweeping views?

Clockwise from top: **Great Langdale, fungi at Ennerdale, and Wasdale – all in Cumbria**

Stunning views and ancient history

In West Cheshire explore the very special Sandstone Ridge, with splendid views of the Cheshire Plain and Welsh Mountains from Alderley Edge, Bickerton Hill and nearby Bulkeley Hill Wood; while Helsby Hill has views across the Mersey Estuary to Liverpool.

Both Bickerton and Helsby have Bronze Age forts at their summits, while Bulkeley, part of the Peckforton range of hills, has acres of ancient woodland and the Sandstone Trail running its length.

Views of the Peak District and Welsh Mountains, with wide expanses of the great Cheshire Plain, can be seen from The Cloud, a great rocky heathland near Timbersbrook in Cheshire.

We love food!

All our tea-rooms, restaurants, farm tea-rooms and pubs use local, seasonal produce to create mouthwatering dishes. So you'll always find something scrumptious, be it spring Herdwick lamb and fresh peas, a strawberry cream tea at the height of summer, a warming soup or stew to take away the autumn chill, or mince pies and mulled wine with the smell of cloves in the air to get you into the Christmas spirit.

Regional specialities include damson dishes at Sizergh, venison from the parks at Lyme, Dunham and Tatton, and Herdwick lamb from Trust farms in Cumbria. Acorn Bank's lovely garden gives us home-grown herbs and loads of rhubarb varieties.

There are also endless delicious cheeses to savour in Cheshire, which just happens to be the gooseberry centre of Britain. And if all that were not enough, many of our tenants now also supply Booths supermarkets in the region with Trust meat, so look out for it while shopping.

Ruins with a story

Further south lies the folly of Mow Cop; built in 1754, it is famed as the birthplace of Primitive Methodism and stands in romantic ruin. To the west of the county is the site of Lewis Carroll's birthplace near Daresbury – kindly donated to the Trust by the Lewis Carroll Birthplace Trust. Here you can find the 'footprint' of Daresbury Parsonage, in which Carroll was born in 1832, while nearby Daresbury Church has a stained-glass window featuring Carroll and his Wonderland characters.

South Cumbria and Lancashire's flora and fauna

Arnside Knott on the Cumbrian coast and Eaves and Waterslack Woods in Lancashire are home to a fantastic variety of wild flowers and butterflies.

Holme Park Fell, on the other side of the M6 as you approach Junction 36, is covered with heather and wild flowers and is home to numerous birds and bees, all thriving in its craggy and majestic limestone nooks and crannies.

Natterjack toads, a nationally rare species, live happily at Sandscale Haws in Cumbria, and at Formby in Lancashire you can hear their extraordinary mating calls on May and June evenings. Sandscale is also home to a rich variety of birds, including shelducks, eider ducks, goldeneyes and plovers, and the high, grass-covered sand dunes are perfect for a day's exploring. Formby also has one of the last remaining colonies of red squirrels in the country.

Green lungs of Manchester, Liverpool and Lancashire

Escape from the city to our open countryside, parkland and gardens – much of which is open all year round. The Stubbins Estate and Holcombe Moor provide open space to the north of Bury, Lancashire, with Dunham, Lyme and Quarry Bank Mill offering acres of parkland and walking trails for you to get away from the urban sprawl. Speke Hall, near Liverpool, offers greenery and space to play, while Rufford and Gawthorpe in Lancashire are set in tranquil gardens.

Right: **Borrowdale, Cumbria** Below: **Derwentwater, as seen from Friar's Crag, Cumbria**

Lake District car parks

Lanthwaite Wood	NY 149 215
Buttermere	NY 172 173
Honister Pass	NY 225 135
Seatoller	NY 246 137
Rosthwaite	NY 257 148
Bowderstone	NY 254 167
Watendlath	NY 276 164
Kettlewell	NY 269 196
Great Wood	NY 272 213
Aira Force	NY 401 201
Glencoyne Bay	NY 387 188
Wasdale Head	NY 182 074
Old Dungeon Ghyll	NY 285 062
Stickle Ghyll	NY 295 064
Elterwater	NY 329 047
Tarn Hows	SD 326 995
Ash Landing	SD 388 955
Sandscale Haws	SD 199 758
Blea Tarn	NY 295 043

Camp in the Lake District with the Trust

Low Wray Campsite
Lying on the quiet western shore of Windermere, this site has spectacular lake and fell views. There is lake access for non-powered boating activities, a new campsite visitor welcome area and shop, and newly refurbished toilet and shower blocks. Set in the heart of Beatrix Potter country, you can enjoy beautiful walks to Hill Top at Near Sawrey, Potter's home, as well as to the Beatrix Potter Gallery at Hawkshead and around Wray Castle's grounds.

Great Langdale Campsite
In the heart of the Lake District mountains, this is an ideal location for climbing and fell walking.

Just a few miles from Ambleside and convenient for the other Lakes' attractions, this is a great base from which to climb Scafell Pike, England's highest mountain, after which you should reward yourself with a pint in one of the nearby traditional Lakeland hostelries.

Wasdale Campsite
This site is a mere stone's throw from beautiful Wastwater, the deepest lake in England and one which has a distinctive Nordic character. The pyramidal peak of Great Gable is reflected in its waters.

Arguably the most dramatic location in England, Scafell Pike and numerous high fell walking routes are within striking distance. This is a remote place where peace and tranquillity reign.

Camping pods
For those who prefer something a little bit more luxurious than a tent...
For details and terms and conditions telephone 015394 63862 or visit **www.ntlakescampsites.org.uk**

Above left:
our campsite at Wasdale Head, Cumbria
Left:
wooden camping pod

Why not try...?

Something new in the Lake District
We've a fantastic new range of 'experiences' leaflets – from rugged coastal walks at Whitehaven to exhilarating cycle rides in the Yewdale Valley, and short walks through woodland at Aira Force and Tarn Hows to bouldering in the Langdale Valley. Visit the website to see what our virtual rangers have to recommend and download your 'experience'. Alternatively pick one up from our Information Points. Look out for our new Information Hub and Shop in Grasmere village, just opposite the church, or Claife Courtyard, just below Claife Station on the west shore of Windermere.

The Grasmere Gallop
Are you free on the second weekend in June? If so then this 6-mile trail run in the stunning setting of the Vale of Grasmere and Rydal could be just the challenge for you. For details visit **www.grasmeregallop.co.uk**

A car-free day
Enjoy leaving your car behind and catch the local bus, train or boat. Just sit back and enjoy the view. Or try a bike trail and feel at one with nature. For details telephone Traveline (see page 10 for details).

Tents and pods
Get back to nature by camping at one of our campsites in the Lake District, the perfect base for a holiday. Set in the most perfect countryside, you have the choice of traditional canvas or funky pods. For details see above.

Acorn Bank Garden and Watermill

Temple Sowerby, near Penrith,
Cumbria CA10 1SP

Map (6) E7   🏰🔧✿🏠 1950

'My visit to Acorn Bank was sheer bliss! An idyllic and peaceful oasis with aromas to calm the senses.'
V. Dawson, Knutsford

Best known for its comprehensive herb collection and traditional fruit orchards, Acorn Bank is a tranquil haven with an almost forgotten industrial past. Visit the tea-room, where culinary herbs and fruit from the garden are used daily in soups, salads and puddings. Wander along the Crowdundle Beck to the watermill, enjoying wildlife in the woods on the way, and discover more about the history of gypsum mining on the estate. Views across the Eden Valley to the Lake District from the magnificent backdrop of the sandstone house, which although not generally open to the public, is available as holiday apartments. **Note**: access to fragile grass paths in the garden may be restricted after wet weather.

Exploring
– Relax in the tranquil and sheltered walled gardens.
– Discover fascinating stories behind the plants in the herb garden.
– Find great crested newts in the garden pond.

Exploring
– Watch the waterwheel turning at the mill (most weekend afternoons).
– Listen to birdsong as you stroll beside Crowdundle Beck.
– See the salads for your lunch growing in the hotbeds.

Eating and shopping: enjoy local produce and the garden's herbs and fruit in the tea-room, where delicious cakes and scones are freshly made in our kitchen. Browse among the plants for sale in the courtyard and local and national products in the shop.

Making the most of your day: Apple Day, 14 October, is a great day out for the whole family (charge, including members). **Dogs**: welcome on leads on woodland walk/garden courtyard. Apple Day: assistance dogs only.

Access for all: 🅿️ 🅿️ 🚻 🔧 🔧 💻 🔧 ⠿ 📷
Watermill 🔧🔧 **Shop and admission point** 🔧🔧
Grounds 🔧🔧🔧➡️🔧

Getting here: 91:NY612281. 6 miles east of Penrith. **Foot**: public footpath from Temple Sowerby. **Cycle**: NCN7, 6 miles. **Bus**: Penrith to Kirkby Stephen, to within 1 mile. **Train**: Langwathby 5 miles; Penrith 6 miles. **Road**: 1 mile from A66. **Parking**: free.

Finding out more: 017683 61893 or acornbank@nationaltrust.org.uk

Acorn Bank		M	T	W	T	F	S	S
Garden, watermill, woodland walks and shop								
11 Feb–4 Mar	10–5	·	·	·	·	·	S	S
10 Mar–4 Nov	10–5	M	·	W	T	F	S	S
Tea-room								
11 Feb–4 Mar	11–4:30	·	·	·	·	·	S	S
10 Mar–4 Nov	11–4:30	M	·	W	T	F	S	S

A colourful herbaceous border in the tranquil and sheltered Acorn Bank Garden, Cumbria

Alderley Edge

Nether Alderley, Macclesfield, Cheshire

Map ⑤ D8 🏛️⛴️⚓ 1946

Walk the dramatic red sandstone escarpment of Alderley Edge, with views over the Cheshire Plain and the Peak District. Explore woodland paths or walk to Hare Hill Garden. Bickerton Hill, Bulkely Hill Wood, Mow Cop, Thurstaston Common, the Cloud and Helsby Hill offer a variety of landscapes with stunning views.

Exploring — Alderley Edge is designated an SSSI for its geological interest.
— A history of copper mining since the Bronze Age.
— Derbyshire Caving Club opens the mines twice a year.
— Bickerton Hill and Thurstaston Common are both designated SSSI sites.

Eating and shopping: why not try the Wizard Country Inn or Wizard tea-room (weekends only), both Alderley Edge (neither National Trust).

Making the most of your day: series of guided walks takes place at Alderley Edge through the summer. **Dogs**: under close control. On leads where livestock is present (particularly during bird-nesting season).

Access for all: 🅿️♿🏷️ Grounds 🏞️➡️

Alderley Edge, Cheshire: impressive views

Getting here: Alderley Edge 118:SJ860776. The Cloud 118:SJ905637; Mow Cop 118:SJ857573; Bickerton Hill 117:SJ498529; Bulkeley Hill 117:SJ527553; Helsby Hill 117:SJ492754; Lewis Carroll's Birthplace 118:SJ593805; Maggoty Wood 118:SJ889702; Burton Hill Wood SJ317743; Caldy Hill SJ223855; Heswall Fields SJ245824; Thurstaston Common SJ248845; Mobberley Fields SJ789801. **Parking**: at some properties (roadside elsewhere); pay and display at Alderley Edge (closing time displayed at entrance).

Finding out more: 01625 584412 or alderleyedge@nationaltrust.org.uk. c/o Cheshire Countryside Office, Nether Alderley, Macclesfield, Cheshire SK10 4UB

Alderley Edge		M	T	W	T	. F	S	S
Countryside								
Open all year		M	T	W	T	F	S	S
Car park								
1 Jan–31 Mar	8–5	M	T	W	T	F	S	S
1 Apr–31 May	8–5:30	M	T	W	T	F	S	S
1 Jun–30 Sep	8–6	M	T	W	T	F	S	S
1 Oct–31 Dec	8–5	M	T	W	T	F	S	S

Site open all year from dawn until dusk. Tea-room (not National Trust) also open Bank Holidays but closed 24 and 25 December.

The Beatles' Childhood Homes

Woolton and Allerton, Liverpool

Map ⑤ C8 🏛️ 2002

A combined tour to Mendips and 20 Forthlin Road, the childhood homes of John Lennon and Paul McCartney, is your only opportunity to see inside the houses where the Beatles met, composed and rehearsed many of their earliest songs. Walk through the back door into the kitchen and imagine John's Aunt Mimi cooking him his tea, or stand in the spot where Lennon and McCartney composed 'I Saw Her Standing There'. Join our custodians on a fascinating trip down memory lane in these two atmospheric period houses, so typical of Liverpool life in the 1950s. **Note**: access to these houses is by National Trust minibus tour only (charge including members).

The kitchen at Mendips, Liverpool

Getting here: 108:SJ422855. No direct access by car or on foot to either house. Access is via minibus tour (advance booking essential) from Liverpool city centre or Speke Hall. **Parking**: for morning tours numerous public pay and display car parks in city centre (not National Trust). For afternoon tours, parking at Speke Hall.

Finding out more: 0844 800 4791 (Infoline). 0151 427 7231 (booking line) or thebeatleshomes@nationaltrust.org.uk

The Beatles' Childhood Homes	M	T	W	T	F	S	S
25 Feb–25 Nov	*			W	T	F	S	S

*Admission by guided tour only. Times and pick-up locations vary. Please visit www.nationaltrust.org.uk/beatles or telephone booking line for details and to book tickets in advance.

Exploring
- Original family photographs by Mike McCartney on display.
- Visit the bedroom where John Lennon did his dreaming.
- Walk in the footsteps of these musical legends.
- Listen to original audio commentary by Mike and Paul McCartney.
- Experience two very different 1950s houses.

Eating and shopping: guidebooks and postcards for sale at both houses and Speke Hall shop. Local produce served at Speke Hall's Home Farm restaurant.

Making the most of your day: departures from convenient pick-up points (city centre and Speke Hall). Our comfortable minibus and easy online booking service allow you to relax, as we take the strain out of visiting.

Access for all: 🦽🔊🖥🔆👁📷 Building 🏠

Beatrix Potter Gallery

Main Street, Hawkshead, Cumbria LA22 0NS

Map ⑥ D8   🏠 1944

This unique gallery space occupies the charming 17th-century building which served as the office of Beatrix Potter's solicitor husband and contains the highlights of our collection of Beatrix Potter artwork. Now, for the first time, we are displaying all of Potter's original ink drawings for the privately published first edition of *The Tale of Peter Rabbit*. Delight in the illustrated letter in which Peter makes his first appearance! Through these rarely seen items from the National Trust collection, you can gain a fascinating insight into Peter's development as one of the world's favourite children's characters. **Note**: nearest toilet 300 yards in main village car park (not National Trust). Timed ticket entry.

Beatrix Potter Gallery, Cumbria: Mr Heelis's office

Exploring
- Peter Rabbit ink drawings, displayed together for the first time!
- Delight in highlights from the National Trust Beatrix Potter collection.
- Discover the illustrated letter in which Peter first appeared.
- Children will love the gallery trail and activities.
- Discover the picturesque and historic Hawkshead village.
- Visit website to download local walks.

Eating and shopping: visit our National Trust shop at Hawkshead, only 50 yards from the Gallery, or shop online at www.shop. nationaltrust.org.uk/beatrixpotter. Enjoy the meals and refreshments available in Hawkshead village (not National Trust).

Making the most of your day: visit Hill Top House to find out more about the amazing life of Beatrix Potter and the places which inspired her. **Dogs**: assistance dogs only.

Access for all: ▯▯▯▯▯▯▯▯ Building ▯

Getting here: 96:SD352982. In Main Street in Hawkshead village, next to Red Lion pub. **Bus**: Windermere ⮞ to Coniston. Cross Lakes shuttle from Bowness to Hawkshead. **Train**: Windermere 6½ miles via ferry. **Road**: B5286 from Ambleside (4 miles); B5285 from Coniston (5 miles). **Parking**: 300 yards (pay and display), not National Trust.

Finding out more: 015394 36355. 015394 36471 (shop) or beatrixpottergallery@nationaltrust.org.uk

Beatrix Potter Gallery		M	T	W	T	F	S	S
Gallery								
11 Feb–31 Mar	11–3:30	M	T	W	T	.	S	S
1 Apr–2 Jun	11–5	M	T	W	T	.	S	S
3 Jun–1 Sep	10:30–5	M	T	W	T	.	S	S
2 Sep–4 Nov	11–5	M	T	W	T	.	S	S
Shop								
7 Jan–5 Feb	10–4	.	.	.	.	.	S	S
11 Feb–4 Nov	10–5	M	T	W	T	F	S	S
7 Nov–30 Dec	10–4	.	.	W	T	F	S	S

Open Good Friday and Fridays 17 February, 8 June and 2 November. Limited number of timed tickets available daily. Shop: closes at 1 on 23 and 30 December; closed 24, 25 and 26 December.

Borrowdale

near Keswick, Cumbria

Map (6) D7 ▯▯▯▯▯▯▯ 1902

Spectacular landscape around Derwentwater, where the Trust cares for much of the valley, including Derwentwater – its islands and Georgian Manor, Watendlath hamlet, Bowder Stone, Friar's Crag, Ashness Bridge and Castlerigg Stone Circle. Explore Brandelhow Park, the first piece of the Lake District to be safeguarded by the Trust from development.

Exploring
- Amble from Keswick to Friar's Crag for breathtaking views.
- Float in a boat across Derwentwater, then walk up Catbells.
- Wander at Watendlath, location of Walpole's *Herries Chronicles*.
- Explore the mined landscape of the Coledale Valley.

Eating and shopping: visit our lakeside shop for inspired local souvenirs. Enjoy refreshment at one of the Trust tenant cafés: Rosthwaite, Watendlath, Seathwaite and Stonethwaite. Taste local Herdwick lamb at the Flock Inn, Rosthwaite, or purchase free-range eggs at Ashness or Stonethwaite farm.

View from Castle Crag, Borrowdale, Cumbria

Making the most of your day: tours and events throughout the season. Family Discovery Days on Derwent Island five times a year – unique opportunity to meet those who live on and care for this fascinating island. **Dogs**: welcome under close control (particularly at lambing time).

Access for all: P♿ D♿ WC Grounds ♿

Getting here: 90:NY250160. 3 miles south of Keswick. **Cycle**: NCN71 (C2C). **Ferry**: Keswick Launch Company service to various National Trust sites around Derwentwater, 017687 72263. **Bus**: frequent local buses from Keswick to Seatoller. **Train**: Penrith 18 miles. **Road**: B5289 south from Keswick. **Parking**: car parks (pay and display) at Great Wood GR273214, Watendlath GR274163, Kettlewell GR266196, Bowder Stone GR253167 , Rosthwaite GR257148, Seatoller GR246138, Honister GR225135. Coach parking by prior arrangement at Seatoller car park only. Limited parking at Catbells; park at Keswick and take boat or bus.

Finding out more: 017687 74649 or borrowdale@nationaltrust.org.uk. Bowe Barn, Borrowdale Road, near Keswick, Cumbria CA12 5UP

Borrowdale	M	T	W	T	F	S	S
Countryside							
Open all year	M	T	W	T	F	S	S
Shop and information centre							
11 Feb–4 Nov 10–5	M	T	W	T	F	S	S

Borrowdale: Force Crag Mine

near Braithwaite, Coledale Valley, Keswick, Cumbria

Map ⑥ D7   🏠🏛♿♿ 1979

Last mineral mine to be worked in the Lake District. Explore the processing mill and landscape with a guide. **Note**: suitable for children over ten years old only. Charges include members.

Access for all: P♿ ♿♿ Building ♿ Grounds ♿

Force Crag Mine in Borrowdale, Cumbria

Getting here: NY200217. 2¾ miles west of Braithwaite near Keswick. Transport available from Noble Knott car park (grid reference 224 244) on Open Days.

Finding out more: 017687 74649 or forcecragmine@nationaltrust.org.uk. Bowe Barn, Borrowdale Road, Keswick, Cumbria CA12 5UP

Borrowdale: Force Crag Mine
Entry by guided tour during open days. Contact National Trust Borrowdale for dates.

Bridge House

Rydal Road, Ambleside, Cumbria LA22 9AN

Map ⑥ D8   🏠 1926

This tiny but iconic building has 400 years of fascinating history: from an apple store to a family home. **Note**: top floor not open to public, due to steep slate steps.

Getting here: NY:374047. Bridge House Information Centre is located in Ambleside, adjacent to Rydal Road car park on A591.

Finding out more: 015394 32617 or bridgehouse@nationaltrust.org.uk

Bridge House
Telephone for opening arrangements.

Buttermere, Ennerdale and Whitehaven

near Cockermouth, Cumbria

Map ⑥ C7   1935

The beautiful lakes of Buttermere, Crummock Water and Loweswater are surrounded by dramatic high fells, in some of Lakeland's most stunning scenery. Over the fells lie 'Wild Ennerdale' and the Whitehaven coast, where the National Trust and our partners are working to allow a wilder landscape to evolve.

Exploring — Walk and picnic around all the lakes.
— Go boating: available to hire on Crummock Water and Loweswater.
— Fishing on Crummock Water, Buttermere and Loweswater by permit.
— Enjoy the extensive off-road cycling in Ennerdale and around Whitehaven.

Eating and shopping: pubs and cafés in Buttermere, Loweswater, Ennerdale villages and Whitehaven town.

Stunning scenery at Ennerdale, Cumbria

Making the most of your day: enjoy the wide variety of lowland and high fell walks from Buttermere and Ennerdale Water (walking guides available from Keswick and Cockermouth shops). Dramatic coastal walks and views at Whitehaven. **Dogs**: on leads near stock grazing.

Access for all: Grounds 🖼️

Getting here: 89:NY180150. 8 miles south of Cockermouth. **Bus**: from Keswick and Cockermouth to Buttermere; and Whitehaven to Ennerdale. **Train**: Whitehaven. **Road**: off the A595. **Sat Nav**: enter CA28 or Whitehaven. **Parking**: at Honister Pass, Buttermere village, Lanthwaite Wood to Crummock Water and by Ennerdale Water (not National Trust) and Whitehaven.

Finding out more: 017687 74649 or buttermere@nationaltrust.org.uk. Bowe Barn, Borrowdale, Keswick, Cumbria CA12 5UP

Buttermere and Ennerdale	Open every day all year

Cartmel Priory Gatehouse

The Square, Cartmel, Grange-over-Sands, Cumbria LA11 6QB

Map ⑥ D9   🏠 1946

Interesting 14th-century gatehouse of medieval priory. **Note**: mainly in private residential use. The Great Room is open several days a year.

Access for all: 🖼️🖼️ Building 🖼️

Getting here: 96:SD378788. In the square in village centre.

Finding out more: 015395 60951 or cartpriorygatehouse@nationaltrust.org.uk

Cartmel Priory Gatehouse

Visit website, email or telephone the property for opening times. Small charge for events.

Coniston and Tarn Hows

near Coniston, Cumbria

Map (6) D8    1930

Coniston covers a large area of some of the Lake District's most scenic woodland, water and fells. One of many lovely places is the iconic Tarn Hows beauty spot, with its magnificent mountain views. The readily accessible Blea Tarn in Little Langdale also has superb views and fine walking.

Exploring — Visit Blea Tarn for spectacular views of the Langdale Pikes.
— There is access to much of Coniston Water shoreline.
— Visit the restored Monk Coniston walled garden.
— Explore the Norse settlement site at Fell Foot.

Eating and shopping: ice-cream van at Tarn Hows during peak season. Numerous places to eat in the area, particularly Coniston – some linked with National Trust tenants. National Trust shop in nearby Hawkshead.

Making the most of your day: superb network of paths and bridleways at Coniston. Cruise on Steam Yacht *Gondola*, disembarking at Monk Coniston jetty for a walk through Monk Coniston grounds to Tarn Hows. **Dogs**: on leads (stock grazing).

Access for all: 🅿♿ Grounds ♿➡

Getting here: OL7:SD326995. Tarn Hows 2 miles north-east of Coniston. OL6:SD295043, Blea Tarn, Little Langdale, 5 miles north of Coniston. **Bus**: from Windermere to Coniston. **Parking**: pay and display at Tarn Hows OL7:326995, Glen Mary OL7:321998 and Blea Tarn OL6:295043.

Finding out more: 015394 41456 or coniston@nationaltrust.org.uk. Boon Crag, Coniston, Cumbria LA21 8AQ

Coniston and Tarn Hows	Open every day all year

Walkers explore the paths surrounding the iconic Tarn Hows beauty spot, Cumbria

Dalton Castle

Market Place, Dalton-in-Furness,
Cumbria LA15 8AX

Map (6) D9 | 1965 |

Eye-catching 14th-century tower built to assert
the authority of the Abbot of Furness Abbey.
Note: opened on behalf of the National Trust
by the Friends of Dalton Castle.

Access for all: ☷☷☷ Building ☷

Getting here: 96:SD226739. In market place at
top of main street of Dalton.

Finding out more: 015395 60951 or
daltoncastle@nationaltrust.org.uk

Dalton Castle
Visit the website, email or telephone the property for
opening times.

Dunham Massey

Altrincham, Cheshire WA14 4SJ

Map (5) D8 ☷☷☷☷☷☷☷ | 1976 |

'A very enjoyable day spent in what feels like
a warm, very well-loved home.'
Ruth Curtis, Reading

Set in a magnificent 121-hectare (300-acre)
deer park, this Georgian house tells the story
of the owners and the servants who lived here.
Discover the salacious scandals of the 7th Earl
of Stamford, who married Catherine Cocks, a
former bare-back circus rider, and the 2nd Earl
of Warrington, who was so enamoured with
his wife that he wrote a book anonymously on
the desirability of divorce! Uncover these and
other fascinating stories when you explore
this treasure-packed house, then take a stroll
in one of the North's great gardens, including
Britain's largest winter garden. **Note**: all visitors
require a white entry ticket (free to members),
available from visitor reception.

Exploring
– Play the piano or Edwardian
games in the Gallery.
– Enjoy a game of croquet on a
summer's afternoon.
– Wine coolers to potties –
the Trust's greatest silver
collection.
– Feed the chickens or water the
edible garden.
– Discover more about the
family's sporting adventures
through their costumes.
– Explore Britain's largest
winter garden.

Eating and shopping: enjoy a seasonal lunch
made with the best of local ingredients, or
treat yourself to one of our delicious home-
baked cakes in the Stables Restaurant. Visit the
shop for a beautiful gift or a tasty local treat.

Making the most of your day: join our guides
on a free tour. Family fun in the house and
garden, school holiday activities. Free guided
walks. Cycling for under fives. **Dogs**: welcome
on leads in deer park and walks around
the estate.

Access for all: ☷☷☷☷☷☷☷☷☷☷☷☷
☷☷ House ☷☷☷ Restaurant ☷☷☷
Park and garden ☷☷☷☷

The Canal Border at Dunham Massey, Cheshire

Getting here: 109:SJ735874. 3 miles south-west of Altrincham. Foot: close to Trans-Pennine Trail and Bridgewater Canal. Cycle: NCN62, 1 mile. Bus: from Altrincham and Warrington, stops at main gates. Train: Altrincham 3 miles; Hale 3 miles. Road: off A56: M6 exit 19; M56 exit 7. Parking: 200 yards. March to October shuttle buggy service operates most days between car park and visitor facilities.

Finding out more: 0161 942 3989 (Infoline). 0161 941 1025 or dunhammassey@nationaltrust.org.uk

Dunham Massey		M	T	W	T	F	S	S
House*								
25 Feb–4 Nov	11–5	M	T	W	.	.	S	S
Garden**								
1 Jan–24 Feb	11–4	M	T	W	T	F	S	S
25 Feb–4 Nov	11–5:30	M	T	W	T	F	S	S
5 Nov–31 Dec	11–4	M	T	W	T	F	S	S
Restaurant and shop								
1 Jan–24 Feb	10:30–4	M	T	W	T	F	S	S
25 Feb–4 Nov	10:30–5	M	T	W	T	F	S	S
5 Nov–31 Dec	10:30–4	M	T	W	T	F	S	S
Park*								
Open all year	9–5	M	T	W	T	F	S	S
Mill								
25 Feb–4 Nov	12–4	M	T	W	.	.	S	S
White Cottage**								
26 Feb–4 Nov	2–5	.	.	.	.	.	.	S

*11 to 12 visit to house by guided taster tours only (11 and 11:30), places limited. Open Good Friday. **Winter: closes 4 or dusk if earlier. ***March to October: gates open to 7:30. Property closed 21 November for staff training and 25 December (including park). ****Open last Sunday of the month, by guided tour only – all visits must be booked by email at dunmasswhite@nationaltrust.org.uk or telephone 0161 928 0075.

Fell Foot Park

Newby Bridge, Windermere, Cumbria LA12 8NN

Map (6) D9   🏠🌳🛶🏡🍴 1948

The views of Lake Windermere from the park will captivate you. They are truly breathtaking! Lawns and paths sweep down to picnic and barbecue areas towards the lakeshore. Enjoy a lunch with family and friends on the boathouse terrace, then maybe explore the lake using one of our rowing boats. Note: launch/slipway facilities available for a wide variety of craft (charge including members).

Exploring   – Hire a rowing boat for family fun.
– Stroll around the grounds and enjoy the magnificent views.
– Let the children loose on our adventure playground.
– Picnic or barbecue in designated areas of the park.

Eating and shopping: our boathouse café offers a selection of hot and cold beverages and snacks made with fresh seasonal ingredients. Our local Cumbrian producers include bakers, butchers and ice-cream makers. There is a limited retail offer for our visitors.

Making the most of your day: rowing boats and kayaks available for hire April to October (weather permitting). Special events, please see website for details. Dogs: on leads welcome.

Access for all: 🅿️🅳♿🚾🚶 Grounds 🚶

Getting here: 96/97:SD381869. South end of Lake Windermere. Ferry: Fell Foot to Lakeside (seasonal). Bus: services from Ambleside to Barrow and Kendal, alight Newby Bridge 1 mile south of Fell Foot. Train: Grange 6 miles; Windermere 8 miles. Road: entrance off A592. Parking: charges for non-members apply. Coach access difficult (booking essential).

Lake Windermere, seen from Fell Foot Park, Cumbria

Finding out more: 015395 31273 or fellfootpark@nationaltrust.org.uk.
Fell Foot Park, Newby Bridge, Ulverston, Cumbria LA12 8NN

Fell Foot Park		M	T	W	T	F	S	S
Park								
2 Jan–31 Jan	9–3	M	T	W	T	F	S	S
1 Feb–23 Mar	9–5	M	T	W	T	F	S	S
24 Mar–30 Sep	8–8	M	T	W	T	F	S	S
1 Oct–31 Dec	9–5	M	T	W	T	F	S	S
Catering facilities								
3 Feb–23 Mar	11–3	M	T	W	T	F	S	S
24 Mar–4 Nov	10–4	M	T	W	T	F	S	S

Later closing when events in park. Boat hire available from 24 March to 4 November, daily, 11 to 4. Weather permitting. Times of opening for catering facilities may vary in adverse weather conditions.

Formby

near Freshfield, Liverpool

Map (5) B7 1967

This ever-changing sandy coastline set between the sea and Formby town offers miles of walks through the woods and dunes. Glimpse a rare red squirrel or see a historic landscape levelled for asparagus. Prehistoric animal and human footprints can sometimes be found in silt beds on the shoreline. **Note**: toilets close at 5:30 in summer, 4 in winter.

Exploring
- Enjoy a bracing walk on the sandy beaches.
- Explore Formby's historic asparagus landscape.
- Follow the fascinating Formby Point audio guide trail.
- Search for secretive red squirrels in the pine woods.

Eating and shopping: ice-creams, soft drinks and coffee from mobile van.

Making the most of your day: guided walks and awareness days. Circular and longer walks linked to the Sefton Coastal Path. Formby Point audio guide trail. **Dogs**: under close control (vulnerable wildlife).

Access for all:
Accessible toilet **Grounds**

Getting here: 108:SD275080. 2 miles west of Formby, 6 miles south of Southport. **Foot**: Sefton Coastal Footpath. **Cycle**: NCN62, 3 miles. **Train**: Freshfield 1 mile. **Road**: 2 miles off A565. Follow brown signs from roundabout at north end of Formby bypass. **Sat Nav**: entrance at grid reference SD281082: use postcode L37 1LJ. **Parking**: width restriction 3 yards. Minibuses: £10, coaches: £25.

Finding out more: 01704 878591 or formby@nationaltrust.org.uk

Formby
Open every day all year from dawn to dusk

Closed 25 December. Long queues for car parks in peak season. Booking essential for minibuses and coaches. Group bookings: 01704 874949.

Strolling on the beach at Formby, Liverpool

Gawthorpe Hall

Burnley Road, Padiham, near Burnley,
Lancashire BB12 8UA

Map ⑤ D6   1972

This imposing house is set in the heart of urban Lancashire. In the 19th century Sir Charles Barry created the opulent interiors we see today. The Hall displays more than 500 textiles from the Rachel Kay-Shuttleworth collection, including needlework, lace and embroidery. The grounds are popular with dog walkers. **Note:** financed and run in partnership with Lancashire County Council.

Exploring – Admire the fantastic interiors, furniture and portraits in the house.
  – Enjoy displays from the nationally important textile collection.

Eating and shopping: enjoy light snacks in the tea-room.

Making the most of your day: events throughout the year, including open-air theatre in July and Victorian Christmas in December. **Dogs**: under close control in grounds.

Access for all: 🔲🔲🔲🔲🔲🔲
Building 🔲 Grounds 🔲🔲🔲➡

The south front of Gawthorpe Hall, Lancashire

Getting here: 103:SD806340. On outskirts of Padiham. **Foot**: driveway from Burnley Road (no footpath). **Bus**: frequent buses from Burnley bus station. **Train**: Rose Grove, Burnley Barracks and Burnley Manchester Road stations nearby. **Road**: on A671. From M65 exit 8 towards Clitheroe then Padiham. **Parking**: 150 yards, access road narrow with passing places.

Finding out more: 01282 771004 or gawthorpehall@nationaltrust.org.uk

Gawthorpe Hall		M	T	W	T	F	S	S
House								
31 Mar–4 Nov	12–5		·	·	W	T	F	S	S
Tea-room								
21 Mar–4 Nov	11–5		·	·	W	T	F	S	S
Grounds								
Open all year	8–7	M	T	W	T	F	S	S

Hall and tea-room also open Bank Holidays. Opening times and prices for Hall are controlled by Lancashire County Council and subject to change.

Grasmere and Great Langdale

near Ambleside, Cumbria

Map ⑥ D8    1925

The iconic Langdale Pikes stand majestic in the landscape. The Trust owns most of the valley farms, Trust campsite, the glaciated valley of Mickleden, a Victorian garden at High Close and the dramatic Dungeon Ghyll. In and around Grasmere, the Trust owns the lake bed and parts of Rydal Water.

Exploring – A wonderful opportunity to walk up to the Langdale Pikes.
  – Wide range of low-level circular routes in both valleys.
  – Breathtaking scenery.
  – Old Dungeon Ghyll is a popular area for rock climbing.

Eating and shopping: The Old Dungeon Ghyll hotel at head of Great Langdale. Numerous cafés, restaurants and hotels in Grasmere.

Peaceful Grasmere in Cumbria

Making the most of your day: don't miss our Grasmere Information Centre and shop in the centre of the village. Visit our website for the June annual Grasmere Gallop (www.grasmeregallop.org.uk). **Dogs**: welcome under control.

Access for all:
Grasmere Information Centre ⛰⛰ Grounds ⛰

Getting here: 89/90:NY290060. Great Langdale valley starts 4 miles west of Ambleside. Grasmere is 4 miles north of Ambleside. **Foot**: network of local footpaths as well as the Coast to Coast route cross both valleys. **Cycle**: NCN37, then links from Skelwith Bridge to Elterwater. **Bus**: services from Ambleside to Grasmere and Langdale. **Road**: A591 to Ambleside, continuing to Grasmere. A593 to Skelwith Bridge, B543 to Great Langdale. **Parking**: three National Trust car parks in the Langdale valley. Three car parks in Grasmere village (pay and display), none National Trust.

Finding out more: 015394 63823 (Property Office). 015394 35665 (Grasmere Information Centre) or grasmere@nationaltrust.org.uk. Central and East Lakes Property Office, The Annexe, The Hollens, Grasmere, Cumbria LA22 9QZ

Grasmere and Great Langdale	Open every day all year

Grasmere Information Centre open during the season, 9:30 to 5.

The Hardmans' House

59 Rodney Street, Liverpool, Merseyside L1 9EX

Map ⑤ B8   2003

Step back in time and experience the 1950s. In this time capsule of post-war years, you will glimpse the life of an extraordinary couple. Renowned photographer E. Chambré Hardman and his talented wife Margaret lived and worked together in this remarkable Georgian house for 40 years, keeping everything, changing nothing. **Note**: admission by guided tour only – booking not required but advised to avoid disappointment.

Exploring – Spot the unopened food rations and admire glamorous period clothing.
– Listen to the reminiscences of former members of staff.
– Enjoy evocative original photographs taken by this talented couple.
– Explore Liverpool through the lens of a remarkable photographic partnership.

Kitchen at The Hardmans' House, Liverpool

Eating and shopping: unique photographic prints and postcards available from our shop, along with property guidebooks.

Making the most of your day: book your place on a tour in advance to avoid disappointment. Virtual tour of the house available. Children's quiz trail.

Access for all: 🅿️🅳♿🆆🅲🏮📺♿😊🅰️
Building 🏛️🏛️

Getting here: 108:SJ355895. ¾ mile north of Liverpool city centre. Rodney Street is off Hardman Street and Upper Duke Street. **Foot**: follow fingerposts '59 Rodney Street'. Visitor entrance on Pilgrim Street, near Anglican Cathedral. **Bus**: frequent services from surrounding area. **Train**: Liverpool Lime Street ½ mile. **Parking**: no onsite parking. Offsite parking most days at Anglican Cathedral (pay and display). Slater Street NCP.

Finding out more: 0151 709 6261 or thehardmanshouse@nationaltrust.org.uk

The Hardmans' House		M	T	W	T	F	S	S
14 Mar–28 Oct	11–3:30	·	·	**W**	**T**	**F**	**S**	**S**

Admission by timed ticket only, including members (places limited). Visitors advised to book in advance (by telephone or email to property) to avoid disappointment, as tickets on the day are subject to availability. Open Bank Holiday Mondays and for the Queen's Diamond Jubilee (5 June).

Hare Hill

Over Alderley, Macclesfield, Cheshire SK10 4PY

Map ⑤ D8 🌼♣ 1978

This charming woodland garden provides the ideal habitat for a wide variety of native wildlife while also boasting ornamental ponds, impressive collections of rhododendrons, azaleas and other fine specimen shrubs and waterside plantings. At its heart is the delightful walled garden – currently being restored to recapture its Victorian character.

Exploring – Walk through landscaped park past the lake to Alderley Edge.
– Bring your binoculars and a picnic.

Exploring – Relax in the beautiful setting of the walled garden.
– Views from a rural to urban landscape.

Eating and shopping: hot drinks vending machine.

Making the most of your day: enjoy glorious walks, explore the hare sculpture trail, spot birdlife from the hide and picnic in the walled garden. **Dogs**: under close control on the estate only.

Access for all: 🅰️♿😊 Grounds 🏛️🏛️

Getting here: 118:SJ873763. 2½ miles from Alderley Edge and Prestbury. **Train**: Alderley Edge and Prestbury, both 2½ miles. **Road**: between Alderley Edge and Macclesfield (B5087). **Parking**: not suitable for coaches.

Finding out more: 01625 584412 or harehill@nationaltrust.org.uk

Hare Hill		M	T	W	T	F	S	S
18 Mar–28 Oct	10–5	·	**T**	**W**	**T**	**F**	**S**	**S**

Open Bank Holiday Mondays. Last admission one hour before closing. **Car park closes at 5.**

The walled garden at Hare Hill, Cheshire

Always remember your current membership card

Hawkshead and Claife

near Hawkshead, Cumbria

Map (6) D8 1929

Hawkshead village, home to the Beatrix Potter Gallery, is surrounded by beautiful countryside for walks and exploration. Claife Station and courtyard, new for this year, on Windermere lakeshore, is a great place to start your adventure. The grounds of Wray Castle are open all year for you to explore.

Explore Wray Castle's grounds, Cumbria

Exploring
– Discover Claife Station, see the views, learn about the history.
– Enjoy wonderful low-level walks with great views.
– Leave the car behind – visit by boat, bus and boot.
– Explore the grounds at Wray Castle, join in our events.

Eating and shopping: there are plenty of catering options and shopping opportunities available in and around Hawkshead village, including the Hawkshead National Trust gift shop. Visit our internet shop at www.shop. nationaltrust.org.uk/beatrixpotter.

Making the most of your day: experience the wonderful countryside that inspired Beatrix Potter; why not visit Hawkshead and the gallery there? National Trust campsite on lakeshore at Low Wray (90:NY372012). Visit website for details. **Dogs**: allowed in countryside, under close control. Assistance dogs only on guided walks and tours.

Access for all:

Getting here: 96/97:SD352982. Hawkshead 6 miles south-west of Ambleside. **Foot**: many footpaths in the area. **Ferry**: Windermere car and passenger ferry; Ferry House to Ferry Nab. **Bus**: from Windermere ≡ to Coniston. **Parking**: pay and display at Ash Landing (near ferry) and Harrowslack, near Lake Windermere.

Finding out more: 015394 41456 or hawkshead@nationaltrust.org.uk. Boon Crag, Coniston, Cumbria LA21 8AQ

Hawkshead and Claife	Open every day all year
Hawkshead Courthouse (not staffed): access by key from the National Trust shop or the Beatrix Potter Gallery ticket office in Hawkshead. Free admission but no parking facilities. Wray Castle grounds open all year, some access to the castle. Claife Station and courtyard free entry, not always staffed.	

Hill Top

Near Sawrey, Hawkshead, Ambleside, Cumbria LA22 0LF

Map (6) D8 1944

Enjoy the tale of Beatrix Potter – Hill Top is a time capsule of this amazing woman's life. Full of her favourite things, the cottage appears as if Beatrix had just stepped out for a walk. Every room contains a reference to a picture in a 'tale'. The lovely cottage garden is a haphazard mix of flowers, herbs, fruit and vegetables. Hill Top is a small house and a timed-ticket system is in operation to avoid overcrowding and to protect the interior. Hill Top can be very busy and visitors may sometimes have to wait to enter the house. **Note**: tickets cannot be booked and **early sell-outs** are possible, especially during school holidays.

Beatrix Potter's delightful cottage home, Hill Top in Cumbria, is a fascinating time capsule

Exploring — Don't miss the children's garden trail.
— Explore the traditional English country garden throughout the seasons.
— Enjoy the views which inspired Beatrix's tales and illustrations.
— See website for details of Beatrix Potter walks and events.
— Downloadable local walks.

Getting here: 96/97:SD370955. 2 miles south of Hawkshead, in Near Sawrey hamlet; 3 miles from Bowness via ferry. **Foot**: off-road path from ferry (2 miles), marked. **Ferry**: seasonal service from Bowness Pier 3 (telephone 01539 448600 for details). **Bus**: regular service, plus seasonal service from Bowness Pier 3. **Train**: Windermere 4½ miles via vehicle ferry. **Road**: B5286 and B5285 from Ambleside (6 miles), B5285 from Coniston (7 miles). **Parking**: limited.

Eating and shopping: visit our internet shop www.shop.nationaltrust.org.uk/beatrixpotter or use our mail-order service (contact hilltop. shop@nationaltrust.org.uk or 01539 436801). Treats available in the shop. Sawrey House Hotel and Tower Bank Arms serve meals and refreshments.

Making the most of your day: leave the car behind to visit by boat, bus, boot or bike – see 'Windermere Cross Lakes Experience' website (not National Trust); include a visit to the Beatrix Potter Gallery. **Dogs**: assistance dogs only in garden and house.

Finding out more: 015394 36269 or hilltop@nationaltrust.org.uk

Hill Top		M	T	W	T	F	S	S
House								
11 Feb–31 Mar	10:30–3:30	M	T	W	T		S	S
1 Apr–2 Jun	10:30–4:30	M	T	W	T		S	S
3 Jun–1 Sep	10–5	M	T	W	T		S	S
2 Sep–4 Nov	10:30–4:30	M	T	W	T		S	S
Shop and garden								
11 Feb–31 Mar	10:15–4	M	T	W	T	F	S	S
1 Apr–2 Jun	10–5	M	T	W	T	F	S	S
3 Jun–1 Sep	9:45–5:15	M	T	W	T	F	S	S
2 Sep–4 Nov	10–5	M	T	W	T	F	S	S
5 Nov–24 Dec	10–4	M	T	W	T	F	S	S

House open Good Friday, and also Fridays 17 February, 8 June and 2 November. Entry by timed ticket (limited). Small car park. Access to garden and shop free during opening hours. Shop closes at 1 on 24 December.

Access for all: 🗎 ▢ 🖉 ⠿ Ⓐ
House ♿ 🏔 Garden ♿ ➡

Little Moreton Hall

Congleton, Cheshire CW12 4SD

Map (5) D9   1938

A Cheshire icon not to be missed! This quirky black and white Tudor Hall, surrounded by a moat, is brought to life through free guided tours and family activities throughout the year. Find out what Tudor life was like as you explore this charming and intimate property. Our small orchard, pretty knot garden and large front lawn provide the perfect setting for relaxing and enjoying time with friends and family. Our new visitor facilities include a larger shop located in the car park and extended catering facilities within the Hall. **Note**: new facilities due to open in April.

Exploring
- Learn about the fascinating history on a free guided tour.
- Climb the stairs to the breathtaking Long Gallery.
- Enjoy delicious food in the Brewhouse Restaurant or coffee shop.
- Play Tudor games or try on a Tudor costume.
- Discover the writing on the walls of the chancel.
- Relax in the orchard and admire the pretty knot garden.

Eating and shopping: enjoy delicious food in the Brewhouse Restaurant or new coffee shop. Sample homemade puddings, cakes and scones from our own bakery. Locally made ice-cream available. Treat yourself to a souvenir, including local gifts, from our friendly, welcoming shop.

Making the most of your day: regular living history and musical events bring the Hall to life. Exhibitions, displays, open-air theatre and family activities throughout year. Yuletide celebrations in December. **Dogs**: on leads in car park and short estate walk only.

Access for all: ⓟ Ⓓ 💺 wc ♿ 🐕 ⑂ 🖼 vd Ⓙ
∴ Ⓐ Building 🦽🦽🦽♿ Grounds 🦽🦽➡

Getting here: 118:SJ832589. 4 miles south-west of Congleton. **Foot**: leave the Macclesfield canal at bridge 86. Map to Hall displayed on towpath. **Bus**: services from Alsager to Congleton (passing close to Kidsgrove), infrequent (not Sundays). **Train**: Kidsgrove 3 miles; Congleton 4½ miles. **Road**: on east side of A34. From M6 exit 17 follow signs for Congleton and join A34 southbound (signed Newcastle) from Congleton. **Parking**: 100 yards.

Finding out more: 01260 272018 or littlemoretonhall@nationaltrust.org.uk

Little Moreton Hall		M	T	W	T	F	S	S
4 Apr–4 Nov	11–5	·	·	W	T	F	S	S
10 Nov–16 Dec	11–4	·	·	·	·	·	S	S

Closed until 4 April due to building works. Open Bank Holiday Mondays and for the Queen's Diamond Jubilee (5 June).

The Tudor Little Moreton Hall in Cheshire

Lyme Park, House and Garden

Disley, Stockport, Cheshire SK12 2NR

Map (5) E8 1947

At Lyme there is a painting of a servants' ball, which was painted at the height of the Edwardian age when this great sporting estate was enjoying a golden era. It captures a moment when Lyme was at its best, however life would never be the same again after the tragedy of the Great War. Explore lavish interiors, celebrations, treasures and beautiful gardens set against sweeping moorland. Enjoy a relaxed visit, and dip into experiences of a vanished age. What was life like before the ball had ended? **Note:** owned and managed by the National Trust but partly financed by Stockport Metropolitan Borough Council.

Exploring
- CD sets the scene as you drive to the house.
- Relax among luxurious borders and sweeping lawns.
- Discover untold stories.

Lyme Park, House and Garden, Cheshire

Exploring
- Get carried away in the children's playscape, Crow Wood.
- Toys to play with, costumes to try, books to read.
- Enjoy stunning views and peaceful walks.

Eating and shopping: quick snacks in the park, leisurely lunches in the house. Why not grow your own souvenir from the plant shop or browse in our well-stocked bookshop?

Making the most of your day: plenty for families, from Crow Wood to fun activities. New walks leaflets exploring undiscovered areas. Be the first to experience untold stories of people who lived and worked here. **Dogs**: under close control and in park only (on leads in some areas).

Access for all:
House 🔲🔲 Garden 🔲🔲🔲 Park 🔲

Getting here: 109:SJ965825. 1 mile west of Disley. **Foot**: northern end of Gritstone Trail. **Bus**: frequent bus services to entrance from Stockport and Buxton. **Train**: Disley ½ mile from entrance. **Road**: entrance on A6 only. **Sat Nav**: stay on A6. **Parking**: 1 mile from entrance. Limited coach parking. Grass overflow parking.

Finding out more: 01663 762023 or lymepark@nationaltrust.org.uk

Lyme Park		M	T	W	T	F	S	S
Garden, 'Beatrix Potter' exhibition and shop								
1 Jan–19 Feb	11–3	·	·	·	·	·	S	S
House, restaurant and shop								
25 Feb–28 Oct	11–5	M	T	·	·	F	S	S
Garden								
25 Feb–28 Oct	11–5	M	T	W	T	F	S	S
Park								
Open all year	8–6	M	T	W	T	F	S	S
Coffee shop								
Open all year	11–4	M	T	W	T	F	S	S
Plant sales and shop								
1 Jan–19 Feb	11–4	·	·	·	·	·	S	S
25 Feb–28 Oct	10:30–5	M	T	W	T	F	S	S
3 Nov–30 Dec	11–4	·	·	·	·	·	S	S
Garden, 'Nuffin like a Puffin' exhibition and shop								
3 Nov–16 Dec	11–3	·	·	·	·	·	S	S
17 Dec–31 Dec	11–3	M	T	W	T	F	S	S

Closed 25 December. Last entry to house and garden 4.

We welcome dogs assisting visitors with disabilities

Nether Alderley Mill

Congleton Road, Nether Alderley, Macclesfield, Cheshire SK10 4TW

Map (5) D8   1950

This charming rustic mill is one of only four virtually complete corn mills in Cheshire. **Note**: undergoing major roof restoration (telephone Quarry Bank Mill for update on progress and likely date for opening).

Access for all: Building 🏠

Getting here: 118:SJ844763. 1½ miles south of Alderley Edge, on east side of A34.

Finding out more: 01625 527468 or netheralderleymill@nationaltrust.org.uk

Nether Alderley Mill
Telephone for opening arrangements.

Quarry Bank Mill and Styal Estate

Styal, Wilmslow, Cheshire SK9 4LA

Map (5) D8   1939

Quarry Bank Mill, Cheshire, seen from the garden

Visit Quarry Bank at Styal and discover the compelling story of mill workers, entrepreneurs and the Industrial Revolution. Watch hand-spinners at work, experience the clatter of machinery and the hiss of steam engines, and marvel at Europe's most powerful working waterwheel. Take a guided tour of the Apprentice House, which housed the pauper children who worked in the mill. Visit the stunning garden, and follow our progress with our Upper Garden Project. Stroll to Styal village, built by the Gregs to house the mill workers and still a thriving community, or walk through beech woods along the beautiful River Bollin.

Exploring
– Experience demonstrations on how cotton was processed into cloth.
– Be amazed by our waterwheel and steam engines.
– Enjoy the beautiful garden and discover our new Upper Garden.
– See how apprentices lived and worked and visit Styal village.
– Bring a picnic before exploring our new natural play area.
– Family tours of the Apprentice House in the summer season.

Eating and shopping: browse in the shop for gifts, mementoes and glass cloths produced in the mill. Plants for sale in the mill yard. Enjoy lunch or afternoon tea in our Mill Café, and fresh coffee or delicious ice-cream from the Pantry.

Making the most of your day: programme of events, guided walks and open-air theatre. School holiday activities and trails for all the family. Children's play areas. Picnic facilities. Cycle route. **Dogs**: under close control on estate. On lead only in mill yard.

Access for all:
Building 🏠 Grounds

Getting here: 109:SJ835835. 1½ miles north of Wilmslow. **Cycle**: NCN6, 1½ miles. RCR85, ½ mile. **Bus**: regular service from Manchester Airport train station and Wilmslow stations. **Train**: Manchester Airport 2 miles; Wilmslow 2 miles. **Road**: off B5166, 2 miles from M56, exit 5. Heritage signs from A34 and M56. **Parking**: 200 yards.

Finding out more: 01625 445896 (Infoline). 01625 527468 or quarrybankmill@nationaltrust.org.uk

Quarry Bank Mill and Styal Estate		M	T	W	T	F	S	S
Mill and Apprentice House								
1 Jan–24 Feb	11–3:30	·	·	W	T	F	S	S
25 Feb–4 Nov	11–5	M	T	W	T	F	S	S
7 Nov–30 Dec	11–3:30	·	·	W	T	F	S	S
Shop, café and ticket/information office								
1 Jan–24 Feb	10:30–4	·	·	W	T	F	S	S
25 Feb–4 Nov	10:30–5	M	T	W	T	F	S	S
7 Nov–30 Dec	10:30–4	·	·	W	T	F	S	S
Garden								
25 Feb–4 Nov	10:30–5	M	T	W	T	F	S	S

Open every day during school holidays, including half-terms. Open Monday 2 January, but closed 3 to 6 January for essential maintenance. Mill and garden: last admission one hour before closing. Apprentice House guided tours: timed tickets only, available from ticket office (early arrival advised). In winter Mill closes at 3:30 during week and 4 at weekends. Garden open winter weekends, weather permitting. Popular destination for schools.

Rufford Old Hall

200 Liverpool Road, Rufford, Near Ormskirk, Lancashire L40 1SG

Map (5) C6   1936

Admire Lancashire's finest Tudor building, where a young Will Shakespeare once performed. His stage, the 16th-century Great Hall with its 'movable' screen (the only surviving example of its type), is as spectacular today as when the Bard was performing for the owner, Sir Thomas Hesketh, and his raucous guests. Wander around the house and enjoy its collection including furniture, paintings and armour. Then step outside and enjoy the charming gardens, topiary, sculpture and a walk in the woodlands alongside the canal. **Note**: charges for special events such as the Christmas Fair (including members).

Exploring   – Marvel at the angels in the Great Hall's hammerbeam roof.
            – Enjoy Ellen Stevens' botanical watercolours, wonderfully intricate and detailed.

Eating and shopping: complete your visit with fresh local food in the tea-room. Enjoy a family picnic in the grounds. Browse in the shop and our plant centre.

Making the most of your day: discover fascinating facts from room guides and see conservation in action. Family events programme, outdoor and house quizzes for children. **Dogs**: on leads in woodland only.

Access for all: ⬚⬚⬚⬚⬚⬚⬚⬚⬚⬚
Building ⬚⬚⬚⬚ Grounds ⬚⬚⬚➡⬚⬚

Getting here: 108:SD462161. ½ mile from Rufford. **Foot**: on towpath of Leeds to Liverpool Canal. **Bus**: services from Southport to Chorley and Preston to Ormskirk. **Train**: Rufford ½ mile; Burscough Bridge 2½ miles. **Road**: on A59. From M6 junction 27, follow signs for Parbold then Rufford. **Parking**: onsite.

Finding out more: 01704 821254 or ruffordoldhall@nationaltrust.org.uk

Rufford Old Hall		M	T	W	T	F	S	S
House, garden, shop and tea-room*								
25 Feb–7 Mar	11–4	M	T	W	·	·	S	S
10 Mar–4 Nov	11–5	M	T	W	·	·	S	S
Garden, shop and tea-room								
10 Nov–16 Dec	11–4	·	·	·	·	·	S	S

*Access to Hall may be from 1 occasionally. Open 13 to 15 and 20 to 22 February for half-term, 11 to 4 (house closed). Open Good Friday, also Thursdays during August.

Topiary at Rufford Old Hall, Lancashire

Sizergh Castle and Garden

Sizergh, near Kendal, Cumbria LA8 8DZ

Map (6) E8  1950

This imposing house, at the gateway to the Lake District, stands proud in a rich and beautiful garden, which includes a pond, lake, National Collection of Hardy Ferns and a superb limestone rock garden. Still lived in by the Strickland family, Sizergh has many tales to tell and certainly feels lived in, with centuries-old portraits and fine furniture sitting alongside modern family photographs. The exceptional wood panelling culminates in the Inlaid Chamber, returned here in 1999 from the Victoria & Albert Museum. The 647-hectare (1,600-acre) estate includes limestone pasture, orchards and ancient, semi-natural woodland.

Sizergh Castle and Garden, Cumbria

Exploring
- Admire some of England's finest Elizabethan wood carving and panelling.
- Relax in the National Trust's largest limestone rock garden.
- See the kitchen garden, orchard and herbaceous border.
- Follow footpaths to stunning viewpoints of Morecambe Bay/Lakeland hills.
- Visit the Strickland Arms pub and Low Sizergh farm shop.

Eating and shopping: savour local, seasonal food in our contemporary licensed café. Buy a picnic to enjoy while relaxing in the garden. Plants and local products from our shop. Sample the food at the pub and farm tea-room.

Making the most of your day: varied programme of events throughout the year. Explore the estate with a walks leaflet. Garden trail and house quizzes for children. **Dogs**: welcome in car park and estate footpaths. Assistance dogs only in house and garden.

Access for all:
Building ⬚⬚⬚ Grounds ⬚➡⬚⬚

Getting here: 97:SD498878. 3½ miles south of Kendal. **Foot**: adjacent to footpaths 530002 and 530003. **Cycle**: NCN6, 1½ miles. RCR20 passes main gate. **Bus**: regular services. Keswick to Kendal/Lancaster (passing close Lancaster ⬚), Kendal to Arnside (passing close Arnside ⬚). All pass Kendal ⬚. **Train**: Oxenholme 3 miles. **Road**: M6 exit 36 then A590 towards Kendal, take Barrow-in-Furness turning and follow brown signs. From Lake District take A591 south then A590 towards Barrow-in-Furness. **Parking**: 250 yards.

Finding out more: 015395 60951 or sizergh@nationaltrust.org.uk

Sizergh Castle and Garden		M	T	W	T	F	S	S
House*								
11 Mar–4 Nov	1–5	M	T	W	T	·	·	S
Garden, café and shop*								
1 Jan–10 Mar	11–4	·	·	·	·	·	S	S
13 Feb–17 Feb	11–4	M	T	W	T	F	·	·
11 Mar–4 Nov	11–5	M	T	W	T	F	S	S
5 Nov–31 Dec	11–4	M	T	W	T	F	S	S

*Two guided house tours also available 12 to 1 (places limited, £1 per person – can be booked or taken on the day, if available). A timed-ticket system will be in operation on Sundays, school and Bank Holidays. **Some parts of garden are closed Fridays and Saturdays and January, February, November and December. Café, shop and garden closed 25 December.

Speke Hall, Garden and Estate

Speke, Liverpool L24 1XD

Map (5) C8 🏠🏠⭐🌸🔔 1944

Speke Hall is a rare example of a Tudor manor house with Victorian interiors and original William Morris wallpaper. Situated in a most unusual setting, it is surrounded by attractive gardens and woodland. Constructed by a devout Catholic family, who were keen to impress visitors with their home's grandeur (the Great Hall, in particular, is spectacular), this beautiful building has witnessed more than 400 years of turbulent history. Uncover the hidden Tudor secrets, play billiards, explore the maze or enjoy a bracing walk with stunning views of the Welsh hills. A perfect oasis from modern life. **Note**: administered and financed by the National Trust, assisted by a grant from National Museums Liverpool.

Exploring
- Join a Victorian or Tudor costumed guided tour.
- Take your cue from us – have a go at billiards.
- Explore the gardens and woodland walks.
- Children can burn off energy in the playground.
- Solve the puzzle of the maze.
- Discover the restored kitchen garden.

Eating and shopping: browse in our well-stocked shop for local gifts, products and plants. Why not use our free plant babysitting service? Relax in the Home Farm restaurant and enjoy freshly made regional specialities, such as Scouse Pie and Wet Nelly.

Making the most of your day: highlights of our year include Easter, Hallowe'en, the Christmas season, open-air theatre and themed Tudor and Victorian events. Families will enjoy our all-weather play areas and special activities. **Dogs**: on leads in woodland and on signed estate walks.

Access for all: 🅿️🅳♿�{}🧍🦽🖼️📷
⚫🅰️ Hall ♿🏠🦽 Grounds 🦽➡️♿

Getting here: 108:SJ419825. 8 miles south of city centre. **Cycle**: NCN62, 1¾ miles. **Bus**: services to Liverpool Airport and Liverpool Lime Street ≋ to Liverpool Airport. All within 1 mile of entrance (then ½ mile to reception). Additional service planned, telephone for details. **Train**: Liverpool South Parkway 2 miles; Southport to Hunt's Cross line. **Road**: adjacent to Liverpool Airport. 1 mile off A561. Follow airport signs from M62 exit 6, A5300; M56 exit 12. Brown signs from city centre. **Parking**: large car park.

Finding out more: 0844 800 4799 (Infoline). 0151 427 7231 or spekehall@nationaltrust.org.uk

Speke Hall, Garden and Estate		M	T	W	T	F	S	S
25 Feb–11 Mar	11–4						S	S
14 Mar–22 Jul	11–5			W	T	F	S	S
24 Jul–2 Sep*	11–5		T	W	T	F	S	S
5 Sep–28 Oct	11–5			W	T	F	S	S
3 Nov–9 Dec	11–4						S	S

House: entry 11 to 12:30 by guided tour only (places limited); free-flow from 12:30. *During summer, access to the house on Tuesdays is by guided tour only (places limited). Speke Hall is open on Bank Holiday Mondays and the Queen's Diamond Jubilee (5 June). Some rooms under covers 25 February to 11 March with conservation cleaning demonstrations taking place during this period. Car park closes 30 minutes after times stated above.

Fine 16th-century timberwork at Speke Hall, Liverpool

Entry is still possible at most places up to 30 minutes before closing

Stagshaw Garden

Ambleside, Cumbria LA22 0HE

Map (6) D8   ⊕ 1957

A fine collection of shrubs, including rhododendrons, azaleas and camellias; best viewed April to June. Skelghyll Woods are close by. **Note**: no facilities.

Access for all: Grounds 🖳

Getting here: 90:NY380029. ½ mile south of Ambleside on A591. Nearest car parks at Waterhead (pay and display).

Finding out more: 015394 46027 or stagshaw@nationaltrust.org.uk

Stagshaw Garden		M	T	W	T	F	S	S
1 Apr–30 Jun	10–6:30	M	T	W	T	F	S	S

Steam Yacht Gondola on Coniston, Cumbria

Exploring — For a grand Victorian day out, disembark at Brantwood House.
— Enjoy a *Swallows and Amazons*-type adventure.
— Combine your cruise with a circular walk to Tarn Hows.
— Disembark at Parkamoor to enjoy stunning walks.

Eating and shopping: local, freshly prepared food at the Bluebird Café, Coniston Pier. Disembark at Brantwood jetty for Jumping Jenny's tea-room. Catering provided for private hires. *Gondola* souvenirs available on board.

Steam Yacht Gondola

Coniston Pier, Lake Road, Coniston, Cumbria LA21 8AN

Map (6) D8   1980

The original Victorian Steam Yacht *Gondola*, first launched in 1859 and now completely rebuilt by the National Trust, gives passengers the chance to sail in her sumptuous, upholstered saloons. This is the perfect way to view Coniston's spectacular scenery. Sail to Monk Coniston jetty at the north of the lake, then walk through the Monk Coniston garden on to Tarn Hows. Circular walk four miles or disembark at Brantwood to visit Ruskin's home. **Note**: all sailings are subject to weather conditions. No toilet on scheduled sailings. Fares (including members) as *Gondola* is an enterprise.

Exploring — Explorer cruises – hear about Coniston's famous connections!

Making the most of your day: look out for cruises and guided walks, evening Campbell and *Bluebird* talks and more. **Dogs**: in outside areas only.

Access for all: 🅿️🚻😊♿ Gangway 🐾🖳

Getting here: 96:SD307970. Sails from Coniston Pier (½ mile from Coniston village). **Bus**: from Windermere ➡. **Train**: Foxfield, not Sunday, 10 miles; Windermere 10 miles via vehicle ferry. **Road**: A593 from Ambleside. Pier is at end of Lake Road, turn immediately left after petrol station if travelling south from centre of Coniston village. **Parking**: 50 yards, pay and display, at Coniston Pier (not National Trust).

Finding out more: 01539 432733 or sygondola@nationaltrust.org.uk. Low Wray Campsite, Low Wray, Ambleside, Cumbria LA22 0JA

Steam Yacht *Gondola*

Daily sailing 1 April to 2 November. For sailing timetable and fares, visit www.nationaltrust.org.uk/gondola or telephone 015394 32733. Piers at Coniston, Monk Coniston, Parkamoor and Brantwood (not National Trust).

The spectacular Japanese garden at Tatton Park, Cheshire: just one among many exotic garden themes

Tatton Park

Knutsford, Cheshire WA16 6QN

Map ⑤ D8

This is one of the most complete historic estates open to visitors. The early 19th-century Wyatt house sits amid a landscaped deer park and is opulently decorated, providing a fine setting for the Egerton family's collections of pictures, books, china, glass, silver and specially commissioned Gillows furniture. The theme of Victorian grandeur extends into the garden, with its Fernery, Orangery, Rose Garden, Tower Garden, Pinetum, Walled Garden with its glasshouses, Italian and Japanese gardens. Other features include a 1930s working rare breeds farm, a children's play area, speciality shops, restaurant and 400-hectare (1,000-acre) deer park. **Note**: managed and financed by Cheshire East Council. For tours and special events supplementary charges may apply (including members).

Exploring
   – The mansion has one of the finest Gillows furniture collections.
   – Enjoy the landscaped deer park, including a new bird hide.
   – The gardens contain 250 years of garden design and history.

Exploring
   – Explore 500 years of history at the Old Hall.
   – Visit one of over 100 events held throughout the year.
   – Feed rare-breed animals at the 1930s working farm.

Eating and shopping: Tatton's Stableyard is perfect for shopping and dining. Our shops showcase the best in local and estate produce and carefully selected gifts and souvenirs reflecting the history and character of Tatton Park. The Stables Restaurant offers quality local dishes.

Making the most of your day: visit www.tattonpark.org.uk for events. Members – free admission to house and gardens only, half-price entry to farm, car entry charge. Old Hall special openings. Tatton Park Biennial 2012: contemporary art event. **Dogs**: on leads at farm and under close control in park only.

Access for all: 🅿️ 🅿️ ♿ 🚻 🅿️ 🔳 ♿ 📷
Building ♿♿♿♿ Grounds ♿♿➡️♿

Getting here: 109/118:SJ745815. 2 miles north of Knutsford, 4 miles south of Altrincham. **Cycle**: Cheshire Cycleway passes property. **Bus**: buses from surrounding areas to Knutsford, then 2 miles. **Train**: Knutsford 2 miles. **Road**: 5 miles from M6, exit 19; 3 miles from M56, exit 7, well signposted on A556; entrance on Ashley Road, 1½ miles north-east of junction A5034 with A50. **Sat Nav**: follow directional signs to Tatton Park rather than using satellite navigation systems. **Parking**: £5 car entry charge applies (including members).

Finding out more: 01625 374435 (Infoline). 01625 374400 or tatton@cheshireeast.gov.uk. www.tattonpark.org.uk. Tatton Park, Knutsford, Cheshire WA16 6QN

Tatton Park		M	T	W	T	F	S	S
Parkland								
1 Jan–23 Mar	11–5		T	W	T	F	S	S
24 Mar–28 Oct	10–7	M	T	W	T	F	S	S
30 Oct–30 Dec	11–5		T	W	T	F	S	S
Mansion								
24 Mar–30 Sep	1–5		T	W	T	F	S	S
2 Oct–28 Oct	12–4		T	W	T	F	S	S
Gardens and restaurant								
1 Jan–18 Mar	11–4		T	W	T	F	S	S
24 Mar–28 Oct	10–6	M	T	W	T	F	S	S
30 Oct–30 Dec	11–4		T	W	T	F	S	S
Farm								
1 Jan–23 Mar	11–4						S	S
24 Mar–28 Oct	12–5		T	W	T	F	S	S
3 Nov–30 Dec	11–4						S	S
Shops								
1 Jan–23 Mar	12–4		T	W	T	F	S	S
24 Mar–28 Oct	11–5	M	T	W	T	F	S	S
30 Oct–30 Dec	12–4		T	W	T	F	S	S

Open Bank Holiday Mondays. Closed 25 December. Attractions: last admission one hour before closing. Mansion also open for Christmas events during December, check for details. Guided mansion tours Tuesday to Sunday 24 March to 30 September at 12 by timed ticket available from garden entrance after 10:30. Places limited, small charge including members. Old Hall special opening arrangements: telephone for details. Advisable to check opening times before visiting.

kitchen, which has a real fire burning most days and a quirky collection of domestic tools. Exploring further, you can marvel at the intricately carved furniture and discover why the collection of books belonging to a farming family is of international importance.

Exploring
- Discover more about life as a Lake District farmer.
- Have a go at making a rag rug.
- Relax in the pretty cottage garden.
- Find out more on a guided tour in the mornings.
- Download a circular walk taking in Townend and Troutbeck Valley.

Eating and shopping: look through our small selection of postcards and souvenirs. Warm up with a hot drink from our vending machine. Treat yourself to a second-hand book. Buy a plant from our selection, grown in the garden.

Making the most of your day: have a go at making a rag rug or enjoy our live interpretation. Our children's trail helps to bring the house to life.

Access for all: 🅿️🔖📖⋮🅰️
Building 🔖 Grounds 🔖🔖

Townend

Troutbeck, Windermere, Cumbria LA23 1LB

Map (6) D8   🏠 ❉ 1948

'Fascinating – so much history in one house. A truly inspiring visit.'
Nick Turner, Grasmere

The Brownes of Townend were just an ordinary farming family, but their home and belongings bring to life more than 400 years of extraordinary stories. You will understand why Beatrix Potter described Troutbeck Valley as her favourite as you approach this traditional stone and slate farmhouse. Once inside, you are welcomed into the farmhouse

Townend, Cumbria: traditional stone farmhouse

Getting here: 90:NY407023. 3 miles south-east of Ambleside at south end of Troutbeck village. **Bus**: services from Windermere ☒, alight Troutbeck Bridge, 1½ miles. **Train**: Windermere 2½ miles. **Road**: off A591 or A592. **Parking**: free, 300 yards. Not suitable for coaches or campervans.

Finding out more: 015394 32628 or townend@nationaltrust.org.uk

Townend		M	T	W	T	F	S	S
House tours*								
10 Mar–4 Nov	11–1	·	·	**W**	**T**	**F**	**S**	**S**
House								
10 Mar–4 Nov	1–5	·	·	**W**	**T**	**F**	**S**	**S**

*11 to 1 entry by hourly guided tour only (places limited). Tours at 11 and 12, then 1 to 5 free-flow. Open Bank Holiday Mondays. May close early due to poor light. Property less busy at weekends.

Ullswater and Aira Force

near Watermillock, Penrith, Cumbria

Map (6) D7

Dramatic walks around Aira Force waterfall and picturesque pleasure grounds, renowned in Victorian times as a beauty spot. Beyond Aira Force there are four farms, beautiful woodlands and acres of wild fell. Wordsworth's famous daffodils can be found on the shores of the lake.

The waterfall at Aira Force in Cumbria

Exploring
– Enjoy the breathtaking waterfalls at Aira Force.
– Relax among Wordsworth's daffodils on the shore of Ullswater.
– Enjoy the new level path around Brotherswater.
– Take in stunning views from the summit of Gowbarrow.

Eating and shopping: Aira Force tea-room (not National Trust) by car park. Walk from Glenridding to Side Farm tea-room (Trust farm).

Making the most of your day: delight in the stunning scenery. **Dogs**: under close control (stock grazing).

Access for all: Grounds ⬇️➡️

Getting here: 90:NY401203. 7 miles south of Penrith. **Cycle**: NCN71, 2 miles. **Bus**: from Penrith ☒ to Patterdale. **Train**: Penrith 10 miles. **Parking**: two car parks at Aira Force and Glencoyne Bay (pay and display).

Finding out more: 017684 82067 or ullswater@nationaltrust.org.uk. Tower Buildings, Watermillock, Penrith, Cumbria CA11 0JS

Ullswater and Aira Force	Open every day all year

Wasdale, Eskdale and Duddon

Cumbria

Map (6) C8

From Scafell Pike, England's highest mountain, look down on Wastwater, England's deepest lake, with its majestic screes. The National Trust owns the valley farms, campsite, lake, surrounding mountains and the nearby Nether Wasdale Estate. Walk the delightful paths of Upper Eskdale or explore the ever-changing Duddon Valley.

Exploring
- Visit Hardknott Roman fort.
- Camp at the head of Wasdale at our Trust site.
- Admire the amazing stone walls at Wasdale Head.

Making the most of your day: explore the many paths in these spectacular valleys. **Dogs**: under close control (stock grazing).

Access for all: Grounds 🦽

Getting here: NY152055. **Train**: Ravenglass for Eskdale; Foxfield for Duddon; Seascale for Wasdale. **Road**: Wasdale 5 miles east of A595, turning at Gosforth. Eskdale, 6 miles east of A595, turning at Eskdale Green. Duddon 3 miles north of A595, turning at Duddon Bridge near Broughton-in-Furness. **Parking**: at Wasdale Head.

Finding out more: 019467 26064 or wasdale@nationaltrust.org.uk. The Lodge, Wasdale Hall, Wasdale, Cumbria CA20 1ET

Wasdale, Eskdale and Duddon	Open every day all year

Windermere and Troutbeck, Cumbria: pastoral scene

Windermere and Troutbeck

near Windermere, Cumbria

Map ⑥ D8 🏠🏛♿ 1927

Take a footpath from Ambleside over Wansfell to the Troutbeck Valley, admire tiny Bridge House or visit the Roman fort in Ambleside. Stroll through Cockshott Point on the lakeshore at Bowness-on-Windermere or walk to Orrest Head, Adelaide Hill or Miller Ground, just some of our sites around Windermere. **Note**: no facilities.

Exploring
- Enjoy breathtaking views from the summit of Wansfell.
- Relax by the lake on Cockshott Point.
- Visit Bridge House, Ambleside's smallest building.
- Follow in the footsteps of Romans at Galava Roman Fort.

Making the most of your day: exciting events around Windermere. Make a day of it and visit nearby Townend and Fell Foot. **Dogs**: welcome under close control (stock grazing).

Access for all: Bridge House 🦽

Getting here: 90:NY407023. **Ferry**: from Newby Bridge to Ambleside and Bowness. **Bus**: services from Windermere ➡. During the season open-top buses run regularly from Bowness to Ambleside. **Road**: Troutbeck is signposted east of A591 Windermere to Ambleside road.

Finding out more: 015394 46027 or windermere@nationaltrust.org.uk. St Catherine's, Patterdale Road, Windermere, Cumbria LA23 1NH

Windermere and Troutbeck	Open every day all year

Wordsworth House and Garden

Main Street, Cockermouth, Cumbria CA13 9RX

Map ⑥ C7 1938

'Absolutely fab. So much to do for my grandchildren as well as interest for us. Superb café. Very highly recommended.'
A. Carlin and M. Brown, Sudbury, Suffolk

Step back to the 1770s and experience life as William and his sister Dorothy might have at this beautiful, homely property. Enjoy a warm welcome from the Wordsworths' servants and find out more about the restoration of the house and garden, including our recently opened cellars. William's beloved garden inspired many of his poems and contains 18th-century flowers, fruit and vegetables – all used in the house. Relax in our beautiful new summerhouse on Wordsworth's famous terrace, walk and listen to his poetry and accounts of the great flood of 2009. Enjoy daily recipe tastings and children's holiday activities.

Exploring – Explore our hands-on rooms with toys, costumes and books.
– Meet the servants and enjoy a gossip.
– Come along for a talk, tour or special event.
– Listen to music from the harpsichord.
– Enjoy the garden and meet our Scots Dumpy hens.
– Write with quill pen and ink, or do some baking.

Eating and shopping: browse for Wordsworth and local souvenirs in our shop. Enjoy superb home-baked cakes in our café.

Making the most of your day: costumed servants, family activities every school holiday, talks, harpsichord music, garden tours, cooking demonstrations, original Wordsworth items, Georgian tastings and games, plus craft activities. **Dogs**: on leads in front garden only.

Access for all: [icons] Building [icons] Grounds [icon]

Getting here: 89:NY118307. In centre of Cockermouth. **Foot**: close to town car parks and bus stop. Entrance on Main Street, not side gate on Low Sand Lane. **Cycle**: NCN71 (C2C) and NCN10 (Reivers) pass door. **Bus**: from Penrith to Workington and Workington to Cockermouth. **Train**: Workington 8 miles; Maryport 6½ miles. **Road**: off A66, on Cockermouth Main Street. **Parking**: in town centre car parks. Long stay car park signposted as coach park (not National Trust), 300 yards on Wakefield Road, walk back over footbridge to house.

Finding out more: 01900 820884 (Infoline). 01900 824805 or wordsworthhouse@nationaltrust.org.uk

Wordsworth House and Garden		M	T	W	T	F	S	S
House, garden and café*								
10 Mar–4 Nov	11–5	M	T	W	T	.	S	S
Shop								
4 Jan–14 Jan	10–4	.	T	W	T	F	S	.
10 Mar–4 Nov	10–5	M	T	W	T	F	S	S
5 Nov–22 Dec	10–4:30	M	T	W	T	F	S	.

*Café open 10:30 to 4:30. Last entry 4. Timed tickets may operate on busy days.

The kitchen at Wordsworth House and Garden, Cumbria

Yorkshire

Delicate plasterwork and ice-cool colours
provide classic Georgian comfort at
Ormesby Hall

Outdoors
in Yorkshire

Above: **pretty heather bells**
Above right: **visitors enjoying Brimham Rocks in North Yorkshire**

Yorkshire contains some of the country's finest landscapes – boasting acres of green fields, drystone walls, moorland heaths and wildflower-rich hay meadows. It also has an important industrial heritage, stunning views and is a haven for wildlife and heaven for walkers.

The National Trust owns land in the Yorkshire Dales, North York Moors, Marsden Moor and the Yorkshire coast, including part of the Cleveland Way. There are also the hidden gems of Brimham Rocks, Hardcastle Crags and the Bridestones.

Challenge yourself in this ancient landscape
Formed more than 320 million years ago, the fantastically shaped formations at Brimham Rocks are home to a huge variety of wildlife, and present an intriguing challenge for ramblers, climbers and those seeking the perfect day out.

There are more than 470 climbs, and the Trust offers taster days for beginners, as well as harder climbs for the more experienced.

With imaginative names, including the Dancing Bear, Castle Rock and the Anvil, the site was created by geological movement, ice ages and weather erosion.

www.nationaltrust.org.uk/coastandcountryside

Left:
Upper Wharfedale, Yorkshire Dales, North Yorkshire
Below:
Malham Tarn Estate, also in the Yorkshire Dales, North Yorkshire

In the heart of the North York Moors, the Bridestones nature reserve is also home to rock formations, including the Pepper Pot – so named because of its unusual shape. This is a wonderful place to visit, with views over moorland, woodland and sheltered valleys.

On the edge of the North York Moors you'll find the iconic Roseberry Topping. Walk – or even run – the 350 yards to the summit and take in the spectacular views across industrial Teesside, rural farmland and moorland and the meandering Yorkshire coastline.

Explore meadows and dales
The endless drystone walls, green fields and meadows of the Yorkshire Dales have created a landscape emblematic of this wonderful corner of Yorkshire.

The estates at Malham Tarn and Upper Wharfedale contain some of the finest upland landscapes in the Dales, with limestone pavements, waterfalls and flower-rich hay meadows criss-crossed with stone walls and studded with traditional field barns.

The Trust cares for nearly 3,000 hectares (7,500 acres) in Malhamdale, and we have waymarked walks throughout the Dales – from Malham Cove to Fountains Fell. So go for a ramble, or follow a circular trail across the ancient limestone pavements. Alternatively take a route around Malham Tarn, which, with its adjacent areas of raised bog, fen and woodland, is protected as a National Nature Reserve.

We've got leaflets listing several routes around the tarn and surrounding area. Either request these in advance, or pick one up from the leaflet dispensers around the estate.

You can also enjoy a family bike ride around the tarn on fairly flat paths and quiet roads, or stroll to the shore and picnic.

A moorland bird haven
The windswept landscape of Marsden Moor may at times appear bleak and inhospitable, but it is home to many colonies of birds – such as golden plover, red grouse, curlew, snipe and twite. In fact the birdlife is so rich, that the estate has been designated an international Special Protection Area for birds.

For a taste of the estate's past, follow one of the footpaths across the moor. Many of these follow ancient pack-horse routes, from where it is possible to glimpse evidence of the estate's industrial history.

Discover the Yorkshire coast

There is so much to discover along the Yorkshire coastline. Go exploring and take in the Ravenscar Coastal Centre and Peak Alum Works, then The Old Coastguard Station at Robin Hood's Bay.

Nestling on the edge of the North Sea, The Old Coastguard Station is now an interpretive visitor centre. Find out about the hidden history of an ancient landscape and hear how the building has been an important focus of village life, then savour the panoramic views across the bay – from Ness Point in the north, to Ravenscar in the south.

There are also commanding views to be enjoyed at Ravenscar, where you can see the complete sweep of the bay from a vantage point 200 metres high.

The Trust cares for a wealth of features in and around the village, including the remains of a Second World War radar station, a reinstated rocket post – once used by local coastguards – flower-rich meadows, farmland and bluebell woods.

Always something to see and do

Whatever the time of year, the Yorkshire Moors, Dales and the coastline offer something to do. There are so many activities on offer. Choose from walking, climbing, cycling, horse riding, or just simply playing and enjoying the great outdoors.

For the more adventurous, there is rock climbing at

Why not try...?

Staying longer and getting closer

We have holiday cottages in some stunning locations. You can stay in the deer park at Fountains Abbey and Studley Royal Water Garden or in The Old Coastguard Station at Robin Hood's Bay. Or, for a wilder location, why not book one of our cottages in the Yorkshire Dales or the North York Moors?

Taking two wheels instead of four

Bring your bicycle when you visit and explore Yorkshire in a whole new way. Cycling gives you a completely different perspective and allows you to discover parts of the countryside inaccessible to cars. More and more of our places are opening new cycling routes and

linking in with national ones. For example, the Way of the Roses coast-to-coast route passes several places – Beningbrough Hall and Gardens, Treasurer's House, Fountains Abbey and Studley Royal Water Garden, as well as the weird and wonderful Brimham Rocks.

Getting your walking boots on

Walking in Yorkshire offers so much variety – from vast swathes of purple heather, to atmospheric woodland and magnificent hills, with stunning views over the surrounding countryside. Our walks range from short rambles, suitable for anyone from health groups to families with young children, to longer Ranger-guided adventures or challenging hikes.

Above: a view of Ravenscar from the beach at Boggle Hole

Brimham, mountain biking in the Dales, hang gliding over at Marsden Moor or climbing Roseberry Topping, where you will be rewarded by breathtaking views from the summit.

For families, our countryside places offer events such as Easter lambing and farm open days, as well as numerous organised activities, including pond dipping and den building.

Beningbrough Hall and Gardens

Beningbrough, York,
North Yorkshire YO30 1DD

Map ⑤ G4 🏚🏤🌼🌺🏡🔔🍴 1958

Beningbrough Hall and Gardens, North Yorkshire

'If walls could talk what would they say about gorgeous Georgians, industrious Victorians and brave airmen at this extraordinary hall?'
Mrs Susan Frith, Southport

Each visit to Beningbrough is a friendly, relaxed and inspiring journey. There is so much to explore; walking though pear arches and hidden gateways to reveal labyrinthine paths through new apple trees, grand Italianate borders and hidden woods. Stepping inside the cool and reflective Great Hall, uncover scandalous stories behind the National Portrait Gallery paintings, brought to life in real costumed splendor, or reveal your inner Georgian with costumes, virtual portraits and by sculpting your own nose. Or you could just bring a rug and enjoy a cream tea on the cherry tree lawn watching the clouds drift by.

Exploring
– Discover the 'Making Faces' galleries and commission your own portrait.
– Explore acres of beautiful gardens and the wilderness play area.
– Working walled garden supplies produce to the Walled Garden Restaurant.
– Get involved with our range of events and Artrageous! workshops.
– Beningbrough Home Farm Shop run by National Trust tenant farmers.
– Fully equipped Victorian laundry, with wet and dry rooms.

Eating and shopping: enjoy hot lunches and snacks in the Walled Garden Restaurant, made with local, seasonal produce. The shop and plant centre stock a selection of quality goods.

Making the most of your day: large enough for a quiet picnic and stimulating enough to get involved with; living history, interactive galleries, Artrageous! Hidden House tours, Laundrymaids and guided garden walks on selected days. **Dogs**: welcome in parkland. Assistance dogs only in gardens and grounds.

Access for all: 🅿️🅳♿️🚻🔈🎧📷👓🎨
Georgian mansion ♿🦽🔼🅱️ Stable block 🦽🅱️
Grounds 🦽🦽➡️🅱️

Getting here: 105:SE516586. 8 miles north-west of York. **Foot**: footpath from York, along River Ouse, 10 miles. **Cycle**: NCN65. **Bus**: York to Easingwold, alight Shipton, 1 mile. **Train**: York, 8 miles. **Road**: signposted off A59 and A19. **Parking**: free, disabled parking at main entrance. Coaches via A19.

Finding out more: 01904 472027 or beningbrough@nationaltrust.org.uk

Beningbrough Hall and Gardens		M	T	W	T	F	S	S
House, galleries, gardens, shop and restaurant								
3 Mar–1 Apr	11–5:30	M	T	W	·	·	S	S
2 Apr–15 Apr	11–5:30	M	T	W	T	F	S	S
16 Apr–3 Jun	11–5:30	M	T	W	·	·	S	S
4 Jun–10 Jun	11–5:30	M	T	W	T	F	S	S
11 Jun–1 Jul	11–5:30	M	T	W	·	·	S	S
2 Jul–2 Sep	11–5:30	M	T	W	T	F	S	S
3 Sep–28 Oct	11–5:30	M	T	W	·	·	S	S
29 Oct–4 Nov	11–5:30	M	T	W	T	F	S	S
Galleries, gardens, shop and restaurant								
1 Jan–5 Feb	11–3:30	·	·	·	·	·	S	S
10 Nov–23 Dec	11–3:30	M	T	W	·	·	S	S

House: March to October opens at 12; November to 31 December, opens 11:30. Galleries, gardens, shop and restaurant: also open 11 to 19 February, 11 to 3:30. Visit website for Christmas and New Year opening.

Braithwaite Hall

East Witton, Leyburn, North Yorkshire DL8 4SY

Map ⑤ E3   1941

A striking 17th-century tenanted farmhouse in Coverdale. The hall, sitting room and carved staircase are on show to visitors. **Note**: no toilet.

Access for all: Building 🏠

Getting here: 99:SE117857. 1½ miles south-west of Middleham, 2 miles west of East Witton (A6108). Narrow approach road.

Finding out more: 01969 640287 or braithwaitehall@nationaltrust.org.uk

Braithwaite Hall	
June to September by arrangement in advance with the tenant, Mrs Duffus. Please contact well in advance to arrange a mutually convenient time for your visit.	

Bridestones, Crosscliff and Blakey Topping

Staindale, Dalby, Pickering, North Yorkshire YO18 7LR

Map ⑤ I3   1944

Spectacular all-year round, the Bridestones are a geological wonder and natural playground. Enjoy moorland vistas, woodland walks and grassy valleys. **Note**: Dalby Forest drive starting 2½ miles north of Thornton le Dale – toll charges apply (including members). Nearest toilets at Staindale Lake car park.

Access for all: 🅿️♿🚻♿ Grounds 🏠

Getting here: 94:SE877906. In North York Moors National Park.

Finding out more: 01723 870423 or bridestones@nationaltrust.org.uk. c/o Peakside, Ravenscar, Scarborough, North Yorkshire YO13 0NE

Bridestones	Open every day all year

Brimham Rocks

Summerbridge, Harrogate, North Yorkshire HG3 4DW

Map ⑤ F4   1970

An amazing collection of weird and wonderful rock formations which makes a great day out for families, climbers and those wanting to enjoy the simple pleasures of fresh air and magnificent views over Nidderdale. Let your imagination run wild as you explore the labyrinth of paths through this unique landscape. **Note**: beware of changes in height and cliff edges.

Exploring
 – Marvel at the fantastically shaped rock formations.
 – Let children explore this natural playground.
 – Enjoy magnificent views over Nidderdale and beyond.
 – Great for walking over moorland and through woodland.

Eating and shopping: excellent range of Yorkshire products for sale in our shop. Great value picnic food from our refreshment kiosk. Why not treat yourself to a hot chocolate or ice-cream?

Making the most of your day: discover the rocks' geological and social history and how we conserve this special place in the visitor centre. Regular guided walks. Tracker Packs available for five to eleven year olds. **Dogs**: under control and on leads on moorland April to June (ground-nesting birds).

Access for all: 🅿️♿🚻♿🔊📷♿ ⬜⬜🅿️
Building 🏠♿ Grounds ➡️

Getting here: 99:SE206650. 10 miles south-west of Ripon. **Foot**: Nidderdale Way passes through. **Cycle**: welcome on main track. **Bus**: Harrogate ▣ to Pateley Bridge, alight Summerbridge, 2 miles. Extra service Sundays and Bank Holidays, May to October, Harrogate to Brimham Rocks. **Road**: 11 miles from Harrogate off B6165, 4 miles from Pateley Bridge off B6265. **Sat Nav**: only gives approximate location. **Parking**: pay and display (coins only), £4 up to three hours, then £5. Motorcycles free; minibuses £8; coaches £15.

Finding out more: 01423 780688 or brimhamrocks@nationaltrust.org.uk

Brimham Rocks		M	T	W	T	F	S	S
Countryside								
Open all year	8–12	M	T	W	T	F	S	S
Visitor centre, shop and kiosk								
1 Jan–2 Jan	11–5	M	·	·	·	·	·	S
11 Feb–19 Feb	11–5	M	T	W	T	F	S	S
25 Feb–25 Mar	11–5	·	·	·	·	·	S	S
31 Mar–15 Apr	11–5	M	T	W	T	F	S	S
21 Apr–27 May	11–5	·	·	·	·	·	S	S
2 Jun–30 Sep	11–5	M	T	W	T	F	S	S
6 Oct–28 Oct	11–5	·	·	·	·	·	S	S
29 Oct–4 Nov	11–5	M	T	W	T	F	S	S
10 Nov–30 Dec	11–4	·	·	·	·	·	S	S

Visitor centre, shop and kiosk open Bank Holiday 7 May. Also open 26 December.

Brimham Rocks, North Yorkshire: sculptural shapes

East Riddlesden Hall

Bradford Road, Riddlesden, Keighley, West Yorkshire BD20 5EL

Map ⑤ E5   🏠 🏠 ✿ 🍴 ♿ ☂ 1934

'**Superb. I have never been anywhere ever where the guides were so friendly, helpful and knowledgeable.**'
Mrs Merrett, Suffolk

East Riddlesden Hall boasts an excellent story of survival. For generations, the East Riddlesden Hall Estate was a hive of farming activity. Today, visitors can wander through the house and discover some of the property's fascinating stories, furniture and textiles. The intimate award-winning gardens are the perfect place to relax and unwind. For younger visitors, the natural play areas are ideal for letting off steam. The mud pie kitchen offers the chance for budding chefs to get creative, and the new bird hide is a must for those who like getting up close to nature.

Exploring
- Absorb the tranquillity of our romantic award-winning gardens.
- Visit one of the finest 17th-century barns in northern England.
- Go wild in our children's natural play areas.
- Seek out the ghostly grey lady among our exquisite embroideries.
- Spy on local birdlife from our new bird hide.
- Step into the shoes of a 17th-century merchant.

Eating and shopping: indulge yourself with homemade soups, made using herbs from the garden, and our delicious afternoon tea. Get horticultural inspiration from our plant sales area and shop.

Making the most of your day: explore our herb interpretation area and discover our new composting area. Follow one of our fun trails to find out more. **Dogs**: assistance dogs only.

East Riddlesden Hall, West Yorkshire: tumultuous past

Access for all: [icons] Building [icons] Grounds [icons]

Getting here: 104:SE079421. 1 mile north-east of Keighley. **Bus**: Bradford Interchange ⊞ to Keighley, alight Granby Lane. **Train**: Keighley 1½ miles. **Road**: on south side of the Bradford Road in Riddlesden, close to Leeds & Liverpool Canal. A629 relief road from Shipley and Skipton signed for East Riddlesden Hall. **Parking**: free, 100 yards. Narrow entrance.

Finding out more: 01535 607075 or eastriddlesden@nationaltrust.org.uk

East Riddlesden Hall		M	T	W	T	F	S	S
House, shop and tea-room								
11 Feb–19 Feb	10:30–4:30	M	T	W	·	·	S	S
25 Feb–18 Mar	10:30–4:30	·	·	·	·	·	S	S
19 Mar–4 Nov	10:30–4:30	M	T	W	·	·	S	S
Shop and tea-room								
10 Nov–23 Dec	11–4	·	·	·	·	·	S	S

Open Good Friday. Entry to the house may be by guided tour. Last admission to tea-room 15 minutes before closing.

Fountains Abbey and Studley Royal Water Garden

Fountains, Ripon, North Yorkshire HG4 3DY

Map ⑤ F4 [icons] [icons] 1983

'What a beautiful place, even in the rain! The children enjoyed the freedom and we enjoyed the "potter".'
V. Powell, York

Come and discover for yourself why Fountains Abbey and Studley Royal is a World Heritage Site. Enjoy exploring the 323 hectares (800 acres) of beautiful countryside, where you'll find dramatic 12th-century abbey ruins, stunning Georgian water gardens, a high Gothic Victorian church, medieval deer park, Jacobean Hall and the only surviving Cistercian corn mill. Take a stroll along the banks of the

River Skell and find the perfect spot for a picnic. Play hide and seek along the high ride, and see how the colours of the garden and parkland change throughout the seasons. **Note**: cared for in partnership with English Heritage.

Exploring — Uncover the Abbey's history at the Porter's Lodge exhibition.
— Climb, swing, jump and run in the children's play area.
— Dare yourself to walk through the serpentine tunnel.
— Spot the differences between the red, fallow and sika deer.
— Have a go at grinding corn at Fountains Mill.
— See the splendour of the snowdrops in February.

Eating and shopping: tempt your taste-buds with our local and seasonal menu, including our estate-reared venison, and buy local produce in the shop. Enjoy the views from our lakeside and new abbey tea-rooms. Find the perfect gift in our shop and plant area.

Making the most of your day: find out more on guided tours and wildlife walks throughout the year. Enjoy open-air theatre, Christmas entertainment, medieval re-enactments and changing exhibitions. School holiday children's trails and craft workshops. **Dogs**: on short leads only.

Access for all: ⬛⬛⬛⬛⬛⬛⬛⬛⬛
Building ⬛⬛⬛ Grounds ⬛➡️⬛⬛

Getting here: 99:SE271683. 4 miles west of Ripon. **Foot**: public footpaths and bridleways. **Cycle**: signed on-road cycle loop. On Way of the Roses coast-to-coast route. **Bus**: services from Leeds, York, Yorkshire Dales and Harrogate to Ripon and Fountains Abbey. Daily from Ripon to Fountains, April to October. **Road**: off B6265 to Pateley Bridge, signed from A1, 12 miles north of Harrogate (A61). **Parking**: free at visitor centre, pay and display at Studley Royal deer park. Access from B6265.

Finding out more: 01765 608888 or fountainsabbey@nationaltrust.org.uk

Fountains Abbey		M	T	W	T	F	S	S
1 Jan–31 Jan	10–4	M	T	W	T	·	S	S
1 Feb–31 Mar	10–4	M	T	W	T	F	S	S
1 Apr–30 Sep	10–5	M	T	W	T	F	S	S
1 Oct–31 Oct	10–4	M	T	W	T	F	S	S
1 Nov–31 Dec	10–4	M	T	W	T	·	S	S
St Mary's Church								
1 Apr–30 Sep	12–4	M	T	W	T	F	S	S
Deer park								
Open all year	7–9	M	T	W	T	F	S	S

Estate closes dusk if earlier. Whole estate closed 24 and 25 December. Studley Royal shop opening times vary.

The dramatic and iconic ruins of Fountains Abbey in North Yorkshire

Goddards Garden

27 Tadcaster Road, York,
North Yorkshire YO24 1GG

Map (5) H5   1984

Visit the former gardens of Noel Goddard Terry, of the famous York chocolate-making firm. Designed by George Dillistone, the garden complements the house's Arts and Craft style. With yew-hedged garden rooms, bowling green, wilderness gardens and plants for every season, it is also an oasis for wildlife. **Note**: house not open to public (offices).

Exploring   –   An excellent example of a late Arts and Crafts garden.
       –   Formal terraces, gardens and herbaceous borders enclosed by yew hedges.
       –   Explore the garden and see the restored greenhouse.

Making the most of your day: enjoy a picnic in this tranquil garden, surrounded by lovely scenery and the sound of one of the few British colonies of midwife toads. **Dogs**: on leads only.

Access for all: Grounds 🏛️➡️

Getting here: 105:SE589497. 1½ miles from York. **Bus**: services from York ➤. **Train**: York 1½ miles. **Road**: take A1237/A64, then A1036 Tadcaster Road, signed York city centre, turn right after St Edward's Church, through brick gatehouse arch. **Parking**: free.

Finding out more: 01904 702021 or goddardsgarden@nationaltrust.org.uk

Goddards Garden		M	T	W	T	F	S	S
1 Mar–31 Oct	11–5	M	T	W	T	F	·	·

For opening arrangements visit the website or telephone.

Hardcastle Crags

near Hebden Bridge, West Yorkshire

Map (5) E6    1950

'**What a beautiful place! We really enjoyed our visit, particularly the Easter Egg trail.**'
Debbie Parnaby, Bradford

Explore this beautiful wooded valley with its deep ravines, tumbling streams and glorious waterfalls. Walk through woodland rich in wildlife, with more than 25 miles of footpaths and see the striking seasonal changes in the plants and trees. Nestling alongside the river is Gibson Mill, a former cotton mill and entertainment emporium, now a visitor centre using sustainable energy, where you can discover more about the valley's 200-year history with dressing up, exhibitions and tours. There are also guided walks, events and family activities to enjoy throughout the year. **Note**: steep paths and rough terrain.

Exploring   –   Enjoy 25 miles of walks through spectacular changing scenery.
       –   Stunning autumn colours, springtime bluebells and ever-changing birdsong.
       –   Visit our flagship sustainable property, Gibson Mill.
       –   Discover 200 years of industrial and social history.
       –   Guided walks, events and family activities throughout the year.

Eating and shopping: the Weaving Shed Café offers a selection of freshly made sandwiches, seasonal soups, local cakes and award-winning ice-cream. Visit our shop and browse through the tempting selection of books, hand-picked gifts, cards and sweet treats.

Making the most of your day: four circular walks, ranging from three to seven miles; downloadable walks on the website. Year-round varied programme, including guided and themed walks, events and family activities. **Dogs**: under close control at all times.

Access for all: ⬚⬚⬚⬚⬚⬚⬚⬚ ⬚
Building ⬚⬚ Grounds ⬚

Getting here: 103:SD988291. 1½ miles north-east of Hebden Bridge. **Foot:** via Walkers are Welcome trail from Hebden Bridge. Pennine Way passes nearby. **Cycle:** NCN68 passes nearby. Cycling restricted. **Bus:** local services. **Train:** Hebden Bridge. **Road:** at end of Midgehole Road, off A6033 **Sat Nav:** Midgehole car park: HX7 7AA. Clough Hole car park: HX7 7AZ. **Parking:** nearest 1 mile (pay and display). Disabled badge holders only allowed access to mill (book space). 25 spaces at Clough Hole car park, Widdop Road (steep walk).

Finding out more: 01422 844518 (weekdays). 01422 846236 (weekends) or hardcastlecrags@nationaltrust.org.uk. Hollin Hall, Crimsworth Dean, Hebden Bridge, West Yorkshire HX7 7AP

Hardcastle Crags		M	T	W	T	F	S	S
Countryside								
Open all year		M	T	W	T	F	S	S
Gibson Mill								
7 Jan–26 Feb	11–3	·	·	·	·	·	S	S
1 Mar–31 Oct	11–4	·	T	W	T	·	S	S
3 Nov–23 Dec	11–3	·	·	·	·	·	S	S
Weaving Shed Café								
7 Jan–26 Feb	11–3	·	·	·	·	·	S	S
1 Mar–31 Oct	11–4	·	T	W	T	·	S	S
3 Nov–23 Dec	11–3	·	·	·	·	·	S	S

Weaving Shed Café open daily in local school holidays (31 March to 15 April, 2 to 10 June, 21 July to 2 September and 20 to 28 October), Gibson Mill open Saturday to Thursday. Also open Good Friday, 26 December and all Bank Holiday Mondays. 1 May to 30 September: café open to 5 on Saturday and Sunday.

Looking across the still, mirror-like mill pond at Gibson Mill, Hardcastle Crags, West Yorkshire

Maister House

160 High Street, Hull, East Yorkshire HU1 1NL

Map (5) J6 | 1966 |

A merchant family's tale of fortune and tragedy is intertwined with the intriguing history of Maister House. **Note**: staircase and entrance hall only on show. No toilet.

Access for all: Building

Getting here: 107:TA102287. In Hull's Old Town.

Finding out more: 01723 870423 or maisterhouse@nationaltrust.org.uk. c/o Peakside, Ravenscar, Scarborough, North Yorkshire YO13 0NE

Maister House	M	T	W	T	F	S	S
2 Jan–31 Dec 10–4	M	T	W	T	F	·	·

Closed Bank Holidays.

Malham Tarn Estate

Waterhouses, Settle, North Yorkshire BD24 9PT

Map (5) D4    | 1946 |

This stunning area of limestone pavements, upland hill farms and flower-rich hay meadows provides a marvellous setting for walking, cycling or just enjoying the great outdoors. The National Nature Reserve is home to a unique community of rare plants and animals, with a glorious display of flowers in summer. **Note**: nearest toilet at National Park car park in Malham, or Orchid House exhibition (weekends only).

Exploring – Excellent walking and cycling opportunities around the tarn.
– Stroll from Malham to the beautiful Janet's Foss waterfall.
– Awe-inspiring, far-reaching views around the estate.

Exploring – Walk-in exhibition and group classroom at the Orchid House.

Eating and shopping: tea-rooms and facilities in Malham village.

Making the most of your day: guided walks and events throughout the year; summer holiday activities for the kids. **Dogs**: on leads only.

Access for all: Town Head Barn   Grounds

Getting here: 98:SD890660. Estate extends from Malham village, north past Malham Tarn. **Foot**: Pennine Way and Pennine Bridleway crosses property. **Bus**: Skipton to Malham (passing Skipton ☰), limited service, 1 mile. Telephone to confirm whether Malham Tarn shuttle bus is running. **Train**: Settle 7 miles. **Parking**: in Malham village, not National Trust (pay and display). Free parking at Watersinks car park on south side of Malham Tarn.

Finding out more: 01729 830416 or malhamtarn@nationaltrust.org.uk

Malham Tarn Estate	M	T	W	T	F	S	S
Countryside							
Open all year	M	T	W	T	F	S	S
Town Head Barn							
11 Feb–31 Oct 10–4	M	T	W	T	F	S	S

Malham Tarn Estate, North Yorkshire

Marsden Moor Estate

Marsden, Huddersfield, West Yorkshire

Map (5) E7   1955

The estate, covering nearly 2,248 hectares (5,553 acres) of uninterrupted moorland, spans the South Pennines and Peak District National Park. The landscape supports large numbers of moorland birds and is important for carbon storage and water provision. The estate is an SSSI and a site of European importance. **Note**: nearest refreshments and toilets in Marsden village.

Exploring – Miles of footpaths for walkers.
– A place to be alone with your thoughts.
– Dramatic scenery and visible industrial heritage.
– Varied programme of guided walks and events throughout the year.

Making the most of your day: explore this dramatic countryside on the Marsden Heritage Trail, with walks of four, eight or ten miles (leaflet available to use in conjunction with downloadable walk or OS map). **Dogs**: on leads only.

Access for all: Exhibition 🧑‍🦽 Grounds 🧑‍🦽

Getting here: 109:SE025100. Surrounding Marsden village. **Foot**: Kirklees Way, Pennine Way, Huddersfield Narrow Canal towpath and Colne Valley Circular all run onto the estate. Pennine Bridleway crosses estate. **Bus**: services from Huddersfield and Oldham. **Train**: Marsden. **Road**: between A640 and A635. **Parking**: free, around the estate, including Marsden village (not National Trust) and Buckstones and Wessenden Head.

Finding out more: 01484 847016 or marsdenmoor@nationaltrust.org.uk. Estate Office, The Old Goods Yard, Station Road, Marsden, Huddersfield, West Yorkshire HD7 6DH

Marsden Moor Estate	Open every day all year

Middlethorpe Hall Hotel, Restaurant and Spa

Bishopthorpe Road, York, North Yorkshire YO23 2GB

Map (5) H5    2008

Built in 1699, this quintessentially William and Mary house next to York Racecourse was once the home of the 18th-century diarist Lady Mary Wortley Montagu. Furnished with antiques and fine paintings and set in eight hectares (20 acres) with manicured gardens and parkland beyond, Middlethorpe Hall's country-house character remains unspoilt.

The house and gardens are already accessible to the public as a hotel, and welcome guests to stay, to dine in the restaurant and to have afternoon tea (booking strongly advised). Contact hotel direct for best available offers. **Note**: paying guests to the hotel only are able to walk in the garden and park. Children above the age of six are welcome.

Finding out more: 01904 641241. 01904 620176 (fax) or info@middlethorpe.com. www.middlethorpe.com

The elegant Middlethorpe Hall Hotel, North Yorkshire

Moulton Hall

Moulton, Richmond,
North Yorkshire DL10 6QH

Map (5) F2   1966

Elegant 17th-century manor house with a
beautiful carved staircase. **Note**: no toilet.

Access for all: 🅿️ Building 🏚️ Grounds 🏚️

Getting here: 99:NZ235035. 5 miles east
of Richmond; turn off A1, ½ mile south of
Scotch Corner.

Finding out more: 01325 377227 or
moultonhall@nationaltrust.org.uk

Moulton Hall
By arrangement in advance with the tenant, Viscount Eccles.
Please give as much notice as possible in order to arrange a
mutually convenient time for your visit.

Mount Grace Priory

Staddle Bridge, Northallerton,
North Yorkshire DL6 3JG

Map (5) G3   ✝️ 1953

England's most important Carthusian ruin. The
individual cells reflect the hermit-like isolation
of the monks. Entry via 13th-century manor
house. **Note**: operated by English Heritage;
members free, except on event days. Visit
website for directions.

Access for all: 🅳🚻🔊🎧📷🎞️
Building 🏚️🪜 Grounds 🪜

Getting here: 99:SE449985. 6 miles north-east
of Northallerton, ½ mile off A19, ½ mile south
of junction with A172.

Finding out more: 01609 883494 or
mountgracepriory@nationaltrust.org.uk

Mount Grace Priory		M	T	W	T	F	S	S
7 Jan–31 Mar	10–4	·	·	·	·	·	**S**	**S**
1 Apr–30 Sep	10–6	**M**	·	·	**T**	**F**	**S**	**S**
4 Oct–28 Oct	10–4	·	·	·	**T**	**F**	**S**	**S**
3 Nov–30 Dec	10–4	·	·	·	·	·	**S**	**S**

Closed 1 January and 24 to 26 December.

Nostell Priory and Parkland

Doncaster Road, Nostell, near Wakefield,
West Yorkshire WF4 1QE

Map (5) G6   🏠🍴➕🏛️❄️♣️
🦽🔔🍵 1954

Power, pleasure and prestige. Nostell Priory
and Parkland has been the home of the Winn
family for more than 300 years. The Georgian
mansion was built to show off the family's
wealth, using the best that money could buy.
Inside the house, see our largest collection
of Chippendale furniture, made specially
for Nostell, paintings by Brueghel, Hogarth
and Kauffmann, as well as a John Harrison
(longitude) longcase clock and 18th-century
doll's house. You can also explore over
121 hectares (300 acres) of garden and
parkland – find a place to picnic or simply sit
and watch the world go by. **Note**: conservation
work on stables due to be completed by Easter.

Exploring
- Find the mouse in the
18th-century doll's house.
- Discover masterpieces by
Chippendale, John Harrison
and Brueghel.
- Enchanting menagerie
garden, pleasure gardens and
developing vegetable garden.
- Wear the children out on the
play trail.
- Lose yourself in the extensive
rolling parkland.
- Take a guided walk through
the park – Wednesdays,
Saturdays, Sundays.

Lose yourself in the glorious grounds of Nostell Priory and Parkland, West Yorkshire

Eating and shopping: enjoy fresh, local, seasonal food and snacks in the new café and Bite to Eat outlet. New shop stocking larger range of tempting gifts and souvenirs. Weekend barbecue in the garden, weather permitting. Ice-cream bicycle around the grounds in summer.

Making the most of your day: family activities, craft fairs, theatre, concerts, upstairs-downstairs tours (booking essential). Guided parkland walks, Wednesdays, Saturdays and Sundays, house trails. House tours 11:15, 11:45, 12:15, Wednesday to Sunday. **Dogs**: on leads in park only.

Access for all: P D WC A
House Stable block
Grounds ➡

Getting here: 111:SE407172. 5 miles south-east of Wakefield. **Foot**: via pedestrian entrance on the A638. **Cycle**: NCN67, 3 miles. **Bus**: services from Wakefield to Doncaster. **Train**: Fitzwilliam 1½ miles. **Road**: on A638 towards Doncaster. **Sat Nav**: use WF4 1QD. **Parking**: £2.50 for non-members.

Finding out more: 01924 863892 or nostellpriory@nationaltrust.org.uk. Doncaster Road, Wakefield WF4 1QE

Nostell Priory and Parkland		M	T	W	T	F	S	S
Parkland								
Open all year	9–7	M	T	W	T	F	S	S
House*								
3 Mar–4 Nov	1–5	.	.	W	T	F	S	S
1 Dec–9 Dec	1–4	.	.	W	T	F	S	S
5 Dec–7 Dec	5–8	.	.	W	T	F	.	.
Gardens**								
1 Jan–12 Feb	11–4	.	.	.	.	.	S	S
13 Feb–19 Feb	11–4	M	T	W	T	F	S	S
22 Feb–30 Dec	11–5:30	.	.	W	T	F	S	S
Shop and tea-room***								
1 Jan–12 Feb	11–4	.	.	.	.	.	S	S
13 Feb–4 Nov	10–5:30	M	T	W	T	F	S	S
5 Nov–31 Dec	11–4	M	T	W	T	F	S	S

*House open 11 to 1 for guided tours at 11:15, 11:45 and 12:15 (not bookable, places limited), then free-flow 1 to 5. Open Bank Holiday Mondays: house, 11 to 5, gardens, shop and tea-room, 11 to 5:30. Parkland closes dusk if earlier. Rose garden may close occasionally for private functions. Closed 25 December. **Gardens open seven days during local school holidays, visit website for details. ***Shop open seven days a week from Easter dependent on completion of new facilities. Please telephone to confirm opening times before visiting Monday or Tuesday.

Nunnington Hall

Nunnington, near York,
North Yorkshire YO62 5UY

Map ⑤ H4   🏠 ♿ 1953

The south front of Nunnington Hall, North Yorkshire

The sheltered walled garden, with spring-flowering organic meadows, orchards and flamboyant peacocks, complements this beautiful Yorkshire house, nestling on the quiet banks of the River Rye. Enjoy the atmosphere of this former family home. Explore period rooms while hearing the Hall's many tales, and then discover one of the world's finest collections of miniature rooms in the attic. The Hall also holds a series of important art and photography exhibitions during the year. Why not make a day of it? Its proximity to Rievaulx Terrace (only 7½ miles) makes it an ideal double visit in one day.

Exploring
 — Visit our art and photography exhibitions.
 — Discover the amazing Carlisle Collection of miniature rooms.
 — Enjoy a stroll in the organic walled garden.

Eating and shopping: licensed tea-room with waitress service, serving local and seasonal produce. Special diets catered for including gluten-free options. Lovely picnic spots and tea-garden. Look for the local ranges in the shop.

Making the most of your day: full events programme throughout the year, including art and photography exhibitions, family activities, food events, concerts and much more.
Dogs: welcome in the car park only.

Access for all: 🅿 ♿ 🚽 ⚡ 👓
Building 🔆 ♿ 🚶 Grounds ♿ 🚶

Getting here: 100:SE670795. 4½ miles south-east of Helmsley. **Bus:** from Hovingham to Helmsley. **Road:** A170 Helmsley to Pickering road; 1½ miles north of Malton to Helmsley road (B1257); 21 miles north of York, via B1363. **Parking:** free, 50 yards.

Finding out more: 01439 748283 or nunningtonhall@nationaltrust.org.uk

Nunnington Hall		M	T	W	T	F	S	S
11 Feb–4 Nov	11–5			T	W	T	F	S	S
10 Nov–16 Dec	11–4		.	.	.	.	.	S	S
Open Bank Holiday Mondays.									

The Old Coastguard Station

The Dock, Robin Hood's Bay,
North Yorkshire YO22 4SJ

Map ⑤ I2   🏠 🖼 🏠 1998

A visitor centre at the edge of the sea. Our hands-on exhibition shows how the power of the tides, waves and wind have shaped the coastline and tells the story of local life, from dinosaurs to the present day. Come face to face with rock-pool inhabitants in our tank. **Note:** steep walk from car park.

Exploring
 — Be fascinated by our interactive exhibition.
 — See shoreline creatures up close in the rock-pool aquarium.
 — Explore the Dinosaur Coast.
 — Don't miss our historic village trail.

Eating and shopping: our shop offers a wide range of gifts and books to suit all interests, as well as local information.

Making the most of your day: follow the village trail, join a guided walk or go rock-pooling. Arts and crafts exhibitions. **Dogs**: allowed in building if carried.

Access for all: ⬛🔲🔲🔲
Old Coastguard Station 🔲🔲🔲

Getting here: 94:NZ953049. On slipway at bottom of village. **Foot**: Cleveland Way passes alongside the building. Coast-to-Coast Path finishes at building. **Cycle**: NCN1 nearby. **Bus**: from Middlesbrough, Guisborough, Whitby and Scarborough. **Train**: Whitby 5 miles. **Road**: off A171 Whitby to Scarborough, signposted Robin Hood's Bay. No access for cars down the steep hill to the old village. **Parking**: at top of hill, not National Trust (charge including members).

Finding out more: 01947 885900 or oldcoastguardstation@nationaltrust.org.uk

The Old Coastguard Station		M	T	W	T	F	S	S
1 Jan–12 Feb	10–4						S	S
13 Feb–26 Feb	10–4	M	T	W	T	F	S	S
3 Mar–1 Apr	10–4						S	S
2 Apr–4 Nov	10–5	M	T	W	T	F	S	S
10 Nov–23 Dec	10–4						S	S
27 Dec–31 Dec	10–4	M			T	F	S	S

The Old Coastguard Station, North Yorkshire

Ormesby Hall

Ladgate Lane, Ormesby, near Middlesbrough, Redcar & Cleveland TS3 0SR

Map ⑤ G2   🔲🔲🔲🔲🔲🔲 1962

Victorian laundry at Ormesby Hall, Redcar & Cleveland

Home of the Pennyman family for nearly 400 years, this classic Georgian mansion, with its Victorian kitchen and laundry, attractive gardens and estate walks, provides lively resources for local schools and community groups, and a unique venue for wedding ceremonies and corporate events. Weekend visitors can experience the spirit of the intimate home of Colonel Jim Pennyman, the last of the Pennyman line, and his arts-loving wife Ruth, as well as the stylish legacy of the 18th-century character 'Wicked' Sir James Pennyman – so named due to his extravagant lifestyle and his gambling with the family fortune.

Exploring
- Celebrate with us our Golden Jubilee year here at Ormesby.
- Enjoy beautiful gardens in an 18th-century landscape setting.
- Marvel at the astonishing detail in the model railway layouts.
- Admire the working stables, home to Cleveland Mounted Police horses.
- Discover more in the 'Cache in the Attic' stores.

Eating and shopping: enjoy tea in the servants' hall or on the terrace. Taste scones and cakes baked at the Hall. Pick up a souvenir from our reception.

Making the most of your day: weekday programme of special-interest activities and events, including lunchtime lectures and conservation tours. Enjoy the only model railway layouts owned by the National Trust. **Dogs**: on leads in park only.

Access for all: 🅿♿🚾♿🌀💻♪👓📷
Building 🏛♿ **Grounds** ➡♿

Getting here: 93:NZ530167. 3 miles south-east of Middlesbrough. **Cycle**: NCN65, 2¼ miles. **Bus**: services from Middlesbrough (passing close Middlesbrough ≢). **Train**: Marton 1½ miles; Middlesbrough 3 miles. **Road**: west of A171. From A19 take A174 to A172. Follow signs for Ormesby Hall. Entrance on Ladgate Lane (B1380). **Parking**: free, 100 yards.

Finding out more: 01642 324188 or ormesbyhall@nationaltrust.org.uk. Church Lane, Ormesby, Middlesbrough TS7 9AS

Ormesby Hall		M	T	W	T	F	S	S
10 Mar–8 Apr	1:30–5	·	·	·	·	·	S	S
12 Apr–15 Apr	1:30–5	·	·	·	T	·	S	S
21 Apr–29 Jul	1:30–5	·	·	·	·	·	S	S
2 Aug–2 Sep	1:30–5	·	·	·	T	·	S	S
8 Sep–28 Oct	1:30–5	·	·	·	·	·	S	S

Open Bank Holiday Mondays and Good Friday. Gates open 12:45. Property may close 7 and 8 July for concert. Please contact property for confirmation of opening. April and August: Thursday visits by guided tour only.

Rievaulx Terrace

Rievaulx, Helmsley, North Yorkshire YO62 5LJ

Map ⑤ H3   🏠♿♿ 1972

Discover one of Ryedale's true gems – the 18th-century landscape of Rievaulx Terrace. Stroll through woods, then out onto the terrace, with its stunning views down over the Cistercian ruin of Rievaulx Abbey. In spring the bank between the temples is awash with wild flowers, in summer the lawns are the perfect spot for picnics, while in autumn the beech woods are a mass of rich hues. Rievaulx Terrace's close proximity to Nunnington Hall makes it an ideal double visit in one day. **Note**: no access to Rievaulx Abbey from terrace.

Exploring
- Take your time and enjoy the scenic walk.
- Bring a hamper and have a picnic.
- Join in the family activities.
- Find out more by joining a guided tour.
- Spot the fascinating flora and fauna.

The distinctive Roseberry Topping, North Yorkshire

Eating and shopping: treat yourself to an ice-cream, drinks and snacks. Don't miss the shop selling National Trust ranges.

Making the most of your day: events programme throughout year, including family activities in school holidays and programme of guided tours. Free batricars available to book at specific times. **Dogs**: welcome on leads.

Access for all: [icons]
Visitor centre [icon] Temples [icon] Grounds [icons]

Getting here: 100:SE579848. 2½ miles north-west of Helmsley. **Foot**: Cleveland Way within ¾ mile. **Bus**: from Helmsley. April to October, Sundays and Bank Holidays. August, daily. **Road**: on B1257. **Parking**: free, 100 yards. Unsuitable for trailer caravans. Tight corners and no turning space beyond coach park.

Finding out more: 01439 798340 (summer). 01439 748283 (winter) or rievaulxterrace@nationaltrust.org.uk

Rievaulx Terrace		M	T	W	T	F	S	S
11 Feb–4 Nov	11–5	M	T	W	T	F	S	S

Last admission one hour before closing or dusk if earlier.

Roseberry Topping

Newton-under-Roseberry, North Yorkshire

Map (5) G2   [icons] 1985

Layers of human and geological history have shaped this distinctive and iconic landmark, with its bluebell woods and heather moorland. **Note**: nearest toilet at Newton-under-Roseberry car park (not National Trust).

Access for all: [icon]

Getting here: 93:NZ575126. 1 mile from Great Ayton, next to Newton-under-Roseberry village on A173.

Finding out more: 01723 870423 or roseberrytopping@nationaltrust.org.uk. c/o Peakside, Ravenscar, Scarborough, North Yorkshire YO13 0NE

Roseberry Topping	Open every day all year

Treasurer's House

Minster Yard, York, North Yorkshire YO1 7JL

Map (5) H5 [icons] 1930

Only a few yards from York Minster, this was the first house ever given to the National Trust complete with a collection – and it is not all that it first seems! It has a history spanning 2,000 years, from the Roman road in the cellar to the Edwardian servants' quarters in the attics, and 13 period rooms in between. These house one man's remarkable collection of antique furniture, ceramics, textiles and paintings spanning a 300-year period. Infamous ghost stories are another of the many quirky attributes of this property. Outside is an attractive formal sunken garden. **Note**: cellar and attic tour charges (including members).

Exploring
– Take the attic tour and learn about Edwardian servant life.
– Join the cellar tour; hear about sightings of Roman ghosts.
– Relax in the quiet walled garden.
– Enjoy refreshment in the table service tea-room.
– Trails for children available daily.
– Listen to our engaging room guides.

Eating and shopping: enjoy home-cooked local food in our tea-room. Visit our gift shop, including work for sale by local artists, or get a bargain from our range of second-hand books. Check out the website for our food-themed events.

Making the most of your day: daily tours of the Roman ghost cellar or Edwardian servants attics. Themed house tours in February and November. Family trails and activities every school holiday. Events throughout the year. **Dogs**: on leads in formal garden only.

Access for all: [icons]
Building [icons] Grounds [icons]

Getting here: 105:SE604523. In city centre adjacent to Minster (north side, at rear). **Cycle**: NCN65, ⅓ mile. Close to city cycle routes. **Bus**: from surrounding areas. **Train**: York ½ mile. **Parking**: nearest in Lord Mayor's Walk. Park and ride service from city outskirts.

Finding out more: 01904 624247 or treasurershouse@nationaltrust.org.uk

Treasurer's House		M	T	W	T	F	S	S
House, garden, tea-room and shop								
11 Feb–29 Feb*	11–3	M	T	W	T	·	S	S
1 Mar–31 Oct	11–4:30	M	T	W	T	·	S	S
1 Nov–29 Nov*	11–3	M	T	W	T	·	S	S
Tea-room only								
1 Dec–20 Dec	11–3	M	T	W	T	·	S	S

*11 to 29 February and 1 to 29 November: guided tour only (to selected rooms, some of the collection covered). 1 March to 31 October: whole property open.

The history of Treasurer's House, North Yorkshire, spans 2,000 years

Upper Wharfedale

near Buckden, North Yorkshire

Map (5) E4 1989

Along the Upper Wharfe Valley the characteristic drystone walls and barns of the Dales, important flower-rich hay meadows and beautiful riverside and valleyside woodland combine to create a wonderful place to relax and explore the great outdoors.

Exploring
- Spectacular scenery to explore and enjoy.
- Excellent walking and cycling opportunities.
- Beautiful picnic spots along the banks of the River Wharfe.
- Picturesque villages and hamlets to stroll around.

Eating and shopping: village tea-rooms, shops and pubs, farm shops (not National Trust).

Making the most of your day: guided walks and events throughout the year; summer holiday activities for the kids. **Dogs**: on leads only.

Access for all: Town Head Barn Grounds

Getting here: 98:SD935765. Extends from Kettlewell village north to Beckermonds and Cray. **Foot**: Dales Way runs through property, following the River Wharfe from Ilkley to Bowness in Windermere. **Cycle**: Kettlewell lies on the Yorkshire Dales Cycleway (Sustrans Regional Route 10) between Coverdale and Skipton. **Bus**: Skipton to Buckden. **Train**: Skipton, 12 miles. **Road**: B6160 runs along Upper Wharfedale through Cray, Buckden and Kettlewell, towards Grassington (7 miles) and Ilkley in the south. **Sat Nav**: use BD23 5JA. **Parking**: in Kettlewell and Buckden, not National Trust (pay and display).

Finding out more: 01729 830416 or upperwharfedale@nationaltrust.org.uk. Yorkshire Dales Estate Office, Waterhouses, Settle, North Yorkshire BD24 9PT

Upper Wharfedale		M	T	W	T	F	S	S
Countryside								
Open all year		**M**	**T**	**W**	**T**	**F**	**S**	**S**
Town Head Barn								
11 Feb–31 Oct	10–4	**M**	**T**	**W**	**T**	**F**	**S**	**S**

Characteristic drystone walls in Upper Wharfedale, North Yorkshire

Yorkshire Coast

near Ravenscar, North Yorkshire

Map (5) I2   🏛️🅿️♿🚂🚻🏠 1976

Along the Cleveland Way National Trail is

Making the most of your day: wildlife activities and guided walks at Ravenscar, Boggle Hole and Saltburn. Boat trips from Whitby. Industrial heritage exhibition at Ravenscar Visitor Centre. **Dogs**: on leads allowed.

Access for all: ♿🚻🅿️🔁📖
Ravenscar Visitor Centre 🔁 Grounds ♿

Looking from Ravenscar towards Robin Hood's Bay, North Yorkshire, on a perfect, crisp winter's day

a diverse collection of coastal properties stretching south from Saltburn to Newbiggin Cliffs at Filey. Discover breathtaking clifftop views and coastal wildlife from seabird colonies to rock-pool inhabitants. Ravenscar Visitor Centre offers a welcoming and informative introduction to the area.

Exploring
   – See how the elements have created this stunning landscape.
   – Discover more about Britain's first chemical industry.
   – Spot wildlife in bluebell woods and clifftop meadows.
   – Explore your very own Jurassic Park.

Eating and shopping: enjoy the exhibition at the Ravenscar Visitor Centre and shop for all your walking and cycling requirements, local gifts and light refreshments.

Getting here: 94:NZ980016. On the North Yorkshire coast. **Foot**: Cleveland Way passes through property. **Cycle**: NCN1. **Bus**: regular local services. **Train**: Saltburn, Whitby, Scarborough, Filey for access to coast. **Road**: Saltburn to Whitby A174, Ravenscar signposted off Whitby to Scarborough A171. **Parking**: free on roadside at Ravenscar. Also at Saltburn and Runswick Bay (not National Trust).

Finding out more: 01723 870423 or yorkshirecoast@nationaltrust.org.uk. Peakside, Ravenscar, Scarborough, North Yorkshire YO13 0NE

Yorkshire Coast	M	T	W	T	F	S	S
Countryside							
Open all year	M	T	W	T	F	S	S
Ravenscar Visitor Centre							
2 Apr–4 Nov 10–4:30	M	T	W	T	F	S	S

North East

So much to explore: the woodland and lakes at Cragside prove irresistible to all adventurers

Outdoors in the North East

Some of the finest stretches of coast and countryside in Northumberland, Durham and Tyne & Wear are cared for by the National Trust. With unspoilt moorland, magnificent scenery and a dramatic coastline, this is arguably one of the finest places in Britain.

Clockwise from top left: **looking towards Dunstanburgh Castle, Northumberland, from Greymare Rock. The Durham coast and tern**

Spot the rare wildlife

The North East is a haven for wildlife, offering one of the few sanctuaries in England for our threatened native red squirrels. If you are out walking, keep your eyes open for a rare sighting. Red squirrels live in wooded areas and can be seen at Allen Banks, Cragside and Wallington – the latter has a wildlife hide that is perfect for spotting these special animals.

As well as squirrels, there is an abundance of birdlife in the North East. The Farne Islands, for example, are home to more than 100,000 nesting birds and their chicks during the breeding season (May to July). Lying just off the north-east coast from Seahouses, the Farnes are not to be missed if you are interested in wildlife.

Both Inner Farne and Staple Island are accessible only by boat, and can be landed on when the weather permits. Their very special inhabitants include puffins, terns, guillemots, eider ducks and a colony of grey seals.

St Cuthbert died on Inner Farne in 687, and the chapel built in his memory can be visited today.

Beaches, rock pools and dunes

The Trust cares for 16 miles of sandy beaches, dunes and tidal rock pools along the Northumberland coast, as well as five miles of the Durham coast. For many years, the Durham beaches were a dumping ground for the local collieries; however, now they have been cleaned up and this beautiful area has Heritage Coast status.

Near Horden in County Durham, in the south of the region, a piece of coast marks the 500th mile acquired through the Trust's Neptune Coastline Campaign. Once an industrial mining hotspot, this stretch of coastline has since been dramatically restored, and while even today it may be some time before the beaches return to golden sands, the seeds have been sown for the future.

Paradise for walkers

Inland Northumberland offers the natural beauty and tranquillity of Allen Banks and Staward Gorge – a walker's paradise with many miles of footpaths – while both Ros Castle and the World Heritage Site of Hadrian's Wall boast breathtaking views. There are also numerous beautiful woodland walks, including one along the banks of the River Wear at Moorhouse Woods, north of Durham City, and another beside the Derwent at Ebchester.

The unique Holy Island

Accessible by a causeway at low tide, Holy Island is a treasure that has as its centrepiece Lindisfarne Castle. Once a Tudor fort, the castle sits on a rocky crag that can be seen for miles along the sweeping coastline. Converted into a holiday home in 1903, this enchanting place, with its small rooms full of intimate decoration and design, is totally charming. Don't miss the lovely walled garden just below the castle. This was planned by Gertrude Jekyll and dates back to 1922.

Also be sure to stroll along the headland and explore the village – just remember to keep an eye on the tides which cover the causeway.

Right:
Hadrian's Wall,
Northumberland

A Roman wonder

One of the most rugged stretches of countryside in the North East is home to Hadrian's Wall. Snaking across the landscape, the wall was built around AD122 when the Roman Empire was at its height. A World Heritage Site, it remains one of Britain's most impressive ruins.

The Trust protects six miles of Hadrian's Wall, including Housesteads Fort, one of the best-preserved sections of the ramparts and a place which conjures an evocative picture of Roman military life.

Why not try...?

One of our cottages

Why not decide to stay a little longer and rent one of our unique holiday cottages? You can stay in the old lighthouse keepers' cottages at Souter Lighthouse, or among the dunes and sandy beaches of the Northumberland coast. Alternatively you could choose the cosy garden cottage at Cragside or spend time in our cottage near Hadrian's Wall. At Gibside you even have the opportunity of sleeping under canvas in one of the comfy yurts.

Birdwatching on the Northumberland coast

With thousands of birds returning to the Farne Islands each year, take a boat from Seahouses harbour and explore their world. As you near the islands, enjoy the thrill of puffins diving past you and, if you're lucky, finding a seal bobbing along beside the boat. At Lindisfarne Castle, stand on the Upper Battery and watch the fulmars swooping silently by as they return to their nests.

A cycling adventure

If you really want to discover the countryside, then nothing beats cycling. And as more of our places open up new cycling routes and link in with the national ones, the opportunities are endless. In Northumberland, for example, you could join the northern section of the Pennine Cycleway, which runs close to Hadrian's Wall.

Allen Banks and Staward Gorge

Bardon Mill, Hexham, Northumberland

Map (6) F5  1942

This extensive area of spectacular gorge and river scenery forms the largest area of ancient woodland in the county, with miles of waymarked walks to explore. Look out for the remains of a medieval pele-tower and a reconstructed Victorian summerhouse. All sitting within the North Pennines AONB.

Exploring – Home to red squirrels, dormice and woodland birds and plants.
– Explore miles of tranquil and beautiful walks.
– See spectacular views from the medieval pele-tower.

Eating and shopping: there are so many opportunities for you to enjoy a picnic, either at Allen Banks car park, in the woodland or by the river.

Moralee Wood by the River Allen, Northumberland

Making the most of your day: enjoy the peaceful surroundings of Allen Banks and Staward Gorge. Guided walks and family activities including Forest Schools, tree trail and workshops on fungi and woodland birds. **Dogs**: welcome under close control.

Access for all: 🚻♿ Grounds ♿

Getting here: 86:NY799640. 1½ miles from Bardon Mill. **Foot**: numerous public and permitted rights of way. **Cycle**: NCN72, 2½ miles. **Bus**: services from Carlisle to Newcastle upon Tyne, stop within ½ mile. **Train**: Bardon Mill 1½ miles. **Road**: 5½ miles east of Haltwhistle, 3 miles west of Haydon Bridge, ½ mile south of A69. **Sat Nav**: avoid using. **Parking**: at Allen Banks (pay and display), members free. Cars £3. Two coaches at a time maximum (all coaches must book). 3.3-metre height restriction on approach road. Coaches £10 full day.

Finding out more: 01434 344218 or allenbanks@nationaltrust.org.uk. Housesteads Farm, Haydon Bridge, Hexham, Northumberland NE47 6NN

Allen Banks and Staward Gorge	Open every day all year

Cherryburn

Station Bank, Mickley, Stocksfield, Northumberland NE43 7DD

Map (6) G5  1991

Thomas Bewick is perhaps Northumberland's greatest artist: a wood engraver and naturalist who revolutionised print art in Georgian England. Discover his tiny birthplace cottage and farmyard, with glorious views over the Tyne Valley, plus a traditional 19th-century farmhouse (the later home of the Bewick family), containing an unrivalled collection of his work and an exhibition about his life. Follow Bewick's wood blocks on their journey to the print room, where regular Sunday afternoon demonstrations bring alive this intricate craft. Explore the delightful cottage gardens and paddock walk – perfect for picnicking or playing with the children.

Cherryburn, Northumberland: this simple house is the birthplace of artist Thomas Bewick

Exploring
- Newly acquired wood blocks by one of Bewick's leading apprentices.
- Meet alpacas on the paddock walk and friendly farmyard hens.
- Enjoy panoramic picnics or stroll down to the River Tyne.

Eating and shopping: buy prints from original Bewick engravings, plus other gifts and books. Enjoy hot and cold drinks and snacks in the farmhouse kitchen.

Making the most of your day: events for all the family, including popular 'Folk in the Farmyard', first Sunday of the month, May to October.

Access for all:
Building **Grounds**

Getting here: 88:NZ075627. Close to south bank of River Tyne. **Bus**: Newcastle to Hexham (passes Newcastle), alight Mickley Square, ¼ mile. **Train**: Stocksfield 1½ miles; Prudhoe 1½ miles. **Road**: 11 miles west of Newcastle and east of Hexham; follow brown sign off A695 at Mickley Square on to Station Bank. **Parking**: free, 100 yards.

Finding out more: 01661 843276 or cherryburn@nationaltrust.org.uk

Cherryburn		M	T	W	T	F	S	S
1 Mar–4 Nov	11–5	**M**	**T**		**T**	**F**	**S**	**S**

Cragside

Rothbury, Morpeth, Northumberland NE65 7PX

Map (6) G3 1977

'We have highly recommended our visit to everyone. There is something for all at Cragside and we will definitely return.'
Kathy Ogden, Prudhoe, Northumberland

Enter the world of Lord Armstrong – Victorian inventor, innovator and landscape genius. Cragside house was a wonder of its age. It was the first house in the world to be lit by hydro-electricity and is crammed full of ingenious gadgets. The gardens are incredible. One of the largest rock gardens in Europe leads down to the Iron Bridge, which in turn leads across to the formal garden. Children will love our adventure play area and exploring Nelly's Labryrinth, a network of paths and tunnels cut out of a vast area of rhododendron forest. **Note**: challenging terrain and distances. Stout footwear essential.

Exploring
- Visit the first house to be lit by hydro-electricity.
- Enjoy superb views from the iron bridge.
- Stroll around Tumbleton Lake.
- Get lost in the labyrinth.
- Take a peek from our wildlife hide.

Eating and shopping: our licensed tea-rooms offer refreshments to tempt all tastes, from hot meals to frothy coffee. Treat yourself to a sweet indulgence: cream teas, home bakes, ice-cream. Browse through our plants or take home a bottle of Armstrong Ale.

Making the most of your day: free minibus shuttle service between key features. Family activities, special events and activities throughout the year. Family strolls or strenuous hikes to stunning viewpoints. **Dogs**: welcome on estate, on leads at all times.

Access for all: 🅿️🎫♿🚻♿♿🔊📷
📷 House ♿♿ Visitor centre ♿♿♿
Estate ♿➡️

Getting here: 81:NU073022. 13 miles south-west of Alnwick. **Bus**: to nearby Rothbury, with connections from Newcastle, Monday to Saturday. Special summer Sunday service to property. **Road**: on B6341, 15 miles north-west of Morpeth on Coldstream road (A697). Turn left on to B6341 at Moorhouse Crossroads, entrance 3 miles on left. **Parking**: free, nine car parks throughout estate.

Finding out more: 01669 620333 or cragside@nationaltrust.org.uk

Cragside		M	T	W	T	F	S	S
House								
3 Mar–4 Nov	11–5						S	S
6 Mar–2 Nov	1–5		T	W	T	F		
31 Mar–15 Apr	11–5	M	T	W	T	F	S	S
2 Jun–10 Jun	11–5	M	T	W	T	F	S	S
21 Jul–9 Sep	11–5	M	T	W	T	F	S	S
29 Oct–4 Nov	11–5	M	T	W	T	F	S	S
Gardens and woodland								
3 Mar–4 Nov*	10–7		T	W	T	F	S	S
9 Nov–16 Dec	11–4					F	S	S

House open 11 to 5 Northumberland school and Bank Holidays. Last admission one hour before closing. House entry is controlled (queueing at busy times). *Gardens and woodland open Mondays in Northumberland school holidays but closed Mondays all other weeks. Last admission 5. 11 to 19 February half-term: house (ground floor only) open 11 to 4 (closed Monday), weather permitting.

Crossing the Iron Bridge below the precipitously sited Cragside, Northumberland

Dunstanburgh Castle

Craster, Alnwick, Northumberland NE66 3TT

Map (6) H3   🏛️📷 1961

An iconic castle ruin, on one of the most beautiful stretches of Northumberland coastline. An exhilarating walk from Craster. **Note**: managed by English Heritage.

Getting here: 75:NU258220. 9 miles north-east of Alnwick, approached from Craster to the south or Embleton to the north (on foot only).

Finding out more: 01665 576231 or dunstanburghcastle@nationaltrust.org.uk

Dunstanburgh Castle
Closed 1 January and 24 to 26 December.

Looking towards Dunstanburgh Castle, Northumberland

Farne Islands, Northumberland: puffin

Farne Islands

Northumberland

Map (6) H2   ✝️📷🐦 1925

Possibly the most exciting seabird colony in England with unrivalled views of 23 species – including 37,000 pairs of puffins. Large grey seal colony with more than 1,000 pups born every autumn. Strong links with Celtic Christianity and St Cuthbert. A short boat journey to a different world! **Note**: toilet on Inner Farne only. Access by boat from Seahouses (charge including members).

Exploring
- View seabirds at unbelievably close range.
- Excellent photographic opportunities.
- Chapel of St Cuthbert, with fine stained-glass windows.
- Unrivalled views of the Northumberland hinterland.

Eating and shopping: visit our shop in Seahouses for beautiful local crafts. Fantastic puffin range, with fleeces, socks, mugs and coasters.

Access for all: 🚻📋🎵👓 Grounds ♿

Getting here: 75:NU230370. 2 to 5 miles off the Northumberland coast. **Cycle**: NCN1, ¾ mile, from Seahouses harbour. **Ferry**: trips every day from Seahouses harbour, weather permitting.

Bus: Newcastle 🚃 to Alnwick 🚃 and to Berwick, alight Seahouses, 1½ miles. **Train**: Chathill, 4 miles (not Sundays). **Parking**: in Seahouses opposite harbour (pay and display), not National Trust.

Finding out more: 01665 721099 (Infoline). 01665 720651 or farneislands@nationaltrust.org.uk

Farne Islands		M	T	W	T	F	S	S
Both Islands								
1 Apr–30 Apr	10:30–6	M	T	W	T	F	S	S
1 Aug–31 Oct	10:30–6	M	T	W	T	F	S	S
Staple island								
1 May–31 Jul	10:30–1:30	M	T	W	T	F	S	S
Inner Farne Island								
1 May–31 Jul	1:30–5	M	T	W	T	F	S	S

Only Inner Farne and Staple Islands can be visited. Seahouses information centre and shop open all year, 10 to 5.

Making the most of your day: extend your visit by strolling along the banks of the River Tyne.

Access for all: Building 👥

Getting here: 88:NZ126650. ½ mile east of Wylam. **Foot**: access through country park. **Cycle**: NCN72 (level riverside ride). **Bus**: Newcastle to Ovington, alight Wylam. **Train**: Wylam ½ mile. **Road**: 8 miles west of Newcastle, 1½ miles south of A69. **Parking**: in village by war memorial, ½ mile, not National Trust (pay and display).

Finding out more: 01661 853457 or georgestephensons@nationaltrust.org.uk

George Stephenson's Birthplace		M	T	W	T	F	S	S
10 Mar–4 Nov	11–5	·	·	·	T	F	S	S

Open Bank Holiday Mondays.

George Stephenson's Birthplace

Wylam, Northumberland NE41 8BP

Map ⑥ G5   1949

Discover the humble birthplace of railway pioneer George Stephenson – whose family lived in just one room. Our costumed guide tells the story of how challenging life was for mining families, such as George's, which once squeezed into this now charming cottage, nestled in a pretty garden near the River Tyne.

Exploring
 – Step back into 1781, the year of Stephenson's birth.
 – Tread on the same flagstones as young George.
 – Learn about the pioneering steam locomotive the *Rocket*.
 – Cycling the old Wylam Waggonway? Pop in for a snack.

Eating and shopping: enjoy a light snack in the cosy Stephenson tea-room. Buy a souvenir book on the Stephenson family. Look out for the Geordie Food day in June.

Gibside

near Rowlands Gill, Burnopfield, Gateshead, Tyne & Wear NE16 6BG

Map ⑥ H5 🏠➕⛰️🔭✳️🚩 🐟🚶🔔⛏️ 1974

For a taste of the country on the edge of the city, escape to this stunning landscape park and nature reserve. Gibside is a forest garden created by one of the richest men in Georgian England, offering fantastic Derwent Valley views, miles of walks and wide open spaces. Our chapel is an architectural gem, the stables are a vibrant discovery centre, and the once-grand hall is a dramatic shell. See red kites soar above our famous tree-lined avenue, enjoy our ever-changing walled garden, or bring the family for outdoor adventures – including a new adventure play area and rope-climbing challenge.

Exploring
 – Get close to nature with wildlife hide and viewing cameras.
 – Discover Column of Liberty or Skyline Walk for stunning panorama.

The Column to Liberty in the stunning landscape park of Gibside, Tyne & Wear

Eating and shopping: savour breakfast butties, homemade lunches and afternoon teas inspired by our kitchen garden in the Potting Shed café or Renwick's coffee and bookshop. Make a picnic with food from Gibside Larder farm shop. Treat yourself to gifts and plants.

Making the most of your day: events every weekend and school holidays inspired by our wildlife, food and history, from family adventures to guided walks, twice monthly farmers' market and open-air music. **Dogs**: welcome on leads.

Access for all: ▱▱▱▱▱▱▱▱▱▱▱
Chapel ▱▱▱ Stables ▱▱
Landscape garden ▱▱▱▱▱

Getting here: 88:NZ172583. 6 miles south-west of Gateshead and Newcastle. **Foot**: ½ mile from Rowlands Gill. **Cycle**: NCN14, ½ mile. **Bus**: frequent services from Newcastle (passing ≋ and Metrocentre) to Consett, alight Rowlands Gill, ½ mile. **Train**: Blaydon 5 miles; Metrocentre 5 miles; Newcastle 8 miles. **Road**: entrance on B6314 between Burnopfield and Rowlands Gill; follow brown signs from A1, taking exit on to A694 at north end of Metrocentre. **Parking**: free, 100 yards.

Finding out more: 01207 541820 or gibside@nationaltrust.org.uk

Gibside		M	T	W	T	F	S	S
Landscape garden and stables								
1 Jan–29 Feb	10–4	M	T	W	T	F	S	S
1 Mar–31 Oct	10–6	M	T	W	T	F	S	S
1 Nov–31 Dec	10–4	M	T	W	T	F	S	S
Chapel								
1 Jan–26 Feb	10–3:30	.	.	.	.	.	S	S
1 Mar–31 Oct	10–5	M	T	W	T	F	S	S
3 Nov–30 Dec	10–3:30	.	.	.	.	.	S	S
Café, gift shop and farm shop								
1 Jan–29 Feb	10–4	M	T	W	T	F	S	S
1 Mar–31 Oct	10–5	M	T	W	T	F	S	S
1 Nov–31 Dec	10–4	M	T	W	T	F	S	S

Estate closed 24 and 25 December. Last entry: winter 3:30, summer 4:30.

Exploring
– See the shrubbery borders come back to life.
– Uncover Mary Eleanor Bowes' dramatic story of torture and abduction.
– Enjoy exhibitions, events and our milkable cow at the Stables.
– Relax in our summer evening beer garden.

Hadrian's Wall and Housesteads Fort

Bardon Mill, Hexham,
Northumberland NE47 6NN

Map ⑥ F5   🏛️♿🌿🏠 1930

Running through an often wild landscape with vast panoramic views, the wall was one of the Roman Empire's most northerly outposts. Built around AD122, it has 16 permanent bases, of which Housesteads Fort is one of the best preserved, conjuring up an evocative picture of Roman military life. **Note:** fort is owned by the National Trust and maintained and managed by English Heritage.

Exploring – Enjoy walking alongside the wall.
– Wander through the extensive archaeological remains.
– Take in panoramic views of Hadrian's Wall country.
– Look out for different flora and fauna.

A sweep of Hadrian's Wall, Northumberland

Eating and shopping: small shop selling local and 'Roman' souvenirs. Refreshment kiosk with limited indoor seating. **Making the most of your day**: family trail available, and main events organised by English Heritage at Housesteads. **Dogs**: welcome on leads.

Access for all: 🅿️♿🚻🔦👁️ Visitor centre ♿
English Heritage museum ♿ Fort ♿♿

Getting here: 87:NY790688. 6 miles north-east of Haltwhistle. **Foot**: Hadrian's Wall Path and Pennine Way. **Cycle**: NCN72. **Bus**: Hadrian's Wall service, April to November daily, Newcastle ➡️ to Hexham ➡️ to Carlisle (passing Haltwhistle ➡️). Check before journey. **Train**: Hexham or Haltwhistle connect with bus. **Road**: best access from car parks at Housesteads, Cawfields and Steel Rigg. **Parking**: pay and display (not National Trust), charge including members. Car and coach parks operated by National Park Authority at Housesteads (½-mile walk to the Fort), Steel Rigg and Cawfields.

Finding out more: 01434 344525 (visitor centre). 01434 344363 (English Heritage museum) or housesteads@nationaltrust.org.uk

Hadrian's Wall
Closed 1 January and 24 to 26 December. Telephone for details or visit www.english-heritage.org.uk.

Holy Jesus Hospital

City Road, Newcastle upon Tyne,
Tyne & Wear NE1 2AS

Map ⑥ H5

Holy Jesus Hospital survives amid 1960s city-centre developments, displaying features from all periods of its 700-year existence. The National Trust's Inner City Project is now based here, working to provide opportunities for inner-city dwellers to gain access to and enjoy the countryside on their doorstep. **Note**: owned by Newcastle City Council but managed by the National Trust.

Exploring
- Visit our exhibition room on weekdays.
- Listen to voices from the past in our interactive displays.
- Take a guided tour on first Saturday of every month.
- Don't miss the plant fair at our June open day.

Eating and shopping: tea, coffee and biscuits available on Saturday open days.

Making the most of your day: discover the site's fascinating history and learn about the remains of the 14th-century Augustinian friary, Tudor tower, 17th-century almshouse and Victorian soup kitchen.

Access for all: ⃞⃞⃞⃞⃞
Building ⃞⃞⃞

Getting here: 88:NZ253642. In the centre of Newcastle upon Tyne. **Cycle**: close to riverside routes. **Bus**: local services from city centre. **Train**: Newcastle, ½ mile. **Underground**: Monument Metro, ¼ mile. **Road**: close to Tyne Bridge and A167. **Parking**: nearest in city centre, 30 yards (pay and display).

Finding out more: 0191 255 7610 or holyjesushospital@nationaltrust.org.uk

Holy Jesus Hospital		M	T	W	T	F	S	S
10 Jan–28 Jun	12–4	·	**T**	**W**	**T**	·	·	·
2 Jul–31 Aug	12–4	**M**	**T**	**W**	**T**	**F**	·	·
4 Sep–13 Dec	12–4	·	**T**	**W**	**T**	·	·	·

Open for guided tours (no booking required) on the first Saturday of every month (except January), 10 to 4 (last tour 3:30). Closed Bank Holiday Mondays and Good Friday.

Lindisfarne Castle

Holy Island, Berwick-upon-Tweed,
Northumberland TD15 2SH

Map ⑥ G1

Location has always been the main attraction for the owners and occupiers of Lindisfarne Castle on Holy Island. Whether it be the original Tudor builders looking for a strong position to protect the island harbour, or the wealthy Edwardian bachelor seeking a quiet retreat from London, the situation of the castle has intrigued and inspired for centuries. Lutyens' renovation both hides and emphasises the old fort, all the while overlooking Gertrude Jekyll's enchanting walled garden and the often-missed grandeur of the Lime Kilns, magnificent evidence of Lindisfarne's industrial past. **Note**: emergency toilet only. Holy Island accessed via a tidal causeway, check crossing times before visiting.

Exploring
- Discover how old the castle is – Elizabethan or Edwardian?
- Specialist Gertrude Jekyll garden, explore the 1911 planting plan.
- See the castle's internal wind indicator, which still works.
- Don't miss the massive 19th-century lime kilns on the headland.
- Invigorating seaside walks, with rock pools to explore.
- Search for wild flowers and spot seabirds and seals.

Eating and shopping: visit our shop in the village for a selection of local produce, including delicious Doddington ice-cream and Loopy Lisa Fudge. We also have a fantastic range of cards by photographer Joe Cornish and exquisite glass art from Seahouses.

Making the most of your day: children's quizzes make family visits more memorable. Specialist Gertrude Jekyll garden talks, monthly May to August. Dogs: assistance dogs only.

Access for all: 🅳🅰🆒🆅🆃🅹⋮🅿 Castle 🅰
Shop 🅰 Grounds 🅰🅰

Getting here: 75:NU136417. On Holy Island, off Northumberland coast. Foot: from main Holy Island village. Cycle: NCN1. Coast and Castles cycle route. Bus: from Berwick-upon-Tweed 🚇, with connecting buses at Beal to and from Newcastle. Times vary with season and tides. Also private island minibus from Holy Island car park to castle. Train: Berwick-upon-Tweed 10 miles from causeway. Road: 5 miles east of A1 across a tidal causeway. Parking: 1 mile, not National Trust (pay and display), charge including members.

Finding out more: 01289 389244 or lindisfarne@nationaltrust.org.uk

Lindisfarne Castle		M	T	W	T	F	S	S
Castle								
14 Jan–15 Jan	10–3						S	S
28 Jan–29 Jan	10–3						S	S
11 Feb–19 Feb	10–3	M	T	W	T	F	S	S
25 Feb–26 Feb	10–3						S	S
10 Mar–31 Jul	Times vary		T	W	T	F	S	S
1 Aug–31 Aug	Times vary	M	T	W	T	F	S	S
1 Sep–31 Oct	Times vary		T	W	T	F	S	S
3 Nov–4 Nov	10–3						S	S
17 Nov–18 Nov	10–3						S	S
1 Dec–2 Dec	10–3						S	S

10 March to 31 October: castle open either 10 to 3 or 12 to 5, due to tides. Check opening times in advance. Open Bank Holiday Mondays (including Scottish Bank Holidays) and every day during August. National Trust flag flies only when the castle is open. Castle winter opening: two weekends a month from 10 to 3, depending on tidal access. For tide tables and detailed opening times send sae to Lindisfarne Castle stating which month you wish to visit or visit www.lindisfarne.org.uk.

Visitors stroll beneath the imposing walls of Lindisfarne Castle, Northumberland

Parking charges for non-members may apply

Seaton Delaval Hall

The Avenue, Seaton Sluice,
Northumberland NE26 4QR

Map (6) H4 2009

Dizzying spirals at Seaton Delaval Hall, Northumberland

Come and take part in the unfolding story of this gem of the North East. This great English baroque villa, built between 1719 and 1732, for Admiral George Delaval, was designed by Sir John Vanbrugh. It has formal gardens with colourful borders and is much more than an architectural masterpiece. For 900 years, the estate has been a stage for drama, intrigue and romance, while the surrounding landscape fuelled the Industrial Revolution. The Hall has survived terrible fires, military occupation and potential ruin. It now provides an amazing space for arts, heritage and the community to come together. **Note:** ongoing building works. Parking and toilet facilities may be limited.

Exploring
— Marvel at Vanbrugh's central hall, gutted by fire in 1822.
— Imagine horses Admiral, Julius and Peacock in the magnificent stables.
— Relax in Lady Hastings' captivating gardens, with striking sculptures.
— Enjoy great portraits and furniture in the family collection.
— Imagine what life was like in the atmospheric cellars.
— Discover how industry shaped the Delavals' fortunes.

Eating and shopping: visit the East Wing café for a light lunch or snack, taste the famous Seaton Delaval ice-cream in the West Pavilion, or chill out while taking tea at the summerhouse. Buy a souvenir at the shop in the ticket hut.

Making the most of your day: an events programme runs throughout the year, with arts and crafts, outdoor fun, lectures and more. Also activity days and trails are available during most school holidays. **Dogs**: welcome on leads in designated areas. Assistance dogs only in house and formal garden.

Access for all: [icons] Central Hall [icon]
Stables [icon] Gardens and grounds [icons]

Getting here: NZ321766. 2 miles from Whitley Bay, between Seaton Delaval and Seaton Sluice. **Foot**: network of footpaths: Seaton Sluice (¾ mile), Seaton Delaval (1 mile), Blyth and North Tyneside. **Cycle**: NCN1, cycle paths to local towns, villages, old mining waggonways, coastal paths. **Ferry**: North Shields Ferry Terminal 8 miles. **Bus**: services from Newcastle centre to Blyth every 30 minutes, stopping at Seaton Delaval Hall (connects with services to Whitley Bay and North Tyneside). **Train**: West Monkseaton Metro 3 miles. **Road**: A190 passes, linking to A193 coast road and A19; 5 miles from A1.

Finding out more: 0191 237 9100 or seatondelavalhall@nationaltrust.org.uk

Seaton Delaval Hall		M	T	W	T	F	S	S
Whole property								
2 Jan–29 Apr	11–3	M	·	·	·	F	S	S
30 Apr–30 Sep	11–5	M	·	·	·	F	S	S
1 Oct–31 Dec	11–3	M	·	·	·	F	S	S
Grounds, café and shop								
1 May–27 Sep	11–5	·	T	·	T	·	·	·

Last entry 45 minutes before closing.
Closed 23 to 26 December.

Souter Lighthouse and The Leas

Coast Road, Whitburn, Sunderland, Tyne & Wear SR6 7NH

Map (6) I5 1990

Souter Lighthouse, Tyne & Wear: iconic beacon

Souter is an iconic beacon, hooped in red and white and standing proud on the coastline midway between the Tyne and the Wear. It's a special place all year and was the first purpose-built lighthouse in the world powered by electricity. Opened in 1871 and decommissioned in 1988, the machinery remains in working order. To the north, The Leas is a 2½-mile stretch of magnesian limestone cliffs, wave-cut foreshore and coastal grassland. The cliffs and rock stacks of Marsden Bay are home to nesting kittiwakes, fulmars, cormorants, shags and guillemots. **Note**: steep stairs (ground-floor CCTV shows views from the top for those unable to climb).

Exploring

- Climb the 76 steps to the top for spectacular views.
- Explore the fully working engine room.
- Discover the Victorian keeper's cottage.
- Become a pirate or princess using the dressing-up box.
- Stretch your legs in Whitburn Coastal Park.
- Take a dramatic clifftop walk.

Eating and shopping: relish the seasonal menu, which uses homegrown and local produce, in our tea-room or coffee shop. Our guidebook is a great souvenir of your visit. Don't leave without a bottle (or two) of our very own Souter Lighthouse Best Bitter.

Making the most of your day: enjoy hands-on family activities, foghorn demonstrations, open-air play area, trails and the picnic and garden areas. Ask about our full programme of events and activities, including rock-pool rambles. **Dogs**: on leads in grounds only.

Access for all:
Building **Grounds**

Getting here: 88:NZ408641. North-east coast, on River Tyne 2½ miles south of South Shields and 5 miles north of Sunderland. **Foot**: South Tyneside Heritage Trail. **Cycle**: NCN1, adjacent to property. **Ferry**: Shields Ferry crosses River Tyne from North Shields to South Shields twice hourly. **Bus**: services from Sunderland to South Shields (passes Sunderland and South Shields). One bus passes lighthouse, others pass close by. **Train**: East Boldon and South Shields (Tyne & Wear Metro) both 3 miles. **Road**: on A183 coast road. **Parking**: free.

Finding out more: 0191 529 3161 or souter@nationaltrust.org.uk

Souter Lighthouse and The Leas		M	T	W	T	F	S	S
11 Feb–19 Feb	11–5	**M**	**T**	**W**	**T**	·	**S**	**S**
10 Mar–4 Nov	11–5	**M**	**T**	**W**	**T**	·	**S**	**S**
10 Nov–16 Dec	11–4	·	·	·	·	·	**S**	**S**

Open Good Friday 11 to 5. July and August: open Fridays, 11 to 4. November and December: weekend openings subject to restrictions due to events.

Wallington

Cambo, near Morpeth, Northumberland NE61 4AR

Map (6) G4 1941

Dating from 1688, Wallington was home to many generations of the Blackett and Trevelyan families, who all left their mark. The result is an impressive, yet friendly, house with a

Imposing Wallington, Northumberland

Eating and shopping: browse in the shop for gifts and treats. Tuck into Wallington Estate produce in the Clocktower Café, or enjoy a cream tea from the potting shed kiosk in the walled garden. Visit our farm shop for a tasty souvenir.

Making the most of your day: year-round programme of events for all ages, including open-air theatre, food and craft festival, themed weekends, guided walks, music, dancing and hands-on activities. Adventure playground and children's trail. **Dogs**: on leads in grounds and walled garden only.

Access for all: 🅿️🔯🚻♿️🔯🗺️🖼️🎵📷
House 🔯🔯🔯♿️ Café and shop 🔯
Grounds 🔯➡️🔯♿️

magnificent interior and fine collections. The remarkable central hall was decorated to look like an Italian courtyard and features a series of paintings of Northumbrian history by William Bell Scott. The formality of the house is offset by the tranquil beauty of the surrounding landscape – with lawns, lakes, parkland and woodland. The beautiful walled garden, with its colourful plant collection and charming conservatory, is an enchanting must-see.

Exploring
- Relax, picnic or play in the grassy courtyard.
- Marvel at Lady Wilson's Cabinet of Curiosities.
- Look out for woodpeckers at the wildlife hide.
- See our fascinating collection of dolls' houses.
- Stretch your legs with a walk on the extensive estate.
- Let off steam in the adventure playground.

Getting here: 81:NZ030843. 6 miles north-west of Belsay. **Bus**: services from Morpeth (Wednesdays and Fridays plus Sundays and Bank Holiday Mondays from June to mid-October). **Road**: A1 north to Newcastle then 20 miles north-west (A696, airport/Ponteland road), and turn off on B6342 to Cambo. A1 south to Morpeth (A192) then 12 miles west (B6343). **Parking**: free, 200 yards.

Finding out more: 01670 773967 (Infoline). 01670 773600 or wallington@nationaltrust.org.uk

Wallington		M	T	W	T	F	S	S
House								
3 Mar–4 Nov	12–5	M		W	T	F	S	S
Walled garden								
1 Jan–31 Mar	10–4	M	T	W	T	F	S	S
1 Apr–30 Sep	10–7	M	T	W	T	F	S	S
1 Oct–31 Dec	10–4	M	T	W	T	F	S	S
Gift shop and café								
1 Jan–10 Feb	10:30–4:30	M	T	W	T	F	S	S
11 Feb–4 Nov	10:30–5:30	M	T	W	T	F	S	S
5 Nov–31 Dec	10:30–4:30	M	T	W	T	F	S	S
Farm shop (outside turnstile)								
1 Jan–10 Feb	10:30–4	M	T	W	T	F	S	S
11 Feb–4 Nov	10:30–5	M	T	W	T	F	S	S
5 Nov–31 Dec	10:30–4	M	T	W	T	F	S	S

Last admission to house one hour before closing. Garden closes 6 in March and October, or dusk if earlier. Café last orders 30 minutes before closing. Gift shop, café and farm shop closed some days over Christmas period (check before visiting).

Wallington, Northumberland: conservatory

Washington Old Hall

The Avenue, Washington Village, Washington,
Tyne & Wear NE38 7LE

Map (6) H5 🏠 ❄ ♠ ⊤ 1956

'Steeped in history. Very interesting
information, especially to keep kids
interested. Staff lovely and nice cakes.'
Elizabeth Bell, West Malling, Kent

Eating and shopping: refresh yourself in the
tea-room, run by the Friends of Washington
Old Hall. Pick up a souvenir of your visit from
our reception. Seek out bargains from the
Friends' bric-a-brac display.

Making the most of your day: picnic in
the gardens, and enjoy a game of croquet.
Seasonal garden trails, events and activities,
including Fourth of July Independence Day
ceremony. **Dogs**: on leads in garden only.

Access for all: 🅿️ 🚻 ♿ 📷 ♿ ∴ 🅰️
Building 🔼 ♿ 🔽 Grounds 🔼 ♿ ➡️ 🔽

Washington Old Hall stands as a testimony
to Anglo-American friendship. Due to be
demolished in 1933 this historic landmark,
with links to the first President of the United
States of America, is a delightful and charming
gem, well worth a visit. It is from here that the
Washington family took their surname. The
house, predominantly dating from the 17th
century, incorporates a large portion of the
original 12th-century building, home to the
Washington family. By 1860 the house had slid
down the social scale. It became a tenement
until 1933, when it was saved from demolition
by Frederick Hill.

Exploring
– Enjoy the tranquillity of the
Jacobean garden.
– Soak up the wildlife in the
wildflower fruit orchard.
– 'What's in a name'? Follow the
link to George Washington.
– Living history – chat to Stan
about life at number five.
– Sample the delights of our
very own honey beer.
– Discover 17th-century room
settings with robust yet tactile
oak furniture.

Looking towards the 17th-century Washington Old Hall,
Tyne & Wear

Getting here: 88:NZ312566. In Washington
village, 7 miles south of Newcastle.
Cycle: NCN7, 1 mile. **Bus**: services to
Washington Galleries and Washington village.
Train: Heworth (Metro) 4 miles; Newcastle
7 miles. **Road**: take A1 junction 64 (A195),
continue over Princess Anne Interchange
roundabout. Left at Biddick Lane roundabout,
then follow brown signs. From A19 and other
routes follow 'Washington', join A1231 until
pick up brown signs. **Parking**: free, small car
park. Other parking on The Avenue.

Finding out more: 0191 416 6879 or
washingtonoldhall@nationaltrust.org.uk

Washington Old Hall		M	T	W	T	F	S	S
House								
1 Apr–31 Oct	11–5	M	T	W	·	·	·	S
Gardens								
1 Apr–31 Oct	10–5	M	T	W	·	·	·	S
Tea-room								
1 Apr–31 Oct	10–4	M	T	W	·	·	·	S

Open Good Friday and Easter Saturday.

Wales

The powerful waterwheel at Aberdulais Tin Works and Waterfall stands out among the site's rich industrial heritage

Outdoors in Wales

Spectacular beaches, high mountains, deep valleys, rolling estates and a coastline that goes on for miles. The National Trust cares for many of the most dramatic landscapes in Wales. These are places of inspiration, relaxation and challenge that will stay long in the memory.

Right:
the magnificent
sandy beach at
Rhossili, Gower
Below:
Hafod y Llan
farm, Snowdonia

Beautiful and rugged

Geologically fascinating, beautiful and rugged, 60 miles of Pembrokeshire's coastline is cared for by the Trust. Wales's patron saint, St David, was born here, on a Pembrokeshire clifftop.

The restoration of traditional cattle and sheep grazing has seen Pembrokeshire's coastal heaths and inland commons bloom again. But the real star of the Pembrokeshire coast is the chough; there are now more than 60 breeding pairs here. Other sights not to be missed are the seal pups on a number of beaches, and the guillemots at Stackpole.

Walkers are spoilt for choice with hundreds of miles of footpaths on the coast and inland. Fine circular walks can be found at Stackpole (lakes and cliffs), Marloes, St David's Head, Dinas Island, near Fishguard, Little Milford and Lawrenny Woods on the secluded River Cleddau.

A dazzling jewel

The Llŷn Peninsula is a dazzling jewel of a place with sparkling seas, sandy beaches and vast skies. Multicoloured beach huts are a vibrant backdrop to the long, sweeping beach at Llanbedrog. In the sheltered bay at Porthor the sand famously whistles underfoot. The fishing village of Porthdinllaen, huddled into the cliff in a sandy cove, is an unforgettable place.

Enjoy a drink at the pub on the beach, while the children build sandcastles. Stroll to the Coastguards' Hut on top of Mynydd Mawr, and on a clear day you will be rewarded with one of the finest views in Wales – stretching all the way to Ireland. Look out for the rare chough flying overhead, dolphins swimming in the bay and seals basking in the sun. A coastal path now skirts the whole peninsula.

Witness the power of nature to reclaim its own at Llandanwg. The beautiful sandy beach has half buried the medieval church in its sand. Above Barmouth is Dinas Oleu, a special place in our history. This coastal hillside, with spectacular views of the sea, was the first property passed to the Trust, in 1895. Nearby, Egryn is also a special place. A home for more than 5,000 years, the medieval hall-house and outbuildings have been newly restored. The award-winning house is now an unforgettable place to stay. Visit **www. nationaltrustcottages.co.uk**

Mae'r wybodaeth sydd yn y llawlyfr hwn am feddiannau'r Ymddiriedolaeth Genedlaethol yng Nghymru ar gael yn Gymraeg o Swyddfa'r Ymddiriedolaeth Genedlaethol, Sgwar y Drindod, Llandudno LL30 2DE, ffôn 01492 860123.

Above: **campion on the Llŷn Peninsula, Gwynedd**
Right: **Pennard, Gower**

Myth and majesty
The Trust cares for 11 of Snowdonia's majestic peaks and many hectares of upland in this land wreathed in myth and legend. These include a wheelchair-accessible, riverside path in the village of Beddgelert, home to the legendary heroic dog.

At Craflwyn the walking choices are limitless – from riverside strolls to a full-scale ascent of Snowdon. Nearby is Llyndy Isaf, the farm and estate at the centre of the Trust's £1 million nationwide appeal to secure it. This unspoiled estate is rich in wildlife, archaeology and history. The red dragon of Wales was born here too! From towering Tryfan, to the dramatic Carneddau mountain range and the waters of Llyn Idwal, the peaks and valleys of Eryri deliver on their promise of challenge, relaxation and inspiration.

An ancient haven
Witness the wonder of migration at Cemlyn's lagoon, a haven for wildlife and nesting birds. In late spring a colony of Arctic and common terns returns to nest. The rocky sea cliffs here are among the oldest in Britain. Some are a mind-bending 1,000 million years old.

Drama and history
The Brecon Beacons is a distinctive landscape of deep valleys and flat-topped summits. Around 250,000 pairs of walking boots climb and ramble on these slopes each year. Some of the most popular summits – Pen y Fan, Sugar Loaf, Skirrid and Henrhyd Falls – are cared for by the Trust.

This is an ancient land and clues to its history are all around. Keep a look out for the fossils of some of the first land plants, which look like smudges on the rock.

Below: **Brecon Beacons National Park in South Wales**

Romantic falls

Henrhyd Falls, the highest waterfall in South Wales, can be found tumbling and falling on the Nant Llech. There are others: a series of beautiful falls is created by the narrow, steep-sided gorges at the heads of the Neath and Tawe rivers.

Historic parkland

A stroll through the parkland at historic Dinefwr, a designated National Nature Reserve, may bring you up close to some of this area's oldest inhabitants. The resident fallow deer and stunning White Park cattle have been in Dinefwr for more than 1,000 years.

There are three walks in the upland 1,000-hectare (2,500-acre) Dolaucothi Estate, home to a Roman gold mine, and all have fabulous views across the Cothi Valley. Another vista that's hard to match is from Paxton's Tower – built in 1811 by Sir William Paxton as a memorial to Lord Nelson.

History at every turn

In terms of sandy bays, secluded coves, sand dunes, salt-marsh, grassy clifftops and commons, Gower has few rivals. Miles of paths make walking a great way to explore the huge variety of habitats and wildlife here.

It is hardly surprising that the Old Rectory at Rhossili Bay is the most popular Trust holiday cottage, given its away-from-it-all situation and enviable view of the lovely bay. Walk to the top of Rhossili Down for panoramic views, or, when the tide is out, cross the rocky causeway to the tidal island of Worm's Head, where grey seals laze on the rocks.

Farming started on Gower in the Stone Age and has continued to change its landscape ever since. There are reminders of this tradition and the life of our ancestors everywhere. Look out for archaeological features, including Neolithic burial chambers, Iron Age forts and the Vile at Rhossili (a medieval open-field strip system).

Unspoilt coastline

There's an intimate charm to Ceredigion's unspoilt coastline. Gently rolling, it has striking rocky outcrops and steep wooded river valleys running inland.

For an unforgettable experience head for Mwnt. This small horseshoe-shaped bay is one of the best places to spot bottlenose dolphins. The lovely, sandy beach at Penbryn is a popular destination for families with their buckets and spades, windbreaks and picnics. There's a timeless quality to life in Ceredigion thanks to the relative lack of development. It is a quality that the Trust is working hard to preserve.

Car parks in Wales

Ceredigion		Pembrokeshire	
Mwnt	SM 193 519	Broadhaven	SR 977 938
Penbryn	SM 296 520	Bosherston	SR 968 947
		Marloes	SM 770 085
Gower		Martin's Haven	SM 758 091
Pennard	SS 553 872	Stackpole Quay	SR 992 958

Llŷn Peninsula		Snowdonia	
Aberdaron	SH 174 264	Craflwyn	SH 599 489
Llanbedrog	SH 331 335	Cregennan	SH 660 140
Porthdinllaen	SH 284 408	Nantmor	SH 597 463
Porthor	SH 166 296		
Uwchmynydd	SH 155 264		

Above: **wild flowers** Below: **a wren,** both on the **Llŷn Peninsula, Gwynedd,** North Wales

Why not try...?

Surfing at Gower
Catch that seventh wave on our glorious sandy beaches or lie on them and watch others ride the surf. Still beside the sea, we have some of Britain's most important colonies of seabirds, while Worm's Head is a great place to see grey seals.

Ceredigion wildlife spotting
Mwnt Bay is one of the best spots in the UK for dolphin watching. In season families of bottlenose dolphins are a regular sight. If you like to be active beside the seaside, the lovely coastline is a great – and quiet – place to stretch your legs.

Holidaying at Llŷn
Home to picture-postcard beaches, sparkling seas and campsites with a view, this is the perfect place for a traditional family holiday. We even have sand that whistles while you walk at Porthor. The sailing's great here, too, and a good way to explore the coastline.

Exploring Snowdonia
Snowdonia's mountains need little introduction for walkers and climbers. For bouldering fans, our ancient, glaciated boulders are the best place to train. Campsites come with splendid scenery attached, and while the cycling here is strenuous, it's something to boast about afterwards!

Birdwatching on Anglesey
Bring your binoculars for the best views of our choughs, puffins and porpoises. Also to be seen on the 1,000-million-year-old sea cliffs are the rock climbers who flock here each summer. The inland lagoon at Cemlyn is a birdwatchers' paradise with its colony of Arctic and common terns.

Riding at Brecon
For a thrilling view of the Brecon Beacons, saddle up and tour on horseback. The network of horse-friendly trails mean you'll really get off the beaten track. On the hoof or on foot are also the best ways to spot Brecon's peregrines and red kites.

Going wild in Pembrokeshire
Pembrokeshire is the UK's coasteering capital, the ultimate place to throw yourself off a cliff (while wearing a wetsuit) and into the waves! On dry land wildlife lovers can watch birds and spot butterflies to their hearts' content. Just want to chill out? We've miles of sandy beaches...

Aberconwy House

Castle Street, Conwy LL32 8AY

Map ④ E2 🏠 1934

This is the only medieval merchant's house in Conwy to have survived the turbulent history of the walled town over nearly six centuries. Furnished rooms and an audio-visual presentation show daily life from different periods in its history. **Note**: nearest toilet 50 yards on quay.

Exploring — Explore how people lived from Tudor to Victorian times.
— Follow the stories of centuries from room to room.
— Discover what the walls are made of.
— Let the introductory footage bring old Conwy to life.

Eating and shopping: stock up on souvenirs in the shop. Conwy is full of great places to eat.

Making the most of your day: live music in the house. Ghost stories. Children's trail. Easter and Hallowe'en activities. Lace demonstrations. Guided tours. **Dogs**: assistance dogs only allowed.

Detail of Aberconwy House, Conwy

Access for all: ☐🖼 Building 🖼

Getting here: 115:SH781777. At junction of Castle Street and High Street. **Cycle**: NCN5. **Bus**: from surrounding areas. **Train**: Conwy railway station 300 yards. **Parking**: no onsite parking.

Finding out more: 01492 592246 or aberconwyhouse@nationaltrust.org.uk

Aberconwy House		M	T	W	T	F	S	S
House								
11 Feb–19 Feb	11–5	M	T	W	T	F	S	S
25 Feb–11 Mar	11–5	·	·	·	·	·	S	S
17 Mar–28 Oct	11–5	M	·	W	T	F	S	S
1 Jul–31 Aug	11–5	M	T	W	T	F	S	S
29 Oct–4 Nov	11–4	M	·	W	T	F	S	S
10 Nov–30 Dec	12–3	·	·	·	·	·	S	S
17 Dec–24 Dec	12–3	M	T	W	T	F	S	S
Shop								
3 Jan–16 Mar	11–5	·	·	T	W	T	F	S	·
17 Mar–4 Nov	11–5:30	M	T	W	T	F	S	S
5 Nov–31 Dec	11–5	M	T	W	T	F	S	S
Closed 25 December.								

Aberdeunant

Taliaris, Llandeilo, Carmarthenshire SA19 6DL

Map ④ E8 🏠🖼🖼 1996

Traditional Carmarthenshire farmhouse in an unspoilt setting. **Note**: administered on the National Trust's behalf by a resident tenant. No toilet.

Access for all: 🅿 Building 🖼 Grounds 🖼

Getting here: 146:SN672308. Full details are sent on booking.

Finding out more: 01558 650177 (Dolaucothi Gold Mines) or aberdeunant@nationaltrust.org.uk

Aberdeunant
Admission by guided tour and appointment only. Tours take place April to September, first Saturday and Sunday of each month, 12 to 5. Telephone Dolaucothi Gold Mines to book. Last booking taken at 5 on Thursday prior to opening.

We welcome dogs assisting visitors with disabilities

Aberdulais Tin Works and Waterfall

Aberdulais, near Neath,
Neath Port Talbot SA10 8EU

Map (4) E9 1980

Set in a steep gorge, this picturesque spot demonstrates the power of water and its impact on industry. Our film, *Reflections on Tin*, tells its 400-year-old story from 1584 to the present, including visits by artists like J. M. W. Turner. An early water-powered tinplate works is the main feature. Today, the waters of the River Dulais are used to help make Aberdulais self-sufficient in environmentally friendly energy, with its waterwheel – the largest in Europe generating electricity. Lifts enable visitors to access the upper levels for excellent views of the falls. **Note**: waterwheel and turbine subject to water levels and maintenance.

Exploring
- 'The Tinworks Exhibition': about adults and children who worked here.
- Check out our summer guided tours.
- Explore with a Tracker Pack or a quiz trail.
- Look out for kingfishers. What other wildlife can you spot?
- Relax with a family picnic; play games on the grass.
- Wonder at the spectacular waterfall – best when it rains!

Eating and shopping: don't miss the National Trust shop. Enjoy Welsh cakes and bara brith in the tea-room. Experience our famous welcome and savour our lemon drizzle cake.

Making the most of your day: Conservation in Action; activity days, demonstrations and family quiz trails, painting, photography and archaeology days. Look out for exciting developments – we're working hard to make your visit even more enjoyable. **Dogs**: welcome on leads.

Aberdulais Waterfall, Neath Port Talbot

Access for all:
Stable and Tin Exhibition
Turbine House
Grounds

Getting here: 170:SS772995. 3 miles north-east of Neath. **Foot**: via Neath to Aberdulais Canal footpath. **Cycle**: NCN47 passes property. Access near B&Q Neath to Neath Canal towpath and Aberdulais Canal Basin. **Bus**: services from Swansea to Brecon, Swansea to Aberdare and Banwen, Neath to Aberdulais and Neath to Aberdulais. **Train**: Neath 3 miles. **Road**: A4109, 3 miles north-east of Neath. Exit 43 off M4 (Llandarcy), take A465 signposted Vale of Neath. **Sat Nav**: follow brown signs, not Sat Nav. **Parking**: outside site on opposite side of road.

Finding out more: 01639 636674 or aberdulais@nationaltrust.org.uk

Aberdulais		M	T	W	T	F	S	S
7 Jan–4 Mar	11–4	·	·	·	·	·	**S**	**S**
13 Feb–17 Feb	11–4	**M**	**T**	**W**	**T**	**F**	·	·
10 Mar–28 Oct	10–5	**M**	**T**	**W**	**T**	**F**	**S**	**S**
2 Nov–23 Dec	11–5	·	·	·	·	**F**	**S**	**S**

Open Bank Holidays (excluding 1 January, 25 and 26 December).

Bodnant Garden

Tal-y-Cafn, Colwyn Bay, Conwy LL28 5RE

Map ④ F2 🏠 ❖ ♠ 1949

Marvel at plants from all over the world grown from seed and cuttings collected over a century ago on plant-hunting expeditions. Created by five generations of one family, this 32-hectare (80-acre) garden is superbly located, with spectactular views across Snowdonia. With expansive lawns and intimate corners, grand ponds and impressive terraces, a steep wooded valley and stream, awe-inspiring plant collections and continually changing glorious displays of colour, there's always something to enjoy. Paths throughout allow you to explore, discover and delight in the garden's beauty – enjoy the clean, fresh fragrances of nature. Note: the garden and tea-rooms are managed on behalf of the National Trust by Michael McLaren.

The Canal Terrace at Bodnant Garden, Conwy

Exploring – Spectacular displays of daffodils, magnolias and camellias in early spring.
– 180-foot long laburnum arch flowers in late May.
– Discover the magical Dell, with towering 200-year-old trees.
– See the tallest coastal redwood in the UK.
– Learn the history of our heliochronometer, and how it works.
– Superb summer colours melt into an explosion of autumnal tints.

Eating and shopping: sample delicious home-baked cakes in our two tea-rooms; in the Pavilion tea-room try locally produced wine and beer. Buy plants and gifts in the adjacent garden centre or find that special bespoke gift in the craft shops (neither National Trust).

Making the most of your day: varied programme of walks and tours, family events, open-air theatre, evening plays. Family trails and Explorer Backpacks. Waymarked route for wheelchairs and pushchairs. Poem open last Tuesday of each month. **Dogs**: assistance dogs only.

Access for all: 🅿 🚻 ♿ 🔄 📷 ♿ ∷
Grounds 🚶 🏛 ➡ ♿

Getting here: 115/116:SH801723. 8 miles south of Llandudno and Colwyn Bay. **Bus**: from Llandudno. **Train**: Llandudno Junction. **Road**: off A470. Signposted from A55, junction 19. **Parking**: 150 yards from garden entrance. Limited mobility parking.

Finding out more: 01492 650460 or bodnantgarden@nationaltrust.org.uk

Bodnant Garden		M	T	W	T	F	S	S
Garden								
1 Mar–28 Oct	10–5	M	T	W	T	F	S	S
29 Oct–11 Nov	11–3	M	T	W	T	F	S	S
27 Dec–31 Dec*	11–3	M			T	F	S	S
Tea-room								
1 Mar–28 Oct	10–5	M	T	W	T	F	S	S
29 Oct–24 Dec	11–3	M	T	W	T	F	S	S
27 Dec–31 Dec	11–3	M			T	F	S	S

*Garden open, weather permitting.

Bodysgallen Hall Hotel, Restaurant and Spa

Llandudno, Conwy LL30 1RS

Map (4) F2    2008

Bodysgallen Hall Hotel, Conwy: view from the gardens

This Grade I-listed 17th-century house has the most spectacular views towards Conwy Castle and Snowdonia. It's set in 89 hectares (220 acres) of award-winning romantic gardens, highlights of which include a rare parterre – filled with sweet-smelling herbs – several follies, a cascade, walled garden and formal rose gardens. Beyond, the hotel's parkland offers miles of stunning walks.

The house and gardens are already accessible to the public as a hotel and welcome guests to stay, to dine in the restaurants and to have afternoon tea (booking strongly advised). Contact hotel direct for best available offer. **Note**: all paying guests to the hotel are welcome to walk in the garden and park. Children above the age of six are welcome.

Finding out more: 01492 584466. 01492 582519 (fax) or info@bodysgallen.com. www.bodysgallen.com

Chirk Castle

Chirk, Wrexham LL14 5AF

Map (4) G3   1981

'A fun, interesting, enjoyable and very memorable experience for us and our children; a fantastic spectacle and performance.'
Mrs Mayall, Flintshire

Completed in 1310, Chirk is the last Welsh castle from the reign of Edward I still lived in today. Features from its 700 years include the medieval tower and dungeon, 17th-century Long Gallery, grand 18th-century state apartments, servants' hall and historic laundry. The award-winning gardens contain clipped yews, herbaceous borders, shrub and rock gardens. A terrace with stunning views looks out over the Cheshire and Shropshire plains. The parkland provides a habitat for rare invertebrates, wild flowers and contains many mature trees. From September, new rooms depict the life of Lord Howard de Walden during the 1930s. **Note**: all visitors, including members, need to obtain tickets before going to castle, tower or garden.

Exploring
- Meet the medieval guards and discover life 700 years ago.
- Try on armour and join in guard duty.
- Be awestruck by over 400 years of elegant family living.
- Explore new areas, like the kitchen garden, dovecote and orchard.
- Encounter Berkshire pigs, ancient trees and bluebells in the woods.
- Savour peace and quiet in the award-winning gardens.

Eating and shopping: be tempted by local fresh produce in the farm shop and sample seasonal menus in the tea-room and coffee shop – all use produce grown in the kitchen garden. Browse through the gift shops, plant sales and second-hand books.

Making the most of your day: our new leaflets tell you all about the many places to explore (including the fortress, gardens and woods), plus fascinating stories about servants' life and the Myddelton family home. **Dogs**: on leads welcome everywhere outdoors, except formal gardens. Please note, no shady parking.

Access for all: ▣ 🅿 🔠 🔠 🔠 🔠 ▣ 🔠 ∴
State rooms 🔠 🔠 🔠 Adam Tower 🔠
Gardens 🔠 🔠 ➡ 🔠

Getting here: 126:SJ275388. 2 miles west of Chirk village, 7 miles from Wrexham and Llangollen. **Foot**: driveways 1½ miles to visitor centre and castle. Permitted footpaths open April to September. 1½ miles from Llangollen Canal to moor near Chirk Tunnel. **Bus**: from Wrexham to Oswestry. **Train**: Chirk, 1½ miles. **Road**: signposted off A483. **Parking**: at home farm, 200 yards to castle and garden via steep hill. One-way system on driveway.

Finding out more: 01691 777701 or chirkcastle@nationaltrust.org.uk

Chirk Castle		M	T	W	T	F	S	S
Estate*								
Open all year	7–7	M	T	W	T	F	S	S
Whole property**								
1 Mar–31 Mar	10–4	M	T	W	T	F	S	S
1 Apr–30 Sep	10–5	M	T	W	T	F	S	S
1 Oct–4 Nov	10–4	M	T	W	T	F	S	S
Garden, tower, shops and tea-rooms								
1 Feb–29 Feb	10–4	M	T	W	T	F	S	S
10 Nov–16 Dec	10–4	M	T	W	T	F	S	S
State rooms* **								
3 Nov–2 Dec	11–3	·	·	·	·	·	S	S
State rooms								
8 Dec–16 Dec	10–4	M	T	W	T	F	S	S

Open Bank Holiday Mondays. *Closes dusk if earlier and open until 9, June to August. **State rooms by guided tour only 11 to 12, free-flow 12 to closing. ***Guided tours only.

Cilgerran Castle

near Cardigan, Pembrokeshire SA43 2SF

Map ④ C7 🏛 1938

This striking 13th-century castle is in a stunning location overlooking the Teifi Gorge and has inspired many artists, including Turner. **Note**: in the guardianship of Cadw – Welsh Assembly Government's historic environment service. Dogs on leads allowed.

Access for all: 🔠 🔠 🔠

Getting here: 145:SN195431. On rock above left bank of the Teifi. 3 miles south-east of Cardigan, 1½ miles east of A478.

Finding out more: 01239 621339 or cilgerrancastle@nationaltrust.org.uk

Cilgerran Castle		M	T	W	T	F	S	S
2 Jan–31 Mar	10–4	M	T	W	T	F	S	S
1 Apr–31 Oct	10–5	M	T	W	T	F	S	S
1 Nov–31 Dec	10–4	M	T	W	T	F	S	S

Closed 1 January and 24 to 26 December.

History comes to life at Chirk Castle, Wrexham

Colby Woodland Garden

near Amroth, Pembrokeshire SA67 8PP

Map ④ C8   🚽❄️🔔🛶🏛️🏠 1980

Set in a tranquil and secluded valley, this glorious informal woodland garden with a fascinating industrial past is always bursting with colour and wildlife. Whatever the season, there's something to delight. Spring brings carpets of bluebells and a vivid display of camellias, rhododendrons and azaleas. Enjoy shady woodland walks, the wildflower meadow and colourful walled garden in summer followed by the marvellous colours of autumn. Explore the meadow with its meandering stream and abundance of dragonflies, butterflies and other insects. Discover more about the garden's wildlife and its history and take a virtual tour of Pembrokeshire in the Bothy exhibition. **Note:** the house is not open.

Gazebo at Colby Woodland Garden, Pembrokeshire

Exploring
– Wander the woodlands and enjoy the peace and tranquillity.
– Have family fun pond-dipping or duck racing on the stream.
– Climb to our sea-view summerhouse or walk to the beach.
– Discover the walled garden and unusual paintings in the gazebo.
– Picnic among the wildflowers, play games in the meadow.
– Don't miss the new waterfall walk in the West Wood.

Eating and shopping: buy a souvenir at the Trust shop or a plant from the walled garden. Visit the Bothy tea-room for a freshly prepared treat. Browse local arts and crafts in the gallery. Visit Summerhill Farm Shop for award-winning lamb and beef.

Making the most of your day: full events programme, including Easter trails, twilight wildlife and bat walks, family fun days, children's quiz, wildlife events, summer holiday activities, guided walks and cream teas with the Head Gardener. **Dogs**: on leads in woodland garden only.

Access for all: 🅿️🔆♿️🚾🔆🔆🔆📷🔆 🔆🔆
Grounds 🔆➡️♿️

Getting here: 158:SN155080. 1½ miles inland from Amroth beside Carmarthen Bay. **Foot**: from beach via public footpath in Amroth (beside Amroth Arms). **Bus**: from Tenby (passing Kilgetty ➿). **Train**: Kilgetty 2½ miles. **Road**: follow brown signs from A477 Tenby to Carmarthen road or off coast road at Amroth Castle caravan park. **Parking**: free, 50 yards. Please note that from January to mid-February, plus November and December, car park is pay and display. Telephone for route map for coaches and cars.

Finding out more: 01834 811885 or colby@nationaltrust.org.uk

Colby Woodland Garden		M	T	W	T	F	S	S
Woodland and walled gardens and bothy exhibition*								
2 Jan–10 Feb	10–3	M	T	W	T	F	S	S
5 Nov–31 Dec	10–3	M	T	W	T	F	S	S
Woodland and walled gardens, shop and bothy exhibition*								
11 Feb–4 Nov	10–5	M	T	W	T	F	S	S
Tea-room								
7 Jan–25 Mar	11–3						S	S
31 Mar–4 Nov	10–5	M	T	W	T	F	S	S
10 Nov–30 Dec	11–3						S	S
Gallery								
31 Mar–4 Nov	11–5	M	T	W	T	F	S	S

*Car park open as woodland and walled gardens.
Closed 1 January and 24 to 26 December.

Conwy Suspension Bridge

Conwy LL32 8LD

Map (4) E2   [icons] 1965

See how trade and travel brought Conwy to life and discover how a husband and wife kept Thomas Telford's bridge open every day of the year, whatever the weather. **Note**: no toilet.

Exploring
- Marvel at Thomas Telford's graceful bridge design.
- Enjoy the stunning views over the Conwy estuary.
- Visit the beautifully restored tiny toll house.

Eating and shopping: bring your own picnic to enjoy on the grassed area.

Making the most of your day: guided talks on Thomas Telford. **Dogs**: allowed.

Access for all: Building [icon] Grounds [icon]

Getting here: 115:SH785775. 100 yards from town centre, adjacent to Conwy Castle. **Cycle**: NCN5. **Bus**: services from surrounding areas. **Train**: Conwy ¼ mile; Llandudno Junction ½ mile. **Parking**: no onsite parking.

Finding out more: 01492 573282 or conwybridge@nationaltrust.org.uk

Conwy Suspension Bridge		M	T	W	T	F	S	S
17 Mar–4 Nov	11–5	**M**	**T**	**W**	**T**	**F**	**S**	**S**

Graceful Conwy Suspension Bridge, Conwy

Dinefwr Park and Castle

Llandeilo, Carmarthenshire SA19 6RT

Map (4) E8   [icons] 1990

'So much to do. The boardwalk was really cool. I caught bugs, saw the deer and had fun outdoors.'
Rebecca Mitchell (aged 12), Llanboidy

A magical place of power and influence for more than 2,000 years, Dinefwr holds an iconic position in the history of Wales. The spirits of Welsh princes still inhabit this magical landscape, with 323 hectares (800 acres) to explore – from the ruined castle to bogland walk, deer park and woodlands to hay meadows and streams. In the Middle Ages Lord Rhys held court at Dinefwr and influenced decisions in Wales. The visionaries George and Cecil Rice designed the superb 18th-century landscape that you see today. Newton House is set in 1912 and gives visitors an atmospheric and hands-on experience. **Note**: castle owned by Wildlife Trust – in guardianship of Cadw, Welsh Assembly Government's historic environment service.

Exploring
- Be amazed at the National Nature Reserve at Dinefwr.
- Be thrilled by views from the top of the castle.
- Let off steam in the children's play area and boardwalk.
- Get close to the rare and historic White Park cattle.
- Help with servants' tasks and hear them chatting about life.
- Learn about and see the herd of fallow deer.

Eating and shopping: buy local Welsh produce and gifts in the atmospheric shop. Eat local fare in the Billiard Room tea-room. Taste local wines and beers overlooking the croquet lawn. Stay at one of our two holiday cottages.

Making the most of your day: daily tours of house and White Park cattle. Seasonal tours of the National Nature Reserve and fallow deer herd. School holiday and family activities. Varied programme of events throughout year. **Dogs**: welcome on leads, in outer park only.

Newton House, Dinefwr, Carmarthenshire

Access for all: 🅿️🅳️🚻🎧🛗📷🎨♿👁️🅰️
Building 🛗🅰️♿ **Grounds** 🅰️

Getting here: 159:SN625225. On west outskirts of Llandeilo. **Bus**: services to Llandeilo, 1 mile. **Train**: Llandeilo, 1 mile. **Road**: on A40(T); from Swansea take M4 to Pont Abraham, then A48(T) to Cross Hands and A476 to Llandeilo. **Sat Nav**: problems, do not use. **Parking**: 50 yards. Narrow access.

Finding out more: 01558 824512 or dinefwr@nationaltrust.org.uk

Dinefwr Park and Castle		M	T	W	T	F	S	S
1 Jan–25 Mar	11:30–4	M	T	W	T	F	S	S
26 Mar–30 Jun	11–5	M	T	W	T	F	S	S
1 Jul–31 Aug	10–6	M	T	W	T	F	S	S
1 Sep–28 Oct	11–5	M	T	W	T	F	S	S
29 Oct–31 Dec	11:30–4	M	T	W	T	F	S	S

Boardwalk, deer park and play area: 29 October to 25 March close 3:30, 4:30 at other times (except July and August, when they close at 5:30). Closed 24 and 25 December. Tea-room open all year.

Dolaucothi Gold Mines

Pumsaint, Llanwrda,
Carmarthenshire SA19 8US

Map ④ E7   1941

Dolaucothi Gold Mines are set amid the wooded hillsides overlooking the beautiful Cothi Valley. More than 2,000 years ago the Romans mined for gold here, and mining continued in the 19th and 20th centuries. The mine yard is preserved as it was in the 1930s – when gold mining ceased. Go back in time on a guided tour and experience the harsh working conditions underground. See and hear the 1930s mine machinery, have a go at gold panning and experience the frustrations of searching for real gold. Stay on our caravan site opposite the Gold Mines for a relaxing break. **Note**: underground tours involve steep slopes, stout footwear is essential.

Exploring
- Experience the thrill of an underground guided tour.
- Try gold panning in the sifting troughs.
- Interpretive history of gold mining at Dolaucothi.
- Enjoy the walks around this beautiful upland estate.
- Overground mine tours of Roman adits.

Eating and shopping: visit our gift shop, featuring Welsh gold jewellery. Taste local cooking in our gold mine tea-room.

Making the most of your day: daily underground tours, charge including members (please note younger children may not be carried). Regular school holiday and family activities. Self-guided walks around the estate. **Dogs**: on leads only.

Access for all: 🅿️ ♿ 🚻 🏢 🔊 ⠿
Building ♿ ♿ ♿

Getting here: 146:SN662403. Between Lampeter and Llanwrda. **Bus**: from Lampeter. **Train**: Llanwrda, 8 miles. **Road**: on A482. **Parking**: free. Overflow car park opposite main entrance.

Finding out more: 01558 650177 or dolaucothi@nationaltrust.org.uk

Dolaucothi Gold Mines		M	T	W	T	F	S	S
Mines, shop and tea-room								
10 Mar–30 Jun	11–5	M	T	W	T	F	S	S
1 Jul–31 Aug	10–6	M	T	W	T	F	S	S
1 Sep–4 Nov	11–5	M	T	W	T	F	S	S
Caravan site								
31 Mar–28 Oct	12–5	M	T	W	T	F	S	S
Christmas shop (Coach House Pumsaint)								
24 Nov–23 Dec	11–4	·	·	W	·	F	S	S

Pumsaint Information Centre and estate walks open all year. Underground tours last one hour approximately (helmets with lights provided). Smaller children will only be allowed on tours at the discretion of staff (please telephone for advice).

Dolaucothi Gold Mines, Carmarthenshire

Dyffryn Gardens

St Nicholas, Vale of Glamorgan CF5 6SU

Map (4) G10

Discover one of our latest additions in Wales. The Grade I gardens cover 22 hectares (55 acres) and feature a stunning collection of intimate garden rooms, formal lawns and an extensive arboretum. Designed by eminent landscape architect Thomas Mawson, the gardens are the early 20th-century vision of industrialist John Cory and his son Reginald Cory. The spectacular symmetry of Mawson's lawn is best appreciated from the terrace of the Grade II* late Victorian house, reminiscent of a French château. The tiered garden rooms are overlooked by a reinstated glasshouse that houses an impressive collection of cacti and orchids. **Note**: due to open early summer (visit website for opening arrangements). Building work is underway on the interior and therefore closed to the public. Parking/toilet facilities may be limited. New place, may be very busy.

Eating and shopping: tea-rooms with indoor and courtyard seating. Shop offers a range of gifts, from garden to kitchenware and jewellery to books. Don't miss out on the seasonal plant sales. Take home your own pick from the walled garden's organic produce.

Access for all: Grounds

Getting here: 171:ST09657217. 7 miles from Cardiff city centre. **Train**: Cardiff Central. **Road**: from M4 take junction 33 on to A4232 (to Barry). Exit second slip road, at roundabout take the fourth exit A48 (to Cowbridge). In St Nicholas village follow signs for Dyffryn. **Parking**: onsite.

Finding out more:
dyffryn@nationaltrust.org.uk
www.nationaltrust.org.uk/wales

Dyffryn Gardens
Visit website for opening arrangements.

Erddig

Wrexham LL13 0YT

Map (4) H3

Described as 'the jewel in the crown of Welsh country houses', Erddig is a fascinating yet unpretentious early 18th-century country house which reflects a gentry family's 250 years of upstairs-downstairs life. The extensive downstairs area contains Erddig's unique collection of servants' portraits, while the upstairs rooms are an amazing treasure trove of fine furniture, textiles and wallpapers. Outside, an impressive range of outbuildings includes stables, a smithy, joiners' shop and sawmill. It's set within a superb 18th-century formal garden and romantic landscape park – which are the starting points for walks, bicycle and carriage rides through the estate.

Exploring
– Gain a fascinating insight into life below stairs.
– An amazing miscellany of treasures and trivia within the house.
– Enjoy the outstanding formal gardens and country estate.
– Look out for the themed country walking routes.
– Take a horse and carriage ride around the grounds.
– Hire a bicycle: tracks criss-cross the estate.

Eating and shopping: pick up gifts in the shop. Take home a selection of peat-free plants. Enjoy refreshments in the restaurant, ice-cream parlour and tea garden. Try a bottle of our own cider.

Making the most of your day: full events programme, including open-air theatre, festivals, craft fairs, Christmas markets and family fun days. Guided walks, tree trails and discovery tours. **Dogs**: on leads in country park only.

Access for all: [icons]
Building [icons] **Grounds** [icons]

The superb 18th-century formal garden at Erddig, Wrexham

Getting here: 117:SJ326482. 2 miles from Wrexham. **Bus**: Arriva 2 from Wrexham, alight Felin Puleston, 1 mile walk through Erddig Country Park. **Train**: Wrexham Central 2½ miles; Wrexham General 3½ miles via Erddig Road and footpath. **Road**: signposted A525 Whitchurch road. A483 exit 3. **Parking**: free, 200 yards.

Finding out more: 01978 355314 or erddig@nationaltrust.org.uk

Erddig		M	T	W	T	F	S	S
House*								
1 Jan–9 Mar	11–3:30	M	T	W	T	F	S	S
House**								
10 Mar–4 Nov	12:30–4:30	M	T	W	T	F	S	S
House*								
5 Nov–31 Dec	11–3:30	M	T	W	T	F	S	S
Garden, restaurant and shop								
1 Jan–9 Mar	11–4	M	T	W	T	F	S	S
10 Mar–4 Nov	11–5:30	M	T	W	T	F	S	S
5 Nov–31 Dec	11–4	M	T	W	T	F	S	S

*Bakery, kitchen and laundry rooms only. **Themed tours at 11:30 and 12; free-flow from 12:30; last admission to house at 3:30. House and gardens closed 25 December. No electric light in the house; for close study of pictures and textiles avoid dull days, especially March and October.

Gower: Rhossili Shop and Visitor Centre

Coastguard Cottages, Rhossili, Gower, Swansea SA3 1PR

Map (4) D9    1933

Overlooking the spectacular Rhossili Bay, the National Trust shop and visitor centre offers everything you need to enjoy fully this beautiful area of outstanding natural beauty; as well as a wide range of gifts and tempting treats to take home afterwards.

Exploring
— Lose yourself on the vast expanse of Rhossili beach.
— Explore Gower's rich heritage and stunning scenery.
— Walk to the iconic Worm's Head (accessible low tide only).

Eating and shopping: treat yourself to a Joe's Ice Cream, an essential part of any visit to Gower. Available from the shop along with many other tempting tastes of the area, including laverbread.

Making the most of your day: events and guided walks are held throughout the year (details from the shop or gower.admin@ nationaltrust.org.uk). **Dogs**: welcome on leads near livestock.

Access for all: 🅿️🔠♿⚫👁️📖 Shop 🅰️
Visitor Centre 🔠 **Grounds** ♿♿

Getting here: 159:SS414881. South-west tip of Gower Peninsula. **Bus**: services from Swansea to Rhossili. **Road**: approached from Swansea via A4118, then B4247. **Parking**: 50 yards (not National Trust), charge including members.

Finding out more: 01792 390707 or rhossili.shop@nationaltrust.org.uk

Sweeping sands at Rhossili Bay, Gower

Rhossili Visitor Centre		M	T	W	T	F	S	S
6 Jan–12 Feb	11–4	·	·	·	·	F	S	S
13 Feb–19 Feb	11–4	M	T	W	T	F	S	S
24 Feb–26 Feb	10:30–4	·	·	·	·	F	S	S
29 Feb–29 Mar	10:30–4:30	·	·	W	T	F	S	S
30 Mar–2 Sep	10:30–5	M	T	W	T	F	S	S
3 Sep–4 Nov	10:30–4:30	M	T	W	T	F	S	S
5 Nov–23 Dec	10:30–4	M	T	W	T	F	S	S
28 Dec–30 Dec	11–4	·	·	·	·	F	S	S

Shop and Visitor Centre closes 6 on Saturdays and Sundays during August.

The Kymin

The Round House, The Kymin, Monmouth, Monmouthshire NP25 3SF

Map ④ H8   🏠👁️♿🔔⛋ 1902

Picnic spot amongst woods and pleasure grounds, visited by Nelson. Spectacular views across Wales. Attractive Georgian banqueting house and temple.

Access for all: 🅿️🔠♿ Round House 🔠♿
Naval Temple ♿ **Grounds** ♿

Getting here: 162:SO528125. 2 miles east of Monmouth and signposted off A4136.

Finding out more: 01600 719241 or kymin@nationaltrust.org.uk

The Kymin		M	T	W	T	F	S	S
Round House								
24 Mar–29 Oct	11–4	M	·	·	·	·	S	S
Grounds								
Open all year	7–9	M	T	W	T	F	S	S

Open Good Friday. Round House: last admission 15 minutes before closing (croquet set and other games for hire and toilet available when open). Car park open during daylight hours only.

Picnicking at The Kymin, Monmouthshire

Llanerchaeron

Ciliau Aeron, near Aberaeron,
Ceredigion SA48 8DG

Map ④ D6 1989

Making friends at Llanerchaeron, Ceredigion

'I've visited this house several times and I'm still fascinated by it. There's always something new to see.'
Mrs Tennant, Pontypridd

This rare example of a self-sufficient 18th-century Welsh minor gentry estate has survived virtually unaltered. The villa, designed in the 1790s, is the most complete example of the early work of John Nash. It has its own service courtyard with dairy, laundry, brewery and salting house, and walled kitchen gardens (with all its produce for sale when in season). The pleasure grounds and ornamental lake and parkland provide peaceful walks. The Home Farm complex has an impressive range of traditional, atmospheric outbuildings and is a working organic farm with Welsh Black cattle, Llanwenog sheep and rare Welsh pigs.

Exploring – Discover and experience the main residence and staff quarters.
– Wander through the pleasure grounds and ornamental lake.
– Explore the working walled gardens.
– Learn about the farm – the buildings and inhabitants.
– Special events days and activities throughout the year.
– Experience self-sufficiency at its best.

Eating and shopping: enjoy light meals and cakes, or bring a picnic. New shop in visitor building sells local crafts, cards, gifts and new books as well as meat and produce from the estate. Don't miss the second-hand bookshop.

Making the most of your day: activities at 2 every day during local school holidays. Special events days. Cycle hire from car park. Newly opened historic woodland walks.

Dogs: river and parkland walks for dogs on leads.

Access for all: [icons]
Visitor building [icons] Villa [icons]
Grounds, farm and gardens [icons]

Getting here: 146:SN480602. 2½ miles east of Aberaeron. **Foot**: 2½ miles foot/cycle track from Aberaeron to property along old railway line. **Bus**: service from Aberystwyth ☒ to Carmarthen ☒, alight New Inn Forge, about ½ mile. **Road**: off A482. **Parking**: free, 50 yards.

Finding out more: 01545 570200 or llanerchaeron@nationaltrust.org.uk

Llanerchaeron		M	T	W	T	F	S	S
Entire property*								
20 Feb–26 Feb	11:30–3:30	M	T	W	T	F	S	S
19 Mar–4 Nov	10:30–5	M	T	W	T	F	S	S
Farm, garden, woodland walks and shop**								
1 Jan–18 Mar	11:30–3:30	M	T	W	T	F	S	S
5 Nov–31 Dec	11:30–3:30	M	T	W	T	F	S	S
Christmas Fair***								
1 Dec–2 Dec	11–4	·	·	·	·	·	S	S
Christmas villa***								
3 Dec–7 Dec	11:30–3:30	M	T	W	T	F	·	·

First entry to villa 11:30, last entry one hour before closing. Full café open mid-February to end October. *Geler Jones Collection open Fridays 12 to 4. **Billiard room and service courtyard area of the villa also open. ***Ground floor of villa open and dressed for Christmas. Closed 25 December. Bad weather can cause access problems (telephone for up-to-date information before visiting between November and March). Parkland open daily dawn till dusk.

Penrhyn Castle

Bangor, Gwynedd LL57 4HN

Map ④ E2 🏠 ➕ ⛴ ✦ ☂ 1951

Set in the breathtaking countryside of Snowdonia, the picturesque Penrhyn Castle stands in 24 hectares (60 acres) of grounds. Built by famed architect Thomas Hopper in the 19th century, the site is brimming with history and splendour. The castle holds a myriad of treasures and artefacts, many dating back hundreds of years. These include a one-ton slate bed, made for Queen Victoria's famous visit, elaborate carvings, wallpaper and plasterwork, and an exceptional collection of paintings. The grounds contain beautiful gardens and a huge variety of plants and wildlife, including an exotic bog garden and stunning Victorian walled garden.

Exploring
- Enjoy majestic views of Snowdonia and the Menai Strait.
- See behind the scenes with our hidden tours.
- Explore the castle and see carefully preserved rooms.
- Discover the history of the Pennant family.
- Roam the extensive grounds, forest, or exotic gardens.

Eating and shopping: after an enjoyable day exploring Penrhyn Castle indulge yourself in our inviting tea-room. Fully licensed, it offers freshly prepared, locally sourced food, including an array of traditional treats – from Teisen Berffro to our delicious Penrhyn cream tea.

Making the most of your day: find out more about our Victorian kitchen or join in the many events throughout the season, including summer fun days (packed with children's activities) and our Victorian Christmas. **Dogs**: on leads in grounds only.

Access for all: 🅿️ 🅳 ♿ 🚻 📶 🔊 🎧 💺 🖼️ ⬚ ⬚
Mansion 🦽 🅗 ♿ Stable block 🅗 ⬚
Grounds 🦽 🅗

Getting here: 115:SH602720. 1 mile east of Bangor. **Cycle**: NCN5, 1¼ miles. **Bus**: services from Bangor and Caernarfon to Llandudno, alight castle driveway. **Train**: Bangor 3 miles. **Road**: at Llandygai on A5122. Signposted from junction 11 of A55 and A5. **Parking**: free, 500 yards.

Finding out more: 01248 363219 (Infoline). 01248 353084 or penrhyncastle@nationaltrust.org.uk

Penrhyn Castle		M	T	W	T	F	S	S
Castle								
17 Mar–4 Nov	12–5	M	·	W	T	F	S	S
1 Jul–31 Aug	11–5	M	·	W	T	F	S	S
Tea-room and grounds								
17 Mar–4 Nov	11–5	M	T	W	T	F	S	S
1 Jul–31 Aug	10–5	M	T	W	T	F	S	S
Shop								
17 Mar–4 Nov	11–5	M	T	W	T	F	S	S
Shop, tea-room, Victorian kitchen and grounds								
2 Jan–16 Mar	12–3	M	·	W	T	F	S	S
5 Nov–24 Dec	12–3	M	T	W	T	F	S	S
26 Dec–31 Dec	12–3	M	·	W	T	F	S	S

Last audio tour 4. Whole property open for the Queen's Diamond Jubilee (5 June). Closed December 25.

Penrhyn Castle, Gwynedd: the Grand Staircase

Plas Newydd Country House and Gardens

Llanfairpwll, Anglesey LL61 6DQ

Map ④ D2 1976

Plas Newydd, the ancestral home of the Marquess of Anglesey, bears witness to a turbulent history: noble beginnings during Henry VIII's reign, triumphant success at Waterloo, bankruptcy at the turn of the 20th century and the revival of the family fortunes in the 1930s. The house is famous for its association with Rex Whistler, and contains his exquisite romantic mural and the largest exhibition of his works. Located on the Menai Straits, with glorious views across Snowdonia, you can stroll through an Australasian arboretum, Italianate summer terrace or follow a woodland path leading to the marine walk along the Straits.

Exploring — Discover portraits and landscapes in the Angleseys' home.

The Music Room at Plas Newydd, Anglesey

Exploring
- Enjoy crafted timber shelters, bird hides and stunning views.
- Wander in the landscaped grounds and along the marine walk.
- Find the rhododendron garden – spectacular in April, May and June.
- Children: enjoy playing in the family room and adventure playground.
- Look out for red squirrels in the woodlands.

Eating and shopping: our restaurant serves delicious local food and drinks. Browse in our two gift shops for great ideas and inspiring offers. Don't miss the second-hand bookshop in our coffee shop at the house.

Making the most of your day: take a stroll through the rhododendron garden and the marine walk. Also why not join us at weekends in December for our Christmas Craft and Food Fair? **Dogs**: in the car park only.

Access for all: ⬛⬛⬛⬛⬛⬛⬛⬛⬛⬛
Building ⬛⬛⬛ Grounds ⬛

Getting here: 114/115:SH521696. 2 miles south-west of Llanfairpwll. **Cycle**: NCN8, ¼ mile. **Bus**: Bangor to Llangefni (passing Bangor ≋ and close Llanfairpwll ≋). **Train**: Llanfairpwll 1¾ miles. **Road**: from A55 take junctions 7 and 8a, or A4080 to Brynsiencyn; turn off A5 at west end of Britannia Bridge. **Parking**: free, 400 yards.

Finding out more: 01248 715272 (Infoline). 01248 714795 or plasnewydd@nationaltrust.org.uk

Plas Newydd		M	T	W	T	F	S	S
House								
17 Mar–7 Nov	11–5	M	T	W	·	·	S	S
Guided tours only*								
17 Mar–7 Nov	11–1	M	T	W	·	·	S	S
Garden and coffee shop**								
17 Mar–7 Nov	10–5:30	M	T	W	·	·	S	S
Rhododendron garden								
31 Mar–6 Jun	10–5:30	M	T	W	·	·	S	S
Shop, restaurant and adventure playground								
1 Jan–16 Mar	11–4	M	T	W	T	F	S	S
17 Mar–7 Nov	10–5:30	M	T	W	T	F	S	S
8 Nov–31 Dec	11–4	M	T	W	T	F	S	S

*Limited places. **Closed 25 December. Picnics in area by car park only.

Places may occasionally close for conservation, safety or events

Quirky electric fire in Honora Keating's bedroom at Plas yn Rhiw, Gwynedd

Plas yn Rhiw

Rhiw, Pwllheli, Gwynedd LL53 8AB

Map ④ C4   🏠⚹♨🏠 [1952]

The house was rescued from neglect and lovingly restored by the three Keating sisters, who bought it in 1938. The views from the grounds and gardens across Cardigan Bay are among the most spectacular in Britain. The house is 16th-century with Georgian additions, and the garden contains many beautiful flowering trees and shrubs, with beds framed by box hedges and grass paths. It is stunning whatever the season.

Exploring
– Find out how the Keating sisters lived in the 1930s.
– Explore the meandering paths and enjoy the stunning views.
– Discover the two-seater garden privy!
– See for yourself what inspired Honora Keating's delightful landscape paintings.

Eating and shopping: enjoy a hot or cold drink and ice-cream from the shop. Plant sales and gifts.

Making the most of your day: plant sales. Guided tours by arrangement. Easter Egg hunt. **Dogs**: on woodland walk below car park only (on leads).

Access for all: 🅿️♿🚾♿📖♿👶
Building 🔼🔼 Grounds 🔼🔼

Getting here: 123:SH237282. 12 miles south-west of Pwllheli. **Foot**: easily accessed from Llyn coastal path. **Bus**: Pwllheli to Aberdaron (passing Pwllheli ☒), alight at gate. **Train**: Pwllheli 10 miles. **Road**: B4413 to Aberdaron (drive gates at bottom Rhiw Hill). **Parking**: small car park, 80 yards. Not suitable for large vehicles. Narrow lanes.

Finding out more: 01758 780219 or plasynrhiw@nationaltrust.org.uk

Plas yn Rhiw		M	T	W	T	F	S	S
29 Mar–29 Apr	12–5				T	F	S	S
2 May–3 Sep	12–5	M		W	T	F	S	S
6 Sep–1 Oct	12–5	M			T	F	S	S
4 Oct–4 Nov	12–4				T	F	S	S

Open Bank Holidays. Garden and snowdrop wood open occasionally at weekends in January and February.

Powis Castle and Garden

Welshpool, Powys SY21 8RF

Map ④ G5 [icons] 1952

The world-famous garden, overhung with clipped yews, shelters rare and tender plants. Laid out under the influence of Italian and French styles, it retains its original lead statues and an orangery on the terraces. High on a rock above the terraces, the castle, originally built *circa* 1200, began life as a medieval fortress. Remodelled and embellished over more than 400 years, it reflects the changing needs and ambitions of the Herbert family – each generation adding to the magnificent collection of paintings, sculpture, furniture and tapestries. A superb collection of treasures from India is displayed in the Clive Museum. **Note**: all visitors (including members) need a ticket from reception. Assistance dogs only allowed (deer park).

Exploring
- Relax in the sumptuous 10.5-hectare (26-acre) garden.
- Delight in the grandeur of the Elizabethan Long Gallery.
- Be amazed by the exquisite collection of Indian treasures.
- Go behind the scenes with castle and garden tours.
- Travel back in time with our themed events.

Eating and shopping: locally sourced seasonal produce served in the restaurant. Try our bara brith, made with our own secret recipe. Take home your own Powis plant, propagated in our nursery. Gifts and products from Wales on sale in the shop.

Making the most of your day: children's activities during school holidays, tours and lectures about the castle and garden during autumn and winter. Weekly talks and tours about caring for the collection. **Dogs**: assistance dogs only.

Access for all: [icons]
Building [icon] Grounds [icons]

Getting here: 126:SJ216064. 1 mile south of Welshpool. **Foot**: 1-mile walk from Park Lane, off Broad Street in Welshpool. Access from High Street (A490). **Bus**: services from Oswestry to Welshpool and Shrewsbury to Llanidloes. On both alight High Street, 1 mile. **Train**: Welshpool, 1¼ miles on footpath. **Road**: signed from main road to Newtown (A483); enter by first drive gate on right. **Parking**: free.

Finding out more: 01938 551944 (Infoline). 01938 551929 or powiscastle@nationaltrust.org.uk

Powis Castle and Garden		M	T	W	T	F	S	S
Castle and Clive Museum								
1 Mar–31 Mar	12–4	M	T	W	T	F	S	S
1 Apr–30 Sep	12–5	M	T	W	T	F	S	S
1 Oct–31 Dec	12–4	M	T	W	T	F	S	S
Garden, restaurant and shop								
1 Mar–31 Mar	11–4:30	M	T	W	T	F	S	S
1 Apr–30 Sep	11–5:30	M	T	W	T	F	S	S
1 Oct–31 Dec	11–4	M	T	W	T	F	S	S

Last admission to castle 45 minutes before closing.
Closed 25 December. 1 November to 31 December: limited number of castle rooms open.

The monumental Powis Castle, Powys

St David's Visitor Centre and Shop

Captain's House, High Street, St David's, Pembrokeshire SA62 6SD

Map (4) A8   1974

Opposite The Cross in the centre of St David's, Wales's smallest historic city, the Visitor Centre and Shop is open all year. Try out our new interactive technology for a complete guide to the National Trust in Pembrokeshire – places to visit, beaches and walks – and browse in the well-stocked shop. **Note**: no toilet.

Exploring
– Take a virtual tour of Pembrokeshire.
– Pick up a leaflet and plan where to visit next.
– Discover more about the coast and countryside in our care.

Eating and shopping: comprehensive range of merchandise, including books, cards and maps. Treat yourself to locally made gifts and produce.

Making the most of your day: walks and evening talks throughout the year (ask staff for information).

Access for all: Building 🏛

Getting here: 115:SM753253. In the centre of St David's. **Foot**: Pembrokeshire Coast Path within 1 mile. **Bus**: from Haverfordwest ➤. Additional services during main holiday season. **Parking**: no onsite parking.

Finding out more: 01437 720385 or stdavids@nationaltrust.org.uk

St David's Visitor Centre		M	T	W	T	F	S	S
2 Jan–17 Mar	10–4	M	T	W	T	F	S	
18 Mar–31 Dec	10–5:30	M	T	W	T	F	S	S

Closes 4 on Sunday. Closed 25 and 26 December.

Segontium

Caernarfon, Gwynedd

Map (4) D2   🏛 1937

Fort built to defend the Roman Empire against rebellious tribes. **Note**: in the guardianship of Cadw – Welsh Government's historic enviroment service. Museum not National Trust.

Access for all: Grounds 🦽

Getting here: 115:SH485624. On Beddgelert road, A4085, on south-east outskirts of Caernarfon, 500 yards from town centre.

Finding out more: 01286 675625 or segontium@nationaltrust.org.uk

Segontium	
Museum (not National Trust) open Tuesday to Sunday, 12:30 to 4:30 (open Bank Holiday Mondays). Closed end of November.	

Skenfrith Castle

Skenfrith, near Abergavenny, Monmouthshire NP7 8UH

Map (4) H8   1936

Remains of early 13th-century castle, built beside the River Monnow to command one of the main routes from England. **Note**: in the guardianship of Cadw – Welsh Government's historic enviroment service.

Access for all: Building 🦽

Getting here: 161:SO456203. 6 miles north-west of Monmouth, 12 miles north-east of Abergavenny, on north side of the B4521.

Finding out more: 01874 625515 or skenfrithcastle@nationaltrust.org.uk

Skenfrith Castle	
Open every day all year from dawn to dusk	

Stackpole

Stackpole, near Pembroke, Pembrokeshire

Map ④ B9   1976

Broadhaven South beach, Stackpole, Pembrokeshire

Once owned by the Cawdor family, who transformed much of the natural landscape, this beautiful and varied stretch of coastline is famous for its award-winning sandy beaches, wooded valleys, dramatic cliffs and lily ponds. The Bosherston Lakes and Stackpole Warren are part of Stackpole National Nature Reserve, managed in partnership with the Countryside Council for Wales. Wildlife includes otters, herons, wintering wildfowl and dragonflies, as well as breeding seabirds and choughs. Also on the estate is the recently refurbished Stackpole Outdoor Learning residential eco-centre for schools and universities with a multipurpose theatre venue and classrooms.

Exploring
— Relax on excellent sandy beaches at Broadhaven South and Barafundle.
— Enjoy the spectacular clifftop scenery – look out for choughs.
— Visit Bosherston Lily Ponds, home to otters, wildfowl and dragonflies.
— Walk miles of footpaths – linking lakes, woods, cliffs and beaches.
— See where Stackpole Court once stood and admire the views.
— Coarse fishing – permits available. Conditions apply.

Eating and shopping: the Boathouse tea-room at Stackpole Quay serves a wide range of freshly prepared dishes. Mencap Walled Garden produces and sells plants, fruit and vegetables. Stay in one of our holiday cottages at Stackpole Quay.

Making the most of your day: guided coast and lake wildlife walks. Family activities throughout the year. Theatre and music concerts.

Dogs: under control on the estate.

Access for all: 🅿️ 🚻 ♿ 🏛
Building ♿ Grounds ♿ 🚶

Getting here: 158:SR992958. 6 miles south of Pembroke. **Foot**: via Pembrokeshire Coast Path. **Bus**: Pembroke ➡ to Angle. **Train**: Pembroke 6 miles. **Road**: B4319 from Pembroke to Stackpole and Bosherston (various entry points onto estate). **Parking**: at Stackpole Quay, Broadhaven South and Bosherston Lily Ponds (charge applies). Access via narrow lanes with passing places.

Finding out more: 01646 661359 or stackpole@nationaltrust.org.uk. Old Home Farm Yard, Stackpole, near Pembroke, Pembrokeshire SA71 5DQ

Stackpole		M	T	W	T	F	S	S
Estate								
Open all year		M	T	W	T	F	S	S
Boathouse tea-room								
11 Feb–19 Feb	10:30–5	M	T	W	T	F	S	S
24 Feb–1 Apr	11–4					F	S	S
2 Apr–4 Nov	10:30–5	M	T	W	T	F	S	S
9 Nov–23 Dec	11–4					F	S	S
24 Dec–31 Dec	11–4	M	T	W	T	F	S	S

Boathouse tea-room closed 24 and 25 December.

Tredegar House

Newport, Newport NP10 8YW

Map ④ G9  2012

One of the finest Grade I 17th-century restoration houses in Britain is now yours to visit. For over four centuries it was the country estate of the flamboyant Morgan family. The fascinating narrative of the family is told throughout the house, from ancestral portraits adorning the walls to the cosmopolitan craftsmanship of the State Rooms. The Morgans' enthusiasm for racing and hunting is reflected by the impressive Grade I 17th-century stables that flank the courtyard. It is surrounded by 36 hectares (90 acres) of parkland and includes the great lake, three walled gardens, an orangery and farm buildings. **Note**: due to open early summer (visit website for opening arrangements). Building work may be underway on house exterior. New place, so may be very busy.

Eating and shopping: pop in for afternoon tea or enjoy a light lunch and refreshments at our tea-rooms. Our shop offers a range of souvenirs, gifts and snacks.

Access for all: 🚾 ♿ 🔊 Grounds ♿ ♿

Getting here: 171:ST28828524. 2 miles west of Newport. **Train**: Newport (south-east Wales). **Road**: from M4 take junction 28, then exit roundabout A48 (to St Mellons). **Parking**: onsite pay and display (charge including members).

Finding out more:
tredegar@nationaltrust.org.uk.
www.nationaltrust.org.uk/wales

Tredegar House
Visit website for opening arrangements.

Tudor Merchant's House, Pembrokeshire: step back in time to 1500

Tudor Merchant's House

Quay Hill, Tenby, Pembrokeshire SA70 7BX

Map ④ C9 🏠 1937

Step into the world of a successful merchant and his family in 1500 when this fine three-storey house had just been built. Discover the merchant's shop and working kitchen on the ground floor. The first-floor Hall is newly transformed for this year with colourful wall hangings and replica Tudor furniture. **Note**: no toilet.

Exploring
 – Sit on the furniture – imagine you're back in Tudor times.
 – Discover fascinating facts about Tudor family life from our guides.
 – Touch and smell the exotic spices and the merchant's wares.
 – Don't miss the small herb garden, open weather permitting.

Eating and shopping: treat yourself to a Tudor replica gift from the merchant's shop. There's specially made pottery based on finds at the house, pewterware, glass, beeswax candles and also books about the Tudors.

Making the most of your day: kitchen fire lit at weekends. Tudor costumes for children and replica toys. Staff wear Tudor costumes on Bank Holidays. Easter and Hallowe'en family events. Children's quiz.

Access for all: 🔲🖥️🚻👁️ Building 🔗

Getting here: 158:SN135004. In the centre of Tenby, between Tudor Square and Tenby harbour. **Foot**: follow finger post from Tudor Square by Lifeboat Tavern, or from Bridge Street or Crackwell Street. **Bus**: local services from surrounding areas, drop off at town walls, ¼ mile. **Train**: Tenby ½ mile. **Parking**: very limited parking on streets within town walls. July to August: parking in pay and display car parks only or via park and ride (charge including members).

Finding out more: 01834 842279 or tudormerchantshouse@nationaltrust.org.uk

Tudor Merchant's House		M	T	W	T	F	S	S
11 Feb–19 Feb	11–3	M	T	W	T	F	S	S
25 Feb–25 Mar	11–3	·	·	·	·	·	S	S
26 Mar–22 Jul	11–5	M	·	W	T	F	S	S
23 Jul–2 Sep	11–5	M	T	W	T	F	S	S
3 Sep–4 Nov	11–5	M	·	W	T	F	S	S
10 Nov–30 Dec	11–3	·	·	·	·	·	S	S

Open Tuesdays of Bank Holiday weeks, 11 to 5.

Tŷ Mawr Wybrnant, Conwy: Bishop Morgan's birthplace

Tŷ Mawr Wybrnant

Penmachno, Betws-y-Coed, Conwy LL25 0HJ

Map (4) E3 🏠♿ 1951

Explore centuries of Welsh living in this traditional stone-built upland farmhouse. Set in the heart of the beautiful Conwy Valley, it's one of the most important houses in the history of the Welsh language, and was once the home of Bishop William Morgan. A gem definitely worthy of a visit.

Exploring
– View the impressive Bible collection in nearly 100 languages.
– Discover how people survived without electricity or other creature comforts.
– New: explore the woodland animal trail.

Eating and shopping: bring your own picnic and relax by the stream.

Making the most of your day: introductory talks. Woodland walks. Exhibition room. Families will enjoy the children's art packs, family activity sheet and woodland animal trail. **Dogs**: under close control.

Access for all: 🅿️🚻♿
Building 🔗♿ Grounds ♿

Getting here: 115:SH770524. 2½ miles north-west of Penmachno, at the head of the Wybrnant Valley. **Bus**: Llanrwst to Cwm Penmachno (passing Betws-y-Coed 🚂), alight Penmachno, then 2-mile walk. **Train**: Pont-y-Pant 2½ miles. **Road**: from A5 6 miles south of Betws-y-Coed, take B4406 to Penmachno, then take forest road. **Parking**: free, 500 yards.

Finding out more: 01690 760213 or tymawrwybrnant@nationaltrust.org.uk

Tŷ Mawr Wybrnant		M	T	W	T	F	S	S
29 Mar–4 Nov	12–5	·	·	·	T	F	S	S

Open Bank Holiday Mondays.

Northern Ireland

Intrepid visitors demonstrate their head for
heights on the rope bridge at Carrick-a-Rede

Outdoors in Northern Ireland

Above:
the haunting green drumlins at Strangford Lough, County Down

Northern Ireland is famed for its outstanding natural beauty and remarkable diversity of landscape. The scenery is spectacular, ranging from the granite peaks of the Mourne Mountains and the bizarre shapes of the basalt columns of the Giant's Causeway, to the drumlin landscape of Strangford Lough and the haunting Fermanagh lakeland. With miles and miles of beautiful coastline, spectacular landscapes and panoramic views, Northern Ireland has a wealth of treasures to share.

Enjoy the majesty of Down
Visit the wildly beautiful Strangford Lough, Britain's largest sea inlet and one of Europe's key wildlife habitats, and discover its tidal treasures. The rock pools brim with marine life and there is some of the best birdwatching in the UK and Ireland. Or take a bracing coastal walk and spot delicate wild flowers as well as numerous varieties of butterflies.

Right:
**White Park Bay,
County Antrim**
Far right:
**Rathlin Island,
off the coast of
County Antrim**

Explore Slieve Donard
and neighbouring Slieve
Commedagh in the Mourne
Mountains, and follow the
intriguingly named Brandy
Pad – an ancient smugglers'
route which runs from the
shore deep into the heart of
the mountains.

Enjoy the circular walk to
Port Kelly, Barhall Bay and
Barhall Hill at Ballyquintin on
the southern tip of the Ards
Peninsula. Here you will find
yourself surrounded by the
Irish Sea, with views in
every direction.

On the Irish Sea coast of
the Ards Peninsula, a long
narrow road runs through
green drumlins to the sandy
beach of Knockinelder and the
charming village of Kearney,
where a choice of attractive
walks start at the little cluster
of 14 cottages. Meanwhile the
wilder Ballymacormick Point,
with its gorse scrub, shingle
beaches, rocky islets and
coves, offers an escape from
the crowds.

Marvel at the Antrim coast
For quiet relaxation, stroll
along the spectacular sandy
beach at White Park Bay. A
beautiful white arc running
between two headlands, this
idyllic beach is backed by
ancient dunes, which provide
a range of rich habitats for
birds, mammals and plants.

Set on a wonderful stretch of
coastline on the Islandmagee
Peninsula, Portmuck and
Skernaghan Point offer
spectacular views over
Muck Island towards
Scotland. This is a Site of
Special Scientific Interest
and has some of Northern
Ireland's largest colonies of
cliff-nesting seabirds.

Look out for the impressive
30-foot waterfall in a deep
gorge in the small village of
Glenoe. Or visit Cushendun,
a charming historic village of
immense character which has
numerous folk tales associated
with it. There is also a circular
walking trail which boasts the
most breathtaking scenery.

Murlough Bay and Fair Head
is an idyllic corner of County
Antrim. The sheer cliffs of Fair
Head rise 600 feet above sea
level (in fact it is Northern
Ireland's tallest cliff face) and
contrast strongly with the lush
green slopes of Murlough Bay.

Rathlin is a peaceful and
beautiful island with a
distinctive landscape and

way of life. The land at
Ballyconagan is a mosaic of
heaths, grasslands, mires and
ponds, and offers fabulous
walks and birdwatching.

Seek out gems in the city
Close to the city yet at the
same time in the heart of the
country – that's the paradox
of Minnowburn. Riverbank,
meadow and woodland walks
link the landmarks of Shaw's
Bridge and the Giant's Ring,
while the Terrace Hill rose
garden has glorious views
across the Lagan Valley.

Cregagh Glen and Lisnabreeny
is an easily overlooked haven
in the heart of Belfast. Climb
up alongside a tumbling
stream through mixed
woodland and farmland, and
you will find magnificent views
across Belfast Lough, Lagan
Valley, Strangford Lough and
the Ards Peninsula.

Meanwhile, tucked away in the
heart of West Belfast, between
Collin Hill and Black Mountain,
is the wonderful Collin Glen.
Look out for the impressive
carpets of bluebells in spring.

Explore the rolling hills of mid-Ulster

The mixed woodland of Ballymoyer has the atmosphere and mystery of a fairy glen. Surrounded by the wild and dramatic scenery of the Fews Mountains, it was once the haunt of robbers and highwaymen.

Tiny Coney Island in Lough Neagh is only 2.8 hectares (seven acres) and it is believed there have been people here since 8000BC. Originally connected to the mainland by a causeway, which can be easily seen in summer when it is under less than two feet of water, the island is notable for its variety of bats.

Further information

Euro notes are accepted by the Trust's Northern Ireland places.

Under the Ulster Gardens Scheme, a number of private gardens are generously opened to the public to provide income for Trust gardens in Northern Ireland. For the 2012 programme telephone 028 9751 0721.

To find out what is happening in Northern Ireland this year, see our 2012 *Events Guide*.

Left: **walking on the clifftop at the Downhill Demesne, County Londonderry**

Why not try...?

Losing yourself outdoors
With more than 120 miles of coastline and 40 square miles of scenic countryside in our care in Northern Ireland, we've got a world of outdoors waiting to be explored and enjoyed.

Putting your best foot forward
You don't have to be an expert to go walking, and we cater for a wide range of abilities and experience, offering everything from short circular routes to more challenging hill walks. With more than 35 accredited 'Quality Walks' across Northern Ireland (assessed by the Countryside Access and Activities Network, Northern Ireland Tourist Board and Northern Ireland Environment Agency) there's a walking trail to suit everyone. For more information visit **www.walkni.com**

Pedal power
Hire a bike at Florence Court through our partners Wildflower Bike Hire and see parts of this lovely place that you would probably never venture to on foot. While at Castle Ward, the new cycle trails are about 12 miles long and run through atmospheric woodlands and around the boundary walls of Castle Ward demesne. A wide range of bicycles is available for hire, including tandems and wheelchair tandem bicycles – unique in Ireland.

A night under the stars
Our camping and touring sites are located in some of the most beautiful areas of Northern Ireland and are a great base from which to explore nearby Trust coast and countryside or built places. The camping and caravan park at Castle Ward, for example, is in a secluded location on the shores of Strangford Lough, while the breathtaking Crom demesne is set amid the romantic and tranquil landscape of Upper Lough Erne. Alternatively, experience the charming spirit of Springhill, with its walled garden and parklands, full of tempting paths and trails.

So what are you waiting for – let's go outdoors!

Ardress House

64 Ardress Road, Annaghmore, Portadown,
County Armagh BT62 1SQ

Map (7) D7   1959

This charming 17th-century farmhouse, elegantly remodelled in Georgian times, offers fun and relaxation for all the family. Set in 40 hectares (100 acres) of countryside, there are apple orchards and beautiful woodland walks. The atmosphere of a working farmyard has been rekindled with the return of small animals.

Exploring – Enjoy 'The Ladies' Mile' walk through trees and shrubs.
– Children will love feeding the chickens in the farmyard.
– Attractive garden, with scenic woodland walks.
– Elegant Neo-classical drawing room, with plasterwork by Michael Stapleton.

Eating and shopping: drinks and ice-cream available. Picnic in the attractive garden and charming woodlands.

Making the most of your day: see miniature Shetland ponies, pygmy goats, Soay sheep, ducks and chickens. Events include Country Capers and Ghostly Hallowe'en. Children's play area. **Dogs**: on leads in garden only.

Access for all: [WC] Building [stairs][access] Grounds [access]➡

Getting here: H914561. Portadown 7 miles.
Bus: Portadown to Tullyroan Bridge (passing close Portadown ▣), to within ¼ mile.
Train: Portadown 7 miles. **Parking**: free, 10 yards.

Finding out more: 028 8778 4753 or ardress@nationaltrust.org.uk

Ardress House		M	T	W	T	F	S	S
Farmyard and house								
11 Feb–12 Feb	12–5						S	S
10 Mar–30 Jun.	1–6						S	S
6 Apr–15 Apr	1–6	M	T	W	T	F	S	S
1 Jul–31 Aug	1–6				T	F	S	S
1 Sep–30 Sep	1–6						S	S
Lady's Mile Walk								
Open all year	Dawn–dusk	M	T	W	T	F	S	S

House: admission by guided tour (last admission one hour before closing). Open Bank Holiday Mondays and all other public holidays in Northern Ireland **including 17 March.**

The Argory

144 Derrycaw Road, Moy, Dungannon,
County Armagh BT71 6NA

Map (7) C7   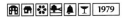 1979

Built in the 1820s, this handsome Irish gentry house is surrounded by its 130-hectare (320-acre) wooded riverside estate. The former home of the MacGeough Bond family, a tour of this Neo-classical masterpiece reveals it is unchanged since 1900 – the eclectic interior still evoking the family's tastes and interests. Outside there are sweeping vistas, superb spring bulbs, scenic walks and fascinating courtyard displays. A gift shop, second-hand bookshop, adventure playground and award-winning tea-room provide retreats for children and adults alike.

Exploring – Garden, woodland and riverside walks with wonderful sweeping views.
– Snowdrop walks and superb spring bulbs.

The Argory, County Armagh: this Neo-classical masterpiece remains unchanged since 1900

www.nationaltrust.org.uk

Exploring – Discover the rejuvenated walled garden and its produce.
– Children's adventure playground and play areas.
– House is a treasure trove of Victorian and Edwardian interests.
– Hear stories of Captain Shelton's heroism at sea.

Eating and shopping: enjoy afternoon tea in Lady Ada's tea-room. Light lunches and snacks available. Browse the gift shop and second-hand bookshop.

Making the most of your day: lively programme of events – craft fairs, children's events, musical events. The house is a particular delight at Christmas. **Dogs**: on leads in grounds and garden only.

Access for all: ⬚⬚⬚⬚ Grounds ⬚⬚

Getting here: H871577. 4 miles from Charlemont. **Cycle**: NCN95, 7 miles. **Bus**: Portadown to Dungannon (passing close Portadown ≋), alight Charlemont, 2½-mile walk. **Road**: 3 miles from M1, exit 13 or 14 (signposted). Coaches must use exit 13; weight restrictions at Bond's Bridge. **Parking**: 100 yards.

Finding out more: 028 8778 4753 or argory@nationaltrust.org.uk

The Argory		M	T	W	T	F	S	S
Grounds								
1 Jan–29 Feb	10–4	M	T	W	T	F	S	S
1 Mar–30 Apr	10–5	M	T	W	T	F	S	S
1 May–30 Sep	10–6	M	T	W	T	F	S	S
1 Oct–31 Oct	10–5	M	T	W	T	F	S	S
1 Nov–31 Dec	10–4	M	T	W	T	F	S	S
House								
10 Mar–30 Jun	12–5	·	·	W	T	F	S	S
6 Apr–15 Apr	12–5	M	T	W	T	F	S	S
1 Jul–31 Aug	12–5	M	T	W	T	F	S	S
1 Sep–30 Sep	12–5	·	·	W	T	F	S	S
6 Oct–28 Oct	12–4	·	·	·	·	·	S	S

Admission to house by guided tour (last admission one hour before closing). Open Bank Holiday Mondays and all other public holidays in Northern Ireland, **including 17 March**. Tea-room, shop and bookshop open as house, and also 27 to 31 December (when house not open). February snowdrop walks: weekends 11 to 4 (house not open). Closed 25 and 26 December.

Carrick-a-Rede

119a Whitepark Road, Ballintoy,
County Antrim BT54 6LS

Map ⑦ D3   ⬚⬚⬚ | 1967 |

Take the exhilarating rope bridge to Carrick-a-Rede island and enjoy a truly unique clifftop experience. This 30-metre deep and 20-metre wide chasm is traversed by a rope bridge traditionally erected by salmon fishermen. Visitors bold enough to cross to the rocky island are rewarded with fantastic views. **Note**: maximum of eight people on bridge at once. Suitable clothing and footwear recommended.

Exploring – Fantastic birdwatching and unrivalled coastal scenery.
– Uninterrupted views of Rathlin and the Scottish islands.
– Site of Special Scientific Interest: unique geology, flora and fauna.
– Stay in Carrick-a-Rede holiday cottage.

Eating and shopping: the Weighbridge tea-room and gift shop offers a delicious array of light lunches, snacks and sweets; including wonderful gifts and souvenirs.

Making the most of your day: guided tours (by prior arrangement). Breathtaking coastal path experience – part of the Causeway Coast Way from Portstewart to Ballycastle and the Ulster Way. **Dogs**: on leads (not permitted to cross bridge).

Access for all: ⬚⬚⬚⬚⬚
Grounds ⬚⬚⬚

Getting here: D049446. 5 miles from Ballycastle, ½ mile from Ballintoy village. **Foot**: North Antrim Coastal Path and road. **Cycle**: NCN93. **Bus**: services from Coleraine and Belfast. **Road**: on B15, 7 miles from Bushmills and Giant's Causeway. **Parking**: free.

Finding out more: 028 2076 9839 or
carrickarede@nationaltrust.org.uk

Carrick-a-Rede		M	T	W	T	F	S	S
Bridge								
1 Jan–26 Feb	10:30–3:30	M	T	W	T	F	S	S
27 Feb–27 May	10–6	M	T	W	T	F	S	S
28 May–2 Sep	10–7	M	T	W	T	F	S	S
3 Sep–28 Oct	10–6	M	T	W	T	F	S	S
29 Oct–31 Dec	10:30–3:30	M	T	W	T	F	S	S

Last entry to rope bridge 45 minutes before closing. Car park and North Antrim Coastal Path open all year. Bridge open weather permitting. Closed 25 and 26 December.

Castle Coole

Enniskillen, County Fermanagh BT74 6JY

Map A7    1951

Castle Coole, County Fermanagh: stately grandeur

Experience the stately grandeur of this stunning 18th-century mansion set in a beautiful wooded landscape park – which is ideal for family walks. Castle Coole is one of Ireland's finest Neo-classical houses: the sumptuous Regency interior and the State Bedroom prepared for George IV provide a rare treat for visitors, allowing them to glimpse what life was like in the home of the Earls of Belmore. Discover the story of the people who lived and worked below stairs as you explore the extensive basement. Celebrate our Diamond Anniversary with a variety of themed events throughout the year.

Exploring
– Tour one of Ireland's finest Neo-classical houses.
– Take a guided tour of the historic basement.
– Enjoy a walk in the historic landscape and woodlands.
– Explore the Grand Yard and see the Belmore Coach.
– Discover the wildlife that lives in and around Lough Coole.
– Attend one of our Diamond Anniversary celebration events.

Eating and shopping: relax and unwind over lunch in the Tallow tea-room. Souvenirs and gifts can be purchased in the shop.

Making the most of your day: enjoy a stroll around the Lake Walk, with breathtaking views and the opportunity to catch a glimpse of the vast variety of wildlife. Musical events throughout the year. **Dogs**: on leads in grounds only.

Access for all: 🅿🅳♿🚻🔼📷
Building 🔼♿🔼 Grounds ♿➡

Getting here: H245431. 1½ miles south-east of Enniskillen. **Cycle**: NCN91. **Bus**: Enniskillen to Clones (connections from Belfast). **Road**: on Belfast to Enniskillen road (A4). **Parking**: walkers' car park. Main car park, 150 yards.

Finding out more: 028 6632 2690 or castlecoole@nationaltrust.org.uk

Castle Coole		M	T	W	T	F	S	S
Grounds								
1 Jan–29 Feb	10–4	M	T	W	T	F	S	S
1 Mar–31 Oct	10–7	M	T	W	T	F	S	S
1 Nov–31 Dec	10–4	M	T	W	T	F	S	S
House, tea-room and shop								
10 Mar–27 May	11–5	·	·	·	·	·	S	S
6 Apr–15 Apr	11–5	M	T	W	T	F	S	S
1 Jun–31 Aug	11–5	M	T	W	T	F	S	S
1 Sep–30 Sep	11–5	·	·	·	·	·	S	S

House: admission by guided tour (last tour one hour before closing). Open Bank Holiday Mondays and all other public holidays in Northern Ireland **including 17 March**.

Castle Ward

Strangford, Downpatrick,
County Down BT30 7LS

Map (7) F7

'The glorious view from the Gothic terrace overlooking Strangford Lough is something I will always remember.'
John and Caroline Sullivan,
Westcliff-on-Sea, Essex

Sitting boldly on rolling hillside overlooking Strangford Lough, the magnificent, eccentric 18th-century house oozes personality, boasting two very different styles of façade – one classical and the other Gothic. History meets recreation throughout the 332-hectare (820-acre) walled demesne. A 16th-century tower-house stands firmly in the farmyard, while the working cornmill is a fine example of Irish industrial heritage, and the exotic garden and 21 miles of walking, cycling and equestrian trails through woodlands and along the lough shore are exceptional. An impressive laundry, tack room, children's Victorian play centre, gift shop, second-hand bookshop and tea-room complete the picture. **Note**: 1 March to 30 November visitor access to livestock grazing areas may be restricted.

Exploring
- Hire a bicycle and explore the miles of new trails.
- Indulge in cream teas in Lord Bangor's sitting room.
- Relax in the stableyard with a coffee and a book.
- Compare the two architecturally different façades of the house.
- Attempt the 'mega slide' in the adventure playground.
- Visit the barn and children's Victorian indoor play area.

Why not visit us on foot or by public transport? See pages 10 and 380

Eating and shopping: local produce and Castle Ward giftware available from our gift shop. Bargain buys can be found in the bookshop. The stableyard tea-room has a family menu with homemade cakes. A stay in our caravan park will complete your visit.

Making the most of your day: variety of events throughout the year, including Pirate's Picnic, Pumpkinfest, Turkey Trot Fun Run, Book Fair and Santa's House. Children can explore with Tracker Packs. Guided house tours. **Dogs**: on leads in grounds only. Livestock grazing areas out of bounds.

Access for all: [icons]
Building [icons] Grounds [icons]

Getting here: J573484. 7 miles north-east of Downpatrick. **Foot**: on Lecale Way. **Ferry**: from Portaferry. **Bus**: Downpatrick to Strangford, bus stop at gates. Summer bus service weekends only. **Road**: 1 mile from Strangford on A25. **Sat Nav**: follow signs for Castle Ward only. **Parking**: free.

Finding out more: 028 4488 1204 or castleward@nationaltrust.org.uk

Castle Ward		M	T	W	T	F	S	S
Parkland, woodland and garden								
1 Jan–31 Mar	10–4	M	T	W	T	F	S	S
1 Apr–30 Sep	10–8	M	T	W	T	F	S	S
1 Oct–31 Oct	10–5	M	T	W	T	F	S	S
1 Nov–31 Dec	10–4	M	T	W	T	F	S	S
House, laundry, pastimes centre, tea-room and gift shop								
10 Mar–31 Oct	11–5	M	T	W	T	F	S	S
Second-hand bookshop								
10 Mar–31 Oct	12–5	M	T	W	T	F	S	S
The Barn								
31 Mar–22 Apr	12–5	M	T	W	T	F	S	S
5 May–27 May	12–5						S	S
30 Jun–2 Sep	12–5	M	T	W	T	F	S	S
Trailhead and refreshments								
10 Mar–31 Oct	10–5	M	T	W	T	F	S	S

Last admission to house one hour before closing. Timed tickets apply to guided house tours. Open Bank Holiday Mondays and all other public holidays in Northern Ireland **including 17 March**. The Barn is open throughout the year when primary schools are closed. The cornmill operates on Sundays from Easter to September, 2 to 5. Tea-room and shop also open 27 to 31 December.

The magnificent and eccentric Castle Ward in County Down

Crom

Upper Lough Erne, Newtownbutler, County Fermanagh BT92 8AP

Map ⑦ A8 [icons] 1987

Escape to this breathtaking 810-hectare (2,000-acre) demesne, set amid the romantic and tranquil landscape of Upper Lough Erne. One of Ireland's most important nature conservation areas, Crom's ancient woodland and picturesque islands are home to many rare species. Stay for longer at one of our holiday cottages or campsite. **Note**: the 19th-century castle is private and not open to the public.

Lough Erne at Crom, County Fermanagh

Exploring — Hire a boat and explore the islands.
— Look out for wildlife from our bird hide.
— Enjoy woodland walks and nature trails.
— Have a go at coarse angling or pike fishing.

Eating and shopping: treat yourself to afternoon tea in the visitor centre, then browse through the many gifts and souvenirs.

Making the most of your day: regular guided walks by our conservation warden. Visit the historic castle ruins. Enjoy a Cot Trip on Bank Holiday Mondays. **Dogs**: on leads only.

Access for all:
Building 🦽♿ Grounds 🦽➡️💺

Getting here: H380255. 3 miles west of Newtownbutler. **Cycle**: NCN91. **Ferry**: from Derryvore church (must be booked 24 hours in advance). **Bus**: Enniskillen to Clones (connections from Belfast), alight Newtownbutler, 3 miles. **Road**: on Newtownbutler to Crom road, or follow signs from Lisnaskea (7 miles). Crom is next to the Shannon to Erne waterway. Public jetty at visitor centre. **Parking**: 100 yards.

Finding out more: 028 6773 8118 or crom@nationaltrust.org.uk

Crom		M	T	W	T	F	S	S
Grounds								
10 Mar–31 May	10–6	M	T	W	T	F	S	S
1 Jun–31 Aug	10–7	M	T	W	T	F	S	S
1 Sep–31 Oct	10–6	M	T	W	T	F	S	S
Visitor centre								
10 Mar–30 Sep	11–5	M	T	W	T	F	S	S
6 Oct–28 Oct	11–5						S	S

Open Bank Holiday Mondays and all other public holidays in Northern Ireland **including 17 March**. Last admission one hour before closing. Tea-room open as visitor centre (closed October).

Derrymore House

Bessbrook, Newry,
County Armagh BT35 7EF

Map ⑦ D8

An elegant 18th-century thatched cottage with its peculiar gentrified vernacular style. A rich history and delightful walks. **Note**: no toilet.

Access for all: 🅿️ Grounds 🦽➡️

Getting here: J057275. 1½ miles from Newry, on A25 off the Newry to Camlough road at Bessbrook.

Finding out more: 028 8778 4753 or derrymore@nationaltrust.org.uk

Derrymore House	
Grounds	
Open every day all year from dawn to dusk	

Treaty Room open 7 May, 4 June, 12 and 13 July, plus 27 August, 2 to 5:30.

The Crown Bar

46 Great Victoria Street, Belfast,
County Antrim BT2 7BA

Map ⑦ E6 🏛️♿ 1978

Wonderful atmospheric setting, with period gas lighting and cosy snugs. Ornate interior of brightly coloured tiles, carvings and glass. **Note**: run by Mitchells and Butlers.

Getting here: J336737. In the centre of Belfast, on Great Victoria Street.

Finding out more: 028 9024 3187 or info@crownbar.com

The Crown Bar		M	T	W	T	F	S	S
1 Jan–30 Dec	12:30–10							S
2 Jan–31 Dec	11:30–11	M	T	W	T	F	S	

Closed on some Bank and public holidays (telephone 028 9024 3187 for details).

Divis and the Black Mountain

Divis Road, Hannahstown, near Belfast,
County Antrim BT17 0NG

Map ⑦ E6

The mountains rest in the heart of the Belfast Hills, which provide the backdrop to the city's skyline, while the rich, varied archaeological landscape is home to a host of wildlife. There are walking trails along a variety of terrain – through heath, on stone tracks, along boardwalks and road surface. **Note**: cattle roam freely during summer months.

Exploring – Panoramic views across Northern Ireland, Donegal and Scotland.

Looking towards Divis Mountain, County Antrim

Exploring – Home to a wealth of flora, fauna and archaeological remains.
– Fantastic viewpoint for Hallowe'en firework displays.
– Ten-mile trail – Divis Mountain to Lady Dixon Park.

Eating and shopping: tea and coffee available in the Long Barn.

Making the most of your day: a haven for those seeking the wild countryside experience. Programme of guided walks to discover the wealth of biodiversity and archaeological remains. 'Changing Places' toilet and accessible toilets available. **Dogs**: welcome but please note cattle roam freely during summer.

Access for all: ⛶ 🚻 ♿ 🅿️ ♿
Visitor centre ♿ Mountain ♿

Getting here: J266741. 1 mile west of Belfast. **Bus**: alight at Divis Road. **Road**: minor road west of A55. **Parking**: free.

Finding out more: 028 9082 5434 or divis@nationaltrust.org.uk

Divis and the Black Mountain	Open every day all year
Car park open 9 to 8.	

Downhill Demesne and Hezlett House

Mussenden Road, Castlerock,
County Londonderry BT51 4RP

Map ⑦ C3

Visit the stunning landscape of Downhill Demesne, with its beautiful gardens and magnificent clifftop walks, affording rugged headland views across the awe-inspiring North Coast. Discover the striking 18th-century mansion of the eccentric Earl Bishop that now lies in ruin, then explore Mussenden Temple, perched on the cliff edge. As an extra treat you can learn about the reality of life in the rural 17th-century cottage of Hezlett House, told through the people who once lived in one of Northern Ireland's oldest surviving buildings.

Exploring – Enjoy a stroll around the inspiring gardens.
– Take in the panoramic views from Mussenden Temple.
– Children's Tracker Packs – include binoculars, compass and bird identification cards.
– Visit the garden restoration project at the Bishop's Gate.
– Take part in the archaeology project at Downhill Demesne.

Whitewashed Hezlett House, County Londonderry

Pretty Mussenden Temple, County Londonderry

Exploring – Hezlett House is also home to the Downhill Marbles Collection.

Eating and shopping: tea and coffee facilities offered at reception of Hezlett House. Perfect for a picnic in the sheltered gardens.

Making the most of your day: programme of events. Beautiful orchard to explore at Hezlett House. **Dogs**: on leads only.

Access for all: [P&] [WC] Building [♿] Grounds [♿]

Getting here: C757357. 1 mile west of Castlerock. **Cycle**: NCN93. **Ferry**: Magilligan to Greencastle ferry (8 miles). **Bus**: Coleraine to Londonderry. **Train**: Castlerock ½ mile. **Road**: 1 mile from Castlerock and 5 miles from Coleraine (A2). **Parking**: at Lion's Gate. Coach parking at Bishop's Gate entrance or Hezlett House.

Finding out more: 028 7084 8728 or downhilldemesne@nationaltrust.org.uk. 107 Sea Road, Castlerock, County Londonderry BT51 4TW

Downhill and Hezlett	M	T	W	T	F	S	S
Downhill Demesne grounds							
Open all year	M	T	W	T	F	S	S
Hezlett House and facilities							
24 Mar–30 Sep 10–5	M	T	W	T	F	S	S

Florence Court

Enniskillen, County Fermanagh BT92 1DB

Map (7) A7  1954

There is something for all the family at this warm and welcoming 18th-century property, the former home of the Earls of Enniskillen. The house enjoys a peaceful setting in West Fermanagh, with a dramatic backdrop of mountains and forests. This classical Irish house is brought to life on fascinating guided tours. Outside there are glorious walks to enjoy in the estate and numerous places to explore, including the icehouse, sawmill and charming walled garden. Don't miss the Rock Hound Room, where children can enjoy activities based around the 3rd Earl's fossil collection.

Exploring – Take a guided tour of this fine 18th-century house.
– Enjoy spectacular views and discover flora and fauna.
– Visit the mother tree to all Irish yews.
– Have a browse in the second-hand bookshop.
– Discover the kitchen garden project in the walled garden.
– Relax in the summerhouse, overlooking the pleasure grounds.

Eating and shopping: enjoy homemade delights in the Stables restaurant. The Coach House shop offers an excellent range of gifts.

Making the most of your day: range of events throughout the year. Children's Tracker Packs available. Licensed civil wedding venue, with a number of historic rooms to hire for that special occasion. **Dogs**: on leads in garden and grounds only.

Access for all: [P&] [D&] [WC] [♿] [♿] [♿] [□] [•••] [Ⓐ] Building [♿] [♿] [♿] Grounds [♿] [➡] [♿]

Getting here: H176349. 8 miles south-west of Enniskillen. **Cycle**: NCN91. Entrance on Kingfisher Trail. **Bus**: Enniskillen to Swanlinbar, alight Creamery Cross, 2-mile walk.

Giant's Causeway

44 Causeway Road, Bushmills,
County Antrim BT57 8SU

Map (7) D3   1962

Northern Ireland's iconic World Heritage Site and Area of Outstanding Natural Beauty is home to a wealth of local history and legend. Explore the basalt stone columns left by volcanic eruptions 60 million years ago and search for distinctive stone formations fancifully named the Camel, Harp and Organ. **Note**: the new Giant's Causeway Visitor Experience opens this summer.

Florence Court, County Fermanagh: Georgian charm

Road: by A4 Sligo road and A32 Swanlinbar road, 4 miles from Marble Arch Caves.
Parking: 200 yards.

Finding out more: 028 6634 8249 or florencecourt@nationaltrust.org.uk

Florence Court		M	T	W	T	F	S	S
Gardens and park								
1 Jan–29 Feb	10–4	M	T	W	T	F	S	S
1 Mar–31 Oct	10–7	M	T	W	T	F	S	S
1 Nov–31 Dec	10–4	M	T	W	T	F	S	S
House, tea-room and shop								
10 Mar–29 Apr	11–5	·	·	·	·	·	S	S
6 Apr–15 Apr	11–5	M	T	W	T	F	S	S
1 May–31 May	11–5	M	T	W	T	·	S	S
1 Jun–31 Aug	11–5	M	T	W	T	F	S	S
1 Sep–30 Sep	11–5	M	T	W	T	·	S	S
6 Oct–28 Oct	11–5	·	·	·	·	·	S	S

House: admission by guided tour (last admission one hour before closing). Open Bank Holiday Mondays and all other public holidays in Northern Ireland **including 17 March**. Open Irish Bank Holiday 29 October. Gardens and park, Colonel's Room, tea-room and gift shop also open 27 to 31 December.

Exploring – Beautiful coastal path extends 11 miles to Carrick-a-Rede Rope Bridge.
– Geology, flora and fauna of international importance.
– Runkerry Head provides a spectacular two-mile walk.
– Some of Europe's finest cliff scenery, with fantastic birdwatching.

Eating and shopping: during building works for the new visitor facility, temporary facilities are available at the Causeway Hotel, including retail outlet and tourist information. New visitor facilities open this summer, including a café, shop and tourist information.

Making the most of your day: open for walking all year, with stunning coast and cliff paths for exploration. Finn MacCool's Causeway is steeped in legend and folklore. **Dogs**: on leads only.

Access for all: ⟨wc⟩ ⟨⟩ Grounds 🦽🏔️➡️

Getting here: C944439. 2 miles from Bushmills. **Foot**: Causeway Coast Way. **Cycle**: NCN93. **Bus**: services from Coleraine and Belfast. **Train**: from Belfast and Londonderry to Coleraine or Portrush (onward via bus). **Road**: on B146. **Parking**: limited. Park and ride at Bushmills.

Finding out more: 028 2073 1855
(Tourist Information) or
giantscauseway@nationaltrust.org.uk

Giant's Causeway		M	T	W	T	F	S	S
Stones and coastal path								
Open all year		M	T	W	T	F	S	S
Visitor information and shop								
1 Jan–29 Feb	9:30–4	M	T	W	T	F	S	S
1 Mar–31 May	9:30–5	M	T	W	T	F	S	S
1 Jun–30 Jun	9:30–6	M	T	W	T	F	S	S

New Giant's Causeway Visitor Experience offering
state-of-the-art interpretation and facilities opens in
the summer. During the construction period, limited
temporary visitor facilities – including tourist information,
shop, catering and toilets – are available at adjoining
Causeway Hotel. For information and opening times
from June visit www.nationaltrust.org.uk or telephone
028 2073 1855. Closed 24, 25 and 26 December.

**Sunset at the Giant's Causeway,
County Antrim: this iconic World
Heritage Site, with its intriguing
basalt stone columns, is home to a
wealth of local history and legend**

Gray's Printing Press

49 Main Street, Strabane,
County Tyrone BT82 8AU

Map ⑦ B5   🏠 ⬇T 1966

A treasure trove of galleys, ink and presses
hidden behind an 18th-century shop front in
the heart of Strabane.

Access for all: ♿ 🅿 Building 👟 ♿

Getting here: H345976. On Main Street,
Strabane.

Finding out more: 028 8674 8210 or
grays@nationaltrust.org.uk

Gray's Printing Press

Press Room: open 4 June, 4, 12 and 13 July, plus 27 August,
2 to 5:30. Also open for booked tours (minimum 15 people;
must be booked one week ahead).

Mount Stewart House, Garden and Temple of the Winds

Portaferry Road, Newtownards,
County Down BT22 2AD

Map ⑦ F6  1976

Mount Stewart is one of the most unique and unusual gardens in the National Trust's ownership. The garden reflects a rich tapestry of design and great planting artistry that was the hallmark of Edith, Lady Londonderry. The mild climate of Strangford Lough allows astonishing levels of planting experimentation. The formal areas exude a strong Mediterranean feel and resemble an Italian villa landscape; the wooded areas support a range of plants from all corners of the world, ensuring something to see whatever the season. Engaging tours of the opulent house reveal its fascinating heritage and historic world-famous artefacts and artwork. Note: a major conservation project starts this year – house will remain open.

Exploring – Explore garden rooms recreated using diaries of Edith, Lady Londonderry.

Exploring – Discover the fascinating history of Mount Stewart mansion.
– Magnificent views of Strangford Lough from Temple of the Winds.
– Follow in footsteps of kings, queens, Prime Ministers and poets.
– Picturesque lake surrounded by beautiful swathes of woodland.
– Dinosaurs and duck-billed platypuses jostle on Dodo Terrace.

Eating and shopping: buy the best of local craft products in our shop. Visit our plant shop, a haven for gardeners, and buy a plant grown at Mount Stewart. Enjoy a meal in our award-winning Bay Restaurant and taste unique Mount Stewart ice-cream.

Making the most of your day: programme of events, including jazz in the garden, craft fairs, guided walks, garden tours, children's events and Santa's Grotto. Family activity packs also available. **Dogs**: on leads in grounds and garden only.

Access for all: [symbols]
Building [symbols] Grounds [symbols]

Mount Stewart House, Garden and Temple of the Winds, County Down: looking across the Italian Garden

Getting here: J555694. 5 miles south-east of Newtownards. **Bus**: Belfast to Portaferry, alight at gates. **Train**: Bangor 10 miles. **Road**: on Newtownards to Portaferry road, A20, 15 miles south-east of Belfast. **Parking**: free, 100 yards.

Finding out more: 028 4278 8387 or mountstewart@nationaltrust.org.uk

Mount Stewart		M	T	W	T	F	S	S
House								
10 Mar–4 Nov	12–6	M	T	W	T	F	S	S
Formal gardens								
10 Mar–4 Nov	10–6	M	T	W	T	F	S	S
Lakeside gardens								
1 Jan–9 Mar	10–4	M	T	W	T	F	S	S
10 Mar–4 Nov	10–6	M	T	W	T	F	S	S
5 Nov–31 Dec	10–4	M	T	W	T	F	S	S
Temple of the Winds								
11 Mar–4 Nov	2–5	·	·	·	·	·	·	S

Open Bank Holiday Mondays and all other public holidays in Northern Ireland **including 17 March**. House: admission by guided tour (timed tickets only) and free-flow on Bank and public holidays. Last admission to house and gardens one hour before closing. Lakeside gardens closed 25 and 26 December. Telephone for shop and restaurant opening times.

Murlough National Nature Reserve, County Down

Murlough National Nature Reserve

Keel Point, Dundrum, County Down BT33 0NQ

Map (7) E8  1967

Murlough is an extraordinarily beautiful dune landscape, fringing one of Northern Ireland's most popular beaches and overlooked by the rounded peaks of the Mourne Mountains to the south. The fragile 6,000-year-old sand dunes, Ireland's first nature reserve, are an excellent area for walking and wildlife. **Note**: limited toilet facilities.

Exploring   – Most extensive example of dune heath within Ireland.
            – Over 330 species of butterflies and moths, including marsh fritillary.
            – Dune flowers, common and grey seals, wintering wildfowl and waders.

Exploring   – Evidence of human habitation from Neolithic times to present day.

Eating and shopping: enjoy a latte in the beach café. Picnics in the car park or on the beach.

Making the most of your day: explore the network of paths and boardwalks through the dunes, woodland and heath. Self-guided nature walk, series of guided walks, volunteer events and family activities throughout the year. **Dogs**: welcome, restrictions apply when ground-nesting birds are breeding or cattle are grazing.

Access for all: 🏻

Getting here: J401350. 1 mile south of Dundrum village, 10 miles east of Downpatrick. **Foot**: from Dundrum, 1 mile, or Newcastle, 2-mile beach walk. **Cycle**: NCN99 passes entrance. **Bus**: Belfast to Newcastle, alight Lazy BJ Caravan Park (main entrance to reserve). **Road**: signposted off A2, between

    Members may have to pay on special events days

Dundrum and Newcastle. **Parking**: open all year, pay and display. Admission charge when facilities open.

Finding out more: 028 4375 1467 or murlough@nationaltrust.org.uk

Murlough		M	T	W	T	F	S	S
Facilities								
10 Mar–27 May	10–6	·	·	·	·	·	S	S
2 Apr–15 Apr	10–6	M	T	W	T	F	S	S
1 Jun–30 Sep	10–6	M	T	W	T	F	S	S
6 Oct–28 Oct	10–6	·	·	·	·	·	S	S
Nature reserve								
Open all year		M	T	W	T	F	S	S

Open Bank Holiday Mondays and all other public holidays in Northern Ireland **including 17 March**.

Access for all: 📇 🚻 ♿ 🚹
Building ♿ ♿ Grounds ♿

Getting here: J261854. 2 miles north-east of Templepatrick. **Bus**: services from Belfast to Cookstown, bus stop at gates. **Train**: Antrim 8 miles. **Road**: on Antrim to Belfast road, A6; M2 exit 4. **Parking**: free, 50 yards.

Finding out more: 028 9443 3619 or pattersons@nationaltrust.org.uk

Patterson's Spade Mill		M	T	W	T	F	S	S
6 Apr–15 Apr	11–4	M	T	W	T	F	S	S
21 Apr–27 May	11–4	·	·	·	·	·	S	S
2 Jun–30 Aug	11–4	M	T	W	T	·	S	S
1 Sep–30 Sep	11–4	·	·	·	·	·	S	S

Admission by guided tour. Open Bank Holiday Mondays and all other public holidays in Northern Ireland **including 17 March**. Last admission one hour before closing.

Patterson's Spade Mill

751 Antrim Road, Templepatrick, County Antrim BT39 0AP

Map ⑦ E6      1991

Hear the hammers, smell the grit and feel the heat of traditional spade-making. Guided tours vividly capture life during the Industrial Revolution and dig up the history and culture of the humble spade. Find the origin of the phrase 'a face as long as a Lurgan spade'.

Exploring
– Last working water-driven spade mill in the British Isles.
– See red-hot billets of steel fashioned into spades.
– Listen to the thunder of the massive water-powered trip hammer.
– Travel back in time to a bygone industrial era.

Eating and shopping: handcrafted spades on sale and made to specification. Tea and coffee available from drinks machine.

Making the most of your day: enjoy a 'Slippery feast' on St Patrick's Day and full steam ahead at the fascinating Stationary Engine Day. Guided tours and demonstrations for all the family with the Spade Maker.
Dogs: on leads only.

Spade-maker at Patterson's Spade Mill, County Antrim

Portstewart Strand

118 Strand Road, Portstewart,
County Londonderry BT55 7PG

Map ⑦ C3   🏖️🏕️🦆 | 1981 |

The magnificent two-mile strand of glistening golden sand is one of Northern Ireland's finest and most popular beaches with all ages. It is the perfect spot to spend lazy summer days and take long walks into the sand dunes, which are a haven for wild flowers and butterflies.

Exploring   –   Explore the magnificent sand dunes and waymarked nature trail.
     – Many species of butterflies and moths, and colourful wild flowers.
     – Visit the Barmouth bird hide for fantastic birdwatching.
     – Enjoy family picnics, building sandcastles and swimming.

Eating and shopping: beach toys and light refreshments are available in the visitor centre.

Making the most of your day: relax and enjoy the sea and sand, or meander through the dunes to see the wildlife – look out for the common blue butterfly, six-spot burnet moth and rare orchids. **Dogs**: on leads only.

Access for all: 🚾♿ Beach ➡️

Getting here: C811366. Just outside the centre of Portstewart. **Cycle**: NCN93 runs nearby. **Bus**: service from Coleraine (connections from Belfast route 218). **Train**: Coleraine. **Parking**: on beach.

Finding out more: 028 7083 6396 or portstewart@nationaltrust.org.uk

Portstewart Strand		M	T	W	T	F	S	S
Beach								
Open all year		M	T	W	T	F	S	S
Facilities								
25 Feb–1 Apr	10–4	M	T	W	T	F	S	S
2 Apr–29 Apr	10–5	M	T	W	T	F	S	S
30 Apr–3 Jun	10–6	M	T	W	T	F	S	S
4 Jun–2 Sep	10–7	M	T	W	T	F	S	S
3 Sep–30 Sep	10–5	M	T	W	T	F	S	S
1 Oct–28 Oct	10–4	M	T	W	T	F	S	S

2 April to 30 September: barrier closes two hours after facilities.

Portstewart Strand, County Londonderry: two miles of glorious golden sands

Rowallane Garden

Saintfield, County Down BT24 7LH

Map (7) E7 [emoji icons] 1956

Be inspired by this enchanting garden's dazzling array of exotic species from the four corners of the globe. Created in the mid-1860s by the Reverend John Moore, this informal plantsman's garden reflects the beautiful natural landscape of the surrounding area. There are spectacular displays of shrubs, including a large collection of rhododendron species, and several areas managed as wildflower meadows. It is also home to a notable natural Rock Garden Wood, with shade-loving plants. The outstanding walled garden includes spectacular displays of herbaceous plants, shrubs and bulbs.

Exploring
- Browse for gardening ideas in the newly opened garden shop.
- Watch the master potter at work in the Secret Garden.
- Take a tranquil walk around the famous Rock Garden Wood.
- Book a gardening tour with the Head Gardener.
- Discover exotic and rare species of rhododendron.
- Follow the farmland trail to the summit of Trio Hill.

Eating and shopping: pick up a bargain book from the second-hand bookshop. Purchase a unique Rowallane Garden glazed stoneware pot. Explore the garden shop for inspirational ideas. Due to enhancement of visitor facilities, tea-room unavailable early this year.

Making the most of your day: wide range of events, spring and autumn plant fair, Ghosts and Gourds and Yuletide market. Children's activity sheets available. **Dogs**: on leads in garden only.

Access for all: [icons] Grounds [icons]

Getting here: J412581. 1 mile south of Saintfield, 11 miles south-east of Belfast. **Bus**: Belfast to Downpatrick (passing Belfast Great Victoria Street ➔). **Road**: on Downpatrick road (A7). **Parking**: free.

Finding out more: 028 9751 0131 or rowallane@nationaltrust.org.uk

Rowallane Garden		M	T	W	T	F	S	S
1 Jan–29 Feb	10–4	M	T	W	T	F	S	S
1 Mar–30 Apr	10–6	M	T	W	T	F	S	S
1 May–31 Aug	10–8	M	T	W	T	F	S	S
1 Sep–31 Oct	10–6	M	T	W	T	F	S	S
1 Nov–31 Dec	10–4	M	T	W	T	F	S	S

Closed 25 and 26 December. Telephone 028 9751 2315 for shop and tea-room opening times.

Discovering Rowallane Garden, County Down

Springhill

20 Springhill Road, Moneymore, Magherafelt,
County Londonderry BT45 7NQ

Map (7) C6  1957

Eating and shopping: delicious cream teas in the Servants' Hall tea-room. Look for presents in our little gift shop. Select a book in our 'Well Read' bookshop. Enjoy a picnic in the garden.

Making the most of your day: meet the family from long ago, enjoy the walks and then relax in the Servants' Hall tea-room with a delicious cream tea of homemade scones and raspberry jam. **Dogs**: on leads in grounds only.

Experience the beguiling spirit of this inimitable 17th-century 'Plantation' home, with its walled gardens and parkland, full of tempting waymarked paths. Informative tours breathe life into the fascinating past of this welcoming family home. There are ten generations of Lenox-Conyngham family tales to enthral you, as well as numerous portraits and much furniture to admire – not forgetting Ireland's best-documented ghost, Olivia, and the family's maritime heritage with links to the *Titanic*. The old laundry houses the celebrated Costume Collection, which features some fine 18th- to 20th-century pieces that highlight its great charm and enthralling past.

Exploring
 – Captivating tours with intriguing links to world-famous ship, the *Titanic*.
 – Fun for all the family, with new trails for children.
 – Fascinating new costume exhibition every year.
 – Enjoy short walks around the charming estate.
 – Relax in the herb garden with a chamomile lawn.
 – Admire the 1,000-year-old yew tree.

Springhill, County Londonderry: 'Plantation' home with a beguiling spirit (and ghost)

Access for all: [symbols]
Building [symbols]

Getting here: H866828. 1 mile from Moneymore village. **Foot**: from Moneymore village, 1 mile. **Cycle**: NCN94/95, 5 miles. **Bus**: services from Belfast to Cookstown, alight Moneymore village, 1 mile. **Road**: on Moneymore to Coagh road, B18. **Parking**: 50 yards.

Finding out more: 028 8674 8210 or springhill@nationaltrust.org.uk

Springhill		M	T	W	T	F	S	S
Grounds								
Open all year	Dawn–dusk	M	T	W	T	F	S	S
House and costume collection								
10 Mar–30 Jun	12–5	·	·	·	T	F	S	S
6 Apr–15 Apr	12–5	M	T	W	T	F	S	S
1 Jul–31 Aug	12–5	M	T	W	T	F	S	S
1 Sep–30 Sep	12–4	·	·	·	·	·	S	S

House: admission by guided tour. Last admission one hour before closing. Open Bank Holiday Mondays and all other public holidays in Northern Ireland **including 17 March**. Tea-room open as house and also for snowdrop walks in February (Sundays only 12 to 4). Closed 25 December.

Places may occasionally close for conservation, safety or events

Wellbrook Beetling Mill

20 Wellbrook Road, Corkhill, Cookstown,
County Tyrone BT80 9RY

Map (7) C6   1968

Nestling in an idyllic wooded glen that offers lovely walks and picnic spots, this, the last working water-powered linen beetling mill, offers a unique experience for all the family. Try some scutching, hackling and weaving as you take part in hands-on demonstrations, set against the thundering cacophony of beetling engines.

Making the most of your day: tour the mill and find out about its history and historic linen-making processes. Experience Living History days. Walk up the head-race and then relax with a picnic on the lawn. **Dogs**: on leads in grounds only.

Access for all: 🅓 🔲 🔲 🔲 🔲
Building 🔲 🔲 Grounds 🔲 🔲

Getting here: H750792. 4 miles west of Cookstown. **Cycle**: NCN95. **Bus**: from Cookstown, with connections from Belfast, ½ mile. **Road**: ½ mile off Cookstown to Omagh road (A505): from Cookstown turn right at Kildress Church or follow Orritor Road (A53) to avoid the town. **Parking**: free, 10 yards.

Finding out more: 028 8675 1735 or wellbrook@nationaltrust.org.uk

Exploring
- Follow the head-race to the source of the power.
- Lovely walks and picnic opportunities by the Ballinderry River.
- Watch the massive water-powered wheel as it turns.
- Look out for pearl mussels in the mill race.

Eating and shopping: tea and coffee are available on request. Delicious afternoon teas on Living History days. Irish linen and gifts are for sale in the small cottage shop. Picnic tables near the river.

Wellbrook Beetling Mill, County Tyrone: still working

Wellbrook Beetling Mill		M	T	W	T	F	S	S
10 Mar–30 Jun	2–5						S	S
6 Apr–15 Apr	2–5	M	T	W	T	F	S	S
1 Jul–31 Aug	2–5				T	F	S	S
1 Sep–30 Sep	2–5						S	S

Admission by guided tour. Open Bank Holiday Mondays and all other public holidays in Northern Ireland **including 17 March**. Last admission one hour before closing. Telephone for shop opening arrangements.

Your visit

Welcoming families
We offer various facilities to help your visit run smoothly, as well as many activities and events to make your day with us truly memorable.

Facilities: parking is made easy and most places have baby-changing and baby-feeding areas – some also have parent and baby rooms. Restaurants and cafés have highchairs, children's menus, colouring sheets and some have play areas. Unfortunately it is usually difficult to accommodate prams and pushchairs, because they impede other visitors and can cause accidental damage. You may be asked to leave them at the entrance; however, front-carrying slings for smaller babies and hip-seat carriers or reins for toddlers are often available to borrow. We welcome baby back-carriers wherever we can, although where space is limited (and at very busy times) it may not be possible to admit them.

Activities: many places have guides, trails or quizzes for children and families, and we are trying to find ways to tell the stories of our places through more hands-on activities, such as Tracker Packs (bags packed with activities to do as you explore). These are free to borrow, although some places will require you to leave a deposit. Many sites have discovery activity rooms and play areas too. Visit **www. nationaltrust.org.uk/ familyactivities** for inspiring ideas, and we would love to hear how these places have helped you rekindle your childhood memories.

Shopping and eating
Every time you buy something in our shops, restaurants, tea-rooms and coffee shops, your purchase helps our work.

Shops: our many property-based shops offer a wide range of relevant merchandise, much of which is exclusive to the National Trust. We also have some 20 shops in towns and cities. Times vary, so please telephone for details if you are making a special journey. You can buy many National Trust gifts online at **www. nationaltrust.org.uk/shop**

Restaurants and tea-rooms: we open about 150 tea-rooms and cafés, which are often located in very special buildings, such as stable blocks or hothouses. There are many autumn, winter and Christmas events.

Dogs
We always try to provide facilities such as water, areas where dogs can be exercised and shady spaces in car parks (though dogs should not be left alone in cars). Dogs are welcome at most countryside places, where they should be kept under close control at all times. Please observe local notices on the need to keep dogs on leads, particularly at sensitive times of year, such as during the bird breeding season, at lambing time or when deer are calving. Dogs should be kept on a short lead on access land between 1 March and 31 July, and at any other time when near livestock.

In some areas, particularly on beaches, we have found it necessary to introduce restrictions, usually seasonal. Where access for dogs is restricted, we attempt to identify suitable alternative locations nearby.

Enjoying a day out at Clumber Park, Nottinghamshire

Please clear up dog mess and dispose of it responsibly. Where dog-waste bins are not provided, please take the waste away with you.

Learning

We welcome visitors from across the educational sector and from special interest groups. We recommend that teachers make a preliminary visit before they bring their group. This can be arranged free of charge. Frequent visitors will find it worthwhile to consider Educational Group Membership. For more information telephone 0844 800 1895.

Events

We offer a variety of events throughout the year, from wildflower walks, to family fun at Easter and Hallowe'en. There are live summer concerts, living history events, countryside open days and open-air theatre productions. Our lecture lunches and 'behind-the-scenes' tours explain the work of our gardeners and house staff, while our 'Conservation in Action' events provide opportunities for you to see conservation specialists at work and talk to them about their techniques. The year ends with Christmas craft fairs, carol concerts and winter walks.

For details telephone 0844 800 1895 or visit **www.nationaltrust.org.uk/ events**

Weddings and private functions

The bell and glass symbols at the top of entries indicate that the place is licensed for civil weddings (bell symbol) and/or available for private functions (glass symbol), such as wedding receptions, family celebrations and so on. For more information, contact the place, the Supporter Services Centre on 0844 800 1895 or visit **www.nationaltrust.org. uk/hiring**

Access Guide

We welcome all visitors to our properties. Most of our places have a good degree of access, and we are committed to developing and promoting inclusive access solutions that are creative and sensitive to the surroundings.

This *Handbook* provides just a brief indication of the access facilities at our places. More detailed information on access provision is available in our free *Access Guide*, which is available in both standard and large print, and can be downloaded from **www.nationaltrust.org.uk/accessforall**

The *Access Guide* can be obtained from our Supporter Services Centre. Telephone 0844 800 1895, email enquiries@nationaltrust.org.uk or write to FREEPOST NAT9775, Warrington WA5 7WD.

Both the *Access Guide* and *National Trust Magazine* are available free on CD or tape. If you would like to receive these regularly, please contact SoundTalking direct by emailing admin@soundtalking.co.uk or telephoning 01435 862737.

For details of our admission policy and how to obtain an Access for All Admit One Card for an essential companion, please see page 9.

Walk, cycle or drive

Walking

Long-distance walking routes, including 13 National Trails, link many Trust places, on top of a scenic web of local paths and access land.

- Hundreds of guided walks take place at our sites each year. They are a great way to find out more about our conservation work, wildlife, history, farming and so much more, while enjoying a healthy stroll. Many places also offer waymarked trails, leaflets and maps.

- Hundreds of walks sheets are available free on the Trust website to download, print and take on your day out.

Before setting out visit www. nationaltrust.org.uk/walks for a route map and description of our interesting walks.

Handbook entries give information on pedestrian access from the nearest town or railway station and details of routes passing through or nearby.

Your safety

At all our sites the responsibility for visitor safety should be seen as one that is shared between the National Trust and the visitor. We take reasonable measures to minimise risks in ways that are compatible with our conservation objectives – but not to eliminate all risks. This is especially the case at our coastal and countryside sites, where we aim to avoid measures that might restrict access or affect people's sense of freedom and adventure.

As the landscape becomes more rugged or remote, the balance of responsibility between you and us shifts. There will be fewer safety measures and warning signs, and you will need to rely more on your own skills, knowledge, equipment and preparation. For more information see page 9.

Cycle hire venues
Onsite:

Blickling Estate, Norfolk (01263 738015)

Castle Ward, County Down, Northern Ireland (028 4372 3933)

Clumber Park, Nottinghamshire (01909 544911)

Devils Dyke, West Sussex (01234 567890)

Dunstable Downs, Chilterns Gateway Centre and Whipsnade Estate, Bedfordshire (01582 500920)

Florence Court, County Fermanagh, Northern Ireland (00353 499 523923)

Ickworth, Suffolk (01284 735350)

Llanerchaeron, Ceredigion, Wales (01545 570200)

Wicken Fen National Nature Reserve, Cambridgeshire (01353 720274)

Nearby:
Long Mynd, Shropshire (01694 720133)

Lydford Gorge, Devon (01837 861141)

Walkers at Hadrian's Wall and Housesteads Fort, Northumberland

Car-free days out

In support of car-free travel, a growing number of places offer incentives for visitors arriving without a car, such as a tea-room voucher. Visit **www.nationaltrust.org.uk/carfreedaysout**

Car parks

Visitors use car parks at Trust places entirely at your own risk. You are advised to secure your car and not to leave any valuable items in it during your visit. Parking in Trust car parks is free for members displaying current stickers, although a valid membership card should always be shown to a member of staff on request. Individual members' stickers cannot be used to gain free parking for coaches.

Car-parking sticker

This year your car-parking sticker can be found on the inside front cover of this *Handbook*, lightly glued to a bookmark which can also be easily removed.

If you need a replacement or additional sticker, please ask a member of staff at the visitor reception at your next visit.

You will need to show your current membership card, which should continue to be shown to staff on request whenever you enter Trust places and pay and display car parks.

The sticker is not a substitute or alternative to a current membership card – it's just for use in pay and display car parks.

Top ten places to get to without a car

Cotehele, Cornwall (page 39). Make a 1½-mile walk beside the River Tamar part of the pleasure of your visit to this medieval house. The footpath is signposted from Calstock station on the scenic railway line between Plymouth and Gunnislake.

Tyntesfield, Somerset (page 93). Frequent buses from Bristol bus station reach this North Somerset house. A local bus driver raised £1,500 to help save this Victorian jewel.

Ightham Mote, Kent (page 130). This idyllic moated manor house can best be reached on Thursday and Friday by the service from Sevenoaks. On other days it's a ¾-mile walk from the Ivy Hatch stop.

Osterley Park and House, Middlesex (page 173). It's only a 1-mile walk from Osterley underground station on the Piccadilly Line to the verdant sanctuary that surrounds Adam's exquisitely decorated house.

Anglesey Abbey, Cambridgeshire (page 181). Take the Harcamlow Way to reach this individualistic house about 6 miles from Cambridge. Alternatively there are buses with good links from the railway station.

Sunnycroft, Shropshire (page 253). There's just ½ mile between this Edwardian time capsule and Wellington railway station, on the line between Birmingham and Shrewsbury.

Lyme Park, Cheshire (page 282). Frequent buses from Stockport and Buxton deliver you to the gates of this largely classical house, surrounded by the grounds made famous by the BBC's adaptation of *Pride and Prejudice*.

Seaton Delaval Hall, Northumberland (page 327). NCN72 and NCN1 provide a largely traffic-free link between Newcastle and this majestic baroque house designed by Sir John Vanbrugh, which has quickly become an intrinsic part of the local community since its recent acquisition.

Aberdulais Tin Works and Waterfall, Neath Port Talbot (page 337). Traffic-free sections of NCN47 along the Neath Canal link Neath with this tinplate works. Buses also arrive from Swansea, Brecon and Neath railway station.

Rowallane Garden, County Down (page 375). This informal plantsman's garden can be reached by buses from Belfast and Downpatrick.

Your questions answered

Where can I take photographs? We welcome amateur photography out of doors at our places and – without flash or tripods – indoors when houses are open, at the discretion of the Property/General Manager and where owners of-loan items have granted permission.

The use of mobile phones with built-in cameras is similarly permitted indoors (again, no flash please). At most places special arrangements can be made for interested amateurs (as well as voluntary National Trust speakers, research students and academics) to take interior photographs by appointment outside normal opening hours. Requests to arrange a mutually convenient appointment must be made in writing to the place concerned, giving your address. This facility isn't offered everywhere and we may make an admission charge (including Trust members).

All requests for commercial, non-editorial filming and photography go through the Broadcast and Media Manager (020 7799 4547).

Is there somewhere to leave large or bulky bags? When visiting historic buildings you will be asked to leave behind large items of hand luggage. This is to prevent accidental damage and to improve security. The restriction includes rucksacks, large handbags, carrier (including open-topped) bags, bulky shoulder bags and camera/camcorder bags. You can safely leave such items at the entrance, just as is standard practice at museums and galleries worldwide. See the Welcoming families section on page 378 for information on back-carriers and pushchairs.

What types of footwear are restricted? Any heel which covers an area smaller than a postage stamp can cause irreparable damage to floors, carpets and rush matting. So sharp-heeled shoes aren't allowed. Ridged soles also trap grit and gravel, which scratch fine floors, so overshoes may be provided and boot-scrapers and brushes are available, as well as plastic slippers for visitors with unsuitable, wet or muddy footwear.

What may I touch? We'd love you to be able to touch as much as possible, but many objects and surfaces are simply too fragile or important to be handled without the possibility of causing irreparable damage and loss.

Volunteer room guides and staff will guide you on what can be handled. At some places you will be welcome to play a piano or even try your hand at snooker.

Why is it dark inside some historic rooms? This is to prevent – or at least slow down – the deterioration of light-sensitive contents, especially textiles and watercolour paintings. Light levels are carefully controlled using blinds and sun-curtains. We recommend that you allow time for your eyes to adapt to these darker conditions.

What happens during winter? Many historic houses offer special tours during the winter months, when house staff share the secrets of their traditional housekeeping practices and explain why we have to close many of our houses during at least part of the winter.

Why is it so cold inside some houses in winter? The heating systems in National Trust houses are just not designed for the levels of domestic heating that we have become used to in our own homes. We suggest that you dress warmly – just like our hardy staff and volunteers! – when you visit during the winter.

May I use my mobile? We'd be really grateful if you could take a moment to turn off your mobile or put it on silent before going into one of our houses. Just as in a theatre, mobiles can really disrupt the atmosphere and detract from other people's experience.

Where may I sit down? We want you to be able to rest and relax, so we are increasing the seating in our houses and gardens. In show rooms most historic furniture is too fragile to use, often indicated by token barriers (such as ropes, ribbons, teasels and fir cones). Room guides will be happy to show you where it is safe to sit.

Joining in with the Trust

As a charity we rely greatly upon additional support, beyond membership fees, to help us to protect and manage the coastline, countryside, historic buildings and gardens in our care. You can help us in several ways, such as making a donation or leaving a gift to us in your will, or by volunteering.

Volunteer with us

During 2010 we enjoyed the support of nearly 62,000 volunteers, who together contributed a truly remarkable 3.6 million hours of combined effort in a hugely diverse range of roles – such as bringing our historic houses to life through room guiding and story telling, tackling vital countryside conservation tasks, running workshops in schools and welcoming visitors of all ages to special events throughout the year. Volunteers are involved behind the scenes at our places too, working alongside staff on strategic projects and managing and training other volunteers. You could also enjoy a working holiday (see page 388), join a supporter group (see below) or take part in our voluntary internship programme. We even have roles which families can take on together. By volunteering you could make new friends, gain work experience, use and develop your skills and see behind the scenes at our beautiful places. And with your help we'll make a real difference to those places, and to the people who love to visit them. Whatever your interests and motivations there's bound to be something to suit you – so if you'd like to get involved we'd love to hear from you. To find out more contact your local place, telephone 01793 817632 or visit **www.nationaltrust.org. uk/volunteering** or **www. nationaltrustjobs.org.uk/ other_ways_in/internships**

Voluntary talks service

Enthusiastic and knowledgeable volunteer speakers are available to give illustrated talks to groups of all sizes. Subjects range from the Neptune Coastline Campaign to garden history, conservation, individual places and regional round-ups. They can also tailor talks to meet your group's particular interests. To find out more contact 01793 817632.

Join your local Trust supporter group

Join your local supporter group and experience the fresh air, hidden depths and new views of the National Trust while helping to conserve our heritage for ever, for everyone.

Getting together with people who feel passionate about the same things as you do is priceless. Sharing experiences and finding out more about the places you visit is just part of the pleasure of joining a local National Trust supporter group. You'll also enjoy learning from expert speakers, going on behind-the-scenes tours and taking holidays. Our supporter groups promote the National Trust within their local area and raise money through all kinds of events.

You could also join one of our local friends or advisory groups; imagine getting to see what really goes on behind the scenes at your favourite Trust place, not to mention ensuring its healthy future. As a part of a friends group, you'll develop a unique relationship with the place which is most special to you. You can get involved with their volunteering team, learn about conservation, organise events and fundraising and work on ideas for the future.

If you can see yourself in the great outdoors (or the great indoors), a National Trust Volunteer Group could be the perfect choice for you. You might be constructing a footpath, building a fence or helping to restore natural coastal habitats, but whatever you're doing, you'll be in the company of a great bunch of like-minded people.

Supporter groups play a vital role in bringing our places to life for everyone to enjoy. Get involved with your local supporter group today and enjoy a deeper and more rewarding experience with the National Trust.

To find out more telephone 01793 817636, email sglo@nationaltrust.org.uk, or visit **www.nationaltrust.org.uk/supportergroups**

How you can support us

Gift Aid on Entry

The Gift Aid on Entry scheme gives non-members a choice between paying the standard admission price or paying the Gift Aid Admission, which includes a 10 per cent voluntary donation. Gift Aid Admissions enable the Trust to reclaim tax on the whole amount – currently an extra 25 per cent – potentially a very significant boost to a place's funds.

Gift Aid donations must be supported by a valid Gift Aid declaration, and a Gift Aid declaration can only cover donations made by an individual for themselves or for themselves and members of their family.

Admission prices are shown on our website, and are available on request from our Supporter Services Centre. Both the standard admission price and the Gift Aid Admission are displayed onsite and on our website.

Most Trust members already pay their subscriptions using Gift Aid, helping the Trust to the tune of many millions of pounds every year at no extra cost to themselves. If you would like to know more about Gift Aid, please contact the Supporter Services Centre on 0844 800 1895.

Donations and gifts

You can help us protect the special places in our care by donating to appeals, such as the work to secure the future of Knole, the forgotten palace. Or perhaps you would like to give to the ongoing work in the Lake District, or the appeal to save and protect the coastline – the Neptune Coastline Campaign. You will find all of these appeals and more at **www.nationaltrust. org.uk/donations**

You could also support your favourite place by buying a raffle ticket when you visit. Properties often have a specific conservation project which will be funded by money raised from the property raffle.

If you're stuck for ideas for a present, why not give a virtual gift: help plant a fruit tree in an orchard, protect the habitat of an endangered red squirrel or save a foot of coastline. Visit **www. nationaltrust.org.uk/ whatagreatgift** to see the full range of our imaginative and original gifts.

National Trust places mean so much to so many people that supporting us makes an ideal way to remember someone you've loved, or to celebrate a special occasion. To find out more about our Commemorative Giving Programme visit **www. nationaltrust.org.uk/ tributegiving**

We also organise several programmes to give donors the opportunity to see at first hand the work they support, such as the Guardian, Benefactor, Patron and Quercus Supporter Programmes. These include special behind-the-scenes events and the opportunity to talk to our experts. To find out

more email enquiries@ nationaltrust.org.uk or telephone 0844 800 1895.

Legacies

By making provision for the National Trust with a legacy in your Will, you would be providing a lasting gift for future generations. Every sum, whatever the size, will make a positive difference to our work across England, Wales and Northern Ireland in permanently safeguarding our natural and built heritage. No legacy income is spent on overheads or general administration – it is used right at the heart of the work of the Trust. Choose where you would like your gift to be directed – the project, place or region which means most to you.

Find out more by requesting our legacies guide or by attending a legacy event. Telephone our Supporter Services Centre on 0844 800 1895 or visit us today at **www. nationaltrust.org.uk/legacies**

National Gardens Scheme

ngs gardens open for charity

Each year many of the National Trust's gardens are opened in support of the National Gardens Scheme (NGS). If this is on a day when the garden is not usually open, National Trust members will have to pay for entry. All money raised is donated by the NGS to support nurses' and garden charities, including the National Trust garden careership training scheme.

The Trust acknowledges with gratitude the generous and continuing support of the National Gardens Scheme Charitable Trust.

How you can support the National Trust in the US – join The Royal Oak Foundation

The Royal Oak Foundation inspires Americans to learn about, experience and support places of historic and natural significance in the UK in partnership with the National Trust. Through the generous, tax-deductible support of its members and donors across the US, Royal Oak makes grants that advance the Trust's mission. Royal Oak members receive free entry and parking at all properties and the Trust's magazine, together with Royal Oak's newsletter.

Members' exploration continues in the US, where Royal Oak sponsors a national lecture series that informs Americans about the places, people and practices of the Trust and related topics in British architecture, art, garden and landscape design, and history.

The Royal Oak Foundation, 35 West 35th Street, Suite 1200, New York, NY, 10001-2205, USA.

Telephone 001 212 480 2889
Fax 001 212 785 7234
email general@royal-oak.org
website www.royal-oak.org

And thank you to…

ArtFund°

Art Fund
The National Trust is grateful to the Art Fund (www. artfund.org) for its continuing generous support in the acquisition of historic contents (a Brueghel painting for Nostell Priory and Seaton Delaval Hall are recent examples). We warmly welcome Art Fund members, who may visit places which have benefited directly, free of charge.

National Trust books, guidebooks, electronic newsletter and prints

We publish a range of books and guidebooks that promotes our work and the great variety of places and collections in our care. To buy any of these books or other titles about Trust places, please visit the National Trust Bookshop. Details of selected new titles can be found in the members' magazine or online. Visit **www.nationaltrustbooks.co.uk** or telephone 0845 672 0012.

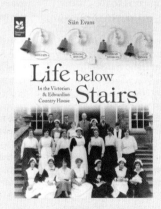

To subscribe to the Trust's free quarterly electronic newsletter, *ABC* (Arts, Building and Conservation), email abc@nationaltrust.org.uk. Past copies of this critically acclaimed publication – full of fascinating material and news – are posted on the Trust's website.

The official decorative print sales website of the National Trust is **www.ntprints.com** The collection of images available to buy (including prints of those appearing in this *Handbook*) vividly illustrates the rich diversity and historical range of properties and collections in the Trust's care. These include images by some of the country's leading photographers of works of fine art, sumptuous interiors and exteriors, gardens and landscapes. A range of print sizes and finishes is available, including art paper and canvas. Prices start at as little as £12.

Have your say

Governance
A guide to the Trust's governance arrangements is available on our website **www.nationaltrust.org.uk** and on request from the Secretary. Copies of our Annual Report and Accounts are available from the Supporter Services Centre.

Annual General Meeting
It is a crucial part of the governance of the Trust that once a year its members have the chance to meet their officers and senior staff at the Annual General Meeting (AGM). It is an opportunity for you to comment and make suggestions, to make your views known to the Trustees and the staff through questions and putting forward and debating resolutions of real interest to the charity.

You will receive the formal papers for our AGM – including voting papers – with the autumn magazine. We hope you will consider attending this year's AGM. However, you don't need to come to the meeting to take part. You can listen to the meeting and take part in the debates on our webcast (see **www.nationaltrust.org.uk/ agm**). You can also let us know your views by returning your voting papers – or voting online – ahead of the meeting.

In addition, you have the opportunity to elect members of our Council. The Council is made up of 52 members, 26 elected by you and 26 elected by organisations whose interests coincide in some way with those of the National Trust. This mix of elected and appointed members ensures that the Trust takes full account of the wider interests of the nation for whose benefit it exists. The breadth of experience and perspective which this brings also enables the Council to act as the Trust's conscience in delivering its statutory purposes.

Privacy Policy
The National Trust's Privacy Policy sets out the ways in which we process personal data. This Privacy Policy only relates to personal data collected by the National Trust via our website, membership forms, fundraising responses, emails and telephone calls.

The full Privacy Policy is available on our website **www.nationaltrust.org.uk**

The Data Protection Act 1998
The National Trust makes every effort to comply with the principles of the Data Protection Act 1998.

Use made of personal information
Personal information provided to the National Trust via our website, membership forms, fundraising responses, emails and telephone calls will be used for the purposes outlined at the time of collection or registration in accordance with the preferences you express.

Consent
By providing personal data to the National Trust you consent to the processing of such data by the National Trust as described in the full Privacy Policy. You can alter your preferences as follows.

Verifying, updating and amending your personal information
If, at any time, you want to verify, update or amend your personal data or preferences please write to:

National Trust,
Supporter Services Centre,
PO Box 39,
Warrington,
WA5 7WD.

Verification, updating or amendment of personal data will take place within 28 days of receipt of your request.

If subsequently you make a data protection instruction to the National Trust which contradicts a previous instruction (or instructions), then the Trust will follow your most recent instruction.

Subject access requests
You have the right to ask the National Trust, in writing, for a copy of all the personal data held about you (a 'subject access request') upon payment of a fee of £10.

To access your personal data held by the National Trust, please apply in writing to:

The Data Controller,
National Trust,
Heelis, Kemble Drive,
Swindon,
Wiltshire,
SN2 2NA.

Your membership

Through your membership of the National Trust you not only have free access to visit more than 400 places listed in this *Handbook*, as many times as you like all year, and the right to park free of charge in Trust car parks on coast and countryside sites, but reassurance that your subscription forms a significant part of the financial bedrock of the Trust. As an independent registered charity this support is absolutely vital to us – thank you very much indeed.

Here are some important messages about your membership; please take a moment to read them.

- Membership of the National Trust allows you free parking in Trust car parks and free entry to most Trust places open to the public during normal opening times and under normal opening arrangements, provided you can present a current valid membership card.

- **Remember to display your current car-parking sticker.**

- **Please check that you have your card with you before you set out on your journey. Without it, we regret that you may not be admitted free of charge, nor will we subsequently be able to refund any admission charges.**

- Membership cards are **not transferable**.

- If your card is lost or stolen, please contact the Supporter Services Centre (address opposite), telephone 0844 800 1895.

- A temporary card can be sent quickly to a holiday address or emailed to you.

- Members wishing to change from one category of life membership to another, or requiring information on pensioner membership, should contact the Supporter Services Centre for the scale of charges.

- In some instances an entry fee may apply. Additional charges may be made:

  • when a special event is in progress;

  • when we open specially for a National Gardens Scheme open day;

• where the management of a place is not under the National Trust's direct control, for example Tatton Park, Cheshire;

• where special attractions are additional and/or separate elements of the property, for example Steam Yacht *Gondola* in Cumbria, Dunster Watermill in Somerset, the model farm and museum at Shugborough in Staffordshire and the Tudor Old Hall and farm at Tatton Park in Cheshire;

• where special access conditions apply, for example The Beatles' Childhood Homes in Liverpool, where access is only by minibus from Speke Hall and Liverpool city centre, and all visitors (including Trust members) pay a fare for the minibus journey.

Reciprocal visiting

National Trust members enjoy reciprocal visiting arrangements with certain overseas National Trusts, including Australia, New Zealand, Barbados, Bermuda, Canada, Italy and – closer to home – Jersey and Guernsey. A similar arrangement is in place with the Manx Museum and National Trust on the Isle of Man (your current membership card is always needed). A full list is on our website and may be obtained from the Supporter Services Centre.

Entry to places owned by the Trust but maintained and administered by English Heritage or Cadw (Welsh Historic Monuments) is free to members of the Trust, English Heritage and Cadw.

National Trust for Scotland (NTS)

Members of the National Trust are also admitted free of charge to properties of the NTS, a separate charity with similar responsibilities. NTS places include the famous Inverewe Garden, Bannockburn, Culloden and Robert Adam's masterpiece, Culzean Castle. Full details are contained in *The National Trust for Scotland Guide to Properties* (£5, including post and packaging), which can be obtained by contacting the NTS Customer Service Centre, telephone 0844 493 2100. Information is also available at **www.nts.org.uk**

National Trust Holiday Collection

Want to holiday independently, with family and friends, or travel with like-minded people? The National Trust Holiday Collection has holidays to suit all tastes – from our own holiday cottages set in stunning locations and our hands-on working holidays, to a programme of cruises, escorted tours, activity holidays or short breaks operated by carefully selected tour operators.

National Trust Holiday Cottages

Nearly 400 unique properties in outstanding locations. Individual and intriguing, each is furnished traditionally and tastefully to complement period features. By staying with the National Trust, you can look forward to stunning locations and quality accommodation, ideal for celebrating special occasions, escaping from everyday life or simply enjoying heritage at first hand, whether it's for two nights or two weeks. To book telephone 0844 800 2070 or visit **www. nationaltrustcottages.co.uk**, quoting ref NTHBK.

National Trust Working Holidays

The National Trust Working Holidays programme provides great opportunities to make new friends, socialise and work together in a team. You can get away from the day-to-day distractions of modern living to achieve a worthwhile objective and make a significant difference to the preservation of our

The quirky Round House, Ickworth: one of nearly 400 fabulous holiday cottages

coast, countryside and historic houses. We also offer Youth Discovery holidays for 16 to 18 year olds (to find out more email working.holidays@ nationaltrust.org.uk) and family holidays. Each holiday is run by Trust staff and trained volunteer leaders, so experience is not necessary – just plenty of energy and enthusiasm.

To book telephone 0844 800 3099 or visit **www.nationaltrust.org.uk/ workingholidays**

Bed and Breakfast on National Trust Farms, Camping and Caravan Sites

Enjoy some of the best of our countryside and coastal areas and a warm welcome by

staying with National Trust tenant farmers or at one of our camping and caravan sites. For details visit **www.nationaltrust.org.uk/ holidays** or telephone 0844 800 1895 for a bed and breakfast leaflet.

Historic House Hotels

Treat yourself to a break at Hartwell House Hotel, Restaurant and Spa near Aylesbury (page 126), Middlethorpe Hall Hotel, Restaurant and Spa in York (page 305) or Bodysgallen Hall Hotel, Restaurant and Spa in North Wales (page 339) – all generously given to the National Trust in 2008. Please note all paying guests to the hotels are welcome to walk in the gardens and parks.

Holidays with National Trust partners

National Trust Cruise Collection

The National Trust Cruise Collection is operated by National Trust Discover Hebridean Island Cruises, Swan Hellenic and Voyages of Discovery, all of which are part of the largest British-owned cruise company, All Leisure Holidays Ltd.

All three brands combine the chance to relax at sea or on rivers on small ships, enjoy stylish onboard amenities and hospitality, with the opportunity to discover the world's great sites and cultures in the company of experts. Specific cruises are National Trust themed and Trust speakers will be on board to share their knowledge.

For more details, please telephone 0844 822 0830, quoting National Trust, Voyages of Discovery 0844 556 8190, Swan Hellenic 0844 822 0693, Hebridean Island Cruises 01756 704704. Or visit **www.nationaltrustcruises.co.uk**

National Trust supporters booking from a Trust promotion will be entitled to a five per cent discount on all cruises, and ten per cent of the purchase price will be donated to the Trust.

National Trust Active Holiday Collection

Discover walking and activity holidays that will invigorate, inspire and relax you. HF Holidays offers guide-yourself breaks, or you can be accompanied by one of their expert guides every step of the way to stunning backdrops, hidden pathways, new friendships and a nice cup of tea. With more than 300 different holiday ideas to choose from, there is something for everyone.

For a brochure telephone 0845 458 0120 or visit **www.nationaltrust.org.uk/activeholidays**

HF Holidays will donate £10 to the National Trust for each holiday booked. This does not affect the price you pay.

National Trust Coach Breaks

Visit our beautiful places the relaxing way – by coach. Just Go! Holidays offers an inspiring collection of four- and five-day coach breaks to some of our most interesting houses and gardens.

Members benefit from special prices, as your membership entitles you to free entry at most properties. In addition, Just Go! will donate £10 for each holiday booked.

For a brochure telephone 0844 822 3460 or visit **www.nationaltrust.org.uk/coachbreaks**

Pride of Britain Hotels

Privately owned luxury hotels in 40 locations around the UK reflecting a mix of traditional and contemporary styles, all offering excellent cuisine, comfortable accommodation and outstanding service. Many have spa facilities too. Pride of Britain Hotels is the official hotel partner to the National Trust.

For your 2012 directory please telephone 0800 089 3929. To book, telephone the same number or visit **www.nationaltrust.org.uk/hotels**

Pride of Britain will donate five per cent of the value of each booking to the National Trust. This does not affect the price you pay.

Sail away on Swan Hellenic's sleek *Minerva* and enjoy impeccable hospitality

Heritage Lottery Fund

Using money raised through the National Lottery, the Heritage Lottery Fund (HLF) sustains and transforms a wide range of heritage for present and future generations to take part in, learn from and enjoy. From museums, parks and historic places to archaeology, natural environment and cultural traditions, we invest in every part of our diverse heritage. The HLF has supported 33,900 projects, allocating £4.4 billion across the UK. We have supported the following National Trust projects:

Beningbrough Hall and Gardens, North Yorkshire
Biddulph Grange Garden, Staffordshire
Birmingham Back to Backs, West Midlands
Chedworth Roman Villa, Gloucestershire
Clumber Park, Nottinghamshire
Dinefwr Park and Castle, Carmarthenshire
Divis and the Black Mountain, Belfast
Giant's Causeway, County Antrim
Gibside, Tyne & Wear
Greenway, Devon
Hardcastle Crags, West Yorkshire
The Hardmans' House, Liverpool
Hardwick Hall, Derbyshire
Holy Jesus Hospital, Newcastle

Ickworth, Suffolk
Llanerchaeron, Ceredigion
Lyme Park House and Garden, Cheshire
Morden Hall Park, London
Nostell Priory and Parkland, West Yorkshire
Prior Park Landscape Garden, Bath
Springhill, County Londonderry
Stowe, Buckinghamshire
Sudbury Hall and the National Trust Museum of Childhood, Derbyshire
Tyntesfield, North Somerset
Wordsworth House and Garden, Cumbria
The Workhouse, Southwell, Nottinghamshire

LOTTERY FUNDED

Awarding funds from
The National Lottery®

If you would like to find out more please visit **www.hlf.org.uk**

Visitors to Stowe this year can enjoy not only the extraordinary Temple of British Worthies, seen here, but also approach these fantasy gardens from the newly opened visitor facilities at New Inn – restored and converted thanks to substantial grant-aid from the HLF and donations to a successful National Trust appeal

Area maps

This key shows how England, Wales and Northern Ireland are divided into ten areas for the purposes of this *Handbook*, and displayed on seven maps. The maps show those places which have individual entries as well as many additional coast and countryside sites in the care of the National Trust.

In order to help with general orientation, the maps show main roads and population centres. However, the plotting of each site serves only as a guide to its location. (Large-scale maps can be purchased from National Trust shops.) Please note that some countryside places, for example those in the Lake District, cover many thousands of hectares. In such cases the symbol is placed centrally as an indication of general location.

KEY:

Map 1	South West
Map 2	South East and London
Map 3	East of England Midlands (east)
Map 4	Wales Midlands (west)
Map 5	Yorkshire North West (south)
Map 6	North West (north) North East
Map 7	Northern Ireland

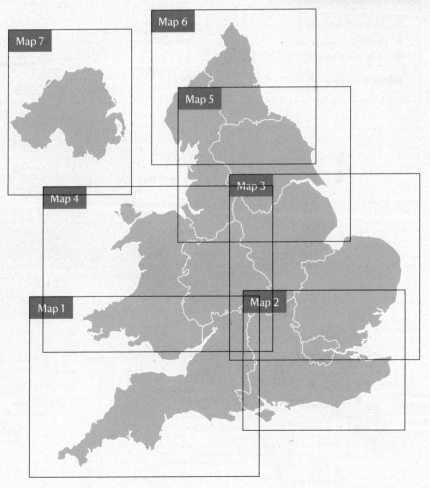

Map 1

South West page 11

▲ Buildings and gardens

■ Coast and countryside

0   10   20 miles
0   10   20   30 kilometres

South West

Grid references (by column A–F, row 1–10):

Pen Anglas
Dina Island
Ynys Barri
Cilgerran Castle ▲
Newcastle Emlyn
Dolau Gold M
Cardigan
Fishguard
St David's Head ■
St David's ▲
Carmarthen
Aberdeunant ▲
Llandeilo
Dinefwr P and Castl ▲
St Bride's Bay ■
Haverfordwest
Narberth
St Clears
Paxton's Tower ■
Ammanford
Henr
Martin's Haven ■
Milford Haven
Neyland
Colby Woodland Garden ▲
Kidwelly
Marloes Deer Park ■
Marloes Sands ■
Ragwen Point ■
Burry Port
Llanelli
Freshwater West ■
Pembroke
Tenby
Tudor Merchant's House ▲
Swansea
Gower Peninsula
Stackpole ■
Broadhaven ■
Lydstep Headland ■
Rhossili ▲
Port Einon
Pennard Cliffs ■
Port Talbo
Barafundle Bay ■

Countisbury
Watersmeet
Lundy ■
Ilfracombe
Heddon Valley ■
Lynmouth
Morte Point ■
Woolacombe ■
Baggy Point ■
Braunton
Arlington Court ▲
Barnstaple
East Titchberry ■
Abbotsham ■
Bideford
South Molton
South Hole ■
Buck's Mills ■
Great Torrington
Sandy Mouth ■
Dunsland ▲
Bude
Crackington Haven ■
Holsworthy
Okehampton
Boscastle ■
Barras Nose ■
Tintagel Old Post Office ▲
Launceston
Finch Foundry ▲
Castle Drogo ▲
Teign Valley
Port Quin ■
Lydford Gorge ■
The Rumps and Pentire Point ■
Camelford
Lawrence House ▲
Widecombe in the Moor
The Church House ▲
Padstow
Wadebridge
Rough Tor ■
Holne Wood
Park Head ■
Tavistock
Trowlesworthy ■
Carnewas and Bedruthan Steps ■
Bodmin
Liskeard
Cotehele ▲
Buckland Abbey ▲
Hembury Woods
Newquay
Lanhydrock ▲
Crantock and Holywell Bay ■
Saltash
Plym Bridge Woods ▲
Chapel Porth and Wheal Coates ■
Trerice ▲
Antony ▲
PLYMOUTH
Zennor Head ■
Godrevy ■
Truro
St Austell
Fowey
Bodigga Cliff ■
Saltram ▲
Bosigran ■
East Pool Mine ▲
St Ives
The Gribbin ■
Wembury ■
Overbeck's ▲
Levant Mine ▲
Trelissick Garden ▲
The Dodman ■
South Milton Sands ■
Bolt Tail ■
Botallack Count House ■
Trengwainton Garden ▲
Camborne
Nare Head ■
Bolberry Down ■
Cape Cornwall ■
Penzance
Falmouth
St Anthony Head ■
Soar Mill Cove ■
Bolt Head ■
Mayon Cliff ■
Godolphin ▲
Helston
Glendurgan Garden ▲
Portlemouth Down ■
Porthcurno ■
St Michael's Mount ▲
Helford ■
Poldhu ■
Penrose Estate: Gunwalloe and Loe Pool
Mullion Cove ■
Kynance Cove ■
Lizard Point ■

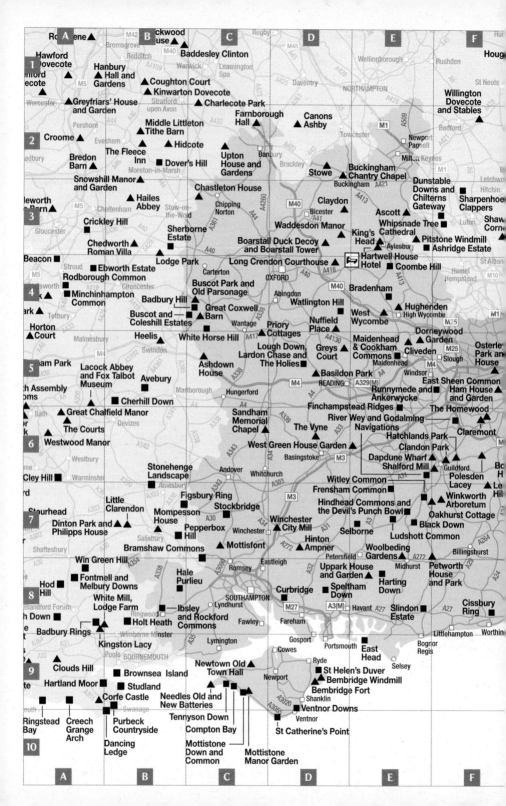

Mill

Dunwich Heath Coastal Centre and Beach

Theatre Royal

Waterbeach
Histon
CAMBRIDGE
Burwell
Newmarket
Bury St Edmunds
Saxmundham
Leiston
Aldeburgh

Anglesey Abbey, Gardens and Lode Mill

Ickworth
Stowmarket

Wimpole Estate
Haverhill
Royston

Melford Hall
Lavenham Guildhall
Long Melford
Sudbury
IPSWICH
Woodbridge

Kyson Hill
Sutton Hoo
Orford Ness

Saffron Walden

Flatford: Bridge Cottage
Pin Mill

Bishop's Stortford
Halstead

Coggeshall Grange Barn and Paycocke's
Colchester
Dedham Vale
Harwich
Felixstowe

Braintree
Bourne Mill
Clacton-on-Sea

Ware
Hertford

Hatfield Forest
Witham
Copt Hall Marshes
West Mersea

Harlow
Chelmsford
Blakes Wood
Maldon

London

Danbury and Lingwood Commons
Northey Island
Burnham-on-Crouch

Fenton House and Garden
2 Willow Rd
Sutton House
Brentwood Rayleigh
Rayleigh Mount
Basildon
Southend-on-Sea

Eastbury Manor House
eighton House
Rainham Hall
Canvey Island

George Inn
Red House
Blewcoat School
St John's Jerusalem
Sheerness
Margate

Carlyle's House
Rochester
Whitstable
Herne Bay
Ramsgate

Morden Hall Park
Cobham Wood and Mausoleum
Faversham
Canterbury
A257

Selsdon Wood
Owletts
Coldrum Long Barrow

Vatermeads
Quebec House
Knole
Old Soar Manor
Maidstone
Stoneacre

South East

Deal

Chartwell
Ightham Mote
Emmetts Garden
Ashford
South Foreland Lighthouse

Reigate Fort
Toys Hill
Chiddingstone Village
Sprivers Garden
Sissinghurst Castle
Dover
White Cliffs

Tunbridge Wells
Folkestone

Standen
Scotney Castle
Tenterden
Hythe

Wakehurst Place
Smallhythe Place
Royal Military Canal

Nymans
Haywards Heath
Sheffield Park and Garden
Bodiam Castle
New Romney

Bateman's
Rye
Lamb House

Saddlescombe Farm and Newtimber Hill
Battle

Devil's Dyke
Lewes
Hailsham
Hastings
Bexhill-on-Sea

Brighton
Monk's House
Alfriston Clergy House

Newhaven
Frog Firle Farm
Eastbourne

Birling Gap and the Seven Sisters
Chyngton Farm

Crowlink

Map 2

South East page 99

London page 167

▲ Buildings and gardens

■ Coast and countryside

⌂ Historic House Hotel

0   10   20 miles
0   10   20   30 kilometres

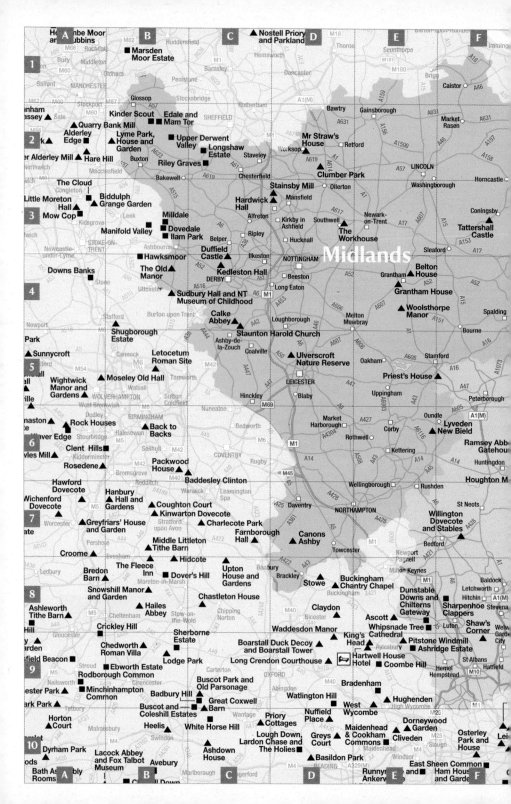

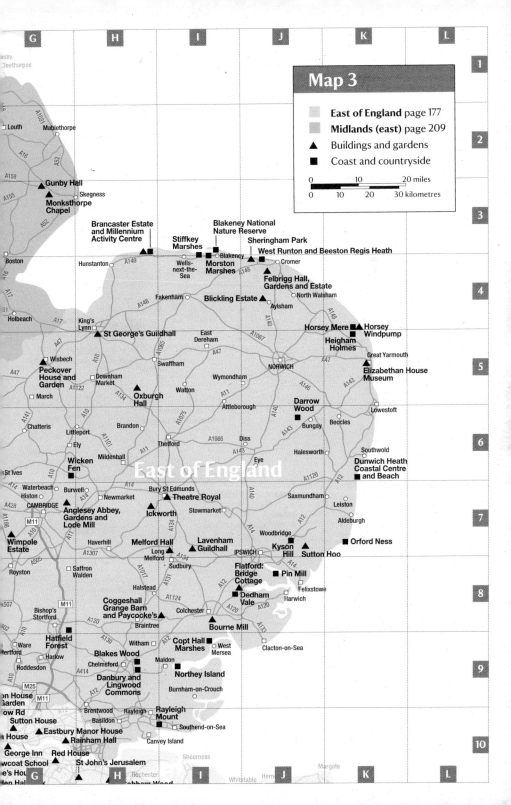

Map 3

East of England page 177
Midlands (east) page 209
▲ Buildings and gardens
■ Coast and countryside

0   10   20 miles
0   10   20   30 kilometres

G H I J K L

1 2 3 4 5 6 7 8 9 10

asby
Cleethorpes

Louth   Mablethorpe
A1031
A16
A52
A158
A155   Gunby Hall
        Skegness
        Monksthorpe
        Chapel
A52

Boston

Hunstanton   A149
A16
A17

Holbeach   A17   King's
                    Lynn   St George's Guildhall

Wisbech
Peckover
House and   Downham
Garden   A1122   Market
March   A134

Chatteris
Littleport   Brandon
Ely
St Ives   Wicken   Mildenhall
A10   Fen
Waterbeach   Burwell
Histon   A14   Newmarket
CAMBRIDGE
M11   Anglesey Abbey,
A1198   Gardens and
M10   Lode Mill

Wimpole   Haverhill
Estate   A1307
Royston   Saffron
          Walden

Ware
Hertford   Harlow
Hoddesdon   A414
M25
on House   M11
Garden
ow Rd
Sutton House
▲
House   ▲ Eastbury Manor House
         ▲ Rainham Hall   Canvey Island
George Inn   Red House
wcoat School   St John's Jerusalem
en Hal

Brancaster Estate
and Millennium   Stiffkey
Activity Centre   Marshes

Wells-   Blakeney
next-the-   Morston
Sea   Marshes   A148

Fakenham   Blickling Estate ▲

Blakeney National
Nature Reserve   Sheringham Park
                West Runton and Beeston Regis Heath
        Cromer
Felbrigg Hall,
Gardens and Estate
North Walsham

East
Dereham   A140
A47
A1065
Swaffham
A10   Wymondham
Watton   A11
        Attleborough
A1075

Aylsham   A149
        Horsey Mere ■▲ Horsey
                Windpump
        Heigham
        Holmes
NORWICH   A47   Great Yarmouth
A146   Elizabethan House
A143   Museum
        Lowestoft
Darrow
Wood   Beccles
A143   Bungay
Halesworth   Southwold
                Dunwich Heath
                Coastal Centre
Eye   A143   ■ and Beach
A1120

Oxburgh
Hall

Thetford   A1066   Diss

Mildenhall   A11

A14   Bury St Edmunds   A140   Saxmundham   Leiston
                    ▲ Theatre Royal   Aldeburgh
Anglesey Abbey,   A134   Stowmarket
Gardens and   Ickworth
Lode Mill   Woodbridge   A14
Melford Hall   Lavenham   Kyson   Orford Ness
Long ▲ Guildhall   Hill   Sutton Hoo
Melford   A134   IPSWICH
Sudbury   Flatford:
         Bridge   ■ Pin Mill
         Cottage   Felixstowe
Halstead   A12   ■ Dedham   Harwich
Coggeshall   A1124   Vale   A120
Grange Barn   Colchester   A120
and Paycocke's   ▲
Braintree   Bourne Mill   A133
A120
Hatfield   A130   Witham   Copt Hall   West
Forest   Marshes   Mersea   Clacton-on-Sea
Bishop's
Stortford   Blakes Wood
Chelmsford   Maldon
Danbury and   Northey Island
Lingwood
Commons   Burnham-on-Crouch

Brentwood   Rayleigh   Rayleigh
Basildon   Mount
            Southend-on-Sea

Sheerness

Margate
Whitstable   Hern
Rochester

East of England

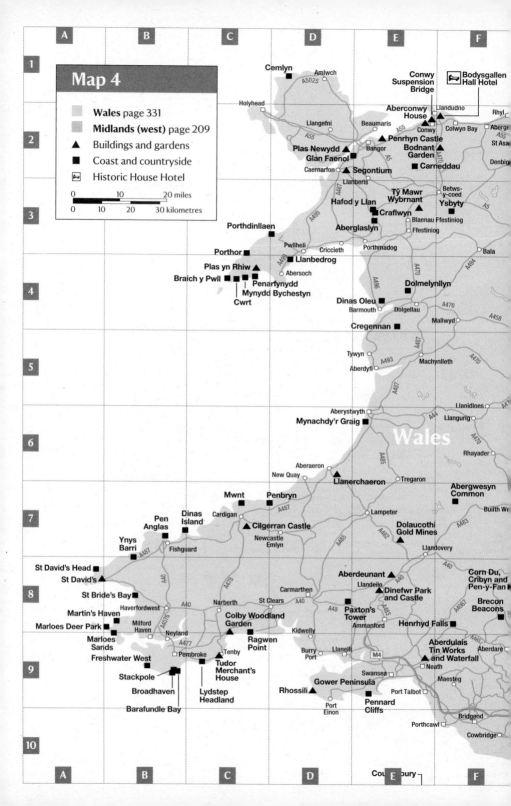

Map 4

- Wales page 331
- Midlands (west) page 209
- ▲ Buildings and gardens
- ■ Coast and countryside
- 🏠 Historic House Hotel

0   10   20 miles
0   10   20   30 kilometres

Wales

Cemlyn

Amlwch

Conwy Suspension Bridge

Bodysgallen Hall Hotel

Holyhead

Aberconwy House

Llandudno

Rhyl

Llangefni

Beaumaris

Conwy

Colwyn Bay

Abergele

Penrhyn Castle

St Asaph

Plas Newydd
Glan Faenol

Bangor

Bodnant Garden

Carneddau

Denbigh

Caernarfon

Segontium

Llanberis

Betws-y-coed

Tŷ Mawr Wybrnant

Hafod y Llan

Craflwyn

Ysbyty

Porthdinllaen

Aberglaslyn

Blaenau Ffestiniog

Ffestiniog

Pwllheli

Criccieth

Porthmadog

Bala

Porthor

Llanbedrog

Plas yn Rhiw

Abersoch

Braich y Pwll

Penarfynydd

Mynydd Bychestyn

Cwrt

Dinas Oleu

Barmouth

Dolgellau

Dolmelynllyn

Mallwyd

Cregennan

Tywyn

Aberdyfi

Machynlleth

Aberystwyth

Mynachdy'r Graig

Llanidloes

Llangurig

Wales

Rhayader

Aberaeron

New Quay

Llanerchaeron

Tregaron

Abergwesyn Common

Mwnt

Penbryn

Cardigan

Lampeter

Builth Wells

Pen Anglas

Dinas Island

Cilgerran Castle

Newcastle Emlyn

Dolaucothi Gold Mines

Ynys Barri

Fishguard

Llandovery

St David's Head

St David's

Carmarthen

Aberdeunant

Llandeilo

Corn Du, Cribyn and Pen-y-Fan

St Bride's Bay

Dinefwr Park and Castle

Brecon Beacons

Martin's Haven

Haverfordwest

Narberth

St Clears

Paxton's Tower

Marloes Deer Park

Milford Haven

Neyland

Colby Woodland Garden

Ammanford

Henrhyd Falls

Marloes Sands

Kidwelly

Aberdulais Tin Works and Waterfall

Freshwater West

Pembroke

Ragwen Point

Burry Port

Llanelli

Neath

Stackpole

Tenby

Tudor Merchant's House

Swansea

Maesteg

Broadhaven

Lydstep Headland

Rhossili

Gower Peninsula

Port Talbot

Barafundle Bay

Port Einon

Pennard Cliffs

Bridgend

Porthcawl

Cowbridge

Cou...bury

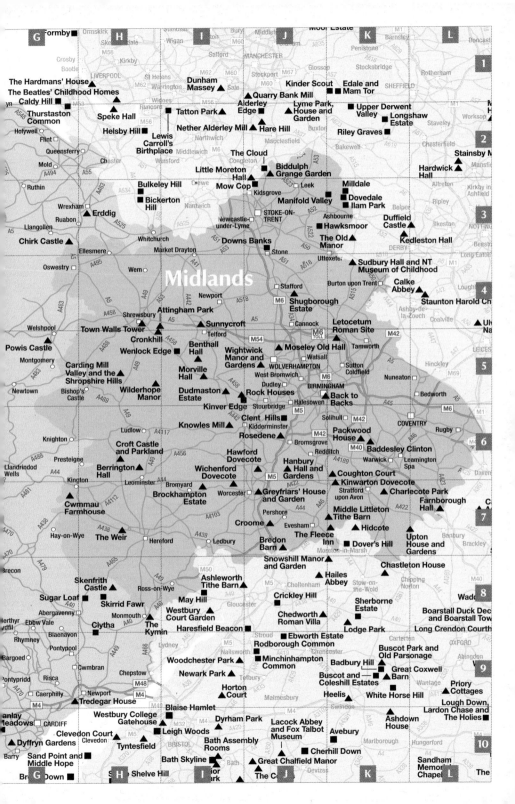

North West

Grid reference labels (left margin, top to bottom): A, B, C, D, E, F
Grid reference labels (rows, left margin): 1, 2, 3, 4, 5, 6, 7, 8, 9, 10
Grid reference labels (bottom margin): A, B, C, D, E, F

Moor...se ■
Woo...
Brandon
Durha...

Derwent Island House
North House and Garden ▲
Penrith
Acorn Bank Garden ▲
Spennymoor
Bishop Auckland
A1(M

Friar's Crag
Bassenthwaite Lake
Keswick

Castlerigg Stone Circle ■
Appleby-in-Westmorland
Newton Aycliffe

Force Crag Mine ▲
Crummock Water
Derwentwater
Ullswater and Aira Force
A66
Barnard Castle
Darlington

Ennerdale
Borrowdale ■
Keld Chapel ▲
Brough

Buttermere
Grasmere and Great Langdale
Haweswater
M6

Wasdale
Coniston and Tarn Hows ■
Bridge House ▲
Moulton Hall ▲

Scafell Pike ■
Wastwater
Stagshaw Garden
A685
A66

Eskdale ■
Townend ▲
Hudswell Woods ■
Richmond

Beatrix Potter Gallery ▲■
Windermere and Troutbeck ■
Catterick
A1

Steam Yacht 'Gondola' ▲
Hawkshead and Claife
Sedbergh
Leyburn
A68

Duddon ■
Coniston Water
Hill Top ▲
Bedale

Fell Foot Park ▲
Sizergh Castle and Garden ▲
Hawes
A684
Braithwaite Hall ▲

Cartmel Priory Gatehouse ▲
Arnside Knott ▲
Holme Park Fell ▲

Millom
Ulverston
Kendal

Sandscale Haws ■
Grange-over-Sands
Heald Brow ■
Upper Wharfedale ■
Ripon

Dalton Castle ▲
Eaves and Waterslack Woods ■
Malham Tarn ■
Fountains Abbey and Studley Royal ▲

Barrow-in-Furness
Jack Scout ▲
Settle

Morecambe
Heysham ■
Lancaster
Brimham Rocks ■

M6
Knaresborough
Skipton
A59
Harrogate

Fleetwood
North West
A682

Garstang
Ilkley
A65

Clitheroe
A6068
Keighley
A650
Yeadon

Blackpool
Gawthorpe Hall ▲
Burnley
Hardcastle Crags ■
Shipley
LEEDS

Kirkham
Preston
A59
BRADFORD
M621

Lytham St Anne's
Warton
A59
Blackburn
M65
Accrington
Rawtenstall
Todmorden
Halifax
Batley
Wakefield

Leyland
Rufford Old Hall ▲
Chorley
Holcombe Moor and Stubbins ■
A58
Huddersfield

Southport
M6
M61
Standish
Bury
Rochdale
M62
Marsden Moor Estate ■
M1

Formby ■
Ormskirk
Wigan
Bolton
Middleton
M60
Oldham
A635
Barnsley

Skelmersdale
M58
Salford
MANCHESTER
Penistone
A629

Crosby
Kirkby
M62
M60
Stockport
M67
Glossop
Stocksbridge

Bootle
LIVERPOOL
St Helens
Dunham Massey ▲
Kinder Scout ■
Edale and Mam Tor ■
SHEFFIE...

The Hardmans' House ■
Warrington
Sale
M60
The Beatles' Childhood Homes ▲
Quarry Bank Mill ▲
Lyme Park, House and Garden ▲
Upper Derwen... Valley ■

Caldy Hill ■
M53
Widnes
Runcorn
Alderley Edge ▲
Buxton
Long... Estat...

Thurstaston Common
Speke Hall ▲
M56
Tatton Park ▲
Nether Alderley Mill ▲
Hare Hill ▲
Riley Graves ■

Helsby Hill ■
Lewis Carroll's Birthplace
Northwich
Macclesfield

Queensferry
Chester
Winsford
Middlewich
M6
The Cloud ▲
Congleton
Bakewell
A619

Denbigh
Mold
Little Moreton Hall ▲
Biddulph Grange Garden ▲
Milldale

Ruthin
Bulkeley Hill ■
Crewe
Mow Cop ▲
Leek
Dovedale ▲
Ilam Park ■

Bickerton Hill ■
Nantwich
Kidsgrove
Manifold Valley ▲

Erddig ▲
STOKE-ON-TRENT
Ashbourne
Duffield Castle ▲

Chirk Castle ▲
Ellesmere
Whitchurch
Market Drayton
Downs Banks ■
Hawksmoor ■
The Old Manor ▲
Ke...
DERBY

Oswestry
Wem
Stone
Uttoxeter
Sud... Mus... ▲
Hall a... h of Ch...

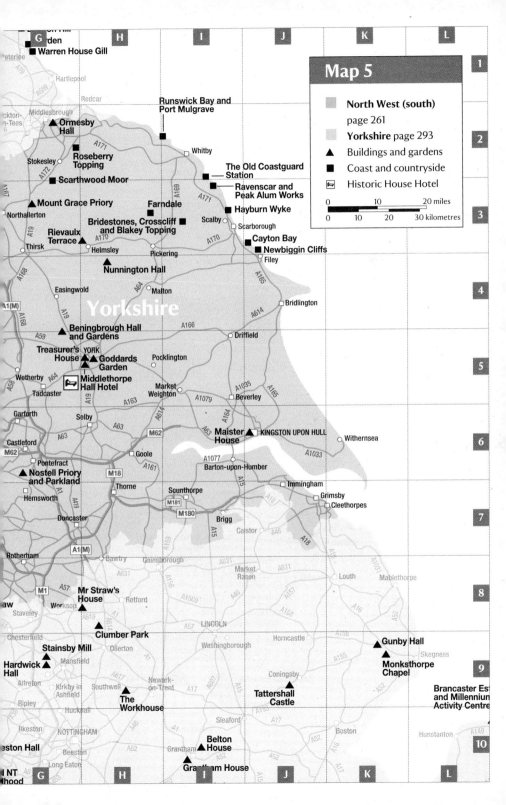

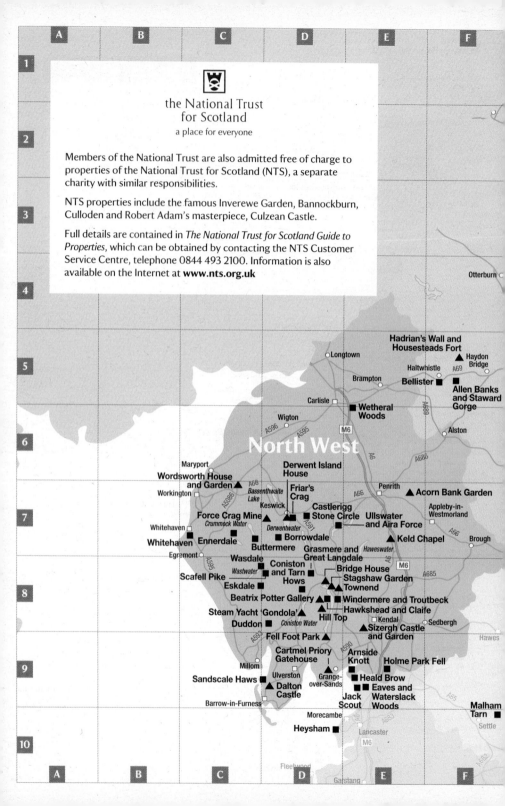

the National Trust for Scotland
a place for everyone

Members of the National Trust are also admitted free of charge to properties of the National Trust for Scotland (NTS), a separate charity with similar responsibilities.

NTS properties include the famous Inverewe Garden, Bannockburn, Culloden and Robert Adam's masterpiece, Culzean Castle.

Full details are contained in *The National Trust for Scotland Guide to Properties*, which can be obtained by contacting the NTS Customer Service Centre, telephone 0844 493 2100. Information is also available on the Internet at **www.nts.org.uk**

North West

Hadrian's Wall and Housesteads Fort

Longtown
Haltwhistle   A69   Haydon Bridge
Brampton   Bellister
Carlisle   Wetheral Woods
Allen Banks and Staward Gorge
Wigton
A596   A595   M6
Alston
Otterburn

Maryport   Derwent Island House
Wordsworth House and Garden
Workington   A66   Bassenthwaite Lake   Friar's Crag
Keswick
Penrith   Acorn Bank Garden
Castlerigg Stone Circle   Ullswater and Aira Force
Appleby-in-Westmorland
Force Crag Mine   Crummock Water   Derwentwater
Whitehaven
Whitehaven   Ennerdale   Borrowdale
Keld Chapel   Brough
Egremont
Buttermere   Grasmere and Great Langdale   Haweswater
Wasdale   Coniston and Tarn   Bridge House   M6
Scafell Pike   Wastwater   Hows   Stagshaw Garden
Eskdale   Townend
Beatrix Potter Gallery   Windermere and Troutbeck
Steam Yacht 'Gondola'   Hawkshead and Claife
Duddon   Coniston Water   Hill Top   Kendal   Sedbergh
Fell Foot Park   Sizergh Castle and Garden   Hawes
Cartmel Priory Gatehouse   Arnside Knott   Holme Park Fell
Millom   Ulverston   Grange-over-Sands   Heald Brow
Sandscale Haws   Dalton Castle   Eaves and Waterslack Woods
Barrow-in-Furness   Jack Scout
Malham Tarn
Morecambe   Settle
Heysham   Lancaster   M6
Fleetwood   Garstang

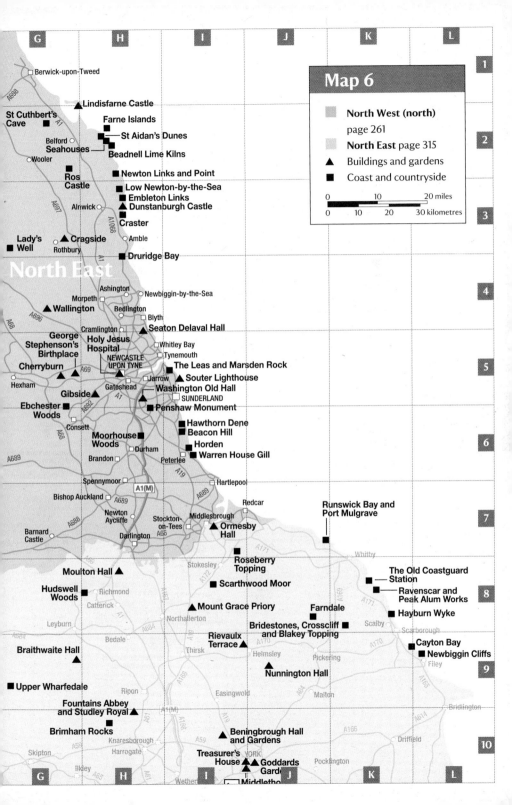

G   H   I   J   K   L

1

Berwick-upon-Tweed

Lindisfarne Castle

St Cuthbert's Cave

Farne Islands

St Aidan's Dunes

Belford
Seahouses
Wooler

Beadnell Lime Kilns

2

Ros Castle

Newton Links and Point

Low Newton-by-the-Sea
Embleton Links
Dunstanburgh Castle
Alnwick
Craster

3

Lady's Well
Cragside
Rothbury

Amble

Druridge Bay

North East

Ashington
Newbiggin-by-the-Sea

Morpeth
Wallington
Bedlington
Blyth

4

Cramlington
Seaton Delaval Hall

George Stephenson's Birthplace
Holy Jesus Hospital
Whitley Bay
Tynemouth

NEWCASTLE UPON TYNE

Cherryburn

The Leas and Marsden Rock

5

Hexham
Jarrow
Souter Lighthouse
Gibside
Gateshead
Washington Old Hall
Ebchester
Woods
SUNDERLAND
Penshaw Monument

Consett
Hawthorn Dene
Beacon Hill
Moorhouse Woods
Durham
Horden
Brandon
Warren House Gill
Peterlee

6

A689
Spennymoor
Hartlepool

A1(M)

Bishop Auckland
Redcar

Newton Aycliffe
Stockton-on-Tees
Middlesbrough
Runswick Bay and Port Mulgrave

7

Barnard Castle
Darlington
Ormesby Hall

Stokesley
Whitby

Roseberry Topping

Moulton Hall

The Old Coastguard Station

Hudswell Woods
Richmond
Scarthwood Moor
Ravenscar and Peak Alum Works

8

Catterick
Mount Grace Priory
Farndale
Hayburn Wyke

Leyburn
Northallerton
Bridestones, Crosscliff and Blakey Topping
Scalby
Scarborough

Braithwaite Hall
Bedale
Rievaulx Terrace
Thirsk
Helmsley
Pickering
Filey
Cayton Bay
Newbiggin Cliffs

9

Upper Wharfedale
Ripon
Easingwold
Malton
Bridlington

Fountains Abbey and Studley Royal

Brimham Rocks
Knaresborough
Beningbrough Hall and Gardens
Driffield

10

Skipton
Harrogate
Treasurer's House
YORK
Goddards Garden
Pocklington

Ilkley
Wetherby
Middleton

G   H   I   J   K   L

Map 6

North West (north) page 261

North East page 315

▲ Buildings and gardens

■ Coast and countryside

0   10   20 miles

0   10   20   30 kilometres

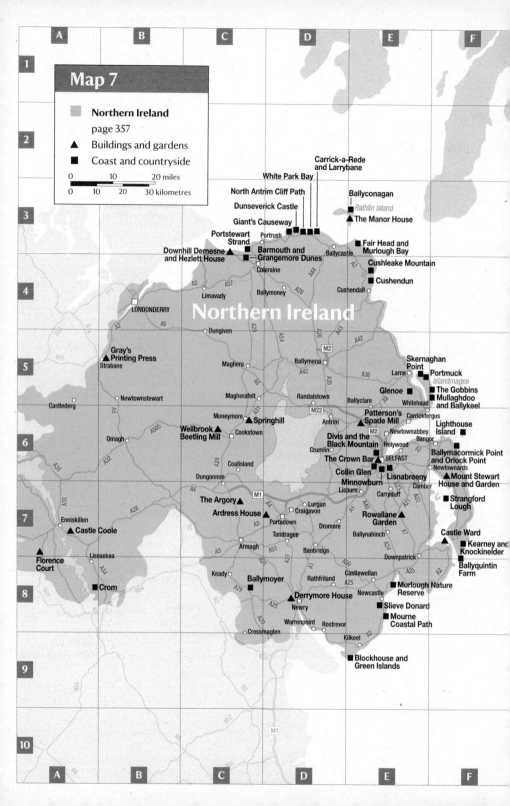

Map 7

- Northern Ireland
  page 357
- ▲ Buildings and gardens
- ■ Coast and countryside

0   10   20 miles
0   10   20   30 kilometres

Carrick-a-Rede
and Larrybane

White Park Bay

North Antrim Cliff Path   Ballyconagan

Dunseverick Castle   ■ Rathlin Island

Giant's Causeway   ▲ The Manor House

Portstewart   Portrush
Strand   ■ Fair Head and
Downhill Demesne ▲   Barmouth and   Murlough Bay
and Hezlett House   Grangemore Dunes   Ballycastle
                     Coleraine   ■ Cushleake Mountain

                                                ■ Cushendun

            Limavady   Ballymoney   Cushendall

LONDONDERRY

            Dungiven

Gray's   Skernaghan
▲ Printing Press   Maghera   Ballymena   Point
Strabane   Larne ■ Portmuck
                                                      Islandmagee
                                         A36   ■ The Gobbins
   Newtownstewart   Magherafelt   Randalstown   Glenoe ■ Mullaghdoo
Castlederg   Ballyclare   Whitehead and Ballykeel

                     Moneymore ▲ Springhill   Antrim   Patterson's Carrickfergus
            Wellbrook ▲   Spade Mill
Omagh   Beetling Mill   Cookstown   Lighthouse
                                                   Divis and the Newtownabbey Island ■
                                          Crumlin Black Mountain Holywood Bangor
                                                                          ■ Ballymacormick Point
                            Coalisland   BELFAST   and Orlock Point
                                          The Crown Bar ▲   Newtownards
            Dungannon   Collin Glen ■ Lisnabreeny ▲ Mount Stewart
                                          Minnowburn   Comber House and Garden
                                          Lisburn   Carryduff
            The Argory ▲   Lurgan   ■ Strangford
            Ardress House ▲   Craigavon   Rowallane ▲ Lough
Enniskillen   Portadown   Dromore   Garden
▲ Castle Coole   Tandragee   Ballynahinch   Castle Ward ▲
                     Armagh   Banbridge   Downpatrick   ■ Kearney and
            Lisnaskea   Knockinelder
▲
Florence   Ballyquintin
Court   Keady   Ballymoyer   Rathfriland Castlewellan Farm
■ Crom   Newcastle ■ Murlough Nature
                              ▲ Derrymore House   Reserve
                              Newry   ■ Slieve Donard
                         Warrenpoint Rostrevor   ■ Mourne
                                                           Coastal Path
                     Crossmaglen   Kilkeel

                                          ■ Blockhouse and
                                          Green Islands

Index of properties by county/administrative area

Properties with no individual entries are shown in italics.
* Denotes properties shown only on maps.

Swansea
Gower Peninsula (4:D9)   334, 346
Gower: Rhossili Shop and
    Visitor Centre (4:D9)   346
Pennard Cliffs (4:E9)   *398

Wrexham
Chirk Castle (4:G3)   339
Erddig (4:H3)   345

Northern Ireland

County Antrim
Ballyconagan (7:E3)   359
Carrick-a-Rede (7:D3)   362
Cushendun (7:E4)   359
Cushleake Mountain (7:E4)   *404
Dunseverick Castle (7:D3)   *404
Fair Head (7:E3)   359
Giant's Causeway (7:D3)   369
Glenoe (7:E5)   359
The Gobbins (7:F5)   *404
Larrybane (7:D3)   *404
The Manor House,
    Rathlin Island (7:E3)   *404
Mullaghdoo and Ballykeel (7:F5)   *404
North Antrim Cliff Path (7:D3)   *404
Patterson's Spade Mill (7:E6)   373
Portmuck (7:E5)   359
Rathlin Island (7:E3)   359
Skernaghan Point (7:E5)   359

White Park Bay (7:D3)   359

County Armagh
Ardress House (7:D7)   361
The Argory (7:C7)   361
Ballymoyer (7:C8)   360
Derrymore House (7:D8)   366

Belfast
Collin Glen (7:E6)   359
The Crown Bar (7:E6)   366
Divis and the Black
    Mountain (7:E6)   359, 366
Lisnabreeny (7:E6)   359
Minnowburn (7:E6)   359

County Down
Ballymacormick Point (7:F6)   359
Ballyquintin Farm (7:F7)   359
Blockhouse Island (7:E9)   *404
Castle Ward (7:F7)   360, 364
Green Island (7:E9)   *404
Kearney (7:F7)   359
Knockinelder (7:F7)   359
Lighthouse Island (7:F6)   *404
Mount Stewart House, Garden and
    Temple of the Winds (7:F6)   371
Mourne Coastal Path (7:E8)   *404
Murlough National Nature
    Reserve (7:E8)   372
Orlock Point (7:F6)   *404
Rowallane Garden (7:E7)   375, 381

Slieve Donard (7:E8)   359
Strangford Lough Wildlife
    Centre (7:F7)   358, 360

County Fermanagh
Castle Coole (7:A7)   363
Crom (7:A8)   360, 365
Florence Court (7:A7)   360, 368

County Londonderry
Barmouth (7:C4)   *404
Downhill Demesne
    and Hezlett House (7:C3)   367
Grangemore Dunes (7:C4)   *404
Portstewart Strand (7:C3)   374
Springhill (7:C6)   360, 376

County Tyrone
Gray's Printing Press (7:B5)   370
Wellbrook Beetling Mill (7:C6)   377

Northern Ireland's North Coast
Carrick-a-Rede (7:D3)   362
Downhill Demense
    and Hezlett House (7:C3)   367
Dunseverick Castle (7:D3)   *404
Giant's Causeway (7:D3)   369
Murlough Bay
    and Fair Head (7:E3)   359, 372
Portstewart Strand and
    the Bann Estuary (7:C3)   374
Rathlin Island (7:E3)   359
White Park Bay (7:D3)   359

Tourist areas

For information on the
properties below, please visit
www.nationaltrust.org.uk and
follow links to the new website.

North Devon
Arlington Court and the National
    Trust Carriage Museum
Bideford Bay and Hartland
Croyde, Woolacombe and Mortenhoe
Dunsland
Heddon Valley
Lundy
Watersmeet

Somerset Countryside
Brean Down
Cheddar Gorge
Fyne Court
Glastonbury Tor
Holnicote Estate
King John's Hunting Lodge
Mendip Hills

South Downs
Birling Gap and the Seven Sisters
Black Cap
Black Down
Cissbury Ring
Ditchling Beacon
Uppark House and Garden
Woolbeding Gardens

Isle of Wight
Bembridge and Culver Downs
Bembridge Windmill
Borthwood Copse
Chillerton Down
Compton Bay and Downs
Mottistone Estate
Mottistone Manor Garden
Newtown National Nature Reserve
St Catherine's Down and Knowles Farm
St Helens Duver
The Needles Headland
    and Tennyson Down
The Needles Old Battery
    and New Battery
Ventnor Downs

The Lake District
Acorn Bank Garden and Watermill
Arnside and Silverdale
Beatrix Potter Gallery
Borrowdale
Bridge House
Buttermere, Ennerdale and Whitehaven
Cartmel Priory Gatehouse
Coniston and Tarn Hows
Dalton Castle
Fell Foot Park
Steam Yacht Gondola
Grasmere
Great Langdale
Hawkshead and Claife
Hill Top
Little Langdale

Sandscale Haws
Sizergh Castle and Garden
Stagshaw Garden
Townend
Ullswater and Aira Force
Wasdale, Eskdale and Duddon
Windermere and Ambleside
Wordsworth House and Garden

Brecon Beacons
Abergwesyn Common
Central Beacons
Lanlay
Sugarloaf and Usk Valley
The Kymin

Snowdonia
Carneddau and Glyderau
Craflwyn and Beddgelert
Eifionydd
South Snowdonia
Tŷ Mawr Wybrnant
Ysbyty Ifan

Pembrokeshire
Abereiddi to Abermawr
Cilgerran Castle
Cleddau Woodlands
Colby Woodland Garden
Marloes Peninsula
Solva Coast
St David's Peninsula
Stackpole
Strumble Head to Cardigan
Tudor Merchant's House

Property and general index

Properties with no individual entries are shown in italics.
* Denotes properties shown only on maps.

© 2012 National Trust

Editor
Lucy Peel

Editorial assistance
Anthony Lambert
Wendy Smith

Production
Graham Prichard

Art direction
Craig Robson
Wolff Olins

Content management
Roger Shapland
Dave Buchanan

Design
LEVEL Partnership

Maps © **Blacker Design**, Maps in Minutes"/Collins Bartholomew 2011

Origination
Zebra

Printed
St Ives, Peterborough

NT LDS stock no: 73801/12
ISBN 978-0-7078-0415-6

Sponsor
Louise McRae

Publisher
John Stachiewicz

Project management
Your Membership Matters Ltd

Image acknowledgements

National Trust Images'
photographers:

Matthew Antrobus
Cristian Barnett
Bill Batten
Don Bishop
Alex Black
Mark Bolton
Daniel Bosworth
Jonathan Buckley
Andrew Butler
Michael Caldwell
Val Corbett
Joe Cornish
Stuart Cox

Eric Crichton
Derek Croucher
Nick Daly
Bill Davis
David Dixon
Rod Edwards
Andreas von Einsiedel
Phil Evans
Geoffrey Frosh
John Garrett
Dennis Gilbert
John Hammond
Jerry Harpur
Paul Harris
Ross Hoddinott
Andrea Jones
Andy Keen
Chris King
David Levenson
Nadia Mackenzie
Marianne Majerus
Leo Mason
Nick Meers
John Millar
Andrew Montgomery
Robert Morris
Alan North
David Noton
Alasdair Ogilvie
Erik Pelham
Nature P. L.
Phil Ripley

Stephen Robson
David Sellman
Ben Selway
Arnhel de Serra
Neil Campbell-Sharp
Ian Shaw
Tim Stephens
Megan Taylor
Rupert Truman
Mike Williams

Additional images supplied by:

Dave Almond
Stuart Banks
Janet Baxter
Janet Bradley
Heather Bradshaw
Mark Bradshaw
Bernie Brown
Mike Cable
CAMS
Martin Charles
Roger Coulam
Gillian Day
David Dixon
Gavin Duthie
Nick Trustram Eve
John Faulkner
Zoe Frank
Simon Fraser

Jason Friend
Jonathan Gardner
Jenna Garrett
David Griffen
David Hardman
Guy Harrop
Catherine Hayburn
Tamsin Hennah
Paul Hewitt
Chris Hill
Hannah Holohan
Historic House Hotels
Steve Hughes
Fisheye images
Mark Ivkovic
Clare Kendall
David Kirkham
Kippa Matthews
Stuart Meopham
John Millar
Kate Mount
Peter Muhly
Katie Piggford
John Rawlinson
John Reaney
John Bigelow Taylor
John Walton
David Watson
Tony West
Dave Wood
Sam Youd

Getting in touch

The National Trust supports the National Code of Practice for Visitor Attractions. We are very willing to answer questions and keen to receive comments. Many National Trust places provide their own comment cards and boxes. All your comments will be read, considered and action taken where necessary, but it is not possible to answer every comment or suggestion individually.

Enquiries by telephone, email or in writing should be made to the Trust's Supporter Services Centre (see opposite), open seven days a week (9 to 5:30 weekdays, 9 to 4 weekends and Bank Holidays). (Our 0844 numbers are charged at 5p per minute from BT landlines, charges from mobiles and other operators may vary.) You can also obtain information from our website **www.nationaltrust.org.uk**

National Trust Supporter Services Centre
PO Box 39, Warrington WA5 7WD.
0844 800 1895, 0844 800 4410 (minicom)

Email **enquiries@nationaltrust.org.uk** for all general enquiries, including membership.

Central Office
The National Trust and National Trust (Enterprises) Ltd, Heelis, Kemble Drive, Swindon, Wiltshire SN2 2NA.
01793 817400, 01793 817401 (fax)

National Trust Holiday Cottages
0844 800 2072 (brochures)
0844 800 2070 (reservations)

To contact the Editor email
lucy.peel@nationaltrust.org.uk